Dreamweaver 4
THE MISSING MANUAL

*The book that
should have been
in the box*

Dreamweaver 4
THE MISSING MANUAL

David Sawyer McFarland

POGUE PRESS™

O'REILLY®

Beijing • Cambridge • Farnham • Köln • Paris • Sebastopol • Taipei • Tokyo

Dreamweaver 4: The Missing Manual

by David Sawyer McFarland

Copyright © 2001 Pogue Press, LLC. All rights reserved.
Printed in the United States of America.

Published by Pogue Press/O'Reilly & Associates, Inc., 101 Morris Street, Sebastopol, CA 95472.

July 2001:   First Edition.

This book is printed on acid-free paper with 85% recycled content, 15% post-consumer waste. O'Reilly & Associates is committed to using paper with the highest recycled content available consistent with high quality.

ISBN: 0-596-00097-9   [7/01]
[M]

Table of Contents

Part Two: Building a Better Web Page

The Missing Credits

About the Author

 **David Sawyer McFarland** is president of Sawyer McFarland Media, a Web development and training company in the San Francisco Bay Area. He's been building Web sites since 1995, when he designed and produced his first Web site, an online magazine for communication professionals. He's served as the Webmaster at the University of California at Berkeley and the Berkeley Multimedia Research Center.

In addition to building Web sites, David is also is a writer, trainer, and instructor. He's taught Dreamweaver at Intuit, UC Berkeley Graduate School of Journalism, the Center for Electronic Art, the Academy of Art College, and Ex'Pressions Center for New Media. He's also written articles about Dreamweaver and the Web for both *Macworld* magazine and CreativePro.com.

He welcomes feedback about this book by email: *missing@sawmac.com*. (If you're seeking technical help, however, please refer to the sources listed in Appendix A.)

About the Creative Team

David Pogue (editor, indexer), weekly personal-technology columnist for the *New York Times* and award-winning former *Macworld* columnist, is the creator of the Missing Manual series. He's the author or co-author of 20 computer, humor, and music books, including four books in the Missing Manual series (*Mac OS 9, iMovie, iMovie 2*, and *Windows Me*); six books in the ...*for Dummies* series (*Macs, The iMac, The iBook, Magic, Opera*, and *Classical Music*); *Macworld Mac Secrets*, now in its sixth edition; and *PalmPilot: The Ultimate Guide*. He and his family live in Connecticut, as copiously photographed at *www.davidpogue.com*.

He welcomes feedback about this book and others in the Missing Manual series: *david@pogueman.com*.

Nan Barber (co-editor, copy editor) hails from Providence and holds a degree in Japanese studies from Brown University. After copy editing the Missing Manual titles on Mac OS 9, AppleWorks 6, iMovie, and Windows Me, she graduated to authoring, having co-written the bestselling *Office 2001 for Macintosh: The Missing Manual*. She is managing editor for *Salamander*, a magazine for poetry, fiction, and memoirs, and lives with her husband near Boston. Email: *nanbarber@mac.com*.

Rose Cassano (cover illustration) has worked as an independent designer and illustrator for twenty years. Assignments have ranged from the nonprofit sector to corporate clientele. She is lives in beautiful Southern Oregon, grateful for the miracles of modern technology that make living and working there a reality. Email: *cassano@cdsnet.net.* Web: *www.rosecassano.com.*

Murray Summers (technical editor) is a biochemist by training, but has spent the last 20 years working in the computer industry. In 1998, he started his own Web site production company, Great Web Sights. As a Macromedia Evangelist, he also participates in the sponsored newsgroups for Dreamweaver and other products. He lives in rural Philadelphia with Suzanne, his lovely wife, their 11-year-old daughter Carly, a Golden Retriever, an Eski-poo, and some goldfish.

Phil Simpson (book design and layout) has been involved with computer graphics since 1977, when he worked with one of the first graphics-generating computers—an offspring of flight-simulation technology. He now works out of his office in Stamford, CT *(pmsimpson@earthlink.net),* where he has had his graphic design business for eighteen years. He is experienced in many facets of graphic design, including corporate identity, publication design, corporate and medical communications.

Acknowledgments

Many thanks to all those who helped with this book. Murray Summers drafted the original version of Chapter 12 and provided fabulous insights into the program during his technical edits. Kelly Lunsford wrote Appendix B, the detailed menu-by-menu analysis of Dreamweaver (so detailed, in fact, it couldn't fit in this book; it's at *www.missingmanuals.com*). Jane Stevens provided the "beginner's mind" needed to make this book's tutorials user-friendly. Renowned Dreamweaver Extension developer Massimo Foti graciously gave permission to use several regular expressions that he created.

Of course, without the hard work of the Dreamweaver team, this book wouldn't have been possible. A special thanks to Eric Ott, Sho Kuwamoto, and Narciso Jaramillo from Macromedia for providing quick and informative answers during the writing of this book.

Finally, thanks to David Pogue whose comments (LOL) kept me motivated; my mom; Mary and David; and Phyllis and Les, whose enthusiasm helped buoy my spirits during this project. Of course, this book and so much more were only possible because of the unfailing love and support of my wonderful wife, Scholle.

—*David Sawyer McFarland*

The Missing Manual series is a joint venture between Pogue Press—the dream team introduced on these pages—and O'Reilly & Associates, one of the most respected publishers on earth. It's only because Tim O'Reilly and his team had the vision to take a gamble on this concept that this book came into existence. Tim, Cathy Record,

Edie Freedman, Allen Noren, Laura Schmier, Sue Willing, Mark Brokering, Dana Furby, Lisa Mann, and Sara Winge were especially critical to this book's birth.

Thanks, too, to agent David Rogelberg, the Missing Manuals' first believer; Elizabeth "Eagle Eye" Tonis, this book's indefatigable beta reader; Scholle Sawyer McFarland, who pinch-hit edited a few chapters; David Sawyer McFarland, who was not only a dream author but who performed an eleventh-hour "beta read" of his own; and the other Pogues—Jennifer, Kelly, and Tia—who make this series, and everything else, possible.

—David Pogue

The Missing Manual Series

Missing Manuals are designed to be authoritative, superbly written guides to popular computer products that don't come with printed manuals (which is just about all of them). Each book features a hand-crafted index; cross-references to specific page numbers (not just "See Chapter 14"); RepKover, a detached-spine binding that lets the book lie perfectly flat without the assistance of weights or cinder blocks; and an ironclad promise never to use an apostrophe in the possessive word *its*.

Recent and upcoming Missing Manual titles include:

- *Office 2001 for Macintosh: The Missing Manual* by Nan Barber & David Reynolds

- *Mac OS 9: The Missing Manual* by David Pogue

- *AppleWorks 6: The Missing Manual* by Jim Elferdink & David Reynolds

- *iMovie 2: The Missing Manual* by David Pogue

- *Windows Me: The Missing Manual* by David Pogue

- *Windows 2000 Pro: The Missing Manual* by Sharon Crawford

- *Mac OS X: The Missing Manual* by David Pogue

- *Windows XP Home Edition: The Missing Manual* by David Pogue

Introduction

T he World Wide Web has evolved quite a bit since its humble beginning in the early Nineties as a simple tool for exchanging scientific information. Back then, beer commercials dominated the Super Bowl. Well, actually, they still do, but these days, ads for E*Trade.com threaten to steal our attention from the King of Beers, Amazon.com has become as familiar as Walgreen's, and the business section of the newspaper isn't complete without a story about the rise or fall of some dot-com startup.

Whatever you may feel about society's thirst for instant access to online stock quotes, sports scores, and dancing hamsters (*www.hampsterdance2.com*), the presence of the Internet is inescapable. It's now an integral part of our economy, if not the lives of over half of the American population.

But even as new technologies like streaming video, 3-D animation, and high-quality audio appear at a Web site near you, the underlying foundation of Web pages has remained pretty much the same. A simple formatting language called *HTML*, or Hypertext Markup Language, forms the basis of most of the world's Web pages. HTML lets you create even complex Web sites just by typing into a simple text editor like the Windows Notepad or SimpleText on the Mac.

But why use a text editor, when Dreamweaver's *visual* page-building approach makes your job of creating beautiful, complex, and useful Web sites much easier? Whether you're new to building Web pages or a hard-core, hand-coding HTML jockey, Dreamweaver is a powerful tool that lets you build Web sites quickly and efficiently, without compromising the quality of your code.

What's New in Dreamweaver 4

If you've never used Dreamweaver before, see Chapter 1 for a grand tour and welcome. If you're upgrading from Dreamweaver 3 or some other version, you'll find in Dreamweaver 4 a host of new features aimed at both the novice Web designer and the seasoned HTML guru:

- **Layout view** provides an intuitive and visual method of building complex table-based page designs. New tools let you easily draw layouts in the document window (see Chapter 6).

- Add crisp text, using almost any fonts you like, and interactive buttons with the **Flash Text** and **Flash Buttons** features. Create simple Flash files directly in Dreamweaver (see Chapter 5).

- The previously confusing and cumbersome process of creating and using external **Cascading Style Sheets** has been simplified to a single click, as described in Chapter 8.

- **Code view** provides syntax coloring and improved editing of HTML, JavaScript, and XML files. If you hand-code your HTML, this feature is probably the single best improvement in the program. Add line numbers, set code indenting, turn on word wrapping, and even highlight invalid HTML within a powerful text-editing environment. Chapter 9 tells all.

- If you enjoy both the creative freedom of Dreamweaver's visual editing view and the precision of working directly in HTML, you can have the best of both worlds. **Split view** lets you simultaneously view (and edit) a visual display of your page *and* the HTML underneath. See Chapter 9.

- Forget those bulky Web books (except this one, of course). Access complete references on HTML, JavaScript, and Cascading Style Sheets directly in Dreamweaver. The **Reference panel** provides comprehensive information on these technologies, excerpted from computer books published by O'Reilly & Associates. See Chapter 9.

- JavaScript programmers will be blown away by the **JavaScript Debugger**. Use traditional debugging techniques like setting breakpoints in scripts and stepping into and out of functions. Debug scripts directly in Internet Explorer or Netscape Navigator. See Chapter 9.

- The new **toolbar** brings many common commands to your fingertips. Adding titles to your pages, previewing in Web browsers, and switching from Code view to Design view have never been easier.

- Thanks to the addition of small identifying tabs, locating editable regions in **Templates** is much easier. See Chapter 17.

- Corporate users and workgroups will be pleased by Dreamweaver's **WebDAV** and **SourceSafe** integration. You can use these file control systems to assure that other people in your workgroup don't work on files at the same time you do. See Chapter 16.

- **Site reports** provide site-wide analysis of your Web pages. These reports let you locate untitled documents, find missing **Alt** properties, and identify sloppy HTML quickly. See Chapter 15.

- Re-using Web page elements—including GIFs, JPEGs, links, colors, and Flash movies—is a snap with the **Assets panel**. You can even identify and organize your favorite assets for easy re-use throughout your site, as detailed in Chapter 14.

- The **Extension Manager** lets you add hundreds of new plug-in features to Dreamweaver—for free. See Chapter 19.

- Powerful **Fireworks** integration let you use Macromedia's image editing and Web development programs together. Optimize graphics within Dreamweaver, and switch effortlessly back and forth from Fireworks.

Tip: Since Dreamweaver 4 was first released, Macromedia has issued an update—version 4.01—that fixes many bugs, especially in the Macintosh version of the program. In addition, all Dreamweaver *behaviors* (see Chapter 12) that come with the updated version now work in the Netscape 6 Web browser. To download this free update, go to *www.macromedia.com/support/dreamweaver/downloads/*.

HTML 101

Underneath the hood of any Web page, whether it's your Uncle's "Check out this summer's fishin'" page or the home page of a billion-dollar online retailer, is nothing more than line after line of ordinary typed text. With its use of simple commands called *tags*, HTML is still at the heart of most of the Web.

The HTML code that creates a Web page can be as simple as this:

```
<html>
<head>
<title>Hey, I'm the title of this Web page.</title>
</head>
<body>
Hey, I'm some body text on this Web page.
</body>
</html>
```

While it may not be exciting, the HTML shown here is all that's needed to make a Web page.

Of Tags and Properties

In the example above—and, indeed, in the HTML code of any Web page you examine—you'll notice that most HTML commands appear in *pairs* designed to surround a block of text or other commands.

These bracketed commands, which constitute the "markup" part of the Hypertext Markup Language (HTML), are called *tags*. Sandwiched between brackets, tags are simply instructions that tell a Web browser how to display the information on a Web page.

The starting tag of each pair tells the browser where the instruction begins, and the ending tag tells it where the instruction ends. Ending tags always include a forward slash (/) after the first bracket symbol (<), which tells the browser that this is a closing tag.

Note that Dreamweaver can generate all of these tags *automatically* behind the scenes; by no means will you ever have to memorize or type out these commands (although some programmers enjoy doing so for greater control). It's important to understand that at its heart, Dreamweaver is a program that converts your visual designs into underlying codes like these:

- The <html> tag appears once at the beginning of a Web page and again (with an added slash) at the end. This tag tells a Web browser that the information contained in this document is written in HTML, as opposed to some other language. All of the contents of a page, including other tags, appear between the opening and closing <html> tag.

  If you were to think of a Web page as a tree, the <html> tag would be its trunk. Springing from the trunk are two branches that represent the two main parts of any Web page: the *head* and the *body*.

- The *head* of a Web page, surrounded by <head> tags, contains the title of the page; it may also provide other, invisible information (such as search keywords) that browsers and Web search engines can exploit.

  In addition, the head can contain information that's used by the Web browser for displaying the Web page and for adding interactivity. *Cascading Style Sheet* information, used for formatting text and other elements, may be defined in the head of the document (see Chapter 8). In addition, JavaScript scripts, functions, and variables can be declared in the head of the document. In fact, Dreamweaver Behaviors (Chapter 11) achieve their interactive effects with the help of JavaScript code placed in the head of the page.

- The *body* of a Web page, as set apart by its surrounding <body> tags, contains all the information that appears inside a browser window—headlines, text, pictures, and so on.

  In Dreamweaver, the body area is represented by the blank white area of the document window (see Figure I-1), and resembles the blank window of a word-processing program.

Most of your work with Dreamweaver involves inserting and formatting text, pictures, and other objects in the body of the document. Many tags commonly used in Web pages appear within the <body> tag. Here are a few:

- You can tell a Web browser where a paragraph of text begins with a <p> (opening paragraph tag), and where it ends with a </p> (closing paragraph tag).

- The <b> tag stands for bold; if you surround some text with it and its partner tag, </b>, you get boldface type on the Web page. For example, the HTML snippet *<b>Hello</b>* tells your visitor's Web browser to display the word "Hello" in bold type on the screen.

- The <a> tag, or anchor tag, creates a link (hyperlink) in a Web page. A link, of course, can lead anywhere on the Web. How do you tell the browser where the link should go? Simply give the browser more instructions inside the <a> tags; for instance, you might type *<a href="http://www.missingmanuals.com"> Click here!</a>*.

The browser knows that when your visitor clicks the words "Click here!," it should go to the Missing Manual Web site. In Dreamweaver, the *href* part of the tag is called a *property* (you may also hear the term *attribute*); the URL (the Universal Resource Locator or Web address—in this example, *http://www.missingmanuals .com)* is the *value* of the Href property.

Figure I-1:
The Document window displays your page as you build it. You can add text, graphics and other elements to it, and–thanks to Dreamweaver's visual approach–see a close approximation of how the page will appear in a Web browser.

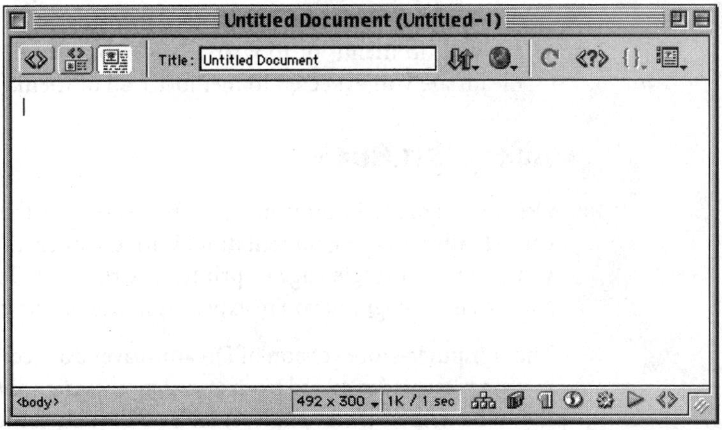

Fortunately, Dreamweaver exempts you from having to type any of these codes, and provides an easy-to-use window called the Property inspector for adding properties to your tags and other page elements. To create links the Dreamweaver way (read: the easy way), turn to page 85.

The Very Basics

You'll find very little jargon or nerd terminology in this book. You will, however, encounter a few terms and concepts that you'll encounter frequently in your computing life:

- **Clicking.** This book gives you three kinds of instructions that require you to use your computer's mouse or trackpad. To *click* means to point the arrow cursor at something on the screen and then—without moving the cursor at all—to press and release the clicker button on the mouse (or laptop trackpad). To *double-click,* of course, means to click twice in rapid succession, again without moving the cursor at all. And to *drag* means to move the cursor while pressing the button continuously.

- **Keyboard shortcuts.** Every time you take your hand off the keyboard to move the mouse, you lose time and potentially disrupt your creative flow. That's why many experienced computer fans use keystroke combinations instead of menu commands wherever possible. Ctrl+B (⌘-B), for example, is a keyboard shortcut for boldface type in Dreamweaver (and most other programs).

  When you see a shortcut like Ctrl+S (⌘-S) (which saves changes to the current document), it's telling you to hold down the Ctrl or ⌘ key, and, while it's down, type the letter S, and then release both keys.

- **Choice is good.** Dreamweaver frequently gives you several ways to trigger a particular command—by choosing a menu command, *or* by clicking a toolbar button, *or* by pressing a key combination, for example. Some people prefer the speed of keyboard shortcuts; others like the satisfaction of a visual command array available in menus or toolbars. This book lists all of the alternatives, but by no means are you expected to memorize all of them.

About this Book

Despite the many improvements in software over the years, one feature has grown consistently worse: documentation. With the purchase of most software these days, you don't get a single page of printed instructions. To learn about the hundreds of features in a program, you're expected to use online electronic help systems.

The computer-store version of Dreamweaver does come with a printed manual; the version you can download from *www.macromedia.com/downloads/* doesn't. But even if you have the official guide, it feels as though something is missing. At times, it assumes you already understand the discussion at hand, and skips over important topics that require an in-depth presentation. In addition, as with many manuals, you don't always get an objective evaluation of the program's features. (Engineers often add technically sophisticated features to a program because they can, not because you need them.) You shouldn't have to waste your time learning features that don't help you get your work done.

The purpose of this book, then, is to serve as the manual that should have been in the box. In this book's pages, you'll find step-by-step instructions for using every Dreamweaver feature, including those you may not even have quite understood, let alone mastered, such as Libraries, Layout view, Behaviors, and Dreamweaver's Site

Management features. In addition, you'll find clear feature evaluations that help you determine which ones are useful to you, as well as how and when to use them.

Dreamweaver 4: The Missing Manual is designed to accommodate readers at every technical level. The primary discussions are written for advanced-beginner or intermediate computer users. But if you're a first-timer, special sidebar articles called Up To Speed provide the introductory information you need to understand the topic at hand. If you're an advanced user, on the other hand, keep your eye out for similar shaded boxes called Power Users' Clinic. They offer more technical tips, tricks, and shortcuts for the experienced computer fan.

Macintosh and Windows

Dreamweaver 4 works almost precisely the same in its Macintosh and Windows versions. Every button in every dialog box is exactly the same; the software response to every command is identical. In this book, you'll see even-handed treatment; half of the illustrations show the Windows version, half show the Mac.

Only the keystrokes are slightly different, because the Ctrl key in Windows is the equivalent of the Macintosh ⌘ key. Whenever this book refers to a key combination, you'll see the Windows keystroke listed first (with + symbols, as is customary in Windows documentation); the Macintosh keystroke follows in parentheses (with - symbols, in time-honored Mac fashion). In other words, you might read, "The keyboard shortcut for saving a file is Ctrl+S (⌘-S)"; now you'll know what that notation means.

About the Outline

Dreamweaver 4: The Missing Manual is divided into five parts, each containing several chapters:

- Part 1, **Building a Web Page**, explores Dreamweaver's interface and takes you through the basic steps of building a Web page. It explains how to add text and format it, how to link from one page to another, and how to spice up your designs with graphics.

- Part 2, **Building a Better Web Page,** takes you deeper into Dreamweaver and explains how to gain greater control of the design of a Web page. You'll learn how to use more advanced features such as tables, layers, Cascading Style Sheets, and frames. In addition, you'll get step-by-step instruction in using Dreamweaver 4's new Layout view, as well as how to view and work with the underlying HTML code of a page.

- Part 3, **Bringing Your Pages to Life,** helps you add interactivity to your site. From using forms to collect information from your site's visitors, to easily adding complex JavaScript programs, this section guides you through adding animation, multimedia, and other interactive effects.

- Part 4, **Building a Web Site,** covers the big picture: managing the pages and files in your Web site, testing links and pages, and moving your site onto a Web server connected to the Internet. And since you're not always working solo, this section also covers features that let you work with a team of Web developers.

- Part 5, **Dreamweaver Power,** shows you how to take full advantage of such time-saving features as Libraries, Templates, and History panel automation. It also covers Dreamweaver's Extension Manager, a program that can add hundreds of new, free features to the program.

At the end of the book, an appendix provides a list of Internet resources for additional Web-design help. At the Missing Manual Web site, you'll find a free, downloadable bonus appendix—a menu-by-menu explanation of the Dreamweaver 4 commands, in both Windows and Macintosh versions (because the menus are organized slightly differently).

About→These→Arrows

Throughout this book, and throughout the Missing Manual series, you'll find sentences like this one: "Open the System Folder→Preferences→Remote Access folder." That's shorthand for a much longer instruction that directs you to open three nested folders in sequence, like this: "On your hard drive, you'll find a folder called System Folder. Open that. Inside the System Folder window is a folder called Preferences; double-click it to open it. Inside *that* folder is yet another one called Remote Access. Double-click to open it, too."

Similarly, this kind of arrow shorthand helps to simplify the business of choosing commands in menus, as shown in Figure I-2.

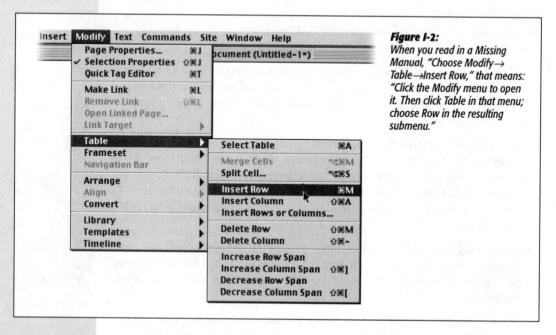

Figure I-2:
When you read in a Missing Manual, "Choose Modify→Table→Insert Row," that means: "Click the Modify menu to open it. Then click Table in that menu; choose Row in the resulting submenu."

Living Examples

This book is designed to get your work onto the Web faster and more professionally; it's only natural, then, that half the value of this book also lies on the Web.

As you read the book's chapters, you'll encounter a number of *living examples*—step-by-step tutorials that you can build yourself, using raw materials like graphics and half-completed Web pages, that you can download from *www.sawmac.com/missing/*. You might not gain very much by simply reading these step-by-step lessons while relaxing in your tree hammock; but if you take the time to work through them at the computer, you'll discover that these tutorials give you an unprecedented insight into the way professional Web pages are built by professional designers.

You'll also find, in this book's lessons, the URLs of the finished pages, so that you can compare your Dreamweaver work with the final result. In other words, you won't just see pictures of Dreamweaver's output in the pages of the book; you'll find the actual, working Web pages on the Internet.

About MissingManuals.com

At the *missingmanuals.com* Web site, you'll find articles, tips, and updates to the book. In fact, you're invited and encouraged to submit such corrections and updates yourself. In an effort to keep the book as up-to-date and accurate as possible, each time we print more copies of this book, we'll make any confirmed corrections you've suggested. We'll also note such changes on the Web site, so that you can mark important corrections into your own copy of the book, if you like.

In the meantime, we'd love to hear your own suggestions for new books in the Missing Manual line. There's a place for that on the Web site, too, as well as a place to sign up for free email notification of new titles in the series.

Part One:
Building a Web Page

1

Dreamweaver Guided Tour

Welcome to Dreamweaver

Dreamweaver is a program for producing and managing Web sites. It lets you build Web pages and Web sites quickly and maintain them with ease. Its graphical user interface lets Web designers create pages in an intuitive, visual manner. In addition, Dreamweaver lets you manage complex Web sites and add interactive behavior, advanced Web technologies like Cascading Style Sheets, and Dynamic HTML.

And you don't need to build your sites from scratch with Dreamweaver, either. Dreamweaver happily opens Web pages and Web sites that were created in another program without destroying any of your carefully handcrafted code. Dreamweaver's *Round-Trip HTML* feature works to ensure that HTML written by hand within Dreamweaver (or any text editing program) stays the way you want it.

Some of Dreamweaver's key benefits include:

- **Visual page building.** If you've spent any time using a text editor to punch out the HTML code for your Web pages, you know the tedium involved in adding even a simple item like a photograph to a Web page. When your boss asks you to add her photo to the company home page, you launch your trusty text editor and type something like this: *<img src="images/staff/bigcheese.gif" width="100" height="150" alt="The Boss" border="0">*.

Not only is this approach prone to typos, but it also separates you from what you want the page to *look* like.

Dreamweaver, on the other hand, takes a visual approach to building Web pages. If you put an image on your page, Dreamweaver shows you the picture on the screen. As in a word processor, which displays documents on screen as they should look when printed, Dreamweaver provides a very close approximation of what your Web page will look like in a Web browser.

- **Complex interactivity, simply.** You've probably seen Web pages where a graphic (on a navigation bar, for example) lights up or changes appearance when you move your mouse over it.

Dynamic effects like this—mouse rollovers, alert boxes, and pull-down navigation menus—usually require programming in *JavaScript,* a programming language that most Web browsers understand. While JavaScript can do amazing things that are not possible with HTML alone, it's a programming language that requires time and practice to learn.

Dreamweaver relieves you of having to learn JavaScript for these purposes; the program makes it easy to add complex interactivity with just the click of the mouse. Chapter 11 explains how you can use these *Behaviors* (ready-made Java-Script programs in Dreamweaver) to bring your pages to life.

- **Roundtrip HTML.** Every now and then, even in Dreamweaver, you may sometimes want to put aside the WYSIWYG (What You See Is What You Get) view and look at the underlying HTML code of a page. You may feel more comfortable creating some of your HTML by hand, for example, or you may want to tweak the HTML that Dreamweaver produces.

Macromedia realized that many professional Web developers still do a lot of work "down in the trenches," typing HTML commands by hand. In Dreamweaver, you

---

UP TO SPEED

Hand-coding Versus WYSIWYG Editors

Creating Web pages in a text editor was long considered the best method of building Web sites. The precise control over HTML available when code is written by hand was (and often still is) seen as the only way to assure quality Web pages.

Hand coding's reputation as the only way to go for pros is fueled by the behavior of many visual page-building programs that add unnecessary code to pages—code that affects how a page appears *and* how quickly it downloads over the Internet.

But hand coding is time-consuming and error-prone—one typo can render a Web page useless. Fortunately, Dreamweaver brings solid code writing to a visual environment. Since its earliest incarnation, Macromedia has prided itself on Dreamweaver's ability to produce clean HTML *and* its tolerance of code created by other programs—

including text editors. In fact, Dreamweaver 4 introduces a new, powerful built-in text-editing mode that lets you freely manipulate the HTML of a page.

But the real story is that the code produced when working in the visual mode is as solid and well written as hand coding. Knowing this, feel free to take advantage of the increased productivity that Dreamweaver's visual-editing mode brings to your day-to-day work with its one-click objects, instant JavaScript, and simplified layout tools. Doing so won't compromise your code, and will certainly let you finish your next Web site in record time.

(And by the way, no Web-design program is really WYSIWYG—What You See Is What You Get. Because every browser interprets the HTML language slightly differently, Web design is more like *WYSIRWYGOAGD*: What You See Is Roughly What You'll Get, On A Good Day.)

---

can edit the raw HTML to your heart's content. Switching back and forth between the visual mode—called the Design view—and the Code view is seamless and, best of all, nondestructive. Unlike many visual Web page programs, where making a change in the WYSIWYG mode stomps all over the underlying HTML code, Dreamweaver respects hand-typed code and doesn't try to rewrite it (unless you ask it to).

See Chapter 9 to learn more about how Dreamweaver handles HTML.

- **Site management tools.** Rarely will you build just a single Web page. More often, you'll be creating and editing pages that work together to form part of a Web site. Or you may be building an entire Web site from scratch.

  Either way, Dreamweaver's site management tools make your job of dealing with site development easier. From managing links, images, pages, and other media to working with a team of people and moving your site onto a Web server, Dreamweaver automates many of the routine tasks every Webmaster faces. Part IV of this book looks at how Dreamweaver can help you build and maintain Web sites.

- **Have it your way.** As if Dreamweaver didn't have enough going for it, the engineers at Macromedia have created a software product that is completely customizable, or as they call it, *extensible*. Anyone can add to or change the menus, commands, objects, and windows in the program.

  Suppose, for example, that you hardly ever use any of the commands in the Edit menu. By editing one text file in the Dreamweaver Configuration folder, you can get rid of any unwanted menu items—or even add new commands of your creation. This incredible flexibility lets you customize the program to fit your work methods, even add features that Macromedia's programmers never imagined. Best of all, the Macromedia Exchange Web site includes hundreds of free extensions to download and add to Dreamweaver. See Chapter 19 for details.

The Dreamweaver Interface

Dreamweaver's floating windows let you add and modify elements of a Web page. Macromedia refers to most of these floating windows as *panels,* and Dreamweaver has an almost overwhelming number of them.

Many of the windows are used to assist with specific tasks, like building style sheets, and are described in the relevant chapters. But you'll frequently interact with four main windows: the document window, the Objects panel, the Property inspector, and the Launcher.

The Document Window

You build your Web pages in the document window. As in a word processor, you can simply click inside the body of the document window and type to add text to the page. In addition to the body, the document window has a title bar, toolbar, status bar, and (in the Windows version of the program) a menu bar.

• **Title bar.** The title bar shows the title of the Web page, and, in parentheses, the name of the underlying *file* and what folder it's in. For instance, in the example shown in Figure 1-1, the Web page called *Cabbage Attacks on the Rise* is saved as an HTML file called *cabbage.html* in a folder called *test_site*.

• **The menu bar** lists Dreamweaver's commands, just as in any program. On Windows, the menu bar appears below the title bar; on Macs, the menu bar appears at the top of the screen.

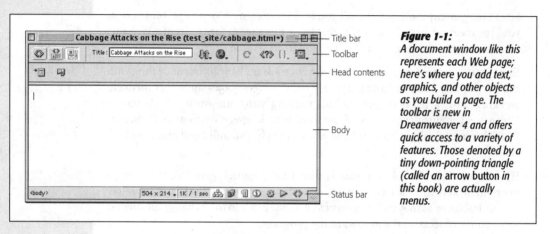

Title bar
Toolbar
Head contents
Body
Status bar

Figure 1-1:
A document window like this represents each Web page; here's where you add text, graphics, and other objects as you build a page. The toolbar is new in Dreamweaver 4 and offers quick access to a variety of features. Those denoted by a tiny down-pointing triangle (called an arrow button *in this book) are actually menus.*

• **Toolbar.** New in Dreamweaver 4, the *toolbar* lets you change the title of a page, toggle between Design and Code views, preview and debug the page in different browsers, access a context-sensitive reference (help) system, and change how the document window looks. To make the toolbar visible if it's not already, choose View→Toolbar. You'll be reading about its various buttons and menus in the relevant chapters of this book.

• **Head content.** Most of what you put on a Web page winds up on the body of the page, but some elements are specific to the region of the page called the *head*. Here you put things like the title of the page, *meta tags* to provide information for some search engines and browsers, JavaScript scripts, and Cascading Style Sheet information (Chapter 8).

This information doesn't appear in your visitors' Web browsers. But while working in Dreamweaver, you can have a look at it by choosing View→Head Content. You'll see a row of icons representing the different bits of information in the head.

• **The status bar** at the bottom of the document window provides useful information about your page. Its mini-launcher bar (see Figure 1-2) lets you open the various windows and panels you use frequently. It duplicates the functions of the regular Launcher (see page 18), but takes up far less screen space.

The tag selector (also shown in Figure 1-2) is also extremely useful; it provides a sneak peek at the HTML codes that compose your Web page. It indicates, based on what you've selected or where the insertion point is, how tags are nested in the document. You can also use the tag selector to select an HTML tag and all of the information nested inside it; clicking <p> selects a paragraph and everything inside it, for example. For experienced Dreamweaver users, the tag selector is one of the program's most used tools.

Tip: Clicking the <body> tag in the tag selector is the same as pressing Ctrl+A (⌘-A)—it selects everything in the document window. After selecting everything this way, for example, you could press the Delete key to quickly get rid of everything in your document.

Figure 1-2:
If the area behind a mini-launcher icon is white, that particular window is open.

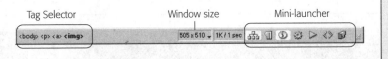

Tag Selector   Window size   Mini-launcher

The Window Size Pop-up Menu

Creating pages that look good on different monitors set to a wide range of resolutions is one of the most difficult tasks facing Web designers. After all, not everyone has a 21-inch monitor or views Web sites with the browser window maximized to fill the whole screen. Nothing is more dispiriting than spending a solid week designing the coolest looking Web page, only to have your client call up to say that your design doesn't fit her 15-inch monitor (a painfully common story).

```
592w
536 x 196  (640 x 480, Default)
600 x 300  (640 x 480, Maximized)
760 x 420  (800 x 600, Maximized)
795 x 470  (832 x 624, Maximized)
955 x 600  (1024 x 768, Maximized)
544 x 378  (WebTV)

Edit Sizes...
```

You can simulate browser windows of different sizes by dragging the resize handle at the lower-right corner of the document window, of course. But Dreamweaver has a better tool for such experiments: the Window Size pop-up menu on the status bar at the bottom of your document window. Clicking the black arrow next to the window size stats lets you choose a different setting for the document window, as shown here. Use this feature to test how your page will look inside different size browser windows. The numbers indicate the width and height in pixels.

The first pair of numbers indicates the amount of usable space in the document window; the numbers in parentheses indicate the resolution of the monitor. The third option shown here, in other words, indicates that if someone has a 640 x 480 monitor and maximizes the browser window, there are 600 by 300 pixels of space to display a Web page. (Even though a monitor's resolution is, say, 800 x 600, after you subtract the space required to display the browser's toolbar, location bar, status bar, and other "chrome," 760 x 420 pixels of space will be visible when a Web page is opened.)

(Note: The Window Size pop-up menu doesn't actually set the size of your *Web page;* Web pages are usually fluid, and can grow or shrink to the size of each visitor's browser window. For techniques that let you exercise greater control of your page presentation, see Chapter 6.)

The Launcher

The Launcher (Figure 1-3) provides one-click access to many of the most important Dreamweaver windows; click a button to open the corresponding window.

Despite the ease of the Launcher, you don't need it. It takes up a fair amount of screen space; furthermore, you can open all of the same windows using either the Window menu or the miniature launcher on the status bar.

Collapse box   Swap orientation

Figure 1-3:
Dreamweaver looks slightly different on the Mac and in Windows; for instance, Mac users see the collapse box which, when clicked, collapses a window down to its title bar.

POWER USERS' CLINIC

Reworking the Launcher

You can add, remove, and change the order of the icons that show up on Dreamweaver's Launcher and Launcher bar. You may as well delete the buttons that open windows you rarely use, and put the ones you use most often in a place where you can get to them easily.

To do so, choose Edit→Preferences, or press Ctrl+U (⌘-U) to open the Preferences dialog box. Click Panels in the Category list.

To *add* a window icon, click the + button. From the pop-up list, select the window you want to access from the Launcher.

To *delete* a window button from the Launcher, select its name from the list, and then click the – button.

You can also rearrange the icons on the Launcher; just select a window button's name in the list, and then click the up or down arrow buttons above the list. (Up moves the icon to the left in the Launcher; down moves it to the right.) Click the next button you want to move, and repeat.

Click OK when you've finished your Launcher surgery.

The Objects Panel

If the document window is your canvas, the Objects panel holds your brushes and paints. While you can add text to a Web page simply by typing in the document window, adding other elements to your page (images, horizontal rules, forms, or multimedia elements) requires the click-to-add approach of the Objects panel. Want to put a picture on your Web page? Just click the Image icon.

Although adding elements to your Web page this way may feel like magic, what Dreamweaver calls an *object* is really just HTML code that gets added to your Web page behind the scenes. Clicking the horizontal rule icon, for instance, simply inserts the <hr> tag into the underlying HTML of your page.

When you first start Dreamweaver, the Objects panel is open. If you ever close it by mistake, you can open it again by choosing Window→Objects or by pressing Ctrl+F2 (⌘-F2). On the other hand, if space is at a premium on your screen, you can close the Objects panel and use the Insert menu in its place. Its commands duplicate all of the objects available from the Objects panel.

Tip: Remembering what all those cryptic icons on the Objects panel stand for can be difficult. Dreamweaver does offer *tooltips*–pop-up caption balloons that appear at your cursor tip if you point to an icon and wait without clicking–but waiting for them can slow you down.

Until you get familiar with what the little icons mean, you can add text labels for them, as shown in Figure 1-4; see step 2 on page 19 for details. (The illustrations in this book assume you've followed this advice.)

Figure 1-4:
Left: The Objects panel displays icons representing the different elements you can place in your Web page. There are seven different sets of objects available; you can move between the different sets using the pop-up menu at the top of the panel (circled). Below the objects is a pair of layout tools and buttons that let you switch between the two table-design modes: Standard view and Layout view (see Chapter 6). Right: The Objects panel with text labels.

There are seven different sets of objects available from the Objects panel; if you open the pop-up menu at the top of the panel, you'll see this list:

- **Common objects.** In addition to objects like images, tables, and horizontal rules, which you'll use frequently in everyday Web design, this "page" of the Objects panel offers multimedia objects that may not be part of your daily routine: Shockwave files and Generator templates, for example.

  (Not surprisingly, these other multimedia objects are all based on other Macromedia software programs. "Hello, Engineering? This is Marketing calling...")

- **Character objects.** These are special symbols you can pop onto your page, such as copyright symbols or trademark symbols (see page 44 for details).

- **Form objects.** Want to get some input from visitors to your Web site? You'll use *forms* when you want to receive visitor feedback, collect credit card information for online sales, or gather any other kind of data on your Web site. The Forms panel lets you add form elements like radio buttons, pull down menus, and text boxes. For more on forms, see Chapter 10.

- **Frame objects.** It's possible to display several Web pages in one browser window at the same time, thanks to an HTML mechanism called *frames;* see Chapter 7 for complete details.

- **Head objects.** The Head objects panel lets you insert objects that don't actually appear on your Web page: its title, what alphabet the browser should use to display the page (Cyrillic or Japanese, for example), or a description of the page for use by search engines.

- **Invisible objects.** This panel offers another collection of Web page elements that never actually show up on your Web page, including anchors (see page 90), scripts, and comments that help you or your collaborators remember why you designed your Web page the way you did.

- **Special objects.** Use the Special objects palette to insert Java applets, plug-ins, and Active X controls. Chapter 13 has the details.

The Property Inspector

After dropping in an image, table, or anything else from the Objects panel, you can use the Property inspector to fine-tune its appearance and attributes. Suppose, for example, that your boss has decided she wants her name to appear in bold, bright red type under her picture. After highlighting her name in the document window, you would then use the Property inspector to change its type characteristics accordingly.

The Property inspector is a chameleon. It's aware of what you're working on in the document window—a table, an image, some text—and displays the appropriate set of properties (that is, options). You'll use the Property inspector extensively while working with Dreamweaver.

Tip: Double-click any blank gray area in the Property inspector to hide or show the bottom half of the palette, where Dreamweaver displays an additional set of advanced options. (It's a good idea to leave the inspector fully expanded most of the time, since you may otherwise miss some useful options.)

The Property inspector appears on the screen the first time you run Dreamweaver. But if you don't see it, you can reopen it by choosing Window→Properties, or by pressing Ctrl+F3 (⌘-F3).

Tip: At its heart, the Property inspector is simply a display of the attributes of HTML tags. The *src* (or source) attribute of the *<img>* (or image) tag, for instance, tells a Web browser where to look for an image file. The best way to make sure you're setting the properties of the correct object is to click its tag in the tag selector (see page 16).

Figure 1-5:
Four controls on the Property inspector never change: The Close box; the Help button, which opens an appropriate help Web page; the Quick Tag editor (see Chapter 9); and the Expander arrow, which shows or hides advanced properties in the bottom half of the inspector.

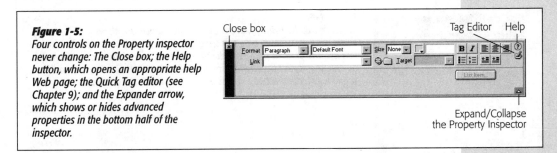

Close box   Tag Editor   Help

Expand/Collapse
the Property Inspector

Window Management

So far, you've read about the Objects panel, Property inspector, and document window. As you learn more advanced features, you'll encounter even more windows. In fact, without too much trouble, you could easily wind up with ten or more windows open on your screen.

Dreamweaver offers several features that are dedicated to helping you manage all of these windows. For example:

• You can combine several windows into one, just by dragging the "file-folder" tab into a similarly designed window, as shown in Figure 1-6.

• When you drag or resize a window, Dreamweaver tries to make it snap neatly against the edge of other windows or the edge of the screen, as though drawn by magnetism. This handy feature, new in Dreamweaver 4, makes it easy to align windows and place them right next to each other.

• If you've really made a mess of your screen, having dragged Dreamweaver windows all over the place, you can make them snap back into a tidy arrangement by choosing Window→Arrange Panels. (Unfortunately, this command doesn't arrange your document windows or the Site window for you—only tool panels and inspector windows.)

• If you want to hide all windows *except* for documents, choose Window→Hide Panels (or press F4)—a useful trick when you want to maximize the amount of your screen dedicated to showing the actual Web page you're working on. To bring back all of Dreamweaver's administrative windows, press F4 again, or choose Window→Show Panels.

• Finally, don't forget that your own computer offers several window management tools. For example, to fit more windows onto your screen, for example, you can make them smaller—in Windows, drag any window edge; on the Mac, drag the

Resize box in a window's lower-right corner. On Windows, you can also minimize all Dreamweaver windows by choosing Windows→Minimize All (or pressing Shift+F4); restore them all to their original sizes by choosing Windows→ Restore All (Alt+Shift+F4 [Option-Shift-F4]).

Figure 1-6:
In this figure, the History, Layers, and Frames panels are all presented in a single window. Clicking on a tab brings that panel forward. If you find that you use one of these panels all the time, you can move it to its own window by dragging its tab beyond the boundaries of the window. To add a panel to a window with other tabbed panels, drag its tab inside the window.

FREQUENTLY ASKED QUESTION

Where Did the Property Inspector Go?

Occasionally, one of the floating windows—the Property inspector, for example—simply disappears. Yet when you visit the Window menu, you still see a checkmark next to the window's name. In other words, that window is actually still open…somewhere.

This problem can result from accidentally dragging a window off the screen or from choosing a smaller screen resolution. Either way, simply choosing the window's name from the Window menu won't help you; you're just hiding or

showing a window that's beyond the boundaries of your monitor. Even quitting and restarting Dreamweaver is no use.

To get out of this predicament, choose Window→Arrange Panels to make the windows snap back to their default— and visible—locations on the screen.

This trick, however, doesn't work for the Site window. If you happen to drag *that* window off the screen, just quit and restart Dreamweaver to bring it back.

The Dreamweaver Test Drive

Although reading a book is a good way to learn the ins and outs of a program, nothing beats sitting in front of the computer and taking a program through its paces. Many of this book's chapters, therefore, conclude with hands-on training: step-by-step tutorials that take you through the creation of a real, working, professionally designed Web site for the fictional online magazine *Cosmopolitan Farmer*.

The rest of this chapter, for example, introduces Dreamweaver by taking you step-by-step through the process of building a Web page. It shouldn't take more than an hour. When it's over, you'll have learned the basic steps of building any Web page: creating and saving a new document, adding and formatting text, inserting graphics, and adding links.

If you're already using Dreamweaver and want to jump right into the details of the program, feel free to skip this tutorial. And if you're the type who likes to read first and try second, read Chapters 2 through 5, and then return to this chapter to practice what you've just learned.

Note: The tutorial in this chapter requires the example files from this book's Web site, *www.sawmac.com/ missing/*. Click the Tutorials link to go to the tutorials page. Download the Test Drive—Mac files link or Test Drive—Win files, depending on the kind of machine you're using (Mac or Windows).

After you've downloaded and decompressed the files, you should have a DWTutorial1 folder on your computer, containing the Web pages and graphics needed for this tutorial. If you're having difficulties, the Web site contains detailed instructions for downloading the files you'll be using with this book.

Phase 1: Creating a Web Site

Whenever you build a new Web site or edit an existing one, you must begin by introducing Dreamweaver to it—a process called *defining a site*. This simple process is the most important first step you should make when you start using Dreamweaver, whether you plan to work on a five-page Web site, build a thousand-page online store, or edit an existing Web site.

During this process—and, indeed, everywhere in Dreamweaver—you'll encounter a few terms frequently heard at Web-designer luncheons:

- **Root folder.** The first basic rule of Web design is that every piece of the site you're working on—all Web-page (HTML) documents, graphic images, sound files, and so on—must sit in one, single, main folder on your hard drive. That master folder is called the *root folder* for your Web site—in fact, it's the *local* root folder. ("Local" means *on your computer,* as opposed to the copies of these Web pages that will ultimately hang on the Internet. "Root" means "the master, outer, main folder, in which there may be plenty of subfolders.")

- **Local site.** The usual routine for creating Web pages goes like this: You first create the page on your own computer, using a program like Dreamweaver; then you upload it to a computer on the Internet called a Web server, where your handiwork becomes available to the masses. In other words, almost every Web site in the universe exists in two places at once. One copy is on the Internet, where everyone can get at it. The other, original copy is on some Web designer's hard drive.

  The copy on your own computer is called the *local site* or the *development* site. Think of the local site as a sort of staging ground, where you build your site, test it, and modify it. Because the local site isn't on a Web server, and can't be accessed by the Web-surfing public, you can freely edit and add to a local site without affecting the pages your visitors are viewing, meanwhile, on the remote site.

- **Remote site.** When you've added or updated a file, you move it from the local site to the *remote site*. The remote, or *live,* site is a mirror image of the local site.

Because you create it by uploading your local site, it has the same organizational folder structure as the local site, and it contains the same files. Only polished, fully-functional pages go online (to the remote site); save the half-finished, typo-ridden drafts for your local site. Chapter 16 explains how to use Dreamweaver's FTP features to define and work with a remote site.

Whenever you want to use Dreamweaver to create or edit a Web site, your first step is always to show the program where the root folder is—the master folder for all your Web site files. You do it like this:

1. **Choose Site→New Site.**

   The Site Definition window opens (see Figure 1-7). Although there are five different categories of options, you only need to give the site a name and designate a local root folder to get started.

2. **Type *Cosmo Farmer* in the Site Name field.**

   The name you type here is solely for your own reference, to help you identify the site in Dreamweaver's Site menu. It won't appear on the Web.

   In the next step, you'll tell Dreamweaver where your master root folder is. In this example, you'll use the folder you downloaded from this book's Web site; in other situations, you'll choose (or create) a folder of your own.

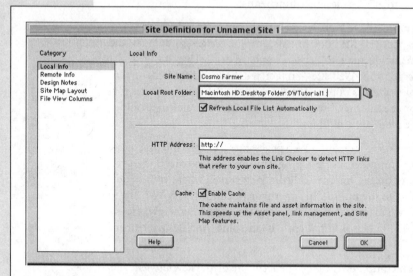

Figure 1-7:
The Site Definition dialog box is where you provide the information that Dreamweaver needs to manage the files in your Web site. To get started, you need to do only two things: Give the site a name and locate the Local Root Folder. Leave Enable Cache turned on; it lets Dreamweaver save information that will help it manage the links and files in your site (details in Chapter 14).

3. **Click the folder icon next to the Local Root Folder field.**

   The Choose Local Folder dialog box opens.

4. **Browse to and select the DWTutorial1 folder.**

The Mac and Windows versions of Dreamweaver handle this ritual a bit differently; see Figure 1-8.

You've just defined the *local root folder:* the folder on your computer where you'll store the HTML documents and graphics files that make up your Web site.

If you were starting a Web site from scratch, you could also create a new empty folder anywhere on your computer from the Choose Local Folder dialog box. You would then save your Web pages and graphics into this folder as you build your site.

For more on root folders and organizing Web sites, see Part IV. For now, the fact to burn into your brain is that all the files that will constitute your Web site must live, while you're working on them, in a single folder—the *local root folder.*

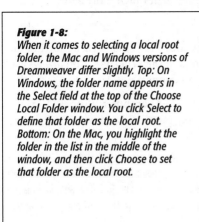

Figure 1-8:
When it comes to selecting a local root folder, the Mac and Windows versions of Dreamweaver differ slightly. Top: On Windows, the folder name appears in the Select field at the top of the Choose Local Folder window. You click Select to define that folder as the local root. Bottom: On the Mac, you highlight the folder in the list in the middle of the window, and then click Choose to set that folder as the local root.

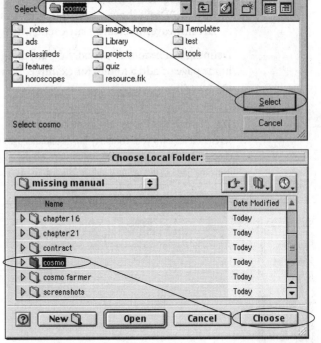

5. **Back in the Site Definition window, turn on Refresh Local File List Automatically.**

This option ensures that the file list in the Site window (a master window that lists every file involved in your Web site) will be automatically updated when you add new files to the site.

If you were creating a Web site for yourself (or a client), you'd take another step here, too: In the HTTP Address field, you would specify the address your site will have once it's on the Internet, staring with *http://*. Adding a URL in this field helps with Dreamweaver's link-checking feature, which is discussed on page 396. (This step is necessary only if your Web site uses *absolute links* to link to pages in your site. See page 82 for more on absolute links.)

6. **Make sure Enable Cache is turned on.**

   Dreamweaver creates a small database (cache) that tracks pages, links, images, and other assets in your site. The cache helps Dreamweaver's site management tools avoid breaking links, warn you when you're about to delete important files, and help you reorganize your site quickly. If you turn off the site cache, Dreamweaver will still track this information—but much more slowly.

7. **Click OK.**

   If a dialog box warns that Dreamweaver is about to create a cache for this site, turn on "Don't show me this message again" and then click OK. You *always* want Dreamweaver to create a site cache when you define a new site.

Defining a site doesn't actually do anything to your computer; it doesn't create a home page or add a folder, for example. It merely prepares Dreamweaver for working on a site.

Tip: Dreamweaver lets you define multiple Web sites, a handy feature if you're a Web designer with several clients, or if your company builds and manages more than one site. To define an additional site, choose Site→New Site and follow the steps on page 24. You can then switch from one site to another using the Site List in the Site window (see Figure 14-3).

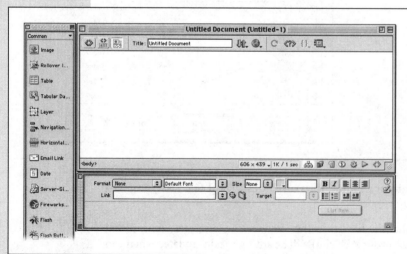

Figure 1-9:
The three most important windows are the document window, Objects panel, and Property inspector. You can close all other windows for now. (If you don't see the Objects panel or Property inspector, choose Window→Objects or Window→Properties. And if you don't see the document window, simply press Ctrl+N [⌘-N] to create a new document.)

Phase 2: Setting Page Properties

As noted at the beginning of this chapter, Dreamweaver has many different windows that help you build Web pages. For this tutorial, though, you'll need only three: the Objects panel, document window, and Property inspector (see Figure 1-9).

Before beginning the Web site construction in earnest, though, you'll help yourself greatly by adjusting a few Dreamweaver preferences like this:

1. **Choose Edit→Preferences.**

   The Preferences dialog box opens (see Figure 1-10).

2. **Make sure the General category is selected; choose Icons and Text from the Object Panel menu.**

   The Objects panel usually appears as a long column of confusing icons. You've just told the program that you want to see not only the icons, but also a short text description that identifies the purpose of each button on the Objects panel, as shown in Figure 1-4.

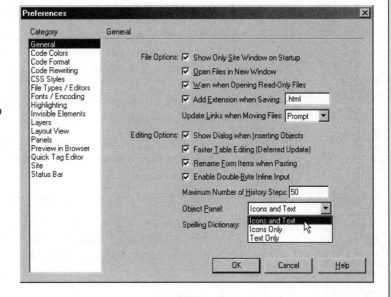

Figure 1-10:
Dreamweaver's Preferences dialog box is a smorgasbord of choices that let you customize the program to work and look they way you want. In this step, you're adding labels to the cryptic icons on the Objects panel, so you'll know what the heck they're for.

3. **Click Invisible Elements in the Category list on the left side of the Preferences dialog box. Make sure the fourth option, Line Breaks, is turned on.**

   You'll see why this option is useful in the coming steps.

4. **Click OK.**

   The dialog box closes; you're ready to start building a Web site.

Phase 3: Saving and Modifying a Web Page

"Enough already! I want to build a Web page," you're probably saying. You'll do that in this phase of the tutorial.

1. **Click inside the document window and choose File→Save.**

   The Save As dialog box opens.

2. **Save the page as *advertise.html* in the folder DWTutorial1.**

   Make sure you save this page into the correct folder. In Phase 1, you defined the DWTutorial1 folder as the *root* of the site—the folder that holds all the pages and files for the site. If you save the page outside of this folder, Dreamweaver will get confused, and its site management features won't work correctly.

Tip: Most operating systems let you save files with long names, spaces and other characters, such as #, $, &, and /. But some browsers and servers have trouble interpreting anything other than letters and numbers; for example, Netscape 4 can't find files with spaces in their names. Play it safe: use only letters, numbers, and—if you want a good substitute for a space—the underline or underscore character _ (Shift-hyphen).

Your Web-page documents also need a filename extension at the end of the file name, such as *index.html*. Web servers rely on file extensions like .htm, .html, .gif, and .jpg to know whether a file is a Web page, graphic, or some other type of file. Windows automatically adds the extension to your saved document names; but on the Mac, which lets you save files without extensions, you need to type the suffix *.html* or *.htm* when you save a Dreamweaver document.

---

3. **If the document window toolbar isn't already open (see Figure 1-1), choose View→Toolbar to display it.**

   The toolbar at the top of the document window, new in Dreamweaver 4, provides easy access to a variety of tasks you'll perform frequently, such as titling a page, previewing it in a Web browser, and looking at the HTML source code.

4. **Click in the Title field in the toolbar; type *Advertise with Cosmopolitan Farmer*.**

   The Title field lets you set a page's title—the information that appears in the title bar of a Web browser. The page title is also what shows up as the name of your Web page when someone searches the Web using a search engine like Yahoo or Google.

Tip: Try this simple experiment: Go to *www.altavista.com* and search for "Untitled Document." You'll find that the Web is strewn with thousands upon thousands of Web pages without titles, many of which were created with Dreamweaver.

That's because, when you create a new Web page, Dreamweaver assigns it the not-so-glamorous title Untitled Document—and all too many people forget to change that dummy text to something more meaningful. Not only does Untitled Document look very unprofessional on a Web page, but since search pages often display page titles in their results, an untitled page looks terrible in a search engine. (Fortunately, Dreamweaver has tool to fix just this problem. Page 405 has the details.)

---

5. **Choose Modify→Page Properties.**

The Page Properties dialog box opens (see Figure 1-11), in which you can define the basic attributes of each Web page you create; it's a good idea to do this as soon as you create and save a page.

You'll notice that the Title of the page is already set; you typed it into the toolbar in the previous step.

6. **Click the small gray box next to the word Background; using the eyedropper cursor, click a black square on the pop-up color palette.**

When you create a new document in Dreamweaver, the page background is white, just as in a word processor. But if white pages don't inspire your design sense, you're not stuck. Using this pop-up palette, you can choose any background color you want (or you can type in the hexadecimal number of the color you want, if you're an HTML guru). Both the palette and the hexadecimal color-specifying field reappear fairly often in Dreamweaver.

In this case, you've just set the background color of the Web page to black.

Tip: You can even fill the background of your page with a graphic—to add a subtle pattern or texture, or to put the company logo in the background as a "watermark."

To choose a background image, click the Browse button shown in Figure 1-11. This opens a window that lets you search for the graphic you want to use. Be careful with background images, however; if there's a lot of contrast and detail in your background image, it can easily obscure the rest of the content on the page.

Figure 1-11:
The Page Properties dialog box lets you set general properties of a Web page, such as the color of text and links. Clicking a color box opens the color selector. You can choose one of the colors in the palette or even use the eyedropper to sample a color from your document window. Mac users can sample colors from anywhere on their screen—even from open documents in other applications.

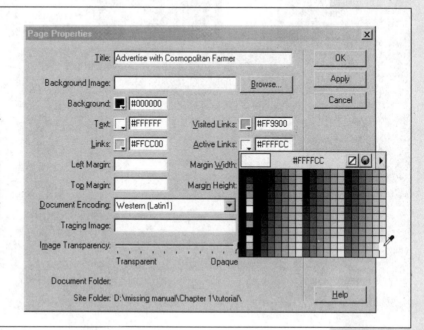

7. **Click the small black box next to the Text label; from the pop-up color palette, choose white (or type** *#FFFFFF* **into the box beside the palette square).**

By default, text appears in black on a Web page. But since you just set the background of this page to black, the text needs to be a light color—white, in this case—to be readable. (White will just be the proposed color; you will be able to override this color on a case-by-case basis, as you'll see later in this tutorial.)

Using Dreamweaver's Color Box

The innocent-looking gray box on the Property inspector and in various Dreamweaver dialog boxes is called the color box. Click it for a pop-up rainbow palette of color choices.

You can choose a color for the selected Web-page element in any of three ways: First, you can click one of the colors available on the color palette.

Second, you can use the eyedropper cursor that appears when you click. This cursor is "loaded"; you can click any color visible on your screen—even outside the dialog box you're in—to select a color, a trick that comes in handy when you want to use a color from a graphic you've placed in

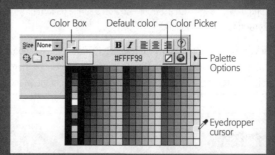

Color Box   Default color — Color Picker

#FFFF99 — Palette Options

Eyedropper cursor

your document. Mac users can even sample a color from another application: just move the eyedropper over the color and click. (This click may take you out of Dreamweaver; just return to Dreamweaver and you'll see that the color you sampled has been applied.)

Finally, you can click the Color Picker icon, identified here, to launch the Mac or Windows color-picker dialog box, which lets you choose from among millions of colors.

If you decide you don't want to add color, or you want to remove a color you've already applied, click the Default Color button. Without a specific color setting, Web browsers will use default colors for the element in question (black for text, for example).

Next to the color box is a blank text field. If you know your Web colors, you can type their *hex codes* into this box, which is sometimes more precise than clicking the palette.

In a hex code, a Web color is represented by a six-digit code like this: #FF0000. (Hexadecimal notation is a system computers use for counting; it's what you'd use for counting, too, if you had 16 fingers. In this system, you count like this: 0, 1, 2, 3, 4, 5, 6, 7, 8, 9, A, B, C, D, F. The # tells the computer that the following sequence is a series of hex numbers, in this case three pairs of them.) The best way to learn a color's hex value is to choose it by clicking it in the palette, and then looking at the code that Dreamweaver writes into the text box next to it.

You can choose a different set of rainbow colors (the ones that appear in the palette), too, if necessary, by using the Palette Options menu. You can choose from among five different palettes: Color Cubes, Continuous Tone, Windows OS, Mac OS, and Grayscale. The first two palettes contain the Web-safe color palette (colors that most browsers on most machines will reliably display in the same shades you pick) in different arrangements. The Windows OS and Mac OS palettes display the colors available on those respective operating systems when in 256 color mode. Finally, the grayscale palette offers 256 somber shades of gray; you'll find them useful primarily when building Ingmar Bergman tribute sites.

8. **In the Links color field, type *#FFCC00;* in the Visited Links field, type *#FF9900;* and in the Active Links color field, type *#FFFFCC.***

   These are *hexadecimal* codes (see the facing page).

   Links come in three varieties. An *active* link is one you're clicking at this moment; a *visited* link is one you've already been to, as noted in a browser's History list. Finally, a *regular* link is a plain old link, unvisited, untouched. You can choose different colors for each of these link states.

   While it may seem a bit like overkill to have three different colors for links, the regular and visited link colors can provide useful feedback by indicating which links your visitors have already followed, and which remain to be checked out.

9. **Check the margins; adjust them, if you like.**

   Most browsers put a little bit of space between the contents of your Web page and the top and left sides of the browser window; the exact amount of this margin varies from browser to browser. If you like, you can change the default setting so that the browser adds more space to the top and left side of the page—or eliminates the margin altogether.

   Unfortunately, Internet Explorer and Netscape Navigator use different terms for the top and left margins, so you need to set all four of the Margin boxes here if you want to see the same size margins in the two browsers. In Internet Explorer, the number you put into Dreamweaver's Left Margin and Top Margin boxes define the distance between your page contents and the left and top of the browser window, measured in pixels.

   In Netscape browsers, Dreamweaver's Margin Width box defines the space from the *left* edge of the window, and Margin Height for the space from the *top.*

Tip: To completely eliminate margins, type *0* in each margin field. That's a useful setup when you want a graphic, such as a banner, to butt directly up to the top and left edges of the browser window.

Setting all four of these options won't cause any problems with the different browsers; Internet Explorer simply ignores the Netscape-specific code, and vice versa.

Figure 1-12:
The title bar reveals both the page title (which appears in the title bar of a Web browser and gets listed as a bookmark or favorite); the file name is the name of the document saved onto your disk drive.

Page title   File name

Advertise with Cosmopolitan Farmer (DWTutorial1/advertise.html)

Title: Advertise with Cosmopolitan Farme

For this tutorial, you don't need to set any margins, but keep this discussion in mind when you start building your own pages.

10. **Click OK to close the window and apply these changes.**

    You return to your document window (see Figure 1-12). If you see an asterisk next to the filename at the top of the window, it means you've made changes to the page since you last saved it.

11. **Choose File→Save (or press Ctrl+S [⌘-S]).**

    Saving your work frequently not only prevents a headache if the power goes out as you finish that beautiful—but unsaved—home page, but also ensures that you won't have problems setting up links later. (Links are often dependent on where a page is saved in the folder structure of a site, as described in Chapter 4.)

Phase 4: Adding Images and Text

Now you'll add the real meat of your Web page: words and pictures.

1. **Click the Image button on the Objects panel.**

    Alternatively, choose Insert→Image. Either way, the Select Image Source dialog box opens.

2. **Browse to the *images* folder in the DWTutorial1 folder; double-click the graphics file called *banner.gif*.**

    The banner picture appears at the top of the page, as shown in Figure 1-13. A thin border appears around the image, indicating that it's selected. The Property inspector changes to reflect the properties of the image.

Figure 1-13:
When an image is selected in the document window, the Property inspector reveals its dimensions. In the top left corner, a small thumbnail image appears, as does the word Image—to let you know an image is selected—and the image's file size (in this case, 10 K). The other image properties are described in Chapter 5.

3. **In the Alt field in the Property inspector, type *Advertising Information*.**

    An image's *Alt* property is a text description of the graphic. It's important to add a text label for each graphic on your Web page. Two populations will thank you:

First, there are the people who deliberately *turn off* pictures in their Web browsers, in exchange for a dramatic speed-up in the appearance of Web pages; second, visually impaired people often use software that reads the text of Web pages aloud. In both cases, Alt labels are all these visitors will have to go on.

4. **Deselect the image by clicking anywhere in the document window outside of the image. Press Enter to create a new paragraph. Type** *Ad Sizes and Rates.*

   The Property inspector now displays text-formatting options.

Note: The key called Enter on a Windows keyboard is called Return on some Macintosh keyboards. If you have a Mac, you can press either Return or Enter.

---

5. **From the Format menu in the Property inspector, choose Heading 1.**

   This Format pop-up menu (Figure 1-14) offers a number of different paragraph types, as described on page 57. Because you're about to type a heading for your page, you've used the Heading 1 style, which makes text big and bold.

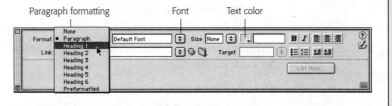

Figure 1-14:
When you're editing text, the Property inspector offers formatting controls for your text.

6. **Press Enter to create another new paragraph. Type this:** *Cosmopolitan Farmer offers 3 sizes and rates for advertisements.*

   Oops—this text is as big as the first line you typed. A quick look at the Property inspector shows you why: this paragraph is also formatted as a Heading 1. But because the insertion point is still in the new paragraph, you can change its style just by choosing from the Format menu again.

7. **From the Format menu in the Property inspector, choose Paragraph.**

   The text shrinks to a smaller size and the bold formatting disappears; you've selected standard Paragraph formatting. It's a bit dull, so you'll spice up its appearance like this:

8. **Highlight the entire sentence you've most recently typed.**

   You can do so by dragging carefully across the entire line. (Unlike the Format menu, which affects an entire paragraph, the Font menu, which you're going to use next, only applies to *selected* text. See page 57 for more on the distinction between paragraph and font formatting.)

9. **From the Font menu in the Property inspector, choose "Arial, Helvetica, Sans-Serif."**

The sentence is now displayed in another font. (Why is more than one font listed for each choice in the Font menu? Turn to page 70 to find out.)

Next, you'll want to italicize the name of your publication:

10. **Select the words "Cosmopolitan Farmer," and then click the button labeled *I* in the top row of the Property inspector.**

The *I* button, of course, means *italics;* Dreamweaver italicizes your selection.

For added attractiveness, you can now add a horizontal line (a *rule,* as designers call it) underneath the text you've typed so far:

11. **Click at the end of the last sentence to place the cursor there. Press Enter to create a blank line, and then click the Horizontal Rule button in the Objects panel.**

(If you can't identify the Horizontal Rule button, turn on text labels for your Objects panel as described on page 27.) Dreamweaver inserts a line across the page. It's highlighted, meaning that the Property inspector is showing its characteristics.

12. **With the horizontal rule still selected, type *580* in the W field of the Property inspector. Press Enter.**

By default, the width of a horizontal line is 100%—meaning that it spans the entire width of a browser window, no matter how wide the window is. You've just changed your selected line's width to 580 pixels wide.

13. **From the Align menu in the Property inspector, choose Left.**

Normally, a horizontal rule is centered in the middle of a page. Now the line is aligned to the left, to match the alignment of the text and graphics on the page.

Next, you'll add a subhead to the page, a graphic, and set of bulleted information points.

14. **Click below the horizontal rule and type *Square Button.* From the Format menu in the Property inspector, choose Heading 2.**

The text for Square Button (one of the online ad sizes your Web site will be offering) changes style. It's now bigger and bolder, though smaller than the first paragraph—the Heading 1—at the top of the page. Now add some additional formatting to this text:

15. **Select the text you just typed; choose "Arial, Helvetica, Sans-Serif" from the Font menu in the Property inspector.**

A quick way to select a paragraph is to click the <h2> that appears in the lower left-hand corner of the document window (the tag selector, which lets you quickly and accurately select HTML tags—in this case, the Heading 2 tag).

To add some visual variety to the page, you'll color this heading.

16. **With the text still selected, click the Color box in the Property inspector. From the pop-up palette, choose a light yellow color.**

    The text changes to the color you selected.

17. **Click at the end of the line of text; press Enter.**

    Notice that the Property inspector shows all of the formatting of the previous paragraph: Heading 2, same font, yellow color. You don't want those settings for this paragraph, so you need to get rid of them.

18. **Choose Window→HTML Styles.**

    The HTML Styles panel window opens. You'll learn about the HTML Styles panel in the next section of this tutorial; but for now, you'll use it to eliminate the current text formatting.

19. **In the HTML Styles panel, click the Clear Paragraph Style button.**

    All of the formatting is gone. You're left with a plain, unformatted paragraph. (If this step didn't work, make sure the Apply checkbox at the bottom of the HTML Styles panel is turned on.)

    Now you'll add another image—a sample advertisement—to the page.

20. **Click the Image button on the Objects panel (or choose Insert→Image). Browse to the *images* folder in the DWTutorial1 folder; double-click the file called *square_ad.jpg*.**

    A square ad for Cosmopolitan Farmer appears. It would look better if it were indented a bit.

21. **Click to the right of the image to deselect it.**

    A tall, blinking insertion point should appear just to the right of the image.

22. **Click the Indent button on the Property inspector (see Figure 1-15).**

    Dreamweaver indents the picture.

23. **Hit the Enter key to create a new paragraph. Click the Bulleted List button in the Property inspector.**

Figure 1-15:
Many of the Property inspector text formatting options are similar to tools you'd find in a word processing program.

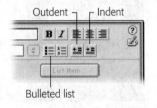

Next, you'll be adding a series of bulleted items that explain the size and cost of a "Square Button" ad in Cosmopolitan Farmer.

24. Type *$100 for one month*; hit Enter. Type *Dimensions: 125 x 125* and hit Enter. Click the Bulleted List button again to end the list.

You can also click the Outdent button to do the same thing.

You've just added a list with two bulleted items and reset the formatting to a regular paragraph—no indent and no fancy formatting. Next, you'll add another horizontal rule.

25. Click the Horizontal Rule button in the Objects panel.

Dreamweaver inserts a line across the page. It's highlighted, meaning that it's selected.

26. Click in the W field of the Property inspector; type *580*. From the Align menu in the Property inspector, choose Left.

As you did once before, you just created a horizontal rule of a specified width and aligned against the left edge of the window.

Your Web page in progress should now look like the one shown in Figure 1-16.

27. Choose File→Save.

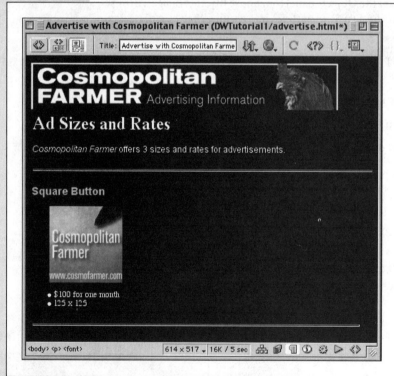

Figure 1-16:
The Web page is starting to come together. You've added graphics, text, and horizontal rules, as well as played with some of the text formatting options available in the Property inspector.

Phase 5: Preview Your Work

Dreamweaver is a *visual* HTML application, meaning that for the most part, what you see in the document window is what you'll get on the web.

At least that's how it's supposed to work. But Dreamweaver may display *more* information than you'll see on the Web (including "invisible" objects, table borders, and other elements that you won't see in a Web browser), and may display *less* (it sometimes has trouble showing complex designs and Cascading Style Sheet information).

Furthermore, much to the woe of Web designers, different Web browsers display pages differently. In some cases, the differences may be subtle (perhaps text may be slightly larger or smaller). Other times, the difference is dramatic; Layers, for example, an advanced design technology discussed in Chapter 12, are notoriously finicky in Netscape 4, while much more predictable in Internet Explorer. Throughout this book, you'll find tips and techniques to deal with this problem.

If you're designing Web pages for use on a company intranet, and only have to worry about the one Web browser your IT department has put on everyone's computer, you're lucky. But most sites must withstand scrutiny by a wide range of browsers; it's a good idea to preview your Web pages using whatever browsers you expect visitors to your Web sites to use. Fortunately, Dreamweaver lets you preview a Web page using any browser you have installed on your computer.

Before you can preview a page, you need to set up your list of browsers:

1. **Choose File→Preview in Browser→Edit Browser List.**

   The Preview in Browser preferences window opens (see Figure 1-17).

2. **Click the + button.**

   The Add Browser or Select Browser window opens.

3. **Click the Browse button. Search your hard drive to find the browser application you most frequently use and select it.**

   Dreamweaver inserts the browser's default name in the Name field of the Add Browser window. If you wish to change its name for display purposes within Dreamweaver, select it and type a new name. (Don't do this *before* selecting the browser, however; Dreamweaver erases anything you might have typed after you select a browser.)

4. **Turn on the Primary Browser box. Click OK.**

   You've just designated the browser as your *primary* browser while working in Dreamweaver. You can now preview your pages in this browser with a simple keyboard shortcut: F12.

   If you like, you can also choose a secondary browser, which you'll be able to launch by pressing the Ctrl+F12 (⌘-F12) key combination.

   Now you're ready to preview your document in a real, bona fide Web browser:

5. **Press the F12 key (or choose Edit→Preview in Browser and select a browser from the menu).**

The F12 key is the most important keyboard shortcut you'll learn. It opens your Web page in your primary browser, letting you preview your work.

Macintosh note: In Mac OS 9, the F12 shortcut in Dreamweaver may not work. OS 9 lets you define the function keys to be launching keys, so that they open programs or documents of your choosing. Unfortunately, this "hot keys" feature intercepts Fkey presses in other applications, including Dreamweaver.

To turn off this feature so that you can use the predefined function-key commands in programs like Dreamweaver, choose ⌘→Control Panels→Keyboard. Turn off the Hot Function Key Settings checkbox and click OK.

---

6. **When you're done previewing the page, go back to Dreamweaver.**

Do so using your favorite way to switch programs on your computer—by using the Windows Taskbar or the Macintosh Application menu, for example.

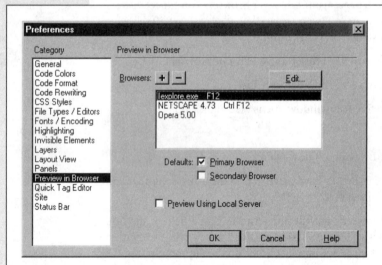

Figure 1-17:
You can tell Dreamweaver which browsers you wish to use for previewing your Web pages in the Preferences window. You can set the browser to be your primary browser, accessible by the F12 key, or your secondary browser, accessible by Ctrl+F12 (⌘-F12). Additional browsers can be added to the list. To preview a page with a browser other than the primary or secondary, choose File→Preview in Browser and select the appropriate browser from the submenu.

Phase 6: Formatting with Style

Dreamweaver 4 is about productivity—doing things quickly and well. The program is crammed with useful tools that streamline the Web production process.

One of these is the HTML Styles tool. It's designed to let you apply lots of individual text formatting steps with a single click. In this next section, you'll add more information to the Web page, taking advantage of Dreamweaver's power to do it more quickly.

1. **Click below the last horizontal rule in the document window; type *Full Banner*.**

   Notice that there's no formatting. Since the text is a heading of the same importance as the "Square Button" paragraph above it, it would be nice to make it look the same. You could follow the same steps as you did for formatting that text, but there's a better way.

2. **If the HTML Styles panel isn't open, choose Window→HTML Styles.**

   The HTML Styles dialog box appears.

3. **Click anywhere in the heading "Square Button," then click the New Style (+) button in the lower-right corner of the HTML Styles panel.**

   The Define HTML Style window opens (see Figure 1-18).

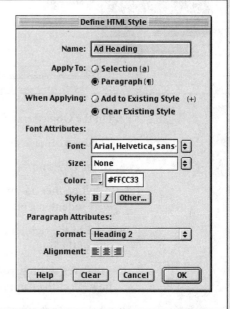

Figure 1-18:
The Define HTML Styles window lets you define a variety of formatting options that you can apply to text with a single click. Chapter 3 discusses HTML Styles in depth.

4. **In the Name field, type *Ad Heading;* click OK.**

   Notice that the HTML Styles panel has a new Ad Heading style listed. You've just defined a *style*—a canned set of predefined formatting characteristics (bold, large type, red, centered, or whatever) based on the formatting you added by hand to the "Square Button" subhead. In the next step, you'll apply all of these formatting traits with a single click to another piece of text.

5. **Click anywhere in the text "Full Banner." In the HTML Styles panel, click Ad Heading. (See Figure 1-19.)**

   Voila! Dreamweaver formats the text instantly. (If not, make sure the Apply checkbox in the HTML Styles panel is turned on.)

Now it's time to add another graphic—a sample full banner ad—and a set of bulleted information points, just as you did for the "Square Button" section.

6. **Click at the end of the paragraph and press Enter to create a new paragraph. On the HTML Styles panel, click the Clear Paragraph Style button.**

   Doing so strips away all formatting in this paragraph, creating a clean slate for adding and formatting new text or images.

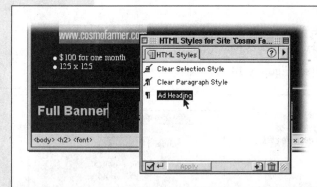

Figure 1-19:
HTML Styles let you apply many text formatting options with a single click. Just make sure the Apply checkbox at the bottom of the HTML Styles panel is turned on.

7. **On the Objects panel, click the Image button (or choose Insert→Image).**

   The Insert Image dialog box appears.

8. **In the DWTutorial1→images folder, double-click the file *full_banner_ad.gif*.**

   A full banner ad for Cosmopolitan Farmer appears. It would look better if it were indented a bit.

9. **Click to the right of the image to deselect it and place the insertion point at the end of the line.**

   Whatever settings you change on the Property inspector, in other words, will now affect the paragraph that contains the graphic.

10. **Click the Indent button on the Property inspector.**

    Dreamweaver indents the paragraph by a preset amount. See page 62 for more on indenting (and reversing indenting) paragraphs in Dreamweaver.

    Finally, you're ready to add the last bit of information about this ad option.

11. **Hit Enter to create a new paragraph; click the Bulleted List button in the Property inspector.**

    You've just added a bullet at the beginning of the paragraph.

12. **Type *$560 for one month*, and then press Enter; type *Dimensions: 468 x 60,* and then press Enter.**

    You've just created two bulleted items.

13. Click the Bulleted List button again to end the list.

   To wrap up, you'll insert another horizontal line beneath your ad rates:

14. Click the Horizontal Rule button in the Objects panel.

   Dreamweaver inserts the line; you'll need to make it look like the other lines.

15. With the rule still selected, click in the W field of the Property inspector and type *580*. From the Align menu in the Property inspector, choose Left.

   The line moves to the left edge of the window, just like the other lines.

16. Choose File→Save.

Phase 7: Finishing the Page

You've covered most of the steps you'll need to finish this Web page. All you need to do now is add the rest of the ad sizes and rates, add some contact information, and add a copyright notice:

1. Click below the last horizontal rule in the document window; type *Half Banner*. Repeat steps 5-16 of the previous instructions to add and format the final ad size and rates.

   You'll use the graphic called *half_banner_ad.gif* located in the Images folder. The two bulleted items of text should read: "$230 for one month" and "Dimensions: 234 x 60."

2. Click below the last horizontal rule on the page; type *Contact Information*. Choose Heading 1 from the Format menu in the Property inspector.

   You've just created a big, bold heading.

3. Press the Enter key; choose Paragraph from the Format menu in the Property inspector. Choose "Arial, Helvetica, Sans-Serif" from the Font menu.

   You've set up the formatting in advance for the typing you're about to do:

4. Type *The sales staff at Cosmopolitan Farmer would be happy to take your money. Contact us and we'll make it so. Call us at 555-768-9090 or email our* (don't type a final period).

   Web pages can contain email links—a link that opens your visitor's email program, and automatically adds an email address to a new message. Dreamweaver has a built-in function for adding this type of link.

5. Click the Insert Email Link button in the Objects panel (or choose Insert→Email Link).

   The Insert Email Link dialog box opens.

7. Type *Advertising Department* in the Text field.

   This is the text that will appear on the Web page.

8. **Type *adsales@cosmofarmer.com* in the Email field, and then click OK.**

   Notice that "Advertising Department" appears on the page underlined and in yellow. This is the formatting for links on this page. The email address *adsales@cosmofarmer.com,* however, is embedded into the link of the page. It may be invisible to your audience, but a Web browser knows it's there.

9. **Press Enter to create a new paragraph.**

   A blank line appears. You'll add some text and a link to another Web site.

10. **Type *For more information on online advertising, visit the Internet Advertising Bureau.***

11. **Select the words "Internet Advertising Bureau."**

    You'll turn these words into a link.

12. **In the Link field in the Property inspector, type *http://www.iab.net;* then press Enter.**

    You've just added an *external link.* When you preview this page and click that link, you'll be taken to the home page for the Internet Advertising Bureau.

13. **Press Enter and add another 580-pixel horizontal rule to the page.**

    In other words, repeat steps 14 and 15 of the previous instructions. This line, like the other ones you've added, helps break up the page into distinct sections.

14. **Click below that last line and type *Copyright 2001, Cosmopolitan Farmer.***

    No page is complete without stamping your legal rights onto it. But that doesn't mean you have to rub it in anyone's face, so you'll make the text a little less noticeable, like this:

15. **Select your copyright-notice text; from the Size menu in the Property inspector, choose 2.**

    The text shrinks one size. (See page 73 for an explanation of why Dreamweaver doesn't offer the traditional list of font point sizes.)

16. **Choose File→Save. Press the F12 key to preview your work in your browser.**

Congratulations! You've just built your first Web page in Dreamweaver, complete with graphics, formatted text, and links. If you'd like to compare your work with an actual, Internet-posted version of the same page, visit the tutorial page for this book, *www.sawmac.com/missing/tutorials.*

Much of the work building Web sites involves the procedures covered in this tutorial—defining a site, adding links, formatting text, and inserting graphics. The next few chapters cover these basics in greater depth and introduce other important tools, tips, and techniques for using Dreamweaver to build great Web pages.

Adding Text to Your Web Pages

Broadband Internet media, like streaming video, audio, and high-res graphics, have been grabbing a lot of headlines lately. After all, it's exciting to speculate about the Web replacing your telephone, or tapping your keyboard to get movies on demand.

But the Web is primarily woven with *words;* Steven King novellas, Sony PlayStation 2 reviews, and tour dates for Britney Spears's upcoming concerts still drive people to the Web. As you build Web pages and Web sites, you'll spend a lot of your time adding and formatting *text*. Understanding how Dreamweaver works with text will take you a long way toward making your next great Web site.

This chapter covers the not-always-simple act of getting text *into* your Dreamweaver documents; in Chapter 3, you can read about formatting this text, so that it looks like the professionally designed Web pages you see every day.

Adding Text in Dreamweaver

In many ways, Dreamweaver works like a word processing program. When you create a new document, the blinking cursor appears at the top of the page; you can begin typing. When you finish a paragraph, press Enter or Return to start a new one. Text, as well as anything else you add to a Web page, starts at the top of the page and works its way down to the bottom.

Adding Special Characters

Using your keyboard to add text in Dreamweaver works well, but many useful special characters, such as copyright or trademark symbols, don't appear on the keys on your keyboard, and are difficult or impossible to type. The Character category of the Objects panel lets you insert a variety of symbols and international characters quickly by clicking an icon.

To open this panel:

1. **Choose Window→Objects to open the Objects panel, if it isn't already open.**

   The keyboard shortcut Ctrl+F2 (⌘-F2) works, too.

2. **Click the arrow at the top of the panel; select Character from the menu.**

   The palette shown in Figure 2-1 appears, offering a wide range of symbols and international characters. Unlike regular Western characters, such as *a* or *z*, these special characters are represented in HTML by a code name or number. For instance, a trademark symbol (™) is written in HTML as *&#153*.

3. **Click a special character's button on the Objects panel.**

   Dreamweaver inserts the appropriate HTML code into your Web page.

Caution: If you set the encoding of your Web page to anything other than Western in the Page Properties window (Modify→Page Properties), you can reliably insert only line breaks and nonbreaking spaces. The other special characters available from the Character category of the Objects panel may not work.

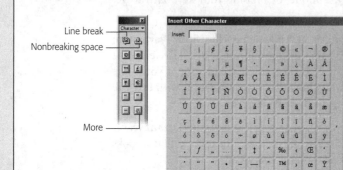

Line break
Nonbreaking space

More

Figure 2-1:
The More button on the Objects panel (left) brings up the Insert Other Character dialog box (right). There are even more characters available than are listed in this dialog box (they're listed at www. ramsch.org/ martin/uni/fmi-hp/iso8859-1.html. *To add a character not shown in the dialog box, type its name or number in the Insert field and click OK.*

Line breaks

Pressing Enter creates a new paragraph, exactly as in a word processor. Unfortunately, Web browsers automatically insert a blank line's worth of extra space above and below paragraphs—which can be a real nuisance if you're trying to create several single-spaced lines of text, like this:

702 A Street
The Dalles, OR 98789
USA

Each part of the address is on its own line, but it's still just a single paragraph (and shares the overall formatting of that paragraph, as you'll learn in the next chapter).

To create this effect, you need to insert a *line break* at the insertion point, using one of these techniques:

- Click the Line Break icon from the Character category of the Objects panel, as described on the facing page.

- Choose Insert→Special Characters→Line Break.

- Press Shift-Enter.

Tip: When you place a line break in Dreamweaver, you may get no visual hint that it's even there; after all, a regular paragraph break and a line break both create a new line of text. At times, this can be a big problem; copying and pasting text from email, for instance, sometimes adds unwanted line breaks. A line break may go unnoticed, too, if it occurs at the end of a long line.

Fortunately, you can bring those line breaks out of hiding. Choose Edit→Preferences, or press Ctrl+U (⌘-U) and click on the Invisible Elements category. Make sure the Line Breaks checkbox is turned on; click OK. Now you'll see each Line Break appear as a small gold shield (⬚).

Nonbreaking spaces

You may have noticed that if you type more than one space in a row, Dreamweaver ignores all but the first space. This isn't a glitch in the program; it's standard HTML. Web browsers ignore any spaces following the first one.

Therefore, a line like "Hello   to   you," which contains ten spaces between each word, would appear on a Web page like this: "Hello to you." Not only do Web browsers ignore multiple spaces, but they also ignore any spaces that aren't *between* words. So if you hit the Space bar a couple of times to indent the first line of a paragraph, you're out of luck; a Web browser won't display any of those spaces.

This may seem like good sense, but there are times when it's useful to add a space before the beginning of a word. For instance, adding spaces at the beginning of a paragraph can simulate a first-line indent, which is otherwise impossible to create using HTML.

There may be times, too, when you *need* more than one space in a row. Consider the text navigation bar at the bottom of a Web page, a common Web-page element that lists the different sections of a Web site. Once they've reached the bottom of the page, visitors can then click one of the section titles and jump to a different area of the site.

To keep the sections visually distinct, some designers like to add multiple spaces between the section titles, like this:

News   Classifieds   Jobs

This is where the *nonbreaking space* can help out. It looks just like a regular space, but it acts as glue that prevents the words on either side from being split apart at the end of a line. (That's why it's called a nonbreaking space.)

But when designing Web pages, you'll probably be interested in this fascinating cousin of the regular Space bar for a different reason: it's the only "text spacer" you can use in HTML text.

To insert a nonbreaking space, click where you want it, and then do one of these:

- Click the Nonbreaking Space icon on the Character category of the Objects panel.

- Choose Insert→Special Characters→Nonbreaking Space.

- Press Ctrl+Shift+Space bar (⌘-Shift-Space bar).

Adding a Date to Your Page

The Common category of the Objects panel offers an icon called Date Object. Clicking on its icon (⊞) or choosing Insert→Date opens the Insert Date dialog box (Figure 2-2). Either step makes Dreamweaver insert today's date (as your computer understands it) onto your Web page in progress. In addition to the date, you can also specify whether to include the day of the week and the current time.

Select the format you wish from the Date Format list. There are thirteen different formats to choose from, such as March 7, 1974 or 3/7/74.

You may wonder why Dreamweaver includes an insert date function anyway. How hard is it to just type *Thursday, July 12?*

But the real value of this feature lies in the Update Automatically on Save checkbox. Turning on this option forces Dreamweaver to *update* the date each time you save the document.

Many designers use this feature to stamp their Web pages with dates that indicate when the contents were last updated. For example, you might type *This page was last*

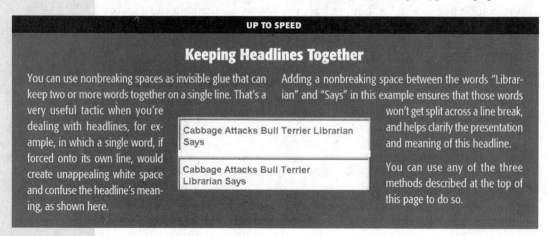

UP TO SPEED

Keeping Headlines Together

You can use nonbreaking spaces as invisible glue that can keep two or more words together on a single line. That's a very useful tactic when you're dealing with headlines, for example, in which a single word, if forced onto its own line, would create unappealing white space and confuse the headline's meaning, as shown here.

> Cabbage Attacks Bull Terrier Librarian Says

> Cabbage Attacks Bull Terrier Librarian Says

Adding a nonbreaking space between the words "Librarian" and "Says" in this example ensures that those words won't get split across a line break, and helps clarify the presentation and meaning of this headline.

You can use any of the three methods described at the top of this page to do so.

revised on: before inserting the date object. Now, each time you make a change to the page, Dreamweaver will automatically change the date to reflect when you saved the document. You never again have to worry about it.

Figure 2-2:
When you insert a date object into a Web page, you have two additional options: If you want to add the day of the week–Thursday, for example– choose the format you want from the Day Format pop-up menu (top). You may also choose to add the current time in hours and minutes–in either military time (22:18) or regular time (10:18 PM)– from the Time Format pop-up menu (bottom).

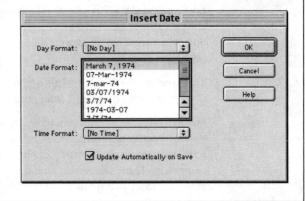

Copying and Pasting Text

If you're building Web sites as part of a team or for clients, your writers may often send you their text in the form of word processing documents (from Microsoft Word, for example). Unfortunately, Dreamweaver falls a bit short when it comes to handling text from other programs. Unlike desktop publishing programs like Quark XPress or Adobe PageMaker, Dreamweaver generally can't import a text file or word processing document.

The section "Importing HTML from Word" on page 49 offers a trick that helps you bring Word documents into Dreamweaver. For text in other formats, however, you'll

Figure 2-3:
When you copy from Word (or any other program), as shown at left, and paste into Dreamweaver, as shown at right, all formatting is lost, and paragraph breaks are replaced with line breaks. The little icon that appears at the end of the first line at right represents the invisible line break (see page 45).

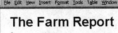

need to resort to copying and pasting, exactly like generations of noble Web designers before you.

Open the document in whatever program created it—Word, AppleWorks, or whatever. Select the text you want (by dragging through it, for example), or choose Edit→Select All (Ctrl+A [⌘-A]) to highlight all text in the document, and then choose Edit→Copy (Ctrl+C [⌘-C]) to copy it. Switch to Dreamweaver, click in the document window where you wish the text to go, and choose Edit→Paste (Ctrl+V [⌘-V]).

This routine pastes the text into place; unfortunately, you lose all text formatting (font type, size, color, bold, italic, and so on) in the process, as shown in Figure 2-3.

Furthermore, you'll find pasted paragraphs separated by line break characters, not standard carriage returns. Strangely enough, this means that when you paste in a series of paragraphs, Dreamweaver treats them as though they're one gargantuan paragraph. These line break characters can pose problems when trying to format what you think is a single paragraph.

Tip: You *can* make Dreamweaver paste separate paragraphs correctly—but only in Windows. The trick: In the word processor, before copying the text, add a blank line by pressing the Enter key an extra time between paragraphs. If you'll be cutting and pasting a lot of text from other programs, ask whoever is writing the text for your Web site to use a double Return to separate paragraphs, saving you a lot of hand formatting. Or just use your own word processor's Replace command to replace single Returns with double ones.

If you work with spreadsheets or need to present numbers and other information within a table, you can import such information directly into a table in Dreamweaver, as described on page 160.

WORKAROUND WORKSHOP

Pasting HTML

Copying and pasting has changed significantly in Dreamweaver 4. In previous versions, you had to use the Edit→Paste as Text command to preserve line breaks when pasting text into Dreamweaver from another program.

In Dreamweaver 4, Paste as Text is gone; now Edit→Paste accomplishes the same purpose. Unfortunately, this change eliminated a nice feature of Dreamweaver 3's Copy command, which copied not only the text but also all of the HTML code of the current selection. In other words, you could copy the HTML from Dreamweaver and paste it directly into another program. To accomplish the same thing in Dreamweaver 4, use the Copy HTML command from the Edit menu. To paste HTML you copied from another program into Dreamweaver, choose Edit→Paste HTML.

By the way, you don't have to use these commands when copying and pasting *within Dreamweaver.* It's smart enough to keep all of the formatting—and HTML tags—when copying and pasting within a Dreamweaver document.

Importing HTML from Word

Pasting text from another program into your Dreamweaver document works, but it's not the most elegant or efficient method for getting text onto a Web page. Not only do you lose formatting, but the resulting line breaks are a real annoyance.

A better alternative is to use Microsoft Word to save documents as Web pages, which then act as an intermediary between Word and Dreamweaver. All recent versions of Word (97, 2000, and XP for Windows; 98 and 2001 for Mac) can save files in HTML format, with formatting like fonts, text colors, and text sizes intact.

Unfortunately, the HTML code that Word produces is hideous. One look at the underlying code, and you'd think that your cat fell asleep on the keyboard. Because it needs to be able to reopen the document as a Word file, Word injects reams of information that adds to the file size of the page. This is a particular problem with Word 2000 and 2001, which add loads of XML and Cascading Style Sheet information. Fortunately, Dreamweaver can strip out most of that unnecessary code and produce leaner Web pages, as described below.

Exporting HTML from Word

From Word 97 (Windows) and Word 98 (Mac), you save a Word document as a Web page by choosing File→Save As HTML. Word 2000, 2001, and XP users do the same by choosing File→Save as Web Page.

Tip: If you have Word XP, when the Save As dialog box appears, choose "Web Page, Filtered" from the "Save as type" pop-up menu. As the resulting message box informs you, this option strips out all the extra XML codes that permit the document to be reopened as a full-fledged Word document—but also strips out the junk for Web page purposes.

Importing the HTML into Dreamweaver

Once you've saved a Word Web page onto your hard drive, you can bring it into Dreamweaver using either of these methods:

The Import Word HTML command

Choose File→Import→Import Word HTML. In the dialog box that appears, navigate to and select the Word HTML file you wish to import. The result is a new, unsaved document that bears at least a passing resemblance to your Word original.

The Open command

You can also open a Word HTML file just as you would any other Web page: by choosing File→Open. Once the file is open, choose Commands→Clean Up Word HTML.

The Clean Up Word HTML dialog box opens; Dreamweaver automatically detects whether the HTML was produced by Word 97/98 or Word 2000/2001/XP. Dreamweaver applies different rules for cleaning up the HTML, depending upon the version.

Note: If Dreamweaver doesn't recognize the version of Word you used, a warning box pops up. You can manually select the version from the pop-up menu.

There are two tabs in the dialog box: Basic and Detailed (see Figure 2-4). The Basic tab is the same regardless of whether the HTML was created by Word 97/98 or Word 2000/2001/XP, and lists actions Dreamweaver can take on the document.

The first four options, for example, fix problems that Word introduces to the HTML it creates. It's usually best to leave these options turned on.

The last three options of the Basic tab work like this:

- **Set background color.** This option lets you choose what color you want for the Web page. By default, Word produces Web pages with a gray background. Dreamweaver sets it to #FFFFFF (white), but you can change this value to another hexadecimal color value (see the sidebar box on page 30).

- **Apply Source Formatting.** To make the HTML of the page look more like other pages produced by Dreamweaver, turn on this checkbox, which makes Dreamweaver rewrite the HTML to fit Dreamweaver's style (which you can define, as described on page 252).

- **Show log on completion.** This option generates a report describing all of the changes Dreamweaver made to the Word HTML.

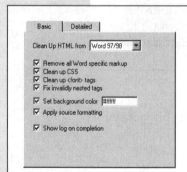

Figure 2-4:
You can access advanced options on the Detailed tab of the Clean Up Word HTML dialog box. Since Word 97/98 and 2000/2001 write such wildly different HTML, the options available in the Detailed tab vary depending on which version of Word created the page. Dreamweaver's default settings do the best job at producing lean pages.

The Cleanup Word HTML feature of Dreamweaver is quite an achievement. Considering the complexity of the code generated by Microsoft Word, it's amazing that Dreamweaver can cut through most of the chaff to get to the wheat.

Unfortunately, it's not perfect. While Dreamweaver does a good job of fixing the HTML produced by Word 97 and 98, the extensive use of Cascading Style Sheets generated by Word 2000, 2001, and XP is often more than Dreamweaver can handle. Even after cleaning up Word 2000 HTML, a Web page may still be filled with unnecessary junk. (On the other hand, if you plan on using Cascading Style Sheets in your site, Word 2000/2001/XP can play a useful role in your Web production workflow. To see how, see the box on page 221.)

Importing HTML
from Word

Selecting Text

After you get text into your Dreamweaver document, you'll undoubtedly need to edit it. You'll delete words and paragraphs, move sentences around, add words, and fix typos.

The first step in any of these procedures is learning how to select your text, which works just as it does in word processors. You can drag across text to highlight it, or just click where you wish the selection to begin and hold down the Shift key as you click at the end of the selection. You can also use shortcuts like these:

- To select a word, double-click it.

- To select a line of text, move your cursor to the left of the line of text until the cursor changes from an I-beam to an arrow; you've reached the left-margin selection strip. Click once to highlight one line of text, or drag vertically in this selection strip to select multiple lines.

- While pressing Shift, use the left and right arrow keys to select one letter at a time. Ctrl+Shift (⌘-Shift) and the left and right arrow keys select one *word* at a time.

- Ctrl+A (⌘-A) selects everything in the body of the page—text, graphics, and all.

Once you've selected text, you can cut, copy, or delete it. To move text to another part of the Web page, or even to another Dreamweaver document, you can use the Cut, Copy, and Paste commands in the Edit menu; you can also move text around by dragging and dropping it, as shown in Figure 2-5.

Figure 2-5:
You can move a blob of selected text simply by dragging it to another location in the document window. Point to a spot inside your highlighted selection; the cursor changes from an I-beam to an arrow; you can now drag the selection. Let go of the mouse button to drop your selection at the spot indicated by the vertical bar, as shown here. This technique works with graphics and other objects you've selected in the document window, too. You can even move a copy of the selection by pressing Ctrl (Option) as you drag-and-drop the selection.

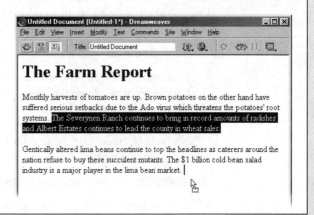

Once copied, the text remains in your computer's Clipboard and can be placed again and again (until you copy something else to the Clipboard, of course). When you cut (or copy) and paste *within* Dreamweaver, all of the formatting you have applied to the text stays intact; if you copy a headline that's in bold green type, and paste it into another document window in Dreamweaver, it stays bold and green.

You can delete any selection by pressing Delete or choosing Edit→Clear.

Spell Checking

You spend a lot of time perfecting your Web pages, making sure the images look great, that the text is properly formatted, and that everything aligns to make a beautiful visual presentation. But one step is often forgotten, especially given the hyperspeed development process of the Web: making sure your Web pages are free of typos.

Spelling mistakes give an unprofessional impression and imply a lack of attention to detail. Who wants to hire a "coppy editur" or "Web dezyner"? Dreamweaver's spell checking feature can help you.

About Dictionaries

Before you start spell checking, you should make sure that the correct *dictionary* is selected. Dreamweaver comes with dictionaries for several different languages, and more are available online (see the box on page 54); when it checks your spelling, it compares the text in your document against the list of words in one of these dictionaries.

To specify a dictionary, choose Edit→Preferences—or press Ctrl+U (⌘-U)—to open the Preferences dialog box; select the General category. The Spelling Dictionary menu at the bottom lets you select the dictionary you want.

Performing the Check

Once you've selected a dictionary, open the Web page whose spelling you wish to check. You can check as much or as little text as you like:

1. **Highlight the text you want (even a single word).**

   If you want to check the entire document, make sure that nothing is selected in the document window. (One good way to make sure nothing is selected is to click in the middle of a paragraph of text.) Unlike spell checkers in other programs, you don't have to place the cursor at the beginning of the document; Dreamweaver always checks spelling starting at the beginning of the document, no matter where the insertion point is.

2. **Choose Text→Check Spelling (or press Shift-F7).**

   The Check Spelling dialog box opens (see Figure 2-6). If the selected word is not in Dreamweaver's dictionary, it appears in the top field of the box, along with a list of suggested alternative spellings.

The first suggestion is listed in the Change To field.

3. **If the Change To field is correct, click Change.**

   If Dreamweaver has correctly flagged the word as misspelled, but the correct spelling isn't in the Change To field, double-click the correct spelling in the list. If the correct spelling isn't in the list, type it yourself in the Change To box.

   Then click the Change button to correct this one instance, or click Change All to replace the misspelled word everywhere it appears in the document.

   Dreamweaver makes the change and moves on to the next questionable spelling.

4. **If the word is actually correctly spelled (but not in Dreamweaver's dictionary), click Ignore, Ignore All, or Add to Personal.**

   If you want Dreamweaver to ignore this word *every* time it appears in the document, rather than just this instance of it, click Ignore All.

   On the other hand, you'll frequently use some words that Dreamweaver doesn't have in its dictionaries. You may, for instance, use a client's name throughout your Web pages. If that name isn't in Dreamweaver's dictionary, Dreamweaver will claim that it's a spelling error.

   To teach Dreamweaver the client's name so that the Check Spelling dialog box won't pop up each time you spell check, click Add to Personal. Dreamweaver adds the word to your personal dictionary, which is a special dictionary file that Dreamweaver also consults when checking your spelling.

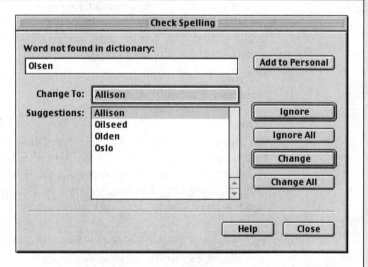

Figure 2-6:
Unfortunately, Dreamweaver's spell checking feature checks words only in the document window. It can't check the spelling of comments, Alt tags, or any text that appears in the head of the document. Nor can you spell check an entire Web site's worth of pages with a single command. You need to check each Web page individually.

Tip: If you click Add to Personal accidentally, you'll probably want to fix your mistake. Unfortunately, there's no obvious way to remove words in your personal dictionary!

There's a trick, though: Your personal dictionary is a file called personal.dat, which is in the Macromedia Dreamweaver 4→Configuration→Dictionaries folder. Make a backup copy of this file just in case, and then open it in a text editor like WordPad or SimpleText and delete the words you no longer want. You can also add words manually by typing them in, if you wish.

Whether you've used the Ignore or Change function, Dreamweaver skips ahead to the next word it doesn't recognize; begin again from step 3.

5. **To end spell checking, click Close.**

POWER USERS' CLINIC

International Dictionaries

While Dreamweaver comes with spell checkers for U.S. English, British English, French, and German, you can download additional dictionaries from the Macromedia site at: *www.macromedia.com/support/dreamweaver/documentation/dictionary.html.* There you can find dictionaries for Spanish, Catalan, Italian, Portuguese, Swedish, and more. After downloading and decompressing the dictionary file, put it in the Dreamweaver→Configuration→Dictionaries folder.

Undo, Redo and the History Panel

One of the great consciousness-altering moments of the twentieth century was the introduction of the Undo command. After a long day in front of the computer, the ability to undo any action seems quite natural. (Unfortunately, reaching for the Ctrl+Z keys after dropping an egg on the floor still doesn't work in the real world.)

Fortunately, most mistakes you make in Dreamweaver can be reversed with the Undo command or the History panel.

Undo

Like most computer programs these days, Dreamweaver lets you undo the last step you took by pressing Ctrl+Z (⌘-Z), or by choosing Edit→Undo. (The command changes to reflect your most recent action; if you just deleted some text, it says Edit→Undo Delete.) Likewise, when you're feeling indecisive, you can *redo* the action you just undid by choosing Edit→Redo, or by pressing Ctrl+Y (⌘-Y).

Tip: Jumping back and forth with the Undo/Redo commands is a good way to compare a change you made to a Web page with its previous appearance. For instance, suppose you're having trouble deciding on a background color for a Web page. You could set it to a dark blue, then set it to a dark purple, and then choose Edit→Undo Set Page Properties to return to the dark blue background. Choose Edit→Redo Set Page Properties to view the purple background. This before-and-after toggling feature of the Undo/Redo combo can be a great aid to your Web-building efforts.

You're not limited to a single undo, either. You can undo multiple steps, up to 50 of them, or whatever number you specify in Preferences. Choose Edit→Preferences to open this dialog box; click the General category from the preferences Category list; and change the number in the Maximum Number of History Steps box. (Note, however, that the more steps Dreamweaver remembers, the more memory the program needs. If you set this preference very high, or your computer doesn't have a lot of memory, you may find your computer acting sluggish.)

Tip: You can even undo actions *after you have saved* a document (although not after you've closed it). Unlike many programs, Dreamweaver doesn't erase the list of actions you've performed when a page is saved. This means you can feel free to save as often as you want—a wise safeguard against crashes and other mishaps—without losing the ability to undo what you've done. Unfortunately, this flexibility doesn't extend to the Redo command. If you undo one or more actions, and then save your document, Dreamweaver forgets any possible redo actions.

History Panel

You may have wondered why the Preferences setting for the Undo command refers to "History Steps." Dreamweaver creates a *history* for a document as you work on it. Each time you add text, insert a graphic, change the background color of the page, or do anything else to a document, Dreamweaver adds a new step to a list of previous actions.

All of these steps are listed in the History panel. To see it, choose Window→History, or press F9 (Shift-F10). Or, depending on how you set up the Launcher and Launcher bar (see page 18), you may also be able to open the History panel by clicking the Open History icon (▷) on the Launcher or Launcher bar.

Each row in the panel represents one action or step, and includes a description. For instance, hitting Return or Enter while typing in the document creates a step called New Paragraph. Steps are listed in the order you perform your actions, with the latest actions at the bottom and earliest action at the top of the list.

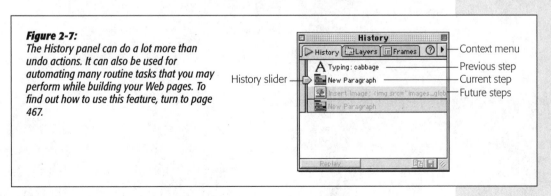

Figure 2-7:
The History panel can do a lot more than undo actions. It can also be used for automating many routine tasks that you may perform while building your Web pages. To find out how to use this feature, turn to page 467.

History slider ―― Context menu / Previous step / Current step / Future steps

But the History panel isn't just a dull document to be examined; it's a living, multiple-step Undo command. Use the History slider to move to any step in the history list. To undo one action, for example, drag the slider up one step. When you do this, you'll notice that the slider's previous position step is grayed out. Steps that are dimmed represent future steps, so moving the slider down one step is the equivalent to choosing Edit→Redo.

You can undo or redo multiple steps by moving the slider up or down the list. Alternatively, if you want to jump to a particular step, click the track to its left. The slider jumps to that spot.

If you want to eliminate all of the history steps for a document, select Clear History from the History Panel's context menu. Be careful; this is one action you can't undo.

Text Formatting

Getting text onto a Web page (Chapter 2) is a good start, but effective communication requires effective design, too. Large, bold headlines can help readers scan a page's important topics. Colorful text focuses attention. Bulleted sentences crystallize and summarize ideas. Just as a monotonous, low-key voice puts a crowd to sleep, a vast desert of plain HTML text is sure to turn visitors away from the important message of your site. In fact, text formatting could be the key to making your *Widgets Online 2001 Sale-a-thon* a resounding success instead of an unnoticed disaster.

To help you get your point across, Dreamweaver provides the tools you need to format your text in compelling and eye-catching ways (see Figure 3-1 for examples of good and bad text formatting).

Paragraph Formatting

Just as you use paragraphs to help organize your thoughts into clear, well-structured and cohesive units when you're writing a paper or letter, you organize content on Web pages into blocks of information within HTML tags (see page 3 for more on tags). The most basic block of information is a simple paragraph, indicated in HTML by a <paragraph> tag, like this:

```
<p>Hello. This is one paragraph on this Web page. </p>
```

To a Web browser, everything between the opening and closing <p> tags is considered part of the same paragraph. Many Dreamweaver formatting options—headlines, lists, indents, and alignment options, for example—can apply only to an entire paragraph at a time, as opposed to individual words. In a word processor, you'd call this kind of formatting *paragraph* formatting; in Web design, it's called *block-level* formatting. The idea is exactly the same: These characteristics affect an entire paragraph (that is, a *block* of text, whether that's just one sentence or several sentences) at a time.

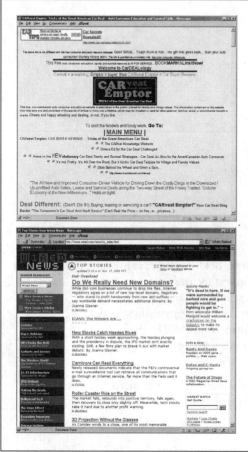

Figure 3-1:
These pages both use different fonts, colors, and sizes to display text, but the one at bottom uses a consistent arrangement of styles to organize the text and guide the reader through the page.

Notice how the headline "Do We Really Need New Domains?" with its larger type size draws your eye to it immediately. Below that, the supplementary articles and their summaries are easy to identify and read. In the page at top, by contrast, the largest type element, "Main Menu," sits in the middle of a scattered, randomly formatted sea of text.

(*Character-level* formatting, on the other hand, can be applied to individual words or even letters; bold and italics fall into this category, as described later in this chapter.)

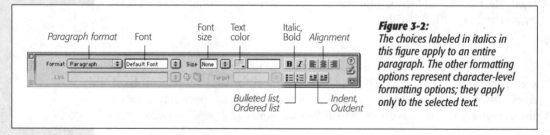

Figure 3-2:
The choices labeled in italics in this figure apply to an entire paragraph. The other formatting options represent character-level formatting options; they apply only to the selected text.

Paragraphs

When you create a new document in Dreamweaver and start typing, the text you type has no paragraph formatting at all, as indicated by the word *None* in the Format menu at the left side of the Property inspector. *None* isn't an HTML tag; it means that there are *no* tags at all surrounding your text.

When you press Enter or Return, you create a new paragraph, complete with opening and closing <p> tags, as shown above; but your newly born paragraph still has no formatting tags. When your Web site visitors look at it, the font and size of your type are determined by their own Web browser preference settings. It may not look anything like the typography you saw in Dreamweaver.

You can add the Paragraph format to any block of text. Since this formatting option affects all of the text in the block, you don't need to select any text as a first step. Simply click inside the block of text and do one of the following:

- Choose Paragraph from the Format menu in the Property inspector.

- Choose Text→Paragraph Format→Paragraph.

- Press Ctrl+Shift+P (⌘-Shift-P).

Tip: Much to the chagrin of Web designers, Web browsers display a line's worth of blank space before and after block-level elements like headings and paragraphs. This visual gap can be distracting, but unfortunately, you can't get rid of it with regular HTML.

However, many of the formatting limitations of HTML, including this one, can be fixed using Cascading Style Sheets. See the tip on page 232 to fix this problem.

Headlines

Headlines announce information (**The Vote Is In!**) and help organize content. Just as this book uses different levels of headings to introduce its topics—from chapter titles all the way down to subsections—the HTML heading tag comes in a variety of sizes used to indicate importance.

Headlines range in size from 1 (largest) to 6 (smallest), as shown in Figure 3-3. HTML's creators intended these headings to be an outlining aid for Web authors, but these days, Web designers use them more frequently simply for basic text formatting.

To turn a paragraph into a headline, click inside the line, or block, of text and then do one of the following:

- Select one of the heading levels (Heading 1 through Heading 6) from the Format menu in the Property inspector.

- Choose Text→Paragraph Format→Heading 1-6.

- Press Ctrl+Shift+1 (⌘-Shift-1), for the Heading 1 style, Ctrl+Shift+2 (⌘-Shift-2) for Heading 2, and so on.

Preformatted Text

Web browsers normally ignore extra spaces, tabs, and other blank-space characters when displaying a Web page. However, using the Preformatted paragraph format, you can override this behavior. Preformatted paragraphs display *every* text character in a paragraph, including tabs, multiple spaces, and line breaks, so you don't have to resort to multiple nonbreaking space characters (see page 45) to insert more than one space in a row.

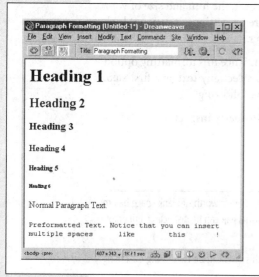

Figure 3-3:
You can apply any of eight basic paragraph formats to a block of text: Headings 1 to 6, Paragraph, and Preformatted. In their default settings, they vary in size, font, and boldness.

The original idea behind the Preformatted format was to display tabular data—as in a spreadsheet—without the use of tables. That's why preformatted paragraphs show up in a *monospaced* font like Courier. In monospaced fonts, each letter of the alphabet, from *i* to *w,* is the same width and takes up the same horizontal space on a page, making it easy to align letters in columns. That's also why, when you use this paragraph style, you can use tabs to align text in columns. (When you use any other paragraph format, Web browsers ignore tabs.) These days, however, Dreamweaver's table feature is a much superior method of creating columns; see Chapter 6.

Nonetheless, the Preformatted format can still be useful, especially when displaying sample HTML or programming code, for example. You can add the Preformatted format to any block of text. Simply click inside the block of text and then take one of these two steps:

• Choose Format→Preformatted from the Property inspector.

• Choose Text→Paragraph Format→Preformatted Text.

Keep in mind that preformatted text appears exactly as you enter it. Unlike normal paragraph text, lines of preformatted text don't automatically wrap if they're wider than the window. To end a line of preformatted text and create another, you must press the Enter or Return key to create a manual line break.

Paragraph Alignment

All text in a Web page starts out aligned with the left edge of the page (or, in the case of tables, to the left edge of a table cell). But there are times when you may want to center text in the middle of the page—perhaps an elegantly centered title—or to the right side. While there are many ways to achieve this effect in Dreamweaver, the Property inspector's word processor-like controls make this a snap (or is that a click?).

To change a paragraph's alignment, click inside a paragraph and do one of the following:

- Click one of the alignment icons in the upper right corner of the Property inspector (see Figure 3-2).

- Choose Left, Center, or Right from the Text→Align menu.

- Use one of the following keyboard shortcuts:

  Left: Ctrl+Alt+Shift+L (⌘-Option-Shift-L);

  Centered: Ctrl+Alt+Shift+C (⌘-Option-Shift-C;

  Right: Ctrl+Alt+Shift+R (⌘-Option-Shift-R).

After you align a paragraph, the Property inspector displays a depressed button for the alignment option you chose, indicating what kind of alignment you've applied to that paragraph.

You can change the alignment of a paragraph by applying a different alignment option, or remove an alignment by reapplying the *same* alignment. For instance, if you've right-aligned a paragraph, clicking the right-align button in the Property inspector removes all alignment information and returns that paragraph to its de-

---

UP TO SPEED

Keep Your Pages Lean

Many of the things that contribute to slow Web page downloads—congestion on the Internet, for example—are out of your control. But you can do your part by making sure your pages are as compact as possible: keep the file size of graphics down and eliminate extraneous lines of HTML code. The more HTML you include in a page, the larger the file, and the slower the download.

For example, text on a Web page aligns to the left of a page *by default*. You'd be pointlessly bloating your Web page, therefore, by specifying left alignment of your text using a paragraph's alignment property. In fact, when you encounter the phrase "by default" describing an HTML property in this book, it's a safe bet that you can get that effect without adding any HTML.

Other ways to keep your pages lean and fast are highlighted throughout this book, but remember this rule of thumb: The less HTML code you create, the faster your Web page will download, and the happier your audience will be.

fault setting. (This is a better solution than clicking the left-align button, which adds extra lines of HTML code to do the same thing.)

Indented Paragraphs

Indenting a paragraph can set it apart from the paragraphs before and after it. It's perfect for adding a small amount of space on either side of a paragraph, and it's frequently used to present a long quote or passage from a book or other source. In fact, an indented paragraph is called a *blockquote* in HTML.

To indent a paragraph or block-level element like a heading, click it and do one of the following:

• Click the Indent button on the Property inspector (see Figure 3-2).

• Choose Text→Indent.

• Press Ctrl+Alt+] (⌘-Option-]).

Unfortunately, since indenting a paragraph simply nests that paragraph in a basic HTML <blockquote> tag, you don't have any control over how *much* space is added to the margins of the paragraph. Most Web browsers insert about 40 pixels of blank space on the left and right side of a blockquote.

You can add additional space to the margins of a paragraph by applying *another* indent, thus creating a nested set of blockquotes. To do so, click an already indented paragraph and repeat one of the indenting procedures described above. You can continue to add multiple indents in this way.

Note: Unfortunately, you're still deprived of the ability to specify exactly how much more indentation you're getting. For the ultimate in margin control, therefore, use Cascading Style Sheets for pixel-level accuracy as described on page 231.

But what if you want to remove indents from a paragraph? Use Dreamweaver to *outdent* it, of course. (Yes, *outdent* is a real word—ever since Microsoft made it up.) To remove a paragraph's indent formatting—that is, remove a <blockquote> tag— click inside the paragraph and do one of the following:

• Click the Outdent button on the Property inspector (see Figure 3-2).

• Choose Text→Outdent.

• Press Ctrl+Alt+[(⌘-Option-[).

You can continue to outdent a paragraph using one of these methods until the paragraph returns to the left edge of the page; at that point, the outdenting commands have no further effect.

Lists

Lists organize the everyday information of our lives: to-do lists, grocery lists, top ten lists, and so on. On Web pages, lists are indispensable for presenting groups of items such as links, company services or employees, or a series of instructions.

HTML offers formatting options for three basic categories of lists (see Figure 3-4). The two most common types of lists are *bulleted* (called *unordered* lists in the HTML language) and *numbered* lists (called *ordered* in HTML). The third and lesser-known list type, a *definition* list, comes in handy for creating glossaries or dictionary-like entries.

Figure 3-4:
HTML has several predefined list formats, including bulleted lists and definition lists, which let you organize information into orderly units. Once you've told Dreamweaver that you intend to create a bulleted or numbered list, it adds the bullets or the numbering for you automatically.

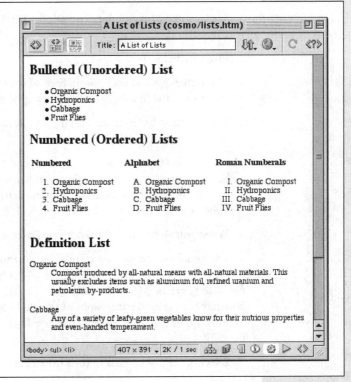

Bulleted and Numbered Lists

Bulleted and numbered lists share similar formatting. Dreamweaver automatically indents items in either type of list, and automatically precedes each list item by a character—a bullet, number, or letter, for example:

- Unordered or bulleted lists, like this one, are good for groups of items that don't necessarily follow any sequence. They're preceded with a bullet.

- Ordered lists are useful when presenting items that follow a sequence, such as the numbered instructions in the paragraph below. Instead of a bullet, a number or letter precedes each item in an ordered list. Dreamweaver suggests a number (1, 2, 3, and so on), but you can substitute Roman numerals, letters, and other variations.

You can create a list from scratch within Dreamweaver, or add list formatting to text already on a Web page.

Creating a new bulleted or numbered list

When making a list in Dreamweaver, you start by choosing a list format, then typing the list items:

1. **In the document window, click where you wish to add a list.**

   See Chapter 2 for full detail on adding text to a Web page.

2. **Apply the list format by clicking the Ordered or Unordered List button in the Property inspector.**

   Alternatively, you can choose Text→List→Unordered List or Ordered List. In either case, the first bullet or number appears in your document automatically.

3. **Type the first list item and then press Return. Repeat until you have added all items in the list.**

   The text you type appears (*Organic Compost,* for example, in Figure 3-4) after the bullet or number. When you press Return, a new bullet or number appears, ready for your next item. (If you just want move to the next line *without* creating a new bullet, insert a line break by pressing Shift-Return.)

4. **When you've finished the list, press Enter or Return twice.**

   The double carriage-return ends the list and creates a new empty paragraph.

Formatting existing text as a list

You may have several paragraphs of text that you've already typed in or pasted from another application. It's a simple process to change any group of paragraphs into a list.

1. **Select the text you wish to turn into a list.**

   The easiest way to select text is to drag from the first list item straight down into the last item of the list. Lists are block-level elements; each paragraph, whether it's a headline or regular paragraph, becomes one bulleted or numbered item in the list. In other words, you don't actually need to select all of the text in either the first or last paragraph.

2. **Apply the list format.**

   As when creating a list from scratch, as described above, click either the Unordered or Ordered List button in the Property inspector or choose from the Text→List submenu. The selected paragraphs instantly take on the list formatting, complete with bullets and automatic numbering.

Whichever way you started making a list—either by typing from scratch or reformatting existing text—you're not stuck with the results of your early decisions. You can add onto lists, add extra spaces, and even renumber them, as described in the following section.

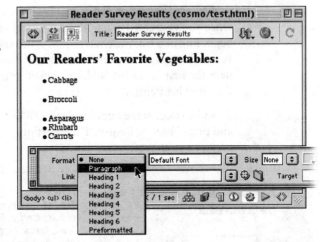

Figure 3-5:
Because each paragraph in HTML starts on a new line, with a certain amount of space after the paragraph above, you can use the paragraph tag to add space between list items, as described below.

Reformatting Bulleted and Numbered Lists

HTML tags define lists, just as they define other Web page features. Making changes to an existing list is a matter of changing those tags, using Dreamweaver's menu commands and Property inspector tools.

Adding space between list items

Usually there isn't any blank space between items in a list, which makes for nice, compact lists. However, sometimes a long list of unspaced, bulleted items can look too congested, especially when each item is itself several lines long.

Figure 3-6:
The tag selector is a great way to quickly and accurately select an HTML tag. Clicking the <ul> (unordered list) tag, for instance, selects the entire bulleted list.

Fortunately, you can take advantage of the spacing provided by the paragraph tag. To add space between one list item and the next, click the first one and then change the paragraph formatting from None to Paragraph. To add space between *all* items in a list, select the entire list—click the <ul> or <ol> tag in the tag selector (Figure 3-6)—and apply paragraph formatting in the Property inspector (Figure 3-5).

Adding new items to a list

Once you've created a list, it's easy to add additional items. To add an item at the beginning of a list, click before the first character of the first list item, type the item you wish to add, and press Enter or Return. Dreamweaver makes your newly typed item the first in the list, adding a bullet or number accordingly (and renumbering the other list items, if necessary).

To add an item at the middle or end of a list, click at the end of the *previous* list item and press Enter or Return. The insertion point appears after a new bullet or number; type your list item on this new line.

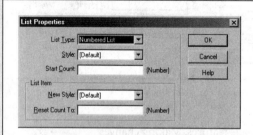

Figure 3-7:
The List Properties dialog box lets you set the type and style of a list. It offers five styles: Number (1, 2, 3), Roman Small (i, ii, iii), Roman Large (I, II, III), Alphabet Small (a, b, c), and Alphabet Large (A, B, C).

Changing bullets and numbers

Bulleted and numbered lists aren't limited to just the default round black bullet or the numbers 1, 2, or 3. You can choose from two bullet types and a handful of different numbering schemes:

1. **Click once inside any list item.**

   Strangely enough, you can't change the properties of a list if you've first selected the entire list, an entire single list item, or several list items.

2. **Open the List Properties dialog box.**

   To do so, either click the List Item button in the bottom half of the Property inspector or choose Text→List→Properties. (If the list is inside a table cell, your only choice is to use the Text menu; in this situation, the List Item button doesn't appear in the Property inspector.)

3. **Choose a type from the List Type pop-up menu.**

   In this way, you can turn a numbered list into a bulleted list, or vice versa. You should avoid the two other options in the menu—Directory List and Menu List; these are old list types that won't work in Web browsers of the future.

4. **Choose a bulleting or numbering style.**

Bulleted lists can have three different styles: default, bullet, and square. In most browsers, the *default* bullet style is the same as the *bullet* style: a simple, solid, black circle. As you might guess, the *square* style uses a solid black square for the bullet character.

Ordered lists, on the other hand, have a greater variety of style options. The default is a simple numbering scheme (1, 2, 3...), but you can choose from any of five styles for ordered lists, as shown in Figure 3-7.

5. **Set the starting number for the list.**

You don't have to begin a numbered list at 1, A, or the Roman numeral I. You can start it at another number, if you wish—a trick that can come in handy if, for example, you're creating a Web page to explain how to rebuild a car's engine:

As part of each step, you want to include a photograph. You create a numbered list, type in the directions for step 1, hit Return, and insert an image (as described in Chapter 5). You hit Return again and type in the text for step 2. Unfortunately, the photo, because it's an item in an ordered list, now has the number 2 next to it, and step 2 is listed as 3!

When you remove the list formatting from the photo to get rid of the 2, you create one list above it and another below it (as described on page 69). Step 2, *below* the photo, now thinks it's the beginning of a new list—and starts over with the number 1!

The solution is to make it think it begins with 2.

To start the list at something other than 1, type the starting number in the Start Count field (Figure 3-7). This must be a number, even if you choose to display the list using letters. So to begin a list at D instead of A, type *4* in the Start Count field.

In fact, you can even change the style of a *single* list item. For instance, you could change the third item in a numeric list from a 3 to the letter C. (Of course, just because you can, doesn't mean you should. Dreamweaver is very thorough in supporting the almost overwhelming combination of options available in HTML, but, unless you're building a Dadaist revival site, how often do you want a list that is numbered 1, 2, C, iv, 1?)

6. **Click OK to apply the changes.**

Nested lists

Some complex outlines require multiple *levels* of lists. Legal documents, for instance, may list major clauses with capital letters (A, B, C, and so on) and use roman numerals (i, ii, iii, and so on) for subclauses (see Figure 3-8).

It's easy to create such nested lists in Dreamweaver; Figure 3-8 shows the steps.

Definition Lists

Definition lists can be used to display items in a dictionary or glossary, or whenever you need to present a term and its definition. Each item in a definition list is composed of two parts: a word or term, and a definition.

As you can see in Figure 3-4, definition lists aren't as fancy as they sound. The first item in the list (the word or term) is presented on its own line with no indent, and the second item (the definition) appears directly underneath, indented.

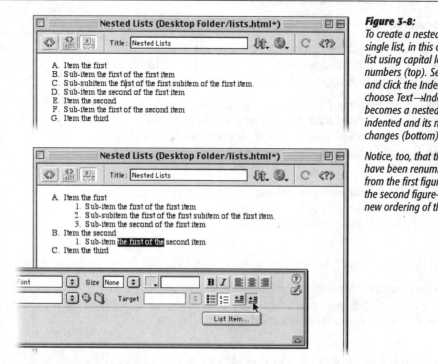

Figure 3-8:
To create a nested list, start with a single list, in this case a numbered list using capital letters instead of numbers (top). Select a subtopic and click the Indent button or choose Text→Indent. The item becomes a nested list; it's indented and its numbering changes (bottom).

Notice, too, that the major points have been renumbered—letter E from the first figure is letter B in the second figure—to reflect the new ordering of the list.

You can't create a definition list using the Property inspector. Instead, start by highlighting the paragraphs that contain the terms and definitions you wish to include in the list; then choose Text→List→Definition List.

To turn a definition list *back* to regular paragraphs, select it and choose Text→List→ None, or click the Outdent button in the Property inspector.

Removing and Deleting List Items

Dreamweaver lets you take items out of a list in two ways: either by removing the list *formatting* from an item or items (and changing them back into normal paragraphs) or by deleting their text outright.

Removing list items

To remove list formatting from one or more list items (or an entire list), highlight the lines in question and then choose Text→List→None (or just click the Outdent button on the Property inspector). You've just removed all list formatting; the text remains on the screen, however, now formatted as standard paragraphs.

If you reformat an item in the middle of a list using this technique, it becomes a regular paragraph; Dreamweaver turns the items above it and below it into separate lists.

Deleting list items

A simple way to delete a list or list item is to use the tag selector in the status bar of the document window (see Figure 3-6). To delete an entire list, click anywhere inside the list, then click its tag in the tag selector—<ul> for a bulleted list or <ol> for a numbered list—and press Delete. (You can also, of course, drag through all the text of the list and then press Delete.)

To delete a single list item, click that item in the document window, click the <li> tag in the tag selector, and then press Delete.

Tip: You can rearrange lists by selecting a list item and dragging it to another position within the list. If it's an ordered list (1,2,3...), Dreamweaver automatically renumbers the list. For example, if you select an item numbered 4 (or D, if it's an alphabetical list) and drag it to the second position in the list, Dreamweaver changes the item to 2 (or B) and renumbers all items that follow.

However, selecting a list item can be tricky. If you simply drag to select the text, you don't actually select the list item itself, with all its formatting and numbering. To be sure you've selected a list item, click the <li> tag in the tag selector in the document window's status bar (see Figure 3-6). Now, when you drag the selection to a new position in the list, the number (or bullet) follows. You can also select a list item in this way, copy or cut it, and paste it back into the list in another position.

Character Formatting

The simple formatting applied by a paragraph format is not much to write home about, much less to advertise on a résumé. Heading 1, for instance, is generally displayed in black and bold using a large Times Roman font. (Yawn.)

Character formatting, on the other hand, introduces another level of typographic control. By assigning different font faces, colors, styles, and sizes to your text, you can bring a Web page to life.

Unlike paragraph formatting, which applies to an entire paragraph or block of text, you can apply character formatting to any selection of text, whether it's a single word, one sentence, an entire paragraph, or your whole Web page. In general, you apply character formatting just as you would in a word processor: Select the text (using any of the methods described on page 51) and then apply a format using the Property inspector or Text menu.

Fonts

Unfortunately, the Web is like a word processor in a bad way, too. If you create some beautiful document in Microsoft Word, using fancy fonts you just bought from a small font company in Iowa, you're in for a rude surprise when you email the document to your boss. He won't see anything resembling what the memo looked like on *your* screen. Because he doesn't own the same fonts you used, he'll see some default font on his computer—Times, perhaps. Fonts show up in a distributed document only if each recipient happens to have the same fonts installed.

Same thing on the Web. Although you're free, as a Web designer, to specify any font you want in a Web page, it won't show up on your viewer's computer unless she's installed the same font in her system. Otherwise, your visitor's Web browser will show your text in a default font, which is usually some version of Times or (if you used the Preformatted format) Courier.

There are several solutions to this dilemma. One is to use Flash Text, which is described on page 115, or to convert your text into graphic images (page 96). Another is to specify the font you'd *like* to use; if your viewer's computer has the specified font installed, that's what she'll see. You can specify secondary or tertiary font choices if the preferred font isn't available; in fact, Dreamweaver offers prepackaged lists of such "first choice, second choice, third choice" fonts, as you'll find out in the following section.

UP TO SPEED

Knowing Your Font Types

You can literally find tens of thousands of different fonts to express your every thought—from bookish, staid, and classical type faces to rounded, cartoonish squiggles.

Most fonts can be divided into two categories: *serif* and *sans-serif.* Serif fonts are best for long passages of text, as it's widely believed that *serifs*—small decorative strokes ("hands" and "feet") at the end of a letter's main strokes—

gently lead the eye from letter to letter, making text easier to read. Examples of serif fonts are Times, Times New Roman, Georgia, and the main body paragraphs of this book.

Sans-serif fonts, on the other hand, lack serifs, and are often used for headlines, thanks to their clean and simple appearance. Examples of sans-serif fonts include Arial, Helvetica, Verdana, and the one you're reading now.

Applying font formatting

Dreamweaver's approach to font formatting is straightforward; just highlight the text whose font you want to change (or click to indicate where you're *about* to type), and then choose the font you want from the Font pop-up menu in the Property inspector. (Or choose Text→Font and select a font from the submenu.)

You'll soon discover that Dreamweaver's font menus aren't quite what you're used to. When you apply a font to text, you have to choose a *list* of fonts like "Arial, Helvetica, sans-serif." You don't just choose a single font, such as Helvetica.

That's because, as noted above, in order for your viewer's computer to display a font correctly on a Web page, it must have the same font installed. If the font's not there, the browser simply replaces the font specified in the Web page with the browser's default font.

In order to control this process, you can specify a list of fonts that look similar to your first-choice font (Arial, for example). Your visitor's Web browser checks if the first font in the list is installed on the computer. If it is, that's what your visitor sees when viewing your Web page.

But if the first font isn't installed, the browser looks down the list until it finds a font that is installed. Different operating systems use different fonts, so it's good practice to list one font that's common on Windows and another, similar-looking font that's common on the Mac. Arial, for instance, is found on all Windows machines, while Helvetica is a similar font for Macs.

Tip: While Mac and Windows used to come with very different sets of preinstalled fonts, there has been some convergence in the past few years. These days, you can count on the average Mac or PC having these fonts available:

Arial, Arial Black, Comic Sans MS, Courier, Courier New, Georgia, Impact, Monotype Sorts, Times, Times New Roman, Trebuchet MS, Verdana, Webdings, Wingdings.

If your audience includes Unix or Linux users, all bets are off. In this case, you should stick to these three fonts: Helvetica (make sure to also specify Arial for Windows users), Times (Times New Roman for Windows), and Courier (Courier New for Windows).

That's it. You're just applied one of Dreamweaver's predefined fonts. If you'd like a greater degree of control of what fonts your page displays, read on.

Creating custom font lists

Dreamweaver comes with six preset "first choice, second choice, third choice" font lists, which incorporate fonts that are standard on both Windows and Mac. But you can easily stray from the pack and create your own font lists for use in your Web pages. If you proceed with the custom approach, make sure you know what fonts your visitors have—easily done if you're designing a corporate intranet and know what computers are used in your company—*and* always specify one font that you *know* is installed. In this way, your page may not look exactly as you intended, but it'll at least be readable.

Here's how you create a new "first choice, second choice, third choice" font list:

Note: Technically, you can specify any number of fallback fonts in one of these lists, not just first, second, and third choices; your list can specify only a single font, or a long list in order of your preference.

---

1. **Open the Edit Font List dialog box.**

Choose Edit Font List from the Property inspector's Font menu. Alternatively, choose Text→Font→Edit Font List. Either way, the Edit Font List dialog box appears (Figure 3-9).

2. **Select a first-choice font from the list of Available Fonts, or type in the font name.**

   All fonts on your computer are listed in the Available Fonts menu. Simply click to select the font you wish to add.

   Alternatively, you can type a font's name into the box that appears directly below the list of available fonts—a handy trick if you want to include a font that *isn't* installed on your computer (a Windows font when you're working on a Mac, for example).

3. **Add the font you've just specified to your new, custom font list by clicking the << button (or just double-clicking the font name).**

   Your first-choice font appears in the Chosen Font list.

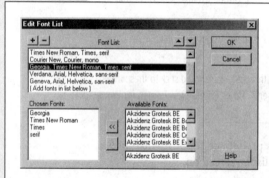

Figure 3-9:
Not only can you create your own font lists, but you can also edit, remove, or reorder the current lists in this dialog box. When you click a list in the Font List, the "first choice, second choice, third choice" fonts appear in the lower-left corner. To remove a font from that list, click the font name and then click the >> button. To add a font to the list, select a font in the Available Fonts menu and click the << button. Finally, to reorder the font lists as they appear in the Property inspector or Text→Font menu, click the arrow keys near the upper-right corner of the dialog box.

4. **Repeat steps 2 and 3 for each font you wish to include in your custom list.**

   The order in which you add the fonts is the order they appear in the list; these become the "first choice, second choice, third choice" fonts.

   Unfortunately, there's no way to change the order of the fonts once you've added them. So if you accidentally put the fonts in the wrong order, you must delete the list by clicking the – button (at the upper-left corner of the dialog box) and start over.

5. **Lastly, add a generic font family.**

   This last step isn't strictly necessary, but it's a good idea. If your Web-page visitor is some kind of anti-font radical whose PC doesn't have *any* of the fonts you've chosen, her browser will substitute the generic font family you specify here. On most systems, for instance, the monospace font is Courier, the serif font is Times, and the sans-serif font is Arial or Helvetica.

Generic fonts are listed at the bottom of the list of Available Fonts and include Cursive, Fantasy, Monospace, Sans-Serif, and Serif. Select a generic font that's similar in type to the fonts in your list. For instance, choose Sans-Serif if your list is composed of sans-serif fonts like Helvetica or Arial; choose Serif if you specify fonts like Times or Georgia.

6. **Click OK.**

Your new font package appears in the Property inspector's Font menu, ready to apply.

Font Size

Varying the sizes of fonts on a Web page is one way to direct a viewer's attention. Large type screams "Read Me!"—excellent for attention grabbing headlines; small type, meanwhile, fades into the background—perfect for necessary but unexciting legal mumbo jumbo like copyright notices.

Unless you specifically define its size, text in a regular paragraph appears at the default size specified by your visitor's Web browser, such as 12 points. (A *point* is a typographic measurement equal to 1/72 of an inch.)

In theory, 12-point lettering is roughly 1/6 of an inch tall. In practice, however, the resolution of the monitor, the font itself, and the operating system drastically affect the size of type on the screen. To the eternal frustration of Web designers who are used to, say, PageMaker or QuarkXPress, text on a Web page viewed in Netscape Navigator for Windows, for instance, appears substantially larger than when viewed

---

FREQUENTLY ASKED QUESTION

Changing Sizes

Why can I apply font sizes like -1 or +2, and what does the Size Change menu do?

Here's another example of Dreamweaver's drive to give you access to almost every possible HTML tag and property setting ever created. Yes, if you select Text→Size Change, you can choose from these options: +1, +2, +3, +4, -1, -2, or -3. In addition, the Property inspector's font size menu offers positive and negative values ranging from 1 to 7.

These settings let you specify a text size that's relative to what is called the *basefont* size of a Web page. That basefont size, unless you indicate otherwise, is equivalent to a text size of 3. So, if you applied the size of -1 to some text, it would display as size 2 text.

You can, if you so desire, change the basefont size of a Web page. Dreamweaver doesn't provide an easy way to do this; you have to enter the code by hand in Code View (see Chapter 9) by adding the following tag to the <head> tag of a Web page: <*basefont size=3*>. Replace the number 3 with any number from 1 to 7; now all text defaults to that size. So if you set the basefont to size 7 and then set some text to a size of -3, it shows up as size 4 text.

Confused by all this math? Don't worry about it; the <basefont> tag is an old HTML tag. It won't be included in future definitions of the HTML language, and may not work in new versions of the popular Web browsers. In other words, don't bother using these relative size options; stick to the standard numbering, 1 through 7.

---

in Navigator on a Mac. Add to this the fact that a user can change her browser's default text size to any size she wishes, and you'll quickly understand that Web design requires a Zen-like acceptance of factors beyond your control.

However, HTML does provide a modicum of control. You can choose from seven different "virtual" font sizes, ranging from 1 (smallest) to 7 (largest). Each size is *relative* to the default text size defined in each visitor's Web browser. (Now you know why Web-design programs don't simply offer a Font Size menu with commands like 12 Point, 14 Point, and so on).

"Standard" text on a Web page is considered size 3. Each size increment represents a 20 percent change in the font's size: size 4 is 20 percent bigger than size 3, while size 2 is 20 percent smaller than size 3. So, for example, if the Web browser's default text size is 12 point, size 3 text is 12 points, size 2 is 10 points, and size 4 is 14 points.

To specify one of these relative text sizes, first select it and then do one of the following:

- Choose a font size, 1 through 7, from the Size menu in the Property inspector (see Figure 3-2)

- Choose Text→Size, and select a size from the submenu.

Tip: Since size 3 is the default size of text anyway, it's a waste of time and precious file size to set text to size 3. Better to just leave the font size set to None, which requires no additional HTML tags.

Font Color

Most color formatting you do in Dreamweaver, whether it's for text or for a table cell, makes use of Dreamweaver's *color box*. For more information on applying color in Dreamweaver and using the color box, see page 30.

To set the color of text, first select it and then take your pick:

- Click the color well in the Property inspector and select a color.

POWER USERS' CLINIC

Be Careful Using the <font> Tag

For years, font faces, sizes, and colors have been specified using HTML's <font> tag. As of HTML 4.0, however, the W3C (World Wide Web Consortium) officially "deprecated" the font tag, meaning that it will no longer be used in future versions of HTML. In the long term, this means that future browser versions may not recognize formatting that relies on the <font> tag.

In reality, since so many Web pages have been built using this tag, browsers will continue to support it for several years at least. However, it's becoming increasingly common to use Cascading Style Sheets—the future formatting standard—to define the look of text and other objects on a Web page instead. To learn how to create and use CSS, see Chapter 8.

- Click the Font Color field in the Property inspector, and type in the *hexadecimal number* (see page 30) of the color you want. (Clearly, this is the option for hard-core HTML geeks. After all, surely you've memorized the hex number of that light shade of blue you always use—#6699FF, isn't it?)

Remember, as part of the properties for a Web page, you can choose a default color for all text on the page—see page 30 for the details. This is a useful shortcut for when you want all or most of the text on a page to be a color other than black.

Text Styles

To add emphasis to your words, you can choose from several text styles. You can apply the two most common emphasis effects, bold and italics, from the Property inspector; for less frequently used styles choose from the Text→Style submenu (see Figure 3-10).

To add bold or italic formatting to text, select the word or words you'd like to make bold or italic, then click the Bold or Italic button on the Property inspector.

Tip: Use italics with care. While italics are frequently used in printed material to add *emphasis* or when referencing a book title, they can be difficult to read on a computer screen, especially at small type sizes.

As shown in Figure 3-10, HTML has a host of different text styles; some fulfill special and sometimes obscure purposes. For instance, the Code and Variable styles are

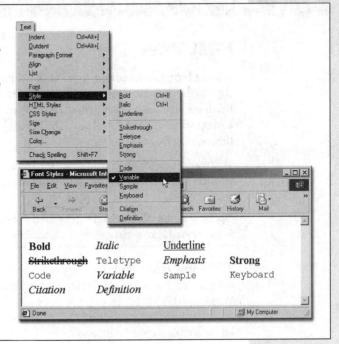

Figure 3-10:
While the Property inspector lets you apply bold and italic styles to text, the Text→Style menu (top) offers a larger selection of text styles. As you can see (bottom), the many different style options are usually displayed in bold, italics, the browser's monospaced font (usually Courier), or some combination of the three. You'll probably rarely use any of these additional styles.

intended for formatting the display of programming code, while the Sample style is used to display the output from a computer program—not exactly styles you'll need often in promoting, say, your Cheeses of the World mail-order company.

In general, you're better off avoiding these styles. But if you think one of these styles might come in handy, you can find more about them and their usefulness from Dreamweaver's new built-in HTML reference; see page 257 for details. However, stay away from the underline and strikethrough styles; both of those have been deprecated in the HTML 4 standard and may produce no effect in future browser versions.

Formatting Is Inherited

Pressing Enter or Return creates a new paragraph; the formatting of that paragraph is based on whatever text formatting you were using *before* you hit Enter or Return.

For example, suppose you just typed a new headline on the page using the Heading 1 format, and you set the font color to blue. Pressing Enter or Return creates another Heading 1 paragraph with blue text.

Changing the format of that new paragraph isn't so hard.

But what if you had lots of formatting applied to that first paragraph, including choices of typeface, text color, and alignment? To select the paragraph and remove all those individual formatting choices would be a pain.

A quick way to get rid of all of that formatting information and start with a basic paragraph is to click inside the paragraph and then click the "Clear Paragraph Style" option on the HTML Styles panel. This button eliminates all formatting from the paragraph.

HTML Styles

Adding formatting options to text can require many clicks of the mouse and many trips to the Property inspector. Suppose, for instance, that you want all of the major headings on a page to be formatted as Heading 1, using the Arial font, in red, italic, and centered. If your page has many headings, this could add up to a lot of formatting work.

To streamline such situations, use Dreamweaver's HTML Style feature. HTML Styles provide a single-click method for applying multiple text formatting options.

Tip: Be aware that HTML Styles are not an "official" Web technology like Cascading Style Sheets or JavaScript. They're a Macromedia creation, a shortcut for completing multiple formatting tasks in one step.

The control center for HTML Styles is the HTML Styles panel (see Figure 3-11). To open it, click the HTML Styles icon in the Launcher bar (see page 17), choose Window→HTML Styles, or press Ctrl+F11 (⌘-F11). The panel lists all styles defined for the current site (see page 23 for full detail on creating sites in Dreamweaver) and lets you create, apply, edit, and delete HTML Styles.

Creating HTML Styles

You can create an HTML Style either by formatting some text by hand first, or from scratch.

Figure 3-11:
To edit, delete, or duplicate a style, you need to select it. Unfortunately, selecting a style while the Auto Apply box is turned on automatically applies that style to any text you've selected. For this reason, make sure this box is not checked when you want to edit or delete an HTML Style.

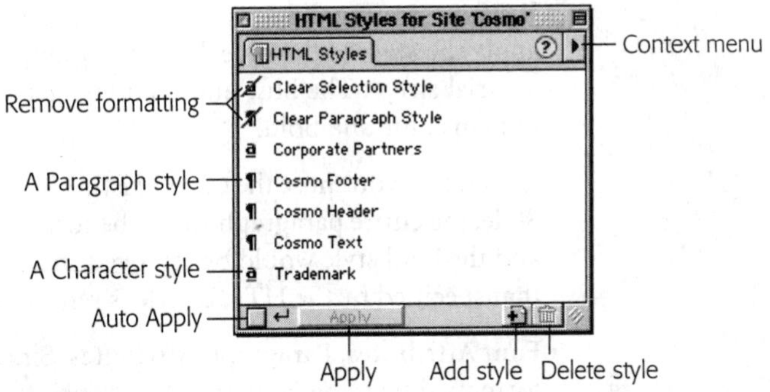

You can, if you like, create an HTML Style from scratch. But you save a lot of time by preformatting some text in your document, and then telling Dreamweaver to base its new style on *that*.

If the HTML Styles panel is open, start by clicking the Add Style button (the + button), or select New from the context menu (shown in Figure 3-11); if not, you can also choose Text→HTML Styles→New Style.

In any case, the Define HTML Style window opens, as shown in Figure 3-12. Set up your new style like this:

- **Name.** Type a name for your new style. For example, you might call it Author Name or Copyright. The name you type appears only in the HTML Styles panel; it won't become part of the Web page itself.

- **Apply To.** If you want the style to apply to a single word or a selection of text, not a whole paragraph—in other words, *character* formatting—choose Selection. If you want your company's name to appear in a different font face and color, for instance, create a selection style. If you choose this option, the Paragraph options—alignment and paragraph formatting—are dimmed and unavailable.

  A paragraph style, on the other hand, affects an entire paragraph or block-level element, such as a heading. (See page 57 for more on the character/paragraph formatting distinction.)

  A small character symbol appears in front of your style's name in the HTML Styles list, indicating how the style will be applied. If you choose Selection, a character symbol (a) appears before the name; if you choose Paragraph, a paragraph symbol (¶) appears. (Both are shown in Figure 3-11.)

- **When Applying.** If you apply an HTML Style to text that you've already formatted, Dreamweaver could easily become confused. Should it remove all previous formatting and *then* apply the HTML Style? Or should it *add* the HTML Style formatting to any formatting that already exists?

For example, say you've selected some blue, bold text, and you've created a paragraph HTML Style with the Arial font set to size 4.

If, when creating this style, you chose the Add to Existing Style option, when you apply the style to the blue, bold paragraph, the entire paragraph gets formatted as Arial size 4. The blue and bold text gets the same paragraph formatting, but remains blue and bold.

However, if you chose the *Clear* Existing Style option when you created the HTML Style, the entire paragraph would be formatted as Arial, size 4, but the blue color and the bold style would be removed from the text. In fact, all formatting *except* that specified by the HTML Style is removed.

- **Font Attributes, Paragraph Attributes.** Since you're basing this style on already formatted text, the Font and Paragraph attributes are already defined. Just click OK to create your style.

To create an HTML Style from scratch, use the HTML Styles panel (Figure 3-11); click the Add Style button. (The long way is to choose Text→HTML Styles→New Style or select New from the context menu on the HTML Styles panel.) In any case, the Define HTML Style window opens, as shown in Figure 3-12.

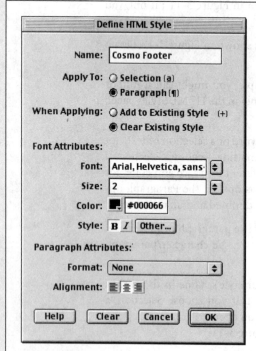

Figure 3-12:
The Define HTML Styles window lets you define the various font and paragraph attributes of an HTML Style. The options are the same as those in the Property inspector or the Text menu. If you need help, you can click the Help button to activate Dreamweaver's Help system. In addition, if you don't like the font and paragraph attributes you've set for the style, you can click Clear to set all attributes of the style to None.

Name and set the basic properties of the style, as described above; then set up the font, size, color, and style you want (if it's a character style). If it's a paragraph style, you can also specify a paragraph format (Heading 1, Paragraph, and so on) and an alignment option (left, centered, or right). (HTML Styles can't include list formatting.) Finally, click OK.

Applying HTML Styles

Once you've defined a style, you can apply it just by selecting some text and then using the HTML Styles panel.

Tip: If you're about to apply a paragraph-level style, you don't have to select the whole paragraph. Simply clicking anywhere inside the text block is enough.

If the Auto Apply checkbox is selected (see Figure 3-11), a single click on the style's name applies it. If Auto Apply is not turned on, you have to click the name of the style to select it, and *then* click Apply. And if all of this is too confusing, you can always apply a style by choosing its name from the Text→HTML Styles submenu.

Editing styles

Editing a style is just as easy. With the Auto Apply checkbox turned off, double-click a style name. The Define HTML Styles window opens (see Figure 3-12). Make any changes to the style, and then click OK.

GEM IN THE ROUGH

Anti-Styles

Even if you don't plan to use HTML Styles, two default styles listed in the HTML Styles panel (Figure 3-11)—and the Text→HTML Styles submenu—can be very useful: Clear Selection Style and Clear Paragraph Style.

Actually, these aren't styles at all. They're more like anti-styles. Both come in handy when you want to remove a bunch of formatting from a selection or paragraph of text.

Suppose you highlight some text that includes both paragraph styles and character styles, as shown here at top. If you click the Clear Selection Style button, Dreamweaver removes all character formatting from the selection, including font face, color, size, align-

ment, and style (center). But it preserves paragraph formatting, such as alignment, and doesn't affect any other formatted text in the paragraph.

If you click Clear Paragraph Style, however, Dreamweaver removes all text *and* paragraph formatting from a block of text as shown here at bottom. It also converts headings and preformatted text to plain paragraphs.

These may not seem like earth-shattering tools, but imagine the alternative: selecting each piece of formatted text and removing text and paragraph attributes one at a time from the Property inspector.

Although HTML Styles may remind you of styles in, say, Microsoft Word, they're not the same thing. Editing a style, for example, affects only *subsequent* applications of the HTML Style; Dreamweaver doesn't automatically update text that you'd *previously* formatted with the style. You have to tell Dreamweaver to update them, as described next.

Updating HTML Styles

As noted above, editing a Dreamweaver style doesn't change the formatting of text to which you'd already applied that style. If you'd created a style called Footer that had a font size of 2 and a color of red, editing the style to make its text purple doesn't affect any Footer text you'd already typed; that text stays red. You have to manually reselect the text and reapply the style to update the formatting.

Tip: On the other hand, Dreamweaver *can* make a formatting change that ripples through and updates all corresponding formatting on a Web page (or even a Web site)—but not with HTML Styles. The trick is to use Cascading Style Sheets instead, as described in Chapter 9.

Removing HTML Styles

If you want to remove an HTML Style that you've defined, make sure the Auto Apply checkbox is turned off, and then select the style you wish to edit from the HTML Styles panel. Click the Trash can icon in the lower right corner of the HTML Styles panel or choose Delete from the panel's context menu to banish the style. (Doing so has no effect on text to which you've already applied that formatting.)

POWER USERS' CLINIC

Sharing Your HTML Styles

You may wonder where Dreamweaver stores all of the HTML Style information you create. After all, the names you give your HTML Styles never appear in the HTML of your pages; yet you can apply the same style to multiple pages, so Dreamweaver must be keeping this information *somewhere.*

Here's where: Dreamweaver records HTML Styles in a file (technically, an XML file) called, logically enough, *styles.xml.* It's in the Library folder in each Web site's local *root folder*—that is, the master folder that con-

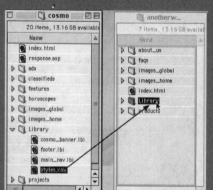

tains all of the files for your Web site. (For more information on local site folders, see Chapter 14).

That's good to know, especially when the day comes when you want to transfer HTML Styles you've created from one site to another. In that case, you simply make a copy of the styles.xml file in the first site folder, and place it the Library folder of the second site folder. Alternatively, drag the file while holding down the Ctrl (Option) key into the new Library folder.

Links

The humble hyperlink may not raise eyebrows anymore, but the notion that you can easily navigate a whole sea of information, jumping from one piece of information to another with a simple click, is a very recent and powerful invention. Interested in a particular band? Go to Yahoo.com, type in the band's name, *click* to go to its Web site, *click* to go to the page that lists its upcoming gigs, *click* to go to the Web site for the club where the band is playing now, and *click* to buy tickets.

Although links are a basic part of building pages, and although Dreamweaver, for the most part, shields you from their complexities, they can be tricky to understand. The following section provides a brief overview of links, including some of the technical distinctions between the different types. If you already understand links, or are just eager to start using Dreamweaver, jump to "Adding a Link" on page 85.

Understanding Links

A link is a snippet of computer code that gives a Web browser directions for how to get from one page to another on the Web. What makes links powerful is the fact that the distance those directions take doesn't matter. A link can just as easily lead to another page on the same site or to a page on a Web server halfway around the globe.

Behind the scenes, a simple HTML tag called the anchor (<a>) tag generates each and every link. Links come in three different flavors: absolute, document relative, and root relative. See page 84 for some examples of each link type in practice.

Absolute Links

When people need to mail you a letter, they ask for your address. Suppose it's 123 Main St., New York, New York 12001. No matter where in the country your friend is, if she writes *123 Main St, NY, NY 12001* on an envelope—and attaches postage—it will get to you. That's because your address is unique—just like an absolute link.

Similarly, every Web page also has a unique address, called a *URL* (most people pronounce it "You Are El"), or Uniform Resource Locator. If you open a Web browser and type *http://www.sawmac.com/missing/index.html* into the address bar, the home page for this book opens.

This URL is an *absolute link*; it's the complete, unique address for a single page. Absolute links always begin with *http://*, and you'll use them any time you link to a Web page *outside of your own site*. Absolute links always lead to the same page, whether the link to it is on a page in the current site or an entirely different site.

The bottom line: Use absolute links when you want to link to a page on another Web site.

Parts of a URL

URLs are made up of different pieces of information, each of which helps a Web browser locate the proper Web page. Take the following URL, for instance: *http://www.sawmac.com/missing/index.html.*

http—This portion specifies the *protocol*—the method the Web browser must use to communicate with the Web server. HTTP stands for hypertext transfer protocol, for what it's worth; it specifies a connection to a Web page (as opposed to protocols like *ftp* [for transferring files] and *mailto* [for email addresses]).

www.sawmac.com—This portion specifies the exact computer that's dishing out the Web site in question—that is, it's the address of the Web *server*.

/missing/—This is the name of a folder (sometimes called a directory) on the Web server.

index.html—This is the name of the actual document or file that the Web browser is supposed to open—the Web page itself. It's these HTML documents that Dreamweaver creates—and that you're reading about.

Document-Relative Links

Suppose you, the resident of 123 Main Street, drop in on a neighbor who just moved into the neighborhood. After letting him know about all the great restaurants nearby, you tell him about a party you're having at your place.

When he asks you where you live, you could, of course, say, "I live at 123 Main St., NY, NY 12001," but your neighbor would probably think you needed a little psychiatric help. More likely, you would say something like, "Just go across the street and turn left; I'm the second house on the right." Of course, you can't use these instructions as your mailing address, because they work only *relative* to your neighbor's house.

When you want to create a link from one Web page to another within the same Web site, you can use similar shorthand: a *document-relative* link. In essence, a document-relative link—like the directions you give your neighbor—simply tells the browser where to find the linked page *relative to* the current page. If two pages are in the same folder, for instance, the path is as simple as, "Go to that page over there." In this case, the link is simply the name of the file you wish to link to: *index.html*. You can leave off all that *http://* and *www.sawmac.com* business, because you're already there.

Document-relative links can be finicky, however, since they're completely dependent on the location of the page containing the link. If you move the page to another part of the site—filing it in a different folder, for example—the link won't work. That's why working with document-relative links has traditionally been one of the most troublesome chores for a Web designer, even though this kind of link is ideal for linking from one page to another in the same site.

Fortunately, Dreamweaver makes working with document-relative links so easy, you may forget what all the fuss is about. For example, whenever you save a page into another folder—a maneuver that would normally shatter all document-relative links on the page—Dreamweaver quietly *rewrites* the links so they still work. Even better, using the program's site management tools, you can cavalierly reorganize your Web site—moving folders and files, for example—without harming the delicate connections between your site's files. Dreamweaver's site management features are discussed in depth in Part IV.

Root-Relative Links

Root-relative links describe, to a Web browser, how to get from one page to another within the same site, just like document-relative links. However, in this case, the path is described relative to the site's *root folder*—the folder that contains the home page and other pages, folders, and files that make up your site. (For a detailed description of the root folder and structuring a Web site, see Chapter 14.)

Imagine you work in a big office building. You need to get to a co-worker's office for a meeting. You call her up for directions. Now, she may not know the precise directions from your office to hers, but she can tell you how to get from your building's entrance to her office. Since you both know where your building's front door is, these directions work well. Think of the office building as your site, and its front door as the *root* of your site.

Root-relative links always begins with a slash /. This slash is a stand-in character for the root folder—the front door—of the site. The same root-relative link always leads to the same page, no matter where it is on your Web site.

There are some major drawbacks to using root-relative links in Dreamweaver. The most apparent is that they don't work when you test them on your own computer; clicking a root-relative link in a Web browser on your own machine produces only a "File Not Found" error. Such links work once they're moved to a Web server—Web servers understand root-relative links—but not on your local computer.

Stick to document-relative links for your pages, but keep this discussion in mind. You'll see later that Dreamweaver's site-management features use root-relative paths to track your site's files.

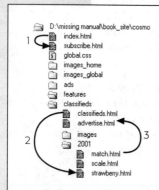

Figure 4-1:
Here are a few examples of links for a fictitious Web site located at www.cosmofarmer.com. Notice that although the root folder (cosmo) is nested inside several other folders—book_site and missing manual—it's still the top-level folder for the site, since it holds the home page and all of the other files that go on the site. Keep this distinction in mind: The site root is not the same as the top level of your hard drive.

Link Types in Action

Figure 4-1 shows a Web site as it lies on a hard drive: folders filled with HTML documents and graphics. Here's a closer look at some links you might find on the pages there, and how they might work:

Links from the Home page (index.html) to the Subscribe page

The home-page document is usually called index.html. You could create a link—identified by the number 1 in Figure 4-1—from it to the subscribe.html page using any of the three link types:

- **Absolute.** *http://www.cosmofarmer.com/subscribe.html.* What it means: Go to the Web site at *www.cosmofarmer.com* and download the page *subscribe.html.*

- **Document Relative.** *subscribe.html.* What it means: Look in the same Web site and folder and download the page *subscribe.html.*

- **Root Relative:** */subscribe.html.* What it means: Go to the top level folder of this site (called cosmo, in this case, but it doesn't matter) and download *subscribe.html.*

Links from the Classifieds page to the Strawberry page

Now imagine that you're building a Web page that you want to link to a page in another folder (called 2001, in this case). Here's how you'd use each of the three link types to create the link identified by the number 2 in Figure 4-1:

- **Absolute.** *http://www.cosmofarmer.com/classifieds/2001/strawberry.html.* What it means: Go to the Web site at *www.cosmofarmer.com,* look in the folder *classifieds,* and then in the folder *2001;* download the page *strawberry.html.*

- **Document Relative:** *2001/strawberry.html.* What it means: From the current page, look into the folder *2001* and download the page *strawberry.html.*

- **Root Relative:** */classifieds/2001/strawberry.html.* What it means: Go to the top level folder of this site, look in the folder *classifieds,* and then in the folder *2001;* download the page *strawberry.html.* (Notice that a root relative link looks just like an absolute link, minus the initial *http://www.cosmofarmer.com.*)

Links from the Match page to the Advertise page

Now suppose you're building a Web page that's in a deeply nested folder; you want it to link to a document that's *outside* of its folder, a link labeled 3 in Figure 4-1:

- **Absolute.** *http://www.cosmofarmer.com/classifieds/advertise.html.* What it means: Go to the Web site at *www.cosmofarmer.com,* look in the folder *classifieds,* and download the page *advertise.html.*

- **Document Relative.** *../advertise.html.* What it means: Go up one level—outside of the current folder—and download the page *advertise.html.* In links, a slash (/) represents a folder or directory. The two dots (..) mean, "Go up one level," into the folder that *contains* the current folder.

- **Root Relative.** */classifieds/advertise.html.* What it means: Go to the top level folder of this site; look in the folder *classifieds,* and download the page *advertise.html.*

The executive summary

To summarize all of this discussion: Use absolute URLs for linking *outside* of your site. Use document-relative links for links *within a site.* And avoid root-relative links.

Adding a link

If all that talk of links got you confused, don't worry. Links *are* confusing, and that's one of the best reasons to use Dreamweaver. If you can navigate to a document on your own computer or anywhere on the Web, you can create a link to it in Dreamweaver, even if you don't know the first thing about URLs and don't intend to learn.

Figure 4-2:
The Property Inspector provides three ways to add links to text or images on a Web page: the Link field, the Point-to-File icon, and the Browse-for-File icon. The Link field includes a pop-up menu listing the most recently used links. Avoid it; Dreamweaver doesn't always use the correct path for links listed in this menu.

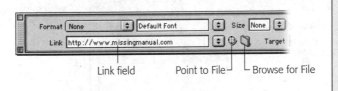

Link field   Point to File ⏌ ⌐ Browse for File

Browsing for a File

To create a link from one a page to another on your own Web site, use the Browse for File button on the Property inspector (see Figure 4-2) or its keyboard shortcut (see the steps below). Browsing for a file in Dreamweaver uses the same type of dialog box that you already use to open or save a file, making this the easiest way to add a link. (To link to a page on another Web site, you'll need to type the Web address into the Property inspector. Turn to page 88 for instructions.)

Note: Before you add any links, *save your Web page.* Not only is saving often good computer common sense, but saving a document means that you've settled on a folder location for it–a requirement if you hope to use document-relative links.

---

1. **In the document window, select the text or image you want to use for the link.**

   You can select a single word, a sentence, or an entire paragraph. When this process is over, the selected words will show up blue and underlined (depending on your visitors' Web-browser settings), like billions of links before them.

   Of course, you can also turn a picture into a link—a great trick for adding attractive navigation buttons.

2. **Click the folder (Browse for File) icon in the Property inspector, or choose Modify→Make Link, or press Ctrl+L (⌘-L).**

   The Select File dialog box opens (see Figure 4-3).

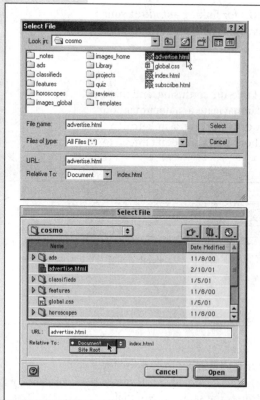

Figure 4-3:
The Select File dialog box looks slightly different in Windows (top) and Mac (bottom), but both let you browse your computer's file system to select the file you wish to link to.

From the Relative To pop-up menu, you can choose what type of link–Document or Site Root relative–to create. Since root-relative links don't work when you preview your pages on your computer, choosing Document from the pop-up menu is almost always your best bet. Whichever you choose, Dreamweaver remembers your selection and uses it the next time you create a link. Keep this quirk in mind if you suddenly find that your links are not working when you preview your pages. Odds are you accidentally selected Site Root at some point, and Dreamweaver happily continued writing site root-relative links.

3. **Choose the type of link—Document or Site Root—from the Relative To menu.**

As noted earlier in this chapter, document-relative links are the best choice. Root-relative links (which is short for Site Root-relative links) don't work when previewing the Web site on your own computer.

4. **Navigate to and double-click the file you want the link to open.**

The file should be a Web page that's part of your Web site; in other words, that's in the local root folder (see page 23), or in a folder therein.

If you try to link to a file outside the root folder, Dreamweaver alerts you to this problem, and offers to copy the file into the root folder. Remember: For a Web site, the root folder is like the edges of the known universe; nothing exists outside it.

In any case, the text or image now links to another Web page. (If you haven't yet saved the Web page, Dreamweaver doesn't know how to write the document-relative link. Instead, it displays a dialog box saying that it will assign a temporary path for the link until you save the page—see the box on page 90.)

After you've applied a link, graphics don't look any different, but linked text appears underlined and colored (using the color defined by the Page Property window, which is described on page 29). If you want to take the link for a spin, press the F12 key to preview the page in your browser (see page 37), where you can click the link.

FREQUENTLY ASKED QUESTION

Targeting Links

What's the Target menu in the Property inspector for?

The Target menu has nothing to do with the accuracy of your links, nor with shooting ranges. Instead, it deals with how the destination page appears when you click a link.

The new page can appear (a) right in the browser window, just the way most links work; (b) in a new browser window (choose the _blank option); or (c) in a different *frame* on the same page (see Chapter 7).

Using the Point-to-File Icon

You can also create links in Dreamweaver by dragging icons, which is one great use of Dreamweaver's Site window (shown in Figure 4-4). If your site involves a lot of links, learning the Point-to-File tool will save you time and energy.

To use this trick effectively, position your document window and Site window side-by-side, as shown in Figure 4-4.

1. **In the document window, select the text or image you want to turn into a link.**

Make sure that both the Property inspector and Site window are open. (To open the Property inspector if it's not on the screen, choose Window→Properties. To open the Site window if *it's* not visible, choose Window→Site Files. Before using the Site window, you need to first create a local site, as described on page 24.)

2. **Drag the Point-to-File icon in the Property inspector *onto* a Web page into the Site window (see Figure 4-4).**

   Alternatively, you can Shift-drag the selected text or image in the document window to a Web page in the Site window—a method that bypasses the Property inspector altogether.

3. **After dragging over the correct Web page, release the mouse button.**

   The selected text or image in your Web page turns into a link to the file you just pointed to.

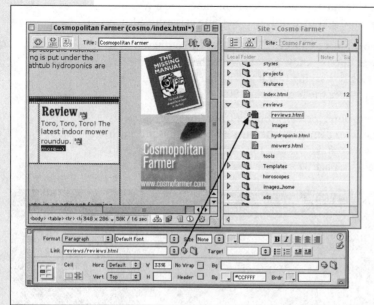

Figure 4-4:
In this figure, the text "more–>" is selected in the document window to the left. To link to another page, drag from the Point-to-File icon in the Property inspector to a Web page in the Site window shown at right. In this example, Dream-weaver creates a link to the Web page called reviews.html. Another method would be to press Shift and drag from the text "more–>" to the page mowers.html in the Site window.

Typing (or Pasting) the URL or Path

If you need to link to another Web site, or you feel comfortable with how document-relative links work, you can also simply type the URL or path to the page in the Property inspector. Note that this is the *only* way to add a link to a page outside of the current Web site.

Start by selecting the text or graphic you want to make into a link. Then, in the Link field in the Property inspector (see Figure 4-1), type the URL or path to the file. (If the link leads to another Web site, type an absolute URL—that is, a complete Web address, starting with *http://*.)

Tip: An easier approach is to copy a complete URL—including the *http://*—from the Address bar in your browser window. Then paste the address into the Link field.

To link to another page on your own site, you can type a document-relative link (see page 84 for some examples). Of course, you'll be less prone to error if you let Dreamweaver write the correct path using the browsing or point-to-file techniques described above. However, typing the path can come in handy, for instance, when you want to create a link to a page you haven't yet created.

Finally, press Enter (Return) to apply the link; the text or image now links to another Web page.

Adding an Email Link

Whenever you want to invite your visitors to email you, an *email link* is the perfect solution. When a visitor clicks an email link, her email program launches automatically; a new message opens with your email address already in the To field. She can then just type her message and send it off.

An email link looks like this: *mailto:bob@cosmofarmer.com.* The first part, *mailto:*, indicates the type of link, while the second part *(bob@cosmofarmer.com)* specifies the email address.

Note: Email links only work if the person who clicks the link has an email account and an email program. If someone visits your site from a computer at the public library, he might not be able to send an email. If this drawback troubles you, remember that you can also collect information using a Form (as discussed in Chapter 10)—a feedback method that has neither the limitations nor the easy setup of an email link.

You can create an email link much the way you'd create any other Dreamweaver link: by selecting some text or image and typing the mailto address, as shown above, into the Link field in the Property inspector. To simplify this process, Dreamweaver has a quick method of inserting an email link.

If you've already typed the text *(Email me!)* on your Web page, select it first. Then choose Insert→Email Link (or click the Email Link icon on the Objects panel).

The Insert Email Link dialog box opens (see Figure 4-4), with these two fields to fill in:

• **Text.** Type the text you want to appear on the Web page. It should give visitors some indication of what the link does, such as *Email the Webmaster.* (If you selected already-typed text before opening this dialog box, it automatically appears in the Text field.)

• **E-Mail.** Type the address that appears in the user's email program when he clicks the link. (You don't have to type *mailto:*; Dreamweaver adds this to the email address automatically.)

When you click OK, Dreamweaver adds the text to the page, complete with a mailto link.

Linking Within a Web Page

Clicking a link usually loads a Web page into the browser window. But what if you want to link not only to a Web page, but to a specific *spot* on the Web page? See Figure 4-6 for an example.

Introducing the *anchor link*, a special link type that's designed to auto-scroll to a particular spot on a particular page.

Phase 1: Creating an anchor

Creating an anchor link is a two-step process: first add and name an anchor, thus identifying the destination for the link; then add a link that goes to that named

Figure 4-5:
The Insert Email Link dialog box lets you specify the text that appears on the Web page and the email address. You can also select some text you've already added to the document and click the Email Link icon on the Objects panel. The text you selected is copied into the Text field in the dialog box.

FREQUENTLY ASKED QUESTION

The Mysterious Triple Slashes

Why do my links start with file:///?

Links that begin with file:/// (for example: *file:///D:/missing manual/book_site/cosmo/subscribe.html*) aren't valid links. Rather, they are temporary addresses that Dreamweaver creates as placeholders for links to be re-written later. (A file:/// path tells Dreamweaver where to look on your computer for the file.) You'll spot these addresses when you add document-relative links to a page that hasn't been saved, or when working with files that are outside of your site's local root folder.

Suppose you're working on a Web page that will contain your company's legal mumbo-jumbo, but you haven't yet saved it. After adding a document-relative link that links to your home page, you notice that the path displayed in the Property inspector's Link field begins with file:///. Since your legal page hasn't yet been saved and therefore doesn't yet have a folder location, Dreamweaver can't create a link telling a browser how to get from it to the home page.

So Dreamweaver creates a temporary link, which helps it keep track of what page to link to. Once you save the page

somewhere in the site, Dreamweaver rewrites the link into a proper document-relative format and the file:/// disappears.

Likewise, when you work with files that are outside of the local root folder, Dreamweaver can't write a proper link. (Any folder outside of the local root folder isn't part of the Web site; and there's no way to write a correct link from nowhere to somewhere.) So, if you save a page *outside* of the local root folder, Dreamweaver writes all document-relative links on that page as file paths beginning with file:/// To avoid this invalid-link problem, always save your Web pages inside of the local root folder or a folder *inside* of the local root folder. To learn more about root folders and Web sites, see Chapter 14.

When you *link* to a page—or add an image, as you'll see in the next chapter—that's outside of the local root folder, Dreamweaver has the same problem. However, in this instance, Dreamweaver gives you the option of copying the out-of-bounds file to a location of your choosing within the root folder.

---

anchor. For instance, in the Answers page example of Figure 4-6, you would place a named anchor at the beginning of each answer.

To create a named anchor, click where you want it to appear (that is, where you want the link to jump to). Now use one of these three methods:

- Choose Insert→Invisible Tags→Named Anchor.

- Press Ctrl+Alt+A (⌘-Option-A).

- Select the Invisibles category (see page 20) from the Objects panel pop-up menu and click the Named Anchor icon.

Now, in the Insert Named Anchor dialog box, type a unique name for the anchor; it should be short and easy to remember. No spaces are allowed, however. Punctuation is illegal, too; stick to letters and numbers (but you can't *begin* an anchor with a number). If you violate any of these regulations, Dreamweaver scolds you.

When you click OK, the text or image you selected becomes a link to the anchor specified in the Link field. You'll see a gold shield with an anchor on it at the anchor point; click this icon to show the name of the anchor in the Properties inspector. (If you don't see it, refer to page 92 for detail on hiding and showing anchors.)

The anchor icon is the key to removing or editing the anchor later: Just click the icon and press Delete to get rid of it, or click it and change its name in the Property inspector. (Deleting the name in the Property inspector deletes the anchor, too.)

Figure 4-6:
Imagine a Web page with a list of Frequently Asked Questions (right). To make it easier to update, all of the answers are listed together on a single page. Adding anchors to the Answers page makes it possible to jump from the Questions page to the precise location of the answer on the Answers page.

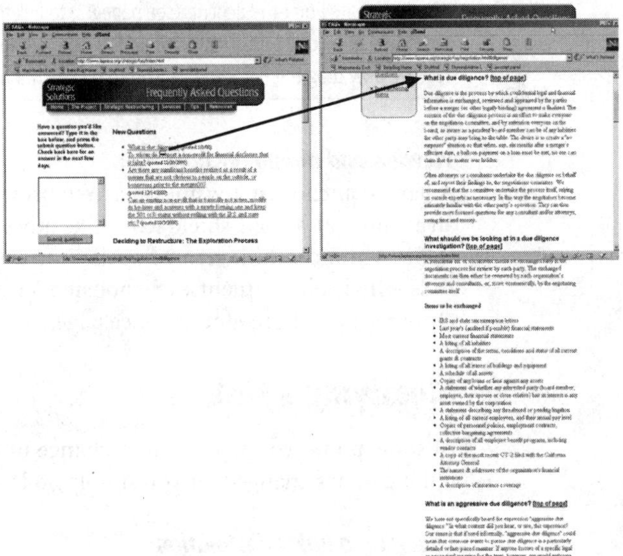

Phase 2: Linking to an anchor

Creating a link to a named anchor is not all that different from linking to a Web page. Once you've created and named an anchor, you can link to it from within the same Web page, or from a different page.

To link to an anchor on the same page, select the text or image you want to make into a link. Now, in the Link field in the Property inspector, type #, followed by the name of the anchor. (Alternatively, use the Point-to-File icon; see Figure 4-7.) That's all there is to it. The # sign indicates that the link goes to a named anchor. In other words, if you wish to link to an anchor named *directions,* the link would be *#directions.*

You can also link from one Web page to a particular location on another Web page in your site. The process is the same as linking to an anchor on the same page, except that you have to specify both the path to the Web page *and* the name of the anchor. In other words, in the Link field of the Property inspector, type or choose the URL or path of the page you wish to link to.

You can use any of the methods described earlier: browsing, point-to-file, or typing the path. Unfortunately, if you *browse* to select the linked file, Dreamweaver doesn't offer any means of listing the anchors on it; therefore, after choosing the page itself by browsing, click at the end of the URL or path in the Property inspector's Link field. Type #, followed by the name of the anchor.

Either way, the Link field should something look like this: *contact.html#directions.*

Tip: To use the Point-to-File icon (see page 87) to link to an anchor on another Web page, just open both pages—the one you're linking from, and the one with the anchor you're linking to—in Dreamweaver, side by side. Now drag the Point-to-File icon to the anchor as shown in Figure 4-7.

Viewing and hiding anchors

A named anchor isn't visible in a Web browser; it's represented in Dreamweaver as an anchor-on-a-gold-shield icon. Like other invisible elements—line breaks, for instance—you can hide named anchors in Dreamweaver by choosing View→Visual Aids→Invisible Elements, or choosing Visual Aids→Invisible Elements from the Options menu in the toolbar (see page 16).

Modifying a Link

At some point, you may need to change or edit a link. Perhaps the URL you were linking to has changed, or you simply no longer need that link.

Changing a link's destination

As you'll read in Part IV, Dreamweaver provides some amazing tools for automatically updating your links so your site stays in working order, even if you move files around your site. But even Dreamweaver isn't smart enough to know when a page on someone *else's* Web site is moved or deleted. And you may decide you simply need to change a link so that it points to a different page on your own site. In both of these cases, you'll need to change the links on your Web pages by hand.

1. **Select the text link or picture link.**

   Do so by clicking anywhere inside of text link, or clicking once on the link image.

   The existing link path appears in the Link field in the Property inspector.

2. **Use any of the techniques described on page 85 for specifying the link's target.**

   For example, click the Browse-for-File button in the Property inspector and locate a different Web page in your site.

   The destination of the link changes to the new URL, path, or anchor.

Removing a link

Sometimes, you want to stop a link from linking—when the Web page you were linking to no longer exists, for example. You want the text or image on your Web

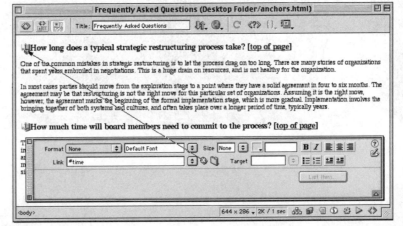

Figure 4-7:
You can use the Property inspector's Point-to-File icon to link to a named anchor on a page. Simply select some text or an image in an open page. Then drag the Point-to-File icon to an anchor on any other open document to set the link. If you can't see the shield icons that mark anchors, see page 92 for instructions on how to make them visible.

FREQUENTLY ASKED QUESTION

Anchors Away

When I click on a link to an anchor, the Web browser is supposed to go to the page and display the anchor at the top of the browser window. But sometimes the anchor appears in the middle of the browser. What's that about?

Web browsers can't scroll beyond the bottom of a Web page, so an anchor near the bottom of a page sometimes

can't move to the top of the browser window. If one of your own Web pages exhibits this problem, the fix is simple: Just add a bunch of empty lines—press the Enter key repeatedly—below the last item on the page. You've just added space at the bottom of the page, so the browser can scroll the page all the way to the anchor.

page to stay the same, but you want to remove the disabled link. In that case, just select the link text or image, and then use one of these tactics:

- Choose Modify→Remove Link.

- Press Ctrl+Shift+L (⌘-Shift-L).

- Delete the text in the Link field of the Property inspector.

The text or image remains on your Web page, but it no longer links to anything. If it's a text link, the color changes from the page's link color (see page 30) to the normal text color for the page.

Of course, if you're feeling particularly destructive, you can also delete the link text or image itself; doing so also destroys the link.

FREQUENTLY ASKED QUESTION

Link Colors

How can I change the color of my links?

To help Web visitors identify links, Web browsers usually display linked text in a special color (blue, for example). Fortunately, you can control which color the browser uses; to do so, begin by choosing Modify→Page Properties to open the Page Properties dialog box. For more information, see page 30.

While we're on the subject, I'm already using a different *color for my links to make them stand out from the other text. Can I get rid of the underline that Dreamweaver automatically puts under links?*

Yes, but not with HTML alone. By default, all text links show up with underlines, and no HTML code can change that. However, Cascading Style Sheets provide a lot more formatting control than plain HTML—including, yes, the ability to remove link underlines. To find out how, see Chapter 8.

Images

Nobody believes that a picture is worth a thousand words more than today's
Web designers, as evidenced by the increasingly visual nature of the Internet.
In fact, it's not difficult to stumble onto a home page these days composed
of nothing but graphics (see Figure 5-1).

Even if you don't want to go that far, understanding how to use graphics effectively
is invaluable. Whether you want to plop a simple photo onto your page, cover it
with clickable "hot spots," or design an interactive set of buttons that light up when
the cursor passes over them, Dreamweaver makes the job—and the underlying
JavaScript programming—easy.

Figure 5-1:
Some Web sites rely almost exclusively on graphics
for both looks and function. The home page for the
PBS Kids Web site, for instance, uses graphics not just
for pictures of their shows' characters, but also for the
page's background and navigation buttons.

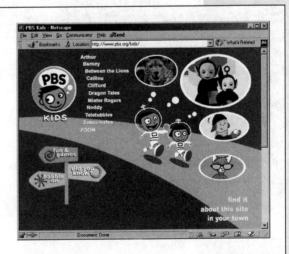

Adding Images

If you were writing out the HTML instructions for your Web page by hand, you'd insert an image into a Web page using the Image tag—<img>. The primary *property* of an image is called the source *(src)*, which is the URL or path to the graphics file.

Fortunately, Dreamweaver can do all of this coding for you automatically when you insert a picture into your fledgling Web page:

1. **Save the Web page that will contain the image.**

   In order to insert an image, Dreamweaver must determine the path from your Web page to that image, which could be anywhere on your hard drive. As with links (see page 85), saving the page before you proceed enables Dreamweaver to correctly determine that path from the image to the page you just saved.

2. **In the document window, click where you want to insert the image.**

   This might be at the beginning or end of a paragraph, or within a cell in a table (see Chapter 6). To set a graphic apart, put it in its own paragraph; that is, click at the end of the preceding paragraph and press Enter before inserting it.

UP TO SPEED

GIFs, JPEGs, and PNGs: The Graphics of the Web

Computer graphics come in hundreds of different file formats. The assorted acronyms can be mind-numbing: TIFF, PICT, BMP, EPS, Amiga IFF, and so on.

Fortunately, graphics on the Web are a bit simpler. There are only three graphics formats—two established formats and one exciting newcomer. All three provide good *compression;* through clever computer manipulation, they reduce the graphic's file size so it can travel more rapidly across the Internet. They differ only in the details.

GIF (Graphics Interchange Format) files provide good compression for images that have areas of solid color: logos, text, simple banners. In addition, GIFs offer single-color transparency, meaning that one color in the graphic can be made to disappear, permitting the background of a Web page to show through part of the image.

Unfortunately, a GIF image can only contain a maximum of 256 shades, generally making photos look blotchy; that radiant sunset photo you took with your digital camera

won't look so good as a GIF.

JPEG (Joint Photographic Experts Group) graphics, on the other hand, pick up where GIFs leave off. A JPEG graphic can contain millions of different colors, making them ideal for photographic images. Not only do JPEGs do a better job on photos, they also compress much better than GIFs, because the JPG compression algorithm considers how the human eye perceives different adjacent color values. When your graphics software saves a JPEG file, it averages the colors of adjacent pixels.

Finally, the **PNG** (Portable Network Graphics) format holds great promise for the future. These files can be compressed even smaller than in GIF format, contain millions of colors, and offer 256 levels of transparency, which means that you could actually see through a drop shadow on a graphic through to the background of a Web page. Unfortunately, only the most recent Web browsers recognize this format, so you'd be well advised to avoid PNG graphics for the moment.

---

3. **Choose Insert→Image.**

Alternatively, if the Objects panel is open, you can click the Image button in the Common category. Or, if you're a keyboard nut, press Ctrl+Alt+I (⌘-Option-I).

In any case, the Select Image Source dialog box opens. This box is identical to the Select File window that appears when adding a link to a page. The only difference is the Preview Images checkbox; turning it on shows a thumbnail of any selected image in the Preview window.

4. **Browse to and select the graphics file you wish to add to the page.**

The graphic file must be in one of the formats that work on the Web: GIF, JPEG, or PNG.

The file should be stored somewhere in the local root folder of your site (see page 23) or in one of its subfolders. If it isn't, Dreamweaver can't add the correct path to your Web page.

That's why, if you select a graphic for insertion that's not already in your site folder, Dreamweaver offers to add a *copy* of it there. If you choose Yes, a Copy File As dialog box opens, so that you can save the file into your local root folder, renaming it if you wish. If you choose No, Dreamweaver uses a file-relative path (beginning with *File:///*—see page 90) for the image's Source property. But clicking No is usually a bad idea; while it allows the graphic to be displayed while you work with Dreamweaver on your computer, the graphic won't appear once you move the document to the Web.

5. **Choose the type of path to create: Document or Site Root.**

When you insert an image into a Web page, you don't actually add the graphics file to the HTML file; instead, you create a *path* to the image, a coded description of where a computer can find the relevant graphics file, so that a Web browser knows where to look for and download the graphic.

In general, Document is the best choice. Site Root-relative paths don't always work when previewing a page. (See page 82 for detail on the difference between document- and root-relative links.)

6. **Click Select (Windows) or Open (Mac).**

The image appears on your Web page.

Modifying an Image

After inserting a graphic, you can work on it in several ways: by attaching a link to the image, aligning it on the page, or adding a border and margin to it, for example. As with most objects on a Web page, you set image properties using the Property inspector (see Figure 5-2).

Naming an Image

Just to the right of an image's thumbnail on the Property inspector is a small field where you can type a *name* for that image. Most of the time, you'll leave this field blank. However, if you plan to add interactive effects to it (such as the rollover effect discussed on page 303, or your own JavaScript programming), you *must* name your picture. Whatever name you choose should only use letters and numbers—no spaces or other punctuation.

Note: JavaScript uses the image name that you type here for its own reference; no one actually sees this name in a Web browser. This isn't, in other words, the place to give your graphic a text label that shows up when your reader has graphics turned off, for example; for that purpose, read on.

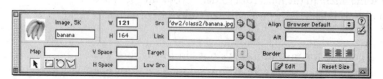

Figure 5-2:
The Property inspector displays the specs for a graphic, plus a mini version in the upper-left corner.

Adding a Text Description to an Image

Not everyone who visits your Web site gets to see those stunning photos of your last summer vacation. Some people deliberately turn off graphics when they surf, enjoying a Web without the wait; graphics-free Web pages appear in a Web browser almost instantly. Other people have vision impairments that prevent them from enjoying the graphic nature of the Web; they rely on special software that reads Web-page text aloud, including any labels you've given your graphics.

To assist Web surfers in both situations, make a habit of setting the *Alt property* of the image. Short for *alternative text,* the Alt property is a text description that Web browsers use as a stand-in for the image (see Figure 5-3).

INFREQUENTLY ASKED QUESTION

The Low Src Property

What's an image's Low Src property, shown in Figure 5-2?

The most important thing to know about the Low Src property is that you shouldn't bother setting it! It's a not-so-useful property that is recognized *only* by Netscape browsers.

But since you asked: This property defines a low-resolution version of the final image. Back when people had 14.4 K modems and it took a long time to download graph-

ics, a designer could create a very small image file—a temporary placeholder—that would download quickly and appear on a Web page, while the browser was busy downloading the much larger final image. Once downloaded, the real image would replace the Low Src graphic.

This property isn't even available from the Property inspector if your graphic was born in Fireworks (see Figure 5-8).

To add a text description to an image, type it in the Alt field in the Property inspector. If you're naming graphics that will be navigation buttons, you could just use the same text that appears on the button, such as *Home* or *Products*. For images that carry greater meaning—such as a photo of the product itself—you might use a more detailed description: "Photo of the Anodyne 3001—the most powerful apartment gardening tool ever devised."

Changing the Size of an Image

The Width and Height properties of a graphic do more than determine its screen size; they also help Web browsers load it quickly and efficiently. Since the HTML of a Web page downloads before any graphics do, a Web browser displays the text on the page first, and then adds the images as they arrive. If width and height statistics are missing, the browser doesn't know how much space on the page to give each image, so it has to redraw the page after each image is downloaded and its dimensions are determined. The stuttering appearance of this redrawing is disconcerting,

Figure 5-3:
The Alt property can be an important aid for those surfing without graphics. Top: On this Web site (at www.designinteract.com), graphics indicate the different sections of the site, such as Features, Site of the Week, and Insights.

Bottom: With graphics turned off, that information is still available, thanks to the alt text. However, graphics without an Alt property simply disappear or display the generic label IMAGE. In the case of an important identifying graphic like the site logo (the "design interact" banner in the first figure), a missing <alt> tag leaves visitors wondering where they are.

makes Web pages appear slowly, and shatters your reputation as a cool, competent Web designer.

Fortunately, you don't have to worry about specifying the picture's dimensions yourself. Whenever Dreamweaver inserts an image into a Web page, it automatically calculates its width and height and enters those values into the W and H fields in the Property inspector (see Figure 5-2).

You can, if you like, shrink a graphic by typing smaller values into the W and H fields, but doing so won't do anything to speed up the download time. You'll make the picture *appear* smaller, but the Web browser will still have to download the entire graphics file. To make your graphic smaller both in appearance and file size, do it in an image-editing program like Fireworks, Photoshop, or ImageReady. Not only will you get an image that's exactly the size you want, but you'll also trim a few bytes off its file size, and maybe even save a second or two in download time.

On the other hand, setting width and height values that are *larger* than the actual dimensions of the graphic merely distorts the image by stretching it, creating an undesirable pixellated effect. If you want a larger image without distortion, start with a larger original image; that is, return to your digital camera or stock photo CD, or re-create the graphic at a larger size in Photoshop or Fireworks.

WORKAROUND WORKSHOP

Watch Those Resize Handles!

After you insert an image in the document window, a thin black border appears around it, indicating that it's selected. In addition, three small black squares—the resize handles—appear on the right edge, bottom edge, and lower-right corner, as shown here.

Dragging these handles changes the width and height of the graphic—or, rather, the Width and Height *properties* in the Property inspector; the graphic file itself remains unchanged.

As noted above, however, dragging one of these handles to make the picture appear bigger is almost always unsuccessful; the result can be distortion and ugly pixellation.

But those pesky resize handles are far too easy to acciden-

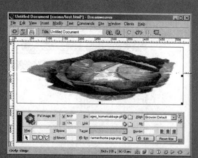

tally grab and drag. In fact, sometimes you might resize a graphic and not know it. Perhaps you accidentally dragged the left resize handle a few pixels, making the graphic wider, but not enough to notice.

Fortunately, the Property inspector provides some subtle feedback to let you know if your graphic is distorted. A boldfaced number in the W or H field tells you that the Width or Height property now differs from the actual dimensions of the graphic.

Clicking the letter W or the letter H *resets* the Width or Height property back to that of the original graphic file, undoing your little slip of the mouse. Clicking the Reset Size button in the lower-right corner of the Property inspector resets both properties.

Tip: You can use the image-distorting properties of the Property inspector's width and height fields to your advantage when working with solid-color shapes. Say you want to insert an orange line (580 pixels wide and 4 pixels tall) to separate two paragraphs on a page. Sure, you could insert a GIF graphic with an orange background that's 580 pixels wide by 4 pixels tall.

But the clever Web designer would save on file size by creating an orange GIF graphic that's only 1 pixel by 1 pixel, inserting it into the page, and using Dreamweaver to change its size to 580 x 4. After all, stretching a solid-color graphic doesn't break it up; it just makes more of the solid color! And the 1-pixel GIF is a far smaller file than the 580 x 4 one. Even better, you can reuse it to make lines of other sizes and take advantage of a Web browser's download-saving cache (see the tip on page 410).

Aligning an Image

Images, like text, appear in the normal flow of HTML in a page. In other words, a picture can appear as a paragraph by itself, or within a sentence or paragraph of text.

The Property inspector has two sets of alignment controls that affect images (see Figure 5-4). Only the Align menu, however, controls alignment specific to an image. (The second set of alignment options applies to the entire paragraph; see page 61.)

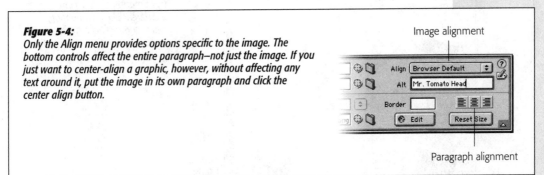

Figure 5-4:
Only the Align menu provides options specific to the image. The bottom controls affect the entire paragraph–not just the image. If you just want to center-align a graphic, however, without affecting any text around it, put the image in its own paragraph and click the center align button.

If you've inserted a graphic into a text paragraph, you can specify exactly how the image relates to the words around it. The Align menu in the Property inspector lets you select ten different options (see Figure 5-5). However, only six of them work in all browsers; you should avoid the other four, as noted below, which work only in some browsers.

To set a graphic's vertical alignment, click the image to select it. Then choose one of the following options from the Align menu at the right side of the Property inspector; you can see each illustrated in Figure 5-5:

• **Browser Default** means that the graphic will sit on the baseline (the bottom of the line of text on which the graphic appears). The effect is identical to choosing **Bottom**.

- **Middle** aligns the text on the current line with the middle of the graphic, but may add an awkward-looking complication. Subsequent lines of text move *below* the graphic. Solve the problem with the wrap options, described below.

- **Top** alignment aligns the image with the top of the line of text in the paragraph. Again, because top alignment can create a gap between the first line and the rest of the text, consider using the Left or Right wrapping options described below.

- **Left** places an image to the left of any text, which then wraps down the right side.

- **Right** moves the image to the right and wraps text along its left edge.

- **Baseline, TextTop, Absolute Middle,** and **Absolute Bottom** are not part of the official HTML standard, and only work in some browsers; avoid them.

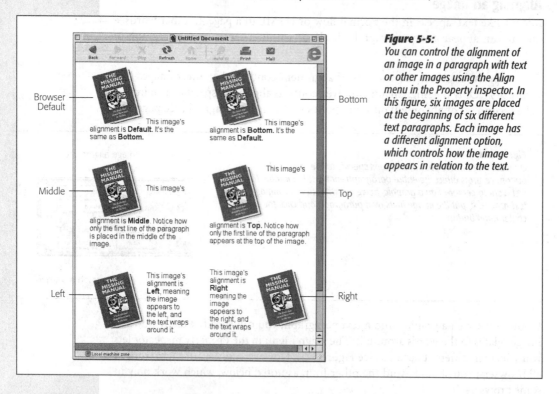

Figure 5-5:
You can control the alignment of an image in a paragraph with text or other images using the Align menu in the Property inspector. In this figure, six images are placed at the beginning of six different text paragraphs. Each image has a different alignment option, which controls how the image appears in relation to the text.

Adding a Margin Around an Image

When you place an image into a paragraph, text butts right up to the edge of the graphic—an invasion of the picture's personal space that's often visually unappealing. Fortunately, you can add a margin of space around your images with the Horizontal Space and Vertical Space properties.

You add a margin around an image by telling Dreamweaver how many pixels of space to add on each side. As shown in Figure 5-6, about 20 pixels makes an attractive amount of space. To add a margin above and below a graphic, type a number of pixels in the V Space field in the Property inspector. To add space to the left and right of an image, type a number in the H Space field. (Unfortunately, you can't specify independent values for each of the four margins.)

Figure 5-6:
The horizontal margin setting is particularly useful when used in combination with an image's Left or Right alignment option (see facing page). When using either of these two wrap alignment options, a horizontal margin setting adds much needed space between an image and any text wrapping around it. (To turn on the onscreen rulers as shown here, choose View→Rulers.)

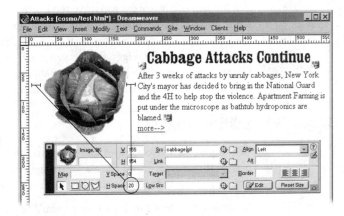

Adding a Border

Dreamweaver offers a quick, easy way to add a border around a graphic using the Border field on the Property inspector (see Figure 5-1).

To add a border, click the image to select it and then type a width, in pixels, into the Border field. One pixel creates a fine, almost invisible border; ten pixels makes a fat one. Press Enter or Return to apply the new border. Click anywhere on your page to remove the selection border and resize handles, the better to see the results of your work.

EASTER EGG HUNT

Meet the Geeks Behind Dreamweaver

Hidden throughout Dreamweaver are amusing diversions programmed by Dreamweaver's engineers: so-called "Easter Eggs," a computer-industry term for buried credits screens that appear only when you stumble onto the secret and unusual combination of words, keystrokes, and mouse-clicks. This book reveals all of them known to man…so far.

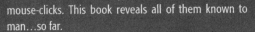

One of these is hidden in the Property inspector. Select an image in the document window. Then Ctrl-double-click (⌘-double-click) the thumbnail of the graphic in the left side of the Property inspector. A picture of one of Dreamweaver's programmers appears, along with his name. Ctrl (⌘)-double-click the thumbnail repeatedly to cycle through the names and pictures of other members of the Dreamweaver team.

Tip: The color of a border you create this way is always the same as the text color you chose in the Modify→Page Properties dialog box (see page 29). However, if you add a link to an image with a border, the color changes to the link colors specified for the page (see page 30).

It's worth noting that if you don't specify *any* border for an image that you've defined as a link (in other words, you leave the Border box empty), most Web browsers add a border around the image anyway. This automatic border is two pixels wide, colored with the link colors defined in the Page Properties dialog box. To remove this distraction, give the image a Border value of 0 (as opposed to leaving the box blank). Dreamweaver usually adds the 0 automatically when you add a link to an image, but occasionally, you may need to do this by hand.

Editing Images

Nothing's ever perfect, especially when you're building a Web site. Corrections are par for the course—not just to a Web page, but to the pictures on it, as well. ("Hey, can you change the text on that button from 'Meet the Bus' to 'Meet the Boss'?")

In the hands of less-capable software, you'd face quite a tedious switching-and-opening task each time you wanted to open a graphic. You'd have to open Photoshop, Fireworks, or whatever graphics program you prefer; choose File→Open; navigate to your Web site folder; find the graphic that needs touching up (if you can even remember its name); then open it to make your changes.

Once again, Dreamweaver proves much more considerate of your time. It lets you specify your favorite graphics program; thereafter, using that program to edit a picture on your Web site is as easy as a couple of clicks.

Setting Up an External Editor

Before you can take advantage of this timesaving feature, you need to tell Dreamweaver which graphics program you want to use.

1. **Choose Edit→Preferences.**

   The Preferences dialog box opens, as shown in Figure 5-7.

2. **In the left pane, click File Types/Editors.**

   The Preferences box now shows your settings for the editing programs you like to use for different types of files. Two columns appear in the bottom half of the box: Extensions and Editors.

3. **Select a graphic extension from the Extensions list.**

   Three types of graphic files are listed: GIFs, JPEGs, and PNGs. You can choose a different editing program for each type of file, if you like. In addition, you can add other filename extensions to this list by clicking the + button above the Extensions list.

4. Click the + button above the Editors list.

The Select External Editor dialog box opens.

5. On your hard drive, find the program you wish to assign as an editor for the selected type of graphics file.

It might be Photoshop, AppleWorks, ImageReady, or whatever.

6. If you wish to make this program the primary program for editing this type of file, click Make Primary.

This *primary* editor will be the one Dreamweaver opens when you choose to edit the graphic. (You can define other, less frequently used, editors as well. See the Tip on the next page.)

7. Repeat steps 3 through 6 for each type of graphics file that you work with.

Dreamweaver treats GIFs, JPEGs, and PNGs as separate file types, so you need to assign an editor to each. Of course, most people choose the same program for all three file types.

8. Click OK to close the Preferences dialog box.

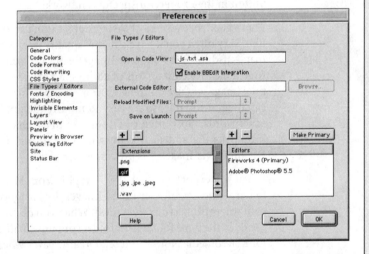

Figure 5-7:
You can select external editors for various types of Web files, including graphics formats such as GIFs, JPEGs, and PNGs, from the File Types/Editors category of the Preferences dialog box.

From now on, whenever you need to touch up a graphic on your Web page, just select it and then click Edit on the Property inspector (see Figure 5-2). Alternatively, press Ctrl+E (⌘-E), or right-click (Control-click) the image and choose Edit→Edit with External Editor from the contextual menu. In any case, your graphic now opens in the graphics program that you set as your primary editor in step 6 above.

Now you can edit the graphic and save changes to it. When you return to Dreamweaver, the modified image appears on the page. (If you're a Fireworks user, you're in even better shape; read on.)

Tip: You aren't limited to just one external editor. The primary editor opens when you click the Edit button on the Property inspector, or double-click a file in the Site Files window (see page 375). But if there's some Fireworks feature you need even though Photoshop is your primary editor, you can still jump to it directly from Dreamweaver.

The trick is to right-click (Control-click) the image you want to edit, whether it's in the document window or the Site Files window. If you've defined more than one image editor (as described on page 105), choose Edit With → [Program Name] from the contextual menu. Otherwise, choose Edit With → Browse; then, in the resulting dialog box, choose the editing program you want to use. That program opens automatically, with the graphic you clicked open and ready to edit.

Editing Images with Fireworks

Fireworks is Dreamweaver's companion graphics program—a powerful image-editing program made specifically to create and optimize Web graphics. You can get it as a stand-alone product, or included with Dreamweaver as part of its Web Design Studio package.

The engineers at Macromedia have made sure that these sibling programs play well together. You can switch back and forth between them with a single click, for example. And instead of simply opening a GIF or JPEG file when you click the Edit button in the Property inspector, Fireworks can open the original Fireworks file.

That's good, because most Web graphics don't start life as compressed GIF or JPEG files. Very often you'll have a higher quality image in your image editor's native format—.psd for Photoshop or ImageReady, for example, or. png for Fireworks. This source file may contain lots of additional information that doesn't need to be in the final image you use on the Web. For example, in most image editing programs, text can remain editable; so it's easy to modify the link description on a button, say. In other words, most often you'll want to make changes to the original Photoshop or Fireworks file and *then* export it as a GIF or JPEG. If you're using Fireworks, Dreamweaver makes this process easier.

When you export a GIF or JPEG graphic from Fireworks, save it into your Web site folder—into a subfolder called Images, for instance (see page 370 for strategies to help you organize your site's files). When you do so, Fireworks creates a folder called _notes in the same folder. This folder contains small files whose names end in .mno— for Macromedia Note—that tell Dreamweaver where to find the original Fireworks PNG file on your computer.

When Dreamweaver opens a Web page, it checks for this folder and any notes that are associated with the graphics on the page. When you select an image created with Fireworks, Dreamweaver displays this information in the Property inspector (see Figure 5-8).

To edit a Fireworks graphic, just click it in the document window, and then click Edit in the Property Inspector. Or, if you're in a hurry, just Ctrl (⌘)-double-click the image, or right-click (Control-click) it and choose Edit With Fireworks 4 from the contextual menu. Either way, Dreamweaver launches Fireworks. (You may be prompted to choose whether to open the source file of the exported GIF or JPEG, depending on how you've set up your Fireworks preferences.)

Figure 5-8:
The Property inspector displays special logos (circled) and options when you're working with a graphic created in Fireworks.

In Fireworks, make any changes you wish to the image. When you're finished, click Done. Fireworks exports the image, closes the file, and returns you to Dreamweaver. The updated graphic appears on your page.

Creating an Image Map

As Chapter 4 makes clear, it's easy to turn a graphic into a clickable link. It's also possible to add *multiple* links to a single image.

Suppose your company has offices all over the country, and you want to provide an easy way for your visitors to locate the nearest state office. One approach would be simply to list all of the state names and link them to separate pages for each state. But that's boring! Instead, you could use a map of the United States—one image—and turn each state's outline into a hotspot that's linked to an appropriate page, listing all of the offices in that state.

The array of invisible link buttons (called *hotspots*) responsible for this magic is called an *image map*. An image map contains two or more hotspots, each leading somewhere else.

Here's how to go about creating an image map:

1. **Select the graphic you wish to make into an image map.**

   The Property inspector displays that image's properties and, in the lower left corner, the image map tools (shown at bottom in Figure 5-9). (These appear in the lower half of the Property inspector, which appears only if the Property inspector is fully expanded [page 20]).

2. **Type a name for the map in the Map field of the Property inspector.**

   The name should only contain letters and numbers, and can't begin with a number. This step is optional; if you don't give the map a name, Dreamweaver automatically gives the map the ingenious name *Map*. If you create additional image maps, Dreamweaver will call them Map2, Map3, and so on.

3. **Select one of the image map tools.**

Choose the rectangle tool, the circle tool, or the polygon tool depending on the shape you have in mind for your hotspot. For instance, in the image in Figure 5-9, the polygon tool was used to draw each of the oddly shaped hotspots.

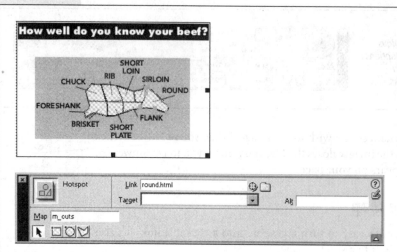

Figure 5-9:
Individual links on an image map—called hotspots—are displayed as a transparent blue in Dreamweaver. When you select a hotspot, the Property inspector displays its Link, Target, and Alt properties. The lower half of the inspector displays the name of the map as well as tools for selecting and drawing additional hotspots.

4. **Draw the hotspot.**

   To use the rectangle and circle tool, click directly on your picture; drag diagonally to form a rectangle or circle. To make a perfect square, press Shift while dragging with the rectangle tool. (The circle tool always creates a perfect circle.)

   To draw an irregularly shaped hotspot using the polygon tool, click once to define one corner of the hotspot. Continue clicking until you've defined each corner of the hotspot; Dreamweaver automatically joins the corners to close the shape.

   Dreamweaver fills in the inside of the hotspot with a light blue tint to make it easy to see; your Web visitors, needless to say, won't see the blue highlighting.

   If you need to adjust the hotspot you've just drawn, click the arrow tool on the Property inspector. You can drag the light blue square handles of your hotspot to reshape or resize the area, or drag inside the hotspot to move the whole thing. If you change your mind about the hotspot, press Delete to get rid of it altogether.

5. **Add a link to the hotspot.**

   After you draw a hotspot, that hotspot is selected; its properties appear in the Property inspector (see Figure 5-9). Use any of the techniques discussed on page 85 to link this hotspot to another Web page or anchor.

6. **If necessary, set the Target property.**

   Most of the options in the Target pop-up menu are useful only when you're working with frames, as discussed in Chapter 7. The _blank option, however, can be useful any time, since it forces your visitor's Web browser to load the linked page into a *new* browser window. The original page remains open, underneath the new window.

7. **Set the Alt property of the hotspot.**

By typing a label into the Alt box in the Property inspector, you provide a written name for this portion of the graphic; as noted on page 98, Alt tags are extremely important to people who surf the Web with graphics turned off, or who use text-to-speech reading software.

8. **Repeat steps 2 through 7 for each hotspot you wish to add to an image.**

As you work, you can see the light-blue hotspots filling in your image map.

Editing a hotspot's properties

As noted in step 4 above, you can change a hotspot's shape by dragging its tiny square handles. But you can also change its other properties—which Web page it links to, for example.

To do so, click to select the image map. Using the black arrow tool—the hotspot selection tool—on the Property inspector (see Figure 5-9), click the hotspot you wish to edit; then use the Property inspector controls to edit the Link, Target, and Alt properties.

If you're having a fit of frustration, you can also press Delete or Backspace to delete the hotspot altogether.

Adding Rollover Images

Rollover images are among the most common user-interface elements on the Web, especially when it comes to navigation buttons. You've almost certainly seen rollovers in action; that's when your mouse rolls over a button on some Web page and it (the button) lights up, or glows, or turns into a frog.

Figure 5-10:
Rollover graphics appear frequently in navigation bars, like the one shown at top. As your cursor touches a rollover button (top), the button changes appearance (bottom) to indicate that the graphic has a functional purpose—in this case, "I'm a link. Click me."

This simple change in appearance is a powerful way to inform a visitor that the graphic is more than just a pretty picture—it's a button that actually does something. Rollovers are usually used to show that the image is a link.

Behind the scenes, you create a rollover by preparing *two different* graphics—"before" and "after." One graphic appears when the Web page first loads, and the other appears when your visitor's mouse moves over the first. If the cursor then rolls away without clicking, the original image pops back into place.

This dynamic effect is achieved with the use of JavaScript, a programming language that most Web browsers use to add interactivity to a Web page. Fortunately, you don't need to be a programmer to take advantage of this exciting technology. Dreamweaver's many prewritten JavaScript programs, called Behaviors, let you add rollover images and other interactivity to your pages. (More about Behaviors in Chapter 11.)

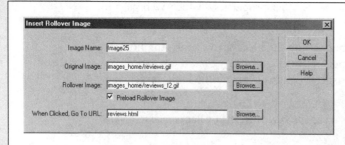

Figure 5-11:
The Insert Rollover Image dialog box lets you specify the name, link, and image files you wish to use to create the rollover effect. Turning on the Preload Rollover Image checkbox forces the Web browser to download the rollover image file along with the rest of the page. If you turn preloading off, the browser doesn't download the file until the user moves her mouse over the original image, causing a disorienting delay; leave this option untouched.

To insert a rollover image, use a graphics program to prepare the "before" and "after" button images. Unless you're going for a bizarre distortion effect, they should be exactly the same dimensions. Store them somewhere in your Web site folder.

Then, in the document window, click where you want to insert the rollover image. Most of the time, you'll use a table to lay out your rollover buttons (see Chapter 6), and insert the image within a table cell.

Choose Insert→Interactive Images→Rollover Image (or click the Insert Rollover Image button on the Objects palette). Either way, the Insert Rollover Image dialog box appears (see Figure 5-11). Fill in the blanks like this:

- **Image Name.** Type a name for the graphic, if you like. JavaScript requires *some* name for the rollover effect. If you leave this blank, Dreamweaver gives the image an unimaginative name—for example, Image2—when you insert a rollover. However, if you plan to later add additional interactive effects (see Chapter 11), you might want to change it to something more descriptive, to make it easier to identify the graphic later.

- **Browse button #1.** When you click the top Browse button, a dialog box appears; Dreamweaver is prompting you to choose the graphic you want to use as the "before" button—the one that first appears when the Web page loads. (See page 96 for more on choosing graphics.)

  Browse button #2. When you click the second Browse button, Dreamweaver prompts you to choose the "after" graphic images, the one that will appear when your visitor's mouse rolls over the first one.

- **When Clicked, Go to URL.** Rollover images are most commonly used for navigation elements that, when clicked, take the user to another Web page. In this box, you specify what happens when your visitor actually falls for the animated bait and *clicks* the rollover button. Type an absolute URL beginning with *http://,* or click the Browse button to select a Web page from your site, as described on page 85, for the rollover image to link to.

When you click OK, you return to your document window, where only the "before" button image appears. You can select it and modify it just as you would any image; in fact, it's just a regular image with a link and a Dreamweaver Behavior (see Chapter 11) attached.

To see your rollover in action, preview it in a Web browser by pressing the F12 key or using the File→Preview in Browser command.

EXTENSION ALERT

InstaGraphics Extensions for Dreamweaver

Ever get tired of the limited number of fonts you can use on your Web pages? How about the appearance of those boring bullets in unordered lists? No problem. Dreamweaver lets you add new commands–called *extensions*–to the program. This great feature makes it possible to add literally hundreds of additional features.

Many are available for free from a Macromedia's Web site in a section called The Exchange–*www.macromedia.com/ exchange/.*

Go there and search for the nifty InstaGraphics extension, which can convert headings and other text in a page to a GIF file using any font you installed on your computer. In addition, this extension can replace HTML bullets with a nicer looking graphic. (Fireworks is required to make this feature work.)

For more on using the Macromedia Exchange, see Chapter 19.

Flash Buttons

While adding graphic rollovers to a Web page is a breeze, Dreamweaver 4's new *Flash button* feature is even easier. Without any additional image-editing program or animation software, you can bring your pages to life with interactive buttons that include animation and sound.

Flash buttons, new in Dreamweaver 4, are predesigned buttons, to which you can add your own labels and links. They can do much more than just change from a "before" look to an "after" look; for example, they may have *three* different looks (a third being a "pushed down" look that shows up when the button is clicked). They may also play music or trigger a little animation.

You can download additional button styles from the Web, and, if you have Flash 5, you can even create your own (see the box on page 115).

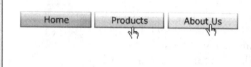

Figure 5-12:
When the button is just sitting on the page, it's in its "up" state (left); when the mouse rolls over it, you see its "over" state (middle). A Flash button usually changes appearance when clicked, showing the "down" state (right).

A Warning About Flash

It's important to understand, however, that Flash buttons (and Flash text, page 115) are based on Macromedia's Flash animation technology. Flash is quickly becoming the standard format for Web animation, thanks to its small file size, crisp graphics, and interactive effects. But Flash files (called Flash movies) require special software to view; they won't work on your Web page unless each of your Web site visitors has installed the Flash plug-in.

Most Macintosh and Windows browsers now come with the Flash plug-in already installed, but Unix browsers and many older browsers may not have the plug-in. (Macromedia says that nearly 95 percent of the Web browsers worldwide have at least the Flash 3 plug-in installed—which is fortunate, since Dreamweaver's Flash buttons work with the Flash plug-in version 3 and above.)

The point is, though, that if you want to ensure that *everyone*, regardless of computer type, can savor your Web site to the same degree (without having to scurry off to another Web site to download the Flash plug-in), steer clear of Flash buttons.

Adding a Flash button to a Web page

If you're undaunted by the fact that not all of your audience may be able to enjoy Flash buttons, you're ready to proceed.

When you add a Flash button to a Web page, Dreamweaver creates and inserts a Flash movie file, ending in the extension .swf, into your Web page. You can preview the button within Dreamweaver and edit it at any time.

You perform most of the work in a single dialog box (Figure 5-13), which appears when you choose Insert→Interactive Images→Flash Buttons (or click the Flash Button icon in the Objects panel). The object now is to choose the correct settings for the lively button you're about to create:

- **Style.** When you click a style name, an interactive sample appears at the top of the window. Try pointing to each sample as well as clicking it (and holding down your mouse button) to see all of its different looks; stop when you find one you like.

- **Button Text.** Most button styles have space for a short piece of text that will appear as a label, right on the button. Into this box, type something informative about the button's function *(Buy Now!)* or its link *(Home)*. Buttons have limited space; Dreamweaver ignores letters that don't fit on the button.

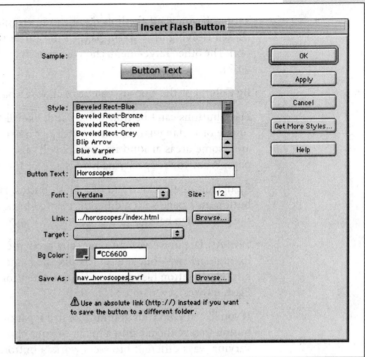

Figure 5-13:
The Insert Flash Button window lets you select a style, set text, and add links and formatting to a Flash button. In addition, you can go onto the Web and collect additional button styles by clicking the Get More Styles button. When you do, your Web browser launches and opens the Macromedia Exchange Web site. To go to the section of the Exchange where you can find additional styles, choose Flash Media from the Browse Extensions pop-up menu. See page 493 for more detail on using Macromedia Exchange.

- **Font, Size.** You can select a font from the Font menu and specify a size (in points) in the Size field. (This time, you're not confined to fonts that each of your Web site visitors is likely to have [see page 70]; Dreamweaver will convert the font that's on your computer into a graphic image.) You can use any TrueType font you have installed on your computer; unfortunately, Flash buttons can't handle Postscript fonts.

- **Link.** If you want your button to link to another page when clicked, you can add either an absolute link or document-relative link (see page 82). Type an absolute link starting with *http://* in the Link field. Alternatively, you can click the Browse button and select a page from your site to create a document-relative link.

  One thing to keep in mind about document-relative links in Flash buttons: the link information is embedded inside the Flash file. As a result, if you save the page you're working on to a different folder, the link won't work any more.

  That's why, if you hope to create one set of Flash navigation buttons and use them over and over on all the pages of your site, you should use *absolute* links. These work regardless of the location of the Flash button file or the Web page the button is on. (*Site root-relative links* [see page 83] don't work at all in Flash movies.)

Tip: For a more advanced solution to this problem, see page 355.

- **Target.** If you want the linked page to open into a new browser window when clicked (leaving the current page in the current window), select the _blank option. The other Target menu choices are useful when working with frames (Chapter 7).

- **Bg Color.** Use this pop-up palette to choose a background color for your button.

  Flash buttons can't be transparent and, like all Web page graphics, can be only square or rectangular. In other words, if your Flash button is rounded (as most are), some areas around its corners will obscure the background of your Web page. What you're specifying here is a color for these exposed corner areas.

  By default, the background of a Flash button is white, but if you plan to use a button on a page with a different colored background, set the button to match the page's own background color.

- **Save As.** Dreamweaver automatically gives the button a file name—something like *button1.swf*—but you can change the name, if you like, by typing it into this box. Flash button files must end in the extension .swf (the file extension used by Flash movies), even on a Macintosh.

  If you like to keep your graphic files in a separate folder, you can click the Browse button to save the file into a folder of your choice. But be careful: Thanks to the varying ways different browsers work, a button to which you've given a document-relative link may not work unless you save the file into the same folder as its Web page.

WORKAROUND WORKSHOP

Broken Flash Buttons on the Macintosh

If you use a Macintosh, you may notice that Flash buttons don't return to their original "up" state once you move your mouse off of them—not just in your Web browsers, but even right there in Dreamweaver.

You're witnessing a bug in the Flash Player plug-in that comes with Dreamweaver. If you notice this problem, download the latest version of the plug-in from the downloads section of Macromedia's Web site: *www.macromedia. com/downloads/*.

Once you've installed the plug-in into your browser, you

should update the plug-in in Dreamweaver's configuration folder. To do so, use Sherlock (choose its name from the menu) to search for a file named *Shockwave Flash NP-PPC* on your Mac. You'll probably find multiple versions of the file.

Select one and choose File→Get Info→General Information (or press ⌘-I) to determine the plug-in's version. Look for Version 5.0r41 or greater. Make a copy of this file; put it inside the Macromedia Dreamweaver 4→Configuration→Plug-Ins folder. The new version plug-in replaces the older version of the plug-in, thus solving the Flash preview problem.

When you click OK, Dreamweaver creates the Flash movie and saves it in the location you specified. Dreamweaver also inserts the movie into the Web page, with all of the appropriate properties set in the HTML of the page.

Editing Flash buttons

Once you've added a button to a Web page, you can edit it by double-clicking it (or by selecting it in the document window and clicking Edit in the Property inspector). The Insert Flash Button dialog box (see Figure 5-13) appears again. Make any changes you wish to the button, and click OK.

And since Flash buttons are simply Flash movies, you can change any of the movie properties, such as height, width, or background color, using the Property inspector (see Chapter 13 for more on using Flash movies in Web pages).

Previewing Flash buttons

You can see the button in action by previewing the page in a Web browser (press F12, as described on page 37); or, if you just want to see the different looks for the button, you can preview the button without leaving Dreamweaver. Select the button and then click Play on the Property inspector. This procedure may sound a little peculiar, but only until you remember that a Flash button is actually a little movie. The Flash button is now "playing"; you can move your mouse over it, click it, and so on, savoring its animated smarts. To stop the button, click Stop in the Property inspector. (You can't double-click the button to edit it when it's playing.)

POWER USERS' CLINIC

Behind Flash Buttons

You may be a little dismayed by either the limited number of styles available for Flash buttons, or the quality of the buttons' designs. You may decide that none of the buttons match your site's look, so why bother?

Fortunately, Flash buttons, like most features in Dreamweaver, are completely customizable. Each Flash button style is actually a *Generator* template. (Generator is a Macromedia product that can incorporate dynamic data,

such as the time or weather, into a Flash movie, providing cutting edge animation with up-to-the-minute information.)

You can create these buttons using the Generator authoring extensions of Flash 5. For information on creating your own Flash Buttons for Dreamweaver, check out Macromedia's Web site at *www.macromedia.com/support/ dreamweaver/assets/flashbutton.*

Flash Text

As noted in Chapter 3, Web browsers simply don't offer a lot of font choices. Even though it's possible to specify *any* font for your text, unless your visitors have the same font installed on their systems, they won't see the font you intended.

For this reason, Web designers either stick to the handful of fonts that are commonly installed on Windows and Macintosh computers, or they render type *as graph-*

ics and insert them in the page. This workaround has its own downsides, of course: Graphics take longer to download, and you can't edit the text once you've frozen it into a picture.

In an effort to give designers greater choices, Dreamweaver 4 introduces a new feature that solves both problems: Flash text. Based on Macromedia's successful Flash technology, Flash text is a text-only Flash movie on your Web page that maintains the shape and quality of any True Type font you have installed on your computer. It offers a number of benefits:

- Your visitors see exactly the same fonts you used when you created the Web page, even if they don't have the same fonts on their machines.

- The resulting Flash file is usually much smaller and of higher quality than the same text rendered as a graphics file.

- Since Flash uses *vectors*—mathematical formulas—to describe an image's shape and color, you can resize Flash text without degrading its quality.

Unfortunately, Flash text has a significant downside, too: Like Flash buttons, Flash text requires the Flash plug-in; as described on page 112, some visitors may not be able to enjoy your handiwork.

Adding Flash text to a Web page

Inserting Flash text is a combination of adding text and creating a Flash movie. Because you have so many choices, it's longer than most Dreamweaver processes, though no harder; once again, it all happens in a single dialog box (see Figure 5-14).

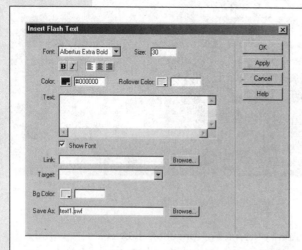

Figure 5-14:
The Flash text tool creates small text-only Flash movies that you can include on your Web pages. As with Flash buttons (see page 111), you can also make the Flash text link to another Web page when clicked, either in your site or elsewhere on the Web.

To make it appear, choose Insert→Interactive Images→Flash Text (or click the Flash Text icon on the Common category of the Objects panel). Now make your settings:

- **Font, Size.** You can select any TrueType font you have installed on your computer. As noted earlier, Flash text doesn't work with Postscript fonts. Type a font size, measured in points, in the Size field.

  Unlike text in a Web page, which, thanks to the quirky HTML language, comes only in *relative* font sizes (1, 2, 3, 4, and so on), Flash text uses the traditional typographic units of measurement, points. 24 points is good for headlines, but you can specify a much larger size if you'd like.

- **B, I, alignment.** Using the tools just below the Font menu, you specify type style attributes. For example, you can apply bold or italics by clicking the B or I buttons. You can also set the alignment of the text—left, right, or centered—by clicking one of the three alignment buttons (see Figure 5-15).

Figure 5-15:
You can align the text within a Flash text file. The alignment you choose here doesn't affect how the text is aligned on your Web page; it determines how the text is aligned inside of the finished Flash movie. If you think of each Flash text file as its own paragraph, the alignment options—shown here, from top to bottom, with Left, Middle, and right alignment—make more sense.

- **Color.** Use this pop-up palette to choose a color for your text. (See page 30 for details on using the Dreamweaver color picker.)

- **Rollover Color.** Flash text can have one basic dynamic effect: It can change color when a viewer moves her mouse over it. This effect can be particularly useful if you wish to use the text as a link, because rollover effects are commonly used to indicate links. Use the Rollover Color pop-up palette to specify the color the text will become when the cursor points to it.

- **Text.** The Text field displays your words in whatever font you've chosen. (If you turn off Show Font, on the other hand, you'll see only some generic font as you edit the text, but the software may feel more responsive as you edit.)

As you type, you must manually enter a line break—by pressing Enter—wherever you want a line of text to end and a new line to begin. If you don't, Dreamweaver will create one wide (perhaps very wide, depending on how much text you have) Flash text movie. That's one reason it's usually better to use Flash text for short pieces of text, like headlines or links.

- **Link.** You can use Flash text as a navigational element by attaching a link to it. In conjunction with a rollover color, you can use this feature to create simple dynamic navigation. In other words, if your Flash text says *Home,* you can set it up so that it's a button link back to your home page.

- **Target.** If you decide to turn your Flash text into a link, you can choose a *target* for that link using the Target pop-up menu, if appropriate. (As noted earlier, select the _blank option if you want the link to produce a new browser window when clicked; otherwise, use this pop-up menu only when working with frames, as described in Chapter 7.)

- **Bg Color.** The Flash text you're creating is a rectangular text block, but the spaces between your lettering and the edge of the block aren't transparent; in fact, they start out white. The result—a bunch of white rectangles—can be pretty goofy-looking if the background of your Web page is, say, fuchsia.

To make it look like the Flash lettering is sitting directly on your Web page's background (without the white rectangles), choose the background color that matches your Web page's background.

- **Save As.** Type a name for your Flash-text movie here. The Flash text tool stores the Flash movie in your site folder, within the folder that contains the Web page it's on. If you wish to save it in some other folder (an Images folder, for example), click the Browse button and navigate to a different folder in the site folder. If you've added a link to the text, however, the warning on page 113 also applies here.

- **Apply.** The Apply button creates the Flash file and shows you the text on the Web page, while leaving the dialog box open. The advantage here is that you can make adjustments before exiting the dialog box.

When you click OK, Dreamweaver creates a Flash file and inserts it on your Web page.

Editing Flash text

To edit Flash text you've created, open the Insert Flash Text dialog box using any of these procedures:

- Double-click the Flash text block in the document window.

- Select the Flash text and then click the Edit button in the Property inspector.

- Right-click (Control-click) the Flash text and choose Edit from the contextual menu.

Once the dialog box is open, you can make any changes you wish to the settings or text.

Resizing Flash text

You can freely resize Flash text in the document window, without ever worrying that it won't look good at one point size or another. Just select the Flash text block, and then use either of these techniques:

- Type new dimensions into the Width and Height fields in the Property inspector. You can set the size using either pixels or percentages.

- Drag one of the square handles on the edges of the Flash object. To avoid distorting the text as you resize the Flash object, Shift-drag the lower right handle.

You can always return the Flash object to its original size by clicking the Reset Size button on the Property inspector.

Tutorial: Adding Rollovers

Adding interactive elements to a Web page can be quite a chore. Unless you're a programmer, learning and using the JavaScript programming language can be time-consuming and frustrating. Fortunately, Dreamweaver does most of the work for you, with its powerful yet easy to use Behaviors.

In this tutorial, you'll add dynamic rollovers to the page you created in the first chapter.

Note: The tutorial in this chapter builds on the page you created in Chapter 1. If you no longer have that page handy, or you'd rather start fresh, you can use download the example files from *www.sawmac.com/ missing/*. Click the Tutorials link. To begin the download, click a link: Images Tutorial–Mac files or Images Tutorial–Win files, depending on the kind of machine you're using (Mac or Windows).

After you've downloaded and decompressed the files, you should have a DWImages folder on your computer, containing the Web pages and graphics needed for this tutorial. If you're having difficulties, the Web site contains detailed instructions for downloading the files you'll be using with this book.

---

1. **Define the DWImages folder as your root folder.**

   If you're working on the page you completed in Chapter 1, use the local site you defined for that tutorial; that is, choose Cosmo Farmer from your Site menu.

   If you're starting fresh, see page 23 for complete instructions on defining a folder as your site folder. In short, this step involves choosing Site→New Site to open the Site Definition window, typing any name you like into the Site Name field, clicking the folder icon next to the Local Root Folder field, and choosing the DWImages folder as your local root folder. Click OK.

Now the Site window (page 387) should be open on your screen.

2. **In the Site window, double-click the file called** *advertise.html*.

The Advertise with Cosmopolitan Farmer page opens. You'll first add a navigation bar.

3. **Click just to the right of the banner at the top of the page.**

You may first need to widen the document window until you see blank space next to the banner. Since the navigation bar will go directly below the banner, as part of the same paragraph, you'll insert a line break.

4. **Press Shift-Enter to insert a line break.**

The insertion point now blinks just below the banner, and a gold shield, representing the line-break character, appears just to the right of the banner. If you don't see the gold shield icon, make sure you turned on invisible characters in the Preferences window as described on page 27.

5. **Choose Insert→Interactive Images→Rollover Image.**

If the Objects panel is open, you may prefer to click the Insert Rollover Image button there. Either way, the Insert Rollover Image dialog box opens (see Figure 5-16.)

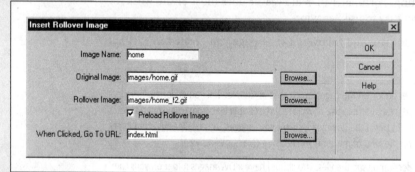

Figure 5-16:
The Insert Rollover Image window lets you define the name, graphics, and link for a rollover. Make sure the Preload Rollover Image checkbox is selected.

6. **In the Image Name field, Type** *home*.

In order for this effect to work, each button must have its own name, which the JavaScript program will use to communicate with and control the graphic. Dreamweaver gives the graphic a generic name like *Image1*, but using a more descriptive name will make it easier for you to change this effect later on.

7. **Click the first Browse button.**

   The Select Image Source dialog box appears. In the next step, you'll select the image for the button that will appear on the page.

8. **Browse to the DWImages→images folder; double-click the graphics file called home.gif.**

   The path to that graphic, images/home.gif, appears in the Original Image field. Next stop: choosing the graphic that will appear when a visitor moves the cursor over the button.

9. **Click the second Browse button; this time, double-click the file called home_f2.gif.**

   Now all you need to do is add a link to turn the graphic into a navigation button.

10. **Click the third Browse button (next to the "When Clicked, Go To URL" field).**

    The "On Click, Go To URL" dialog box opens, awaiting your selection of a Web page that will open when you click your rollover button.

    In this case, your button will link to the home page of the site.

11. **In the DWImages folder, find and double-click the file index.html.**

    At this point, the dialog box should look like Figure 5-16.

12. **Click OK.**

    You're back at your Web page document, where your new, rectangular button, called COSMO FARMER HOME, proudly appears.

    Congratulations! You've made your first rollover. To try it out for yourself, press the F12 key to preview the page in your Web browser. When you move your cursor over the button, the button should glow; when you click the button, it should open the home page.

13. **Return to Dreamweaver.**

    Do so however you switch programs on your computer—by using the Windows taskbar or the Macintosh Application menu, for example.

If you like, you can finish up the navigation bar by adding the six other rollover images. Simply click next to the Home button, and then repeat steps 3 through 10 above. Here are the names, graphics and pages you should use:

- Name: *features*
  Graphics: *features.gif* and *features_f2.gif*
  Page to Link to: *features.html*

- Name: *projects*
  Graphics: *projects.gif* and *projects _f2.gif*
  Page to Link to: *projects.html*

- Name: *horoscopes*
  Graphics: *horoscopes.gif* and *horoscopes _f2.gif*
  Page to Link to: *horoscopes.html*

- Name: *quiz*
  Graphics: *quiz.gif* and *quiz _f2.gif*
  Page to Link to: *quiz.html*

- Name: *reviews*
  Graphics: *reviews.gif* and *reviews _f2.gif*
  Page to Link to: *reviews.html*

- Name: *classifieds*
  Graphics: *classifieds.gif* and *classifieds _f2.gif*
  Page to Link to: *classifieds.html*

When you're finished, choose File→Save, and then preview your new navigation bar (Figure 5-17) in your Web browser. Move your mouse over the buttons to see if they change; click to jump to another page.

Tip: If you like, you can compare your work with the professionally completed version at *www.sawmac.com/ missing/tutorials/*.

Figure 5-17:
Adding interactivity to your site using Dreamweaver's rollover objects is a breeze. No messy JavaScript programming to learn!

Part Two:
Building a Better Web Page

2

Tables

T he Web was invented to help scientists exchange information, not to compete with the sophisticated design of newspapers, glossy magazines, or TV; controlling a page's layout remains one of Web design's greatest challenges. The increasing expectations of the Web's users, however, have forced designers to push HTML into new territories, and the primary weapon in this battle has been the HTML <table> tag.

Though originally intended to display tables of data, today most Web designers use the <table> tag primarily for arranging elements on a Web page, as shown in Figure 6-1.

Figure 6-1:
Underneath many Web pages is an invisible skeleton that gives the page form and structure. HTML tables let you control the placement of graphics, text, and other elements on a Web page with accuracy. Without tables, Web content would simply flow from top to bottom on a page—boring!

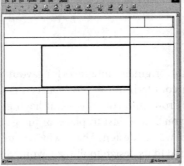 

Of course, trying to force a round peg into a square hole isn't always easy, and creating complex designs with tables often requires clever tricks and workarounds. Fortunately, Dreamweaver 4's advanced table tools anticipate those needs and let you build beautiful table-based layouts. With these tools—and this book—you'll soon be gliding through HTML minefields along the path to attractive, effective Web pages. (If you can't wait to get started using Dreamweaver to create advanced layouts, jump to page 164 and follow the tutorial.)

Table Basics

A table is a grid of rows and columns that intersect to form *cells,* as shown in Figure 6-2. A cell acts like a mini document window, in which you can place images, text, and even additional tables. And because a cell can have a fixed width and height, you can place these items with precision. For example, you can build a table with three cells in a row and fill each cell with a single column of text, thus simulating the column layout of a print publication such as a newspaper.

Tables are also the key to building more complex designs. For instance, you can merge cells together to create larger cells that span columns or rows, nest tables for added versatility, and create flexible designs that expand to fit the browser window. (This should all sound familiar to anyone who's used, for example, the table tool in Microsoft Word.)

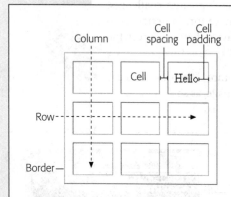

Figure 6-2:
Rows, columns, and cells make up a table. Cell spacing specifies how many pixels of space appear between cells. Cell padding, on the other hand, is the space from the edge of a cell to the content inside the cell. It provides a margin between the four sides of the cell and the cell's content, as described on page 130.

Since tables were not originally intended for layout purposes, many people find working with them counterintuitive. For starters, creating tables usually involves thinking in terms of rows and columns—but having to determine the number of rows and columns you'll need just to place an image at a particular position on a page is not a natural way to design. That's why Dreamweaver 4 adds an additional table-building method to its design toolbox: Layout view. The Layout Table tools let you draw your page layout directly in the document window—a much more natural approach to table design.

But Dreamweaver's original table-building feature, available in Standard view, is still around (you switch to Standard view as shown in Figure 6-3). Layout view and Standard view both produce the same results—an underlying grid of tables and cells that let you control the layout of a page (see Figure 6-1)—and the same HTML code. But although they produce the same table structures, Layout view and Standard view offer different approaches to building them.

Note: When you first enter Layout view, the Getting Started in Layout View window may appear, offering a quick overview of the layout tools. Turn on "Don't show me this message again" to prevent this window from opening every time you switch views; otherwise, it'll get old quick.

Figure 6-3:
You can switch between Standard and Layout views using the buttons at the bottom of the Objects panel. In Layout view, you can take advantage of the Layout Cell and Layout Table drawing tools to draw your page layouts.

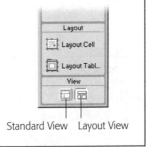

Standard View   Layout View

Standard view requires you to envision most of your design in advance, answering questions like: Where will items go on the page? How many table rows and columns will this require? What size should the table be? In essence, you need to know what the table will look like *before* beginning.

Layout view, on the other hand, lets you work at either the smallest level—a table cell—or the largest—a table. If you use the Cell drawing tool to draw a cell in the document window, Dreamweaver creates the underlying table structure. If you move the cell, resize it, or delete it, Dreamweaver rewrites the code to create a table to fit your design.

This flexibility makes the Layout view a very good place to start when creating a page's design. The changes that Dreamweaver can make to a table's HTML code in Layout view take fractions of a second, while comparable modifications in Standard view could take you hours. Though it's certainly possible to revise a table's structure in Standard view, it can be more difficult (see page 144 for more on modifying tables).

Once the basic design of a page is complete, there's little difference between a page viewed in Layout view and a page viewed in Standard view (see Figure 6-4). In fact, you may well switch out of Layout view for good once the basic page design is complete. Standard view not only hides many of the visual aids included in Layout view (because they sometimes obscure text, images, and other elements on a page), but also lets you access tools that are unavailable in Layout view, such as the basic Table object and Layer tool. In addition, you can set up some properties of a table, like the background image, *only* in Standard view.

The first part of this chapter introduces the Layout view and its associated drawing tools; for a tour of Standard view and its techniques, see page 140. Just keep in mind that, whichever approach you take, you're still only creating basic HTML tables.

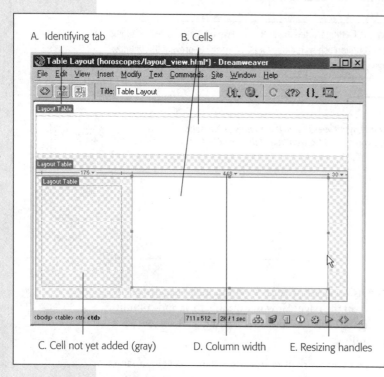

A. Identifying tab   B. Cells

C. Cell not yet added (gray)   D. Column width   E. Resizing handles

Figure 6-4:
Dreamweaver 4's Layout view may take some time to get used to. Tables are identified by small tabs on their top left corners labeled Layout Table (A). You can include more than one table per page, and even put a table inside of another table. Until you add cells to a table (white areas, B), you can't add text, graphics, or anything else; areas of a table without cells have a gray background (C). The width of each column in a table is shown along the top of the table (D). When you select a cell (E), eight resizing handles appear, which you can drag to change the dimensions of that cell.

Layout View

In Layout view, you can start creating a table-based design using either of the two drawing tools—the Layout Cell drawing tool or the Layout Table drawing tool. Both tools await on the Objects panel (see Figure 6-3).

How to Draw a Table in Layout View

Drawing a table is as simple as dragging. Click the Layout Table tool in the Objects panel (see Figure 6-3); the cursor changes to a + sign when you move it over the document window. Drag diagonally to create a rectangular box—the outline of the table. When you release the mouse button, a gray box appears, complete with green borders and a tab in the upper left labeled Layout Table (see Figure 6-4).

Note: Although Dreamweaver uses the words Layout Table and Layout Cell, they're still just HTML tables and cells. In other words, a Layout Table is simply a table viewed in Layout view, and a Layout Cell is just a table cell viewed in Layout view. In Standard view, the same items are just called tables and cells. In this book, you'll see the terms Layout Cell and Layout Table appear when referring to actions you perform while in Layout view.

This Layout Table tool may be a bit confusing until you learn some of Dreamweaver's rules for drawing tables:

- If the document is blank when you draw a table, the table appears in the upper-left corner of the page.

- You can't draw a table over anything that's already on the page. If you move the Table tool over text, the cursor changes to a forbidden (⊘) symbol, and nothing happens when you drag. If there's anything on the page—text, images, tables, even an empty paragraph—you must move the cursor to the bottom of the page in order to draw a table. For this reason, it's usually best to start with a blank document, draw your tables and cells, and only then add content.

- Tables can't overlap each other. The Table tool won't create a table if you drag over the edge of an existing one.

- You can draw a Layout Table *inside* another Layout Table, a technique called nesting tables. However, you can only draw the second table inside the gray area of the Layout Table. In other words, you can't draw a Layout *Table* inside a Layout *Cell*.

Tip: To draw a number of tables one after another without having to keep reselecting the Table tool, hold down the Ctrl (⌘) key when drawing a table. The Table tool remains selected between drags.

Tables are made of rows and columns, a structure Dreamweaver helps maintain by making the edges of tables snap against nearby tables or cells as you draw. If the cursor comes within eight pixels of the edge of a cell or another table, the table edge you're drawing snaps to the other table or cell's edge. This behavior helps you accu-

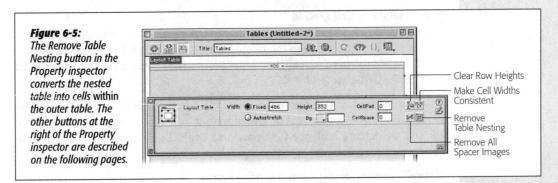

Figure 6-5:
The Remove Table Nesting button in the Property inspector converts the nested table into cells within the outer table. The other buttons at the right of the Property inspector are described on the following pages.

Clear Row Heights
Make Cell Widths Consistent
Remove Table Nesting
Remove All Spacer Images

rately align the borders of your tables; but if it bothers you, turn this snapping feature off by pressing the Alt (Option) key as you draw the table.

Layout Table Properties

After drawing a Layout Table, you'll see a rectangular gray square in the document window. A tab labeled Layout Table appears in the upper-left corner of the table; Dreamweaver indicates the table's width, in pixels, at the top. The Property inspector lists additional properties, such as table height, width, and background color (see Figure 6-5).

Table dimensions

The width and height of the table appear in the Property inspector; you can adjust these values by typing new pixel-measurement values in the Fixed and Height fields. Alternatively, to resize a table, you can drag one of the three handles that appear on the bottom edge, lower-right corner, and right edge of the table in the document window.

Instead of having a fixed width, a table can automatically adjust to fit the available space of your visitor's browser window. To activate this feature, click the Autostretch radio button in the Property inspector. (See page 135 for details on flexible layouts.)

Background color

You can give your table a background color that's independent of the page color. To pick a background color, click the Bg color box in the Property inspector and select from the pop-up palette. (You can actually select any color on your screen using the eyedropper; see page 130.)

After you click, you may wonder if Dreamweaver has gone colorblind; the table's color doesn't match the color you selected. Tables in Layout view have a light gray background to indicate empty areas of the table—places where no cells have yet been drawn. Dreamweaver *mixes* this gray with the color you selected, creating a muddy blend. That gray is just for showing you the table's boundaries in Dreamweaver and doesn't appear in a Web browser.

Cell padding and Cell spacing

When you add a background color to the cells in a table, you may sometimes want to create a visual gap between them—like the grout between tiles (but without the mold). To add this kind of space between cells in a table (see Figure 6-2), type a pixel value in the CellSpace field.

To add margins around all four edges inside of a cell, type a pixel value in the CellPad field. This space keeps the text or graphics *inside* a cell from touching the edges of the cell. By default, both the CellSpace and CellPad values are set to 0, which is appropriate for a design that requires graphics to meet at the edges of cell.

Notice, for example, that the chicken in Figure 6-1 is actually made of four different graphics, each in its own cell. Chopping up a graphic in this way is a typical Web-design trick that lends special flexibility. In Figure 6-1, for example, the chicken graphic appears to jut straight down into the text area of the Web page—a feat that would be impossible if the chicken were a single rectangular image. In this case, if either the CellSpace or CellPad were set above 0, there would be visible gaps between the segments of the image.

How to Draw a Layout Cell

With the Layout Cell drawing tool, you can add cells to any Layout Table on the page. However, you don't need to draw a table before using the Cell drawing tool. In fact, many people use the Cell tool to sketch out the content areas of the page, drawing boxes freehand on the screen, letting Dreamweaver create the rest of the table to fit.

For example, suppose you have a banner ad that must be placed in the upper-right corner of the page. First, you could select the Cell tool in the Objects panel (see Figure 6-3); the cursor changes to a + sign when it's over an empty area of a Layout Table or an empty area of the document window. You create a new cell just by dragging diagonally in the document window or inside an existing Layout Table. (If you draw a cell inside an existing Layout Table, Dreamweaver creates a rectangular cell. If you draw a cell in an empty document window, Dreamweaver creates a cell *and* a Layout Table that encloses it.)

Because tables are organized like a grid, Dreamweaver must organize cells in rows and columns. To indicate this underlying grid, Dreamweaver displays white lines projecting from the sides of a cell to indicate the rows and columns of the table (see Figure 6-6). In addition, as you add more cells to a table, the cursor snaps to these guidelines, as well as to table edges, when it's eight pixels away or closer. This snapping feature helps you accurately align the edges of your cells; once again, you can temporarily override this feature, gaining complete dragging freedom, by pressing Alt (Option) as you draw the cell.

Tip: After you draw a cell, the insertion point blinks patiently inside of the newly created cell, awaiting the text or graphics you're about to type, paste, or import. Creating another cell requires another click on the Layout Cell tool.

As in the previous tip, however, you can draw several cells in sequence without having to re-click the Layout Cell tool after each just by pressing the Ctrl (⌘) key while drawing a cell. The Layout Cell tool remains selected when you release the mouse, ready to draw another cell.

As with Layout Tables, there are some limitations to drawing Layout Cells:

- You can't draw a cell over already existing content. If you move the Cell tool over text, images, or other content on a page, the cursor changes to a ⊘ symbol and won't draw over that area.

- Cells can't overlap each other.

- You can't draw a cell within a cell.

Layout Cell Properties

Like a table, a cell has its own width and height, and can have its own background color. You set these properties in the Property inspector.

To see the properties for a Layout Cell, first select it by clicking any highlighted edge of the cell (the edges appear highlighted in red when your cursor approaches). Resize handles appear around the cell, and the Property inspector displays its attributes (see Figure 6-6).

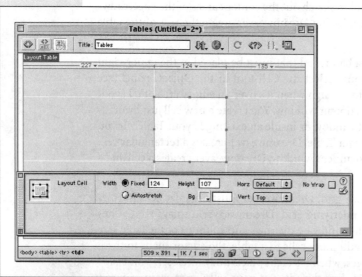

Figure 6-6:
When you select a Layout Cell, resize handles appear at the sides and corners of the cell. Furthermore, the Property inspector changes to reflect the attributes of the cell, including the cell's size and the alignment of the cell's contents. Turning on No Wrap (at the right of the Property inspector) prevents the contents of a cell from wrapping to the next line; the cell instead stretches to fit the contents, no matter how long. Keep No Wrap turned off to avoid such wildly expanding cells.

POWER USERS' CLINIC

Back to the Bad Old Days

Visual HTML editors like Adobe GoLive and Microsoft FrontPage have historically gotten a bad rap from traditional hand-coding HTML programmers—for good reason. These programs sometimes insert special tags or properties into the HTML they create. This extra code adds size to a Web page and only makes the program's life easier, not your site's visitors'.

Macromedia has often held Dreamweaver up as the exception to this phenomenon, and has heralded its "Roundtrip HTML" as lean and hand-coder friendly. As described in Chapter 9, Dreamweaver doesn't rely on secret tricks—special Dreamweaver-only tags, for example—to get the job done.

Unfortunately, the new layout mode is one exception. It sometimes inserts an attribute in the <table> tag: *mm:layoutgroup="true"*. This isn't an HTML property, and it won't help your pages look better in a Web browser; it only exists to help Dreamweaver do its job.

Fortunately, you get this attribute only if you start drawing cells with the Cell tool. To prevent Dreamweaver from adding this extra code, always start by drawing a Layout Table *first,* and then draw cells inside it. (Of course, you can also go into the HTML code itself and manually remove the mm:layoutgroup attribute from the <table> tag. See Chapter 9 for more on editing raw HTML code using Dreamweaver).

Alignment

By default, a cell's contents are aligned with the left side of the cell, and float in the middle of the cell vertically. You can change either or both of these alignment options by setting the horizontal and vertical properties of the cell (see Figure 6-7).

To align the content horizontally inside a cell, select the cell, and then choose an alignment option from the Horz (Horizontal) menu in the Property inspector (see Figure 6-6):

- The **Left** and **Right** options align a cell's contents with its left or right walls. (Since Left is the default, explicitly choosing Left only adds unnecessary code to your page.)

Figure 6-7:
Top: A cell's horizontal (top row) and vertical alignment (bottom row) properties affect how contents are aligned within a cell.

Bottom: The baseline option aligns the bottom of the first line of text in one cell with the other cells in the row. In other words, the first line of text in each cell rests on an invisible line called the baseline—represented in this figure by the black underline.

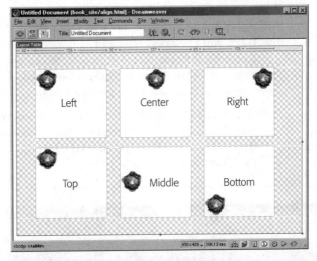

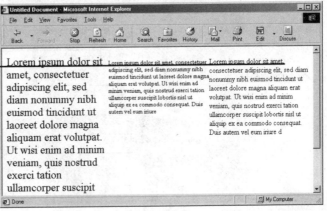

- The **Center** option centers the cell contents between the left and right walls of the cell.

The vertical alignment property works the same way; use the Vert (Vertical) menu of the Property inspector:

- The **Top** and **Bottom** options make the cell contents rest against the cell's top or bottom edge, respectively.

- The **Middle** option makes the cell contents float in the vertical center of the cell. (This is the default behavior of a cell; here again, choosing Middle therefore adds unnecessary code to your page.)

- The **Baseline** option aligns the bottom of the first line of text in the cell with the baseline of text in all the other cells in the row (see Figure 6-7.)

Moving and Resizing Layout Cells and Layout Tables

Once you've drawn cells and tables, you're not locked into that one design. Dreamweaver's Layout view provides several ways to adjust the size and position of cells and tables. As usual, Dreamweaver makes a pleasant task out of a normally time-consuming and error-prone job.

To move a cell, drag one of its edges. Dreamweaver lets you move the cell anywhere within the table; however, you can't move it outside of its Layout Table, into or overlapping another cell, or into another Layout Table. If you try, Dreamweaver displays the ○ symbol.

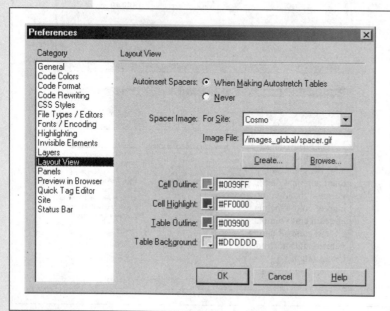

Figure 6-8:
Dreamweaver uses different colors to identify Layout Tables and cells. By default, the outline of a cell is blue; when you move your mouse over a cell, its outline turns red. Table outlines are green by default, and a table's background is gray. You can change any of these colors using the appropriate color boxes in the Edit→Preferences window, as shown here.

Tip: You can nudge a selected cell by one pixel at a time by pressing the arrow keys. Hold down the Shift key, too, to nudge the cell ten pixels per press of the arrow key.

Once you've moved the cell, Dreamweaver redraws the underlying table to accommodate this change.

Resizing a table or cell is easy: For numerical precision, select the table or cell and use the Property inspector to adjust the Width and Height values. You can also resize a table or cell by dragging the handles that appear when you select it. However, since cells can't overlap each other or extend outside of a table, you can't drag the edge of a cell over another cell or out of a table.

Building Flexible Page Layouts in Layout View

When you set a fixed width for a Layout Table, as described on page 130, it remains the same width regardless of your visitor's browser window size. This level of certainty and control is great for making sure elements go where you want them; but at times, fixed-width designs leave large areas of empty space when viewed on larger monitors (see Figure 6-9 for an example).

One solution is to build flexible tables with Dreamweaver's Autostretch option. Flexible tables, sometimes called *liquid HTML*, expand or shrink to fit a browser window's available display area. In this way, your design can accommodate 15-inch *and* 21-inch monitors. (Imagine if newspapers grew or shrank to fit a reader's arm span!)

Figure 6-9:
Flexible table widths provide one solution to Web designers' greatest challenge: designing pages for different monitor and window sizes. A layout that uses a fixed width often has unwanted and distracting white space when viewed on larger monitors. The top two images, for example, show the same fixed-width table viewed on a small screen (left) and a wider one (right). Flexible tables, on the other hand, can shrink or grow to fit the browser window, as shown in the bottom two images.

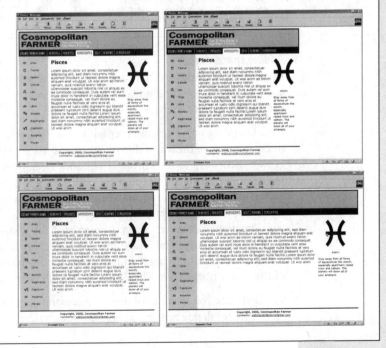

Creating a flexible-width table

Instead of being a certain number of pixels wide, a flexible table always fills the entire window. To achieve this effect, you must set *one* column in the table to Autostretch; that column will expand to fill the page. For instance, in the example in Figure 6-9, the column containing the headline "Pisces" expands, while the left-hand column, containing the navigation bar, remains a fixed width.

To create a flexible column, click the down-pointing triangle next to the pixel width number in the column header (see Figure 6-10) and choose Make Column Autostretch from the contextual menu. You can also select the *cell* you wish to make flexible and click the Autostretch button on the Property inspector. (Although you can also create a flexible table by selecting the *table* and setting its width to Autostretch, it's not necessary to do so. Dreamweaver automatically sets it to Autostretch when you create a flexible column.)

If you want to change the column back to a fixed width size, use the same menu, shown in Figure 6-10, to choose Make Column Fixed Width.

Figure 6-10:
If there are two numbers in the column header—such as "516" (495)—the first is the actual cell width; the second is the width specified in the HTML. To restore the larger size, choose Make Cell Widths Consistent from the column header menu.

Adding spacer images

In order for the Autostretch function to work, Dreamweaver uses a transparent image—an actual, see-through GIF file called a *spacer*—to control the spacing of the columns that *don't* stretch.

Understanding why Dreamweaver adds these invisible spacer images requires some understanding of the way it thinks. When you ask it to make the autostretch column grow as necessary to fill a browser window, Dreamweaver uses a little trick. It sets the column's width to *100 percent*. In other words, the column attempts to take up *all* the space available, even space used by other columns. This greedy behavior, of course, would ordinarily squish the table's other columns into hyper-thinness. That's why Dreamweaver inserts a spacer image (of the width you've specified) into each *fixed*-width column. The image acts like a steel beam across the walls of the fixed-width column, reinforcing it and preventing it from shrinking smaller than the size of the spacer image (see "The Contents Take Priority" on page 152).

The first time you make a column an Autostretcher, Dreamweaver opens a Choose Spacer Image dialog box. It offers you three choices:

- **Create a spacer image file.** If you choose this option, Dreamweaver will create a 1-pixel by 1-pixel, transparent GIF image and prompt you to name the file and save it into any folder of your Web site.

- **Use an existing spacer image file.** If you're already using a 1-pixel by 1-pixel transparent GIF (a standard Web-design tool), choose this option. Dreamweaver then lets you browse to and select the GIF file in your site folder. (For one use for such an image, see "Shrinking Down to a Pixel" on page 154.)

- **Don't use spacer images for Autostretch tables.** This is not a wise choice if you want to use the Autostretch feature. Most likely, your fixed-width columns will appear much smaller than you intended.

WORKAROUND WORKSHOP

When Document Relative Paths Don't Work

Throughout this book, you've been advised to avoid *root-relative* links in your Web pages. Because they don't preview correctly on your computer and work only when viewed from a Web server, root-relative links are usually not a good choice. Unfortunately, if you use the Layout view's Autostretch option and its spacer images, you have no choice.

Whether you let Dreamweaver create a spacer image or you use one already in your site folder, you must choose whether to use a Document or Site Root relative path when adding the image to a Layout Table.

If your first instinct is to choose Document from the Rela-

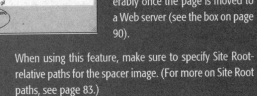

tive To menu, you've been paying close attention to this book—but you'd be wrong. Macromedia dropped the ball on this one; selecting Document *doesn't* create document-relative paths; instead, Dreamweaver inserts the spacer image files as file-relative paths beginning with file:///. While this tactic lets you preview the page accurately on your local computer, it will fail miserably once the page is moved to a Web server (see the box on page 90).

When using this feature, make sure to specify Site Root-relative paths for the spacer image. (For more on Site Root paths, see page 83.)

After you've set the spacer image for the site, Dreamweaver continues to use that file whenever you need one. You can select a different file at any time from the Edit→Preferences→Layout View tab (see Figure 6-8).

While Dreamweaver automatically inserts spacer GIFs, you can also add them manually by choosing Add Spacer Image from the column header menu (see Figure 6-10). This command is grayed out if you turned on the "Don't use spacer images" option in the Choose Spacer Image dialog box.

Removing spacer images

To remove a spacer image from a column, choose Remove Spacer Image from the column header menu. You can also remove *all* of the spacer images on a page by choosing Remove All Spacer Images from the column header menu, or by clicking the Remove Spacer Images button on the Property inspector when a table is selected (see Figure 6-5).

WORKAROUND WORKSHOP

Where Does the Spacer Image go?

When using Layout View's Autostretch feature, Dreamweaver creates a new row at the bottom of the current table. In each fixed-width cell in that row, Dreamweaver inserts a transparent, 1-pixel-tall spacer image set to the width of that cell.

Keep this behavior in mind if you try to place one table on top of another. If the two tables need to touch seamlessly—for example, if they share a color that needs to appear connected—that 1-pixel tall row created by the spacer images creates a 1-pixel gap between the two tables.

Unfortunately, you can't solve this dilemma in Dreamweaver's visually oriented Design view; at only one pixel tall, the new row with the spacer images is practically invisible. You must delve into the HTML code; choose View→Code to open Dreamweaver's Code view (which is described in Chapter 9).

```
<tr>
    <td height="36"></td>
    <td></td>
    <td></td>
</tr>
<tr>
    <td height="1"><img height="1" width="228" src="/cosmo/spacer.gif"></td>
    <td></td>
    <td><img height="1" width="89" src="/cosmo/spacer.gif"></td>
</tr>
</table>
</body>
</html>
```

Last row

Spacer images

You'll need to locate the closing <table> tag for the offending Autostretch table. Directly above that, you'll find a single table row composed of an opening <tr> tag, several lines of <td> (table data or cells) tags, and a closing </tr> tag. Select the entire row, cut it, and paste it directly after the *opening* <table> tag. This essentially moves that bottom row (containing the spacer) to the *top*, and allows the table to rest seamlessly on any table directly below it.

And what if you also want to prevent a gap at the *top* of an Autostretch table? Once again, go in the page's HTML source code and locate the last row of the table. Delete it. Then, back in Design view (View→Design), click inside one cell in each fixed-width column, insert a spacer image (choose Insert→Image), and set its width to match the desired width of that column.

Using a Tracing Image

Layout mode lets you draw your designs directly in the document window, which is a wonderful feature. However, unless you can visualize the layout you want, you may feel that you're just aimlessly drawing boxes on a blank canvas.

Dreamweaver's Tracing Image feature helps you find your way around the dreaded blank screen. With it, you can import a graphic representation of your finished page design—a sketch you've created in a more art-oriented program like, say, Fireworks or Photoshop—and use it as a pattern for tracing the table and cells of your page. In fact, it's very common in the Web-design biz to work up, in a program like Photoshop, a graphic that *looks* like a finished Web page—but it's one giant image, without individual buttons, tables, or editable text (see Figure 6-11).

To add a tracing image to your page, choose Modify→Page Properties (or choose View→Tracing Image→Load); the Page Properties dialog box opens (see Figure 6-11). Click the Browse button near the bottom of the window (next to the Tracing Image field). Finally, find and open a GIF, JPEG, or PNG file to use as the background image.

Now use the Image Transparency slider shown in Figure 6-11: To fade the image into the background of the page, move the slider toward the transparent setting, making it easier to distinguish between the tracing image and the actual content on the Web page.

When you click OK, you return to your Web page with the tracing image in place. (The tracing image appears only in Dreamweaver, never on the Web.)

Figure 6-11:
Top: You can hide or show the tracing image using the Options menu-icon at the top of the document window.

Bottom: In addition to setting the title and color of your page, the Page Properties window lets you add a tracing image to your document and fade it into the background as much as you want. In this example, the tracing image represents a horoscopes page for the Cosmopolitan Farmer Web site. As you can see by the Transparency slider, it's been faded over 50 percent into the background of the page.

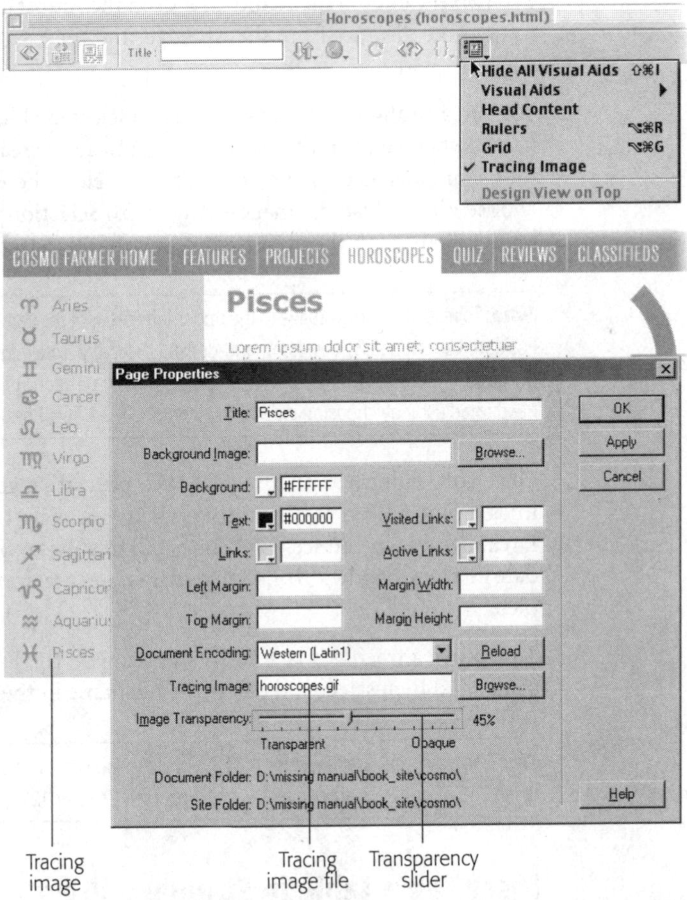

Hiding a tracing image

If you want to temporarily hide a tracing image, choose Tracing Image in the toolbar's Options menu (shown at top in Figure 6-11); choose the same command again to show it. (The long way: Choose View→Tracing Image and turn off the Show option.)

Moving a tracing image

When you first select a tracing image, it appears against the top and left margins, if you've specified them (see page 31). If you didn't specify margins, Dreamweaver places the tracing image several pixels from the left and top edges of the document window—just where it would put text or graphics into a new Web page.

You can't just drag the tracing image elsewhere on the page; if you need it anywhere other than the upper-left corner, choose View→Tracing Image→Adjust Position. Type pixel values in the X and Y fields in the Adjust Tracing Image dialog box; the X value is the distance from the left edge, and the Y value is the distance from the top edge.

You can also align the tracing image to a selected object on the page, which comes in handy when you want to use a tracing image to create a portion of a Web page—a footer or sidebar element, for example. Select the element on the page and then choose View→Tracing Image→Align with Selection. The tracing image's upper-left corner aligns with the upper-left corner of the selected element.

Note: To reset the tracing image to the upper-left corner of the page, choose View→Tracing Image→Reset Position. Unfortunately, this command doesn't place the image in its original position, at the margins of the page; it merely places it at the very corner (the 0,0 position) of the document window. You'll probably need to adjust it by choosing View→Tracing Image→Adjust Position.

Once you've finished building the Web page, it's a good idea to remove the tracing image. Not only is it distracting when you view the page in Dreamweaver, but Dreamweaver introduces extra lines of Dreamweaver-specific HTML to accommodate it. These bandwidth-hogging extra bytes are unnecessary once the page is complete.

To remove a tracing image from a page, open the Page Properties dialog box once again, and then select and delete the file name in the Tracing Image field.

Tip: Tracing images aren't just for the Layout view. You can use a tracing image anytime—a handy feature when you're using Dreamweaver's Layer tools (see Chapter 12).

Inserting a Table in Standard View

While the Layout view is a great way to lay out a page, it can't do certain things. You can't, for instance, add a background image to a table or cell in Layout view. Nor can you add color to a row of cells, or even insert a simple table for displaying data.

Likewise, if you're a former Dreamweaver 3 user and have spent a long time learning to visualize table layouts in your head (or if you find the layout tools cumbersome), you might be more comfortable with the basic approach offered by the Table object in the Objects panel.

Even if you're sold on the Layout view, it's a good idea to familiarize yourself with these steps so that you can troubleshoot tables more easily. To insert a table, first switch to Standard view by clicking the button at the bottom of the Objects panel (or by choosing View→Table View→Standard View). Then proceed like this:

1. **Place the insertion point in the document window where you'd like to insert a table.**

   You can add a table anywhere you can add graphics or text. You can even add a table to another table, by clicking inside a table cell.

2. **Choose Insert→Table.**

   You can also click the Insert Table Button on the Objects panel, or press Ctrl+Alt+T (⌘-Option-T). Either way, the Insert Table dialog box opens (see Figure 6-12).

3. **Using the Rows and Columns fields, specify how many rows and columns you want your table to have.**

   If you're using the table for layout purposes, you might only want two or three columns; if you plan to create a spreadsheet, you could create many rows or columns. (Don't panic about your estimate; you can always add or remove rows or columns later.)

4. **Type the amount of cell padding, in pixels, you want for the table.**

   Cell padding is the margin—the space from the edge of a cell to its contents (see Figure 6-2). Unfortunately, this property applies to *every* cell in a table; you can't add margins to an individual cell in a table.

5. **Type the amount of cell spacing, in pixels, you want for the table.**

   Cell spacing specifies how many pixels of space separate one cell from another (see Figure 6-2). Again, this property applies to every cell in a table. (Note that leaving these fields empty isn't the same as setting them to zero; see Figure 6-12.)

6. **Using the Width field, specify how wide you want the table to be (in units that you specify using the pop-up menu).**

   Tables can have either a specified, fixed minimum width, or they can take up a specified percentage of the space available on the page. To set a fixed width, choose Pixels as the unit of measurement and type a pixel amount in the Width field. Fixed width tables remain the same size regardless of size of the browser window.

   Percentage widths let tables grow or shrink relative to the space available. In other words, the size of a table that's 100 percent wide stretches all the way across your visitor's browser window, no matter how wide or narrow. (You achieve a similar effect with the Autostretch feature in Layout view, as described on page 135.)

Note: Due to differences in the way browsers interpret HTML, the exact pixel dimension of percentage-based tables may differ from browser to browser.

7. **Type a number, in pixels, for the border.**

   If you don't want a border, type *0*. Dreamweaver uses dotted lines to help you identify rows, columns, and cells whose border is 0. (The dotted line won't appear on the finished Web page.)

8. **Click OK to insert the table.**

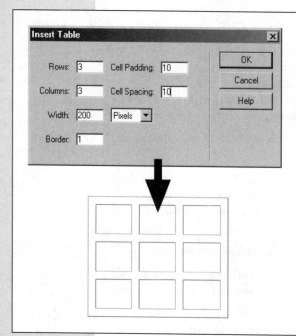

Figure 6-12:
The Insert Table dialog box lets you define the properties of the table. Leaving the Cell Padding and Cell Spacing fields empty isn't the same as setting them to 0. If these properties are empty, most Web browsers insert one pixel of cell padding and two pixels of cell spacing. If you notice unwanted gaps between cells in a table or between content in a table and the cell's edges, empty settings here are the most likely culprit. To truly leave zero space, set Cell Padding and Cell Spacing to 0.

Once you've added a table to a page, you can begin filling the table's cells. A cell works like a small document window; you can click inside it and add text, images, and links using the techniques you've already learned. You can even insert a table inside of a cell (see page 159).

To move the insertion point from one cell to the next, press the Tab key; when you reach the last cell in a row, the Tab key moves the insertion point to the first cell in the row below. And if the insertion point is in the last *cell* of the last row, pressing Tab creates a new row at the bottom of the table.

Shift-Tab moves the cursor in the *opposite* direction—from the current cell to a cell to the left.

Selecting Parts of a Table in Standard View

Tables and their cells have independent properties. For example, a table and a cell can have different background colors. But before you can change any of these properties, you must first *select* the tables, rows, columns, or cells you want to affect.

Selecting a Table

There are a number of ways to select a table in the document window:

- Click the upper-left corner of the table, or anywhere on the bottom edge of the table. (Be careful using the latter technique, however. It's easy to accidentally *drag* the border, resetting the height of the table in the process.)

- Click anywhere inside the table, and then select the <table> tag in the document window's status bar (see page 16 to learn about the tag selector).

- Click anywhere inside the table, and then choose Modify→Table→Select Table.

- Right-click (Control-click) inside a table; choose Table→Select Table from the contextual menu.

Once selected, a table appears with a thick black border and three tiny, square resize handles—at the right edge, bottom edge, and lower-right corner.

Selecting Rows or Columns

You can also select an entire row or column of cells by doing one of the following:

- Move the cursor to the left edge of a row, or the top edge of a column; when it changes to a right- or down-pointing arrow, click (see Figure 6-13).

- Click a cell at either end of a row, or the first or last cell of a column; drag across the cells in the row or column to select them.

- Click any cell in the row you wish to select, and then click the <tr> tag in the tag selector. (The <tr> tag is how HTML indicates a table row; this method doesn't work for columns.)

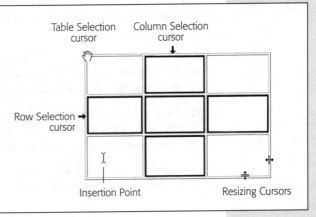

Figure 6-13:
When working with tables, the cursor can take on many different roles. The Table selection cursor lets you select the entire table (in Windows, this looks like a compass.) When the cursor turns into an arrow (either pointing down or to the right), you can click to select a column or row of cells. The insertion-point cursor lets you click to insert content into a cell. When you pass the cursor over a resize handle, it becomes a resize icon, which you can drag to resize rows, columns, or the entire table.

Table Selection cursor   Column Selection cursor

Row Selection cursor

Insertion Point   Resizing Cursors

When a cell is selected, it has a dark border around it. When multiple cells are selected, each cell has a dark border (see Figure 6-13).

Selecting Cells

To select one or more cells:

- Drag over adjoining cells. A solid black border appears around a cell when it's selected.

- To select several cells that aren't necessarily adjacent, Ctrl-click (⌘-click) them one at a time. (You can also Ctrl-click [⌘-click] an already selected cell to deselect it.)

- Click a cell, then Shift-click another cell. Your two clicks form diagonally opposite corners of an imaginary rectangle; Dreamweaver highlights all cells within it.

- Use the tag selector (page 16) to select a cell. Click inside the cell you wish to select, and then click the <td> tag in the tag selector. (The <td> tag stands for Table Data; it's how HTML refers to a cell.)

Formatting Tables

When you first insert a table, you set the number of rows and columns, as well as the table's cell padding, cell spacing, width, and borders. You're not stuck, however, with the properties you first give the table; you can change any or all of these properties, and set a few additional ones, using the Property inspector.

When you select a table in Standard view, the Property inspector changes to reflect that table's settings (see Figure 6-14). You can adjust the table by entering different values for height, width, rows, columns, and so on in the appropriate fields.

In addition, the Property inspector lets you set alignment options and add colors or a background image, as described next.

Aligning Tables

In the normal flow of a Web page, a table acts like a paragraph, header, or any other block-level element: It's aligned to the left of the page, with other elements placed either above it or below it.

But you can make several useful changes to the way a table interacts with the text and other elements around it. After selecting the table, use one of the three alignment options in the pop-up menu at the right of the Property inspector:

- The **Left** and **Right** options align the table with the left or right page margins. Anything you then add to the page, including paragraphs, images, or other tables, wraps around the right or left side of the table.

- The **Center** option makes the table sit in the center of the page, interrupting the flow of the elements around it. Nothing wraps around the table.

Clearing Height and Width Values

Four tools hide behind the obscure-looking buttons in the bottom half of the Property inspector (see Figure 6-14).

- Clicking the Clear Height Values button removes the height property of the table and each cell. Doing so doesn't set the heights to zero; it simply deletes the property altogether.

- Clicking the Clear Width Values button accomplishes the same purpose for the width properties of a table and its cells (see "Setting Cell Dimensions" on page 151).

When creating complex table designs, it's easy to get yourself into a situation where width and height measurements conflict and produce unreliable results. For example, it's possible to set one cell to 300 pixels wide, and later set another cell *in the same column* to 400 pixels wide. Since a Web browser can't do both (how can one column be both 300 *and* 400 pixels wide?), you'll get unpredictable results.

In tables with many cells, these kinds of problems are tough to ferret out. That's when you'll find these timesaving tools handy; you can delete the width and height measurements and start from scratch (see "Tips for Surviving Table Making" on page 152).

Figure 6-14:
When you select a table, you can do everything from adjust its basic structure to fine-tune its appearance in the Property inspector.

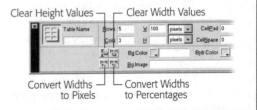

Clear Height Values — ┌ Clear Width Values

Convert Widths to Pixels ┘ └ Convert Widths to Percentages

Decorating a Table

To spruce up a table, you can add color to its background and borders, and even add a background image. As usual in Dreamweaver, you make these changes in the Property inspector; just select the table (see page 143), then click the appropriate box in the Property inspector—Bg Color (background) or Brdr Color (border)—and select a color from the color palette. (See page 30 for more on choosing colors in Dreamweaver.)

To add a graphic image to the background of a selected table, click the folder icon next to Bg Image in the Property inspector. Browse to and open an image in your Web site folder; it appears immediately as a background image for the selected table.

***

Note: Be careful with these properties. Background images for tables work only in 4.0 or later browsers. Early versions simply ignore this property and display no image.

***

Resizing a Table

While you define the width and height of a table when you first insert it, you can always change your mind and modify the width or height later. To do so, first select the table, and then take either of these steps:

- Type a value into the W (width) or H (height) box on the Property inspector, and choose a unit of measurement from the pop-up menu—either pixels or percentage.

- Drag one of the three resize handles on the right edge, bottom edge, or right corner of the table. The corner resize handle adjusts the height and width of the table simultaneously.

You can also, in theory, convert a table from a fixed unit of measurement, such as pixels, to the stretchy, percentage-style width setting—or vice versa—using the bottom two buttons in the Property inspector (see Figure 6-14).

Both of these options depend on the size of the current document window in Dreamweaver. For example, suppose the document window is 700 pixels wide, and you've inserted a table that's 100 percent wide. Clicking the Convert Widths to Pixels button sets the table's width to around 700 pixels (the exact value depends on the margins of the page). However, if your document window were 500 pixels wide, clicking the same button would produce a fixed-width table around 500 pixels wide.

The Convert Width to Percentages button takes the opposite tack. It sets the width of a table and the width of cells to percentages based on the amount of the document window's width they cover at the moment. The bigger the window, the smaller the percentage.

Note that these buttons have no effect on the *height* property of cells or tables. Because the effects of these buttons depend upon the size of the document window, you'll find yourself rarely, if ever, using these two tools.

FREQUENTLY ASKED QUESTION

Floating Images

I want to create a Web page with a single image that floats right in the middle of a user's browser window, no matter what size the window is on the screen. What's the secret?

This little trick is a snap, and it's ideal for giving your Web site an introductory or splash screen page. Insert a one-row, one-column table into an empty document; make sure it has no cell padding, cell spacing, or border. Set the width of the table to *100%* and the height to *100%*.

Now set the horizontal alignment of the cell to Center, and the vertical alignment to Middle. Insert an image into the cell.

When a visitor loads the Web page, no matter what size her browser window is, the table fills the space, and the image floats right in the middle. Of course, you can put anything you want into the cell, not just a graphic: text or even another, smaller table, for instance.

Modifying Cell and Row Properties in Standard View

Cells have their own properties, separate from the properties of the table itself. So do table *rows*—but not columns (see the sidebar box below).

The Dawn of Columns

As far as the standard HTML language is concerned, there really isn't any such entity as a column. Tables are created with the <table> tag, rows with the <tr> tag, and cells with the <td> tag—but there's no column tag. Dreamweaver calculates the columns based on the number of cells in a row. If there are 7 rows in a table, each with 4 cells, then the table has 4 columns; in other words, the number of cells in each row *determines* the number of columns.

But times are changing. Two new tags introduced in HTML 4, the <colgroup> and <col> tags, let you control various attributes of columns in a table. Unfortunately, not all Web browsers understand these tags, and Dreamweaver provides no easy way to add them. You can find out more about them, however, in Dreamweaver 4's new built-in HTML reference (see page 257).

When you click inside of a cell, the top half of the Property inspector displays the cell's text formatting properties; the bottom half shows the properties for that particular cell (see Figure 6-15).

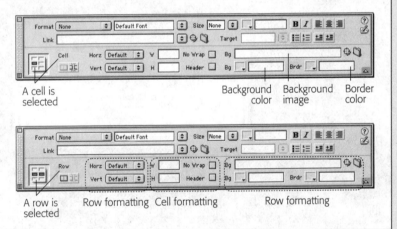

Figure 6-15:
When you select a cell or a row, the bottom half of the Property inspector displays the properties of the selection. While the only apparent differences are the word Cell or Row and the shading on the table icon at the left side of the inspector, rows have their own distinct properties that you can set independently of a cell (background color and border color, for example).

A cell is selected

Background color Background image Border color

A row is selected Row formatting Cell formatting Row formatting

Alignment Properties

By default, a cell's contents hug the left wall of the cell and float halfway between the top and bottom of the cell. After selecting a row, a cell, or several cells, you can change these alignments using the Property inspector. For example, the Horz (Horizontal) menu in the Property inspector (see Figure 6-15) offers Left, Center, and Right alignment options.

Note that these options are separate from the *paragraph* alignment options discussed in Chapter 3. In fact, you can mix and match the two. Suppose, for example, that you have a table cell containing four paragraphs. You want all but one paragraph to be center aligned; you want the last paragraph to be right-aligned. To do so, you could set the alignment of the *cell* to Center, then select just the last paragraph and set its alignment to Right. The paragraph's alignment overrides the alignment applied by the cell.

You can set the vertical alignment property in the same manner. Select the cells and then use one of the four options available in the Vert (Vertical) menu of the Property inspector: Top, Middle (the default), or Bottom.

(The Baseline option aligns the bottom of the first line of text in the cell to the baseline of text in all the other cells in the row. This option can improve the appearance of multiple text columns, as illustrated in Figure 6-7 on page 133.)

FREQUENTLY ASKED QUESTION

Suddenly Jumbo Cells

When I added some text to a cell, it suddenly got much wider than the other cells in the row. What gives?

It isn't Dreamweaver's fault; it's just how HTML works.

Web browsers (and Dreamweaver) display cells to match the content inside. In the example shown here, the first cell of the first row has a little text, the second cell is blank, and the third cell has a 125-pixel-wide image. Since the image is the biggest item, its cell is wider than the other two. The middle cell, with nothing in it, is given the least amount of space.

Usually, you won't want a Web browser making these kinds of decisions. By specifying height and width for a cell (page 151), you can force a Web browser to display a cell with the dimensions you want.

You may also notice that Dreamweaver isn't always terrifically prompt about changing a cell's width as you add to its contents. You may add some text to a cell, click another cell, and add an image—but the cells don't change. However, if you save the file or click outside the table, suddenly the table goes crazy, and *all* of the cells resize.

Actually, Dreamweaver thinks it's doing you a favor; in the interest of speeding your editing along, the program doesn't automatically redraw the table with each change you make.

If you find this behavior disconcerting, choose Edit→Preferences to open the Preferences dialog box. Make sure the General category is selected, and turn off "Faster Table Editing (deferred update)" under Editing Options.

Two Properties to Forget

Two additional properties of a cell, No Wrap and Header, are of such little value that you'll probably go your entire Web career without using them. But for thorough-

ness' sake—and in case you may actually find one of them fits the bill—here's what
they do:

- The **No Wrap** property prevents a Web browser from wrapping a line of text
  within a cell onto multiple lines; the browser instead widens the cell so that it can
  include the line without line breaks. The result is almost never useful or attractive. Furthermore, if you specify a width for the cell, this property doesn't work
  at all!

- The **Header** property converts the HTML tag used for the cell (<td>) into a <th>
  tag—a table header tag—which indicates that a cell is a *headline* for a column or
  row of data. The only noticeable change is that, in most Web browsers, the text
  appears in a header cell in bold type, center aligned.

Cell Decoration

Cells needn't be drab. As with tables, you can give individual cells background colors or even background graphics (see Figure 6-16).

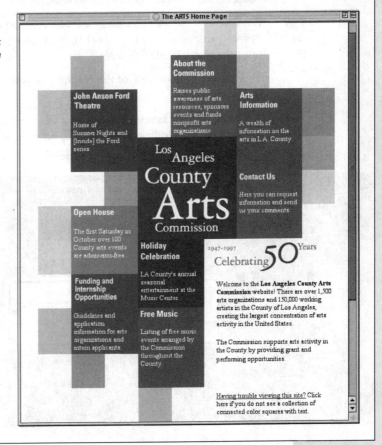

Figure 6-16:
*Add impact with background
color. The home page for the Los
Angeles County Arts Commission
(www.lacountyarts.org) makes a
big visual statement without
being a bandwidth hog. The
trick? There are only a few
graphics on this page; the
colorful squares are simply table
cells with a variety of background colors.*

Adding cell background colors

To set the background color of one or more selected table cells or rows, do one of the following:

- Click the Bg color box in the Property inspector; select a color from the pop-up palette.

- Type a hexadecimal color value into the Bg color field.

You also have the option to set a color for the cell's border using the color box or Brdr field in the Property inspector. However, only Internet Explorer recognizes this property, and, since it is not officially part of HTML, it's unlikely that other browsers will ever support it.

Adding cell background images

You can also add an image to the background of a cell. In this instance, the cell acts much like a miniature document window; the graphic tiles (repeats endlessly) within the cell to completely cover the cell's background.

To add a background image to selected cells, try either of these steps:

- Click the Browse for File icon (the folder icon) to the right of the Bg field in the Property inspector (see Figure 6-15). In the resulting dialog box, navigate to and open the graphics file you want.

- Type the file path or URL of the graphic you want in the Bg field in the Property inspector.

You can also set a background image for a table *row* (<tr> tag) using Dreamweaver, but it involves some coding that isn't officially part of HTML. In fact, only Netscape versions 4 and higher can display a background image for a table row at all.

WORKAROUND WORKSHOP

Beware the Resize Handles

Dreamweaver 4 provides several techniques for resizing tables and cells while in Standard view. Unfortunately, the easiest method—dragging a cell or table border—is also the easiest to do by mistake. Because moving the cursor over any border turns it into the resize tool, almost every Dreamweaver practitioner drags a border accidentally at least once, overwriting carefully calculated table and cell widths and heights.

On occasions like these, don't forget the Undo feature—Ctrl+Z (⌘-Z). And if all is lost, you can always clear the widths and heights of every cell in a table (using the buttons in the Property inspector) and start over by typing new cell dimensions (see Figure 6-14).

Note that this problem only rears its ugly head when resizing a table in Standard view. Layout view provides another, superior method of resizing cell and tables by dragging (see page 134).

Setting Cell Dimensions

Specifying the width or height of a particular cell works just as it does when you set the width or height of a table: select one or more cells and type a value in the W (width) or H (height) field in the Property inspector. This value can be either specified in pixels or percentage. For instance, if you want a particular cell to be 50 pixels wide, type *50*. For a cell that you want to be 50 percent of the total table width, type *50%*. Controlling cell and table dimensions can be tricky business; be sure to read the "Tips for Surviving Table Making" on page 152.

You can also resize a column or row of cells by dragging a cell border. As your cursor approaches the cell's border, it changes shape to indicate that you can begin dragging.

When using this method, however, Dreamweaver automatically calculates the width and height for each cell in the table; as a result, you could wind up with conflicting values. For example, suppose that you drag the border between two cells in a row, changing their widths to 100 pixels and 50 pixels, respectively. Dreamweaver automatically sets the width value of every cell in the first column to 100 pixels, and every cell in the second column to 50 pixels.

So far, so good. But now suppose that you click in the first cell of the first column and change its width value to 200 pixels. The HTML in your page now has a value of 200 pixels set for this cell, but 100 pixels for all other cells in the column. It can't be both; all cells in a column must be equally wide. Since this can lead to random results in different browsers, it's best to avoid mixing the two approaches of setting cell widths and heights. (When madness like this strikes, don't forget you can completely clear the width and height of cells as describe on page 145.)

Figure 6-17:
If you insert a graphic into a cell, and the graphic is larger than the cell's specified width or height, a Web browser won't shrink the image or hide part of it; the cell has to grow to fit. In this figure, although each column was set to a width of 100 pixels, the 174-pixel image stretches the first column's width to 174 pixels. The other two columns must shrink to keep the table's total width to 300 pixels.

Original width settings:

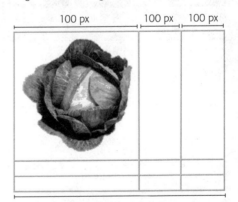

Whole table: 300 pixels

Tips for Surviving Table Making

Nothing can be more confounding than trying to get your tables laid out exactly as you want them. Many beginning Web designers throw their hands up in despair when working with tables, which often seem to have minds of their own. The Layout view eliminates many of the hassles associated with using tables for page layout, but here are a few problems that often confuse designers, and some tips to make working with tables more understandable.

The contents take priority

You've created a 300-pixel-wide table and set each cell in the first row to 100 pixels wide. You insert a larger graphic into the first cell, and suddenly...Kablooie! Even though you set each cell to 100 pixels wide, as shown in Figure 6-17, the column with the graphic is much wider than the other two.

A cell can't be smaller than the largest piece of content inside it. In this case, although you told the cell to be 100 pixels wide, the image is 174 pixels wide, and forces the first column to grow (and the others to shrink) accordingly.

Set each column manually

You've created a 580-pixel-wide table with three columns. You've set the width of a cell in each of the first two columns to 150 pixels and 50 pixels. You assume that the Web browser is smart enough to figure out what size the remaining column should be: 380 pixels, of course, which is exactly what's left over if you subtract the first two column widths from 580. Unfortunately, you'd be wrong, as shown in Figure 6-18.

Web browsers aren't so smart. As you can see in the figure, Netscape Navigator needs more information to display a table correctly.

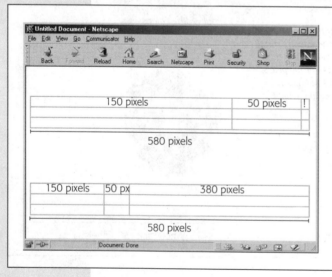

Figure 6-18:
In the top table, the designer set widths for the first two columns; the last column wound up with no width set. In the lower table, the designer manually set the width of the third column to 380 pixels; this time, the browser displays it correctly.

There is no such thing as column width, only cell width

To set the width of a column of cells, you have to set the width of only *one* cell in that column. For example, in the second table in Figure 6-18, the first cell in the top row has a width set to 150. You don't have to set the widths of the two cells below it.

This principle can save a lot of time, and, because it reduces the amount of code on a Web page, makes your pages load and appear faster. For consistency, it's a good idea to pick either the first or last row of a table for width-setting.

The same holds true for the height of a row. You only need to set the height of a single cell to define the height for its entire row. However, if you resize your rows and columns by dragging the cell borders, Dreamweaver automatically sets the width and height value in every cell.

Do the math

Calculators can be really useful when you're building tables. Although you *could* create a 400-pixel-wide table with three 700-pixel-wide columns, the results you'll get on the screen can be unpredictable (700 + 700 + 700 = 400).

As it turns out, Web browsers' loyalty is to *table* width first, then column widths. If you make the widths of your columns add up to the width of your table, you'll save yourself a lot of headache.

The spacer image revisited

Unfortunately, even if you explicitly set cell widths, some browsers still don't do a good job at controlling the width of cells. Remembering that a cell can't be smaller than the largest item inside it, as noted above, is half the battle. For even more control, use a spacer image, just as Dreamweaver does when you use the Autostretch option in Layout view (see page 135).

For example, suppose you want to create a table that's 580 pixels wide, with two rows and three columns. The widths of the columns will be 150 pixels, 20 pixels, and 410 pixels, respectively.

Specifying the widths of each cell in one of the rows would be a good start, but a more reliable approach would be to use a *transparent GIF image* to enforce the column widths:

1. **In a graphics program, create a 1-pixel by 1-pixel transparent GIF graphic.**

   Dreamweaver can do this automatically if you use the Layout view. See page 136.

2. **Create a new row at the bottom of the table.**

   One easy way is to click the lower-right cell of the table, and then press Tab.

3. **Click in the first cell; insert the spacer image by choosing Insert→Image and selecting the spacer file in your site folder.**

   Dreamweaver inserts the image and selects it in the document window.

4. **Using the Property inspector, change the width of the GIF to 150 pixels.**

   Since the first column in the table is 150 pixels wide, this graphic keeps the column from shrinking any smaller—which, in some browsers, it might otherwise do, thanks to an unfortunately common bug.

5. **In the second cell in the row, insert another spacer GIF. Set its width to 20 pixels.**

   Like the previous image, this one helps maintain the 20-pixel width of the column.

6. **Finally, move to the third cell in the row, insert another spacer, and set its width to 410 pixels.**

   Your table is now rock-solid.

Now you can see the advantages of Dreamweaver's Layout mode, which eliminates the need for many of these workarounds. It takes care of a lot of the headaches of building table-based layouts.

WORKAROUND WORKSHOP

Shrinking Down to a Pixel

Suppose you want to make an extremely short table cell. For example, one common trick for overcoming the drab gray quality of HTML's horizontal rule (see page 34) involves assigning a background color to a 1-pixel tall table cell that stretches the entire width of the page. When previewed in a browser, the cell looks like a colorful one-pixel line. Make the cell 2 pixels tall, and you've got a 2-pixel-high line.

But sooner or later, almost every Dreamweaver student runs up against this one: Unfortunately, even when you set the height of an empty cell to 1 pixel, it's still a lot taller than it needs to be. No matter what you try, you can't get that cell any shorter.

When Dreamweaver inserts a table into a document, all of the cells of the table *appear* to be empty. However, Dreamweaver actually inserts a nonbreaking space (see page 45) into each cell—a workaround for a particular display bug in Netscape browsers.

A nonbreaking space takes up space; its height is based on the default font for the Web page. And because a cell can't be smaller than the largest item in it, Web browsers can't shrink the cell down to 1 pixel.

To get around this problem, create a 1-pixel by 1-pixel transparent GIF image and keep it in your site folder. If you insert that image into the cell, Dreamweaver graciously removes its unsolicited nonbreaking space (just as it would for any cell that's not empty). Now the cell can shrink down to a single pixel.

Adding and Removing Rows and Columns

Even after inserting a table into a Web page, you can add and subtract rows and columns from your table. The text or images in the columns move right or down to accommodate their new next-door neighbor.

Adding One Row or Column

To add a single row to the table, you can use any of these approaches:

- Click inside a cell. Choose Modify→Table→Insert Row, or press Ctrl+M (⌘-M), to insert a new row of cells above the current row. Alternatively, you can right-click (Control-click) a cell and choose Table→Insert Row from the contextual menu.

- To add a new row at the end of a table, click inside the last cell in the table and then press Tab.

The new columns inherit the properties (width, height, background color, and so on) of the column you originally clicked.

To add a single *column* of cells:

- Click inside a cell and then choose Modify→Table→Insert Column.

- Click inside a cell and then press Ctrl+Shift+A (⌘-Shift-A).

- Right-click (Control-click) a cell; choose Table→Insert Column from the contextual menu that appears.

In each case, a new column appears to the right of the current column.

Adding Multiple Rows or Columns

When you need to expand your table more rapidly, you can use a special dialog box that lets you add many rows or columns at once.

1. **Click inside a cell. Choose Modify→Table→Insert Rows or Columns.**

   If you're a keyboard lover, you may prefer to press Ctrl+Shift+A (⌘-Shift-A) instead. Either way, the Insert Rows or Columns dialog box appears (see Figure 6-19).

2. **Click either Rows or Columns. Type the number of rows or columns you wish to add.**

   You can also click the tiny up or down arrow buttons next to the Number of Rows (or Number of Columns) field.

Figure 6-19:
The Insert Rows or Columns dialog box lets you add multiple rows or columns to a table; the wording of the options changes depending on whether you're inserting rows or columns. Note that this dialog box offers the only way to add a column to the right *edge of a table.*

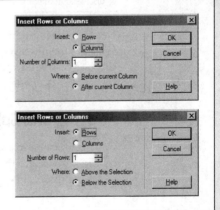

---

3. **Indicate where you wish the new rows or columns to appear, relative to the cell you selected, by clicking Above or Below (for rows) or Before or After (for columns). Click OK to insert them.**

Using the dialog box gives you the advantage of choosing whether you want the new row or column to come *before* or *after* the selected information in your table, as shown in Figure 6-19.

Deleting Rows and Columns

To delete a row from your table, you can use one of the following techniques.

Tip: When you remove a row or column, Dreamweaver also eliminates everything inside. So before you start hacking away, it's a good idea to save a copy of the page with the table.

- Select the row (see page 43); press Delete to delete all of the cells—and everything in them—for the selected row.

- Click a cell. Choose Modify→Table→Delete Row, or use the keyboard shortcut Ctrl+Shift+M (⌘-Shift-M).

- Right-click (Control-click) inside a cell; choose Table→Delete Row from the contextual menu.

Deleting a column is equally straightforward:

- Select the column (see page 143), and then press Delete. You've just eliminated all the selected cells and everything in them.

- Click inside a cell and choose Modify→Table→Delete Column, or use the keyboard shortcut Ctrl-Shift-Hyphen (⌘-Shift-Hyphen).

- Right-click (Control-click) inside a cell; choose Table→Delete Column from the contextual menu.

Note: Dreamweaver doesn't let you delete a row or column if one of its cells is *merged* with another cell, as discussed in the next section.

Deleting a column in this way is actually quite a feat. Since there is no column tag in HTML, Dreamweaver, behind the scenes, has to select individual cells in multiple rows—a task you wouldn't wish on your worst enemy if you had to do it by editing the raw HTML code.

Merging and Splitting Cells

Cells are very basic creatures with some severe limitations. For example, all of the cells in a row share the same height—a cell can't be taller than the cell next to it—which can pose some serious design problems.

Consider Figure 6-20 at top, for example. In the top figure, the left cell containing the gear graphic, is much taller than the top banner to its right. In fact, it's as tall as *both* banners to its right, as shown in the bottom figure. Ideally, you'd want the gear graphic cell to straddle the two cells to its right, as shown in the second banner example. Fortunately, Dreamweaver provides a few such ways of convincing cells to work well together.

The trick is to *merge* cells—combine their area—to create a larger cell that spans two or more rows or columns. In this example, the solution is to merge the two cells in the left column. This single cell holds the image of the gear, while perfectly aligning the two cells in the adjacent column. By using this technique, you can create some very complex designs. In fact, if you view tables created in Dreamweaver's Layout mode, you'll notice that Dreamweaver itself makes extensive use of this technique.

Figure 6-20:
*You can create larger cells that span
multiple rows and columns by merging
adjacent cells. This trick can help solve
some design issues and let you align
items that normally would not line up
(top). The result can join multiple
columns into one, multiple rows, or both
at once (bottom).*

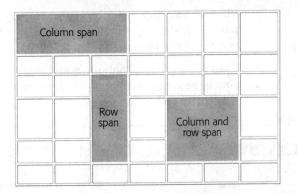

To merge cells, start by selecting the cells you wish to merge, using any of the methods described on page 144. (You can only merge cells that form a rectangle or square. You can't, for instance, select three cells in a column and only one in the adjacent row, as in an L shape. Nor can you merge cells that aren't adjacent; in other words, you can't merge a cell in one corner of the table with a cell in the opposite corner.)

Then, on the Property inspector, click the Merge Cells button (Figure 6-21), or choose Modify→Table→Merge Cells.

Tip: Better yet, use this undocumented keyboard shortcut: the M key. That's it; just select two or more cells and press M. It's much easier than the keyboard shortcut listed in the manual: Ctrl+Alt+M (⌘-Option-M).

Dreamweaver joins the selected cells, forming a single new super cell.

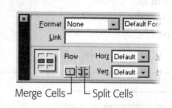

Figure 6-21:
The Merge Cells button is only active when you've selected multiple cells. The Split Cells button only appears when you select a single cell or have clicked inside a cell.

Merge Cells ⌐ └ Split Cells

You may also find yourself in the opposite situation: you have one cell that you want to *divide* into multiple cells. To split a cell, click inside, or select, a single cell. Click the Split Cells button in the Property inspector. (Once again, you can trigger this command in several alternative ways. For example, you can choose Modify→Table→Split Cell. And if you prefer keyboard shortcuts, you can press Ctrl+Alt+S [⌘-Option-S]. You can even right-click [Control-click] the selected cell and then choose Table→Split Cell from the contextual menu.)

When the Split Cell dialog box opens (see Figure 6-22), click one of the buttons to indicate whether you want to split the cell into rows or columns; type the number of rows or columns you wish to create; click OK.

If you split a cell into columns, everything in the cell winds up in the right column, with the new, empty column or columns to the left. When you split a cell into rows, the contents end up in the top row.

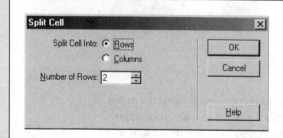

Figure 6-22:
The Split Cell dialog box lets you divide a single cell into multiple cells. You can choose whether to divide the cell into rows (multiple cells on top of each other) or columns (multiple cells side by side).

Nesting Tables in Standard View

By merging cells, you can create complex tables that offer precise control over your layouts. If you use Layout mode to create a detailed, handcrafted design, you'll see how Dreamweaver can generate complex tables using this technique.

But on the Web, simpler is usually better. Sometimes, instead of spending time and effort chopping up and merging cells to create a certain look, the best solution is to *nest* tables—place a table within a table—instead of creating one complex table (see Figure 6-23).

Figure 6-23:
Top: This page looks complicated, but in Dreamweaver (bottom), it breaks down to a series of simple tables. The outside table (A) is a one-row, three-column table with a series of nested tables (B, C, D, E). The first cell contains another basic table (B), which has twelve rows and one column. Using alternating colors for each cell helps set off the information inside.

The third column of the primary table holds the main content of the page; three tables (C, D, E) are placed within the flow of the cell. One nice trick: Use the Align property of a table to create a "floating" sidebar within the normal flow of text. The announcements table here, for instance, is aligned to the right, while text in the cell wraps around it. Note that aligning a table like this is only possible in Standard view.

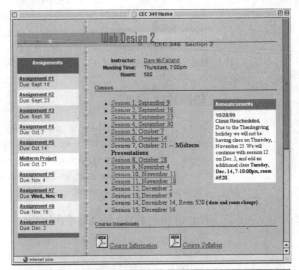

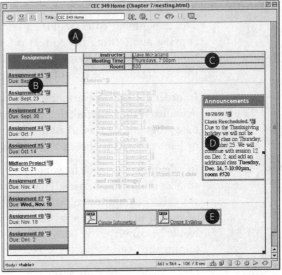

Since a table cell acts just like a mini document, you can put anything that you'd normally place on a page inside a cell—graphics, text, links and, yes, even tables. Simply click a cell and use one of the techniques described above to add and format the table.

You can even place *more* than one table in a single cell. In Figure 6-23, for example, three tables are nested in the right-hand cell of the main table. They're in the flow of the cell contents, separated into individual paragraphs. By compartmentalizing and aligning information, nested tables make complex Web pages easier to both build and edit.

Be aware that there are some limits to nesting tables. For example, it's best to not nest more than three tables deep; in other words, a table inside of a table inside of a table. While most browsers understand and are able to correctly draw tables that are more deeply nested, such complexity can be difficult to render, resulting in pages that are slow to load, especially on slower computers.

Tabular Data

So far, you've learned about using tables for complex Web page designs, using tricks like merging cells, invisible spacer images, and Dreamweaver's Layout view. But what about the original purpose of a table—displaying data in an orderly manner? You can still do that, of course, and Dreamweaver provides a couple of tools to make the process of dealing with tabular data run smoothly.

Importing Data into a Table

Your boss emails you your company's yearly sales information, which includes data on sales, profits, and expenses organized by quarter. She asks you to get this up on the Web for a board meeting she's having in half an hour.

This assignment could require a fair amount of work: building a table and then copying and pasting the correct information into each cell of the table, one at a time. Fortunately, Dreamweaver spares you that headache. It can create a table and import data into the cells of the table's rows and columns, all in one pass.

In order for this to work, the table data you want to display must begin life in a *delimited* format—a task that most spreadsheet programs, including Excel, or database programs, such as Access or FileMaker Pro, can do easily. (Choosing File→Export or File→Save As in these programs usually does it.)

In a delimited file, each line of text represents one table row. Each line is divided into smaller units using a special character called a delimiter—most often a tab, but possibly also a comma or colon. Each unit represents a single cell in the row. In a colon-delimited file, for example, the line *Sales:$1,000,000:$2,000,000:$567,000:$12,500* would be converted by Dreamweaver into a row of five cells, with the first cell containing the word *Sales.*

Once you've saved your boss's spreadsheet as a delimited file, you're ready to import it into a Dreamweaver table:

1. Choose File→Import→Import Tabular Data.

   The Import Table Data dialog box appears (see 6-24).

2. Click the Browse button. In the Insert Tabular Data dialog box, find and open the delimited text file you wish to import.

   A delimited file is no longer a spreadsheet, but a plain text file. Navigate to and double-click the file in the dialog box.

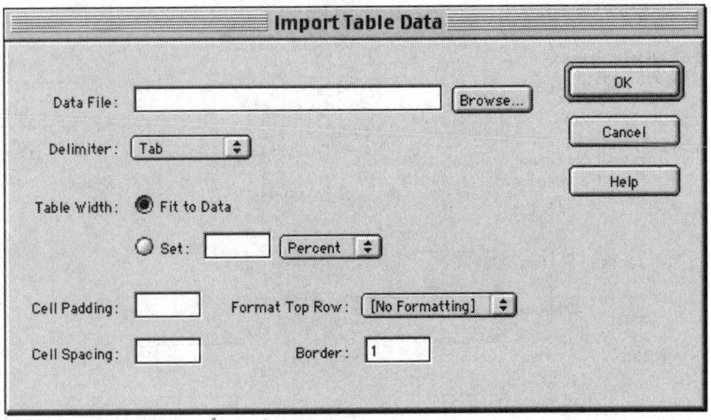

Figure 6-24:
The Import Table Data dialog box lets you select a text file of data to import and choose formatting options for the table.

Import Table Data

Data File: [   ] [Browse...] [OK]

Delimiter: [Tab   ▼] [Cancel]

[Help]

Table Width: ● Fit to Data

○ Set: [   ] [Percent ▼]

Cell Padding: [   ] Format Top Row: [[No Formatting] ▼]

Cell Spacing: [   ] Border: [1]

3. Select the delimiter that was used to separate the data in the text file.

   The choices are Tab, Comma, Colon, Semicolon, or Other. If you select Other, an additional field appears, in which you can type the character you used as the delimiter.

4. Select a table width.

   Choose Fit to Data if you want the table to fit itself to the information you're importing—an excellent idea when you aren't completely sure how much information the file contains. (You can always modify the table once it has been created and the data imported.)

   On the other hand, if your Web page needs a table of a certain size, you can specify it by selecting the Set button and typing a value in the field next to it. Select pixel or percentage value (see page 144).

5. Set Cell Padding, Cell Spacing, and Table Border, if you like.

   See page 144 for details.

6. Select a formatting option for the top row of data.

   If the first line in the text file has column headings—Quarter 1 Sales, Quarter 2 Sales, and so on, for example—Dreamweaver lets you choose Bold, Italic, or Bold

Italic to set this header row apart from the rest of the table. (No Formatting keeps the top row consistent with the rest of the table.)

7. **Click OK to import the data and create the table.**

If you'd like to jazz up your table a bit, but are short on time, you can apply one of Dreamweaver's preinstalled table designs (see Figure 6-25).

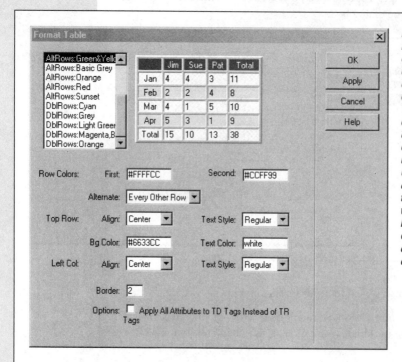

Figure 6-25:
Dreamweaver can apply canned designs to a table of data. Select a table in the document window, and choose Commands→Format Table. You can then select one of the seventeen different designs from the list. You can even create your own design, using the option menus. Unfortunately, you can't save a design you create. While these designs aren't useful when you're using tables to lay out a page as described earlier in this chapter, they are a quick way to spruce up a calendar or spreadsheet.

Sorting Data in a Table

If you have a table that lists employee names, you probably want to present that list in alphabetical order—or alphabetically *and* by department. Dreamweaver's Sort Table command takes a lot of the drudgery out of this task.

1. **Select the table you wish to sort.**

   See page 143 for some table-selection techniques.

2. **Choose Commands→Sort Table.**

   The Sort Table dialog box appears (Figure 6-26).

3. **Using the Sort By pop-up menu, choose the column you wish to sort by.**

   You can choose any column in the table. For example, suppose you have a table listing a bunch of products. Each row has the product name, number, and price.

If you want to see the products listed from least to most expensive, you could sort by the column with the product prices.

4. **Use the next two pop-up menus to specify how you want the data sorted.**

   Data can be sorted alphabetically or numerically. To order the product list by price, choose Numerically from the Order pop-up menu. However, if you're sorting a Name column, choose Alphabetically.

   Use the second pop-up menu to specify that you want an Ascending sort (A ... Z, 1...100) or Descending (Z ... A, 100 ... 1).

5. **If you like, choose an additional column to sort by, using the Then By pop-up menu.**

   This secondary sort can come in handy when several cells in the *first* sorting column have the same value. For example, if several items in your product list are all priced at $100, a sort by price would place them consecutively in the table; you could then specify a secondary sort that would place the products in alphabetical order within each price group. In this way, all of the products would be listed from least to most expensive, *and* products that are the same price would be listed alphabetically within their group.

6. **If the first row of the table contains data to be sorted, turn on Sort Includes First Row.**

   If, however, the first row of the table contains *headings* for each column, don't turn on this box.

7. **Choose whether to keep row formatting with the sorted row.**

   One way to visually organize a table is to add color to alternate rows. This every-other-row pattern helps readers to stay focused on one row of information at a time. However, if you sort a table that you had formatted in this way, you'd wind up with some crazy pattern of colored and non-colored rows.

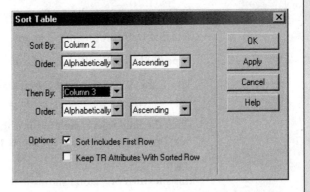

Figure 6-26:
The Sort Table command works well with Dreamweaver's Import Tabular Data feature. Imagine you're given a text file listing all of the employees in your company. You import the data into a table, but realize that the names aren't in any particular order. Use the Sort Table command, as described on these pages, to put the list of names into alphabetical order by last name.

The bottom line: if you've applied colors to your rows, and you'd like to keep those colors in the same order, leave this checkbox turned off.

8. **Click Apply to see the effect of the sort without closing the dialog box.**

   If the table meets with your satisfaction, click OK to sort the table and return to the document window.

Exporting Table Data

Getting data out of a table in Dreamweaver is simple. Just select the table and choose File→Export→Export Table. In the Export Table dialog box that appears, select the type of delimiter (tab, comma, space, colon, or semicolon) and operating system where the file will be used (Mac, Windows, or Unix) and click OK. Give the file a name and save it on your computer. You can then import this delimited file into your spreadsheet or database program.

Tables Tutorial

In this tutorial, you'll learn how to use Dreamweaver 4's exciting new Layout view to build a page for the Cosmopolitan Farmer Web site. In addition, you'll practice adding tables using the Objects panel's Table object, and you'll meet tracing images and Library elements.

Getting Started

Before you begin building the page, download the tutorial files. As always, you'll find them at *www.sawmac.com/missing;* click the Tutorials link to go to the tutorials page. Click either Tables Tutorial—Mac files or Tables Tutorial—Win files, depending on the kind of computer you're using.

When the files have downloaded and decompressed, you should have a folder named DWTables on your computer, containing the Web pages and graphics needed for this tutorial. If you're having difficulties, the Web site contains detailed instructions for downloading the files you'll be using with this book.

1. **In Dreamweaver 4, choose Site→New Site.**

   The Site Definition window opens.

2. **Type *Tables* in the Site Name field.**

   This is the name that Dreamweaver will use while you are working on this tutorial.

3. **Click the Folder icon next to the Local Root Folder field; in the resulting dialog box, browse to and select the folder DWTables. Click OK.**

   If a dialog box appears that says that Dreamweaver is about to create a *cache* for this site, turn on "Don't show me this message again." Click OK.

Now you're all set to begin the tutorial.

Using a Tracing Image

In this tutorial, you'll be building the Pisces page in the Horoscopes section of the Cosmopolitan Farmer Web site. To get your page ready, follow these steps.

1. **Choose File→New to create a new, empty document.**

   Windows users: you can create a new page from the Site window by choosing File→New Window.

2. **Choose File→Save; save this document as *pisces.html*.**

   Save it into the DWTables folder.

3. **Click in the Title field in the toolbar; type *Pisces*.**

   If you don't see the toolbar, choose View→Toolbar.

4. **Choose Modify→Page Properties.**

   The Page Properties window opens.

5. **Click the Browse button next to the Tracing Image field near the bottom of the window.**

   The Select Image Source dialog box appears.

6. **In the DWTables folder, double-click the file called *horoscope.gif*.**

   It's a GIF image of the design for this page.

7. **Move the Page Properties window so that you can see the document window underneath it, and then click Apply.**

   You should see the graphic appear in the document window (see Figure 6-27).

Figure 6-27:
You use the Page Properties dialog box when first setting up a new Web site, but you'll need to come back to it anytime you want to change the page's background color, margins, and so on. Call it up quickly by pressing Ctrl+U (⌘-U). (If you think you might find rulers helpful, as shown here, choose View→Rulers→Show.)

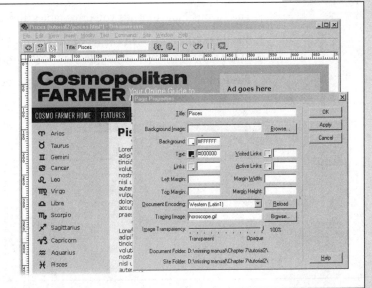

8. **Move the Image Transparency slider to the middle—around 50%—and click OK to close the Page Properties dialog box.**

The image fades into the background of the page. You've just inserted the *tracing image*—a GIF image that you prepared in some graphics program while brainstorming the design of your site, freed from the constraints of actually having to build the Web site while you played around with visual ideas. (You'll notice that the actual horoscope contains fake Latin gibberish; it's just a placeholder until your writing team comes up with the actual text for this Web page.)

You'll use this graphic as a pattern for creating the page layout. This image won't show up in a Web browser; it only appears in Dreamweaver.

9. **Choose File→Save.**

Congratulations! You're well on your way to creating a beautiful new Web site. Next, you'll start to add the details.

Building the Banner in Layout View

You'll use Dreamweaver 4's new Layout view to build a table-based page design.

1. **Click the Layout view button at the bottom of the Objects panel (see Figure 6-3 on page 127).**

Dreamweaver switches to Layout view.

But first, the Getting Started in Layout view window may appear. This window explains how to use the layout tools. Turn on "Don't show me this message again," and then click OK.

2. **Click the Layout Table tool button at the bottom of the Objects panel (also shown in Figure 6-3).**

The Layout Table tool lets you draw tables directly in the document window.

3. **Starting at the upper-left corner of the tracing image, drag diagonally down and to the right, creating a rectangle around the top banner of the tracing image.**

The banner includes the orange and black portions at the top of the page.

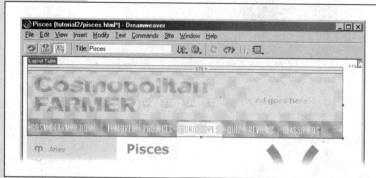

Figure 6-28:
If your Layout Table doesn't exactly fit the tracing image (the Cosmopolitan Farmer banner in this case), you can resize it by dragging any of the three resize handles that appear on the right edge, bottom edge, and right corner of the table.

A light gray box with a green outline appears over the tracing image. The green tab in the upper-left corner indicates that this is a Layout Table (see Figure 6-29).

This page design has so many different areas, you'll need several different tables. While it would be possible to create a single table for the entire page, it's often a better idea to take a modular approach, dividing a page using multiple tables.

4. **Click the Layout Cell tool button at the bottom of the Objects panel.**

   The Layout Cell tool lets you add cells to a Layout Table.

5. **Starting at the top-left corner of the Layout Table, drag diagonally to create a rectangle that includes the entire left half of the orange bar in the banner. Drag from the left edge to just past the word "to" and just above the black area, as shown in Figure 6-29.**

   Cells are indicated by a light blue outline. This cell contains the site's logo.

   When you release the mouse button, the insertion point blinks inside of the cell you just drew; you're ready to fill it up with text or graphics.

Figure 6-29:
The Layout Cell tool lets you drag to create a rectangular cell within a Layout Table.

6. Choose Insert→Image.

   Alternatively, click the Insert Image button on the Objects panel. Either way, the Select Image Source window appears.

7. **Browse to the Images folder inside of the DWTables folder; double-click the file called** *banner.gif.*

   You've just inserted an actual banner heading graphic that neatly fits over the sketch you had made in your tracing image. In the event of an actual Web-creation experience, this is just what you would have done: placing actual graphics over the placeholders you had sketched in the tracing image.(For a refresher on inserting images, turn to Chapter 5.)

Because the tracing image can sometimes obscure what you're doing on the page, it's useful to turn it off occasionally so you can see how your page is coming together:

8. **Choose Tracing Image from the Options menu icon in the toolbar at the top of your document window (shown back in Figure 6-11).**

   The tracing image disappears. If there is no check next to Tracing Image in the menu, the tracing image is already hidden. (You can also show or hide a tracing image by choosing View→Tracing Image→Show.)

9. **Move your mouse over the light-blue outline of the newly created cell until the outline turns red; click to select the cell.**

   If you don't see any red outline, the cell is probably already selected. Eight handles appear around the edges of the cell when it's selected, and the Property inspector changes to indicate the properties of the cell (see Figure 6-30).

Figure 6-30:
The versatile Property inspector changes to show a number of settings for whatever you've selected on your Web page. In this case, a Layout Cell within a Layout Table is selected, as you can tell by the resize handles and the words Layout Cell in the inspector.

10. **In the Bg field of the Property inspector, type #FF9900.**

    The graphic you imported was transparent and didn't include a background color of its own. You've just added an orange background color for the cell.

    Everything looks good so far, so it's time to continue building the page's layout. You should turn the tracing image back on.

11. **Turn the tracing image back on.**

    In other words, choose Options→Tracing Image on the toolbar.

Next, you'll add an additional cell next to the banner image. This cell will hold an advertisement graphic.

12. **Click the Layout Cell tool in the Objects panel; drag to draw a second cell that covers the rest of the orange area of the banner (see Figure 6-31).**

Make this cell the same height as the other cell you drew. Notice that the cursor snaps to the top and right edges of the table. It also snaps to a line created by the bottom edge of the first cell.

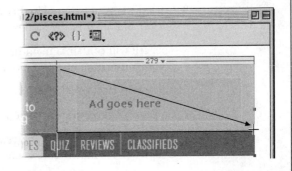

Figure 6-31:
Adding additional cells to a table is as simple as dragging; the sides of a cell snap to other cells already in the table, making aligning the edges of cells a snap.

13. **Choose Insert→Image.**

Or, if you'd rather, click the Insert Image button on the Objects panel. In any case, the Select Image dialog box appears. You're about to choose a graphic that will fill the second cell. Because Web ads often change, it's a file of its own, rather than part of your original logo graphic; this way, you'll be able to swap new ads in as necessary without disturbing the rest of your page.

14. **In the DWTables→Images folder, double-click the file called *ad.gif*.**

The image appears at the upper-left corner of the cell; it would look better if it floated in the middle of the cell.

15. **Move your mouse over the light blue outline of the cell until its color changes to red; click to select the cell.**

The next step doesn't change the *cell's* alignment—its placement on the page— only the alignment of its contents.

16. **In the Property inspector, choose Center from the Horz menu, and Middle from the Vert menu.**

Now the ad floats in the center of its cell.

Next up: Filling the ad cell with the same color orange as the first.

17. **Click the color box next to Bg in the Property inspector.**

The color palette appears, but you'll ignore it; you're more interested in the cursor, which now resembles an eyedropper.

18. **Move the cursor over the orange in the left-side cell; click to "sample" that orange color.**

The new, right-hand cell is now filled with the same orange color as the cell on the left. Although you already know the hexadecimal code for orange (because you typed it in a previous step), the eyedropper technique is handy when you don't know the code for a color that already appears in your layout.

19. **Click the Layout Cell tool in the Objects panel; draw a cell that covers the entire bottom black bar in the banner.**

This cell will contain a main navigation bar for the site. When you release the mouse button, the insertion point blinks inside of the cell you just drew.

In the next step, you'll insert a canned, ready-made navigation bar.

20. **Choose Window→Library to open the site's Library.**

The Library lets you save and reuse frequently needed snippets of HTML; see Chapter 17 for much more detail.

21. **Select Main Navigation from the list in the Library window; click Insert (see Figure 6-32).**

Dreamweaver drops in a row of navigation buttons. Notice that the Property inspector indicates that this is a special type of object called a Library item.

To see how this page is shaping up, you'll temporarily hide the tracing image once again:

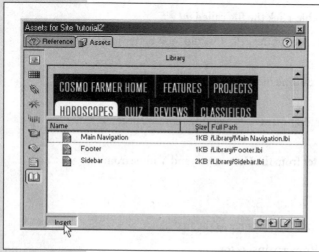

Figure 6-32:
Library items and other site elements such as colors and images can be found and reused from Dreamweaver's Assets panel.

22. Hide the tracing image again (see Figure 6-11).

    The tracing image disappears and you see the nearly completed banner. But notice that the right part of the black row of navigation buttons is still white. To fix this anomaly, you need to give the cell a black background. Move your mouse over the light blue outline of the cell until it turns red; click to select the cell.

    Next, you'll change the background color of the cell. Although the buttons themselves are black, the cell that extends to the right of the buttons has no color, and lets the white of the page show right through.

23. Using the Bg color box in the Property inspector, choose a black swatch from the pop-up color palette.

    If you're a hexy kind of person, you can instead type *#000000*, which means "black" in HTML.

24. Turn the tracing image back on (see Figure 6-11); press F12 to preview the page in your browser.

    Maximize your browser window while viewing the page. If you have a large monitor, you'll notice that there's a large white margin to the right of the table. The page would look much better if the banner could automatically stretch to fill in the gap—a complex bit of HTML programming, but an easy step in Dreamweaver 4.

25. Return to Dreamweaver. Click the first column's header menu (see Figure 6-33); choose Make Column Autostretch.

    The Make Column Autostretch option makes one column in a table stretchy, as described on page 135, so that it can grow or shrink to fill the available space in a browser window.

    As soon as you choose this command, a dialog box appears, asking if you're sure you want Dreamweaver to insert spacer graphics (page 136).

Figure 6-33:
The width of a column is listed at the top of a column in Layout view. Clicking this number reveals a menu of options.

26. In the dialog box, turn on "Create a spacer image file," and then click OK.

    Dreamweaver will use a special trick: it will create a tiny, 1-pixel transparent GIF graphic. That's what Dreamweaver is prompting you to save now.

27. In the Save Spacer Image window, navigate to the DWTables→Images folder; save the image with the name *spacer.gif.*

Dreamweaver adds a 1-pixel tall row at the bottom of the banner table, and inserts the graphic into the right cell. The right column can now stretch to fit the browser window; the spacer prevents the left cell from collapsing down to nothing. (See page 136 for more on this topic.)

28. Choose File→Save to save all your work so far.

Press F12 to view the final banner design in your default browser; it's looking extremely promising.

Building the Content Table

Now that you have the banner, it's time to turn to the actual contents of the page. An important feature of this page in the Cosmopolitan Farmer Web site is a second navigation bar that runs down the left side of the page; it lets your visitors click an astrological sign to read the appropriate horoscope.

1. Make sure the Layout view button is selected in the Objects panel.

Figure 6-3 shows this button.

2. Click the Draw Cell tool on the Objects panel.

You don't have to start with the Table tool when working in Layout view. If you simply draw a cell, the program creates a Layout Table to fit.

3. While pressing the Ctrl (⌘) key, drag to create a cell the size of the beige sidebar in the tracing image.

When you draw a cell while pressing Ctrl (⌘), the Layout Cell tool remains selected, ready to draw another cell. Dreamweaver automatically creates a Table around this cell, making most of your layout turn light gray (to indicate table space where no cells yet exist).

Note: On the Macintosh, you'll smash right into a little Dreamweaver bug on this step. If you try drawing the cell from the bottom of the sidebar area upward to the bottom of the first table, Dreamweaver spits out a nasty error message. But if you draw the cell from just beneath the first Layout Table *downward,* you'll find that Dreamweaver is equally cranky; it doesn't let you draw a cell *exactly* below another table. (You have to begin the cell about ten pixels away.)

There's a quick workaround, however. Don't hold down the ⌘ key for this one. Draw the cell from the bottom up, but not all the way to the top; stop about Aries. Then select the cell by clicking carefully on its edge; finally, drag the resize handle at the top of the cell upward until it touches the bottom of the first table. *C'est la guerre!*

You can release the Ctrl or ⌘ key for the next step.

4. **Starting at the top left corner of the P in the Pisces headline (but not all the way in the corner of its text area), draw a second cell that includes the Alert message (see Figure 6-34).**

   This second cell will hold the main content for the page. Now you'll fill the new cell with text that was written by your crack team of astrologers.

5. **Choose File→Open. In the DWTables folder, double-click the file called *text.html*.**

   This page holds the text for the horoscope page. Dreamweaver doesn't have an Import command like, say, PageMaker or QuarkXPress; you have to copy and paste text into your Web page, like this:

6. **Choose Edit→Select All to select all of the text on the page; then choose Edit→Copy to copy it.**

   Now you'll switch back to your layout and paste the copied text.

7. **Choose Window→pisces.html.**

   A list of all open pages appears at the bottom of the Window menu. You can switch between them by selecting their names; now your Web page reappears.

8. **Click the cell you just drew. Choose Edit→Paste to paste the text into the cell.**

   It may be hard to read, superimposed as it is over the dummy text in your tracing image; you'll take care of that in the following steps.

Figure 6-34:
To precisely place text on your Web page, draw a Layout Cell first; then you can paste in text that you wrote in your favorite word processor. If you did it right, there's a little space between it and the sidebar, and between it and the top of the table. This provides a small margin, allowing a little visual breathing room between the text and other elements around it. (If the new cell isn't quite right, you can always choose Edit→Undo and redraw it.)

9. Choose Modify→Page Properties; select the file name in the Tracing Image field of the Page Properties window, and press Delete. Click OK.

   Since you've finished creating most of the layout of the page, you no longer need the tracing image. Now you'll return to the cell you just added the text to and make it stretchy like the banner.

10. From the column header menu above the cell with the Pisces horoscope, choose Make Column Autostretch.

    This makes the cell flexible, as described in step 25 of the previous instructions; the cell now expands to fill the browser window, so that you can see all the text.

11. Move your mouse over the light blue outline of the sidebar cell until it turns red, and click to select the cell. In the Property inspector's Bg field, type #CCCC99.

    You've just set the cell's background color to a lovely shade of beige.

    In the next steps, you'll insert a graphic into your navigation sidebar—the one that lists the zodiac signs.

12. Click inside the beige sidebar.

    If the Library window isn't open, choose Window→Library; you'll need it in the next step.

13. In the Library window, click the "sidebar" item, then Insert.

    Dreamweaver drops in a table that contains navigation for the Horoscopes section of the site. Notice that the Property inspector indicates that this—like the navigation banner you inserted earlier—is a special type of object called a Library item.

14. Choose File→Save; press F12 to preview your work in your browser.

    It's a good idea to check your work in a browser every time you try something new, because Web pages can look slightly different in browser windows.

Using the Table Object

Like the Layout Table, the Table *object* is a great tool for laying out Web pages; it's also the only way to achieve certain structures, like the nested table you'll be creating in these next steps. The Table object is available only in Standard view, not Layout view.

For the next steps, you'll need the *pisces.html* Web page you were working on in the previous steps; if it's not already on the screen, launch Dreamweaver and open the *pisces.html* file.

Tip: You don't have to choose File→Open; the bottom of the File menu lists the four most recently viewed documents. Choose a file's name to open it.

---

1. **Click the Standard view button in the Objects panel.**

   The Layout Table tabs disappear, and the outlines of the tables and cells change to dotted lines—that's how Dreamweaver displays tables in Standard view.

2. **Click just before the P in the Pisces headline.**

   You've placed the insertion point at the beginning of the cell.

3. **Choose Insert→Table.**

   Or click the Insert Table button on the Objects panel. Either way, the Insert Table dialog box opens.

4. **Type the settings shown in Figure 6-35, pressing Tab to jump from box to box.**

   Don't forget to set the pop-up menu to Percent.

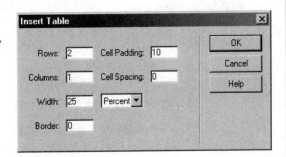

Figure 6-35:
Unlike Layout Tables, which you draw by dragging with the mouse, you create tables in Standard view by typing in dimensions and properties in the Insert Table dialog box. (This command, in fact, is available only in Standard view.)

5. **Click OK.**

   The two-row, one-column Table object appears in your Web page, outlined by transparent (but now highlighted) borders.

6. **Choose Right from the Align menu in the Property inspector (see Figure 6-36).**

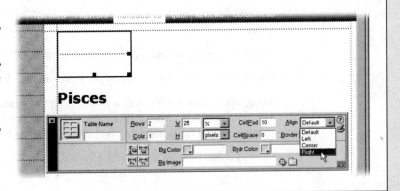

Figure 6-36:
When you choose Right in the Property inspector, the table will jump to the right side of the page. The gold shield that appears just before the Pisces heading—blue when it's selected—indicates where the table actually sits within the flow of the HTML code for the page.

The table jumps to the right side of the Pisces horoscope area, and the text wraps around its left edge.

7. **Ctrl-click (⌘-click) both cells in this new table.**

   Both cells are now selected (surrounded by a black border). The Property inspector reflects the properties of these cells.

8. **Choose Center from the Horz menu in the Property inspector.**

   You've just center-aligned whatever you put into these cells. Now fill them up:

9. **Click the top cell; then choose Insert→Image.**

   Of course, you can also click the Insert Image button on the Objects panel. Either way, the Select Image Source dialog box opens.

10. **Browse to the Images folder in the DWTables folder; double-click the file called** *pisces.gif.*

    The Pisces symbol appears in the cell. (You may see most of the horoscope's text jump below the bottom of the new table you've inserted. Dreamweaver sometimes has trouble keeping up with your design on the screen. Don't worry; it'll look fine in a Web browser.)

11. **Click the bottom cell, and then type** *Alert!*

    Adding text to a cell is as simple as typing it, but there's much more you can do with text in Dreamweaver, as discussed in Chapter 3.

12. **Press Enter to create a new paragraph within the cell, and then type:** *Stay away from all forms of aquaculture this month, especially apartment-raised trout and salmon. The planets will doom all of your attempts.*

    Not the usual horoscope, perhaps, but you get the idea. You're almost done!

13. **Click either to the right or below, outside of the bottom table on the page.**

    You may need to scroll to the far right in order to see the right edge of the table. Clicking outside of this table positions the cursor outside the table.

14. **In the Library window (see step 20 on page 170), click Footer, and then click Insert.**

    Dreamweaver drops in a table containing copyright information for the site.

15. **Choose File→Save; press F12 to preview your work in your default browser.**

    Congratulations: You've built a page with precise layout and a flexible design. If you compare this page with the page you built in Chapter 1, you can see the greater control (and freedom) that tables offer the Web designer.

Feel free to compare with the finished Web page at *www.sawmac.com/missing/tutorials/.*

Frames

The Web-page elements known as *frames* are both alluring and confusing. They're alluring because they provide the unique ability to display multiple Web pages in a single browser window—one independent Web page per frame. Clicking a link may change the page in one frame, while leaving the contents of all the other frames untouched.

At the same time, frames can be confusing to build since they require multiple Web pages—including a special master page called a *frameset*—in order to work. People who create Web pages by typing pure HTML code into a text editor soon discover that building frames-based Web sites can be a frustrating exercise in file management. Dreamweaver, on the other hand, reduces much of this complexity by providing special Frames tools in the Objects panel and letting you preview exactly how the finished frames will look and work.

Frames offer an easy way to compartmentalize different elements within a single browser window. For instance, you can create separate pages for navigation, banners, and content, and display each in its own frame and with its own scroll bars (see Figure 7-1). In addition, using a link's *Target* property, you can even load the link from a page in one frame into a completely different frame. As a result, you can build a navigation bar frame that controls what appears in the other frames on your Web site.

The Frame Page

What your Web page visitor cares about are the text and graphics *within* the frames; but for you, the hard work is creating the special Web page—the frameset page—that gives the frames their structure. The frameset page itself usually doesn't contain text or graphics; it just describes the number, size, and placement of the frames. In addition, this page tells a browser which Web page should load into each frame, whether the frame has borders or scroll bars, and whether the visitor is allowed to resize the frame by dragging its border.

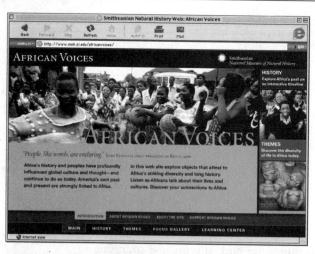

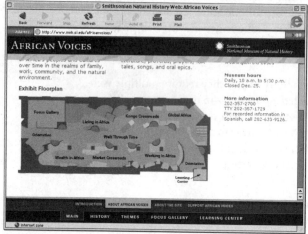

Figure 7-1:
Frames let you keep one element in place–the banner and navigation bars shown here, for example (www.mnh.si.edu/africanvoices)–while other contents of the Web page change. This way, the banner and navigation bar remain visible in one frame, even as your reader scrolls to read a long page full of text in another or even reloads the page.

The frameset page accomplishes all this with the help of two HTML tags: the <frameset> and <frame> tags. A <frameset> tag provides the superstructure of the layout: the number and size of frame rows and columns, as well as the overall border properties of all of the frames. Nested inside the <frameset> tag, a <frame> tag identifies the specifics for each frame: which page loads into the frame, and what visual elements—such as scroll bars—appear within the frame.

When your visitor's Web browser loads a Web page that contains frames, it first loads the frameset page and determines the number, size, and appearance of the frames, as described in the frameset. It then draws each of the frames in the browser window, and finally downloads the Web pages that appear in each frame.

Figure 7-2:
Frames can be obvious and ugly, or subtle and effective. Top: This fictional Web page has five frames; notice the thick border between the frames and the unnecessary scroll bars that appear in the banner and sidebar.

Bottom: This page (bmrc.berkeley.edu) has three frames, but with borders turned off, the three frames merge into a unified presentation. Only a single scroll bar appears in the main content area (middle frame) of the page. This is your only clue that this page uses frames.

In this example, the advantage of using frames is that the site logo and navigation (top frame) and the site tools (bottom frame) always remain visible even if you scroll to read the text contained in the middle frame.

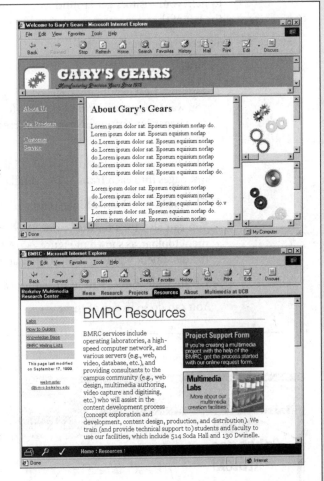

Tip: Since a frameset page is just an empty structure, you also need to create Web pages for each frame you wish to display. So if you add three frames to a page, you're actually creating *four* different Web pages—the frameset page, plus a page for each of the three frames. Because frames create more Web site files for you to manage, you may save yourself some headaches by keeping the number of frames in your site to a minimum.

Creating Frames

Before you begin creating frames, think about how they might best serve your Web site's structure. For instance, if you want a banner with the Web site's logo or name to appear at the top of each page, you could create a frame at the top to hold it. Or, to help your visitors get around, you might include a navigation bar in a frame at the left of the page—that is, a list of links to the site's main sections.

To create frames:

1. **Open or create a Web page.**

   This may be a new, blank page, or a page you've already created. This is the page you want to appear *within* a frame—for example, a page with a banner, or a row of navigation buttons. Next, you'll create a frameset page around the current page.

   This may seem backward—you'd think you'd *start* with the frameset and then put pages into each frame—but you'll quickly get used to Dreamweaver's ways.

2. **Choose View→Visual Aids→Frame Borders.**

   You can also turn on the Frame Borders from the Options menu in the document toolbar, as shown in Figure 7-3. A thick border appears around the edges of the document window, indicating that you're now working with frames.

3. **Create your frames within the window.**

   You can do so in any of three ways.

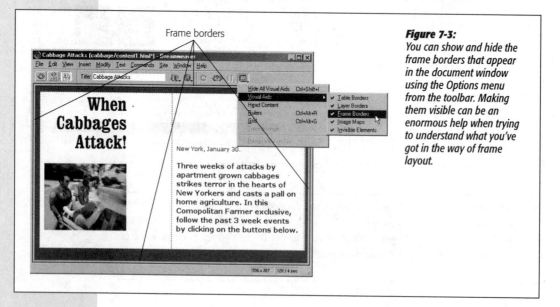

Figure 7-3:
You can show and hide the frame borders that appear in the document window using the Options menu from the toolbar. Making them visible can be an enormous help when trying to understand what you've got in the way of frame layout.

First, you can drag one of the frame borders that now sit at the edges of the document window (Figure 7-4). To create a frame at the left edge of your page, for example, drag the left border inward toward the page center; to add a frame on top, drag the top border down.

Tip: You can create four frames at once—at the top, bottom, and both sides of the current page—by dragging one of the border corners.

Second, you can choose Modify→Frameset→Split Frame Left, Right, Up, or Down. This command may seem confusing at first, but it's worth learning if you want to make more complicated frame designs such as nested frames (page 183). Just remember to make your choice based upon where you want the *current* page to end up. If you want the current page to appear in the left frame, choose Left. If you'd like it to appear at the bottom, choose Down.

Finally, you may prefer to use one of Dreamweaver's one-click, canned frame designs; they're listed on the Objects panel, as shown in Figure 7-5.

When you finish splitting or dragging, borders appear around the frames you've just created. Behind the scenes, some strange things have just happened. First, Dreamweaver has created a frameset page—a new, untitled Web page that describes how a

---

UP TO SPEED

When Frames Aren't the Best Solution

Frames are useful for banner logos, navigation bars, and so on. But if you look around, you'll notice that not many large Web sites use them. The reason: Frames have serious drawbacks.

First, bookmarks and favorites don't always work with frames. When you click a link inside a frame, a new page will load inside that frame; if you click a link on *that* page, yet another page will load. While it looks as if you are on a different page, the URL in the Address Bar remains unchanged. That's because a Web browser uses the address of the *frameset* page.

In other words, suppose you follow several links within a single frame, and then use your browser's Add Bookmark or Add to Favorites command. Later, when you select the bookmark or favorite, you'll see the *original* frameset page and the pages inside its frames—you won't see the page you wound up on.

Printing a Web page with frames can be tricky, too. Since a frames-based page is composed of multiple Web pages, the browser doesn't know which page you want to print. Different browsers handle this problem differently; novice Web surfers who don't understand the frames concept may get confused. (For example, if you're using the Mac version of Internet Explorer 5 to view the second page in Figure 7-2, and you click one of the navigation buttons in the top frame, Internet Explorer thinks you've selected that frame. If you then choose Edit→Print, you'll print only that top frame—a useless row of buttons!)

However, used in moderation and in good taste (see Figure 7-2), frames can be an excellent addition to your bag of Web tricks. Small sites, where users aren't likely to print or bookmark the pages, can make good use of frames. And you needn't use frames everywhere on a site. You can effectively create small presentations within a site—such as an online portfolio—that benefit creatively from frames.

XX

Web browser should draw the frames and which Web pages load into these frames—
around the Web page you started with.

Second, Dreamweaver creates new, untitled documents for each frame you added to
the page. For example, in Figure 7-4, one frame was added above the current page,
and one below. In the process, Dreamweaver created three new documents: the
frameset page, a blank document for the top frame, and a blank document for the
bottom frame.

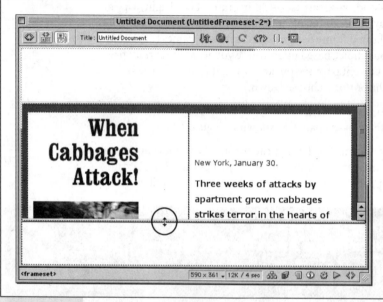

Figure 7-4:
*Dragging one of the frame
borders around the outer
edge of a document is a
quick way to create frames.
When the cursor is correctly
positioned to begin dragging,
it changes shape (circled). To
create additional frames
within the page, Alt-drag
(Option-drag) one of the
inner frame borders. As you
might have guessed, you can
resize your frames by simply
dragging the borders. But for
greater precision, and to
avoid some potential
problems, see "Frame Size"
on page 188.*

For proof, try this experiment: Click a visible portion of the original Web page you
opened in step 1; note that the title bar of your window identifies its original name.

Figure 7-5:
*The Frames category of the Objects panel allows one-click creation of framesets and frames. To
show the Frames category, click the down-pointing triangle at the top of the Objects panel and
select Frames from the menu. Then click the button for the frame design you like. Dreamweaver
creates the frameset and blank pages for any additional frames. Note that one frame in each
button of the Objects panel is light blue; the blue frame shows the position where Dreamweaver
places the current Web page.*

Now, if you click inside one of the blank areas around your original document (that is, one of the other frames), the title bar changes to say *Untitled Document*. That's because you haven't yet saved or named the new Web pages that make up the new frames. You'll do that in a later step (see page 185).

Tip: To eliminate a frame, just drag its border back to the closest edge of the document window.

Nested Framesets

Although there's no limit to the number of frames you can have in a single frameset page, there are some restrictions on how you can arrange them. You can't, for instance, merge one frame into another, setting up a single frame that spans multiple columns or rows. In other words, a design like that pictured in Figure 7-6 is impossible using just a single frameset. In that example, the sidebar navigation spans the entire left side of the window, while the right side has two horizontal frames.

To overcome this limitation, you can insert a frameset *inside* of a frame. Nesting framesets like this gives you much greater flexibility in your designs.

To nest one frameset inside another, just click inside the frame where you wish to insert a new frameset. Then choose Modify→Frameset→Split Frame Up, Down, Left, or Right.

Or, if you'd rather, you can use the Insert menu to insert frames. Choose Insert→Frames and select the location (for example, left or top) where you wish the new frame to go. (You can't drag frame borders to create a nested frameset.)

WORKAROUND WORKSHOP

Don't Leave Anyone Out

Some very old, off-brand Web browsers can't display frames at all. For the unlucky people who use these, a Web site with frames is rather useless. In fact, a browser that doesn't understand frames simply displays a blank page when it loads a frameset.

You don't have to leave these visitors in the lurch, however. The <noframes> tag lets you add Web-page content that's especially for, and can be viewed by, these old browsers; frames-capable browsers simply ignore the <noframes> content. Choose Modify→Frameset→Edit NoFrames Content. The document window changes to an empty window, where you can add text, images, and other HTML.

Remember, what you put here is only for people who can't view frames, so don't feel you have to duplicate your entire Web site. One simple approach is to include a short message—"This site requires a frames-capable browser"—with a link to the Netscape, Microsoft, or Opera Web page, so the person can download a newer browser.

Alternatively, you could link to a non-frames version of your Web site; of course, in that case, you'd have to do the extra work of building an entire frame-free version of the site.

When you're finished adding content for the noframes page, choose Modify→Frameset→Edit NoFrames Content again to return to the document window.

Tip: Dreamweaver offers some common, canned frame designs that you can apply with a click of the mouse; some of these designs include complex, nested framesets. See Figure 7-5. (You can find additional frameset designs on the Macromedia Exchange described on page 493; just search for the extension called More Framesets.)

The new frameset appears inside the original frame. (Because the borders of a nested frame look just like regular frame borders, use the Frames window, as shown in Figure 7-7, to keep track of what you're doing.)

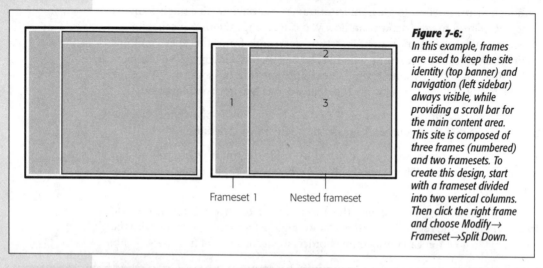

Frameset 1   Nested frameset

Figure 7-6:
In this example, frames are used to keep the site identity (top banner) and navigation (left sidebar) always visible, while providing a scroll bar for the main content area. This site is composed of three frames (numbered) and two framesets. To create this design, start with a frameset divided into two vertical columns. Then click the right frame and choose Modify→ Frameset→Split Down.

Selecting Frames and Framesets

Think of a frame as a mini document window; each frame contains a separate Web page. When you click inside the frame, you can add images, text, and other elements to the page. Click inside another frame to edit *that* frame's Web page.

However, since framesets aren't *visible* elements of a Web page, Dreamweaver provides a special window—the Frames panel—that provides a simple visual overview of frames and framesets, making it easier for you to select and modify them. To open it, choose Window→Frames or press Shift-F2 (see Figure 7-7).

Selecting a frameset lets you save it and modify its properties, such as frame size and borders, as described on page 187. There are several ways to select a frameset:

• Click the thick border around the edges of the frames in the Frames panel. The border becomes a solid black line to indicate the frameset is selected.

• Move the cursor over a frame border in the document window, slowly if necessary, until it changes to a double-headed arrow; then click to select the border. (This works only if frame borders are visible on the page: Choose View→Visual Aids→Frame Borders, or use the View Options menu in the document window's toolbar.) The gray frame borders acquire dashes to show that the entire frameset is selected.

- Click inside a frame in the document window and click the <frameset> tag in the tag selector (which is in the status bar at the bottom of the window; see page 16 for more on the tag selector).

Figure 7-7:
The Frames window shows a thumbnail diagram of the current document's frames. Thick 3-D borders represent a frameset, while thin gray lines represent the borders of frames. Also, a name appears inside each frame to identify it and to target links (see page 193).

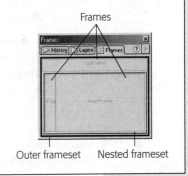

Frames

Outer frameset   Nested frameset

Selecting a frame lets you save it and modify its properties, including margins and scroll bars, as described on page 193. To select a frame, do one of the following:

- Click a frame in the Frames panel.
- Alt-click (Option-Shift-click) a frame in the document window.

Saving Framesets and Frames

It's always a good idea to save Web pages as soon as you create them; for example, you must save them before you can make working links, as described on page 85. Furthermore, you probably do some of your most important formatting, such as choosing a background color, right at the beginning, and you don't want to lose that in a crash or power failure. Finally, you need to save your frameset and all pages contained in it before you can even preview the frameset.

To save a frameset, select it using any of the methods described above; then choose File→Save Frameset (or, to "spin off" a copy of the one you've opened, Save Frameset As). The first time you save a frameset, the Save dialog box opens; name the frameset page and save it in your Web site folder as described on page 85. Although frameset pages have special properties, they're still just Web pages, and they still end in the extension .html. You can save them anywhere in your site folder (see Chapter 14 for some filing tips).

Saving a component page *inside* of a frame works just like saving regular documents: Click the frame in the document window and then choose File→Save Frame, or press Ctrl+S (⌘-S). You can also save all of your frames at once, as described next.

Saving multiple frames

One of the complexities of working with frames and framesets is the fact that you're dealing with many different Web pages at once, and, therefore, many different files. As you modify your frames and framesets, and make changes to the pages in those frames, you'll be saving multiple files.

Fortunately, you don't have to plod through the document window, clicking inside each frame and then saving it independently. To save all the pages in a frameset in one step, choose File→Save All Frames.

However, just after you've created a frameset and frames, Dreamweaver doesn't yet know the component pages' names or folder locations. It therefore shows you the Save As dialog box (see Figure 7-8) *over and over again*, once for each component frame page, so that you can name and file each one.

Clearly, you need to know which frame you're saving each time the Save As dialog box appears. To help you, Dreamweaver provides a visual cue: A thick, crosshatched border appears around the frame you're about to save (see Figure 7-8). Type a name for that page and press Enter; repeat for all pages.

The same thick, crosshatched border appears around the *entire* document window when you're saving the frameset itself.

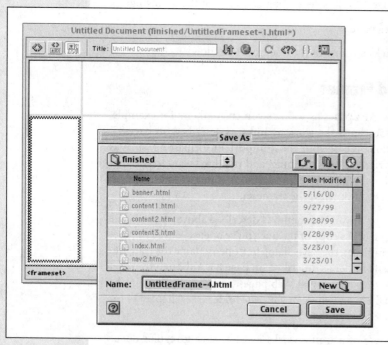

Figure 7-8:
The File→Save All Frames command is a powerful shortcut for quickly saving a frameset and all its pages. The first time you save an entire frameset, Dreamweaver places a thick, crosshatched border around the frame you're about to save, so you can name each page individually.

Frame and Frameset Properties

After creating a frameset, you can control the size, look, and contents of its frames. Dreamweaver treats framesets and frames as separate objects, each with its own set of properties. When you select a frameset or frame, using any of the methods described above, you can view and modify its properties in the Property inspector (see Figure 7-9).

Tip: In general, it's better to set a *frameset's* properties before fine-tuning its *frames,* since some frameset properties affect the properties of individual frames.

Frameset Borders

Borders are intended to visually separate one frame from another, but professional Web designers generally shun their amateurish 3-D appearance and the boxy designs they create (see Figure 7-2).

Fortunately, you can eliminate frame borders entirely. Not only does this free up a few precious pixels of screen real estate, it also lets you create seamless frame designs, so that all your frames appear to be a single, unified Web page.

To control frameset borders, start by selecting the frameset itself (see page 184 for selection techniques). Now consult the Property inspector, where you'll find these options:

- **Borders pop-up menu.** Use this pop-up menu to indicate the visibility status of the borders. To turn off borders, choose No (a good idea, if for tastefulness' sake alone). If you must use borders, select Yes. (The Default setting has the same effect as selecting Yes on most browsers.)

- **Border Width.** Specify the thickness of your border by typing a number (in pixels) into the field; type 0 if you want to completely eliminate borders. (You might think that choosing No from the Borders menu would automatically eliminate any space between frames, but that's not the case; if you don't also set the Border Width to 0, a small gap will appear between frames on the page.)

- **Border Color.** Use this pop-up palette to choose a color for the border (see page 30). Of course, if you've turned off borders, you can leave this option blank.

Figure 7-9:
Even though framesets and frames are treated as separate objects, all of the frames' properties are stored in the frameset file: their size, border, source, and so on. This feature confuses first-time frame builders, who logically assume that since each frame holds a Web page, a frame's properties would be stored with its page.

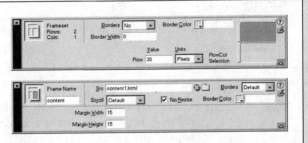

The next time you save your document, Dreamweaver stores all of the new settings into the frameset file (see Figure 7-9).

Note: Nested framesets have their own border settings, but you needn't set them; nested framesets inherit the border settings of the frameset they're in. For example, suppose you created a frameset and turned off the borders. Then you inserted another frameset into one of those frames (see page 183). The borders in the nested frameset are automatically turned off, having inherited the settings of the outer frameset.

Frame Size

You can make your frames bigger or smaller just by dragging the frame borders in the document window. But for more precise, numerical measurement, you'll need to turn to the Property inspector.

Start by selecting frameset containing the frame in question (see page 184). Now consult the Property inspector's controls, which include:

- **Row/Column.** Dreamweaver thinks of a frameset as something like a table: rows and columns. For example, if your frameset has two frames, one on top of the other, Dreamweaver thinks you have *two rows* of frames (one "cell" each). Dreamweaver thinks of a frameset composed of three side-by-side frames as *three columns*. (Beyond this similarity, however, framesets are totally distinct from tables.)

  Use this control (or the thumbnail diagram next to it) to specify the row or column you want to change; Figure 7-10 shows the details.

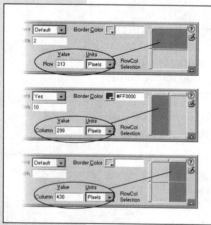

Figure 7-10:
The Property inspector's Row and Column selector shows a thumbnail of the frameset's rows (top), columns (middle), or both (bottom). In the first example—one frame above another—you can only set the height of each row; the width is the entire width of the browser window (or the parent frame, in the case of nested framesets). In the second example—two frames side by side—only the width of each frame can be modified. In the last example—four frames—you can set a mixture of the two: height for each row of frames, width for each column of frames.

- **Value.** Here's where you specify the height or width of the row or column. This can be either a pixel value or a percentage, whichever you specify by using the pop-up menu next to the Value field.

If you set a row height or column width to a *percentage* value, its size will be a percentage of the browser window (or the parent frame, if the frameset is nested inside a frame). That's a handy design safeguard against the fact that every visitor to your Web page may be using a different-sized monitor. You might set up your left-side frame so that it always consumes, say, 25% of the window, no matter how big or small the window is.

• **Units.** Using this pop-up menu, you can choose Pixels, Percentage, or Relative.

Relative is a special unit of measurement that you'll probably want to use for at least one column or row per frameset. To understand its use, imagine this setup: three frames appear one on top of another. The top frame is a banner containing the Web site's name; the middle frame is the main text; the bottom frame holds a navigation bar. If the heights of the top and bottom frames are 30 pixels, and the middle frame is 300 pixels, the page will look just fine if it's viewed in a browser window that's exactly 360 pixels tall (as shown at left in Figure 7-11).

However, if the visitor's browser is much taller, the top and bottom frames won't be the height you wanted (atright in Figure 7-11). You've told it that the total height of the frameset should be 360 pixels (30 + 300 + 30), but the window is actually much bigger—say 900 pixels. In an effort to make the best of a bad situation, the browser just divides the remaining space among the three frames, adding a little height to each of the three frames.

A *relative* measurement, therefore, lets you give a frame a flexible size. It will grow and shrink to accommodate changes in the browser window. In this example, the middle frame should have a *relative* measurement; the top and bottom frames should get *absolute* (fixed) sizes.

Figure 7-11:
You'll usually want to assign a relative width or height to one frame in each frameset. The relative frame grows taller or shorter (or wider or thinner) as the browser window is resized. If you don't, as seen here (before the window is resized, left, and after), all of the frames resize, creating undesirable space in some frames. In this example, both the banner and bottom navigation bar would look much better if they remained the same height. To accomplish this, you would give each of those frames a set height—say 30 pixels— while assigning a relative height to the middle frame.

Tip: If the notion of freely reflowing Web-page contents doesn't sit well with your design sense, and you'd like a bit more control over your visitors' browsers, see page 293 for detail on how to make browser windows open to the exact height and width you want.

Frame Properties

Once you've set the border properties and frame sizes in the *frameset*, you can modify the properties of each *frame*. Select the frame and use the tools in the Property inspector, as shown in Figure 7-10.

Name

Each frame can have its own name, but this isn't the name of the file (or the title of the Web page) that loads *into* the frame. A frame's name exists solely for identification purposes when working in Dreamweaver—specifically, when you want to use a Dreamweaver Behavior (see Chapter 11) or target a link from one frame to another. You'll need frame names, for example, when you wish to use a navigation bar to load pages into another frame (see "Targeting Links," below); otherwise, frame names are optional.

Tip: If you create frames using the Frame Objects panel or the Insert→Frame command, Dreamweaver supplies generic names for the frames it creates. But if you use any of the other methods for creating frames, such as dragging frame borders from the edges of the window, you have to supply frame names yourself.

POWER USERS' CLINIC

Frames from the Inside Out

The Src property also provides an alternative method for building a frames-based design, preferred by some designers.

Imagine that you want to build a page with two frames: top and bottom. You could create a new page, add text and graphics, and then save it as, say, "top.html." Now you create a second page called "bottom.html," and save it for use as the bottom frame.

Finally, you need a third page, one that will serve to hold the first two; split this third page into two frames. Set the source (the Src property) for the top frame to *top.html,* set it to *bottom.html* for the bottom frame, and save the frameset using any name you like (like *frameset.html,* or if it will be the home page to the site, *index.html*).

Using this technique, you make and save the frame pages first, and *then* create and save the frameset page–two frames, three files.

To set the name of a frame, select the frame by clicking it in the Frames window; then type a name in the Frame Name field of the Property inspector.

Src

When you set a frame's *source* (Src) property, you're simply specifying the path to the Web page file that loads into that particular frame. You can change the path—

and the Web page that appears in that frame—by clicking the folder icon and selecting a file from your site folder.

You can, if you like, link to a page that's on somebody else's site; just type the absolute URL here, beginning with *http://*. You won't, however, be able to see the other person's page within Dreamweaver; in the frame, you'll see nothing but the words "Remote File," plus the URL. You have to preview the frameset in a browser connected to the Internet to actually see the remote file appear within the page.

Note: Be careful using the Src property. One common mistake is to add the frameset page itself to one of the frames. In other words, it's possible to click the folder icon next to the Src field, and then select the current frameset page, thus creating a reference to itself.

When you preview the frameset, the browser loads the page—but when it attempts to load pages into each frame, it's trapped: It loads the frameset, which in turn has a frame, which loads the frameset again, which has a frame that loads the frameset again, and so on, and so on. This hall of mirrors continues until the browser crashes and your site's visitors curse your name!

Scroll

To create scroll bars for a frame—or hide them—use the Scroll property. You'll see four options in the Scroll menu in the Property inspector:

- **Yes** adds horizontal and vertical scroll bars to the frame, even if the frame doesn't contain enough material to require them.

- **No** prevents scroll bars from being added to a frame, even if that means some of its contents become inaccessible.

- **Auto** lets the browser determine whether to display scroll bars. If the contents don't fit inside the frame, the browser adds the appropriate scroll bar.

- **Default** works like Auto in most browsers. Since the effect of the Default option can vary from browser to browser, choose Auto instead.

In general, use the Auto option if you know your frame might require some scrolling, or No if not. For example, a frame containing a Web page with a lot of text will probably need a scroll bar, whereas a frame that simply contains the site's logo won't.

No Resize

Usually, your Web site visitors can resize the frames you've created just by dragging their borders right in the Web browser. But if you don't want people monkeying around with your designs, turn on the frame's No Resize checkbox in the Property inspector.

Tip: The No Resize option applies only to manual frame-edge dragging; even with No Resize turned on, your frames may still change size when the *browser window* is resized. If you want to prevent even that layout shift, see page 188.

Margin Width and Margin Height

You can adjust the top and left margins of a frame by setting its Margin Width and Margin Height properties. These settings control the position of the upper-left corner of a page in a frame; they work exactly like page margins in a standard Web page do (see step 9 on page 31).

Margin *width* is the amount of space between the left edge of the frame's border and the left edge of the Web page; margin *height* is the space from the frame's top border and the top of the Web page. These margin settings apply to every page that loads into the affected frame.

Border and Border Color

Using these controls, you can assign a border and border color to each individual frame—giving one important frame a sky-blue border, say, but leaving all other frames borderless.

Unfortunately, Internet Explorer, Netscape Navigator, and Opera all handle this property differently; you can't assume that it will work for all of your visitors. Furthermore, this option has no effect if you've turned off borders in the frameset.

FREQUENTLY ASKED QUESTION

The Underscore Targets

What are the four choices in the Target menu that begin with the "_" character?

If you're working on a frameset page, the link target menu lists all named frames. But even when working in another kind of page, this pop-up menu always offers these four options for a link you've highlighted:

_blank opens a new, second browser window when the link is clicked; the new window loads the linked page. The original window—the one containing the link—remains open. This feature lets you link to another site, for example, leaving your own Web site available in an open window. (To open a new browser window to an exact size, see page 293.)

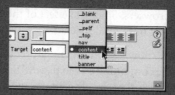

_self loads the linked page into the same window or frame, replacing the current page. Of course, this is how links work normally, so there's little point in choosing this option unless you're trying to get extra exercise.

_top offers a specialized, but very useful feature. Suppose your Web page contains frames—and one of them contains a link to someone else's Web site. If a visitor clicks the link, the "foreign" Web site will appear trapped within one of *your* frames—a strange effect, to be sure, and also one that's considered bad form.

By choosing the _top option for a highlighted link, you force your visitor's browser to load the linked page into the entire browser window, eliminating all frames and framesets, and avoiding the HTML social gaffe of imprisoning someone else's Web site within your own.

_parent replaces the current frameset page with the linked page, exactly like the _top target. The difference is visible only when the frameset page is itself loaded into a frame in *another* frameset page. In that case, this option will replace only the first frameset. (Netscape Navigator's support for this feature is notoriously flaky.)

Targeting Links

Normally, when you click a link, the Web browser replaces the current page with a new Web page; in other words, the entire browser window changes. But when displaying frames, a browser treats each frame as an independent window, which offers some interesting and unique possibilities for linking. Clicking a link on a page merely replaces the contents of *that frame,* leaving the other frames in place.

Using the *Target* property of a link, you can choose, or target, which frame you wish the linked Web page to load in. This option is extremely handy when you use one frame as a navigation bar whose links load pages into *other* frames.

To make a link open in a different frame, create the link as described on page 85; make sure that the link is highlighted. Then, in the Property inspector, choose the name of the frame where you'll want the page to appear, using the pop-up menu next to the Target field.

When you click the link on the finished Web page, the source Web page opens into the frame you just chose.

Tip: Dreamweaver's "Go To Url" behavior lets you really go crazy with linking; using it, you can have a single link target multiple frames at once. Imagine loading four different Web pages with a single click! See page 295 for more information on this powerful feature.

Inserting a Navigation Bar

One of the best reasons to use frames is to keep a *navigation bar* visible on the screen at all times. A navigation bar (called a "nav bar" in the trade) is a set of interactive buttons that let visitors jump to different pages, or load pages into different frames. To make your life easier, Dreamweaver's Navigation Bar object makes quick work of adding complex interactive navigation bars to your frames.

Like the Rollover object described in Chapter 5, nav bar buttons use Dreamweaver Behaviors—JavaScript programs—to dynamically swap graphics files. And nav bar buttons offer two additional styles that help your visitors know where they are in your site (see Figure 7-12).

Figure 7-12:
When a button first appears on a page, it's usually in its up state—ready to be clicked. But when the mouse moves to the button, it changes to its over state. Navigation Bar buttons can also have down and over while down states, as described on step 6, page 195.

To create a navigation bar:

1. Create graphics for the buttons in your navigation bar.

You'll need to create multiple graphic files for each button, using a graphics program like Fireworks or Adobe ImageReady. Since a navigation button can have multiple appearances—states—depending on how the user interacts with it (Figure 7-12), you need a separate graphic file for each state. And, as with rollover images, make sure that each button graphic is *exactly* the same size; otherwise, you'll get distortion (see page 109).

2. Place the cursor in the frame where you'd like to add a navigation bar.

It's usually a sidebar, header, or footer.

3. Choose Insert→Interactive Images→Navigation Bar.

Alternatively, from the Objects panel, click the Insert Navigation Bar object.

Either way, the Insert Navigation Bar window opens (see Figure 7-13). Don't be overwhelmed; there are a lot of options in this window, but they're straightforward.

Just remember that a navigation bar is simply a collection of buttons. You add one button at a time to create a complete navigation system. Each button has a name, up to four different images, and a link.

The window starts out with a single element called *unnamed1*.

4. Type a name for the first button in the Element Name field.

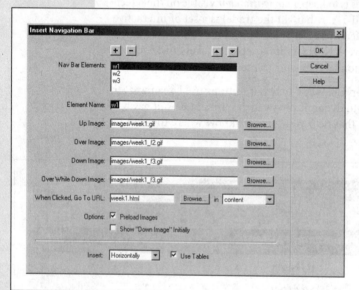

Figure 7-13:
This navigation bar has three buttons so far. The different properties of the button w1—selected in the Nav Bar Elements list—are displayed, including the button's image files, link, and target. This particular navigation bar will be laid out horizontally in the frame. Changing the Insert menu to Vertically would change the orientation of the bar. Unfortunately, this and the Use Tables option are only available when you first insert the Navigation Bar. Once inserted, if you want to orient the buttons in a different direction, you'll have to do it by hand.

This name is just for behind-the-scenes use in the Web page; it won't appear on the button or anywhere on the screen. If you like, you can even skip this step and use Dreamweaver's default names: unnamed1, unnamed2, and so on.

5. **Click the Browser button next to the Up Image field to select a graphics file for the up state of the button.**

This is the image you created in step 1.

6. **Choose graphics for one or more states for the button.**

At a minimum, include an over image, but including images for the other two states of the button will add zing to your navigation bar.

These different state images are good for helping your visitors understand where they are. For example, in Figure 7-11, the frameset loads the first of three pages covering a story about killer cabbages. The Week 1 button in the right corner is in its down state, meaning that "You are at this spot in the story." The Week 2 button is in its up state, meaning that it's clickable, and the Week 3 button is highlighted in its over state, since the mouse is hovering over it. These buttons are just graphic files; you can make their different states look like anything you want.

7. **Using the "When Clicked" field, specify the page you want the button link to open.**

Since this is a *navigation* bar, clicking the button should take the user to another Web page. You can click the Browse button to select a file from your site, type in a path to a page in the site, or, to add a link to a page outside of the current site, type an absolute URL beginning with *http://*.

8. **Select a Target from the pop-up menu.**

Since you're including the navigation bar in a frame of its own, the linked Web page should load into another frame, leaving the nav bar exactly where it was. Select the name of the frame from the menu. The option Main Window makes the Web browser replace the frameset and frames with the linked page.

(The name of the other frames in a frameset appear *only* if the current frameset is open and you're adding the navigation bar to one of the pages in a frame. If, for example, you've opened the navigation bar page by itself, Dreamweaver doesn't know the page is part of a frameset, nor what the other frames names are.)

Note: Take care not to turn off the Preload Images checkbox. As noted in Figure 5-11 (page 110), preloading images prevents a delay when a visitor moves the mouse over the navigation image.

9. **If desired, turn on Show "Down Image" Initially.**

The down image can function like a "You are here" sign, letting visitors know their location in the site. You should select this option only for one button in the navigation bar, and only if that button links back to the original frameset.

For instance, say your home page is a frameset, and one frame contains a navigation bar. Select this option for the Home button on the navigation bar. In this way, when visitors peruse your page, that button is already highlighted—indicating where they are.

10. **Click the + button; repeat steps 4 through 9 for each additional button in the navigation bar.**

The – button deletes the highlighted button; the up and down arrow buttons let you rearrange your buttons by shuffling a highlighted button up or down in the list.

11. **Choose the orientation of the bar from the Insert menu.**

Navigation bars can run horizontally—perfect for headers and footers—or vertically—the right choice for a sidebar.

Tip: To help control layout, turn on the Use Tables checkbox. By containing your graphics within the cells of a table, this feature keeps your graphics together on a page and prevents them from moving around if someone resizes the browser window.

---

12. **Click OK to insert the navigation bar.**

You can insert only one Navigation Bar per Web page; once inserted, you can edit it only by choosing Modify→Navigation Bar. The Modify Navigation Bar dialog box

FREQUENTLY ASKED QUESTION

Nav Bars, No Frames

Can I use the Insert Navigation Bar object without using frames?

Yes, but you'll lose most of the benefits of the Navigation Bar and add unnecessary code to the page.

One of the cool aspects of a Dreamweaver nav bar is its ability to indicate where the visitor is within the site, thanks to the button's down state.

Imagine this scenario. You've built two frames: a top frame for a nav bar, and bottom frame for the main content. The buttons in the nav bar are all in their up states; moving your mouse over the first button causes it to glow, and clicking it loads a new page in the bottom frame.

In addition, the button you just clicked changes to its down state, letting your visitor know what section of the site he's seeing. Only the page in the bottom frame changes; the

top frame with the nav bar simply uses a Dreamweaver behavior to swap the graphics used for the buttons.

Now imagine that you didn't use frames; you just inserted the navigation bar on the same page as the main content. When you click a button in the navigation bar, the browser loads a new page, completely replacing the page that had the navigation bar! You'll have to rebuild the navigation bar on every single page of your site.

Moreover, the down state of the button never appears, because as soon as you click the button, a new page replaces it.

In other words, there's not much point to using the Navigation Bar feature in Dreamweaver unless you're also using frames. If you want to create a frame-free site, it's probably best to just stick with Rollover objects (see page 109) for building navigation buttons.

looks just like the one shown in Figure 7-13, so that you can edit, delete, and rearrange your navigation buttons.

To modify a button, select it in the Nav Bar Elements list; you can then assign new images, settings, and links to it.

Tip: For more advanced navigation bar features, see page 304.

Frames Tutorial

In this tutorial, you'll build an exclusive online story for *Cosmopolitan Farmer* magazine. In the process, you'll learn how to use Dreamweaver's frame building features and add an advanced site-navigation toolbar.

Getting Started

Before you begin building the page, you'll need the tutorial files from this book's Web site. You'll also need to tell Dreamweaver a bit about the site you'll be working on.

1. **Download the files for this tutorial from the companion Web site.**

   Using your Web browser, visit *www.sawmac.com/missing*. Click the Tutorials link to go to the tutorials page.

   Then click the link Frames Tutorial—Mac files or Frames Tutorial—Win files, depending on the computer you're using, to download the tutorial files.

   When the files are downloaded and decompressed, you should have a folder named DWFrames on your computer, containing the Web pages and graphics needed for this tutorial.

   Now launch Dreamweaver and begin:

2. **Choose Site→New Site.**

   The Site Definition window opens.

3. **Type *Tutorial 3* in the Site Name field.**

   This will be the Web-site name Dreamweaver will use while you're working on this tutorial.

4. **Click the Folder icon next to the Local Root Folder field. Navigate to and select the folder DWFrames; click Choose.**

   The path to this folder appears in the box. You've just told Dreamweaver where to find the files that make up your Web site.

5. **Click OK to close the Site Definition dialog box.**

If a dialog box appears, letting you know that Dreamweaver is about to create a *cache* for this site (see page 24), click OK. You *always* want Dreamweaver to create a site cache when you define a new site.

You've now defined the site you'll be working on in this tutorial. Defining Web sites is described in more detail in Chapter 14.

Creating a Frameset and Frames

You'll create this online article by adding frames to a Web page that's already partly made.

1. **Choose File→Open; open the file in the DWFrames folder called *title.html*.**

   The Web page shows the article's headline. You'll start by creating a frameset and adding a single frame.

2. **Choose View→Visual Aids→Frame Borders.**

   If you prefer, you can instead choose Frame Borders and other visual aids from the Options menu (the rightmost icon) in the toolbar.

   A thin, gray border appears around the edges of the page.

3. **Drag the frame border at the top of the document an inch or so down to create a new frame.**

   In this one step, Dreamweaver creates a new, untitled frameset document and a new untitled Web page in the top frame.

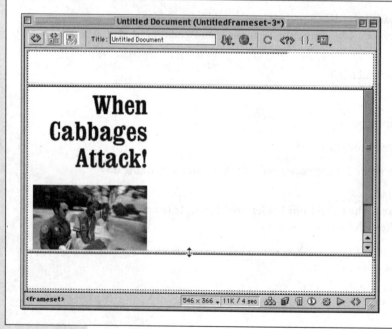

Figure 7-14:
Dreamweaver frees you from the confusing HTML required to build framesets and frames. Instead of messing around with <frameset> and <frame> tags, you can create frames quickly by simply dragging borders on the page.

4. **Drag the bottom frame border upward to create a frame at the bottom of the window.**

   Dreamweaver creates a new, untitled Web page in the bottom frame and adds the necessary HTML code to the frameset document. Your screen should look something like Figure 7-14.

5. **Open the toolbar, if it isn't already open, by choosing View→Toolbar. Type *When Cabbages Attack!* in the Title field of the toolbar.**

   You've just replaced the default title, *Untitled Document.* The new page title appears in the title bar of the document window.

6. **Choose File→Save All Frames.**

   The Save As dialog opens. Since you've just created several new, untitled documents, you'll need to save each one. The first document Dreamweaver saves, as shown by the crosshatched border in the document window, is the frameset page.

7. **Type *cabbages.html* in the Name field; click Save, or press Enter, to save the frameset page.**

   Make sure that you save this page in the proper location: the DWFrames folder, which is the root folder of this site.

   After you click Save, the Save As dialog box appears again. This time, it's prompting you to name and save the bottom page, which you'll later make into a navigation bar for the story.

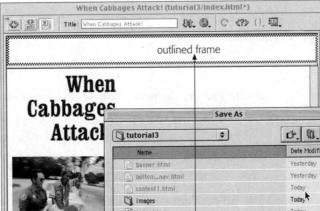

Figure 7-15:
When saving multiple frame pages, one after another, how do you know which page you're saving? Dreamweaver uses a crosshatched border inside the frame to indicate which Web page it is saving.

8. Save the bottom frame as *navigation.html,* also inside the DWFrames folder.

The Save As dialog box appears once again, this time for the page in the top frame (see Figure 7-15). You've already downloaded the page that goes inside this frame, so you don't need to save a new page now.

9. Click Cancel.

Modifying the Frameset and Frames

Although you've got the basic structure of the page in order, each frame needs additional fine-tuning to make it look just right.

1. Open the Frames panel, if it isn't already open, by choosing Window→Frames (or by pressing Shift-F2).

The small Frames panel opens, as shown in Figure 7-16.

2. Select the frameset by clicking the thick border in the Frames panel.

To check what you've selected, look at the document window's status bar; the <frameset> tag appears in bold.

Figure 7-16:
This panel lets you select Framesets and Frames in order to modify their properties. Thick, black borders indicate a selected frameset; a frame has a thin black border when selected. In addition, names of frames appear in each frame in the panel. In this case, none of the frames has been named yet.

3. In the Property inspector, choose No from the Borders menu.

As noted on page 187, frame borders are best avoided for professional-quality Web sites. Eliminating borders lets the frameset and all its frames appear to be a unified whole.

4. Type *0* in the Border Width field in the Property inspector.

As explained on page 187, if you don't do this, some Web browsers will leave space between each frame.

5. In the Property inspector, click the top row of the row selector (see Figure 7-17).

You've just filled in the Property inspector with the current settings for the top frame; now you can modify them.

6. Type *30* in the Row Value field, and make sure Pixels is selected in the Units pop-up menu.

When you press Enter, the top field shrinks.

Figure 7-17:
You specify the size of each frame by selecting a frameset and then using the Property inspector.

7. Click the bottom row of the row selector in the Property inspector, and type *30* in the Row Value field. Make sure Pixel units is selected.

When you press Enter, the navigation field shrinks.

8. In the Property inspector, click the middle row of the row selector and select Relative from the Units pop-up menu.

The top and bottom frames have each been set to a fixed dimension or 30 pixels—they'll contain a thin banner and navigation bar. The middle frame, however, holds the article itself. Because you never know what size browser window your reader is using, you can't reliably specify a size for this middle row. Instead, you've set this row to Relative, meaning that it will take up whatever space is available.

9. Click the top frame in the Frames panel to select it.

The Property inspector displays the properties for that frame.

10. Click the folder icon next to the Src field.

The Select HTML File dialog box appears.

11. Select the file *banner.html* in the DWFrames folder; click Choose.

The page, with the Cosmopolitan Farmer logo, appears in the top frame of the document window.

12. Choose No in the Scroll menu; turn on the No Resize box.

Since this frame contains a simple static banner, scroll bars are unnecessary—and ugly.

13. Type *0* in the Margin Width field, and *0* in the Margin Height field.

Dreamweaver may appear to crop off part of the banner; that's just a bug in the program. Your page looks fine when previewed in a Web browser. (Press F12 whenever you'd like to do that.)

14. Click the bottom frame in the Frames panel to select it.

    This frame will contain the navigation bar for the story.

15. Choose No in the Scroll menu and check the No Resize box. Type *0* in the Margin Width field, and *0* in the Margin Height field.

    This frame will become your navigation bar. Because the nav bar fits completely within the frame, it doesn't need scroll bars or margins.

16. Choose File→Save All Frames.

    Because you've already named the files earlier in the tutorial, Dreamweaver simply saves them now.

Nesting Framesets

The middle frame of the Cosmopolitan Farmer design needs to be subdivided even further. The left side of the frame will hold a photo and title for the article, while the right side will contain the main text of the story. To prepare for this layout, you need to insert a frameset *into* this frame.

1. Click the middle frame in the document window.

   You can also click the middle frame in the Frames panel. Don't click one of the frame *borders* in the document window; doing so selects the entire frameset.

2. Choose Modify→Frameset→Split Frame Left.

   Dreamweaver creates a new frameset with two frames side by side, inside the existing middle frame (see Figure 7-18).

3. Click the thick border of the nested frameset in the Frames panel, as shown in Figure 7-18.

   You've just selected the frameset, so now you can change its settings.

Figure 7-18:
Dreamweaver denotes framesets with thick borders in the Frames panel. When selected, a frameset border turns solid black.

4. In the Property inspector, click the left column of the column selector, then type *200* in the Column Value field. Choose Pixels from the pop-up menu, as shown in Figure 7-19, and press Enter.

You've set the width of the left column to 200 pixels.

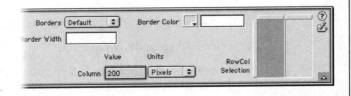

Figure 7-19:
The darkened panel in the thumbnail picture at the right of the Property inspector shows what frame you're currently working on.

5. Click the right column of the column selector in the Property inspector; choose Relative from the Units pop-up menu.

Once again, the Relative setting means that the width of this frame varies depending on the size of the visitor's browser window. That's the ideal setting for the frame that will contain the news story itself.

6. On the Frames panel, click the left frame of this frameset to select it. On the Property inspector, choose No from the Scroll menu and turn on No Resize.

Since there's nothing in this frame but a title and photo, there's no reason to add scroll bars.

7. Click the right frame on the Frames panel. Type *content* in the Frame Name field on the Property inspector; press Enter.

Unlike the other frames, you've named this one. Naming a frame lets you make it the target of links. In other words, you can make a link in another frame load a Web page into *this* frame. Because this frame holds the text of the article, it needs scroll bars and can vary in size.

In the next steps, you'll add a Web page with the first part of the story.

8. Click the folder icon next to the Src field.

The Select HTML File dialog box appears.

9. Double-click the file in the DWFrames folder called *intro.html.*

The page appears in the right frame of the document window.

10. Choose File→Save All Frames. To preview your work, press the F12 key (see Figure 7-20).

Adding the Navigation Bar

The main page of the story is coming together well. But your hapless visitors are stuck here, with no way to view the other pages in the story. In the next step, you'll add a navigation bar to the bottom frame.

1. **Click in the bottom frame of the document window. Choose Modify→Page Properties.**

   The Page Properties dialog box opens, as shown in Figure 1-11 (page 29).

2. **Set the Background color to black.**

   You can leave the page untitled, because only the title of the *frameset page* appears in the browser window's title bar. No one will ever see the title of this page.

3. **Click OK.**

   You return to the document window.

4. **Choose Insert→Interactive Images→Navigation Bar.**

   Alternatively, on the Objects panel, click the Navigation Bar object. Either way, the Insert Navigation Bar dialog box opens (see Figure 7-21). This navigation bar will only have three buttons—one for each week's story.

5. **In the Element Name field, type *w1*.**

   The name of an element is only used as part of the programming of the page and is invisible to visitors. In this case, it's the button for week one.

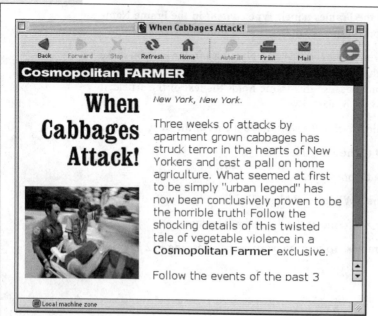

Figure 7-20:
Although this page contains four frames, there are no frame borders, so the page has a clean, unified look. The scroll bar scrolls only the text, leaving the banner, footer, title, and photo in place. The bottom frame is empty, but in the next section, you'll add a navigation bar to it.

6. Click the Browse button next to the Up Image field; in the *images* folder of the DWFrames folder, double-click the file called *week1.gif*.

You've just told Dreamweaver what image to use for the up state of the button. In the next steps, you'll choose the over, down, and over while down images. (See step 6 on page 195 for details on button states.)

7. Click the Browse button next to the Over Image field; in the Open dialog box, double-click the file called *week1_f2.gif*.

Next stop: the button image in its down position.

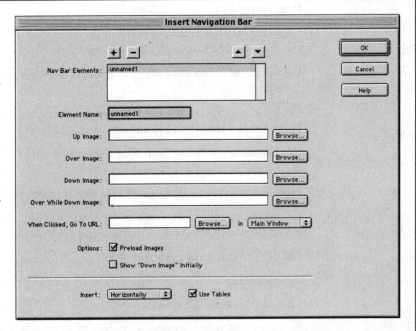

Figure 7-21:
From this one dialog box, you can create a navigation bar with any number of buttons. Just click the + button and type a name to add a new one to the list. You can reorder your navigation buttons anytime using the up and down arrows and delete unwanted ones by clicking the - button.

8. Click the Browse button next to the Down Image field; in the Open dialog box, double-click the file called *week1_f3.gif*.

Finally, you need to choose a graphic for the button's appearance when the mouse passes over it in its down state.

9. Click the Browse button next to the Over While Down Image field; in the Open dialog box, double-click the file called *week1_f3.gif* (yes, the same file you chose in the previous step).

In other words, there isn't any special graphic for this state. When a user moves the mouse over a button in its down state, it will remain unchanged. (If you don't specify a graphic at all, Dreamweaver will use the graphic you specified for the over image, in step 7, as the over while down Image.)

10. **Click the Browse button next to the When Clicked, Go To URL field.**

    The Open file dialog box appears, prompting you to choose the HTML Web-page file that will open when the button is clicked.

11. **In the DWFrames folder, double-click the *week1.html* file.**

    This is the text file for week one of the story—and it's what will appear when your visitors click the week one button link.

12. **Choose Content from the menu to the right of the URL field.**

    "Content" is the name of the frame where each article in the story opens; it's the frame at right in Figure 7-22.

13. **Click the + button in the upper left of the dialog box to add an additional button. Follow steps 5 through 12 to add the Week 2 button.**

    Use the name *w2* for the button, and substitute *week2* where *week1* appears in the instructions.

14. **Click the + button in the upper left of the dialog box to add the last button. Follow steps 5 through 12 to add the Week 3 button.**

    Use the name *w3* for the button, and substitute *week3* where *week1* appears in the instructions. You're almost done.

15. **From the Insert pop-up menu, choose Horizontally; turn on Use Tables.**

    Dreamweaver can automatically create a table to house the navigation graphics, which helps keep the graphics together and prevents possible display problems.

16. **Click OK to insert the navigation bar.**

    You return to your document window, with the nav bar in place.

17. **Choose File→Save All Frames.**

You've completed your masterpiece; press F12 to view it and test it in your Web browser. If you like, you can visit *www.sawmac.com/tutorials* to compare your work with the finished one that's posted online.

Cascading Style Sheets

When you compare the formatting options discussed in Chapter 3 with the text styling in a magazine or book, the Web looks like the ugly duckling of the media world. The handful of options available in HTML—font face, size, and color—doesn't hold a candle to the typographic and layout control you get when creating a document in even the most basic word processing program.

But not anymore. A newer technology called Cascading Style Sheets has begun to address the shortcomings of HTML. Cascading Style Sheets (CSS) allow much greater control over the layout and design of Web pages. Using them, you can add margins to paragraphs (just as in a word processor), colorful and stylish borders to images, and even add dynamic rollover effects to text links. Best of all, Dreamweaver's stream-lined approach lets you combine several of these formats into powerful style sheets with just a few mouse clicks.

Note: Cascading Style Sheets can be one of the most difficult Web-design concepts to grasp. As you read the following pages, resist the temptation to fling your monitor into the hallway until after you've followed the tutorial steps at the end of this chapter, which put all of the tech-talk into context.

Cascading Style Sheet Basics

If you've used styles in word processing programs like Microsoft Word or page lay-out programs like Quark XPress, Cascading Style Sheets (CSS) will feel familiar. A *style* is simply a rule describing how to format a particular piece of HTML. (A style *sheet* is a set of these canned styles.)

You might create a single style, for example, that formats text with the font Arial, colored red, and with a left margin of 50 pixels. You can also create styles specifically for working with images; for instance, a style can center an image on a Web page and place 50 pixels margin between it and the surrounding text.

Once you've created a style, you can apply it to text, images, or other elements on a page. For example, you could select a paragraph of text and apply a style to instantly change the text's size, color, and font. You can also create styles for specific tags, so that all <h1> tags in your site, for example, are displayed in the same style, no matter where they appear.

FREQUENTLY ASKED QUESTION

HTML Styles vs. Cascading Style Sheets

I think you've messed up in your book; I remember reading about this style-sheet business back in Chapter 3. Do I win anything?

Afraid not.

You're probably thinking of Dreamweaver's HTML Styles, which are indeed described on page 76.

CSS may sound like the same idea. However, several important differences separate the two. For example, when you update a CSS style, the changes you've made are instantly applied anywhere the style is used. Your boss doesn't like the blue color of the headings that appear on a page? Just change the style for that heading from red to blue, and all of the red headings suddenly turn blue. Dreamweaver doesn't, on the other hand, automatically

update text you've formatted with HTML styles when you edit the HTML style. You must go back and individually apply the new style to your text (see page 80).

Furthermore, while HTML Styles only apply to text, you can use CSS to format any HTML element, such as a table, image, or even the body of the page.

Most importantly, the underlying technology behind the two approaches is completely different. HTML Styles is simply a Dreamweaver tool that lets you quickly apply basic HTML formatting using paragraph formats and the <font> tag. CSS, however, is not HTML. Although CSS works with HTML (and XML), it has its own language with its own properties and syntax. (Fortunately, Dreamweaver's CSS tools hide all this complexity, so you may never know you're not working in HTML).

Why Use CSS?

Although HTML alone provides basic formatting options for text, images, tables, and other Web page elements, Cascading Style Sheets have many advantages that make it a superior choice for many formatting tasks. In fact, the World Wide Web Consortium (W3C), the organization responsible for defining standards for the Web, plans to phase out the <font> tag in future versions of HTML in favor of CSS. In other words, upcoming Web browser versions may not even understand much of the text formatting you apply with the Property inspector. But they will understand CSS. (For a list of other obsolete tags, see *www.codehelp.co.uk/html/deprecated.html.*)

But even if the threat of obsolescence doesn't motivate you to use CSS, consider this: Style sheets offer far more formatting choices than HTML. With CSS, you can format paragraphs as they appear in a book or newspaper (the first line indented and no space between each paragraph, for example) and control the leading (the space between lines of type in a paragraph). When you use CSS to add a background image to a page, you get to decide how (and whether) it tiles (repeats). HTML can't even begin do any of these things.

Even better, CSS styles take up much less space than HTML's <font> tag formatting. You can usually trim a lot of kilobytes from text-heavy Web pages using CSS while maintaining a high level of formatting control. As a result, your pages look great *and* load faster.

Style sheets also make updating your site easier. As mentioned earlier, when you edit a CSS style, Dreamweaver immediately makes that change ripple through your site, *wherever* that style is used. You can thus completely change the appearance of a site by simply editing a single style sheet.

When Not to Use CSS

Cascading Style Sheets may sound like a cure-all for HTML's anemic formatting powers, but you may pay a price for their convenience.

The first consideration is compatibility. Although the CSS standard has been around for some time, not all Web browsers understand style sheets. And among those that do, some still don't always display style properties correctly (Netscape Navigator 4 is the main culprit here).

Internet Explorer 3 for Windows understood some style sheet properties, but not until the 4.0 versions of Internet Explorer and Netscape Navigator could you count on consistent interpretation of CSS. The bottom line: If you worry that a substantial number of your visitors may still use pre-4.0 browsers, stay away from CSS.

UP TO SPEED

Getting to Know (and Love) CSS

Cascading Style Sheets are an exciting—and complex—addition to your Web building tool kit, worthy of entire books and Web sites on this topic alone. For example:

- For an excellent tutorial on CSS, visit Web Monkey's style sheet tutorial at: *http://hotwired.lycos.com/webmonkey/reference/stylesheet_guide/*

- Ongoing discussions about CSS, and informative articles on this technology can be found at A List Apart: *www.alistapart.com.*

- For the ultimate source of information, turn to the World Wide Web Consortium's Web site:

www.w3.org/Style/CSS/. The W3C is the body responsible for many of the standards that drive the Web—including HTML and CSS.

- If you just love to curl up by the fireplace with a good computer book, *Cascading Style Sheets: The Definitive Guide* by Eric Meyer (O'Reilly) can't be beat.

Finally, you don't have to look any further than your own desktop for the ultimate reference to each CSS property. Dreamweaver 4's new built-in Reference window provides instant access to concise information on Cascading Style Sheets (see the box on page 257).

In fact, even if you're confident that only (or mostly) 4.0-or-later browsers travel to your site, you still need to test your pages thoroughly in a variety of browsers—especially Navigator 4, which tends to have the most trouble with CSS. (By contrast, if you only need to design for Internet Explorer 5, you'll have a much easier time exploiting the powerful design potential of style sheets.)

Finally, as you'll become painfully aware, Dreamweaver's visual display doesn't always work when using Cascading Style Sheets. Many of the formatting properties described in this chapter—such as the border style, custom bullet icon, and word spacing—don't show up in the document window. You'll be forced to preview your pages in a browser frequently, just to get a clear view of how your pages are shaping up.

Internal vs. External Style Sheets

As you create new styles and add them to style sheets, you can then store these style sheets either internally, in the Web page itself, or in another file called an *external style sheet*.

Internal style sheets appear in the <head> portion of a Web page and contain styles that apply to that page. An internal style sheet is a good choice when you have a very specific formatting task for a single page; perhaps you want to create styles to format the text and table of a chart that only appears on a single page.

An external style sheet, on the other hand, contains only styles—no HTML—and can be linked to numerous pages. You can create a single style sheet that affects many pages of your site, creating uniform formatting throughout. For instance, you can put a headline style in an external style sheet and link that sheet to every page in the site. Every headline on the site will then share the same look—instant design consistency! Even better, when the boss (or the interior decorator in you) calls up and asks you to change the color of the headlines, you only need to edit a single file—the external style sheet—to update hundreds or even thousands of Web pages.

You can create both types of style sheets easily in Dreamweaver, and you aren't limited to choosing one or the other; a single Web page can have both an external style sheet (for styles that apply to the whole site) and an internal style sheet (for page-specific formatting). You can even attach multiple external style sheets to a single page.

Types of Styles

Styles come in several different flavors. The two most common are *custom styles* and *redefined HTML tags*.

A custom style is one that you create, name, and attach manually to text or an HTML tag. Custom styles work the most like styles in word processing and page layout programs. For example, if you want the name of your company to be displayed in bold and red wherever it appears in the text of a Web page, you can create a custom style named Company with boldface and red text color formatting. You would then select your company's name on the page and apply this style.

The other major type of CSS style is called an *HTML tag style* and applies globally to HTML tags, as opposed to individual selections. For example, suppose you wanted to display every Heading 1 paragraph (see page 59) in the Arial font. Instead of creating a custom style and applying it to every Heading 1 on the page, you could create a HTML tag style for the <h1> *tag*. In effect, you redefine the tag so that it's displayed in Arial. The main benefit of redefining an HTML tag in this way is that you don't have to apply the style by hand. Since the new style says that *all* <h1> tags must use Arial, wherever a Web browser encounters a <h1> tag, it displays the text in Arial, the specified font.

These HTML tag styles are the easiest way to format a page. For one thing, there's no need to select the tag and apply the style; the page only needs to contain an instance of the tag—<h1> for example—that you've redefined.

Note: In the course of your Web-design career, you may well encounter alternate terms for Custom and HTML Tag styles. In the official terminology of Cascading Style Sheets, custom styles are actually called *classes,* and HTML tag styles are *type selectors.* Since *custom style* and *HTML tag style* are more descriptive terms (and the ones you'll see in Dreamweaver), you'll see those terms used in this book.

Nevertheless, there are times when only a custom style will do, such as when you want to apply different styles to various paragraphs on the same page. Simply redefining the <p> tag won't do the trick; that would affect *all* paragraphs. Instead, you'd have to create a custom style for each paragraph format, and then apply the styles by hand.

Creating Styles

You start most CSS-related tasks in the CSS Styles panel, which is the command center for creating and using styles (see Figure 8-1). To open it, choose Window→CSS Styles (or press Shift-F11). The Launcher bar at the bottom of the document window also includes a button for opening this panel (see page 16).

Figure 8-1:
The CSS Styles panel lists the names of all custom styles available to the page; from its internal style sheet as well as any linked external style sheets. Icons next to the name of each style identify the type of style—internal or external. You use the list to apply styles to selected objects on the page. As a result, only styles you apply yourself (custom styles) appear in the list.

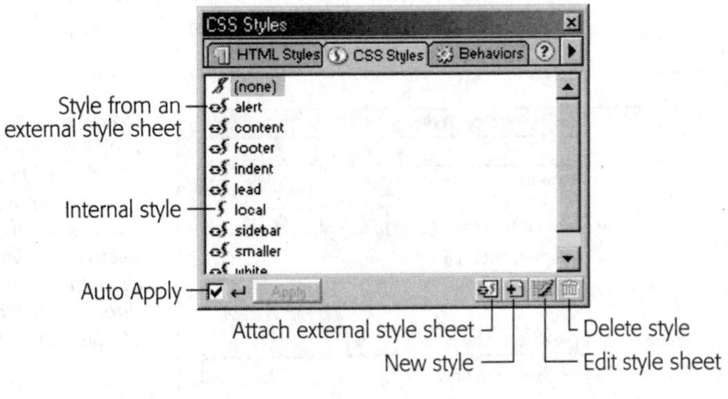

Style from an external style sheet

Internal style

Auto Apply

Attach external style sheet

New style

Delete style

Edit style sheet

Phase 1: Set Up the CSS Type

To create a new style, click the New Style button on the CSS Styles panel (see Figure 8-1), or choose Text→CSS Styles→New Style. The New Style dialog box appears (Figure 8-2), where you begin the process of creating your new style:

- **Type.** Click the appropriate radio button for the kind of style you're creating: *Make Custom Style* (to create your own style from scratch) or *Redefine HTML Tag* (to create a HTML tag style that Dreamweaver will automatically apply to each occurrence of the tag). (See page 210 for a discussion of these two types.)

  The third type offered here, Use CSS Selector, lets you create a style for one of the four *pseudo-classes* Dreamweaver supports or for any valid CSS Selector (see the box on the next page).

- **Name.** If you clicked the Make Custom Style button, type a name for the new style, to replace Dreamweaver's bland default name (*.unnamed1*). All custom styles begin with a period; that's a standard Cascading Style Sheet convention.

Tip: If you're in a desperate hurry, you can leave the period out; Dreamweaver will add it automatically.

Custom style names must *begin* with a letter, too, and can only contain letters and numbers. Dreamweaver lets you know if you use any invalid characters for the name. (It will let you use an underscore like this _ in a name, but some browsers will ignore such a style.)

If you chose Redefine HTML Tag instead, select the HTML tag you want to redefine from the Tag pop-up menu (which appears when you click the Redefine HTML Tag button).

Tip: If you're an HTML guru, you may find it faster to type the tag (minus the brackets) in the Name box. For example, if you want to create a style for all unordered (bulleted) lists, type *ul.*

If you clicked the Use CSS Selector button, Dreamweaver lets you select one of the four CSS pseudo-classes from the menu: a:active, a:hover, a:link, or a:visited (for definitions, see the box on the next page).

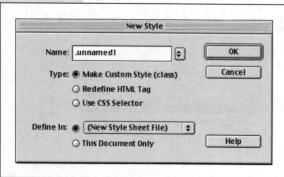

Figure 8-2:
The New Style dialog box is where you choose a type of style and give it a name. Depending on the type of style you choose, the label next to the naming box changes. In this example, since Make Custom Style is selected, the Name label appears. However, if you choose the Redefine Tag option, this changes to (not surprisingly) Tag; or Selector, if you're using the Use CSS Selector option.

- **Define In.** Click This Document Only if you want the styles to apply only to the current Web page (that is, an *internal* style sheet, as described on page 210). To create a new *external* style sheet, choose New Style Sheet File from the Define In pop-up menu. This option not only creates a new external CSS file (which you can save anywhere in your site folder), but adds the necessary code in the current document to link it to that file.

If you've previously linked this document to an external style sheet (see page 210), select that style sheet's name from the pop-up menu; you've just told Dreamweaver to store the new style into this external style sheet file.

Tip: If you create a bunch of internal styles in a particular page, and later realize you'd like to turn them into an external style sheet that you can use in other pages, you're in luck. Dreamweaver has a command for this very task. Open the page containing the internal styles you want to reuse and choose File→Export→Export CSS Styles. A dialog box opens, letting you save the file as an external style sheet. Don't forget to add the .css extension to the end of the file name.

POWER USERS' CLINIC

Pseudo-classes and Other CSS Selectors

When you choose the Use CSS Selector option in the New Style window (Figure 8-3), you aren't actually choosing a third type of style. You're entering the world of *CSS selectors,* where you can access even more advanced style types.

A CSS selector is simply the instruction that tells a Web browser *what* it should apply the CSS formatting rules to. In fact, HTML tag styles and custom styles are *types* of selectors. But there are other, more advanced selectors. For example, an ID selector (which always begins with # symbol like this: *#menu1)* lets you create a style that identifies *one* element on the page. Most people apply it to an object that's controlled by a JavaScript program.

A *contextual selector* is yet another type of CSS selector. Contextual selectors let you create a "smart" style that applies only in certain contexts. For example, you could give a special design to the <b> (bold) tag, but *only* when it appears inside a bulleted (<ul>) list. In this case, the selector would be a combination of the two tags; you would type *ul b* into the Selector box.

You can even create contextual selectors that *combine* a custom style and an HTML tag. For example, you could create a special look for bold words that appear *within* text formatted with a custom style called *.sidebar.* (To create this setup, you'd type *.sidebar b* into the Selector box.)

Clearly, CSS selectors can add plenty of power, but also staggering complexity; to learn how to build them, see one of the references in the sidebar box on page 209.

In addition, Dreamweaver lets you select one of four *pseudo-classes* (a:link, a:active, a:visited, and a:hover) from the Selector menu. The first three correspond to the types of links described on page 30. For example, a:link represents the formatting state of an unvisited link on the page; a:active represents the look of the link it's clicked; a:visited is the link's look after the visitor has already been to the linked page; and a:hover describes the look of the link as the mouse moves over it. This last option works like a rollover image, but for text. (Netscape Navigator 4 doesn't recognize the a:hover style.) To use these pseudo-classes, select each *in this order:* a:link, a:visited, a:hover, and a:active; set the formatting characteristics for each (font color, size, underscore, and so on). For example, you could make your link text appear red and underscored before it's clicked, blinking when the mouse moves over it, purple boldface when clicked, and pale pink after it's been visited. (You might never be hired to do Martha Stewart's Web site, but you could do it.)

If you indicated that you want to create an external style sheet, clicking OK makes a Save Style Sheet As dialog box appear. Navigate to your site's folder and type a name for the new external CSS file. Just as HTML files end in .html, CSS files end in .css.

Tip: If you'll be using this style sheet for all of the pages in your site, you might want to save it in the root folder of your site and give it a general name like *site_styles.css* or *global.css.* (You don't have to type the .css filename extension, by the way; in this case, Dreamweaver adds it.)

No matter what "Define In" option you selected, clicking OK eventually brings you to the Style Definition window.

Phase 2: Defining the Style

The Style Definition window provides access to all of the formatting options available to you and your Web-page text and graphics (see Figure 8-3). A blow-by-blow description of these various options begins on page 224.

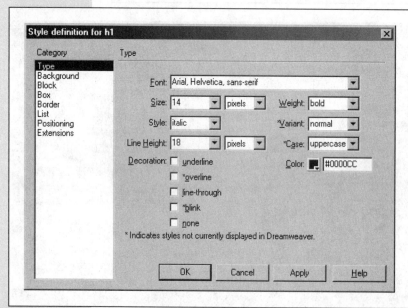

Figure 8-3:
For ultimate formatting control, Dreamweaver lets you set 61 different Cascading Style Sheet properties from the Style Definition window. To learn about these options, see page 224.

Once you've defined the style, click the OK button in the Style Definition window; Dreamweaver adds the style to the specified style sheet, and, if it's a custom style, makes it appear in the CSS panel (Figure 8-1).

The real trick to creating a style is mastering all of the different properties available, such as borders, margins, and background colors, and *then* learning which ones work reliably in the different browsers.

Using Styles

Once you've created styles, applying them is easy. In fact, if you created HTML tag styles, you needn't do anything to apply them, because their selectors (see the box on page 213) automatically dictate which tags they affect.

Linking to an External Style Sheet

Whenever you create an external style sheet, Dreamweaver automatically links it to the current document. To use its styles in a different Web page, however, you must *attach* it to the page.

To do so, open the Web page to which you wish to add the style sheet. Click the Attach Style Sheet button (see Figure 8-1) on the CSS Styles panel. (If the CSS Styles panel isn't open, choose Window→CSS Styles or press Shift-F11.)

In the Select Style Sheet File dialog box that appears, navigate to and double-click the CSS (.css) file you wish to attach to the document; click Yes if Dreamweaver offers to copy the style sheet file into your site's root folder.

POWER USERS' CLINIC

The Parts of a Style

Dreamweaver automatically handles the details of adding the proper CSS code to your pages; but here, if you're looking for something to read in bed, is the behind-the-scenes scoop on how it works.

When you create an internal style sheet, Dreamweaver adds a pair of <style> tags to the head of the page. The opening <style> tag tells a Web browser that the following information is *not* HTML—it's CSS code. When the Web browser encounters the closing </style> tag, it knows the CSS style information has ended.

Each line inside the <style> tag is a single style. An HTML tag style for the Heading 1 tag (<h1>), for example, might look like this:

```
h1 { font-size: 24px; color: #003399}
```

The first part—h1—is called a *selector* (in CSS-speak), and indicates what the style applies to. In this case, wherever the <h1> (heading 1) tag appears, this style will apply.

The information between the braces—{ }—states what formatting the browser should apply. For example, the example above contains two formatting rules for the <h1>

tag. Each rule is called a *declaration* and is composed of a *property* and a *value*. For example, *font-size: 24 px* is one declaration with a property of *font-size* and a value of *24 px*. In other words, this rule tells a Web browser that text inside an <h1> tag should be 24 pixels tall. The second declaration in the example makes the text of all <h1> tags show up using the color #003399.

A custom style looks just like an HTML tag, except that instead of a tag, the selector is a name you've supplied preceded by a dot, like this:

.company { font-size: 24px; color: #003399}

Styles stored in an external style sheet look exactly the same; the only difference is that external style sheets don't include the <style> tags. You can open a page in Code view (choose View→Code) and edit an internal style sheet, just as you would the HTML of the page (see Chapter 9).

To look at the raw style information of an *external* style sheet, however, you'll have to use a text editor other than Dreamweaver. Trying to open a .css file in Dreamweaver simply opens an Edit Style Sheet window (see Figure 8-5).

Dreamweaver adds the necessary HTML code to the head of the Web page, and auto-formats any tags in the document to which the style sheet's HTML Tag styles apply. You'll see the formatting changes take place in the document window immediately after attaching the external style sheet.

If the style sheet contains *custom* styles, on the other hand, you won't see their formatting effects until you apply them to an element on the page, as described next.

Applying a Custom Style

You can apply custom styles to any selection in the document window, whether it's a word, an image, or an entire paragraph. (You can apply any custom style to any element, although doing so doesn't always make sense. If you format a graphic with a style that specifies bold, red Courier type, it won't look any different.)

For example, suppose your company's name appears in a paragraph of text on a Web page that includes a style sheet with a custom style named .company. To format that text using the custom style, you select the name in the document window and apply the style, as described below.

Similarly, to format larger selections, such as an entire paragraph, you'd select the paragraph and apply the custom style. In fact, you can apply a custom style to any HTML tag, such as the <p> (paragraph), <td> (table cell), or <body> tags.

When you apply a custom style (.company, for example) to a tag, Dreamweaver adds a special *class* property to the page's code, like this: <p class="company">. (The leading period disappears when the style shows up in your HTML.) On the other hand, if you apply a class to a selection that *isn't* a tag—a single word you've selected, for example—Dreamweaver wraps the selection within a <span> tag like this: <span class="company">Cosmopolitan Farmer</span>. This tag, in other words, applies a style to a *span* of text that can't be identified by a single tag.

As you can see, it doesn't take much code to add a style to a Web page. A single application of a CSS style might add only 20 characters to your document (for example, <p class="company">). When you compare that instruction with the equivalent HTML code required to produce the same formatted text (such as <font size="5" face="Georgia, Times New Roman, Times, serif" color="#999933">Cosmopolitan Farmer</font>, custom styles look downright petite.

To apply a custom style, select whatever it is you want to style—a single word or an HTML tag, for example. As always, the tag selector in the bottom of the document window is a great way to select a tag (see page 16). Then, in the CSS Styles panel, click the name of the custom style you want. (As shown in Figure 8-1, custom styles are marked by special icons.)

If the Auto Apply checkbox in the CSS Styles panel is turned on (Figure 8-2), Dreamweaver applies the class to the selection (using the <span> tag if it's a small text selection, or using the Class property if it's an HTML tag). If Auto Apply is turned off, you have to click the style name and then click the Apply button.

Tip: You can also apply a class from the document window's tag selector, as shown in Figure 8-4.

It bears repeating: Because Dreamweaver is limited in its display of many CSS properties, the only sure way to see how the page will look is to preview it in a Web browser. (See page 37 for more detail on previewing.)

Figure 8-4:
You can apply a custom style directly to a tag using the document window's tag selector. Just right-click (Control-Click) the tag you wish to format, and then select the custom style from the Set Class submenu. In addition, the tag selector lets you know if a tag has a custom style applied to it. If so, the style's name is added at the end of the tag. For example, in the bottom figure, a custom style named .photo is applied to a graphic (the <img> tag) on the page.

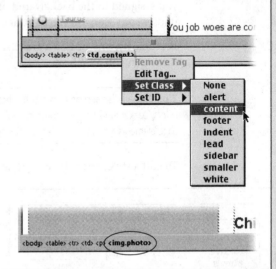

Un-Applying a Custom Style

To remove a style from an object on a Web page, simply select the element and click (none) in the CSS Styles list (see Figure 8-2). You can also choose Text→CSS Styles→None to accomplish the same thing.

Tip: If you've applied a custom style to a selection of text, you don't actually have to select all of the text to remove the style. Just click anywhere inside it and click None in the CSS Styles list (or choose Text→CSS Styles→None). Dreamweaver is smart enough to realize you want to remove the style applied to the text. (If you applied the style to a tag, Dreamweaver removes the Class property. If you applied the style using the <span> tag, Dreamweaver removes the span tag.)

You can't, however, remove *HTML tag* styles from tags. For example, suppose you've redefined the <h1> tag using the steps outlined on page 212. If your page has three Heading 1 (<h1>) paragraphs, and you want the third heading to have no style, you're out of luck. The only way to remove the formatting is to delete the <h1> style altogether (see page 219), which, of course, would remove the formatting from all three headings. In this case, you'd have been better off creating a custom style that you apply to the first two headlines only.

Manipulating Styles

As with anything in Dreamweaver, styles are easy enough to edit, duplicate, or delete; all you need is a map of the terrain.

Editing Styles

While building a Web site, you continually refine your designs. That chartreuse color you assigned to the background of your pages may have looked great at 2 a.m., but it loses something in the light of day.

Fortunately, one of CSS's greatest selling points is how easy it makes updating the formatting on a Web site.

Tip: Although this section talks mostly about text styling, you can also use CSS styles to add background colors, background images, borders, and other options that can apply to images, table cells, and other page elements. For an example of a CSS style applied to an image, see the tutorial on page 242.

To edit a style, open the Edit Style Sheet window using your favorite approach:

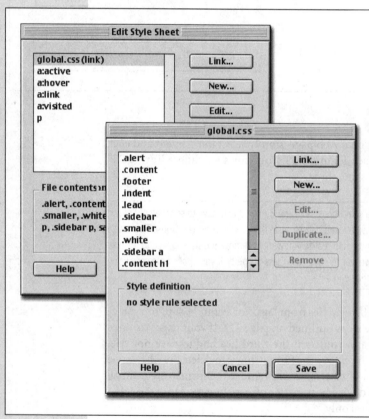

Figure 8-5:
When you open the Edit Style Sheet window, Dreamweaver lists all internal styles (styles added to the current document only) and each external style sheet attached to the page. External style sheets—global.css in the top figure, for example—are indicated by the word link *in parentheses. To edit the styles in the external style sheet, you must first select it in the Edit Style Sheet window and click Edit. There are two shortcuts that let you bypass this two-step process: First, you can double-click a .css file in the Site Files window (see page 375 to learn how the Site window works). Or, press Ctrl (Option) when clicking the Edit Style Sheet button in the CSS Styles panel. In both cases, Dreamweaver automatically opens the list of styles for the external style sheet (bottom).*

- Choose Text→CSS Styles→Edit Style Sheet.

- Click the Edit Style Sheet button on the CSS Styles panel (Figure 8-1).

- Press Ctrl+Shift+E (⌘-Shift-E).

Unlike the CSS Styles panel, the Edit Style Sheet window lists *all* styles—custom, HTML tag, and CSS selector styles. (If you want to edit a style in an external style sheet, you'll need to select that file name in the list and click Edit before proceeding.)

Now just double-click the name of the style in the Edit Style Sheet window.

The Style Definition window opens (see Figure 8-3). This is the same window you used when first creating the style (see page 211). Make your changes to the style and then click OK.

If the style belongs to an external style sheet, Dreamweaver returns you to that sheet's list of styles (see bottom image in Figure 8-5). Click Save to save the changes to the external style sheet and return to the Edit Style Sheet window.

If you're editing an internal style, Dreamweaver saves these changes to the style sheet and returns you to the Edit Style Sheet window.

When you click Done, you return to the document window; Dreamweaver reformats the page to reflect any changes you made to styles used in the current document.

Deleting a Style

At some point, you may find you've created a style that you don't need after all. Maybe you redefined the HTML <code> tag, for example, and realize you haven't even used the tag in your site. There's no need to keep it around; it just takes up precious space in the style sheet.

To delete a style from a style sheet, choose Text→CSS Styles→Edit Style Sheet, or click the Edit Style Sheet button on the CSS Styles panel (see Figure 8-1), or press Ctrl+Shift+E (⌘-Shift-E).

If you want to delete a style in an external style sheet, select the name of the .css file in the list and click the Edit button (or use one of the shortcuts described in Figure 8-5).

Now all you have to do is click the name of the style you want to nuke (any kind of style—custom, HTML tag, or CSS selector) and then click Remove. Dreamweaver removes the style's name from the list. (If the dearly departed style was in an external style sheet, click the Save button to return to the Edit Style Sheet window.) Finally, click Done. Dreamweaver returns to the document window and removes any formatting that was applied by the deleted style.

Unfortunately, deleting a custom style *doesn't* delete any references to the style in the pages of your site. For example, if you've created a style called .company and applied it throughout your site, and you then delete that style from the style sheet, Dreamweaver doesn't remove the <span> tags or class properties that refer to the style. In other words, your pages will still be littered with orphaned code like this— <span class="company">Cosmopolitan Farmer</span>—even though the text loses the styling. (See how to solve this problem using Dreamweaver's powerful Find and Replace tool on page 476.)

Duplicating or Renaming a Style

Dreamweaver makes it easy to duplicate a CSS style, which can be handy when you've created, say, an HTML tag style, and now decide you would actually rather make it a custom style. Or you may want to use the formatting options from one style as a starting off point for a new style. Either way, you start by duplicating an existing style.

To duplicate a style, open the Edit Style Sheet dialog box (choose Text→CSS Styles→Edit Style Sheet, for example), select the style's name, and click Duplicate.

The Duplicate Style window appears (see Figure 8-6), where you can give the duplicated style a new name, reassign its Type setting, use the Define In menu to switch it from an internal to an external style sheet, and so on.

When you click OK, you can edit the new style, just as you would any other style (see page 218).

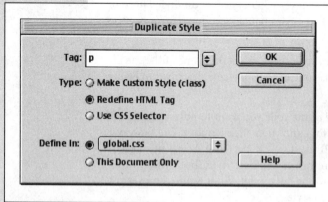

Figure 8-6:
The Duplicate Style dialog box looks and acts precisely like the New Style box (see page 212). You can select a new style type, name it, and add it to an external or internal style sheet. The only difference is that the duplicated style retains all of the CSS properties of the original style.

Tip: This procedure is the only way you can rename a custom style: After you select the custom style in the Edit Style Sheets window, click Duplicate and then type a new name in the Name box.

More About Styles

As you begin to pile styles onto your pages, you may start to notice some peculiar behaviors as styles start to interact. The rules governing these interactions can be complex, but boil down to two main concepts: *inheritance* and *cascading*.

Using Microsoft Word to Prepare Content for CSS

It's easy enough to copy text from a word processing program, paste it into a Dreamweaver document, and then apply paragraph formatting and CSS styles. But when you need to create hundreds of Web pages, this time-consuming ritual can drive you quietly mad.

But if your company or clients use Word 2000, 2001, or XP, and you use Cascading Style Sheets in your site, you can streamline this process. You take advantage of the fact that Word offers style sheets of its own, which it converts to CSS styles when you save a Word document as HTML (see page 49).

When Word exports the document, it records your style information as an internal CSS style sheet in the head of the HTML file. Once in Dreamweaver, you'll find that Word's built in heading styles—like Heading 1, Heading 2, and Heading 3—turn into the appropriate HTML heading tags, <h1>, <h2>, <h3>. Word's Normal style is converted to a plain paragraph—the <p> tag.

Custom styles you created in Word, on the other hand, become custom styles in Dreamweaver. What began life as Word paragraph styles are applied as custom styles to the paragraph tag (<p class="copyright">), and Word's character styles are applied as spans (<span class="company">). (One caution: when creating a character style in Word, don't specify the font. Changing the font of the style adds extra information to the Web page that Dreamweaver can't automatically remove.)

Often, however, the formatting that worked in Word (bold, red, whatever) isn't what you'll want on the final Web page. One way to redefine all of these styles is to edit them one at a time—but life's too short.

A better way is to create an external style sheet filled with styles whose names *exactly* match the style names from Word (and formatted to your taste). Then *delete* the internal style sheet from the imported Web page. When you link the document to your external style sheet, you'll see your preferred formatting magically reappear everywhere a Word style had been applied.

Here's an example. You have a Word document that includes one Heading 1-style paragraph and several paragraphs in a style called Content. You save it as a Word HTML document (page 49) and bring the page into Dreamweaver using the import Word HTML command (page 219). Then delete the internal styles (see page 219) and apply an external style sheet that includes a redefined <h1> tag style and a custom style called .content. Voila: instant formatting.

Using this trick, you free yourself from the tedious process of applying custom styles to every page. You also give the site's content producers—the people creating the text in Word—the responsibility of identifying the different text elements in each page, saving you many a weekends' worth of effort.

Inheritance

Imagine that you've created a new style by redefining the paragraph tag (<p>). This style has a font type of Arial, is red, and is 24 pixels tall. Then you select a single word in a paragraph make it bold. When you use the Property inspector's bold button to do this, Dreamweaver quietly wraps that word in a pair of <b> HTML tags.

When a browser loads the page, it formats all paragraphs in Arial, red, 24 pixels, because that's how you defined the <p> tag. But what happens when the browser suddenly encounters the <b> tag? Since you didn't redefine the <b> tag in red, Arial, 24 pixels, the browser scratches its little silicon head: Should the browser just resort to the *default* font, size, and color when it gets to the <b> tag?

No, of course not. The bolded word should look just like the rest of the paragraph—Arial, red, 24 pixels—but be bold *too*. Fortunately, that's how cascading style sheets work; the <b> tag *inherits* the formatting of the surrounding <p> tags.

In other words, nested HTML tags inherit the properties of tags that surround them. A tag that's nested inside of another tag—that <b> tag inside the <p> tag, for example—is called a *child*, while the enclosing tag is called the *parent*.

Inheritance passes from parent to child; so, in this example, the <p> tag (the parent) passes on the Arial font, red color, and 24 pixel size to the <b> tag (the child). But, just as children have their own unique qualities, the <b> tag adds its own quality—boldness—to the properties of its parent.

Note: Inheritance applies to all styles, not just HTML tag styles. If you apply a custom style, for example, to a <td> (table cell) tag, all tags inside the cell–paragraphs, images, and so on–inherit the properties of the custom style.

Inheritance comes in quite handy at times. For instance, say you want to display *all* text on a page (paragraphs, headings, unordered lists, and links) using the Verdana font. You could, of course, knock off for the week and redefine *every* html tag used to format text—<h1>, <h2>, <p>, <a>, <ul>, and so on, or create a custom style and then manually apply it to all text on the page.

However, a faster technique would be to take advantage of inheritance. Every Web page contains a <body> tag, which contains all the elements of your page. The <body> tag, therefore, is the parent of *all* HTML you see on a page—images, paragraphs, headings, and so on. To quickly format all text, you could create an HTML tag style for the <body> tag using Verdana, or create a custom style using that font and apply it to the <body> tag. Every bit of text inside the body—all children—then inherit the Verdana font property.

Note: Netscape 4 has trouble with inheritance; it doesn't pass properties on to tags inside of tables. So say you created a style for the body tag that uses the font Arial. Text in a table you add to the page won't appear in Arial as it should. The fix: Apply the style to the <td> tags inside each table, as well. Only then does Netscape 4 correctly apply the style to what's inside the table cells.

Cascading

At times, styles can conflict. Let's say you redefine the <h1> tag in an external style sheet, so that all <h1> tags will show up in red, using the Arial font. But now you attach this external style sheet to a Web page that already has an *internal* style sheet, whose <h1> tag style has been set to Times, 24 pixels.

When a Web browser has to display any text formatted as a Heading 1 paragraph, it runs into a little dilemma. The page has two different styles—two sets of formatting rules—for the *same tag*. So which does the browser choose: the style from the internal style sheet or the style from the external style sheet?

The answer is both. The browser merges the two styles into a sort of hybrid, following these rules:

- Properties that don't conflict are applied as usual. In the above example, the red color property only exists in the external style, while only the internal style specifies a font *size*. So far, the browser knows that, for this page, text inside <h1> tags should be both red *and* 24 pixels tall.

- When properties do conflict, a Web browser uses the property from the "closest" or more specific style. External styles (since they're in a separate file) are not as specific as the internal styles, which were created specifically to style this one page. In this case, the font Times (specified in the <h1> tag style in the internal style sheet) wins.

To summarize this example, then, the Web browser determines that text inside an <h1> tag on this Web page should be Times, red, 24 pixels tall.

This cascading effect applies to custom styles, as well. When there's a direct conflict between properties from a custom style and an HTML tag style, the custom style prevails. Because custom styles must be applied directly to a tag—*<h1 class= "specialHeadline">*—they're considered more specific than the HTML tag style. After all, you added the style to a specific instance of the <h1> tag on the page.

Note: In the CSS version of Rock, Paper, Scissors, HTML text formatting beats CSS formatting. Suppose you used the Property inspector to apply a size of 2 to some text and later apply a custom style, defined to have 48-pixel-tall text, to the same words. Web browsers will display the text as an HTML font size of 2, ignoring the CSS style. (The HTML styles panel offers a quick way to remove HTML formatting [page 79].)

These same rules apply when child elements inherit properties from parent elements, as described on the facing page. For example, if you apply a purple, Arial-font custom style to the body of a page, then child elements (anything within the <body> tag) will inherit those properties. If you then redefine the paragraph tag so that paragraph text is green, paragraph text will inherit the Arial font from the body, but will ignore the purple color in favor of the green you specified when redefining its own—paragraph—tag.

If you're still reading, and haven't set this book aside in hopes that the swelling in your brain will subside, you've probably adequately absorbed the notion that the application of style properties can be quite complex. However, this information may come in handy. If you find that the styles you create don't seem to work the way you think they should, look to see if you've applied a style to a parent element, or whether you have two conflicting styles applied to the same text or object.

Style Properties

Cascading Style Sheets are a powerful and complex technology, providing *many* more formatting options than HTML alone, whose formatting options are few enough to fit, for the most part, onto the Property inspector. In fact, Dreamweaver lets you set 61 different CSS properties using the Style Definition window. The following pages cover each of the eight Style Definition categories and the properties available from each. (If you'd prefer an online reference, don't miss the built-in CSS reference available from the Window→Reference command; it's described more completely on page 257.)

Tip: As noted earlier, not all Web browsers can display the many different formatting options available through Cascading Style Sheets. Dreamweaver, in its zeal to give you access to as many options as possible, actually lets you set properties that don't work in *any browser at all* (see the Page Break property on page 235.) It can be frustrating to find a really cool style sheet property, only to realize that it doesn't work in most Web browsers.

There is hope, however. Webreview.com's invaluable Master Compatibility Chart saves you from groping around in the dark. This frequently updated Web page lists which CSS properties work on which browsers, broken down by Mac, Windows, and browser version. You'll find this indispensable guide at *www.webreview.com/style/css1/charts/mastergrid.shtml.*

Type Properties

As the name implies, the Type category of the Style Definition window lets you set formatting options that affect text (see Figure 8-7).

- **Font.** You choose a font for the style from the Font menu. As with the <font> tag (as described on page 70), you choose from *groups* of fonts rather than the specific one you have your heart set on. Unfortunately, your array of choices is no better than in HTML. Dreamweaver also lets you create your own "first-choice, second-choice…" font choices from this menu, exactly as described on page 71.

- **Size.** Unlike HTML, where font size is defined using a number from 1 to 7, CSS offers a dizzying array of size choices.

  If you want to make sure your text appears at the same size regardless of browser or platform, type a number in the Size box and select Pixels from the unit menu to its right. 12 pixels is a good size for regular type.

  There's one downside to this approach: Pixel values prevent visitors from adjusting the size of text on the screen using in most Web browsers' text size up/down controls. To give visitors more control, use one of the relative measurements on the bottom part of the pop-up menu (**small, large,** and so on), which are based on a Web browser's default font size (and *can* be adjusted by your visitors).

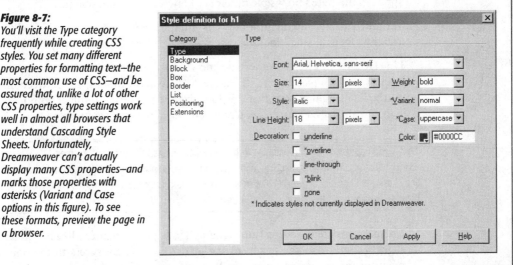

Figure 8-7:
You'll visit the Type category frequently while creating CSS styles. You set many different properties for formatting text—the most common use of CSS—and be assured that, unlike a lot of other CSS properties, type settings work well in almost all browsers that understand Cascading Style Sheets. Unfortunately, Dreamweaver can't actually display many CSS properties—and marks those properties with asterisks (Variant and Case options in this figure). To see these formats, preview the page in a browser.

- **Weight.** Weight refers to the thickness of the font. The Weight menu offers thirteen different choices. Normal and bold are the most common, and work in all browsers that understand CSS. See Figure 8-8 for details.

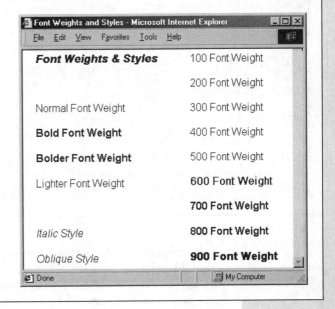

Figure 8-8:
The numeric values 100–900 are intended to work with fonts that have many different weights (ultrathin, thin, light, extra bold, and so on). 400 is normal; 700 is the same as bold. However, in today's browsers, you'll notice no difference between the values 100-500, and only slight changes in the thickness of the type at each higher level. The 900 option results in an extra bold.

- **Style.** In this peculiar instance, Style means **italic, oblique,** or **normal.** Technically, italic is a custom-designed, emphatic version of a type face, *like this.* Oblique, on the other hand, is just a computerized adaptation of a normal font, in which each letter is inclined a certain number of degrees to the right. In practical application, there's no visible difference between italic and oblique.

- **Variant.** This pop-up menu simply lets you specify SMALL CAPS type, if you like—a slightly formal, fancy-looking type style much favored by attorneys' offices.

- **Line Height.** Line height, otherwise known as *leading,* refers to the space between lines of text in a paragraph (see Figure 8-9). To allow more space between lines, set the line height greater than the font size. (If you type a number without a % sign, Dreamweaver assumes you're specifying a line height in pixels.)

Tip: A good approach for line height is to type in a percentage measurement, such as *120%,* which is relative to the size of the text (see "Size" above); if your text is 10 pixels tall, the space from the base of one line of text to the next is 12 pixels (120% of 10). Now, if you change the size of the text, the *relative* space between lines remains the same.

Normal, the default setting (top paragraph in Figure 8-9), uses a line height that's slightly larger than the height of the text. You don't get access to the pop-up menu of measurement units (pixels, points, %, and so on) unless you choose (**value**) from this pop-up menu.

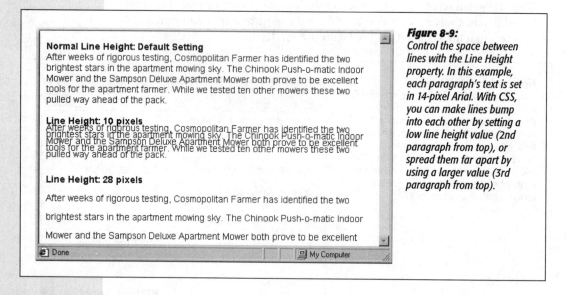

Normal Line Height: Default Setting
After weeks of rigorous testing, Cosmopolitan Farmer has identified the two brightest stars in the apartment mowing sky. The Chinook Push-o-matic Indoor Mower and the Sampson Deluxe Apartment Mower both prove to be excellent tools for the apartment farmer. While we tested ten other mowers these two pulled way ahead of the pack.

Line Height: 10 pixels
After weeks of rigorous testing, Cosmopolitan Farmer has identified the two brightest stars in the apartment mowing sky. The Chinook Push-o-matic Indoor Mower and the Sampson Deluxe Apartment Mower both prove to be excellent tools for the apartment farmer. While we tested ten other mowers these two pulled way ahead of the pack.

Line Height: 28 pixels
After weeks of rigorous testing, Cosmopolitan Farmer has identified the two brightest stars in the apartment mowing sky. The Chinook Push-o-matic Indoor Mower and the Sampson Deluxe Apartment Mower both prove to be excellent

Done — My Computer

Figure 8-9:
Control the space between lines with the Line Height property. In this example, each paragraph's text is set in 14-pixel Arial. With CSS, you can make lines bump into each other by setting a low line height value (2nd paragraph from top), or spread them far apart by using a larger value (3rd paragraph from top).

- **Case.** From this menu, you can set up automatic capitalization of the text in this style. To capitalize the first letter of each word, choose **capitalize.** The **uppercase** option gives you all-capitals typing, while **lowercase** makes all letters lowercase. The default value is **none,** which has no effect on the text.

- **Decoration.** This strange assortment of five checkboxes let you dress up your text, mostly in unattractive ways. **Underline, Overline,** and **Line-through** add horizontal lines above, below, or right through the affected text, respectively. Turning on **Blink** makes affected text blink on and off; unless you want to appear on one of those "worst Web site of the week" lists, avoid it. You can only apply one decorative type per style.

Tip: On certain forward-thinking Web sites these days, text links don't appear underlined; instead, they show up in a different color.

You, too, can perform this trendy design stunt, just by redefining the <a> tag with Cascading Style Sheets, turning on the none option for the Decoration property. Voila! No more underlines.

Use this technique with care, however; most Web surfers have grown accustomed to associating underlines with clickable links. If you do remove an underline, use some other cue—bold and colorful text, for example—to indicate that the text is a link.

- **Color.** Set the color of the style's text using Dreamweaver's color box, which is described on page 30.

Background Properties

While you're probably familiar with changing the background colors of Web pages, tables, and table cells, Cascading Style Sheets provide even more options for adding colors and images to the backgrounds of your styles (see Figure 8-10).

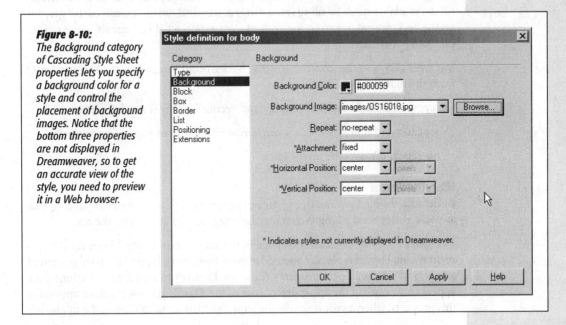

Figure 8-10:
The Background category of Cascading Style Sheet properties lets you specify a background color for a style and control the placement of background images. Notice that the bottom three properties are not displayed in Dreamweaver, so to get an accurate view of the style, you need to preview it in a Web browser.

Background Color

Any object can have a background color: a single word, a paragraph, or the Web page itself. For instance, using this color box, you can redefine the <td> (table cell) tag, for example, using a light blue background color; every table cell on the page gets filled with that light blue color.

Background Image

Add a background image to the style by clicking the Browse button and selecting an image from your site. You can also type an absolute URL, starting with *http://*, to use an image off the Web. (Remember that Dreamweaver can't display images specified with an absolute URL; you'll have to preview the page in a Web browser connected to the Internet to see the effect.)

To fill your entire page background with some repeating graphic, you could either redefine the <body> tag using this property, or create a custom style with a Background Image property and apply it to the <body> tag as described on page 216.

Of course, you can also set up a background image using the Page Properties window (see page 29). The main advantage of the CSS method is that you can control how the image tiles (repeats) and where it's placed on the page (see below). Furthermore, using CSS, you can add background images to any *individual* element on your page: paragraphs, tables, layers, and so on.

Repeat

Background images—either on the background of a page or of a table—normally fill the available space by tiling (repeating) across and down. A small carrot graphic on the background of a page, for example, appears as a field of carrots—one next to each other, row after row.

But with CSS, you can control how the background image repeats. You can select from the following options:

- **repeat** tiles the image horizontally and vertically. This is the default behavior.
- **repeat-x** and **repeat-y** create a single row or column of images, respectively.
- **no-repeat** displays the image once.

Web Attachment

By default, the background image on a page scrolls with the rest of the page, so that as you scroll to read a long Web page, the image scrolls along with the text.

But using CSS, you can lock the image in place by choosing **fixed** from the Attachment menu. For example, say you added your company's logo to the background of a page and set the Repeat property (described above) to no-repeat. The logo now appears only once in the upper-left corner of the page. If you use the *fixed* option for this property, when a visitor scrolls the page, the logo remains fixed in the upper-left corner. (Choosing **scroll** from the Attachment menu means, of course, that the background image will scroll with the page.)

Note: Attachment properties don't work in Netscape 4.

Horizontal and Vertical Position

Using these controls, you can specify a position for the affected Web-page element. The Horizontal position options are **left, center, right** and (**value**); for (value), type an exact number in the box and select a unit of measurement from the menu to the right. Similarly, the Vertical position options include **top, center, bottom** and (**value**).

These positioning options refer to the position of the styled object. For example, suppose you created a custom style that included a background image with horizontal and vertical position both set to *center*. Then you applied that custom style to a paragraph. The background image would appear in the center of that *paragraph*, not in the center of the Web page (see Figure 8-11).

Likewise, if you set the horizontal position of the image to 10 pixels and the vertical position to 20 pixels, the image would start 10 pixels from the left edge of the paragraph and 20 pixels from the top edge.

And if you wanted to place an image in the exact middle of the page, you'd choose *center* from both the Horizontal and Vertical Position menus; set the repeat property to no-repeat; and apply this style to the page's <body> tag (see Figure 8-11).

Figure 8-11:
Background images aren't just for the body of a Web page. You can apply styles that include background images to any selection, even a paragraph of text. Here, a custom style with a background image is set to no-repeat (the image won't tile) and to center horizontally and vertically. The style was applied to the body of the page, resulting in the graphic appearing smack dab in the middle of the window. The same style was applied to a paragraph; this time, the image floats right in the middle of the paragraph.

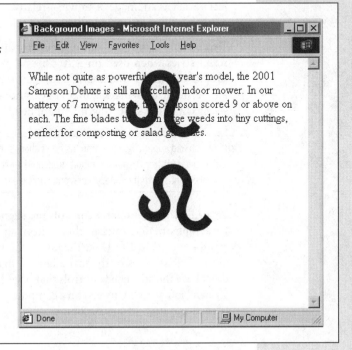

Block Properties

The Block Properties panel is a hodge-podge of CSS settings that affect how letters and words are displayed. Despite this category's name, these properties don't just apply to block-level elements (paragraphs, headlines, and so on). You can also apply a style with these properties to even a single word or two within a paragraph. (The one exception is the Text Align property, which can apply only to paragraphs and other block-level elements.)

- **Word Spacing.** This property helps you clean up text by adding or removing space *between* words. The default value, **normal,** leaves a normal, single space between words; if you want words in a sentence to be spaced apart like this, then type a value of about 10 pixels. (Choose Value from the first pop-up menu, then the units you want from the second one.) The bigger the number, the larger the gap between words. You can also *remove* space between words by using a negative number—agreatchoicewhenyouwanttomakeyourpagesdifficulttoread.

  Unfortunately, only a few Web browsers (Navigator 6, Opera, and the Mac version of Internet Explorer) recognize this property, so you'd be well advised to avoid it for now.

- **Letter Spacing.** This property works just like word spacing, but governs the space between *letters*. To add space l i k e t h i s, type a value of about 5 pixels. The result can make long passages of text hard to read, but a little space between letters can add a dramatic flair to short headlines and movie titles.

- **Vertical Alignment.** With this property, you can control the alignment of an object—such as an image or movie—relative to other items around it. This feature works a lot like the image-alignment options discussed on page 102.

  Two notable additions—**sub** and **super**—also let you create superscript and subscript styles when used on text. This property is a godsend when you want to properly format a trademark, copyright symbol, or footnote reference. For example, in the trademark symbol in Cosmopolitan Farmer™, the letters TM were selected and the super alignment applied.

Tip: The sub and super alignment options don't change the size of text. If you want to create true subscript or superscript (for chemical symbols, trademark or copyright symbols, and so on), you should also use a smaller font size in the style; 75 percent works great.

- **Text Align.** This property controls the alignment of a block-level element like a paragraph or table. You can choose from among the usual suspects—**left, center, right**—or even **justify.** (Like the text in this paragraph, justified text has both the left and right edges of the text aligned.) Just note, however, that Web browsers don't have the advanced controls that page-layout software does; they usually do an awful job of justifying text on a computer screen. The results are usually difficult to read and ugly. Avoid this option.

- **Text Indent.** This useful option lets you indent the first line of a paragraph. If you enter .25 and choose *in* from the pop-up menu, you give each paragraph an attractive quarter-inch first-line indent, exactly as in a real word processor.

  You can also use a *negative* number, which makes the first line extend past the *left* margin of the paragraph, creating a hanging indent (or *outdent*)—a nice effect for bulleted lists or glossary pages. (Beware; some browsers have trouble with negative values for this property.)

- **Whitespace.** This property controls how the browser displays extra white space (spaces, tabs, returns, and so on). Web browsers normally ignore extra spaces in the HTML of a page, reducing them to a single space character between words and other elements (see page 60). The **pre** option functions just like the HTML <pre> tag: Extra white space (like tabs, multiple spaces, and carriage returns) *in the HTML code* appear in the document window (see page 60 for more on this option). The **nowrap** option prevents lines from breaking (and wrapping to the next line) when they reach the end of the browser window.

Note: All versions of Internet Explorer ignore this setting.

Box Properties

CSS lets you control the space that appears around any affected Web page element. You work with those properties in the Box category of the Style Definition window (see Figure 8-12).

- **Width and Height.** You can specify a width and height for any styled object using these properties. Web designers use these settings most often to control layers, using Dreamweaver's Layer tools (see Chapter 12). But they can also affect other Web elements; for example, if you want a paragraph to be 100 pixels wide, create a custom style with the Width property set to 100 pixels and apply it to the paragraph.

- **Float.** If you want to move an object to the left or right of the page and have other content wrap around it, use the Float property. For example, if you want an image to appear at the right side of the page and have text flow around its left and bottom edges, choose **right** from the Float menu. The option behaves just like the right and left alignment options for images (page 102) and tables (page 144).

- **Clear.** Clear *prevents* an element from wrapping around any object with a right or left Float property (see above). You might want, for example, all Heading 1 paragraphs to stand out on their own lines and not wrap around an image with a right float; in that case, you'd choose the **right** option from the Clear menu when you're styling the <h1> tag.

- **Padding.** Padding is the gap that separates the content of the style—such as a paragraph of text or an image—and its border (see Figure 8-12 on page 232). For example, if you put a 1-pixel border around an image and want to add 10 pixels of space between the image and the border, type *10* into each padding box and choose *pixels* from the pop-up menu. You can control the padding around each edge of the style separately.

- **Margin.** The margin is the outermost space surrounding an element (see Figure 8-12). It surrounds the border and padding properties of the style and lets you add space between one element and another. Use any of the values—pixels, percentages, and so on—that CSS supports.

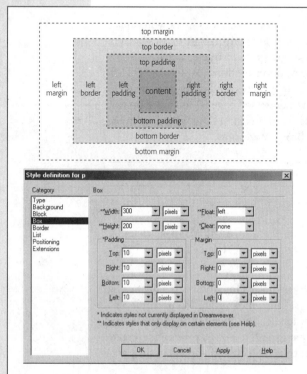

Figure 8-12:
Top: In the CSS Box Model, every style is composed of multiple boxes, one inside the other. Each box controls certain display properties of the style. For example, the outermost box of a style is called the margin. It controls the space between the border of the style and any other objects around the styled object such as images, paragraphs, or tables. Bottom: This dialog box is where you can control the margins and padding around a styled object that uses the Box category. Its fields correspond to the measurements shown in the top diagram.

Tip: You can also use the Margin properties to *eliminate* a margin entirely, if, for example, you don't like the space that browsers automatically insert between paragraphs. Type *0* in the Top margin box and *0* in the Bottom margin box to create a style with no top or bottom margins.

Border Properties

Only a few elements can have borders in HTML: tables, images, and cells. With CSS, however, you can add a border to any object from an image to a paragraph to a single exclamation mark (see Figure 8-13). Even better, you can control each *side* of the border independently with its own width and color settings, or even turn *off* some parts of the border.

- **Border Widths.** You can set the border around each side of a styled object separately. Choose one of the preset widths—**thin, medium, thick,** or **auto**—or, if you choose (**value**) from the pop-up menu, you can type a value into the Width box and select a unit of measurement from the pop-up menu to the right. Again, you can choose from a wide range of types: **pixels, percentage, inches,** and so on. If you want to eliminate the border on one side, type *0* into the appropriate box.

Figure 8-13:
Top: Add colorful and stylish borders to paragraphs, images, tables, and links with the CSS Border properties. Turning on only the bottom border for a paragraph is a great way to add a horizontal rule between paragraphs. While HTML's Horizontal Rule object also does this, only CSS lets you control the color. Bottom: The eight different border styles provide interesting visual diversity to the otherwise plain border. Unfortunately, although Opera and Navigator 6 display these styles well, Internet Explorer displays the last four options as solid lines.

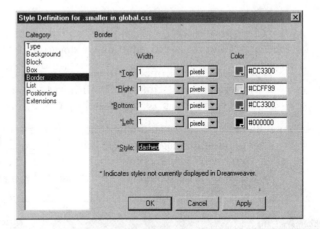

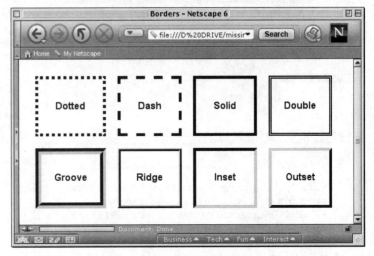

• **Border Colors.** You can color each of the four borders individually using the ubiquitous Dreamweaver color box (see page 30). If you don't assign any colors, but do assign border *widths,* Dreamweaver makes the borders black.

• **Style.** Specify the type of line used for the border with the Style menu. Dreamweaver gives you more options than a frame shop: **none** (the default choice), **dotted, dashed, solid, double, groove, ridge, inset,** and **outset.**

Note: As noted by the asterisks (*) in the dialog box, these borders, like many other CSS elements, don't show up in Dreamweaver itself; you can see them only by previewing your page in a browser. Even then, you may not see the borders even if you set width and color. If that's the case, make sure you selected a Style for the border; you've probably left it on the default setting—none.

List Properties

To exercise greater control over bulleted and numbered lists, use the CSS options on the List panel of the Style Definition window (see Figure 8-14).

- **Type.** Select the type of bullet to be used in front of a list item. Options include: **disc, circle, square, decimal** (1., 2., 3.), **lower-roman** (i, ii, iii), **upper-roman** (I, II, III), **lower-alpha** (a, b, c), **upper-alpha** (A, B, C), and **none** (no bullet at all).

- **Bullet Image.** For the ultimate control of your bullet icon, skip the boring options preprogrammed into a Web browser (like disc, circle, or decimal) and supply your own. Click the Browse button and select a graphics file from your site folder. Make sure the graphic is appropriate bullet material: in other words, small.

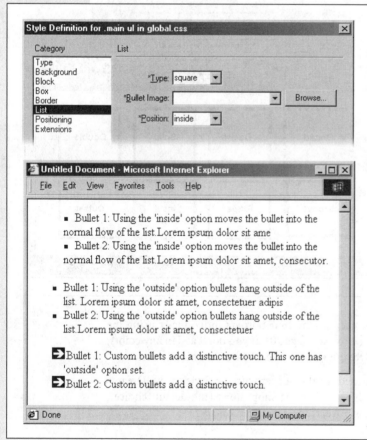

Figure 8-14:
Top: Take control of your bulleted and numbered lists using the Style Definition window's List panel. With Cascading Style Sheets, you can even supply your own graphic bullets.

Bottom: A bullet-crazed Web page, for illustration purposes. Parading down the screen, you can see "inside" bullets, "outside" bullets, and bullets made from graphics.

Note: The bullet image property doesn't work in Netscape 4 (surprise, surprise).

- **Position.** This property controls how the bullet is placed relative to the list item's text. The **outside** option places the bullet outside of the margin of the text, exactly the way bulleted lists normally appear on a Web page. **Inside,** on the other hand, displays the bullet within the text margin, so that the left edge of the *bullet* aligns with the left margin; Figure 8-14 should make the effect clearer.

Positioning Properties

Cascading Style Sheets are also intended as a structural aid for laying out Web pages. But Dreamweaver's own Layer tools achieve the same effects much more easily (Chapter 12). For best results, skip the CSS Positioning settings and use layer tools instead.

Extensions

The final category in the Style Definition window is listed last for a good reason. Only one property in this category works in more than one Web browser, and two of them don't work in *any* current browser.

- **Page Break.** This property specifies, when your visitor makes a printout of your page, whether a page breaks before or after the styled object. You could apply this, for example, to the <h1> in order to make sure each printed page begins with a Heading 1 paragraph—if, that is, any browser recognized this property. None do.

- **Cursor.** Of all the Extension properties, this one holds the most promise. When a visitor moves the mouse over an object with this style applied, this property changes the cursor shape to one of fifteen different designs (a hand, an hourglass, or a crosshair, for example). Internet Explorer 4 and above, Netscape Navigator 6, and Opera 5 all recognize this professional-looking property.

- **Filter.** The Filter property can apply many interesting visual effects to a page; the Filter property, for example, can add a drop shadow to an image. Unfortunately, this Microsoft-only option works in the Windows version of Internet Explorer, and no other browsers.

Cascading Style Sheets Tutorial

In this tutorial, you'll create an external style sheet for a Web page on the Cosmopolitan Farmer Web site.

Note: As usual, this tutorial requires some half-finished starter documents from the Web. Using your Web browser, visit *www.sawmac.com/missing.* Click the Tutorials link to go to the tutorials page. Then click the link CSS Tutorial–Mac files or CSS Tutorial–Win files, depending on the computer you're using.

When the files are downloaded and decompressed, you should have a folder named DWCSS on your computer, containing the Web pages and graphics for this tutorial.

Creating an External Style Sheet

Once you've downloaded the tutorial files and opened Dreamweaver, choose the DWCSS folder as your site folder, using the site-definition routine described on page 24. (In brief, you choose Site→New Site, type something like *CSS Tutorial* into the Site Name field, click the folder icon next to the Local Root Folder field, navigate to and select the folder DWCSS, and then click Choose or Select. Finally, click OK.)

Now you're ready to begin defining a style sheet; in this example, you'll create a collection of styles for the Reviews section of the Cosmopolitan Farmer Web site.

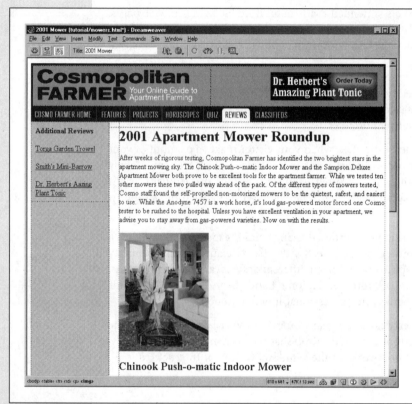

Figure 8-15:
Add style to this rather plain Web page using Cascading Style Sheets. In this tutorial, you'll improve the rather ho-hum appearance of the main section of this page—the white area in this figure.

1. **Choose File→Open; navigate to, and double-click, the file in the DWCSS folder called *mowers.html*.**

   The Web page contains Cosmopolitan Farmer's 2001 Apartment Mower Round-up review (see Figure 8-15). The page's text is a bit boring looking, so you'll use CSS to spiff it up.

   To start, you'll create a style for the Heading 1 paragraph and create an external style sheet at the same time.

2. **Choose Window→CSS Styles (or press Shift-F11).**

   The CSS Styles panel opens.

3. **On the CSS Styles panel, click the Add New Style (+) button .**

   The New Style window opens (see Figure 8-16). You'll first pick the type of style you wish to create.

Figure 8-16:
If you've already attached an external style sheet to a page, you can select its name from the Define In menu. That way, the new style will be added to that file. Your other option, which is what you're doing in this tutorial, is to create the new style sheet when you first create a style.

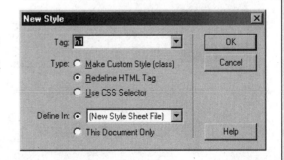

---

4. **Click the Redefine HTML Tag button.**

   This lets you create a style for a particular HTML tag—in this case, the <h1> tag. In other words, you're going to create a formatting rule that applies automatically to every Heading 1 paragraph.

5. **Type *h1* into the Tag box, or choose *h1* from the menu.**

   In the Define In section of the New Style window, the New Style Sheet File option should already be selected (see Figure 8-16).

6. **Click OK.**

   The Save Style Sheet File As dialog box appears. You're about to create the file—an external style sheet—that will store the styles for this page.

7. **Navigate to the DWCSS folder; type *reviews.css* in the name box. Click Save to save the file.**

   Cascading Style Sheet files always end in .css; that's how Web servers and browsers can tell what kind of file it is.

   Having created the external style sheet, you can now create the first style, as suggested by the sudden appearance of the Style Definition window. You'll choose a font, set a size, and assign a color to the <h1> tag.

8. **Choose "Arial, Helvetica, Sans Serif" from the Font menu; type *28* in the Size box; type *#333399* in the Color field.**

   The Style Definition window should look like Figure 8-17.

9. **Click OK.**

The Style Definition window closes and the first headline on the page is now formatted according to the style you just created. As you may have noticed, you didn't have to select the text to apply this style; since it's an HTML tag style, it's applied *automatically* wherever the tag appears on the page.

Now, you'll create a style for the other heading on the page—an <h2> tag.

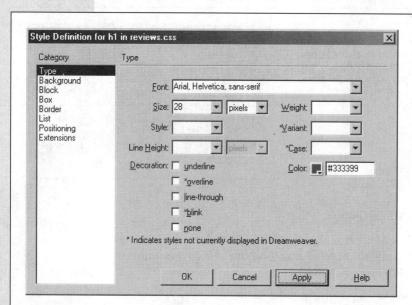

Figure 8-17:
You can set the CSS equivalents of HTML text formatting options from the Type category of the Style Definition window. (If Cadet Blue doesn't do anything for you, click the Color box and choose a color you prefer.)

10. **On the CSS Styles panel, click the New Style button.**

The New Style window opens. The Redefine HTML Tag button is already selected, and the menu in the Define In option lists the new external style sheet—*reviews.css*. In other words, Dreamweaver will add the new style to this external style sheet. All you need to do now is identify which tag you want to redefine.

11. **Type *h2* in the Tag box, or choose *h2* from the menu, and then click OK.**

The Style Definition Window appears.

12. **Choose "Arial, Helvetica, Sans Serif" from the Font menu; type *28* in the Size box; type *#CC0000* in the Color Field; click OK.**

The window closes and the second heading on the page (the Heading 2 heading "Chinook Push-o-matic Indoor Mower") appears in its new formatting. If there had been other Heading 2 headings on this page, you'd see all of them change, too.

Editing a Style

Unfortunately, the second heading you just redefined is the same size as the first heading. In order to make it smaller, to indicate it's a subhead, you'll edit the style you just created.

1. **On the CSS Styles panel, click the Edit Style Sheet button (the icon with a pencil).**

   The Edit Style Sheet dialog box opens. It lists the linked external style sheet that you created—*reviews.css*. You have to open this file to edit the style.

2. **Double-click *reviews.css*.**

   A dialog box that looks a lot like the Edit Style Sheet dialog opens, listing the h1 and h2 styles you've created (see Figure 8-18).

3. **In the Style list, double-click *h2*.**

   The Style Definition window opens. (This is the same window you used when you created the style.)

4. **In the Size box, type *20* to replace the number 28, and then click OK.**

   You've changed the size in the h2 style; now you need to save the external style sheet.

5. **Click Save.**

   The *reviews.css* window closes, leaving the Edit Style Sheet window open.

6. **Click Done to close the window and return to the document.**

   The second headline is now a bit smaller than the first—perfect!

   If you scroll down the page a bit, you'll see the name of one of the mowers—Sampson Deluxe Apartment Mower—below the second photo. This is formatted as a paragraph, but it should be a second-level heading.

Figure 8-18:
Each external style sheet has its own dialog box listing all CSS styles stored in it. To get to it and edit the styles, you need to click the Edit Style Sheet button in the CSS Styles panel (or choose Text→CSS Styles→Edit Style Sheet) and double-click the name of the style sheet file.

7. **Click anywhere in the line "Sampson Deluxe Apartment Mower."**

   You'll change this paragraph to Heading 2 using the Property Inspector. (Because you've already saved CSS formatting for Heading 2, there's no need to go back to the CSS Styles panel.)

8. **From the Format menu in the Property inspector, select Heading 2.**

   If you prefer keyboard shortcuts, press Ctrl+2 (⌘-2); the heading instantly changes to match the other heading. That's the power of HTML tag styles: once created, an HTML tag style's formatting is automatically applied wherever the tag appears.

Creating a Custom Style

Now you'll create a style to highlight the name of products that appear in the review. Notice, for example the phrase "Chinook Push-o-matic Indoor Mower" in the first paragraph. Since the product names consist of just a couple of words *within* the paragraph, you can't redefine an HTML tag to format them globally. Instead, you'll create a custom style, which you can then apply by hand to the text.

1. **Click the New Style button (+) on the CSS Styles panel.**

   The New Style window opens. This time you'll create a custom style rather than an HTML tag style.

2. **Click the Make Custom Style radio button. Type** *.product* **in the Name box.**

   Custom styles, technically called *classes,* always begin with a period.

   Since you want to add the style to the external style sheet, you don't need to do anything else in this dialog box; Dreamweaver already proposes storing it there (see Figure 8-19).

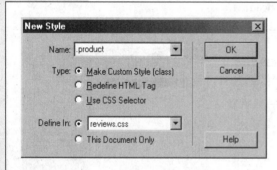

Figure 8-19:
Be careful what you choose in the Define In pop-up menu; if you plan to use the CSS style on other Web pages, save it in an external style sheet–reviews.css, in this case.

3. **Click OK.**

   The Style Definition window appears. You'll add a few new properties to make this style stand out.

4. **From the Weight menu, choose** *bold.*

To make this style even more prominent, you'll add a background color to it.

5. **In the Style Definition window Category list, click Background.**

The background properties appear (see Figure 8-20).

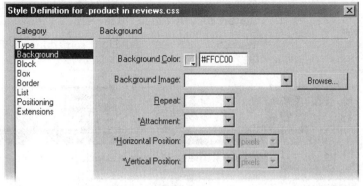

Figure 8-20:
Using Cascading Style Sheet properties, you can add background colors and images as well as more common properties such as text formatting.

6. **Type #FFCC00 into the Background Color box.**

Or, if you don't normally dream in hexadecimal notation, you can select a color using the color box.

Now you'll return to the document and apply your new style.

7. **Click OK.**

The Style Definition window closes, and the CSS Styles window lists the new style (see Figure 8-21). This time, nothing's changed in the document window. Unlike HTML tag styles, custom styles don't show up anywhere until you apply them by hand.

8. **In the first paragraph of the review, drag to select the words "Chinook Push-o-matic Indoor Mower."**

This is the product name you wish to format.

Figure 8-21:
HTML tag styles, such as the redefined <h1> and <h2> tags in this tutorial, aren't listed in the Styles panel. Since this panel is used for applying styles, only custom styles appear here.

9. In the CSS Styles panel, click *product*.

Boom—Dreamweaver formats the text with the bold, colored style. (If it doesn't, make sure the Auto Apply box is turned on [see Figure 8-21].)

Now you'll style a couple more product names.

10. Select "Sampson Deluxe Apartment Mower" in the first paragraph, and apply the .product style to it. Do the same for the words "Anodyne 7457."

Your document text should look something like Figure 8-22.

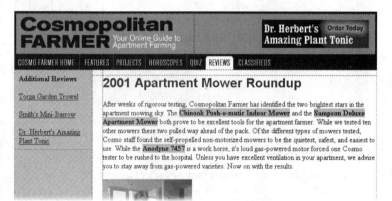

Figure 8-22:
At this point, the text in the page is coming along well. The headlines look distinctive, and you've achieved some effects (like the background color of the product names) that only CSS can accomplish. Next you'll turn your attention to making the images look great.

Formatting the Photos

CSS Styles aren't just for text. You can create styles and apply them to anything on a page—tables, images, or links, for example. In this next section, you'll improve the appearance of the product photos; specifically, you'll bless them with borders and make them hug the right side of the page.

1. Click the New Style button (+) on the CSS Styles panel.

The New Style window opens. You could redefine the <img> (image) tag, but this would affect *every* graphic on your page. Since you only want to create a style for the two product photos, you should create a custom style that you can apply as needed.

2. Type *.photo* in the Name box, make sure the Custom Style button is selected, and then click OK.

The Style Definition window opens. You'll first add a border to this style.

3. Click the Border category in the Style Definition window.

The CSS border properties appear (see Figure 8-23). You'll add a 2-pixel, colored border.

4. **In each of the Width boxes—top, right, bottom, left—type** *2,* **and make sure** *pixel* **is selected in the menus to the right.**

Now for the color:

5. **Select a color for each border by typing** *#CC0000* **in the Color field for each border.**

That's the hex code for a fire-engine red, but you're welcome to choose any color you like (by clicking the color-picker square)—you can even choose *different* colors for the four borders.

You must also select a style for the border; if you leave the *none* option selected, the borders won't appear at all.

6. **From the Style menu, select** *dashed.*

The Style Definition window should look like Figure 8-23.

Next, you'll set an alignment property that will move to the right edge of the page.

7. **Click the Box category at the left side of the dialog box.**

These properties affect margins, padding, and other attributes of a style (see Figure 8-24).

8. **From the Float menu, select** *right.*

This option works like an image's Align right property (see page 102); the graphic will snap against the right side of the browser window.

Figure 8-23:
Unfortunately, as the asterisks in this window indicate, you can't preview Cascading Style Sheet borders within Dreamweaver. To see what your creations look like, you'll have to preview them in a Web browser that understands CSS—most 4+ versions of browsers do.

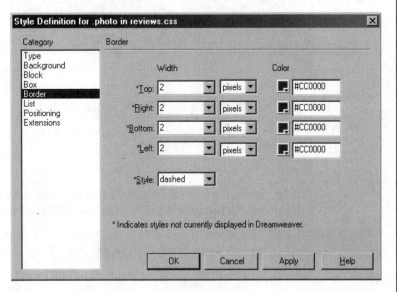

But because text will wrap around the sides of the photos, you should add a little space between the edges of the photo borders and any text around them. The Margin properties are just the ticket.

9. **Type *10* in the Top, Bottom, and Left margin boxes.**

CSS lets you set different margin sizes for each edge of an object. In this case, since the photos will already be aligned to the right edge of the page, there's no reason to add any margin to the right side.

The Style Definition window should look like Figure 8-24. You're done with the style, now it's time to apply it.

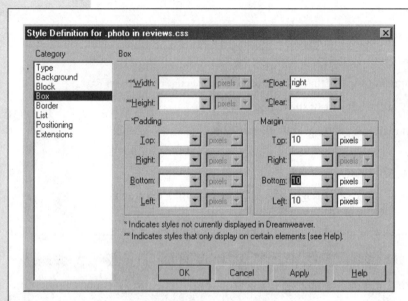

Figure 8-24:
Be careful not to confuse the Padding and Margin properties in the Box category. The Padding settings determine the amount of space between the styled object and its border. The Margins, by contrast, set the amount of space between the borders and other items around the object—in this case, the space between the photos and the text around them.

10. **Click OK to close the Style Definition window.**

The new custom style—*photo*—appears in the CSS Styles panel. To apply it, you'll start by selecting the image.

11. **Click to select the photo—the woman in blue with a lawn mower.**

As you can see in the tag selector at the bottom of the window, clicking the photo automatically highlights the <img> (image) tag to which you'll apply the style.

12. **In the CSS Styles panel, click *photo*.**

If the Auto Apply checkbox is turned off, click Apply, too.

The photo moves to the right edge of the page and the rest of the text flows around it. Dreamweaver can't display the CSS border properties, so you don't see any borders around the photo; but you will in a moment, when you preview the page.

See the large gap between the first paragraph of text and the first subhead? Believe it or not, this distracting space only appears in Dreamweaver. As with borders, Dreamweaver 4 has trouble displaying many CSS properties properly (including margins).

13. **Select the second photo; apply the photo style to it, too.**

    Your photos match, as shown in Figure 8-25. Now you can preview all your hard work.

14. **Choose File→Save to save the page. Press F12 to preview the page in a Web browser.**

    Only 4.0 or later browsers display the CSS properties on this page. (And even they may have trouble, as discussed in Figure 8-25.)

Figure 8-25:
Even browsers that understand Cascading Style Sheets can have a hard time displaying them correctly. This figure shows the completed tutorial page as viewed in Opera 5.11, which does a good job of displaying the styles, including the border and margins around the photo. Mercifully not shown: Netscape Navigator 4.75, which completely botches the border property. Instead of a dashed red line around the photo, Navigator draws a solid red line around some empty space on the page and pushes the photo off the page to the far right.

Attaching an External Style Sheet

Now that you've created these styles, you may be wondering how you can use them on other pages; after all, that's the beauty of external style sheets. Once created, it's a simple process to add a style sheet to other pages in the site.

1. **Choose File→Open; double-click the file *torga.html* in the DWCSS folder.**

   This is another review for Cosmopolitan Farmer. It's not yet formatted, so you'll attach the external style sheet you just created.

2. **Click the Attach External Style Sheet button on the CSS Styles panel (see Figure 8-1).**

   The Select Style Sheet dialog box appears. Navigate to the DWCSS folder and select the *reviews.css* file.

3. **Click Select or Choose to select the file and attach it to the page.**

   Notice that Dreamweaver instantly formats the top headline and two subheads, using the style you created. Pretty cool—and very efficient.

4. **Click the photo to select it.**

   You've simultaneously selected the <img> (image) tag.

5. **Click *photo* in the CSS Styles panel.**

   (If Auto Apply is turned off, click Apply, too.)

   The style is applied to the photo, and it aligns to the right edge of the page.

6. **Press F12 to preview the page.**

   If you'd like to compare your finished product with the professionally completed version, visit *www.sawmac.com/tutorials*.

EASTER EGG HUNT

What is the Frequency, Kenneth?

Ah, where would Dreamweaver be without its Easter eggs? As a reward for mastering the CSS concept, Dreamweaver offers you a special Cascading Style Sheet secret.

It works like this. Open the Styles palette and click the New Style button; create a new style sheet called *.coilA*. When the Style Definition window pops up, click OK; then click Done.

Now click the name of your new style (coilA) in the Styles palette. A box opens, saying: "You have selected coil A. Detact the frequency?"

If you click OK, you'll be taken to www.alexchiu.com (a very strange Web site).

Now then: Wasn't learning CSS worthwhile?

Under the Hood:
HTML

While Dreamweaver is primarily a visual Web page editor, it also includes powerful text-editing features that let you work on your pages' HTML, CSS, and JavaScript code directly. In fact, in recognition of the fact that many of the Web's creators still work deep in the trenches of raw code, Macromedia has added a code editor to Dreamweaver 4 that includes professional features such as syntax highlighting, auto indenting, and line numbering. Now, Dreamweaver may be the only Web page creation program even hardcore code junkies ever need.

Roundtrip HTML

Unlike many other visual HTML editors, Dreamweaver has always graciously accepted HTML written by hand (or even by other programs). In fact, Dreamweaver has always made it easy to jump between it and text-editing programs such as HomeSite (for Windows) and BBEdit (for the Mac).

This ability, called Roundtrip HTML by Macromedia, allows Web developers to write code the way they want, without worrying about Dreamweaver changing it. For example, suppose you have a particular way of formatting your handwritten code; perhaps you insert an extra carriage return after every <td> (table cell) tag or like to use multiple tabs to indent nested tags. Dreamweaver won't try to rewrite that to fit its own style.

Auto-Fixing Your Code

That's not to say that Dreamweaver doesn't *ever* change your code. In fact, the program automatically offers to fix errors when you open a page that was created in another program. By default, Dreamweaver attempts to fix the following errors:

- **Overlapping tags.** Consider this line: <p><b>Fix your tags!</p></b>. This HTML is invalid, because the opening and closing <b> tags should appear *inside* the <p> tag. Dreamweaver will re-write this example as: <p><b>Fix your tags!</b></p>.

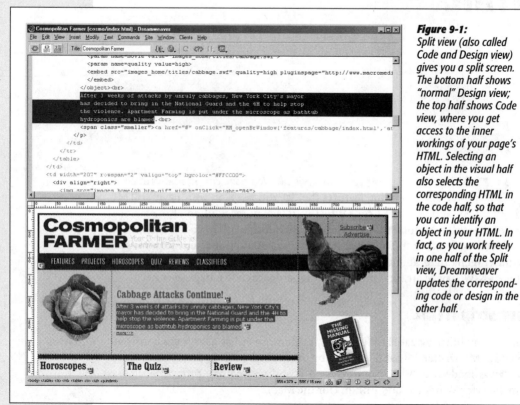

Figure 9-1:
Split view (also called Code and Design view) gives you a split screen. The bottom half shows "normal" Design view; the top half shows Code view, where you get access to the inner workings of your page's HTML. Selecting an object in the visual half also selects the corresponding HTML in the code half, so that you can identify an object in your HTML. In fact, as you work freely in one half of the Split view, Dreamweaver updates the corresponding code or design in the other half.

- **Unclosed tags.** Tags usually come in pairs, like this <i>This text is in italics</i>. But if a page is missing the ending tag (<i>This text is in italics), Dreamweaver adds the closing tag.

- **Extra closing tags.** If a page has an *extra* closing tag (<b>bold</b></b>), Dreamweaver helpfully removes it.

Sure enough, Dreamweaver is touching your page's code; but in this instance, it's a good thing. All of those errors are improper HTML that can cause problems for Web browsers. But if you like, you can turn off this feature in the Preferences window (see Figure 9-2). (Some Web developers, for example, once deliberately omitted closing tags in order to save a few kilobytes in file size. While most Web browsers can still interpret this kind of sloppy code, leaving out tags is asking for trouble.)

Dreamweaver can also change the capitalization (case) of HTML tags and properties, if you want. For example, if you prefer to use lowercase letters for tags and properties like this <a href="nextpage.html">Click here</a>, Dreamweaver can convert uppercase tags (<A HREF="next.html">) to lowercase, or vice versa, when it finds them in pages created by other programs. (You can turn on this feature as described on page 254.)

Web Application Server Pages

Dreamweaver can leave pages with certain filename extensions untouched—pages created for *Web application servers*, for example. Web application servers process Web pages that access databases and other dynamic services, such as shopping cart programs and form processing applications. Many of these systems rely on special code within the HTML of a page—code that Dreamweaver might "fix," interpreting them as HTML errors.

By default, Dreamweaver doesn't rewrite code in pages designed for the leading application server technologies; that is, files whose names end in .asp (Active Server Pages that run on Microsoft's IIS Web Server), .cfm or .cfml (Cold Fusion Markup Language pages that run on Macromedia's Cold Fusion Server), .jsp (Java Server Pages, which run on any Java Server), among others. You can add an extension to this list, as shown in Figure 9-2.

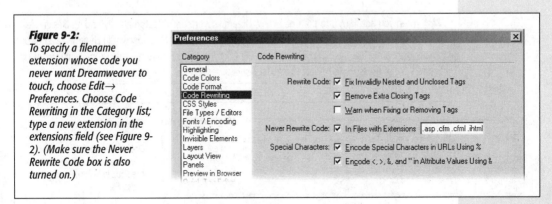

Figure 9-2:
To specify a filename extension whose code you never want Dreamweaver to touch, choose Edit→ Preferences. Choose Code Rewriting in the Category list; type a new extension in the extensions field (see Figure 9-2). (Make sure the Never Rewrite Code box is also turned on.)

Code View

Dreamweaver provides several different ways to view a page's HTML code (see Figure 9-1):

• In **Code view,** Dreamweaver simply displays the raw code of your page.

- **Split view** shows the HTML code and the "regular" Design view simultaneously (Figure 9-1).

- The **Code inspector** is a rather cumbersome editor that can only show the code of one document at a time. Prior to Dreamweaver 4, this window offered the *only* way to view a page's code. To access the Code inspector choose Window→Code inspector; however, the rest of this chapter assumes that you've graduated to Code view for HTML editing purposes.

To move between Dreamweaver's different views, choose a name from the View menu: Code, Design (the "regular," visual mode), or Design and Code (Split view).

Tip: You can quickly jump between Code and Design view by pressing Control+Tab (Option-Tab).

Code view, like the old Code inspector, functions just like a text editor. You can click anywhere inside the window and start typing HTML, JavaScript, or Cascading Style Sheet code.

That doesn't mean you have to type out *everything* by hand; the Objects panel, Insert menu, and Property inspector are at your disposal in Code view, too. Using these sources of canned HTML code chunks, you can combine hands-on HTML work with the easy-to-use, rapid action of Dreamweaver's objects. This trick can be a real timesaver when you need to add a table, which would otherwise be a multiline exercise in typing accuracy. You can also select a tag (an image's <img> tag, for example) in Code view and use the Property inspector to modify it.

Tip: When you add HTML to the Code view, Dreamweaver doesn't automatically update Design view—which can be disconcerting when you're working in Split view. (After all, how would Dreamweaver display a half-finished tag like this: <table border=" ?) Click the Refresh button in the Property inspector (see Figure 9-3), or press F5, to update the visual display.

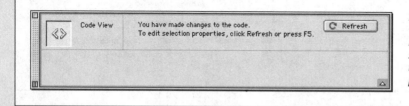

Figure 9-3:
When you want to update Dreamweaver's visual (or split) view, click Refresh on the Property inspector—or press F5.

To help you navigate your code, Code view provides several visual cues:

- **Syntax coloring.** Dreamweaver displays different elements in different colors. Comments, for example, are gray. Text is black, and HTML tags appear in blue. You can change any of these colors, and even specify a unique color for each tag, using the Preferences window (see Figure 9-4).

• **Bad code highlighting.** If you've typed some incorrect code (an opening tag without a closing tag, say), it's highlighted in yellow (see Figure 9-5).

• **Library item shading.** Library items and uneditable regions in pages built from templates appear with a light yellow background; you can't edit them in Code view. (You can change this color, too, as described on page 454. For more on Templates and the Library, see Chapter 17.)

Figure 9-4:
You can control the color Dreamweaver uses to display HTML and script code while in Code view from the Preferences window. Just click a tag in the Tag list, and then use the color box to set a specific color. If you also want everything nested inside the tag the same color, turn on Apply Color to Tag Contents. Note, however, that doing so may make large areas of code the same color, defeating the purpose of color-coded tags. For example, turning on this option for the <table> tag makes everything inside the same color.

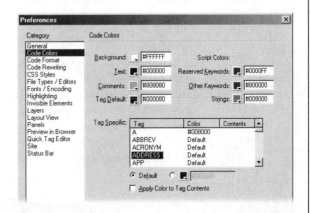

Figure 9-5:
Dreamweaver highlights incorrect HTML code with bright yellow highlighting in Code view (circled). If you click inside the yellow area, the Property Inspector reveals the mistake. In this case, a closing tag is missing. (In Design view, on the other hand, Dreamweaver indicates mistakes by showing the HTML tag—the characters <, b, and >, for example—with a bright yellow background.)

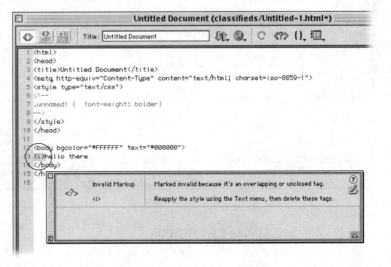

You can also control Code view display using the View options menu in the toolbar (see Figure 9-6), or using the View→Code Options submenu:

• **Word Wrap.** This option makes long lines of code wrap, at the window's edge, to the next line, so you don't have to scroll horizontally to see it all. (This option affects only how Dreamweaver displays the line in the document window; it doesn't actually introduce line breaks.)

- **Line Numbers.** This automatic line numbering can come in handy when debugging JavaScript code (see page 259) or when using Dreamweaver's Check Target Browser command (page 392).

- **Highlight Invalid HTML.** This is the on/off switch for Dreamweaver's friendly tendency to highlight bad HTML in Code view (see Figure 9-5).

- **Syntax Coloring.** This option assigns different colors to tags, comments, and text, to help you tell them apart at a glance.

- **Auto Indent.** When you're working with nested HTML tags, it's often helpful to press the Tab key to indent each level of nested tags, making it easier to identify large blocks of HTML (a table and all its contents, for example). The Auto Indent option carries the same size indent onto the next line when you hit the Return or Enter key. For example, suppose you hit the Tab key twice, type a line of code, and then hit Return. Dreamweaver would place the insertion point on the next line, indented using two tabs just like the line above.

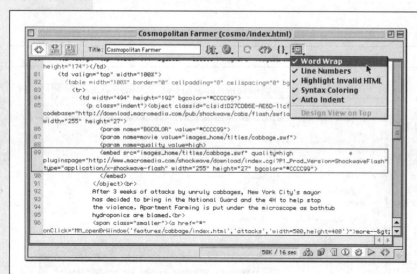

Figure 9-6:
The View Options menu on the toolbar lets you modify the display of code in Code view. The Word Wrap option, for example, forces all code to fit inside the width of the window; if a line of code extends off the page, Dreamweaver wraps it to the next line (the outlined code in this illustration). Your only clue that you're looking at one long line is that the entire glob of text has only a single line number.

Setting Code Formatting

Whenever you use the Object panel, Dreamweaver adds a chunk of HTML that's preformatted for easier reading. The code for table rows, for instance, come indented using two spaces; the code for table *cells* are indented with four spaces. If you're particular about how your HTML is written to the file, and wish to set your own indents and other formatting, Dreamweaver gives you plenty of control.

Note: If you don't work in Code view frequently, you may not care a whit how your HTML is formatted in the file—and that's fine. As long as the underlying HTML is valid (and Dreamweaver always writes valid HTML), Web browsers can display HTML formatted in many different ways. In fact, Web browsers simply ignore multiple spaces, empty lines, and other "white space" characters used to make HTML code more readable.

To control the formatting of the code Dreamweaver produces, open the Preferences window (Edit→Preferences or Ctrl+U [⌘-U]) and click the Code Format category (see Figure 9-7). While the default settings work fine, you can set any of the following options:

Indents

To make your code easier to read, it helps to indent nested tags and other block-level elements. But if you'd rather Dreamweaver quit auto-indenting such elements, turn off Use Indents. This is also your opportunity to specify the use of tabs instead of spaces for indenting lines of code: choose Tabs from the pop-up menu.

You can also set the amount of indentation:

- If Spaces is selected in the Use menu, type the number of spaces you want into the Indent Size field. The default setting is 2, meaning each indent will be two spaces in the code.

- If you selected Tabs in the Use menu, the number in the Tab Size field indicates the size of each tab, measured in spaces. (The size you specify here affects only the display in Code view, in Dreamweaver. In the code itself, Dreamweaver simply inserts a plain tab character.)

Text Wrapping

When a line gets long, Dreamweaver can break it into two or more lines by inserting a hard return, which can make your HTML more readable in Code view and free you from having to scroll to see all of your code. If that's the way you like it, turn on Automatic Wrapping and type a number in the After Column field. The number specifies how many characters long a line must be before Dreamweaver attempts to wrap it.

This option doesn't affect how the page will look to your visitors, only how it looks in a text editor. But unlike the simulated word wrap option shown in Figure 9-6, this option adds real line-break characters to split your code into multiple, shorter lines. If you use the Code view's word wrap, you can skip this (more intrusive) form of text wrapping.

Note: Although Dreamweaver can shorten lines by inserting returns after a specified number of characters, it never does so if the final effect will change the appearance of the Web page. It's smart enough to not sacrifice the quality of a page just to make the code look better in Code view. That's why some lines of HTML may be considerably longer than the limit you specify here.

Line Breaks

Windows, Mac OS, and Unix each uses, and looks for, a different invisible character at the end of each line of code, which can cause problems when you use one kind of computer to create a page, but the remote server that dishes out the page runs on a different OS. Fortunately, Dreamweaver fixes the problem when it transfers a file to a Web server.

But if you plan to use another text editor to edit your Dreamweaver pages later, you should select your operating system from the Line Breaks pop-up menu. Doing so assures that the program on the receiving end will properly read the line breaks in Dreamweaver-produced pages.

Case for Tags and Attributes

You can write tag and property names using either uppercase letters (such as <B>bold</B>) or lowercase (bold); Web browsers don't care. However, *you* may care how they appear in your HTML display; if so, choose your preference from the two Case pop-up menus. Select either the lowercase or uppercase option from the two menus.

Tip: HTML may treat capital and lowercase letters in its tags identically, but XML, an up-and-coming new language, does not. Both it and the hybrid language XHTML require all lowercase tag and property names. That's why many Web developers are getting used to using strictly lowercase characters, even in their HTML.

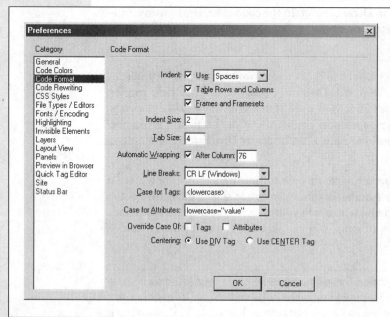

Figure 9-7:
For the ultimate control of the HTML code, Dreamweaver offers the Code Format category in the Preferences window. For most people, this degree of control is overkill; but if the way HTML code appears in a page's file matters to you, go wild. (These settings don't affect how the page looks in a Web browser—only how the code appears when viewed in Dreamweaver's Code view or in another text editor.)

If you also turn on the Override Case checkboxes, you can make Dreamweaver scan tags and properties when opening a page created by someone else (or some other program); if their case doesn't match your preferences, Dreamweaver will rewrite them to fit the wishes of you, its master.

Centering

The Centering buttons let you specify which HTML tag you want Dreamweaver to use when centering block-level elements (like paragraphs) on the page. Leave Use DIV Tag turned on. The CENTER tag won't work in future browser versions.

Quick Tag Editor

Code view is great when you really need (or want) to dig into the trenches and fine-tune your HTML. But if a text editor is all you wanted, you wouldn't have bought

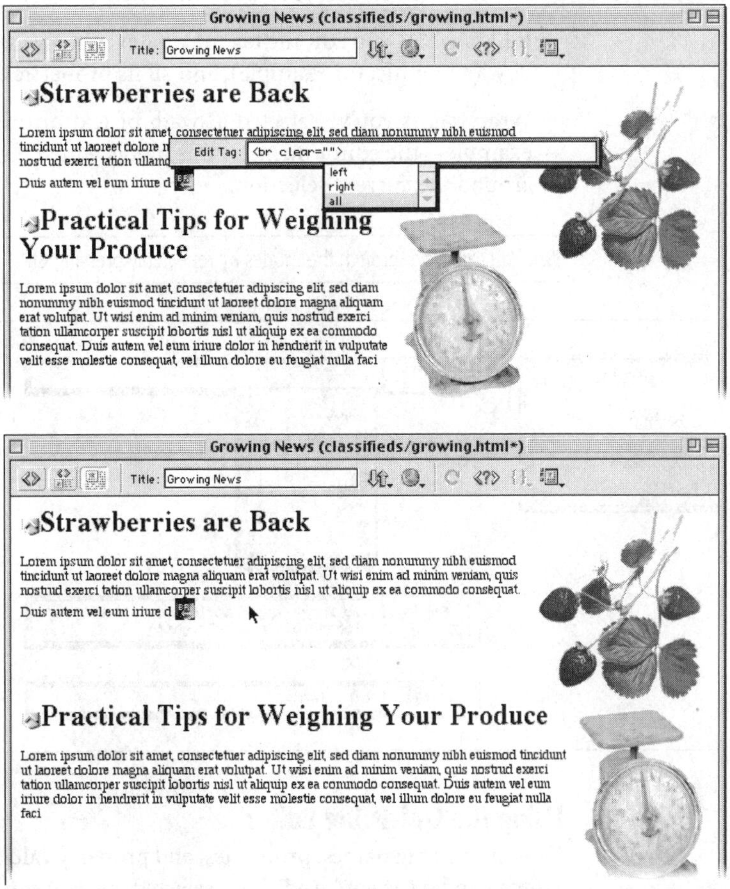

Figure 9-8:
When you align an image with the right side of a page, surrounding material wraps around it—in this case, everything else *(second headline, second blurb, second graphic). Bottom: It's the Quick Tag Editor to the rescue; using it, you can quickly insert the <br clear="all"> tag to the end of the first blurb. This tag and property mean, "Turn off wrapping at this point."*

Dreamweaver in the first place. Most of the time, you'll be working in Dreamweaver's Design view enjoying the pleasures of its visual authoring environment.

Occasionally, however, you'll want to dip momentarily into the HTML pond, especially when you need some HTML that Dreamweaver doesn't make easy to add. You might wish you could type out a quick HTML tag on the spot, right there in Design view, without having to make the mental and visual shift required for a switch into Code view.

That's what the Quick Tag Editor is all about (see Figure 9-8).

To access the Quick Tag Editor, press Ctrl+T (⌘-T)—or, if you're feeling especially mouse-driven, click the Quick Tag editor button in the Property inspector (see Figure 9-9). Depending on what you've got selected in the document window, the Quick Tag Editor opens in one of its three modes (see Figure 9-9):

- **Insert new tag.** Inserts a new tag in the page. You get this mode if nothing is currently selected in your document window.

- **Edit tag.** Lets you edit the tag for whatever you've selected in the document window (a graphic, for example), and all its properties.

- **Wrap tag.** If you've selected a swath of text or other objects—two images, for example—the editor opens in this mode, which makes it easy to wrap a new tag around the current selection.

Tip: You can cycle through the modes by repeatedly pressing Ctrl-T (⌘-T).

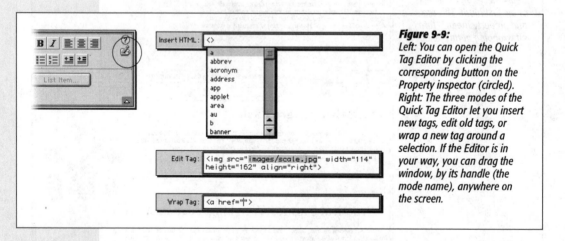

Figure 9-9:
Left: You can open the Quick Tag Editor by clicking the corresponding button on the Property inspector (circled). Right: The three modes of the Quick Tag Editor let you insert new tags, edit old tags, or wrap a new tag around a selection. If the Editor is in your way, you can drag the window, by its handle (the mode name), anywhere on the screen.

Using the Quick Tag Editor

You can type tag names, properties, and property values directly into the Quick Tag Editor window. If you're editing a selected tag, you can change any of the properties listed, and even add new ones. When you're done, press Enter or Return; the Quick Tag Editor closes and the changes take effect.

To make all of this even easier, the Quick Tag Editor sports a helpful list—called tag hints—of HTML tags and properties, for your selection pleasure. When you insert a tag, for example, a menu of available tags appears (top right in Figure 9-9). Use the up and down arrow keys or the scroll bar to move through the list. You can also start typing the first few letters of a tag or property; Dreamweaver jumps to the nearest match in the list.

To choose the highlighted name, press Enter or Return; Dreamweaver adds that tag or property name to the Quick Tag Editor window. If you've selected a tag property, Dreamweaver adds the proper punctuation (href=" ", for example), and the insertion point appears between the quotation marks, waiting for you to type the property's value.

Tip: When editing an existing tag in the Quick Tag Editor, press Tab to select the next property or property value. You can then type a new property or value. Shift-Tab selects the *previous* property or value.

Quick Tag Editor Preferences

If you choose Edit→Preferences and click the Quick Tag Editor category, you can adjust the Quick Tag Editor's behavior in a couple of useful ways:

- **Apply Changes Immediately While Editing.** When this option is on, you can view changes you've just made without even exiting the Quick Tag Editor; just press Tab or Shift-Tab after making the change. Dreamweaver updates your document instantly.

- **Enable Tag Hints.** *Hints* are the tag and properties that appear when using the Quick Tag editor (see top right in Figure 9-9). If they get in your way, turn off this box. Your other option is to leave it on but make the hints take longer to appear, by dragging the slider to the right. In this way, the menu only appears after a certain number of seconds, freeing you to type away, clutter-free.

Reference Panel

When it comes to building Web sites, there's a lot to know; Cascading Style Sheets, HTML, and JavaScript are filled with cryptic terms and subtle nuances. Fortunately, Dreamweaver 4's new Reference panel makes your search for knowledge a little bit easier. It gives you quick access to reference excerpts from Danny Goodman's *DHTML: The Definitive Guide* (O'Reilly and Associates); see Figure 9-10.

To open the Reference panel, choose Window→Reference, or use the keyboard shortcut Ctrl+Shift+F1 (⌘-Shift-F1). The first menu at the top of the panel lets you choose the "book" you want to read: CSS Reference, HTML Reference, or JavaScript Reference. Once you've selected a reference, choose a particular HTML tag, CSS Style, or JavaScript object from the menu directly below the Book menu. A description of that item appears in the main window, complete with sample usage and browser-support details. A secondary menu to the right lets you get additional information about a particular *property* of the selected tag, style or object. For example, in Figure 9-10, to display information about the image tag's Align property, you'd choose IMG from the Tag menu and *align* from the attribute menu next to it.

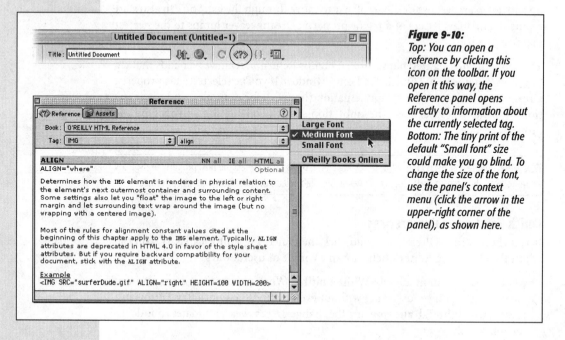

Figure 9-10:
Top: You can open a reference by clicking this icon on the toolbar. If you open it this way, the Reference panel opens directly to information about the currently selected tag. Bottom: The tiny print of the default "Small font" size could make you go blind. To change the size of the font, use the panel's context menu (click the arrow in the upper-right corner of the panel), as shown here.

While you won't spend every waking minute in the Reference panel, it's a good way to keep your HTML, CSS and JavaScript chops sharp.

Inserting JavaScript

As Chapter 11 makes clear, Dreamweaver's Behaviors (prewritten JavaScript programs) let you add exciting interactive effects with very little effort: mouse rollovers, pop-up windows, and animated layers, for example. But they can't do everything; when you, the native JavaScript speaker, need to wade into the depths of JavaScript programming yourself, you'll find two entrances within Dreamweaver.

The most straightforward approach, especially if you're already familiar with JavaScript programming, is to simply switch into code view (Ctrl+Tab [Option-Tab]) and type away. Or, if you prefer, you can use Dreamweaver's Insert Script window to add your JavaScript code (see Figure 9-11).

To do so, click in either the head or body section of the page, and then choose Insert→Invisible Tags→Script. In the Insert Script window (Figure 9-11), choose a language from the menu: JavaScript, JavaScript1.1, JavaScript1.2, or VBScript. (The JavaScript option works with all browsers that understand JavaScript, while JavaScript 1.2 only works in 4+ version browsers. VBScript, on the other hand, works only in the Windows version of Internet Explorer.)

Just type your script into the Content section (you don't need to include <script> tags; Dreamweaver handles that part) and then click OK. If you inserted the script in the body of the document, you'll see a small gold icon (indicating an invisible element on the page) to mark its location.

You can edit your script in Code view, of course; in Design view, select the script icon and then click Edit in the Property inspector.

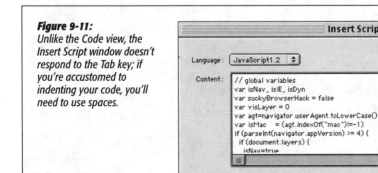

Figure 9-11:
Unlike the Code view, the Insert Script window doesn't respond to the Tab key; if you're accustomed to indenting your code, you'll need to use spaces.

Dreamweaver also lets you open and work on external JavaScript files (.js files) right in Code view. The program doesn't try to interpret the file as an HTML page; it won't attempt to make any of the changes described on page 248. You can just use the built in text editing capabilities of Code view to write your JavaScript programs.

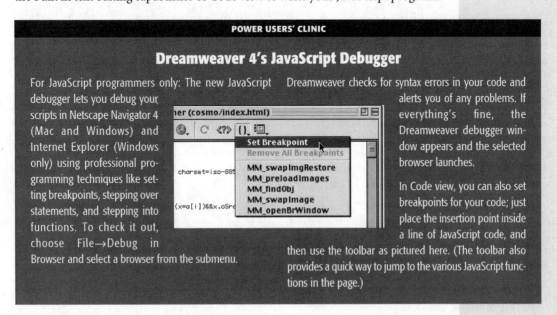

POWER USERS' CLINIC

Dreamweaver 4's JavaScript Debugger

For JavaScript programmers only: The new JavaScript debugger lets you debug your scripts in Netscape Navigator 4 (Mac and Windows) and Internet Explorer (Windows only) using professional programming techniques like setting breakpoints, stepping over statements, and stepping into functions. To check it out, choose File→Debug in Browser and select a browser from the submenu.

Dreamweaver checks for syntax errors in your code and alerts you of any problems. If everything's fine, the Dreamweaver debugger window appears and the selected browser launches.

In Code view, you can also set breakpoints for your code; just place the insertion point inside a line of JavaScript code, and then use the toolbar as pictured here. (The toolbar also provides a quick way to jump to the various JavaScript functions in the page.)

Tip: JavaScript programming is no walk in the park. While it's certainly easier to learn than full-featured languages like Java or C++, it can still be challenging. If you want to get your feet wet, here's a great resource for basic tutorials and information on JavaScript: *www.Webmonkey.com/programming/ javascript/*.

Credit Where Credit's Due

Creating good software involves the tireless work of many dedicated individuals, most of whom never reach the celebrity status of a Bill Gates or Marc Andreesen. Yet they don't get their names on the box or the cover of the manual—so who's to blame them when they try to grab a little credit?

If you'd like to meet the masterminds behind Dreamweaver 4's new JavaScript debugger, you're in luck. This Easter Egg is, in fact, triggered by using that very same debugger and any Web page —with a few minor modifications.

Create a new Web page and save it. Choose view→Code View to see the page's HTML source code. Click after the opening <body> tag and type:

```
<script
debuggercredits=true>
var i;
</script>
```

Next, choose File→Debug in Browser and choose any browser listed in the submenu. The selected browser opens and a different page loads, displaying dancing dots and credits for Dreamweaver's JavaScript debugger creators.

Part Three:
Bringing Your Pages
to Life

3

Forms

A Web site is a great way for you to broadcast a message, announce a new product, post late-breaking news, or just rant about the state of the world. And sure enough, that's exactly how most Webmasters set up their Web pages: as a kind of *one-way* communication.

But you may be curious to get some feedback from your audience. Or you may want to build your business by selling your product through the Internet as well as the traditional channels. Either way, you'll need a way to gather information *from* your visitors. In that situation, it's time to add *forms* to your Web design repertoire (see Figure 10-1 for a simple example). Whatever type of information you need to collect on your site, Dreamweaver's *form objects* make the task easy.

Form Basics

A form begins and ends with the HTML <form> tag. The opening <form> tag indicates the beginning of the form and sets its properties; the closing </form> tag, of course, marks the form's end.

In between these tags, different objects provide the basic user interface elements—the design—of the form. Radio buttons, text fields, and pull-down menus (also called pop-up menus) are just a few of the ways you can gather input. It's perfectly OK to include other HTML elements inside a form, too; in fact, your site's visitors would be lost if you couldn't also add (and format) text that explains the purpose of each form object. And without using a table to control the layout of a form, it can quickly become an unreadable mess (see the box on page 272.)

Every form element, whether it's a text field or a checkbox, has a *name* and a *value*. The name indicates what information the element is intended to collect; for example, if you want your visitors to type their email addresses into a text field, the name of that field might be *email*. The value, on the other hand, is the user's input—what your visitors type into the text field, for example, or the selections they make from a pull-down menu.

After your visitors fill out the form and click the Submit button to transmit their responses, each form element is transmitted as a name/value pair like this: *=bob@bobville.com*. Submitting both pieces of information lets the program that processes the form figure out what the input means. After all, without a name, a value of 39 doesn't mean much (39 what? Potatoes, steps, days until Christmas?). The name/value pair (age=39) provides context for a user's input.

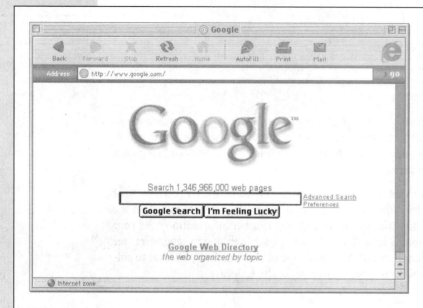

Figure 10-1:
A form can be as simple as a single empty text box (a field) and two buttons for entering a word to search a Web site, or as complex as a 100-question survey composed of fill-in-the-blank and multiple-choice questions.

The Code Backstage

Creating a form is just the first step in collecting information from your Web site's visitors. You also need to connect the form to a computer program that actually *does* something with the information. The program may simply take the data from the form and email it to you; however, it could do something as complex as contacting a bank, processing a credit card payment, creating an invoice item, and notifying a shipping department to deliver the latest Stephen King novel to someone in Nova Scotia. A form is pretty useless without a program like this running on the Web server.

These information-crunching programs can be written in a variety of languages—Perl, C, VBScript, JavaScript, Java—and may be part of a dedicated application server such as Cold Fusion Server or Microsoft's Active Server Page technology. The point is that Dreamweaver, by itself, can only create the front end of your Web site forms; it can't actually collect or process the data that your Web visitors type into it.

Writing the necessary behind-the-scenes processing software can be complex, but the concepts behind forms are straightforward:

1. Someone fills out a form on your Web page and clicks the Submit button.

2. The form data is transmitted over the Internet to a program on your Web server.

3. The program collects the data and does something with it—whatever you and the programmer decide it should do.

4. Finally, the Web server returns a page to the user. It may be a standard Web page with a message like, "Thanks for the info," or a page dynamically generated by the program itself—a detailed invoice page, for example.

So how do you create the processing half of the forms equation if you're not a programmer? If you're part of a Web development team in a company, you may already have programmers in-house who can help you create the processing program.

Furthermore, many Web-hosting companies offer free forms-processing programs as part of their services. Contact your Web host and ask about this. If so, the company will provide instructions on how to use these programs.

Another possibility awaits in Dreamweaver's sibling, Dreamweaver UltraDev. UltraDev provides all the design and page-building power of Dreamweaver, plus added features that let you create dynamic server-side scripts. If your Web server supports Active Server pages, Cold Fusion, or Java Server pages, UltraDev just might be the ticket for creating your own forms-processing programs. For more information on UltraDev, check out Macromedia's Web site at *www.macromedia.com*.

Finally, if you feel adventurous, many forms-processing programs are available for free on the Web; for a thorough sampling, see the CGI Resource Index at *http://cgi.resourceindex.com/*. Using these free programs can be tricky, however; you'll need to download the appropriate program and install it on your Web server. Your Web hosting company may not even permit you to do so.

Creating a Form

In Dreamweaver, you can build forms with one-click ease using the Objects panel. In fact, the Forms category of the panel is dedicated to this one task (shown in Figure 10-3).

To begin, you need to insert a <form> tag to indicate the boundaries of a form.

1. In the document window, click where you wish to insert the form.

    You might decide to place it after a regular paragraph of introductory text, for example.

2. **Click the small down-pointing arrow at the top of the Objects panel and select the Forms category.**

The Objects panel changes to reveal ten form-building tool icons.

3. **Click the Insert Form icon on the Objects panel (the upper-left square).**

Alternatively, if you're a menu-driven kind of person, choose Insert→Form instead.

Either way, a red, dashed-line rectangle appears in the document window, indicating the boundaries of the form (if Dreamweaver's visual aids are turned on; if not, choose View→Visual Aids→Invisible Elements). The top line represents the opening <form> tag; the bottom represents the closing tag. Make sure you always insert form objects, such as buttons and menus, *inside* these lines. (If you don't, Dreamweaver will think you're trying to create a second form on the page. It's perfectly valid to include more than one form per page, but the user can only submit one form—and its data—at a time.)

Since you can place so many other HTML elements inside of a form, it's often easier to insert the form first, adding tables, graphics, text, and form objects later.

4. **If it isn't already selected, click anywhere on the dotted red line to select the form.**

Unlike other objects, such as images, the red line of the form doesn't change appearance when selected. The only way you know you've selected the form is by checking the Property inspector. If it displays the Form Name label at the upper-left corner, as shown in Figure 10-2, you've done it correctly.

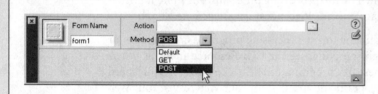

Figure 10-2:
In most cases, you'll want to use the POST method of transmitting data to your Web server.

5. **If you like, type a name for your form into the Form Name field.**

This step is optional. A form doesn't need a name to work, but a name is useful if you use JavaScript or a Dreamweaver Behavior (see the next chapter) to interact with the form or any of its fields.

6. **Type a URL into the Action field, or select a file by clicking the tiny folder icon.**

Your mission here is to specify the location of the program that will process the form; in most cases, figuring out what to type here will require the assistance of whoever wrote your forms-processing application.

It will be a regular Web path—either an absolute URL (one that begins with *http://*) or just the path to the program (see page 81 for more on these different kinds of links).

The major difference is that the file name *doesn't* end in .html. The path might be, for example, *../cgi-bin/forms.pl*. In this case, *pl* is the extension used to indicate a program written in the Perl programming language. Other common file extensions for Web programs include *.asp* (for an Active Server Page), *.cfm* (for a Cold Fusion Markup Language page), *.jsp* (for Java Server Pages), or *.cgi* (for a CGI program).

7. **Using the Method pop-up menu, specify how you want the form data transmitted to the processing program (see Figure 10-2).**

   Here again, you're in fairly technical territory, and the assistance of a programmer may be required.

   In short, however, forms can transmit data to a Web server in either of two ways. The more common method, called POST, is the default method for browsers; this is the one you'll use in most cases. It sends the form data in two steps: First, the browser contacts the form program at the URL you specified in the previous step, and then sends the data to the server. This method provides a bit more security to your data, and can easily handle forms with lots of information.

   The GET method, on the other hand, transmits the form data in the URL like this: *http://search.yahoo.com/bin/search?p=dogs*. The characters following the ? in the address represent the form data. In this instance, a single form field, named *p*, with the value *dogs*, is submitted to the server. As you can see, such a URL could wind up getting extremely long. Because some servers can't handle very long URLs, the GET method is inappropriate for forms that collect a lot of data.

You've laid the foundation for your form; now you're ready to add the input controls to it—menus, checkboxes, and so on, as described in the next section.

Adding Form Elements

Unless you've never used a computer before, the different user-interface elements available for HTML forms should look familiar: text fields where people can type in information (their names, addresses, phone numbers, and so on); checkboxes for making multiple-choice selections that are all visible simultaneously; and menus for making selections from a list. The Objects panel lets you create all of these elements and more.

If you aren't already looking at the Forms panel, click the down-pointing arrow on the Objects panel and choose Forms from the list of categories (see Figure 10-3).

What All Form Elements Have in Common

The routine for adding form elements to your document always follows the same pattern:

1. **In the document window, insert a form (see page 265).**

   Or, if the page already has a form, click inside its red border.

Tip: If the text field is the first element of the form, you can skip this step. As soon as you add a form element to a page, such as a field, checkbox, or pop-up menu, Dreamweaver automatically creates the red dotted-line form boundaries (and, behind the scenes, the corresponding <form> tags).

---

2. **Click the appropriate button on the Objects panel (see Figure 10-3).**

   Alternatively, use the Insert→Form Objects submenu. You'll soon discover that every form object on the Objects panel is also represented by a command in the Insert menu (for example, Insert→Form Objects→Text Field).

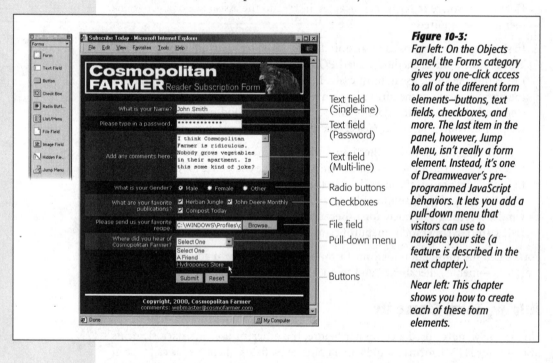

Figure 10-3:
Far left: On the Objects panel, the Forms category gives you one-click access to all of the different form elements—buttons, text fields, checkboxes, and more. The last item in the panel, however, Jump Menu, isn't really a form element. Instead, it's one of Dreamweaver's pre-programmed JavaScript behaviors. It lets you add a pull-down menu that visitors can use to navigate your site (a feature is described in the next chapter).

Near left: This chapter shows you how to create each of these form elements.

Tip: Instead of just clicking a form-element button on the Objects panel, you may prefer to drag it off the panel and into a specific position on your Web page. This trick works with any of the user controls on the Objects panel, not just text fields.

---

3. **Type a name for the freshly minted (and still highlighted) form element into the Property inspector's name box (see Figure 10-4).**

   Dreamweaver automatically names the field—for example, it might propose *textfield* (or *textfield* plus a number if there's more than one field already in the form). It's a good idea, however, to give it a new, unique name, because this name will be submitted with the user's input as a name/value pair.

4. Set the form element's properties.

For example, you may be able to specify its width, height, and other variables; the following descriptions indicate which options are available.

Text Fields

When you need to collect a specific piece of information like a person's name, phone number, or address, you'll use a text field (shown in Figure 10-3). Text fields accept typed responses and are great for open-ended questions. They come in three different flavors: *Single-line* fields for short responses, *Password* fields to hide user input from snooping eyes, and *Multi-line* fields for longer typed replies.

Once you've inserted the text field, you can adjust the following settings in the Property inspector (see Figure 10-4):

- **Char Width.** The width of a text field is measured in characters; so if you type *20* for the Char Width (character width), the text field will be as wide as necessary to hold 20 typed letters. Be aware that the exact size can vary from browser to browser.

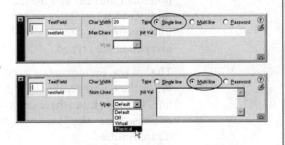

Figure 10-4:
The Property inspector looks slightly different depending on the type of text field you choose. Single-line fields let you specify the field width and the maximum number of permissible characters. Multi-line fields include height (Num Lines) and wrap settings.

- **Type.** A **Single line** text field, of course, holds just one line of text. This is the most common kind of text field; use it for collecting small pieces of information, such as a last name, social security number, or credit card number.

  Multi-line fields provide a larger area for adding multiple lines of text. You'll need to use this kind of text field when offering a place to type longer comments, such as in a "Let us know what you think!" or "Nature of problem:" field.

  Password fields hide the user's input from the prying eyes of passing co-workers and family members. Whatever your Web visitor types appears as asterisks ***
  (Windows) or bullets •••• (Mac) on the screen. (Of course, the information in the password field is still transmitted as plain text, just like any other form field; the masking action takes place only in your visitor's browser.)

- **Max Chars/Num Lines.** The Max Chars (maximum characters) field lets you limit the number of characters that will be accepted—a good way to help ensure that guests type the right information in the right place. For instance, if you use a field to collect the age of the visitor, odds are you won't need more than three characters to do it; very few 1,000-year-olds surf the Web these days.

When you've specified a Multi-line text field, this box's label changes to Num Line; you can't limit the amount of text someone types into one of these fields. You can, however, specify the height of a Multi-line text field on the screen, using the Num Lines (number of lines) field.

Note: The limit you specify here affects only how tall the field will be on the screen. Your visitors can type as many lines of information as they want. (A scroll bar will appear if the typing exceeds the size of the box you've specified with the Num Lines option.)

- **Wrap.** The Wrap property (Multi-line text fields only) can be confusing; it specifies what happens when your visitor types right to the edge of the text box.

  The **Default** value varies from browser to browser; you can't rely on it to produce consistent results for all users.

  The **Off** setting prevents sentences from wrapping inside the text field. When the typed text exceeds the width of the field, a horizontal scroll bar appears at the bottom of the field, and the text scrolls to the left; the text remains on a single line until the user hits Enter or Return. You'll almost never want to use this option; it forces your visitor to scroll not only up and down, but left and right, too, to see everything she's typed.

  The last two options create a text field that works like most people would expect: When the typing reaches the edge of the box, it automatically wraps to the next line. To your visitor, there's no visual difference between the Virtual and Physical options; these wrapping styles differ only in the way they format the text when it's transmitted.

  The **Virtual** setting displays line breaks only on the screen, in your visitor's browser; when the text is actually submitted, it will appear as a single line (unless the user manually inserted line breaks by pressing Enter or Return). If you create the field using the **Physical** setting, on the other hand, the browser inserts line breaks at the end of each line as it wraps. When transmitted, the text maintains these line breaks.

  In general, the Virtual setting is the best approach. It doesn't insert artificial line breaks and maintains the integrity of the user's input.

- **Init Val.** Here, you can specify the Initial Value of the field—starter text that will automatically appear in the field, so that it won't be empty when the visitor begins completing the form. You can use this feature to include explanatory text inside the field itself, such as "Type your name in this box" or "Example: (212) 555-1212."

After you're finished tweaking the text field's properties, don't forget to add a text label next to the field back in your document window. (Add the text just by typing it, as you would any Web-page text.) It's important to let your site's visitors know what the text field is for. Short labels like "First Name," "Phone Number," or "Type your comments here" will let users know what they need to do.

FREQUENTLY ASKED QUESTION

Using the Password Field for Credit-Card Numbers

Can I use the Password field type for credit card numbers and other sensitive information?

Yes, but it won't give the information any extra security.

The Password field does one thing: It hides user input *on the screen.* Someone looking over your visitor's shoulder won't be able to read what he's typing—it'll look like a bunch of dots—but once that information is submitted over the Internet, it's just as visible as a regular text field.

In order to provide real security for forms information, you need an *encrypted connection* between the Web server and the user's computer. Most Web site creators use SSL or Secure Socket Layer technology for this purpose.

Most Web browsers understand this technology, but your Web server must be specially configured to work in this mode. Contact your Web host to see if you can use SSL on your server (the answer is usually Yes). If so, they'll be able to tell you how to set it up.

Checkboxes

Checkboxes (see Figure 10-3) are simple and to the point; they're either selected or not. They're great for multiple-choice questions in which your visitor is allowed to select more than one item in a group. For example, suppose you produce three different email newsletters that you send out each month. In your form, you might include some text—"Check the boxes for the newsletters you'd like to receive"—and three corresponding checkboxes, so that each visitor can sign up for only the newsletters he wants.

Once you've added a checkbox to a form, you can set up these options for it in the Property inspector (Figure 10-5):

- **Checked Value.** You're specifying here the information that, if your visitor turns on this checkbox, will be submitted when the form data is sent to your processing program. It doesn't necessarily have to match the checkbox's label (which you'll create in a subsequent step); it could, instead, transmit some special coded response to your processing application. Your visitors will never actually see this information.

- **Initial State.** Your checkbox doesn't have to start out unselected; if you like, it can be already checked when your Web page first appears. You may have seen this setup on sites that require you to sign up for some service. Usually there'll be a checkbox—already checked—down near the bottom of the form, with fine print like this: "Check here if you want to get daily, unsolicited email from our marketing department."

After adjusting the Property inspector, don't forget to return to the document window to add a text label next to the field. Let people know what the checkbox is for: "Yes, sign me up!" for example. Finally, you may want to insert another checkbox; checkboxes don't necessarily have to come in groups, but they often do.

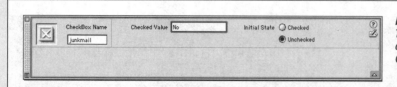

Figure 10-5:
The actual value of a checkbox is defined in its Checked Value property.

Giving Order to Your Forms

If you're not careful, creating forms can quickly lead to visual chaos. The different shapes and sizes of text boxes, radio buttons, and other form objects don't naturally align well with text. Use tables to get a handle on the appearance of your forms.

In the first picture above, form elements were added next to the text on each line, forcing your eye to follow a prominent zigzag pattern created by the form's text boxes. The result is not only ugly, but also hard to read.

In the second picture, a table made of 2 columns and 13 rows (one row for each question) organizes the text and

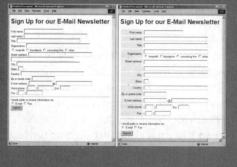

form elements into two columns. Notice that the text next to each form element aligns to the right, creating a clean edge that effectively mirrors the edge created by the form fields.

To make this work most effectively, set each text field to the same width, using the Char Width property.

When using this technique, add the <form> tag first, insert the table inside the form's dotted red boundaries, and then add form elements inside the table. If you insert a table first and then try to insert a form, Dreamweaver will only let you add it to a single cell of the table.

See Chapter 6 for more on creating tables.

Radio Buttons

Radio buttons, like checkboxes, are very simple (see Figure 10-3); they're either selected (represented on screen as a solid circle) or not (an empty circle). But unlike checkboxes, they restrict your visitor to making only one choice from a group, just like the radio buttons on an old-style automobile dashboard. Radio buttons are ideal, therefore, for multiple-choice questions that have only one possible answer. For example, "What is your income?: A. $10-40,000, B. $40-70,000, C. $70-100,000, D. None of your business."

You set up these options for a radio button in the Property inspector (Figure 10-6):

- **Checked Value.** This is the information that will be submitted when your visitor selects this button. Once again, it doesn't necessarily have to match the radio button's on-screen label.

- **Initial State.** Often, when a form page first loads, one radio button in each set is preselected. To do your visitors this timesaving courtesy, turn on Checked for the button that holds the default value, or the one you expect they'll choose most often. Of course, if making any radio-button choice is optional, then you can leave all of the buttons unselected by setting their initial states to Unchecked.

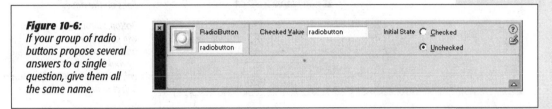

Figure 10-6:
If your group of radio buttons propose several answers to a single question, give them all the same name.

Radio buttons always come in groups; only one button in the group can be selected at the same time. To achieve this effect, every button in the same group shares the same name. If, when testing your page, you notice that you can select more than one radio button at a time, make sure you gave them all the same name. Thus, the buttons should each have different Checked values, but share the same name. (The tutorial at the end of the chapter should make all of this clear.)

The final step in creating radio buttons is to add text labels for the entire group and each button. Dreamweaver offers no special tools for this purpose; simply click in the document window and type, just as you'd add any text to the page. Your whole-group-of-buttons label may take the form of a question ("How would you like to pay?"); the labels for the individual buttons might say, for example, "Visa," "MasterCard," and "I.O.U."

Pull-down Menus and Lists

While both checkboxes and radio buttons provide ways to offer multiple choices, you should consider them only when there are relatively few choices. A form can quickly become overcrowded with buttons and boxes if there are too many options to choose from. The beauty of pull-down menus (pop-up menus) and lists is that they offer your visitors many choices without taking up a lot of screen space. (Figure 10-7 shows an example.)

Once you've inserted a menu or list object onto your document window, here's how to adjust the Property inspector settings:

- **Type.** Menus and lists differ both in appearance (see Figure 10-7) and in function, as described in a moment; click the one you want (Menu or List).

- **Height.** A list can be a single line tall (in which case you may as well use a menu), or many lines (allowing your visitors to see a number of choices at once). The number you type into the Height box (available for lists only) should reflect the amount of space you wish the list to take up on the page. A vertical scroll bar will appear automatically if the height you specify here is smaller than the number of items in the list.

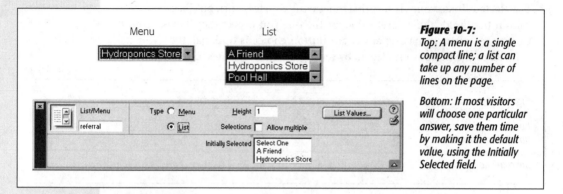

Figure 10-7:
Top: A menu is a single compact line; a list can take up any number of lines on the page.

Bottom: If most visitors will choose one particular answer, save them time by making it the default value, using the Initially Selected field.

- **Allow multiple.** Here's a key difference between menus and lists: If you turn on this option, a user can select more than one item from a list, just by pressing the Ctrl (⌘) key while clicking different options in the list.

- **List Values.** This button opens List Values dialog box (see Figure 10-8), where you build the list of options in your list or menu. Each item is composed of two parts: a *label* (the text that actually appears in the menu or list on the Web page) and the value (the information that will be submitted with the form, which isn't necessarily the same thing as the label).

To use this dialog box, type an item label. Press Tab (or click in the Value column) and then type the value, if you like. (See Figure 10-8 for details.)

Including a value is optional; if you don't specify one, your form will submit the item's label *as* the value. Still, setting up a separate value is often useful. Imagine that you've designed a pull-down menu on an e-commerce site, so that your visitors can choose the month in which their credit cards expire. Figure 10-8 shows what the items for such a pull-down menu might look like: The names of the months would actually appear on the menu, but when a user selects, say, April, the number 4 is what will actually be transmitted to your forms-processing program.

Since computer programs are often more comfortable with numbers than names—and humans often the exact opposite—it can make more sense to use numbers for list values in this case.

Another example: When offering your visitors a pop-up menu of products from which to choose, the label might be the human-friendly name of the product, such as "Blue Wool Cap." The value would be the model number that your forms-processing program can understand, such as XSD1278.

Click OK when you're finished building your menu or list. You can always return to this screen and edit the list of options; to do so, click the menu or list in the document window and then click the List Values button on the Property inspector. You return to the dialog box shown in Figure 10-8.

As with other form elements, you can, and probably should, add some explanatory text alongside it in the document window.

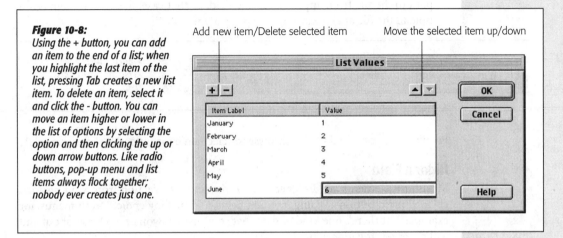

Figure 10-8:
Using the + button, you can add an item to the end of a list; when you highlight the last item of the list, pressing Tab creates a new list item. To delete an item, select it and click the - button. You can move an item higher or lower in the list of options by selecting the option and then clicking the up or down arrow buttons. Like radio buttons, pop-up menu and list items always flock together; nobody ever creates just one.

Add new item/Delete selected item

Move the selected item up/down

File Field

Receiving responses to checkboxes, radio buttons, and pull-down menus is all well and good, but what if you'd like your visitors to submit something a little more meaty—such as an actual file? Imagine a bulletin-board system, for example, that would allow users to post JPEG images of themselves, or upload word processing documents to share with others. They can do just that, thanks to the *file field* field (see Figure 10-3)—and a little magic from your Web server.

Before you get carried away with the possibilities the file field offers, you'll need to do a little research to see if you can use it on your Web site. Although Dreamweaver makes it easy to *add* a field for uploading image files, text files, and other documents, you'll need to check with the administrator of your Web server to see if anonymous file uploads are permitted (some servers don't allow this kind of activity for fear of receiving viruses or overly large files). Then, of course, you'll have to ensure that the program that processes the form is programmed to *do* something with the incoming file—to store it somewhere on the server, for instance.

When you click the File Field button on the Objects panel (or choose Insert→Form Objects→File Field), Dreamweaver inserts a text field *and* a Browse button; together, they constitute a single file field. When you click either one, you highlight both.

The Browse button, once it's posted on the Web and visible in somebody's browser, opens up the standard Windows or Macintosh Open File dialog box, permitting your visitor to navigate to, and select, a file for uploading.

The Property inspector offers only two settings to change (other than specifying a more creative name):

- **Char Width.** The width of a text field is measured in characters; if you type *20* for the character width, the field will be 20 characters wide.

- **Max Char.** This field (Figure 10-9) is intended to limit the number of characters that the field will accept—which could pose a problem if it prevented the full path to the file from appearing in the field. In that case, the browser might not upload the file at all. Leave this property alone.

Figure 10-9:
Avoid the Max Chars Field.

Finally, label your field ("Click Browse to select a file for uploading," for example).

Hidden Field

Most form elements are designed to accommodate interaction from your visitors: clicking radio buttons, typing into text fields, and making choices from menus, for example. But there's one kind of field that your visitors won't even know about and will never set: the *hidden* field.

Why, you're probably asking, would you need to submit a value you already know? In fact, hidden fields are very useful for supplying information to the programs that process forms—information that the program has no other way of knowing. For example, most Web-hosting services offer a generic forms-processing program that collects information submitted with a form and emails it to a selected person. But how does the program know who to email the data to? After all, it's a *generic* program that's used by hundreds of other people. The solution: a hidden field. A hidden field could store the information required for the program to properly process the form—*email=me@mydomain.com,* for example.

To insert a hidden field, click the Hidden Field button on the Objects panel, or choose Insert→Form Objects→Hidden Field. A gold shield icon—Dreamweaver's symbol for HTML that won't be visible in a Web browser—appears on the page. Use the Property inspector to give the field a name and a *value*—the value that will get submitted to your forms-processing program (in example above, your email address).

Buttons

No form is complete without a Submit button, which your Web visitors must click as a final step (see Figure 10-3); only then do their responses set out on their way to your forms-processing application. Another button worth including is a Reset button, which your visitors can click when they've filled out a form and realize they've made an error. The Reset button clears all of the form entries and reset all of the form fields to their original values.

The Property inspector controls (Figure 10-10) for a freshly inserted button are:

- **Label field.** The label is the name that appears on the button. Dreamweaver proposes *Submit*, but you're free to substitute *Do It*, *Make It So*, or *Send my data on its merry way*, if you like.

  For buttons, the label *is* the value that will be submitted like other form data; that's why there's no separate Value field on the Property inspector. This quirk opens up some interesting possibilities. You could, for example, include *several* Submit buttons, each with a different label. Maybe you're creating a form for a database application; one button might say Delete, while another says Edit. Depending on which button gets clicked, the program processing the form would either delete the record from the database or modify it.

- **Action.** These three buttons govern what happens when somebody clicks your button. A **Submit Form** button transmits the form data over the Internet to the form-processing program; a **Reset form** button sets all the fields back to their original values. (This doesn't mean that the fields, checkboxes, or menu items are left blank, unchecked, or unselected; instead, they return to their *initial* values, which you specified when creating these various controls. For example, if you set the Initial State property of a checkbox to Checked, and your visitor unchecks the box and then clicks the Reset button, a checkmark will reappear in the box.)

  Setting the button's action to **None** means that clicking on the button has no effect on the form. "Gee *that's* useful," you're probably thinking.

  But although the button doesn't submit the data or reset the form's fields, you'll need to choose the None option if you want to add interactivity to the button using Dreamweaver's built-in Behaviors (see the next chapter). In this way, you can use a common user-interface element—the 3-D beveled look of a form button—to trigger any of many different actions, like opening a new browser window, starting or stopping a Flash movie, or popping up a message on the screen. If you're a JavaScript programmer, you can use the button to activate your own programs.

Figure 10-10:
Buttons have just three properties: Name, Label, and Action.

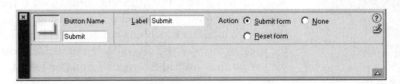

Tip: You can also use a graphic as a Submit button, thanks to something called an *image field*, thus freeing you to be more creative with the look of the button itself. Click the Image Field button on the Objects panel, or choose Insert→Form Objects→Image Field, to select a graphic you want to use as a button. When a Web visitor clicks the image, it submits the form and all its data. (Unfortunately, Image Fields only do one thing: submit form data. They can't be used as form Reset buttons.)

Validating Forms

It can be frustrating to look over feedback that's been submitted via a form on your Web page, only to notice that your visitor failed to provide a name, email address, or some other piece of critical information. That's why, depending on the type of form, you might want to make certain information mandatory.

For instance, a form used for subscribing to an email newsletter isn't much use if the user doesn't type in an email address for receiving it. Likewise, if you need a shipping address to deliver a brochure or product, you'll want to be sure that the user included her address on the form.

Luckily, Dreamweaver provides a Behavior—a ready-made JavaScript program— that accomplishes this exact task. Called Validate Form, this Dreamweaver behavior alerts users when they haven't filled out a form properly. You can specify that a particular field can't be left blank, or that it must contain numbers only, or that it must contain a proper email address. If someone attempts to submit the form without the correct information, a small dialog box pops up identifying the mistake. You'll no longer receive blank forms!

Unfortunately there's a built-in limitation to this Dreamweaver behavior: you can validate only *text fields*. In other words, you can't check to see if a user clicked a particular checkbox or made a selection from a pull-down menu. Nor can you see if they chose a file to upload or clicked a radio button.

Nonetheless, the Validate Form behavior is a great tool for making sure you get the right information from your site's visitors. (Dreamweaver Behaviors are discussed in depth in the next chapter.)

To validate a form:

1. **Select the form or a text field you wish to validate.**

   You can validate form fields in two ways: one field at a time, or all fields at once.

   The first option involves adding the Validate Form behavior to each text field you wish to validate. The form will check to see if the field contents are valid (using one or more of the criteria you set using the steps below) after the user exits the field, either by tabbing out of the field or by clicking anywhere else on the page. In this way, you can validate a particular field immediately, as soon as your visitor has finished entering information into it.

   If you choose to validate the entire form, no checking takes place until your visitor clicks the Submit button. At that moment, the browser will check all the fields you specified; an error message will appear if any of them don't meet the criteria you've specified. To select a form, click on its red dashed border or click <form> in the document window's tag selector.

2. **Choose Window→Behaviors.**

   The Behaviors panel appears.

3. On the Behaviors panel, click the + button; choose Validate Form from the menu.

The Validate Form dialog box appears (see Figure 10-11). Each text field can have its own validation criterion, which shows up in parentheses next to its name.

Figure 10-11:
In this example, the text field "name" must have a value in it; the field "password" is not required, but if the user does fill out this field, it must contain a number. If a field can be left blank— the "email" field, in this example—there's no need to validate it; don't turn on the Required box.

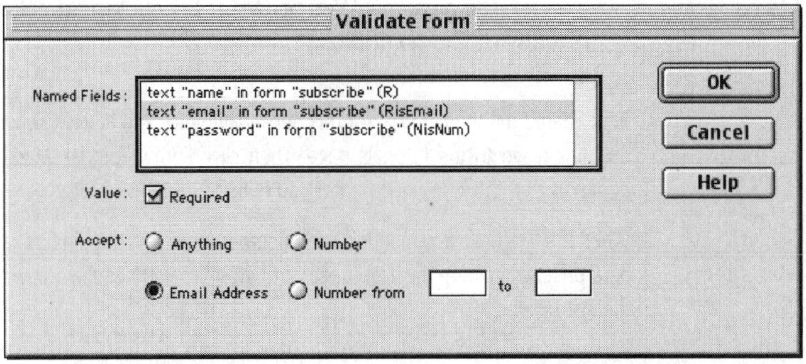

4. Select the field you wish to validate from the list.

You can click it with the mouse, or press the up and down arrow keys to highlight the one you want.

5. Turn on the Required checkbox if completing a certain field is mandatory.

6. Using the Accept radio buttons, choose one of the four validation types.

Anything accepts any value—numbers, letters, or symbols.

Number means that only numbers will be accepted in the field. You might turn this option on, for example, for text fields labeled, "How old are you?" or "How much do you weigh?"

Email Address is for fields that require an email address. Note that this feature checks for the correct email address *format,* not for a *valid* email address—it can't go out on the Internet and determine whether or not your visitor is trying to fool you by typing in a bogus address. In fact, this feature only checks to see if an @ symbol was used in the field.

You can also specify a range of acceptable numbers using the **Number from** option by entering starting and ending numbers. Use this for questions on your form that run along the lines of, "Rate this service from 1 to 10."

As you go, Dreamweaver helps you remember your selections by adding a letter in parentheses after each field name in the dialog box. *R* means that a value is required; *N* means that the field can be left blank; *isEmail* means that the field should contain an email address; *isNum* means that the value should be a number; and *isRange* means the value must be a number within a certain range.

If you're validating the entire form, select additional fields and add the same or different validation criteria, if you like.

7. **Click OK to apply the behavior.**

You return to your document window, where your fields are now ready to use—and to check themselves for accurate entries. To see if it works, press F12 to preview the page in a Web browser. Try clicking the Submit button without filling out any of the text fields.

Tip: There's a bonus tutorial for this book waiting for you at *www.sawmac.com/missing/*. Click the Tutorials link to go to the tutorials page. Then click Forms Tutorial–Mac files or Forms Tutorial–Win files, depending on the kind of computer you're using.

When the files have downloaded and uncompressed, you should have a folder named DWForms on your hard drive, containing the Web pages and graphics you need, along with a PDF (Acrobat) file containing the instructions.

EXTENSION ALERT

Advanced Form Validation

The Validation options Dreamweaver offers are rather rudimentary. The email validation option, for example, doesn't even *really* check for a correctly formatted email address; it just looks for at least one character followed by an @ symbol followed by one more character.

Fortunately, you can find many form-related extensions on the Macromedia Exchange Web site (see page 493); once

you're on the Dreamweaver exchange page, perform a search for the word *validate*.

For example, you'll find three extensions by renowned extension developer Massimo Foti. With these add-ons to Dreamweaver, you can check your form fields for Zip codes, phone numbers, Social Security numbers, and much more.

Dreamweaver Behaviors

C hapter 5 makes clear how easy it is to add mouse *rollover* effects using Dreamweaver's Rollover Image object. That and other interactive features rely on *scripts* (small programs) written in the JavaScript programming language.

You *could* create the same effects without Dreamweaver, but you'd need to take a few extra steps: buy a book on JavaScript, read it from cover to cover, learn about concepts like *array, function,* and *document object model,* and spend weeks discovering the eccentric rules governing how different browsers interpret JavaScript code differently.

Fortunately, Dreamweaver lets you add these dynamic JavaScript programs to your Web pages without doing a lick of programming.

Note: Macromedia's Dreamweaver 4.0.1 update fixes several bugs and also allows the behaviors described in this chapter to work in Navigator 6.0. Download this free update before using Behaviors (see the tip on page 3 for more information).

Understanding Behaviors

Dreamweaver *Behaviors* are powerful, prepackaged JavaScript programs that let you add interactivity to your Web pages with ease, even if you don't know the first thing about JavaScript. By adding behaviors, you can make your Web pages do things like:

• Make layers appear and disappear (see Chapter 12).

• Require users to fill out certain fields in a form (Chapter 10)—as when, for example, you want to make sure that an email address or name is entered before the form is submitted.

• Open a new browser window to a specified size, with or without scroll bars, status bar, location bar, and other Web browser "chrome."

• Let your visitors navigate a Web site using a pop-up menu.

• Give feedback to the visitor in a dialog box or in the browser's status bar.

Tip: Try it yourself. See examples of all of Dreamweaver's Behaviors on the companion Web site for this book: *www.sawmac.com/missing/behaviors/*

FREQUENTLY ASKED QUESTION

Behaviors and Added Code

I hear that the JavaScript that Dreamweaver produces adds excessive lines of code, unnecessarily adding to a page's file size. Is this a reason not to use Behaviors?

In some cases, it's true a JavaScript programmer could write a program that does what a Dreamweaver behavior does using less code.

However, Dreamweaver Behaviors were created to work in as many browsers as possible without producing errors in older browsers. JavaScript doesn't work the same in all browsers or in all versions of browsers; the two main brows-

ers—Netscape Navigator and Internet Explorer—understand JavaScript differently, at times so differently that programmers have to resort to elaborate workarounds, which require a lot of experience, practice, and patience.

Fortunately, the engineers at Macromedia have a vast understanding of JavaScript, HTML, and Web browsers, ensuring that Dreamweaver Behaviors work in as many browsers as possible. At times, this compatibility may lead to larger files with more lines of code, but it also gives you the assurance that your Web pages will work for the broadest audience possible.

Behavior Elements

To use a behavior, you bring together three elements: an action, an event, and an HTML tag:

• The **action** is whatever the behavior is supposed to *do*—open a new browser window or display a message in the browser's status bar, for instance.

• The **event** is the *trigger* that causes the action to happen. It's usually something your visitor does, like clicking a Submit button on a form.

• Finally, both an event and an action are applied to an **HTML tag** to bring interactivity to your Web page.

Let's say you want to let visitors go to different Web pages on your site by using a pop-up menu—a very common Web-page element. This pop-up menu lists the different pages of your site—*About this Company, Contact Us, See Our Products,* and so on.

When a visitor selects one of the options from the menu, his browser opens the Web page for that section of the site. In this case, the *HTML tag* is the pop-up menu itself—a <select> tag; the *action* is opening another Web page in the site; and the *event* brings the two together so that when your visitor makes a selection from the pop-up menu, his browser goes to the selected Web page. Voilà—interactivity!

More About Events

When people visit a Web page, they do more than just read it—they interact with it. You already know that when someone clicks a link, the browser reacts by loading a new Web page or jumping to a named anchor (page 90).

But visitors can also interact with a Web page in a variety of other ways: They may resize the browser window, move the mouse around the screen, make a selection from a pop-up menu, click an image, type inside a form field, or click a form's Reset button. Each of those interactions is an event; Web browsers "listen to" and react to different events with actions.

In JavaScript and Dreamweaver, the names of events always begin with the word "on," which essentially means "when." For example, the onLoad event refers to the moment when an object fully loads into the browser, such as when a Web page, its

---

GEM IN THE ROUGH

Link Events Without Loading a New Web Page

As you start to use Behaviors, you'll quickly notice that there are an awful lot of useful events associated with links. Links can respond to many user interactions, such as moving the mouse over the link, moving it away from the link, or clicking the link.

Clicking a link usually opens a different Web page. But there are times when you may want to use the onClick event to trigger an action without actually leaving the current Web page.

For instance, you might have a Web page with lots of unusual or technical words. It would be great to program the page so that when someone clicks an unfamiliar word, a dialog box displaying its definition pops up on the screen (using the Pop-up Message action, described on page 307). Unfortunately, a Web browser doesn't know when you click on a word—there's no event associated with regular text. However, browsers *do* know when you click a link—and can respond to this action.

But in this case, you don't want to use a real link; that would force a new page to load. You just want to use a

link's onClick event.

Fortunately, you can still take advantage of all of the great events links have to offer without adding links that take you away from the page. Instead of using a real URL or path for the link, you can use a "dummy" link—a link that goes nowhere.

There are two types of "dummy" (also called "null") links. The first uses the pound symbol (#). Simply select the text or graphic to which you want to add the behavior, and then, in the Property inspector, instead of adding a URL in the Link field, simply type in #. (You can also create a dummy link by typing *javascript:;* into the link field. Be sure to include both the colon and semicolon.) This dummy link doesn't load a new Web page, but gives you a link to which you can apply behaviors.

The advantage of the second method is that some browsers scroll to the top of the page when a visitor clicks a link that uses the # symbol, which could be disconcerting if you attached a behavior that appears far down a page.

---

images, and other linked files have been downloaded. Events also include the various ways in which someone can interact with a particular HTML tag (element). For instance, someone can move the mouse over a link or click a link; the corresponding events for links are called onMouseOver and onClick.

Applying Behaviors

Dreamweaver makes adding behaviors as easy as selecting a tag and choosing an action from a pop-up menu in the Behaviors panel.

The Behaviors Panel

The Behaviors panel is mission control for Dreamweaver's Behaviors. On it, you can see any behaviors that are applied to a tag, add more behaviors, and edit behaviors that are already applied.

You can open the Behaviors panel in any of three ways:

- Choose Window→Behaviors.
- Press Shift-F3.
- Click the Open Behaviors Panel button in the Launcher or Launcher bar ().

The panel then appears on your screen.

The currently selected tag is indicated at the top of the Behaviors panel, and a list of all of the behaviors applied to that tag, if any, appears below. Each behavior is listed in two parts: Events and Actions, as described earlier.

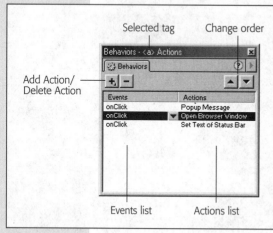

Figure 11-1:
The Behaviors panel lists all of the behaviors attached to the selected HTML tag and lets you add, edit, and delete them. In addition, if you have several behaviors that are triggered by the same event, you can change the order in which they occur with the up and down pointing arrows. Behaviors are grouped by event and listed in the order in which they occur. As you can see here, it's possible to have one event–onClick–trigger multiple actions.

Behaviors, Step by Step

Open the Behaviors panel, and then proceed as follows:

1. Select the object or tag.

You must attach a behavior to an HTML tag, such as a link (indicated by the <a> tag) or the page's body (<body> tag). Take care, however: It's easy to apply a behavior accidentally to the wrong tag. Form elements, like checkboxes and text fields, are easy to select; just click one to select it. For other kinds of tags, consider using the tag selector, as described on page 16, for more precision.

Tip: You can be sure which tag the behavior is applied to by looking at the title bar of the Behaviors panel; the tag's name is listed there.

2. **In the Behaviors panel, add an action.**

   Click the + button in the Behaviors panel and, from the menu, select the action you wish to add (see Figure 11-3). You'll find a complete list of these behaviors and what they do beginning on page 292.

   Some actions are dimmed in the menu because elements necessary for the behavior to work are missing from the Web page. For instance, if you haven't included a form in your Web page, the Validate Form behavior is grayed out. Others are dimmed because they must be applied to a particular page element; for example, Jump Menu is off-limits until you've added a list/menu field to the page and selected it.

3. **In the dialog box that opens, set options for the action.**

   Each action has properties that pertain specifically to it; you set them to your liking in the dialog box that appears. For instance, when you choose the Open URL action, Dreamweaver asks what Web page you want to load. Once again, the following pages describe each of the actions you'll be offered.

4. **Click OK to apply the action.**

   At this point, Dreamweaver adds, to the underlying code of your page, the HTML and JavaScript required to make the behavior work; your behavior's name appears listed in the Behaviors panel.

   Unlike HTML objects, behaviors usually add code to two different places in a document. For behaviors, Dreamweaver usually adds JavaScript code to the head of the document *and* to the body of the page.

5. **Change the event, if desired.**

   When your newly created action shows up in the Behaviors panel, Dreamweaver displays, in the Events column of the panel, a default event (trigger) for the selected tag and action. For example, if you add a Set Text of Status Bar behavior to a link, Dreamweaver suggests the onMouseOver event. (The target browser you select—see Figure 11-2—may affect which event Dreamweaver chooses).

   However, this default event may not be the only event available. Links, for instance, can handle many different events; an action could begin when your visitor's cursor moves *over* the link (the onMouseOver event), *clicks* the link (the onClick event), and so on.

To change the event for a particular behavior, click the Events pop-up menu (the down-pointing arrow) next to the event name (see Figure 11-2); a list of available events for that particular tag appears. Select the event you want. (See page 289 for a list of all available events in the most popular browsers.)

Tip: To make sure that your new behavior works on a particular browser and version, choose a browser's name from the Show Events For submenu (see Figure 11-2). Selecting older browsers from this list limits the number of events you have to choose from. (You don't set this on a behavior-by-behavior basis; it's a global, set-it-and-forget-it choice that applies to all behaviors.)

When you're done, you can leave the Behaviors panel open to add more behaviors to the tag, or to other tags. Select another tag, using the document window or tag selector, and repeat steps 2 through 5.

Adding multiple behaviors

You're not limited to a single behavior per HTML tag. You can, and often will, apply several behaviors to the same tag. For instance, when a page loads—the onLoad event of the <body> tag—it might preload images to be used in rollover effects, open a small browser window displaying a pop-up advertisement, *and* start a DHTML animation (see Chapter 12).

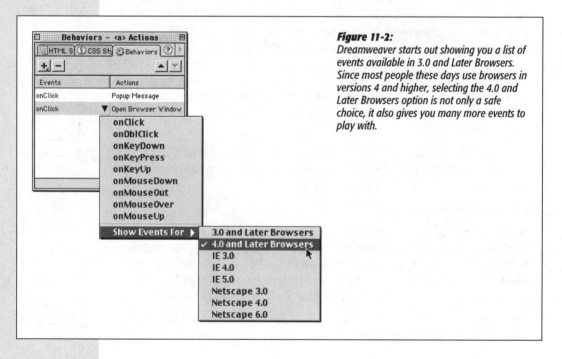

Figure 11-2:
Dreamweaver starts out showing you a list of events available in 3.0 and Later Browsers. Since most people these days use browsers in versions 4 and higher, selecting the 4.0 and Later Browsers option is not only a safe choice, it also gives you many more events to play with.

Nor are you limited to a single *event* per tag. For instance, you can add different actions to a link that are triggered by different events such as onMouseOver, onMouseOut, and onClick.

For example, if you'd set things up for a link as shown in Figure 11-1, when you click the selected link in the browser window, a Pop-up Message appears first, then a new browser window opens, and finally a message appears in the status bar.

Editing Behaviors

Once a behavior is applied, you can edit it at any time. Double-click the behavior in the Behaviors panel to reopen the Settings dialog box that appeared originally, as described in step 3 of the previous instructions. Make any changes you like and click OK.

To remove a behavior from your Web page, select it in the Behaviors panel and click the – button, or press Delete. (If you *accidentally* delete a behavior, just choose Edit→Undo Remove Behavior.)

FREQUENTLY ASKED QUESTION

The Vanishing Events List

I applied a behavior to a link, but the only event available is onMouseOver. What happened to all the other events?

You may have accidentally selected events for 3.0 and Later Browsers in the Events pop-up menu (see Figure 11-2). Browser versions prior to 4.0 don't work with many events.

To make sure your behavior works in as many browsers as possible, check out the Show Events For submenu (also shown in Figure 11-2). The earlier the browser version you choose here, the fewer events you'll see listed. On the other hand, choosing an earlier browser version ensures that your behavior will work for more of your visitors. Keep in mind, however, that the vast majority of Web surfers use *at least* a version 4 browser, making the "4.0 and Later Browsers" option a safe (and rewarding) choice.

A Quick Example

This brief example is designed to give you a clear overview of the behavior-creation process. In it, you'll use a behavior that makes an important message appear automatically when the Web page opens.

1. **Choose File→New to create a new untitled document.**

   You'll start with a new page.

2. **Choose File→Save and save the file to your computer.**

   It doesn't matter where you save the page, since you won't be including any graphics or linking to any pages.

   You'll start the process of adding a behavior by selecting a specific tag—in this case the page's <body> tag.

3. In the tag selector at the lower-left corner of the document window, click <body>.

Once the tag is selected, you can apply one or more behaviors to it. But first, make sure the Behaviors panel is open. If you don't see it, choose Window→Arrange Panels. The Behaviors panel generally appears on the right side of your screen.

4. Click the + button on the Behaviors panel; from the pop-up menu, choose Pop-up Message (see Figure 11-3).

The Pop-up Message dialog box appears.

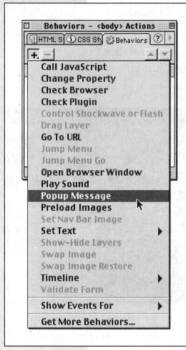

Figure 11-3:
Behaviors you can't currently apply are grayed out. This happens when a necessary object is missing for your page. For example, you can't apply the Control Shockwave or Flash behavior if you don't have a Shockwave or Flash movie on the page.

5. In the message box, type *Attention! Don't miss our big sale: 2 rototillers for the price of 1!* Then click OK.

Dreamweaver adds the required JavaScript code to the page. Notice that the Behaviors panel lists the *action* called Pop-up Message next to the *event* called onLoad. The onLoad event triggers an action *after* a page and everything on it—graphics, and so on—have downloaded.

To see the page in action, preview it in a Web browser:

6. Press the F12 key to preview the page.

See page 37 for more on using this preview function.

Events for 4.0 Browsers

Unfortunately, JavaScript works differently not only in different browsers, but in different *versions* of browsers. Older versions of Netscape Navigator and Internet Explorer don't recognize the same range of events as newer versions. In addition, the latest versions of Netscape Navigator and Internet Explorer differ significantly when it comes to JavaScript (the events available in Netscape Navigator 6 are far fewer than those in Internet Explorer 5). These incompatibilities can make a chore out of developing interactive Web pages that work for the largest possible audience.

If you hope to build successful interactive Web sites, you can't get around having to learn which tag/event combinations work in which browsers. Over 90 percent of Web surfers today, however, use versions 4 or greater of Netscape Navigator or Internet Explorer, so this book concentrates on behaviors that work with those browsers. The following pages list and explain the most useful HTML tags and events that work in those browsers; you can refer to this section whenever you apply a behavior. (Remember: The choice of events for a given tag depends on which option you've selected in the Show Event For menu [see Figure 11-2].)

Each entry shows you the name of the event, as you'll see it listed in the Behaviors panel; a plain-English description of what that event really means; and the list of tags to which this event can be applied. See Figure 11-4 for the visual representations of those HTML tags.

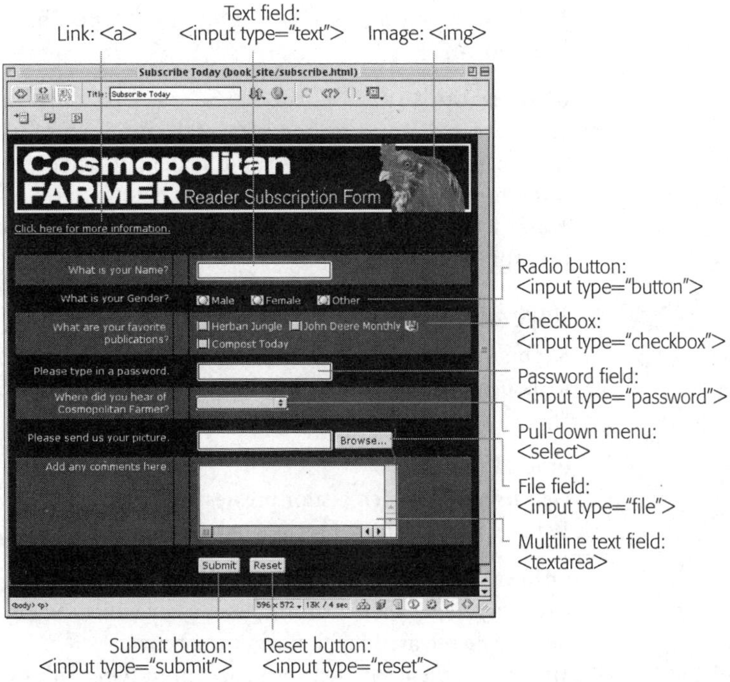

Figure 11-4:
This sample Web page illustrates HTML tags to which you can attach events. Not shown is the body of the Web page (the whole thing, in other words), whose tag is <body>, and the form portion of this page (see Chapter 10), whose tag is <form>. Whenever you set up a behavior, you must attach it to one of these tags.

Text field:
Link: <a>   <input type="text">   Image: <img>

Radio button:
<input type="button">

Checkbox:
<input type="checkbox">

Password field:
<input type="password">

Pull-down menu:
<select>

File field:
<input type="file">

Multiline text field:
<textarea>

Submit button: Reset button:
<input type="submit">   <input type="reset">

Mouse Events

Web designers most often use mouse *movement* events to trigger actions (like the familiar rollover image). But mouse *clicks*—on checkboxes, radio buttons, and other clickable form elements—can be mouse events, too.

onMouseOver

Gets triggered: When the cursor moves over the tag.
Works with these tags: <a>, <area>

onMouseOut

Gets triggered: When the cursor moves off of the tag.
Works with these tags: <a>, <area>

onClick

Gets triggered: When visitor clicks the tag (and releases the mouse button).
Works with these tags: <a>, <area>, <input type="button | checkbox | radio | reset | submit">

onDblClick

Gets triggered: When visitor double-clicks the tag.
Works with these tags: <a>, <area>, <input type="button | checkbox | radio | reset | submit">

onMouseDown

Gets triggered: When visitor clicks the tag. The mouse button doesn't need to be released for this event to occur (note the contrast with onClick).
Works with these tags: <a>, <img>, <input type="button | checkbox | radio | reset | submit">

onMouseUp

Gets triggered: When visitor releases the mouse button while cursor is over the tag. In principle, the effect is the same as the onClick event; but this one works in far fewer browsers.
Works with these tags: <a>, <img>, <input type="button | checkbox | radio | reset | submit">

Keyboard Events

Keyboard events respond to key presses and releases; most Web designers use them in association with form elements that accept text, such as a password or text fields. (See Chapter 10 for more on forms.)

onKeyPress

Gets triggered: When visitor presses and releases a key while the tag is selected.
Works with these tags: <textarea>, <input type="file | password | text">, <a>

onKeyDown

Gets triggered: When visitor presses a key while the tag is selected. The key doesn't need to be released for this event to occur.
Works with these tags: <textarea>, <input type="file | password | text">, <a>

onKeyUp

Gets triggered: When visitor releases a key while the tag is selected.
Works with these tags: <textarea>, <input type="file | password | text">, <a>

Body and Frameset Events

Several events relate to actions involving an entire Web page or frame set:

onLoad

Gets triggered: When a Web page, *and* any embedded elements like images and Flash and QuickTime movies, load. Very often used for triggering actions when visitor first loads the Web page; can also be used with an image tag to signal when just that image has finished loading.
Works with these tags: <body>, <frameset>, <image>

onUnload

Gets triggered: When the Web page is about to be replaced by a new Web page—for instance, just before the Web browser loads a new Web page after visitor clicks a link.
Works with these tags: <body>, <frameset>

onResize

Gets triggered: When visitor resizes the Web browser window.
Works with these tags: <body>, <frameset>

onError

Gets triggered: When an error occurs while a Web page or an image loads.
Works with these tags: <body>, <img>

Selection and Highlighting Events

Some events occur when the visitor focusses on different parts of a Web page, or selects text, or chooses from a menu.

onSelect

Gets triggered: When visitor selects text in a form field.
Works with these tags: <textarea>, <input type="text">

onChange

Gets triggered: When visitor changes the text in a form field.
Works with these tags: <textarea>, <input type="file | password | text | select">

onFocus

Gets triggered: When an element becomes the *focus* of the visitor's attention. For instance, clicking in a form text field gives it the focus.
Works with these tags: <body>, <frameset>, <textarea>, <input type="button | checkbox | file | password | radio | reset | submit | text | select">

onBlur

Gets triggered: When an element loses the focus. For instance, if the visitor is typing into a form text field and then clicks outside of that field, the onBlur event occurs. The onBlur event is also triggered when you, the Web surfer, send a window to the background. For example, suppose you have two windows open: the one you're reading and another in the background. If you click the background window, the current page loses focus and an onBlur event occurs. *Works with these tags:* <body>, <frameset>, <textarea>, <input type="button | checkbox | file | password | radio | reset | submit | text | select">

Form Events

While each element of a form—radio button, text field, checkbox—can respond to a variety of events, the whole form—the entire collection of elements—can respond to only two events:

onSubmit

Gets triggered: When visitor clicks the Submit button on a form.
Tag supported: <form>

onReset

Gets triggered: When visitor clicks the Reset button on a form.
Tag supported: <form>

Tip: You can find out exactly which browsers support which tag/event combinations. In the Macromedia Dreamweaver 4→Configuration→Behaviors→Events folder, you can find files that list the tags and events that work in different browsers, including Netscape Navigator 3.0 and 4.0 and Internet Explorer 3.0, 4.0, and 5.0. In addition, two files—*3.0 and Later Browsers.htm* and *4.0 and Later Browsers.htm*—contain only tag/event combinations that work in both Netscape Navigator and Internet Explorer of the corresponding versions.

The Actions, One by One

While events get the ball rolling, actions are, yes, where the action is. Whether it's opening a 200 x 200 pixel browser window or using HTML to control the playback of a Flash movie, you'll find an action for almost every interactivity need.

Each of the following descriptions lets you know which browsers recognize the corresponding actions. For example, "Netscape Navigator 3+" refers to Netscape Navigator 3.0 and later.

Remember that after you complete each of the sets of steps below, your new action appears in the Behaviors panel, and your Web page is ready to test. At that point, you can click the behavior's name in the Behaviors panel, where—by clicking the Events pop-up menu as shown in Figure 11-2—you can change the event that triggers it.

Navigation Actions

Many of Dreamweaver's actions are useful for adding creative navigational choices to your Web sites, giving you the opportunity to go beyond the simple click-and-load approach of a basic Web page.

Open Browser Window

Windows: Netscape Navigator 3+, Internet Explorer 3+
Macintosh: Netscape Navigator 3+, Internet Explorer 4+

No matter how carefully you design your Web page, chances are it won't look good in every size window. Depending on the resolution of the user's monitor and the dimensions of her browser window, your Web page may be forced to squeeze into a window that's 400 pixels wide, or it could be dwarfed by one that's 1200 pixels wide. Having to design your Web pages so they look good at a variety of different window sizes can be challenging.

It's the Open Browser Window action to the rescue. Using this behavior, you can instruct your visitor's browser to open a new window to whatever height and width *you* desire. In fact, you can even dictate what elements the browser window includes. Don't want the toolbar, location bar, or status bar visible? No problem; this action also lets you include or exclude any such window chrome.

Figure 11-5:
You, too, can annoy your friends, neighbors, and Web site customers with these unruly pop-up browser windows. Just add the Open Browser Window action to the <body> tag of your document. Now, when that page loads, a new browser window opens with the ad, announcement, or picture you specify. Even more annoying, use the onUnload event of the <body> tag to open a new browser window—with the same Web page—when visitors try to exit the page. They won't be able to get to a different page, and may even encounter system crashes. Now that's annoying!

To open a new browser window, you start, as always, by selecting the tag to which you wish to attach the behavior. You can attach it to any of the tags discussed on pages 289–292, but you'll usually want to add this action to a link with an onClick event, or to the <body> tag with the onLoad event.

Once you've selected this action's name from the + button/menu in the Behaviors panel, you see the dialog box shown in Figure 11-6. You have these settings to make:

- **URL to Display.** In this box, type in the URL or path of the Web page, or click Browse and find the Web page on your computer. If you're loading a Web page on somebody else's site, remember to type an *absolute* URL, beginning with *http://* (see page 82).

- **Window Width, Window Height.** Next, type in the width and height of the new window. These values are measured in pixels; in most browsers, 100 x 100 pixels is the minimum size. Also, strange visual anomalies may result on your visitors' screens if the width and height you specify here are larger than the available space on their monitors.

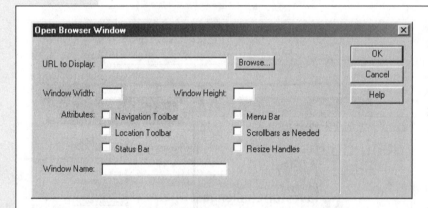

Figure 11-6:
If you leave the window's Width and Height blank, the new window will be the same size as the window it opens from. (Netscape Navigator 4 and earlier ignores the dimension properties if you've specified only one of the dimensions—either height or width.)

- **Attributes.** Turn on the checkboxes for the window elements you want to include in the new window. Figure 11-7 shows the different pieces of a standard browser window.

- **Window Name box.** Give the new window a name here (letters and numbers only). If you include spaces or other symbols, Dreamweaver shows an error message and lets you correct the mistake. This name won't actually appear on your Web page, but it's useful for targeting links or actions from the original window.

Once a new window is open, you can load Web pages into it from the original page that opened the window; simply use the name you give to the new window as the target of the link. For example, you could add this behavior to the <body> tag of a page so that when the page opens, a small new window also appears, showcasing a photo. You could add links to the main page, that, when clicked, load additional photos into the small window.

In addition, if you use more than one open browser window behavior on a single page, make sure to give each new window a unique name. If you don't, you may not get a new window for each Open Browser Window action.

When you click OK, your newly created behavior appears in the Actions list in the Behaviors panel.

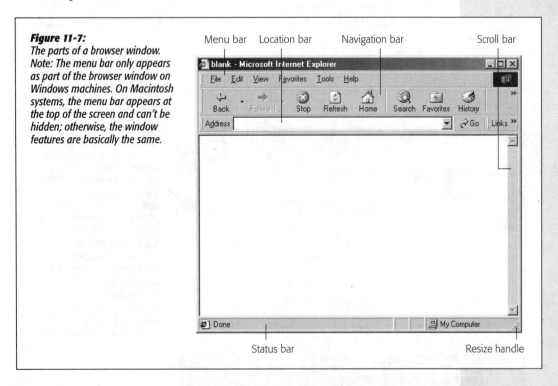

Figure 11-7:
The parts of a browser window. Note: The menu bar only appears as part of the browser window on Windows machines. On Macintosh systems, the menu bar appears at the top of the screen and can't be hidden; otherwise, the window features are basically the same.

Menu bar   Location bar   Navigation bar   Scroll bar

Status bar   Resize handle

Go to URL

Windows: Netscape Navigator 3+, Internet Explorer 3+
Macintosh: Netscape Navigator 3+, Internet Explorer 4+

The Go to URL action works just like a link, in that it simply loads a new Web page. However, while links only work when you click them, this action can load a page based on an event *other than* clicking. For instance, you might want to load a Web page when your visitor's cursor simply moves over an image, or when she clicks a particular radio button.

Once you've selected a tag and chosen this action's name from the + button/menu in the Behaviors panel, you can make these settings in the resulting dialog box:

• **Open in.** If you aren't using frames, only Main Window is listed here. But if you're working in a frameset file (see Chapter 7) and have named each of your frames, they're listed in the "Open in" list box. Click the name of the frame where you'll want the new page to appear.

• **URL.** Fill in the URL of the page you wish to load. You can use any of the link-specifying tricks described on page 85: type in an absolute URL starting with *http://*, type in a path, or click the Browse button and select a page from your Web site.

Note: If you're working in frames and have the frameset file open, you can click each frame listed in the "Open in" list and assign a different URL to it. An asterisk next to the name of a frame indicates that a link points to that frame.

In other words, the same event, such as clicking a link or button, can make more than one frame change; see Figure 11-8 for an example.

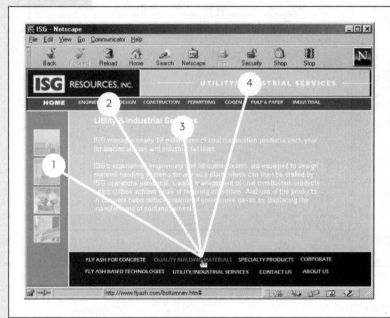

Figure 11-8:
This rather complex Web page is composed of six different frames and uses the Go To URL action with flair. Clicking a single button in the navigation bar at the bottom of the page loads Web pages into four other frames. This feat is impossible using only HTML, but using Dreamweaver Behaviors it's a snap: The Go To URL action was applied to each navigation button, with each action targeting four frames and loading a separate Web page into each.

Jump Menu and Jump Menu Go

Windows: Netscape Navigator 3+, Internet Explorer 4+
Macintosh: Netscape Navigator 3+, Internet Explorer 4+

Conserving precious visual space on a Web page is a constant challenge for a Web designer. Putting too many buttons, icons, and navigation controls on a page can quickly clutter your presentation and muddle a page's meaning. As sites get larger, so do navigation bars, which can engulf a page in a long column of buttons.

One way to add detailed navigation to a site without wasting pixels is to use Dreamweaver's Jump Menu behavior. A *jump menu* is simply a pop-up menu that lets visitors navigate by choosing from a list of links.

The Jump Menu behavior is listed in the Behaviors panel, but for a simpler, happier life, don't insert it onto your page that way. Instead, use the Objects panel or Insert menu, like this:

1. **Click where you want the jump menu to appear on your Web page.**

   It might be in a table cell at the top of the page, or along the left edge of the page.

2. **Click the Jump Menu icon ( ) on the Objects panel, or choose Insert→Form Objects→Jump Menu.**

   If you use the Behaviors panel instead, you first have to add a form and insert a menu into it. The Insert Jump Menu object saves you those steps.

Tip: Even though the jump menu uses a pop-up menu, which is a component of a *form,* you don't have to create a form first, as described in Chapter 10. Dreamweaver creates one automatically when you insert a jump menu.

The Jump Menu dialog box opens, as shown in Figure 11-9.

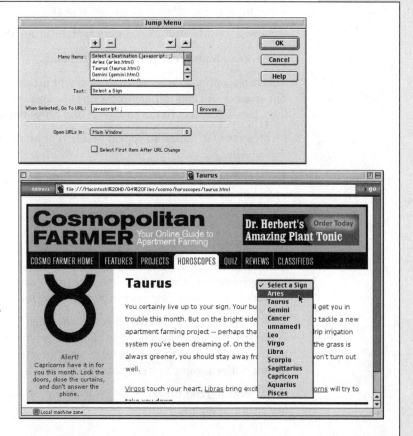

Figure 11-9:
Top: The Jump Menu dialog box shown here is set up so that the onChange event of the <select> tag triggers the Jump Menu action; that is, the Jump Menu behavior works when you select an item other than the one currently listed. Bottom: Unless you include the Insert Go Button After Menu option, the first item of a jump menu should never be used as a link. Instead, use some descriptive text–such as "Select a Destination…"– to let users know what the menu does. Then either leave the URL blank, or, if you are using frames, make the URL a JavaScript "dummy" link: javascript:; (see page 283). When placed on a page, the menu is very compact, but can offer a long list of pages.

3. **Type the name of the first link in the text field.**

You're specifying not just the first command in your pop-up menu, but also the default choice—the first one your visitor sees.

The name you type here, by the way, doesn't have to match the page's title or anchor's name; it's whatever you want your menu to say to represent it. For instance, you can call a menu choice *Home* even if the title of your home page is Cosmopolitan Farmer.

4. **Enter a URL for this link in the When Selected, Go To URL field.**

Use any of the usual methods for specifying a link (page 85).

5. **To add the next command in your pop-up menu, click the + button and repeat steps 3 and 4. Continue until you have added all of the links for this menu.**

If you want to remove one of the links, select it from the Menu Items list and click the – button. You can also reorder the list by clicking one of the link names and then clicking the up- and down-arrow buttons.

6. **If you're using frames, use the Open URLs In pop-up menu to specify a frame in which the indicated Web page should appear.**

Otherwise, the Main Window option loads links into the entire browser window.

7. **In the Menu Name box, give the menu a name.**

This step is optional; you can also just accept the name Dreamweaver proposes. The name doesn't appear anywhere on the page; Dreamweaver uses it only for the internal purposes of the JavaScript that drives this behavior.

8. **If you want a Go button to appear beside your jump menu, turn on "Insert Go Button After Menu."**

You need to use this option only when the jump menu is in one frame, loading pages into another, or when you want to make the first item in your jump menu a link instead of an instruction (see Figure 11-9).

When you include a Go button, Dreamweaver adds a small form button next to the menu, which your visitor can click to jump to whatever link is listed in the menu. But most of the time, your visitors will never get a chance to use this Go button; whenever they make a selection from the menu, their browsers automatically jump to the new page without waiting for a click on the Go button.

The Go button can be handy, however, when there's no selection to make. For example, if the first item in the menu is a link, your visitors won't be able to select it; it's *already* selected when the page with the menu loads. In this case, a Go button is the only way to trigger the "jump."

9. **If you want to reset the menu after each jump (so that it once again shows the first menu command), turn on Select First Item after URL Change.**

Here's another option that's useful only when the jump menu is in one frame, loading pages into another frame. Resetting the menu so that it shows its default command makes it easy for your visitor to make another selection when ready.

10. Click OK to apply the action and close the Jump Menu dialog box.

Your newly created pop-up menu appears on your Web page, and the newly created behavior appears in the Actions list in the Behaviors panel.

Tip: To edit a jump menu, click the menu in your document, and then, in the Behaviors panel, double-click the Jump Menu action in the Actions list. The settings dialog box reappears. At this point, you can change any of the options described in the previous steps, except that you can't add a Go button to a jump menu that didn't have one to begin with. (Click OK when you're finished.)

The Jump Menu *Go* action (available on the Behaviors panel) is only useful if you didn't add a Go menu in step 8 above. In this case, if there's a jump menu on the page and you wish to add a Go button to it, click next to the menu, add a form button, and attach this behavior to it (for more on working with Forms, see Chapter 10).

Check Browser
Windows: Netscape Navigator 3+, Internet Explorer 3+
Macintosh: Netscape Navigator 3+, Internet Explorer 4+

As noted earlier, not all Web browsers work the same way. Prior to version 4, for example, Netscape Navigator and Internet Explorer couldn't handle layers or animation using Dynamic HTML (see Chapter 12 for using Dreamweaver to create DHTML); In addition, Cascading Style Sheets are only available for the more modern 4+ browser vintage.

Instead of confusing users of older browsers with unviewable Web pages in such cases, many Web designers build two separate Web sites: one with advanced capabilities that take advantage of all the latest bells and whistles, and another, simpler site that works with older browsers. This action, called Check Browser, automatically redirects 4.0 and greater browsers to the advanced site, and older browsers to the simpler one.

As usual, assigning this behavior begins with selecting a tag. You'll often add this action to the <body> tag of the first page of your Web site. This "gatekeeper" page determines where to send visitors when they first come to your site.

Tip: It's a good idea to make this gatekeeper page viewable to older browsers—don't load it up with modern behaviors, in other words. In this way, even browsers that don't understand JavaScript can at least access the basic text of your Web site.

Then, when you choose this action's name from the + button/menu in the Behaviors panel, the Check Browser dialog box opens, as shown in Figure 11-10. It offers these controls:

- **Netscape Navigator.** Type the version number of Netscape Navigator you want to check for. Dreamweaver proposes 4.0, but you can change it to any number you want.

  Then, using the first pop-up menu, specify what should happen if the version of Netscape Navigator is *equal to or greater than* the number you specified. You have three choices in the pop-up menu: the browser can go to one of two new Web pages (Go to URL or Go to Alt URL, which you'll specify in step 8) or stay on the same page (Stay on This Page).

  Using the second pop-up menu, specify what to do if the version of Netscape Navigator is *less than* the number you specified.

  Once again, the browser can go to one of two new Web pages (Go to URL or Go to Alt URL) or stay on same page (Stay on This Page).

Tip: If you choose the same option in both pop-up menus, you send users of *all* versions of Netscape Navigator to the same page. In other words, you can use the Check Browser behavior to separate your audience by brand of browser, rather than version—which, when you want to use behaviors that work only in one browser or another, can be equally useful.

- **Internet Explorer.** Type the version number of Internet Explorer you want to check for. Again, Dreamweaver suggests 4.0, but you can change it to any version you wish. This number sorts and redirects Internet Explorers users by version.

  Using the third pop-up menu in the dialog box, specify what should happen if the version of Internet Explorer is *equal to or greater than* the number you specified; using the fourth pop-up menu, specify what to do if the version of Internet Explorer is *less than* the number you specified.

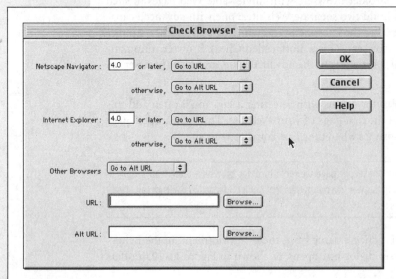

Figure 11-10:
Although the default version number is 4.0, you can enter any decimal number. So say you had a page that worked with Netscape Navigator 4.73 but not version 4.08; just type 4.73 in the Netscape Navigator text field.

As noted in the previous Tip, choosing the same option for both pop-up menus lets you screen out *all* versions of Internet Explorer (to send them to a single alternate Web site, for example).

- **Other Browsers.** If you like, you may choose a Web page for all *other* browsers—Opera, iCab, and so on—using this pop-up menu; fill in the appropriate URL in the appropriate field (probably the Alt URL, described next).

- **URL, Alt URL.** These text boxes let you indicate the URLs for the redirecting commands you specified in the previous steps. For example, if you chose Go to URL from the first pop-up menu, this is where you specify *what* URL you want those Netscape Navigator browsers redirected to. (Choose a link here using any of the techniques on page 85.)

GEM IN THE ROUGH

Using Check Browser as a "Gatekeeper"

One common use of the Check Browser behavior is as a "gatekeeper" that admits only people with certain browsers into your site. For example, suppose you've jazzed up your site with all kinds of features that require a version 4-or-later browser; you want a Welcome page that lets such people proceed to the real site (and directs them there automatically after a moment), but offers everyone else only a note that they'll need a more modern browser (and tells them where they can get it).

To set up this arrangement, add the Check Browser behavior to the opening page of the site (at left in the diagram shown here); in the steps on page 299, add it to the

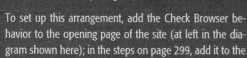

(For 3.0 and older browsers) → (For 4.0 and later browsers)

<body> tag and use the onLoad event.

Then, in the dialog box shown in Figure 11-10, type *4* into both of the top two text boxes; choose Go to URL from the first and third pop-up menus; and type the URL for the fancy, full-fledged page (B) into the URL field.

For the other pop-up menus, labeled "otherwise" and Other Browsers, choose Stay on this Page. And *on* that page (page A), add a note like this: "Sorry, this Web site requires Netscape Navigator or Internet Explorer version 4 or higher. You can download either one for free by clicking these links"—and then add links to the Netscape and Microsoft Web sites.

Image Actions

Images make Web pages stand out. But adding Dreamweaver Behaviors can make those same images come to life.

Preloading Images

Windows: Netscape Navigator 3+, Internet Explorer 4+
Macintosh: Netscape Navigator 3+, Internet Explorer 4+

It takes time for images to load over the Internet. A 16 K image, for instance, takes about four seconds to download over a 56 K modem. However, once a Web browser loads an image, it stores the image in its *cache*, so that it will load extremely quickly if a page requires the same graphic again. The Preload Images action takes advantage of this fact by downloading an image or images and storing them in the browser's cache, *even before* they're actually needed.

Preloading is especially important when using mouse rollover effects on a Web page (see Figure 5-11 on page 110). When a visitor moves the mouse over a particular button, it might, for example, appear to light up. If you couldn't preload the image, then the "lit up" graphic for the "over" state wouldn't even begin to download until the cursor rolled over the button. The resulting delay makes your button feel less like a rollover than a layover.

In general, you won't need to apply this action by hand, since Dreamweaver adds it automatically when you use the Insert Rollover Image (page 109) or insert Navigation Bar (page 193) commands.

But there are exceptions, such as when you use the Preload Images action to load graphics that appear on *other* pages in your site.

For example, suppose you build a graphics-heavy Web site. People hate to wait too long for a Web page to load, but they're slightly more patient when waiting for the *first* page of a site to load. You could capitalize on that fact by adding a Preload Images action to the body of a home page (or even a page that says "Loading Web Site") that preloads most of the site's graphics. (Be careful, though: If any page preloads too many images, even the most patient Web surfer may not stay around to watch the show. Remember to refer to the download stats listed in the document's status bar for the size of your Web page, as discussed on page 409.)

To add the Preload Images action, select the tag to which you want the behavior attached. Most often you'll use the <body> tag, in combination with an onLoad event.

If you've added Rollover Images or a Navigation bar to your page, this behavior may already be in the <body> of the page. In this case, just double-click the Preload Images action that's already listed in the Behaviors panel. If not, just choose this action's name from the + button/menu in the Behaviors panel. Either way, you're now offered the Preload Images dialog box.

Click the Browse button and navigate to the graphics file that you wish to use for preloading purposes, or type in the path or (if the graphic is on the Web already) the absolute URL of the graphic. Dreamweaver adds the image to the Preload Images list. If you want to preload another image, click the + button and repeat the previous step. Continue until you've added all the images you want to preload.

You can also remove an image from the list by selecting it and then clicking the – button. (Be careful not to delete any of the images that may be required for a rollover effect you've already created—the Undo command doesn't work here.)

When you click OK, you return to your document; your new action appears in the Behaviors panel. Here you can edit it, if you like, by changing the event that triggers it; but unless you're trying to achieve some special effect, you'll usually use the onLoad event of the <body> tag.

That's all there is to it. When your page loads in somebody's browser, the browser will continue to load and store those graphics quietly in the background. They'll appear almost instantly when they're required by a rollover or even a shift to another Web page on your site that incorporates the graphics you specified.

Swap Image

Windows: Netscape Navigator 3+, Internet Explorer 4+
Macintosh: Netscape Navigator 3+, Internet Explorer 4+

The Swap Image action exchanges one image on your page for another. (See the end of this section for detail on Swap Image's cousin behavior, Swap Image Restore.)

Simple as that process may sound, swapping images is one of the most visually exciting things you can do on a Web page. Swapping images works something like rollover images, except that a mouse click or mouse pass isn't required to trigger them; in fact, you can use *any* tag and event combination to trigger the Swap Image action. For instance, you can create a mini slide show by listing the names of pictures down the left side of a Web page and inserting an image in the middle of the page. Add a Swap Image action to each slide name, so that the appropriate picture swaps in when your visitor clicks any one of the names.

To make this behavior work, your Web page must already contain a starter image, and the images to be swapped in must be the same width and height as the original graphic. If they aren't, the browser will resize and distort the subsequent pictures to fit the "frame" dictated by the original.

To add the Swap Image behavior, start by choosing the *starter* image file that you want to include on the page. (Choose Insert→Image, or use any of the other techniques described in Chapter 5.) Give your image a name in the Property inspector, so that JavaScript will know which image to swap out. (JavaScript doesn't really care about the original graphic image itself, but rather about the space that it occupies on the page.)

Now select the tag to which you want the behavior attached. When you choose this action's name from the Behaviors panel, the Swap Image dialog box appears, as shown in Figure 11-11:

- **Images.** From the list, click the name of the starter image.

- **Set Source to.** Here's where you specify the image file that you want to swap in. If it's a graphics file in your site folder, click Browse to find and open it. You can also specify a path or an absolute URL to another Web site.

- **Preload Images.** Preloading ensures that the swap action isn't slowed down while the graphic downloads from the Internet (see Figure 5-11 on page 110).

• **Restore Images onMouseOut.** You get this option only when you've applied this behavior to a link. When you turn it on, moving the mouse *off* the link makes the previous image reappear.

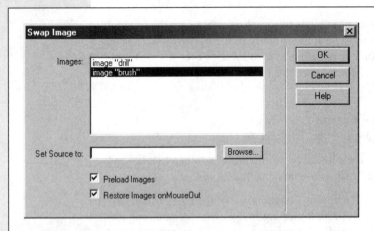

Figure 11-11:
Some actions, like the Swap Image action, can automatically add additional behaviors to a Web page. In this case, the Preload Images and Restore Images onMouseOut options actually add a Swap Image Restore action to the onMouseOut event of the currently selected tag, and a Preload Images action to the onLoad event of the <body> tag.

Swap Image Restore

The Swap Image Restore action returns the last set of swapped images to its original state. Most designers use it in conjunction with a rollover button, so that the button returns to its original appearance when the visitor rolls the cursor off the button.

You'll probably never find a need to add this behavior yourself. Dreamweaver automatically adds it when you insert a rollover image, and when you choose the Restore Images onMouseOut option when setting up a regular Swap Image behavior (see Figure 11-11). But, if you prefer, you can add the Swap Restore Image behavior to other tag and event combinations, using the general routine described on page 284. (The Swap Image Restore dialog box offers no options to set.)

Setting a Navigation Bar Image

Windows: Netscape Navigator 3+, Internet Explorer 4+
Macintosh: Netscape Navigator 3+, Internet Explorer 4+

You can easily modify a navigation bar that you've added to your Web page (see page 193) by choosing Modify→Navigation Bar. However, some advanced features of a navigation bar are only available if you use the Behaviors panel to edit the individual navigation bar images.

The Navigation Bar object specifies different graphics for each state of a navigation button: up, over, down, and over while down. But things can easily get much more complex; this behavior, for example, lets the state of a navigation bar image dictate the state of *other* images on a page, swapping images in response to a visitor's interaction with buttons on the navigation bar. Figure 11-13 shows an example of how this complex behavior might be useful.

Here's how you might proceed:

1. **Place an image on your Web page; type the name for it into the upper-left field of the Property inspector.**

   The name lets JavaScript know which image to swap out.

2. **Insert a navigation bar into the same Web page.**

   See page 193 for full instructions.

3. **Open the Behaviors panel, if it isn't already open (press Shift-F3).**

   You'll notice that the Behaviors panel already lists three Set Nav Bar Image actions: one each for onClick, onMouseOut, and onMouseOver. Dreamweaver created these behaviors automatically when you inserted the navigation bar.

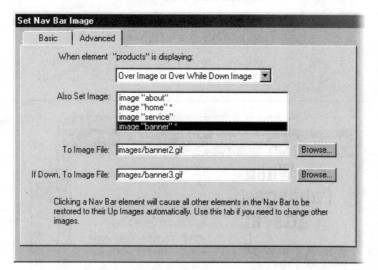

Figure 11-12:
The Advanced tab of the Set Nav Bar Image action can be used to swap other images on a Web page based on the state of a navigation button: over, over while down, or down (but not the up state). This flexibility allows for some very creative and complex interactions. When you add a swap action to an image, Dreamweaver adds an asterisk next to its name. For example, in this figure, both the "home" and "banner" images have actions applied to them.

4. **Click one of the images in the Nav Bar.**

   The image you choose will be able to control other images on the page.

5. **Double-click any of the Set Nav Bar Image actions in the Behaviors panel.**

   All three actions share the same settings, so double-clicking any one of them opens the same Set Nav Bar Image dialog box—a fairly confusing system; no other Dreamweaver behavior works this way.

6. **Click the Advanced tab.**

   If you've looked over page 194, then you've already encountered the Basic tab, but the advanced settings are only available from the Behaviors panel.

7. **Select the state of the navigation button from the menu.**

The behavior you're defining changes one or more images on a page depending on the *state* of the selected navigation button. You can make other images on a page respond to the over, over while down, and down states of the navigation button.

8. **From the Also Set Image list, click the name of the image you want this action to replace with another graphic.**

An asterisk to the right of a name indicates that the image already has an action applied to it.

9. **Specify the image file that you wish to swap in.**

Click the Browse button and navigate to the graphic file, or type in the path or absolute URL of the graphic.

10. **Repeat steps 7 and 8 until you've applied actions to all the images you wish to swap. When you're finished, click OK.**

You can't specify which events trigger this action, making it something of an oddball among the Dreamweaver Behaviors.

Figure 11-13:
Front: In this example, the navigation bar is composed of three graphic buttons: Week 1, Week 2, and Week 3. Back: When a visitor moves the cursor over the Week 2 button, not only does that button change to its over state, but another graphic in the lower-right corner ("The Cabbage Hunt Begins…") is swapped in.

Message Behaviors

Communication is why we build Web sites: to tell a story, sell a product, or provide useful information that can entertain and inform our visitors. Dreamweaver can enhance this communication process with actions that provide dynamic feedback. From subtle messages in a browser's status bar to dialog boxes that command a visitor's attention, Dreamweaver offers numerous ways to respond, in words, to user interaction.

Pop-up Message

Windows: Netscape Navigator 3+, Internet Explorer 3+
Macintosh: Netscape Navigator 3+, Internet Explorer 4+

Use the Pop-up Message behavior to send important messages to your visitors, as shown in Figure 11-14; your visitor must click OK to close the dialog box. Because a pop-up message demands immediate attention, reserve this behavior for important announcements.

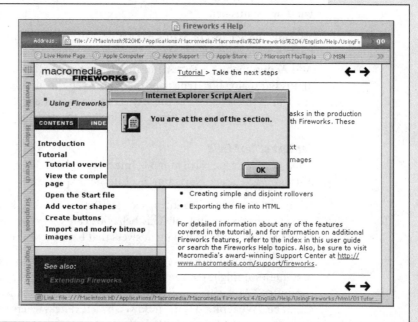

Figure 11-14:
Here a pop-up message signals the end of the online Fireworks 4 tutorial.

To create a pop-up message, select the tag to which you want the behavior attached; for example, adding this action to the <body> tag with an onLoad event will cause a message to appear when a visitor first loads the page.

From the Add Action menu (+ button) in the Behaviors panel, choose Pop-up Message. In the Pop-up Message dialog box, type the message that you'll want to appear in the dialog box. (Check the spelling and punctuation carefully; nothing says "amateur" like poorly written error messages.) Then click OK.

Tip: A note to JavaScript programmers: Your message can also include any valid JavaScript expression. To embed JavaScript code into a message, place it inside braces ({ }). If you want to include the current time and date in a message, for example, add this: *{new Date()}*. If you just want to display a brace in the message, add a backslash, like this: \{. The backslash lets Dreamweaver know that you *really do* want a { character, and not a bunch of JavaScript, to appear in the dialog box.

Set Text of Status Bar

Windows: Netscape Navigator 3+, Internet Explorer 3+
Macintosh: Netscape Navigator 3+, Internet Explorer 4+

Pop-up messages, like those described above, require your visitors to drop everything and read them; for less urgent messages, consider the Set Text of Status Bar behavior. It displays a message in the status bar of a browser window—the strip at the bottom of the window. You can add a message to a link, for example, that lets users know where the link will take them. Or you could set things up so that when a visitor moves the cursor over a photograph, copyright information appears in the window's status bar.

To apply the Set Text of Status bar action, select a tag (a very common example is a link (<a>) tag with the onMouseOver event), choose this behavior's name from the Add Action menu (+ button) in the Behaviors panel, and then, in the Set Text of Status Bar dialog box, type your message. Keep the message short; browsers cut off any words that don't fit in the status bar. Your message can also include any valid JavaScript expression, exactly as described in the previous Tip.

Set Text of Text Field

Windows: Netscape Navigator 3+, Internet Explorer 3+
Macintosh: Netscape Navigator 3+, Internet Explorer 4+

Normally, a text field in a form (see page 269) is blank. It sits on the page and waits for someone to type into it. This behavior can save your visitors time by filling in form fields automatically with answers that have become obvious.

For instance, imagine you've created a Web survey that has a series of questions. The first question might require a yes or no answer, along the lines of: "Do you own a computer?" And you've provided radio buttons for Yes or No. The second question might be, "What brand is it?" followed by a text field where your visitors can type in the computer brand.

But if someone answers "No" to question 1, there's no point in her typing a response to the second question. To help keep things moving along, you can set the second question's text field so that it says: "Please skip to Question 3." To do so, simply add the Set Text of Text Field action to the onClick event of the No radio button of Question 1.

To apply the Set Text of Text Field action, make sure your page includes a form and at least one text field; since this behavior changes the text in a form text field, you won't get very far without the proper HTML on the page.

Select the tag to which you want the behavior attached; in the example above, you'd attach the behavior to the form's No radio button with an onClick event. However, you aren't limited to just form elements. Any of the tags discussed on pages 289–292 will work.

When you choose Set Text of Text Field from the Add Action menu (+ button) in the Behaviors panel, the Set Text of Text Field dialog box opens. Make these changes:

- **Text Field.** The menu lists the names of every text field in the form; choose the name of the text field whose default text you'll want to change. (See Chapter 10 for the full story on building online forms in Dreamweaver.)

- **New Text.** Type the text you'll want that field to display. Take care not to make the message longer than the space available in the field.

   (Once again, your message can include a JavaScript expression, as described in the tip on page 308.)

Tip: Only one action works with forms: the Validate Form action. It can prevent visitors from submitting forms that are missing information, or that contain improperly formatted information. For instance, if somebody leaves the Your Name text field blank, this action opens an error box and asks her to enter her name. This action is described on page 278.

Set Text of Layer

Windows: Netscape Navigator 4+, Internet Explorer 4+
Macintosh: Netscape Navigator 4+, Internet Explorer 4+

Another way to get your message across is to change the text that appears in a layer (see Chapter 12). This action has an added benefit: it lets you use HTML code to *format* the message that appears in the layer. (Actually, the "Set Text" part of this action's name is a bit misleading; this action also lets you include HTML code, images, forms, and other objects in the layer—not just text.)

As always, you start by selecting a tag; in this case, you might select a link, for example, so that moving the mouse over the link changes the text in the layer: "Click here to see our choice of the best tomatoes of the season."

When you choose this action's name from the Add Action menu (+ button) in the Behaviors panel, you get these controls in a dialog box:

- **Layer.** The menu lists the names of every layer on the Web page (see Chapter 12); choose the name of the layer whose text you want to set.

- **New HTML.** In this field, type the text you wish to add to the layer. You can type in a plain text message, for example, or use HTML source code to control the content's formatting.

   For instance, if you want a word to appear bold in the layer, place the word inside a pair of bold tags like this: *important*. Or if you'd rather not mess around with HTML codes, you can also design the content using Dreamweaver's visual

---

design view—that is, right out there in your document window; copy the HTML source from the code view (Chapter 9); and then paste it into this action's New HTML field. You can also include a JavaScript expression, if you know JavaScript, as described in the tip on page 308.

Tip: Dreamweaver provides many prewritten JavaScript programs that let you manipulate layers—animate, drag, hide, or show them, for example. These behaviors are described in Chapter 12.

Set Text of Frame

Windows: Netscape Navigator 3+, Internet Explorer 3+
Macintosh: Netscape Navigator 3+, Internet Explorer 4+

Like the Set Text of Layer action, the Set Text of Frame action replaces the content of a specified frame with the HTML you specify. It's like loading a new Web page into a frame, only faster. Since the HTML is already part of the page that contains this action, your visitors don't have to wait for the code to arrive from the Internet.

To apply the Set Text of Frame action, create frameset and frame pages (see Chapter 7). When you select a tag in any of the frames—even the one whose content you intend to replace—and then choose this action from the Add Action menu (+ button) in the Behaviors panel, the Set Text of Frame dialog box opens:

- **Frame.** The menu lists the names of every available frame. Choose the name of the frame where you'll want the text to appear. (See page 190 for detail on naming frames.)

- **New HTML.** Type the text you want the frame to show. You can type in a plain text message, or use HTML source code to control the content's formatting: *<b> like this </b>* for bold, for example.

  You can also copy the HTML currently in the frame by clicking the Get Current HTML button, which copies the HTML source into the New HTML Field; once it's there, you can then modify it as you see fit. You'd use this technique if, for example, you wanted to keep much of the formatting and HTML of the original page. Be careful, however; this action can only update the *body* of the frame; any code in the <head> of the frame will be lost. You can't add behaviors, meta tags, or other <head> content to the frame.

  Finally, as in most of these message actions, you can include a JavaScript expression as part of the text; see the Tip on page 308.

- **Preserve Background Color.** This option ensures that the background color of the frame won't change when the new text appears.

Multimedia Actions

Multimedia, from background sounds to fully interactive Flash movies, can add a depth of experience that goes well beyond basic HTML. Several Dreamweaver actions let you play sounds, Flash movies, and Shockwave movies. (For more information on incorporating multimedia elements into your Web pages, see Chapter 13.)

Control Shockwave or Flash

Windows: Netscape Navigator 3+, Internet Explorer 4+
Macintosh: Netscape Navigator 3+, Internet Explorer 4+

Flash and Shockwave have become standard elements of many Web sites, and as more and more sites combine Flash and Shockwave movies with regular HTML, it becomes increasingly useful to be able to control how those movies play. With the Control Shockwave or Flash action, regular HTML objects can control the playback of a movie. For example, you could add a set of small VCR-like control buttons—Play, Stop, Rewind—to a page. These graphics—regular HTML on the page—could control the playback of a Flash or Shockwave movie.

1. **Add a Flash or Shockwave movie to the page.**

   See Chapter 13 for details.

2. **Select the movie and name it in the Property inspector.**

   Dreamweaver uses this name to identify the movie in the JavaScript that runs the behavior.

3. **Select the tag to which you want the behavior attached.**

   This might be a dummy link (see page 307) attached to a button graphic. Using the onClick event would help simulate the function of a button.

4. **From the Add Action menu (+ button) in the Behaviors panel, choose Control Shockwave or Flash.**

   The Control Shockwave or Flash dialog box opens, as shown in Figure 11-15.

5. **Choose how you want this action to control the movie.**

   You have four options for controlling a movie: Play (starts the movie from the current frame), Stop, Rewind (to the first frame), or Go to Frame (jumps to a frame you specify by typing its number into the Go to Frame field).

6. **Click OK.**

Figure 11-15:
The Control Shockwave or Flash action lets you control the playback of movie. You can only choose one type of control per action, however, so if you wanted to play a movie from a particular frame you would need to add two actions: the first would use the Go to Frame option, and the second would use the Play option to start the movie.

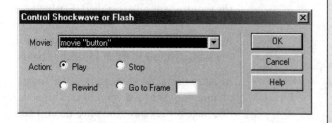

Play Sound

Windows: Netscape Navigator 3+, Internet Explorer 4+
Macintosh: Netscape Navigator 3+, Internet Explorer 4+

The Play Sound action lets you embed a sound file in a Web page and trigger its playback using any available event.

That's the theory, anyway. In practice, this action meets with mixed success. Browsers don't have a built-in sound feature; they rely on plug-ins to play sound files. But JavaScript (that is, Dreamweaver Behaviors) can't control some plug-ins, and some plug-ins can handle only certain types of sound files; the bottom line is that you may wind up with a silent Web page. Therefore, you shouldn't use the play sound action for mission-critical Web pages.

If sound is absolutely essential for your Web page, you're better off using a Flash or Shockwave movie (see Chapter 13) and including a Control Shockwave or Flash Movie behavior (see above).

If, after all of those disclaimers, you still want to try this behavior, follow the usual steps: Select the tag to which you want the behavior attached. (The <body> tag would be the most likely candidate. Using the onLoad event, you could make the sound begin after the page has loaded.)

Then, from the Add Action menu (+) in the Behaviors panel, choose Play Sound; in the resulting dialog box, click the Browse button; navigate to, and double-click, the sound file you want to play. The most common sound formats include WAV (.wav), midi (.mid), AU (.au), and AIFF (.aiff). (If the file isn't already in your Web site folder, Dreamweaver offers to save a copy there.) Finally, click OK.

Check Plug-in

Windows: Netscape Navigator 3+, Internet Explorer 4+ (for Flash and Shockwave plug-ins only)
Macintosh: Netscape Navigator 3+

Flash animations, QuickTime movies, and Shockwave games can add a lot of excitement to any Web site. Unfortunately, they don't work unless your visitors have downloaded and installed the corresponding browser plug-ins (see page 365 for more on this topic).

The Check Plug-in behavior can detect whether or not your visitor's browser has the required plug-in installed (Flash, Shockwave, LiveAudio, Netscape Media Player, or QuickTime)—and if not, to redirect your visitor to a special page for such less-fortunate Web surfers. It has one serious drawback, however, which is described in the Workaround Workshop sidebar below.

Because this action loads a new Web page, starting by selecting a link (<a> tag) with an onClick event is a good idea. This way, when your visitors click the link, they see one page if they have the plug-in, and another if they don't.

Then, when you choose Check Plug-in from the Add Action menu (+) in the Behaviors panel, a dialog box (Figure 11-16) lets you make these settings:

- **Plugin.** From the pop-up menu, choose the plug-in's name, or type its name in the Enter field.

  The plug-in options available in the menu are Flash, Shockwave, LiveAudio, Netscape Media Player, and QuickTime. Only the Flash and Shockwave options work with Internet Explorer (see the box below).

- **If Found, Go To URL/Otherwise, Go To URL.** Using these text fields, specify the Web pages to which your visitor will be directed if the plug-in is, or isn't, installed.

  You can indicate these pages just as you would any link (see page 85); for example, if the Web page is part of the site you're working on, click Browse to locate and open the Web page document.

Tip: If you leave the If Found, Go To URL field empty, the visitor who has the correct plug-in installed will stay right there on the same page. Use this arrangement when you apply the action to a <body> tag with an onLoad event, and the page *contains* the plug-in object.

WORKAROUND WORKSHOP

When Checking Doesn't Check Out

The Check Plug-in action is a great idea, but it doesn't work for everyone.

It works fine in Netscape Navigator. But Internet Explorer can't detect plug-ins using JavaScript; therefore, this action can't detect most plug-ins for Internet Explorer.

If you need to check only for the Flash or Shockwave players, Dreamweaver solves part of the problem by adding some computer instructions in a language that Internet Explorer can understand: VBScript. These instructions let Internet Explorer check for the Flash or Director players in

Internet Explorer *for Windows.*

Unfortunately, those special codes don't work on Internet Explorer prior to version 5 on the Mac. These older versions of Internet Explorer for the Mac are therefore left without any way of detecting whether or not the appropriate plug-ins are installed.

This technical snafu explains why this Dreamweaver behavior isn't actually very useful except to people who care only about Netscape Navigator users.

The Otherwise, Go To URL page could let users know that they need a plug-in to view the site; it should offer a link to the site where the plug-in can be found.

- **Always go to first URL if detection is not possible.** Remember that Internet Explorer can't detect all plug-ins; it wouldn't make sense to send Internet Explorer users to a "You don't have the correct plug-in" page when they might very well have it installed. If you turn on this box, your Web page will assume that the plug-in *is* installed if it can't determine otherwise.

Tip: However you plan to use this action, always make sure that you give users who don't have the plug-in a way to quickly and easily download and install it, so that they can return to your site to bask in the glorious multimedia experience you've created for them.

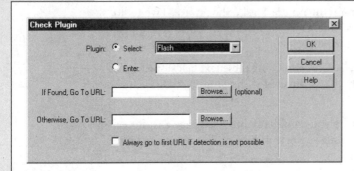

Figure 11-16:
If it isn't listed in the pop-up menu, you can type in the name of the plug-in you wish to check. If you have the plug-in installed in Netscape Navigator, you can find its name by choosing Help→About Plug-ins in Netscape Navigator, which produces a list of currently installed plug-ins and their names.

Advanced Actions

Dreamweaver has two advanced behaviors that let you call custom JavaScript functions and change the properties of various HTML elements. Both of these actions require familiarity with JavaScript and HTML (Chapter 9). Unlike the other Dreamweaver behaviors, these two can easily generate browser errors if used incorrectly.

Call JavaScript

Windows: Netscape Navigator 3+, Internet Explorer 3+
Macintosh: Netscape Navigator 3+, Internet Explorer 4+

You can use the Call JavaScript behavior to execute a single line of JavaScript code, or to call a JavaScript function that you've added to the <head> section of your Web page.

POWER USERS' CLINIC

Closing Browser Windows with the Call JavaScript Behavior

Suppose you've added an Open Browser Window behavior to your home page, so that when visitors come to your site, a small window opens, displaying a Web page that advertises some new feature of your site.

Well, after they've read the ad, your visitors will want to close the window and continue visiting your site. Why not make it easy for them by adding a "Close this Window" button?

To do so, simply add a graphic button—text works fine too—

and add a dummy (null) link to it (that is, in the Property inspector, type *javascript:;* into the Link field). Next, add the Call JavaScript behavior; in step 3 of the instructions on the facing page, type the following line of JavaScript code: *window.close()*.

Finally, after you click OK, make sure that the event is set to onClick in the Behaviors panel.

That's all there is to it; the link you've added to the pop-up window offers a working Close button.

When you select a tag and choose this behavior's name from the Behaviors panel, the Call JavaScript dialog box opens. If you want to execute a single line of JavaScript code, simply type it in. For instance, if you wanted to make the browser window close, you would type *window.close()*. If you want to call a JavaScript function, type the function name, like this: *myFunction()*.

Change Property

Windows: Netscape Navigator 3+, Internet Explorer 3+
Macintosh: Netscape Navigator 3+, Internet Explorer 4+

The Change Property action can dynamically alter the value of a property of any of the following HTML tags: <layer>, <div>, <span>, <img>, <form>, <textarea>, or <select>. It can also change properties for radio buttons, checkboxes, text fields, and password fields on forms (see Chapter 10). As with the previous behavior, this one requires a good knowledge of HTML and JavaScript. Dreamweaver's built-in HTML and JavaScript references (page 257) can help you get up to speed.

Select a tag, choose this behavior's name from the Add Action menu (+ button) in the Behaviors panel, and then fill in the dialog box like this (see Figure 11-17):

- **Type of Object.** The pop-up menu lists the eleven HTML tags that this behavior can control; choose the type of object whose property you wish to change.

- **Named Object.** From this pop-up menu, choose the name of the object you want to modify. (This step shows you how important it is to name HTML objects in advance.)

- **Property.** Choose the property you want to change (or, if you know enough about JavaScript, just type the property's name in the Enter field).

  Because Netscape Navigator and Internet Explorer recognize different properties for many HTML elements, you can use the pop-up menu to the right of the Property menu to specify the browser type and version you're targeting. Unfortunately, you can only select one browser for each Change Property action you apply. If you want to use this action for both browser brands, you'll need to apply it twice: once for each browser.

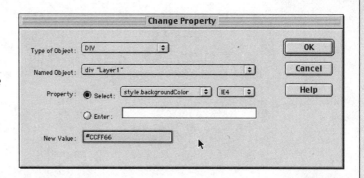

Figure 11-17:
Not only does the Change Property behavior require a good bit of knowledge about HTML, browsers, and JavaScript, its effectiveness is limited to specific browsers. Because Navigator and Internet Explorer differ significantly when it comes to JavaScript, this behavior doesn't always work correctly; you'll often have to apply this action multiple times to target multiple browsers.

• **New Value.** Type the new value you wish to set for this property. This value should be appropriate to the type of property you'll be changing. For example, if you're changing a background color, the value should be a color—*#FF0066*, for example.

Adding More Behaviors

Dreamweaver comes with the 25 preprogrammed behaviors described in this chapter, but you can download many additional behaviors from various Web sites, including Macromedia's Exchange Web site. Once you've downloaded them, you can easily add them to Dreamweaver, as described in Chapter 19.

Dreamweaver's Behaviors can open a new world of interaction for your Web pages. Without having to understand the complexities of JavaScript and cross-browser programming, you can easily add powerful and interesting effects that add spice to any Web visitor's experience.

Layers: Interactivity and Animation

The first MTV generation has grown up—and discovered the Web. Unfortunately, putting the average home page next to the average music video is like pitting a minivan against a Maserati. If you want to keep restless eyes glued to your site, adding attention-grabbing animation and interactivity may do the trick.

Using Behaviors (Chapter 11) and a clever design tool called *layers,* you can make pictures dance across the screen, add pop-up tooltips to your links, and even create Web page sticky notes that visitors can drag around the window. Without Dreamweaver, such animation would require a complex mixture of HTML, programming, and Cascading Style Sheets (Chapter 8) that could leave you crying into your keyboard. You, however, as a Dreamweaver owner, can create these effects without any assistance from therapy or antidepressants.

Tip: As when using any cool new technology, have mercy on your audience when adding interactive effects. Make sure any animations you use contribute to the message of your site and don't become distracting gimmicks whose novelty wears off after the first viewing. Making a news bulletin wiggle across the screen might look neat, but it'll be pretty hard to read.

Creating Layers

A layer is a rectangular container that holds other page material—images, text, form elements, and even other layers. In this regard, it acts like a table cell (page 126). And like a cell, you can define a layer's width and height and give it a background color or image.

But that's where the similarities end. What really sets a layer apart from other page elements is the way you can give it an exact position on a page. Want an image to appear exactly 100 pixels from the top edge of the browser window and 200 pixels from the left? Add a layer at that spot and insert an image in the layer—no jury-rigged table scaffolding required.

Figure 12-1:
Dreamweaver makes it easy to add simple animations to a Web page. Using the program's animation tools you can make items fly—or fall, like this leaf on the www.safetreekids.net Web page—across your pages.

Furthermore, because a layer uses *both* HTML and Cascading Style Sheets, it offers you a much wider range of control and flexibility, from exact screen placement to animation. For example, you can hide or show layers on the screen, nest them, and stack or overlap them. And you can control layers with JavaScript, effortlessly adding live interactive effects like animation.

As you probably know by now, any Web technology this powerful must come at a price: since layers rely on Cascading Style Sheets, only version 4.0 and later Web browsers can display them. Older browsers just ignore layer information and display their contents in the normal flow of the page—no exact positioning, no cool animation. To make matters worse, Netscape Navigator 4 has a notoriously hard time with layers, and often displays them incorrectly (see the box on page 325).

Tip: The members of the W3C, the body that approves Web technology standards, originally envisioned layers as a tool for laying out pages. They hoped that layers, with their exact positioning properties, would let Web designers achieve the level of control found in print design.

But don't rely on layers for layout. Most new browsers can position layers accurately on the screen, but the complexities of complete page designs frequently overwhelm the current browser crop. Use tables (Chapter 6) to lay out your pages instead.

Creating Layers

Dreamweaver wouldn't be Dreamweaver if it didn't give you several ways to perform a certain task, such as creating a layer. You can drag to create one freehand or use a menu command to insert a full-blown, completed layer. Your choices are:

- **Use the Layer tool.** Click the Layer button in the Objects panel (see Figure 12-2). Drag the + cursor diagonally in the document window to create a box—the outline of the layer.

- **Use a menu command.** To insert a layer at the insertion point, choose Insert→ Layer.

  If you don't like the looks of the default layer that Dreamweaver inserts, choose Edit→Preferences and adjust the default layer's properties there. Add a background color, for example, or increase the layer's size. From then on, you can instantly create your favorite kind of layer using the Insert→Layer command.

Note: The Insert→Layer command makes it easy to place a layer inside of a table cell or another layer; however, doing so is not always a good idea. Layers inside table cells cause serious display problems in some browsers; *nested* layers, furthermore, don't work well in Netscape 4 (see page 321 for more on nesting).

Figure 12-2:
The Layer tool on the Objects panel lets you add layers to your pages simply by drawing them in the document window. If you're creating multiple layers, hold down the Ctrl (⌘) key while drawing a layer. When you release the mouse, the Layer tool will remain selected, ready to draw the next layer.

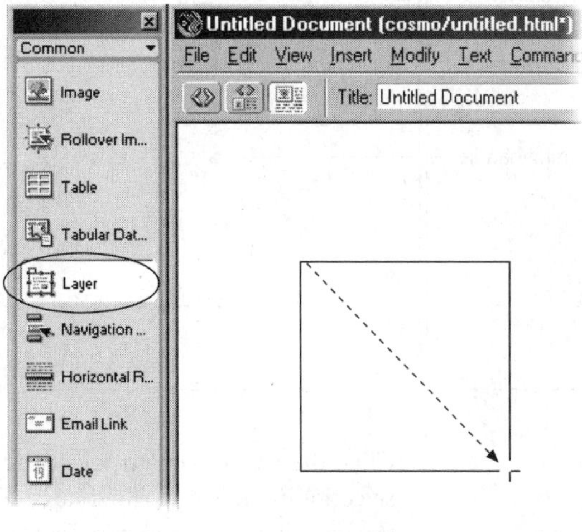

However you create the layer, its outline appears in the document window with a blinking insertion point inside. As with table cells, you can type text into the layer or add other objects, such as images or movies, into it.

Tip: The Layer tool doesn't work in Layout view. If the tool is grayed out in the Objects panel, make sure to switch back to Standard view (see page 127).

Unless you fill it up or add a background color to it, a layer is invisible, like an empty, borderless table. Since it's difficult to identify, select, and modify something that's invisible, Dreamweaver adds visual cues to make working with a layer easier (see Figure 12-3):

- **Layer marker.** The gold shield with the letter C represents the spot within the HTML of the page where the code for the layer actually appears.

While HTML objects generally appear in the document window in a top-to-bottom sequence that mirrors their order in the HTML source code, the position of layers themselves doesn't depend on where the layer-creating code appears in the page's HTML. In other words, it's possible to have a layer appear near the bottom of the page, whose actual code may be the first line inside the body of the page (see Figure 12-3).

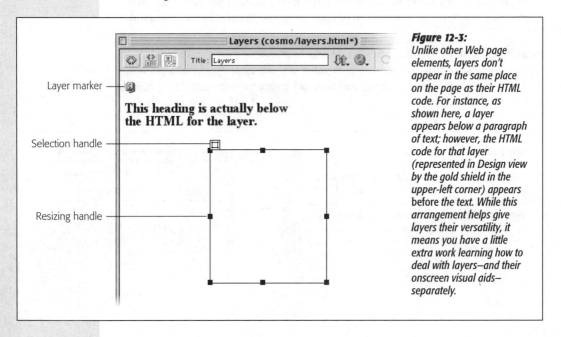

Figure 12-3:
Unlike other Web page elements, layers don't appear in the same place on the page as their HTML code. For instance, as shown here, a layer appears below a paragraph of text; however, the HTML code for that layer (represented in Design view by the gold shield in the upper-left corner) appears before the text. While this arrangement helps give layers their versatility, it means you have a little extra work learning how to deal with layers—and their onscreen visual aids— separately.

Click the shield icon to select the layer. Note, however, the difference from the selection handle described next: when you drag a Layer marker, you don't move the layer in the page layout. Instead, you reposition the layer's code in the HTML of the page.

That quirk can be tricky. For instance, be careful not to drag a Layer marker (which represents the HTML code) into a table. Putting a layer inside a table can cause major display problems in some browsers; the layer's contents may not even appear in Netscape 4.

That said, you *can* draw a layer so that it *overlaps* a table, or even appears to be inside a cell; just make sure the gold Layer marker itself is not inside a cell. If you use the Layer tool to draw a layer (see page 319), you won't have any problem. Dreamweaver won't put the code in a cell.

Tip: The Layer marker takes up room on the screen and can push text, graphics, and other items next to it out of the way. In fact, even the thin borders Dreamweaver adds to tables and layers take up space in the document window, and the space they occupy may make it difficult to place layers precisely. The keyboard shortcut Ctrl+Shift+I (⌘-Shift-I) hides or shows invisible items like Layer markers. The Hide All Visual Aids option from the toolbar does the same thing (see page 16). It's a good idea to hide visual aids while you're drawing layers.

- **Selection handle.** The selection handle provides a convenient handle to grab and move a layer around the page. The handle appears when you select the layer or when you click inside the layer to add material to it.

- **Layer outline.** A thin, gray, 3-D border outlines each layer. Like the Layer marker and selection handle, this border doesn't appear when the page is viewed in a Web browser; it's only there to help you see the boundaries of the layer. You can turn it on and off by choosing View→Visual Aids→Layer Borders. (When you hide the borders, Layer markers remain, but at least hiding borders gives you a quick preview without opening your Web browser.)

Nesting Layers

Later in this chapter, you can read how to animate a layer so that it moves across the screen. But suppose you want a more advanced effect, like a group of layers that move in a synchronized choreography. You could animate each layer independently, of course—or you could harness the power of *nested* layers.

Nesting doesn't necessarily mean that one layer appears inside another layer; it means that the HTML for one layer is written inside the code for another layer. The nested layer itself can appear anywhere on the page (see Figure 12-4). The main benefit of nested layers is that the *parent* layer—the layer containing the HTML of one or more other layers—can control the behavior of its *child* layers.

For example, suppose you create one layer and nest two layers inside it. If you move the parent layer on the screen, the two child layers follow it, which gives you an easy way to move several layers in unison. Furthermore, the parent layer can control the visibility of its children. When you hide the parent layer (see page 331), the nested layers also disappear.

Note: Netscape 4 has big problems displaying nested layers; for example, it often ignores the positioning and visibility you specify. If you need to make your pages compatible for Netscape 4 browsers, it's best to avoid nesting layers or, at the very least, use Dreamweaver's built-in Netscape fix, which is described in the box on page 325.

Here's how to create a nested layer:

- Click inside a layer, and then choose Insert→Layer. You get a new, nested layer inside it.

- Drag the Layer tool from the Objects panel and drop it inside a layer on the page. (Note that this isn't the same procedure described on page 319, in which you click the Layer button and then drag in the document window.)

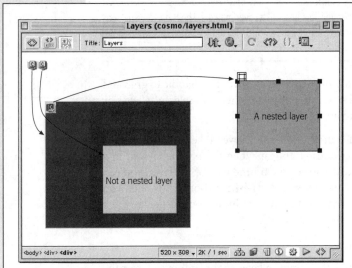

Figure 12-4:
An inner nested layer doesn't necessarily appear inside the outer layer; the HTML code for the layer at the far right, for instance, is nested inside the large gray box layer. On the other hand, a layer that appears inside (on top of) another layer isn't necessarily a nested layer, either; the light gray box inside the darker gray box shown here, for example, isn't nested at all. But the HTML for a nested layer does appear within the code for the outer layer. One sure-fire way of identifying a nested layer is to click a Layer marker (the gold shield) within a layer; the nested layer's selection handle appears, as shown here.

- While pressing the Ctrl (⌘) key, drag one layer in the *Layers panel* (Figure 12-5) onto another layer. The layer you drag becomes the child of the layer you dropped it on. The nested layer appears indented in the Layers panel. To un-nest a layer, drag it above or below the parent layer in the Layers panel.

The Layer marker for a nested layer appears inside the border of the outer layer.

Tip: You can also set Dreamweaver's preferences so that any layer you draw on top of another layer in the document window is automatically nested. Choose Edit→Preferences, click the Layers category, and turn on Nest when Created Within a Layer.

Undoing nested layers

If you later want to un-nest a nested layer, just drag its Layer marker to a new spot in the document window—outside of any other layers.

The Layers Panel

The Layers panel helps you manage the layers in a document (see Figure 12-5). To open it, choose Window→Layers or press F2.

The panel lists all layers in the document, and the three columns provide information on each layer:

- **Visibility.** If left to its own devices, Dreamweaver makes the contents of all layers visible on the page. But there are situations where you may want to make a certain layer (and its contents) invisible in your visitors' Web browsers.

The power of the Visibility property is that, using Dreamweaver Behaviors, you can later make the layer visible again, on cue. Imagine a Web page where you've superimposed many hidden layers on a diagram of a car engine. You could set this up so that moving the mouse over a part of the image reveals a layer, complete with text that describes the corresponding engine part. (Page 331 shows you how to create this effect.)

To change a layer's visibility, click in the Eye column next to the layer's name (see Figure 12-5), or use the Property Inspector. The Property inspector also offers an option not available in the Layers Panel: *inherit,* which lets a nested layer inherit the visibility of a parent layer, so that hiding a parent layer also hides any children whose visibilty property is set to inherit.

Figure 12-5:
The Layers panel lets you name, reorder, and change the visibility of layers. An open eye indicates a layer is visible; a closed eye, hidden. No eye icon at all represents the factory setting (that is, visible).

Turning on or off the Prevent Overlaps checkbox is the equivalent of choosing Modify→Arrange→ Prevent Layer Overlaps.

Visibility indicators

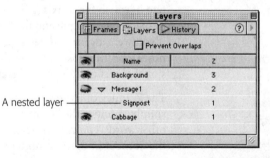

A nested layer

WORKAROUND WORKSHOP

Converting a Layer Grid to a Table

If the Prevent Overlaps box in the Layers panel is turned on, you won't be able to draw one layer on top of another. Nor will you be able to drag a layer onto or over another layer. Dreamweaver 3 aficionados once exploited this feature to create a layer-based design, assembling various rectangles on the screen to hold the different pieces of the Web page, and then converted the finished result into a table. These Dreamweaver veterans took advantage of the fact that the program can convert each layer into a table cell—but only if the layers don't overlap.

The new Layout view in Dreamweaver 4, of course, renders this workaround obsolete (see Chapter 6). But if you're still in the habit of using layers as though they're design tables, turn on the Prevent Overlaps box, draw your page design using the Layer tool, and then choose Modify→Convert→Layers to Tables.

• **Layer Name.** When you create a layer, Dreamweaver gives it a generic name—Layer1, for example. To provide a more descriptive name, one that will make it easier to remember which layer is which, double-click the layer name, and type a new name. (Layer names must start with a letter and can only contain letters and numbers. As Dreamweaver is quick to remind you, spaces and other punctuation aren't allowed.)

Clicking a layer name, by the way, is another way to select a layer in the document window.

Note: Don't rename a layer if you've already used it in a Dreamweaver behavior such as the Show/Hide Layers action (see page 331). JavaScript uses your layer names to "talk" to the layers. If you change a layer's name in the Layers panel, the name isn't automatically updated in the JavaScript code in your page. The behavior, therefore, will no longer work. In that case, you'll need to edit the behavior using the new layer name (see page 287).

• **Z-Index.** Welcome to the third dimension. Layers are unique in the world of Web elements, because they "float" above a Web page and can overlap each other, completely or partially.

If you were awake in high school Algebra, you may remember the graphing system in which the X-axis (a line pointing to the right) specified where a point was in space left-to-right, and the Y-axis specified where the point was vertically. And if you were awake *and* paying attention, you may remember that the Z-axis denotes a point's position in *front-to-back* space. When you draw a three-dimensional object on this type of graph, you need to use all three axes, X, Y, and Z.

The Z-Index of layers doesn't make your Web page *appear* three-dimensional; it simply specifies the "front-to-backness" of overlapping layers. The Z-Index, in other words, controls the stacking order of layers on a page, and is represented by the number in the Z column of the Layers panel (see Figure 12-5).

EASTER EGG HUNT

Franchises Still Available. Call Today.

You'll find a surprise hidden in Dreamweaver's Layers panel. Draw a layer on a page, and open the Layers panel (press F11). Double-click the layer's name, and then type *ToastYourOwn*. The dialog box shown here appears.

If you click Yes (and you're online), you'll be taken straightaway to the home page for Toast Your Own, a promising chain of coffee shops. The twist to this coffee-shop chain: Instead of having the bozos behind the counter serve you burnt, or, even worse, undercooked toast, you take your coffee and fresh-baked bread, sit down at one of the well-lit tables, and pop the bread into one of the many conveniently situated toasters.

Have it your way, indeed.

The page itself lies behind all layers; the layers stack up from there. In other words, the higher the layer number, the higher the layer; a layer with a Z-Index of 4 appears *behind* an overlapping layer with a Z-Index of, say, 7. (These numbers have no relation to the actual number of layers on a page. You could have three layers with Z-Indexes of 2, 499, and 2000, if you chose; you'd just have three layers, one on top of the other in ascending order.)

To change the Z-Index of a layer, click the number in the Z column and type another number. Software veterans will find that Dreamweaver's Layers panel works just as it does in Photoshop or Fireworks; you can drag a layer's name up or down the list to the desired position. The layer at the top of the list (highest number) is in front of all other layers, while the layer at the bottom of the list (lowest number) appears behind all other layers.

Modifying Layer Properties

Once you've drawn a layer, it isn't locked down on the page. Using the Property inspector, you can rename it, resize it, move it, align it with other layers, and set many other properties.

But first, you need to select the layer using one of these methods:

- Click the layer's name in the Layers panel (see Figure 12-5).
- Click the layer's selection handle (see Figure 12-4).
- Click the layer's border.

FREQUENTLY ASKED QUESTION

The Case of the Collapsing Layers

When I preview a page with layers inside Netscape 4, the layers collapse and change size when I resize the browser window. How do I prevent this?

Ahh, Netscape 4: the bane of Web designers the world over.

Due to a bug in that program, resizing the browser window can cause layers to change size and even disappear from the screen. To conquer this problem, Dreamweaver supplies a command that forces Netscape 4 browsers to reload the page whenever the window is resized, redrawing the layers correctly in the process.

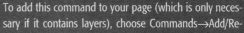

To add this command to your page (which is only necessary if it contains layers), choose Commands→Add/Remove Netscape Resize Fix. This inserts a small JavaScript program in the page, supplying the resize fix. (You can use the same command to remove this JavaScript from your page if you've removed layers entirely. Why weigh down your page with JavaScript that it doesn't need?)

You can also make Dreamweaver insert this command *automatically* whenever you draw a layer. Choose Edit→Preferences to open the Preferences window. Click the Layers category and turn on the "Add Resize Fix" box.

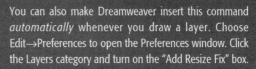

• Click the Layer marker that indicates the HTML code for the layer (see Figure 12-4).

And if that isn't enough ways to select a layer—Macromedia's programmers never sleep—you can also Shift-click a layer, as long as no other layers are currently selected. This technique also lets you select multiple layers, so that you can set the properties of (or align) many layers at once. If you're working in a layer or have a layer selected, Shift-clicking another layer selects them both. You can continue to Shift-click to select additional layers.

Resizing Layers

When you select a layer, eight handles appear around the edges of the layer (see Figure 12-4). You can drag any of these handles to change the layer's dimensions; any of the corner handles resizes both the width and height simultaneously.

You can also use the keyboard to resize a layer. First select the layer, then do one of the following:

• Press the Ctrl (⌘) key and press the arrow keys to change the layer's size by one pixel. The up and down arrow keys adjust the layer's height; the left and right arrows affect its width.

• To change the size *ten* pixels at a time, press Shift+Ctrl (Shift-⌘) and press the arrow keys.

For better precision, use the Property inspector to set an exact width and height for the layer (see Figure 12-6). Type a value in the W and H boxes to change the width and height of the layer, respectively. You can specify any unit of measurement that Cascading Style Sheets understands: px (pixels), pc (picas), pt (points), in (inches), mm (millimeters), cm (centimeters), em (height of the current font), ex (height of current font's x character), or % (percentage). To do this, type a number *immediately* followed by the abbreviation for the unit: for example, type *2in* into the W box to make the layer 2 inches wide.

Another benefit of using the Property inspector is that Dreamweaver lets you resize multiple layers at once. Shift-click two or more layers to select them, and then type new widths and heights; Dreamweaver sets all selected layers to these same dimensions.

Note: If the Prevent Overlaps feature is enabled (see Figure 12-5) you can't drag any of a layer's resize handles over another layer. In other words, layers can't be resized to overlap other layers *when dragging*. But if you use the Property inspector to change the dimensions of a layer, Dreamweaver *always* allows overlaps.

Moving Layers

Moving a layer is just as simple as resizing. Drag any border or the layer's selection handle (shown in Figure 12-4).

For less speed but greater precision, you can move a layer using the keyboard; first select the layer and then do one of the following:

- To move a layer one pixel at a time up, down, left, or right, press the corresponding keyboard arrow key.

- Press Shift while using an arrow key to move a layer ten pixels at a time.

As you'd guess, you can also control a layer's placement using the Property inspector (see Figure 12-6). Dreamweaver measures a layer's position relative to the left and top edges of the page (or, for nested layers, from the left and top edges of the parent layer). The Property inspector provides two boxes for these values: L specifies the distance from the left edge of the page to the left edge of the selected layer; T specifies the distance from the top edge of the page to the top of the selected layer.

To position a layer using the Property inspector, select the layer, using any of the methods described on page 325, and type distances in the L and T boxes. You can use any of the units of measurement mentioned above. You can even use negative values to move part or all of a layer off the page entirely (offstage, you might say), which is something you'd do if you intended a subsequent animation to bring it *onstage*, into the document window (see page 337).

For example, if you drew a 100-pixel tall and 50-pixel wide layer, you could move it to the very top-left corner of the page by selecting it and typing *0* in both the L and T boxes. To position that same layer so that it's just off the left edge of the page, type *-50px* in the L box.

Tip: You can't move a layer completely off the screen by dragging it. If you try, Dreamweaver rudely snaps the layer back to its previous position when you release the mouse. To completely move a layer out of sight, you must use the keyboard or Property inspector.

Aligning Layers

At times you may want to align several layers so that their left, top, bottom, or right edges line up with each other. Dreamweaver's Align command will do just that; it can even make the width and height of selected layers the same.

The layer you select *last* dictates how Dreamweaver aligns the layers. For example, say you have three layers—A, B, and C, and select them in order from A to C. You then align them to Left. Dreamweaver uses the left edge of layer C (the last one you selected) as the value for the other layers.

To use this feature, select two or more layers (by Shift-clicking them), choose Modify→Align, and then select one of the following options from the submenu:

- **Left** aligns the left edges of all selected layers. In other words, it gives each layer the same L property.

- **Right** aligns the *right* edges.

- **Top** aligns the top edges, so that the T properties are all set the same.

- **Bottom** aligns the bottom edges of the layers.

- **Make Same Width** sets the width of all selected layers (the W box in the Property inspector) the same; while **Make Same Height** does the same for the height of the layers.

FREQUENTLY ASKED QUESTION

Decoding DHTML

I've heard people talk about DHTML. What is it, and how is it different from HTML?

DHTML, or Dynamic HTML, is a combination of Web technologies that, among other things, let you animate elements on a page; hide (and then show) text, graphics and other objects; and even make an object draggable within your browser window (imagine a Web page that's a functional jigsaw puzzle). HTML, JavaScript, and Cascading Style Sheets make these kinds of effects possible.

HTML, of course, provides the framework and content for any Web page. It includes the tags that let you insert tables, graphics, and text. Cascading Style Sheets provide exact pixel-level positioning of content on a page; it's what makes layers possible. Finally, JavaScript (the programming language behind Dreamweaver Behaviors) brings the D to DHTML by providing interactive controls for the page's elements, including layers' properties. In short, DHTML is nothing more than the use of these three Web technologies to produce interactive and dynamic Web pages.

Layer Properties

Dimensions, Z-Index, and positioning aren't the only aspects of layers you can adjust using the Property inspector. To see the other options available to you, first select a layer using any of the techniques described on page 325—click its name in the Layers panel, for example—and then inspect the Property inspector:

Background Image and Color

You can set a layer's background in the same way you would for a table or table cell. To add a background image to the layer, click the folder icon next to the Bg Image field, and then select an image from your site folder. As usual, Dreamweaver tiles the image, if necessary, until the entire layer is filled with repeating copies of the graphic.

Setting a background color is even easier: just use the Bg Color box (see page 30) to select a color or sample a color off the screen.

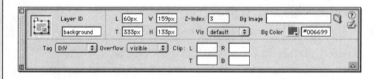

Figure 12-6:
You can set most layer properties in the Layers panel or the Layers category of the Preferences box. The Overflow and Clipping properties, however, are available only in the Property inspector.

Tag

Information about the size, position, visibility, and other properties of a layer is, behind the scenes, described using Cascading Style Sheets, but it's actually stored in an HTML tag within the page. The Tag pop-up menu lets you choose which kind of tag you'll want to store your layer's properties. (Here's another example of Dreamweaver's overachieving excess: two of the tags work only in a single browser version; in real life, you'll only use one of these options: the DIV tag.)

- **DIV** is the best choice. A <div> tag indicates a block-level element, like a paragraph or header. But unlike other block-level elements, the <div> tag has no intrinsic formatting—it's an empty vessel waiting to be filled with formatting information (in this case, layer properties).

- **SPAN** is used for formatting chunks of text *within* a paragraph—a few words on a line, for example. Although using the <span> tag works with layers, the block-level <div> tag is a more logical choice; a layer really is like a block, sitting on the page in all its square glory.

- The **LAYER** and **ILAYER** options work only in Netscape Navigator 4; Navigator 6 doesn't even recognize them. Consider these tags refugees of the browser war—gone and soon to be forgotten.

Overflow

Suppose you draw a square layer, 100 x 100 pixels. You fill it with a graphic that's 150 x 162 pixels—that is, larger than the layer itself.

You've already seen how a table cell reacts to this situation: it simply grows to fit the content inside it. Layers, however, are more (or less) flexible, depending on your choice of Overflow option in the Property inspector. These choices let you decide how browsers handle the excess part of the image:

- **Visible** makes the layer grow to accommodate its contents. This is the default setting.

- **Hidden** chops off the excess. In the example, only the top-left 100 x 100 pixels of the image are visible.

- **Scroll** adds scroll bars to the layer, so that a visitor can scroll to see all of the layer's contents. This feature offers an interesting way to add a small, scrollable window within a Web page; it's like a frame, but without requiring a frameset. Imagine a small "Latest Company News" box; visitors can scroll and read the text without disturbing anything else on the page. Unfortunately, this option doesn't work in Netscape 4 or Opera.

- **Auto** adds scroll bars to a layer *only* if necessary to accommodate its oversize contents. This feature doesn't work in Netscape 4 or Opera, either.

Dreamweaver can display only the Visible option; if you want to see the effect of any other Overflow setting, you must test the effect in a Web browser (see page 37).

Note: Various Web browsers handle the Overflow property differently. For example, Netscape Navigator 4.73 for Windows can't display scroll bars; the Mac version of Internet Explorer 5 often doesn't display the contents of a layer at all when the Overflow option is set to scroll. Test your design thoroughly if you use the Overflow setting.

Clipping

The Clipping property can hide all but a rectangular piece of a layer (see Figure 12-7). In most cases, you should avoid this property; not only is it rarely useful, but it's also a waste of precious bandwidth.

For example, say you put a large graphic into a layer, but only wanted to display one small area—like the single strawberry shown in Figure 12-7. You could use the Clipping property, but the Web browser still has to download the *entire* graphic—not just the clipped area. You're much better off just preparing the smaller graphic at the right size to begin with (see Chapter 5); the kilobytes you save may be your own.

(In theory, you could use JavaScript to *move* the clipping area, creating an effect like a spotlight traveling across the layer. Although that might be a more useful purpose for the Clip property, Dreamweaver unfortunately offers no tools for doing it.)

Figure 12-7:
A layer's Clip property lets you display only a selected section of the layer. In this example, the layer to the left has no clipping set; while the layer to the right has a clipping box that hides all but a single strawberry from sight. Notice that the layer itself remains the same size—as indicated by the gray outline. Only the visible portion of that layer is changed.

If you're not convinced, and you still want to clip a layer in Dreamweaver, here's a sure-fire technique:

1. **Click inside a layer whose contents you wish to clip.**

   The layer should already contain an image.

2. **Choose Insert→Layer.**

Dreamweaver adds a nested layer. You'll use this layer to determine the coordinates of the clipping box.

3. **Drag and resize the nested layer until it exactly covers the part of the layer you wish to show.**

   This is easy to do, because Dreamweaver lets you see the contents of the underlying layer. In Figure 12-7, a nested layer was positioned and sized so it precisely covered the strawberry. For better precision, hide all invisible elements in the page (View→Visual Aids→Hide All).

4. **Select the nested layer and note its L, T, W, and H properties, which you can read in the Property inspector.**

   You can write them on scrap paper, for example. These numbers will let you calculate the exact dimensions of the clipping box.

5. **Delete the nested layer.**

   You needed it only to get the measurements in step 4.

6. **Select the first layer and fill in the Clip boxes in the Property inspector, using the numbers from the nested layer as a guide.**

   In the Clip's L box, enter the nested layer's L value; in the T box type the T value you wrote down in step 4. Add the nested layer's L and W values and type the result in the R box. Finally, in the B box, type the total of the T and H values you wrote down in step 4.

Only the area covered by the nested layer now appears.

Hiding and Showing Layers

Do you ever stare in awe when a magician makes a handkerchief disappear into thin air? Now you, too can perform sleight-of-hand, right on your very own Web pages, making layers disappear and reappear with ease. Although it's not magic, Dreamweaver's Show-Hide Layers behavior is undoubtedly a nifty piece of JavaScript programming.

Show-Hide Layers takes advantage of the Visibility property of layers on your page. You can use it for things like adding pop-up tooltips to your Web page; when a visitor's mouse moves over a link, a layer appears with a more detailed explanation of where the link goes (see Figure 12-8).

The following steps show you how to create this remarkable special effect. Note, however, that the process requires some familiarity with Dreamweaver Behaviors, which are described in Chapter 11. For example, there you'll find out that behaviors are special effects that require you to specify an *event* (something your visitor does that triggers the effect) and an *action* (the effect itself), and that you must attach a behavior to a specific *tag*.

1. Add layers to your Web page using the techniques described on page 319. Use the Visibility setting (page 323) to specify how you want each layer to look when the page loads.

   If you want a layer to be visible at first, and then to disappear when your visitor does something specific, set the layer to visible; if you want it to appear only after some specific event, set it to hidden.

Figure 12-8:
Using Dreamweaver's Show-Hide Layers behavior, you can make layers appear and disappear. In this example at www.safetreekids.net/ awesome/parts.html, several layers lie hidden on the page. When your mouse moves over different parts of the tree cross-section, informative graphics, each placed in a hidden layer, suddenly appear. Moving the mouse away returns the layer to its hidden state. Notice how the information bubble overlaps the tree image and the text above it–a dead giveaway that this page uses layers.

2. In the tag selector, click the tag to which you want the behavior attached.

   Web designers often attach behaviors to link tags (<a> tags); but you can also attach them to images or, as in Figure 12-8, to an image map (see page 107), which defines hotspots on a single graphic. To create this effect, you'd attach two behaviors to each hotspot in the document window (that is, to each <area> tag in HTML): one to show the layer, using the onMouseOver event, and one to hide the layer, using the onMouseOut event.

   Note: If this is all Greek to you, see page 107 for more on image maps and hot spots; page 284 for more on attaching behaviors to tags; and page 289 for details on event types.

   ---

3. If it isn't already open, choose Window→Behaviors to open the Behaviors panel.

   The Behaviors panel (as pictured on page 284) appears. It lets you add, remove and modify behaviors.

4. Click the + button on the panel; select Show-Hide Layers from the menu.

The Show-Hide Layers dialog box appears (see Figure 12-9). You'll use this box to tell Dreamweaver what layer you intend to work with first.

5. **Click a layer in the list of named layers.**

Here's an example of why it's useful to give your layers descriptive names. It's difficult to remember which layer is which when all have the Dreamweaver default names (Layer1, Layer2, and so on).

6. **Choose a Visibility setting for the layer by clicking one of the three buttons, Show, Hide, or Default.**

You're now determining what will happen to the layer when someone interacts with the tag you selected in step 2. Show makes the layer visible; Hide hides the layer; and Default sets the layer's Visibility property to the browser's default value, which is usually the same as the Inherit value described on page 323.

The choice you selected appears in parentheses next to the layer's name, as shown in Figure 12-9.

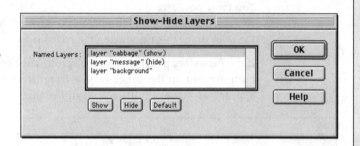

Figure 12-9:
The Show-Hide Layers dialog box lets you hide or show any layer on the page. In fact, you can control multiple layers at once. In the example here, the layer "cabbage" will appear, and the layer "message" will disappear, when the behavior is triggered. The third layer, "background," is unaffected by this particular action.

7. **If you like, select another layer and apply another visibility option.**

A single Show-Hide Layers action can affect several layers at once; a single action can even make some visible and others invisible. (If you apply an action to a layer by mistake, select the same option again to remove it from the layer.)

8. **Click OK to apply the behavior.**

The Show-Hide Layers action is now listed in the Behaviors panel, as is the event that triggers it. For more information on using and setting events, see page 284.

Once you've added Show-Hide Layers, you can preview the behavior in a Web browser (Dreamweaver can't display behaviors by itself). Like other Dreamweaver Behaviors, you can edit or delete this action; see page 287.

Creating Draggable Layers

For a truly interactive Web experience, you can create *draggable* layers that let your visitors rearrange Web page elements themselves. Imagine taking last year's Christmas photo and turning it into a Web-based picture puzzle, which your kids and friends can try to piece together. You could even create a magnetic poetry page, where visitors can drag words around the screen to create their own stream-of-consciousness rants.

Dreamweaver's Drag Layer behavior lets you free a layer from its normally sedentary existence. You can control how the layer is dragged, make it snap into a predefined position, and even have it trigger other exciting JavaScript commands.

Once again, you'll have to slog through Chapter 11 to learn something about Behaviors before proceeding. Once you've grasped the concepts of events, actions, and attached HTML tags, you're ready to begin.

Start by adding a layer to a Web page, using the techniques described on page 319. You may want to give it a name that fits—*puzzle1,* for instance.

You must now attach a behavior to an HTML tag (see page 284). Very often, you'll add this behavior to the <body> of the page, so that the Drag Layer behavior makes the layer draggable right when the page loads.

If the Behaviors panel isn't on the screen, choose Window→Behaviors. From the + button/menu on the panel, choose Drag Layer to make the Drag Layer dialog box appear (see Figure 12-10). Fill it out like this:

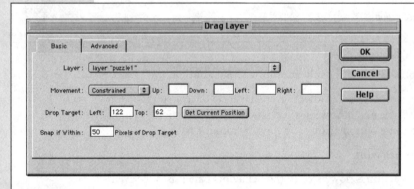

Figure 12-10:
The Drag Layer dialog box lets you set many different properties for a draggable layer, including setting a Drop Target—a location on the page where the layer is supposed to end up.

- **Layer.** Select the layer you want to manipulate. You can only select one layer per Drag Layer action. If you want to make several layers draggable, you'll have to apply this behavior once for each layer. (The exception is nested layers. Add the Drag Layer behavior to the parent layer; when your visitor drags that layer, the nested layers follow along.)

- **Movement.** You can control where the layer can be dragged by selecting one of two options from the Movement menu:

Unconstrained puts no limits on the layer. Visitors can freely drag the layer anywhere on the page; they can even drag most of the layer past the edges of the browser window. **Constrained** lets you limit the area the layer can move in. Four fields—Up, Down, Left, and Right—define the limits of the drag area. Each field accepts a pixel value that indicates how far in a particular direction the layer can move.

For example, suppose you've put a layer smack-dab in the middle of the window. If you type *50, 20, 100,* and *150* in the Up, Down, Left, and Right boxes, visitors will be able to drag the layer no more than 50 pixels up, 20 pixels down, 100 pixels to the left, and 150 pixels to the right. Leaving a field blank means there's no constraint in that direction. For example, if you leave the Up field empty, visitors will be able to drag the layer all the way to the top (and almost out) of the browser window.

Tip: If you want to limit a layer's movement so it can only move left and right (like a slider on a control panel), choose Constrained from the Drag Layer dialog and type *0* in both the Up and Down boxes. To limit its movement to up and down—like an elevator—type *0* in both the Left and Right boxes.

• **Drop Target.** Setting a Drop Target is optional. But it can be useful when your goal is to have visitors drag the layer to a *specific place* on the page. For example, you could create a jigsaw-puzzle Web page where each piece of the puzzle is placed in its own layer. When the page loads, all of the pieces are spread around the page, and your visitor's challenge is to put the pieces together. Each puzzle piece must go in a specific place, so each layer gets its own drop target. (This option works well with the Snap option described next. It can also trigger *another* JavaScript program, as described below.)

The value in the Left field represents the distance, in pixels, from the left edge of the browser window to the top-left corner of the layer. The value in the Top field is the distance from the top of the browser window to the top-left corner of the layer. For example, say you want the top-left corner of the layer to end up 50 pixels from the left of the browser edge and 100 pixels down from the top; in this case, you'd type *50* and *100* in the Left and Top boxes, respectively.

To help you figure all this out, the Get Current Position button calculates the current coordinates of the layer on the page. This may not seem so useful: After all, why would you want to create a drop target in the first place, if the layer is already there?

But the trick is to start by moving the layer you want to make draggable to the position on the page where you'll want it to *end up* (that is, where the visitor should drag it). Then apply the Drag Layer behavior and *then* click the Get Current Position button. Later, after you've finished setting the other properties and clicked OK, you can move the layer to its *starting* position (where it will appear before the visitor drags it).

- **Snap if Within.** One problem with the Drop Target feature is that the drop area is marked by a *single pixel* on the page. Dragging a layer *exactly* to that spot would require that your audience have the patience of Job and the hand of a neurosurgeon.

  Fortunately, you can bend your visitors in the right direction with the help of the Snap if Within option. When a visitor drags the layer within a certain distance of the drop target, this option makes the layer snap right into place. If you type *100,* for example, when a visitor drags the layer and releases the mouse button when the layer's upper-left corner is within 100 pixels of the drop target, that's close enough for government work; it will immediately pop into place.

The previous settings are all you need to create a basic draggable layer; if you click OK, you close the dialog box and apply the action. But if you want to give your draggable layer even more sophisticated and professional features, click the Advanced tab to set additional properties (see Figure 12-11).

- **Drag Handle.** By default, Entire Layer is selected, meaning that a visitor can click *anywhere* on the layer to drag it. But in some cases, you may want to specify that users must click a specific portion of the layer—a handle—in order to drag the layer. For example, perhaps your layer contains a picture of a tool box. You could define the part of the picture with the tool box's handle as the layer's drag handle.

  Choose Area Within Layer from the Drag Handle menu to define the handle area. Four fields (L, T, W, and H) appear on the Advanced tab. You specify the draggable area relative to the layer itself; L represents the distance from the left edge of the layer, T the distance from the top of the layer, and W and H represent the width and height of the handle.

- **While Dragging.** As discussed on page 324, layers can overlap each other in a stack. A layer's Z-Index determines where it belongs in the front-to-back stacking order of the page. By default, the Bring Layer to Front option is turned on, so that the layer doesn't get hidden behind other layers as someone drags it around the page. If you want to leave the layer behind other layers as it's dragged, turn off this option.

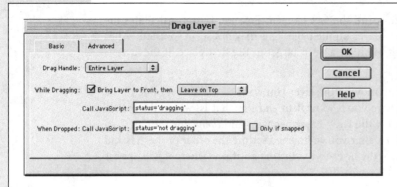

Figure 12-11:
In this example, a simple JavaScript statement—status='dragging'—makes the word dragging *appear in the status bar of the Web browser when a visitor drags the layer. If the user lets go of the layer, the words* not dragging *appear instead.*

In addition, you can control whether the layer stays on top or returns to its place in the stacking order when it's dropped after dragging. The Leave on Top option is selected by default, meaning that when the visitor drops the layer, it stays on top; in fact, it jumps to the very top Z-Index level of the page, above even the layers it *doesn't* actually overlap. (If you turned off Bring Layer to Front, this option has no effect.)

If you want to return the layer to its original level in the stacking order, choose "Restore z-index." Now the layer can appear on top while it's being dragged, but once released, it returns to its original order.

- **Call JavaScript.** These final settings are fun and powerful, but require solid knowledge of JavaScript. The first Call JavaScript box is where you type a JavaScript command or *function call* that you want to run while the layer is dragged. The second box lets you specify a command or function that's called when the layer is dropped.

  Turn on "Only if snapped" if you want the command to run only if the layer is dropped on a target. For example, you could make a dialog box that says "Bullseye!" appear when your visitor drops a layer directly over a target on the page. For another example of these options, see Figure 12-11.

Once you've added your fancy new behavior, you can test it by pressing F12 and previewing it in a Web browser. Like any other Behavior, you can edit the Drag Layer behavior using the directions on page 287.

Animating Layers

Nobody looks at banner ads anymore, but how about a banner ad that flies across the top of the page—towed by a tiny airplane graphic? The latest crop of Web browsers lets you move layers around the screen to produce exciting animated designs.

This kind of dynamic behavior generally requires a deep knowledge of JavaScript and Cascading Style Sheets, as well as the experience and patience to deal with the differences between the various browser brands.

Fortunately, all of the required programming skill and Web development experience is built right into Dreamweaver. With Dreamweaver's Timeline tools, you can create elaborate and complex animations, and even time-based actions like automated slide shows.

Tip: If you've used Macromedia's animation driven programs, Flash and Director, picking up Dreamweaver's tools is a snap. Dreamweaver uses an animation interface very similar to those programs.

Understanding Animation

Programming animation requires that you specify two things: *movement* and *time*. Imagine a ball moving across the screen; it takes the ball two seconds to travel from

---

the left side to the right. A Web browser creates animation by drawing the ball in several different positions over several fractions of a second, so that you see the effect of smooth motion across the screen.

Each of these drawings occurs in a moment of time, referred to as a *frame*—the fundamental building block of computer (or Disney) animation. A collection of frames makes up a *timeline*. Think of a timeline as a strip of movie film; each frame in the filmstrip contains one picture. When the strip is played back from beginning to end, you have a movie.

A Dreamweaver timeline can play back either when the page first loads or when your visitor does something that you specify. For instance, you can add a button to a page that, when clicked, plays an animation on the screen.

Animation The Easy Way

To create an animation, you'll place a graphic into a layer, and then direct that layer to move around the Web page, carrying the image on its back. Animating a layer involves some very sophisticated JavaScript programming code. In fact, the code required to animate a layer can take up more lines of code than the actual HTML of the page. Trying to create such a program yourself could take weeks. But Dreamweaver can do it in seconds by recording the movement of your mouse as you drag a layer around the document window.

To draw an animation on the screen, select a layer to animate, using one of the techniques described on page 325. Now choose Modify→Timeline→Record Path of Layer; the Timelines panel appears, and Dreamweaver is ready to record your animation. (The Timeline is described in detail on page 340.)

Grab the layer by its selection handle or border and drag around the page. A trail of gray dots follows your cursor, indicating the path your animation will follow. Dreamweaver doesn't record the timing of your drag, just the path, so take your time to make sure that the motion is exactly what you want. You'll specify the speed of the animation later, as described in see Figure 12-12.

When you release the mouse, a particularly chatty dialog box appears. It tells you that you can animate the following layer properties: Left, Top, Width, Height, Z-Index, and Visibility. You'll learn how to do all of this shortly. In addition, you're told that Netscape Navigator 4 (that infernal bottleneck to innovation) *can't* animate the width and heights of layers.

Click OK (and, while you're at it, turn on the "Don't show me this message again" box). A gray line appears across the document window, winding its way along the path you just created; and a line with a series of hollow dots appears in the now-open Timelines panel, as shown in Figure 12-12.

If you turn on the Autoplay box (shown in Figure 12-12), your animation will play as soon as the page loads. This is a common choice, since it plays your breathtaking animation immediately upon your visitor's arrival. You can however, start the animation by other means using the Play Timeline behavior, as described on page 347.

In addition, if you want to repeat your animation over and over again—perhaps making an animated bee fly incessantly around your page, in hopes of distracting your visitor from studying your site's privacy policy—turn on the Loop box.

Tip: Because looping immediately jumps from the end of the animation to the beginning, make sure whatever you're animating starts and ends at roughly the same place on the page. Otherwise, it will look as if the layer suddenly disappeared from one area of the page and then reappeared somewhere else.

At this point, you can press F12 to preview your animation in a browser. You can also preview it right in the document window using the Timelines panel (see Figure 12-13). Click the Rewind button, and then click and hold the Forward button; Dreamweaver plays each frame of the animation. Or grab the playback head and drag it back and forth to move backwards and forwards through the animation.

Once you've added an animation to the timeline, you can edit many of the animation's properties, such as its speed or movement; see "Animating with key frames" on page 347.

Figure 12-12:
The easiest method of creating an animation simply requires you to drag a layer along the route you want the animation to take. Dreamweaver can record this path and save it as an animation.

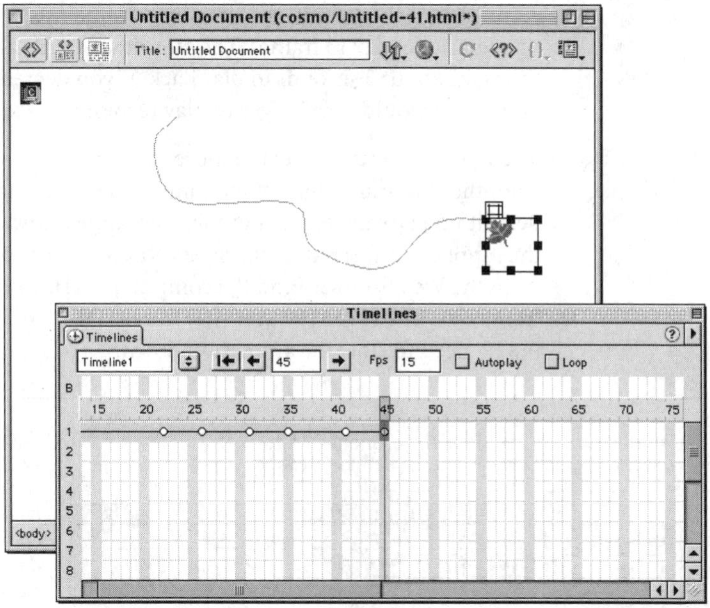

Understanding Timelines

The Timelines panel is the control center for your Dreamweaver animations (see Figure 12-13). Choose Window→Timelines to open it, or press Shift-F9.

Note: Timelines, frames, key frames, and other terms associated with Dreamweaver's animation tools are not a part of HTML, JavaScript, or CSS. There's no tag called *key frame* and no JavaScript command called *play.* Dreamweaver's Timelines panel and animation capabilities are the result of sophisticated programming on the part of the program's engineers, and as such, are specific to Dreamweaver.

The bottom half of the panel displays numbered rows called *channels,* which denote individual layer animations. For example, in Figure 12-13, a single animation sits in channel 1; it's the solid color bar with a line running through it (called the *animation bar*). The numbers along the top of those rows indicate the frames; the animation bar pictured here is 40 frames long. Since a frame is an individual drawing of a layer at a specific time and position, a Web browser would move the layer 40 times to complete this animation.

You can add multiple animations to a timeline, too, so that two or more layers move simultaneously across the screen. Each would appear in its own Timelines channel.

While the number of frames in a channel determines the number of times the Web browser will move the layer, it doesn't directly dictate the *speed* at which the animation plays. The speed is determined by the *frame rate* shown in the Fps (frames per second) box. By default, the timeline's frame rate is 15 fps; in other words, it takes one second to play 15 frames. The sample 40-frame animation in Figure 12-13 would thus take about 3 seconds to play back. If you decreased the speed to 8 fps, the same animation would take longer to play (around 5 seconds).

The lower the frame rate, the more the animation stutters; the higher the rate, the smoother the animation. While compared to a feature film, which runs at 24 fps, the default rate Dreamweaver supplies may appear low. However, it's wise to stick with the supplied 15 fps; redrawing layers is a complex process that requires a lot of power from the Web browser (and the computer it's running on). You can specify a higher frame rate, but a Web browser may not be able to obey. In order to draw each frame, it may need to slow the animation down.

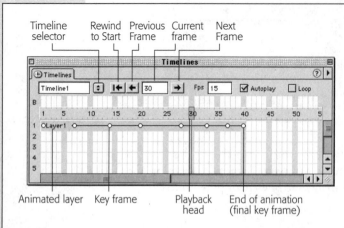

Figure 12-13:
While working in Dreamweaver, you can view different frames of any timeline by using the playback head and the arrow buttons. You can go directly to any point in the animation by dragging the Playback head left or right. The Current Frame box indicates which frame you're currently viewing. You can move forward or backward one frame by clicking the right or left arrows. Holding down either button plays the animation (either forward or in reverse). Click the Rewind button to jump to the first frame in the timeline.

Tip: Although it's possible to tell Dreamweaver to animate, say, 17 different layers at a frame rate of 36 frames per second, you probably won't see the effect you want. In fact, most likely, the Web browser will slow to a crawl and your animation will look like it's moving in slow motion as the Web browser dutifully draws every frame in the timeline, regardless of how long it takes and no matter what speed you specified.

Be careful when creating complex animations. Test them in a variety of browsers, and, if possible, on slower computers. That's the only way to make sure that your stunning animations don't wind up resembling paint-drying contests.

Adding a timeline

Dreamweaver automatically creates a timeline when you animate a layer by recording its path. But you can also add a timeline manually by choosing Modify→Timeline→Add Timeline in the Timelines panel. A new, empty timeline appears, to which you can add layers and create animations.

Adding layers to the timeline

As noted earlier in this chapter, there's an Easy Way to animate a layer—just by dragging it. Unfortunately, at times, you'll find the Easy Way to be less than accurate; as has been noted many times before, drawing with a mouse is like using a bar of soap to paint the Sistine Chapel. Furthermore, you can't create a straight line using this method.

Fortunately, there's also a Harder But More Precise way: selecting a layer (or several) and choosing Modify→Timeline→Add Object to Timeline.

Tip: A quick way to add a layer to the timeline is to drag it from the document window into one of the Layer channels on the Timelines panel.

When you add a layer, a new animation bar appears in one of the channels of the Timelines panel. The animation bar starts out as a solid blue span of 15 frames (one second) that contains the layer's name and begins and ends with a white dot. To extend the animation's length, drag the white dot in frame 15 to the right. For example, if you wanted to make a 10-second-long animation, you'd drag the dot out to frame 150.

You can also move the entire animation bar by dragging the bar along the timeline—a useful tactic when you want to add a slight delay to an animation, or stagger several different animations in the same timeline. For example, imagine you wanted to make two snowflakes (two layers, each with an image of a snowflake) appear at the top of the browser window and float down the page; but you also want the second snowflake to enter the scene about one second after the other. Drag the animation bar with the second snowflake animation so it *begins* on frame 16, one second after the first snowflake falls.

Animating with key frames

The white dots in the animation bar, called *key frames,* are your main tool for controlling an animation. In fact, when you add a layer to the timeline by using the Modify→Timeline→Add Object to Timeline command (or by dragging the layer onto a channel), key frames are the *only* way to give the frame a movement path.

Each animation begins life with two key frames, one each for the animation's beginning and ending positions. So far, the layer is in the same position in both key frames; in other words, it doesn't go anywhere when the animation plays.

By adding and manipulating key frames, you can tell Dreamweaver where you want your layer to wind up at certain points in its motion; the program automatically calculates the layer's position in all of the intermediate frames, saving you endless tedium and grief.

For example, on a brand-new animation with only two key frames (beginning and ending positions), click the second key frame, which selects the corresponding layer in the document window. Drag the layer to the spot on the page where you wish the animation to *end* and let go. Now when you play the animation, the layer travels from its starting position to the *new* ending location. Similarly, you can change the beginning position of the layer by selecting the first key frame and dragging the layer.

Tip: For compulsive precision, you can also specify a new position for a layer by clicking the key frame in the timeline and setting the layer's L and T properties in the Property inspector (see page 327).

Adding key frames to a timeline

Of course, you won't get far in life just making your layers fly from point A to point B. If you add more key frames between the starting and ending ones, you can define new spots for your layer-in-motion to hit at certain times as it putters on its way to the ending spot. (In fact, when you create an animation the Easy Way, by dragging a layer around the screen, Dreamweaver automatically generates dozens of key frames; see Figure 12-12.)

To manually add a key frame, click a frame in the Timelines panel animation bar (one that's not already a key frame). When you click, the playback head (the red box that appears among the frame numbers) moves to the frame.

Now choose Modify→Timeline→Add Keyframe. A hollow circle appears in the animation bar at the frame you selected. You can also press F6 to add a new key frame at the selected point in the animation bar.

Tip: You can conserve a few precious calories by Ctrl-clicking (⌘-clicking) the frame you wish to turn into a key frame. The cursor turns into a tiny hollow circle and instantly creates a new key frame.

Having created a new key frame, you're ready to specify the layer's new position at this point, confident that Dreamweaver will automatically regenerate its movement from the key frames before and after the one you just added; read on.

Tip: To delete a key frame, select it in the timeline and press Shift-F6, or choose Modify→Timeline→Remove Keyframe.

Modifying layers at key frames

Key frames define the position of a layer at a particular moment in the animation. Once you've created a new key frame, the corresponding layer is selected in the document window; you can then drag it to a new location. When you release the mouse, Dreamweaver redraws the gray path line to indicate the new path the animation follows, leading up to, and away from, your new key frame.

Similarly, you can adjust your moving layer's position at any *existing* key frame just by clicking the corresponding spot in the timeline and then dragging the layer on your screen.

But you can do more than change a layer's *position* at each key frame; you can also change other properties at each spot, like this:

- **Visibility.** Use the Property inspector to set the visibility property of a layer at a particular key frame (see page 323 for information on setting the Visibility property). You'll therefore make the layer disappear (or reappear) on cue. Unfortunately, there is no way to fade the layer out gradually; it's either visible or hidden.

WORKAROUND WORKSHOP

Straight-Line Animation

When an animation has more than one key frame, Dreamweaver always creates a curved path from one key frame position to the next—a real problem if you want to create a straight zigzag motion. There's only one way to create a sure-fire, straight-line path: Create an animation with only two key frames. If you try to introduce a third point between them, Dreamweaver goes right back to curving your path.

The workaround, therefore, involves creating a new animation bar for *each* straight-line motion segment. After adding the layer to the timeline, in other words, define its starting position on the screen using the first key frame. Now click the ending-point key frame, and then define the

ending position of the first straight line (the end of the "zig").

Now you're ready to create another animation bar, which will create the "zag." Click the frame just after the last key frame; select the layer on the screen; and choose Modify→Timeline→Add Object to Timeline. Now that the second animation bar has appeared, you can click *its* first and last key frames, positioning the layer on each.

To create a third straight-line movement, choose Modify→Timeline→Add Object to Timeline *again,* and set the starting and ending positions for *its* key frames. Continue this process until you've added animation bars for each stroke in the zigzag path.

To make a layer disappear and reappear later in the animation, click a key frame and set Visibility to hidden; Ctrl-click (⌘-click) consecutive frames to create a series of hidden key frames. Change the last key frame to visible at the point when you want the frame to reappear.

- **Z-Index**. You can also change the stacking order of the layer at a particular key frame. Click the key frame and use either the Property inspector or Layers panel to set the layer's Z-Index (page 324).

Imagine a moon, for instance, flying around a planet. It moves from behind the planet at first, orbits around the front of the planet, and then eventually disappears back behind it. In this example, the planet would be in one layer, the moon in another.

At first, the Z-Index of the planet would be greater than that of the moon. After the moon moves from behind the planet, you would add a key frame, and increase the moon's Z-Index so that it's larger than the planet's, putting the moon layer in front of the planet.

After the moon crosses the face of the planet, you would add another key frame and set its Z-Index back to its original setting—lower than, and behind, the planet.

- **Width and Height**. You can also change the dimensions of a layer at a key frame by changing the W and H fields in the Property inspector (see page 326). The effect is very interesting: Not only does the layer change size when it reaches that key frame, but it automatically and gradually changes size in each frame in between. (Unfortunately, this feature doesn't work in Netscape Navigator 4 or any version of Opera.)

GEM IN THE ROUGH

Create an Automated Slide Show

Most people think of Dreamweaver's Timeline feature in terms of moving *layers* around the screen. But there's one other thing you can add there: graphics. You can't make them fly around unless they're in a layer, but you can make their *properties* change over time. And that's just the feature you need if you want to create an automated presentation of your photos.

Here's how to do it. Add an image to the timeline, either by dragging it to the timeline or by selecting the image in the document window, and choose Modify→Timeline→Add Object to Timeline.

Then decide how frequently you want the image to change.

For example, maybe you want a new image to appear every two seconds. If the timeline's frame rate is 15 fps, you'll want to change the image every 30 frames. Create as many key frames as you have images, spaced 30 frames apart.

Then select each key frame; use the Property inspector to change the Src property for each. The Src property, of course, identifies the graphics file in your site folder; in other words, you can swap one image in for another at a specified time. (Make sure all the images you use are the same size.)

When you play the timeline, a new image appears every other second.

Controlling animation speed using key frames

Once you create a key frame, you can move it in the timeline by dragging it (see Figure 12-14). This is how you control the *pace* of movement between key frames. The more frames between key frames, the slower the movement; fewer frames means faster movement.

For example, in Figure 12-14, a 25-frame animation of a leaf moving along a path has three key frames. The second key frame is selected, showing that the leaf is only about halfway along the path (the gray line). As you can see in the timeline, there are 19 frames from the first key frame to the midpoint. There are only 3 frames, however, from the second key frame until the final one. In other words, it takes about 20 frames (a little over 1 second) for the leaf to travel halfway along the path. The last half goes much faster—only about 4 frames, or less than 1/4 second.

In this example, the leaf will travel leisurely along the screen, until it reaches the midway mark in its path, and will then scream quickly to its destination. If you drag the middle key frame to the center of the animation bar, the leaf would travel at the same speed throughout the animation.

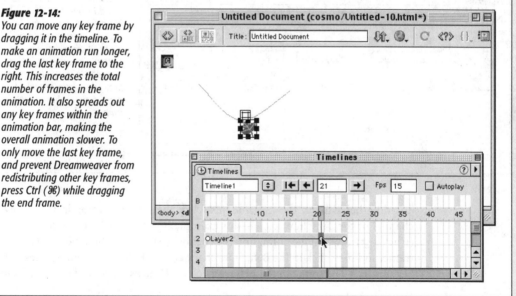

Figure 12-14:
You can move any key frame by dragging it in the timeline. To make an animation run longer, drag the last key frame to the right. This increases the total number of frames in the animation. It also spreads out any key frames within the animation bar, making the overall animation slower. To only move the last key frame, and prevent Dreamweaver from redistributing other key frames, press Ctrl (⌘) while dragging the end frame.

The Behaviors channel

Directly above the frame numbers that appear in the Timelines panel, you'll find another row of frames labeled B. It's the Behaviors channel. You can use this channel to trigger a Dreamweaver Behavior at a particular frame in the timeline. (See Chapter 11 for the exhaustive, and exhausting, story on behaviors.)

In fact, you may have already used the B channel without even knowing it. When you turn on the Loop box in the Timelines panel, Dreamweaver inserts a Go To Timeline Frame behavior into the Behaviors channel in the last frame of your animation (see Figure 12-15). This behavior (see page 349) causes the animation to return to the first frame in the timeline and play again.

Suppose you want an alert box with the word "Boom!" to appear at the instant when one animated layer touches another. All you'd have to do is select the frame where the two layers meet, and then add a Pop-up Message action to the Behaviors channel.

Tip: You don't actually have to have *any* animation on the page to take advantage of the Behaviors channel. Say, for example, you want a new browser window to appear exactly four seconds after a Web page loads–a delayed pop-up ad, perhaps. You'd just add an Open Browser Window action to frame 60 in the Behaviors channel, and then turn on the Autoplay checkbox in the Timelines panel.

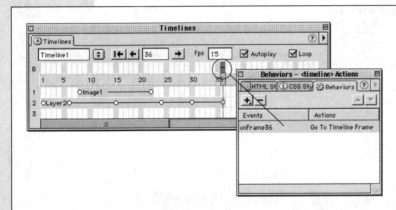

Figure 12-15:
The Behaviors channel lets you add time-based behaviors to your page. Change the text in a layer every 10 seconds, for example, or write a new message to the Web browsers' status bar when an animation reaches its last frame.

To add a behavior to the timeline, just click the relevant frame in the Behaviors channel of the Timelines panel—for example, the frame where two layers collide. (Click key frames in the animation bars below to see where the action is at any given frame, and *then* click in the Behaviors channel. The Behaviors channel doesn't have key frames.) The frame in the Behaviors channel turns black to show it's selected.

Now open the Behaviors panel (Windows→Behaviors), click the + button, and choose a behavior from the menu. For example, you could make a new browser window pop up by selecting the Open Browser Window behavior. (See Chapter 11 for a complete list of Behaviors.)

After you've added a behavior to the channel, a dash appears in the frame, and the Behaviors panel lists the event (it should look something like this: *onFrame36*). Unlike a regular behavior, you can't select an event yourself (page 283). The frame itself acts as the event; the action is triggered when the timeline reaches the specified frame.

You can move your newly created Frame behavior by dragging it left or right in the Behaviors channel, or remove it altogether by clicking its frame, clicking its name in the Behaviors panel, and then clicking the – button in the Behaviors panel.

Tip: Once you click inside the Behaviors channel, Dreamweaver will only let you *add* Behaviors to that channel. If you try to add a behavior to another object in the page (by selecting a link or the <body> tag, for instance, and adding a behavior), Dreamweaver insists on adding it to the Timeline instead. To get past this little bug, click one of the animation layers inside the Timelines panel to deselect the Behaviors Channel.

Adding and deleting timelines

You can create several different animations on one page, each on its own timeline, and control them using the behaviors described below. For example, you might want to have a layer fly onto the page when your visitor's mouse moves over a navigational button, and fly off screen when the mouse moves off the button. The fly-on, fly-off layer might supply information about where the button leads, or even contain a submenu of additional buttons.

To add an additional timeline, open the Timelines panel (Shift-F9); then choose Modify→Timeline→Add Timeline. A new timeline appears in the Timeline field in the upper left of the panel.

Dreamweaver proposes generic names like Timeline1 and Timeline2, and so on; to provide a more recognizable name—*fly* or *submenu1,* for example—select the name of the timeline from the menu in the Timelines panel. Choose Modify→Timeline→ Rename Timeline. A dialog box appears; type the new name and click OK.

It's a good idea to name a timeline immediately after creating it. If you change its name after applying Behaviors that control the timeline, they won't work. You'll then need to edit each behavior to give it the timeline's new name.

If you decide you don't want a timeline any longer, you can delete it; select a timeline from the Timelines panel, and choose Modify→Timeline→Remove Timeline. (Doing so removes all animations and actions in that timeline, but doesn't delete the layers themselves.)

Controlling Playback

Suppose you've created an automated slide show (see page 344). The page loads, and every few seconds a new slide appears. But what if you wanted to let the viewer control the slide show—pausing it, for example, when a particularly interesting image appears, and then restarting it when ready? Or what if you wanted to give your audience the option to rewind back to the beginning or jump to a particular slide?

Special Dreamweaver Behaviors give you this kind of playback flexibility.

Note: If you haven't created at least one timeline, these behaviors are grayed out in the Behaviors panel.

Starting and Stopping Timelines

As mentioned earlier in this chapter, the Autoplay box in the Timelines panel makes a timeline play automatically when the page loads. You might, however, want to start a timeline based on some other action, such as when your viewer clicks a Play button.

Tip: When using Behaviors to *control* a layer, don't apply the behavior *to* the layer. In fact, if you select a layer, these behaviors are grayed out in the Behaviors panel. Behaviors are attached to items that *cause* something to change—for example, a link, that when clicked, starts an animation on the page—and not the thing you wish to change (in this case, a layer).

To give your visitors this push-button control, use the Play Timeline behavior, which you might attach to a Play-button graphic. (For best effect, add a dead link to an image on the page [as described on page 283] and then attach the behavior to that link.) Select a tag, click the + button on the Behaviors panel, and choose Timeline→Play Timeline. The Play Timeline window appears (see Figure 12-16). There's only one option: select a timeline to play from the menu. Click OK, and change the triggering event from the Behaviors panel.

Figure 12-16:
Top: Start any timeline on the page with the Play Timeline behavior. This behavior plays a timeline from its current frame—not necessarily its beginning. So, if you applied a Stop Timeline action, and later used a Play Timeline, the specified timeline would begin playback from the point it was last stopped. Bottom: Stop any or all timelines dead in their tracks with the Stop Timeline behavior. Use it to add a Pause button to an animated page.

If you let someone start an animation on the page, it's only courteous to let him stop it, too. You apply the Stop Timeline behavior just like the Play Timeline action. The dialog box looks similar, too (see Figure 12-16). The one difference: in addition to selecting any one timeline to stop, the Stop Timeline menu also includes the ** ALL TIMELINES ** option, which stops playback of all timelines at once.

Again, this action works well when attached to a Pause-button graphic. Add the button to the page, wrap it in a dead link (see page 283), and then attach this behavior to that link, using the onClick event.

Go to Timeline Frame

You can also jump to a specific point in a timeline with the Go To Timeline Frame behavior. You could use this, for example, to jump to the end of an animation (Fast Forward), or jump back to the beginning (Rewind).

Apply it as you would any Dreamweaver behavior (for detailed directions, see page 284): select a tag, click the + button in the Behaviors panel, and choose Timeline→Go To Timeline Frame. A dialog box appears (see Figure 12-17). Choose a timeline from the menu, and then type a frame number in the Go to Frame box. For example, to rewind to the beginning of a timeline, select the timeline and type *1* in the box.

Tip: The Go To Timeline Frame behavior goes to the specified frame *and stops* the animation. If you want to go to a particular frame and then continue the animation, you'll need to add a Play Timeline behavior. Add it to the same tag as the Go To action, and select the same event for both. Finally, make sure the Play Timeline action is listed *below* the Go To action in the Behaviors panel, so that it occurs *after* the timeline moves to the proper frame.

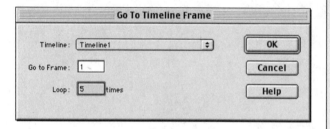

Figure 12-17:
The Loop box in the Go To Timeline Frame dialog box lets you specify the number of times you wish to play a timeline. This option only works when the behavior is attached to a frame in a timeline's Behaviors channel (see page 345).

Flash, Shockwave, and Other Multimedia

With Cascading Style Sheets (Chapter 8), Dreamweaver Behaviors (Chapter 11), and Images (Chapter 5), you can bring your Web pages to life with interactivity and animation. But as you may have noticed, more and more Web pages these days blink, sing, and dance with sound, video, and advanced animation.

You can create these effects too, but they require outside help from other programs like Flash, Director, or Java; all of them let you create complex multimedia presentations. Dreamweaver provides powerful tools for adding these external media files and embedding them within your Web pages.

Four warnings, however. First, while all of the technologies discussed in this chapter let you expand your Web pages into new and exciting territory, they also require external applications (not just a Web browser). These programs, usually called plug-ins, are controversial in the Web development community, mainly because they limit your audience. Not all Web site visitors have the necessary plug-ins installed on their computers. Those guests must choose from three equally unpalatable options: go to a different Web site to download the plug-in; skip the multimedia show (if you've built a second, plug-in-free version of your site); or skip your Web site entirely. All media types in this chapter require a plug-in of some kind; see each section for more detail.

Second, it's worth noting that these effects can bulk up your Web page considerably, making it slower to load—and making it still more likely that some of your visitors (especially those using dial-up modems) won't bother sticking around.

Third, these flashy multimedia effects are easy to overuse. Blink and flash too much, and you'll find your audience beating a hasty retreat for the cyber-exits.

Finally, creating external movies, animations, or applications is an art (and a book or two) unto itself. This chapter is a guide to *inserting* such add-on goodies into your Web page; it assumes that a cheerful programmer near you has already *created* them.

Figure 13-1:
External multimedia files like this Flash movie can add a dimension of sound, animation, and interactivity that brings new life to a site, and makes possible a complexity that's difficult to emulate using HTML alone. In this case (at www.safetreekids.net/ hidden_dangers/ index.html), clicking the man on the pole adjusts your score and lets you play for bonus points.

Flash

Flash is quickly becoming the standard for Web animation, and with good reason: Macromedia's Flash technology produces high-quality, animated images—known as Flash movies—at a relatively small file size. Its drawings and animations are *vector graphics;* they use mathematical formulas to describe objects on the screen. By contrast, bitmap technology like GIF and JPEG graphics include data for every pixel of an image, gobbling up precious bytes and adding download time. Flash's vector graphics, on the other hand, save file size with their compact mathematical expressions.

Furthermore, Flash can also handle MP3 audio and advanced programming features, providing an added dimension of sound and interactivity that can make a plain HTML page look dull by comparison. For example, advanced Flash gurus can build automatic score tracking into an online game, or add a cannon-firing animation each time the player clicks the mouse. While Dynamic HTML (see Chapter 12) can do some of these things, Flash movies are easier to create and less likely to contain programming errors. An intriguing advantage of Flash movies is that they look and work exactly the same on every browser, whether on Windows or Mac. (Don't try *that* with HTML.)

Of course, all of this power comes at a price. Although Dreamweaver has some limited Flash-creation abilities (such as Flash buttons, as discussed on page 111), you need another program, such as Macromedia Flash or Adobe Live Motion, to produce full-fledged movies. These programs aren't difficult to learn, but they're more programs to buy and more technologies to get under your belt.

In addition, your visitors can't play Flash movies without the Flash Player plug-in. If they don't have it, they'll have to download and install it—a sure spontaneity-killer. Fortunately, chances are your visitors already have it—all major browsers (even Opera) now come with the Flash plug-in installed. In fact, Macromedia says that (insert grain of salt here) over 90 percent of Web browsers in use now have some version of the player (only 55 percent have the *latest* version of Flash).

Inserting a Flash Movie

To insert a Flash movie into a Web page, click where you want to insert the movie; choose Insert→Media→Flash (or click the Flash button on the Objects panel). Either way, a Select File dialog box appears; navigate to the Flash movie file (look for a .swf extension) and double-click it. Dreamweaver automatically determines the width and height of the movie and generates the appropriate HTML to embed it into the page. The movie appears as a gray rectangle with the Flash logo in the center; you can adjust its settings as described in the next section.

Note: As with other files you include in a Web page, such as graphics or external Cascading Style Sheets, you can keep Flash movies anywhere inside your site. However, if your Flash movie contains links—for instance, if it's an animated navigation bar—keep the Flash movie file in the same folder as the Web page itself; otherwise, links in the movie may not work. For a workaround to this problem, see the sidebar box on page 355.

POWER USERS' CLINIC

The <object> and <embed> Tags

If you choose View→Code after inserting a Flash movie, you may be surprised by the amount of HTML Dreamweaver deposits in your page. You may also encounter some HTML tags you've never heard of, including <object>, <embed>, and <param>. These tags provide browsers with the information they need to launch the Flash Player and play a Flash movie. These tags are also used for other embedded media (Shockwave, for example).

The <object> and <embed> tags do the same thing in different browsers. Netscape uses <embed> to insert movies and other plug-in media, while Internet Explorer uses the <object> tag to insert ActiveX controls. For maximum browser compatibility, Dreamweaver adds *both* tags; browsers ignore HTML tags that they don't understand, so this method doesn't cause problems.

To preview Flash files directly in Dreamweaver, just select the movie and then click the Play button on the Property inspector. To stop the movie, click the same button, which has become a Stop button.

If your page has lots of Flash movies—numerous animated buttons, perhaps—you can play all of them at once by pressing Ctrl+Shft+Alt+P (⌘-Shift-Option-P). Sit back and watch the show. To stop all running movies, press Ctrl+Shift+Alt+X (⌘-Shift-Option-X). (You can also preview Shockwave movies [see page 358] in Dreamweaver. And no wonder: Macromedia makes Shockwave, too.)

Flash Movie Properties

You'll rarely have to change the default properties created by Dreamweaver. But if you ever want to change the margin of space around a movie, restore it to original size after resizing it, or swap in a different movie, the Property inspector is the place to do it.

Naming a Flash movie

As with images and navigation buttons, you can use JavaScript to control Flash movies. For example, Dreamweaver's built-in Control Shockwave or Flash behavior lets you start, stop, or jump to a specific frame in a Flash movie (see page 311).

As noted on page 311, however, if you plan to use JavaScript with your Flash movie, you need to give the Flash element a name. To do that, type the name you wish to use in the Name field (the box directly below "Flash Text" in the Property inspector). JavaScript uses this name to identify the movie in its code.

Note: As shown in Figure 13-2, all of the plug-in technologies described in this chapter let you set additional parameters governing the embedded media's behavior. You can find about additional HTML properties for Flash in the Flash manual. See the box on the facing page for an example.

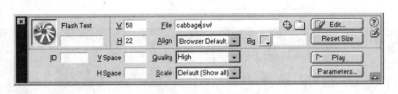

Figure 13-2:
The Parameters button opens a dialog box that offers additional technical controls (see the Flash manual).

The movie file

The File field specifies the path to the Flash movie file on your hard drive. To select a different file, type a new path into the File field, or click the folder icon to access your site folder's contents.

Movie size

Although dragging to enlarge a GIF or JPEG image can turn it into a pixellated mess, you can usually resize Flash movies without problems, since their vector-based images are based on mathematical formulas that scale well. (The exception is when you've included bitmap images, such as GIFs or JPEGs, in your Flash movie. Then, as when resizing an image in a Web page, you'll see distortion and pixellation in the movie.)

POWER USERS' CLINIC

Overcoming the Limits of Links in Flash Movies

When you create Flash movies in Macromedia Flash or Adobe LiveMotion, you can embed links in the movie itself. You can create navigation bars, for instance, or animated pushbuttons that open Web pages.

But links in a Flash movie add a great deal of complexity to your site; when you link from a Flash movie to a Web page, the link is stored in the movie itself, not in the Web page that *contains* the movie. So if the Flash file isn't in the same older as the Web page containing it, a browser may get confused: Should it follow a path relative to the *Web page* or relative to the *Flash file?* In fact, different browsers handle this differently. That's why it's often suggested that you use absolute links (page 82) instead of document-relative links (page 83) in Flash movies.

You could avoid the problem by simply storing the Flash movie in the same folder as the Web page. But doing so can be limiting; for example, you won't be able to use a single animated Flash navigation bar on many different pages of your site, filed in different folders.

Fortunately, you can use a little trick to make your document-relative links work no matter where you file your Flash movies. First, when creating your Flash movie, make sure that any document-relative links in it are spelled out relative to the Flash movie's folder location. For instance, if you save your movie in a folder called *flash,* and you wish it to link to a page called *welcome.html* located one level up from the *flash* folder, the correct link, relative to the movie, would be *../welcome.html.*

Next, after you insert the Flash file into your Web page, click Parameters on the Property inspector. The Parameters window opens, as shown here; now you can add additional properties for plug-in media. In this case, you'll use the BASE property to instruct the Flash Player to use a different URL as the starting location for any links in the Flash movie. In other words, instead of following the link in the movie, the player first appends the path specified by the BASE property's value.

Here's an example: Suppose the Flash movie mentioned above—the one that links to the welcome.html page—is on

a page in the same folder as welcome.html. The document-relative path from that page to the welcome page is *welcome.html*—but *../ welcome.html* relative to the Flash movie. Since the link is in the Flash movie, the path relative to it should work. But some browsers try to follow the path relative to the *Web page,* leading to broken links.

Using the BASE parameter, you can specify that *all* links in the movie should be followed relative to the movie. Here's one instance where a root-relative path comes in handy. Since document-relative links in Flash movies can confuse browsers, a root-relative path is the only way to indicate the exact location of a file within a site. In this case, suppose the "flash" folder is stored in the site's root folder; a root-relative path to the folder with the Flash movie would be */flash/.* (For more detail on document- and root-relative links, see page 82; also see Chapter 14.)

To resize a movie, do one of the following:

- Select the movie in the document window; drag one of the three resizing handles that appear at the edges of the movie. To avoid changing the movie's proportions in the process, press Shift as you drag the lower-right corner handle.

- Select the movie in the document window; type new width and height values into the W and H boxes in the Property inspector. You can also use percentage values; this way, Web browsers scale your movie to fit the window.

If you make a complete mess of your page by resizing the movie beyond recognition, just click Reset Size in the Property inspector.

Alignment

You can align Flash movies relative to the paragraphs around them, just as you do with images. In fact, the alignment options in the Property inspector work exactly the same as image-alignment properties discussed on page 101. For example, choosing Right from the Align menu positions the movie at the right of the screen and wraps text around its left side. (If the movie is inside a layout cell, Align Right moves it all the way to the right of the cell.)

Background Color

To set a background color for a Flash movie, use the Bg Color box in the Property inspector. This color overrides any background color set in the movie itself; it fills the space where the movie appears when the page first loads (and the movie hasn't).

ActiveX ID

The ID field at the left of the Property inspector holds the movie's ActiveX ID parameter (see page 363 for more on ActiveX). The Flash Player—in Internet Explorer for windows—is actually an Active X control itself. If you use other ActiveX controls on a page, you can use this ID to pass information between them. This very technical property is optional; furthermore, since ActiveX controls only work on Windows *and* only in Internet Explorer, you may never need to use it.

Margins

Flash-movie *margins* are especially useful if you've wrapped text around the movie on the page; they determine how much buffer space falls between the movie and the text.

To add space above and below a selected movie, type a number of pixels into the V space field in the Property inspector; press Enter to see the results of your change. To add space to the left and right, type a pixel measurement in the H space field. Ten or 20 pixels usually provides an attractive amount of space. Unfortunately, you can't specify independent values for each of the four margins—only top/bottom and side/side.

Quality settings

If your Flash movie's heavy data requirements overwhelm a visitor's computer, it may run slowly and appear choppy, especially if the animation is action-packed and complex. Until the day when everyone has a one-gigahertz computer with two gigabytes of RAM, you may need to adjust the quality settings of your Flash movies to help them look better on all computers, from the sluggish to the speedy.

By default, Dreamweaver sets the quality to High, but you can choose any of the following four settings from the Quality menu in the Property inspector:

- **High** provides the greatest quality, but the movie may run slowly on older computers.

- **Low** looks terrible. This setting sacrifices quality by eliminating all *anti-aliasing* (edge smoothing) in the movie, leaving harsh jaggy lines on the edges of every image. Movies set to Low quality look bad on *all* computers; to accommodate both the fast and the slow, use Auto High or Auto Low.

- **Auto Low** forces the movie to start in Low quality mode, but to switch automatically to High if the user's computer is fast enough.

- **Auto High** makes the movie switch to low-quality mode only if the user's computer requires it. In this way, you can deliver a high-quality image to most users, while still letting those with slow computers view the movie. This is the best choice if you want to provide a high-quality image, but still make your movie accessible to those with older computers.

Scaling

When you resize a Flash movie (see page 355), changing its original proportions, your visitors' Web browsers will scale or distort the movie to fit the newly specified dimensions. Scaling becomes an issue particularly when, for example, you give a Flash movie *relative* dimensions (setting it to, say, 90 percent of the browser window's width), so that it grows or shrinks as your visitor's browser window grows or shrinks.

The Scale property lets you determine *how* the Flash Player plug-in scales your movie. For example, in Figure 13-3, the top movie's original size is 200 pixels wide and 50 pixels tall. But if you resize the movie so that it's *300* x 50 pixels, one of three things may happen, depending on the choice of Scale setting you make:

- **Show All.** This setting, the default, maintains the original aspect ratio of the movie (second from top in Figure 13-3). In other words, although the overall size of the movie may go up or down, the movie's width-to-height proportion remains the same. This keeps the movie from distorting, but it may also cause borders to appear on the top, bottom, or either side of the movie. (To hide the borders, match the movie's background color to the color on the page, as described on the facing page.)

- **No Border.** This setting resizes the movie according to your specifications *and* maintains its aspect ratio, but may also crop the sides of the movie. Notice how the top and bottom of "Cosmopolitan Farmer" are chopped off (third from top in Figure 13-3).

- **Exact Fit.** This option may stretch your movie's picture either horizontally or vertically. In Figure 13-3 (bottom), "Cosmopolitan Farmer" is stretched wider.

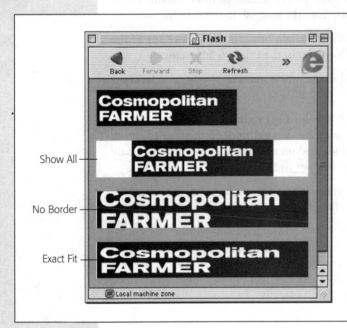

Show All

No Border

Exact Fit

Figure 13-3:
A Flash movie's Scale property specifies how a movie should be scaled when its Width and Height properties are set differently than the original movie. If you've resized a movie, press F12 to see how it looks in a Web browser, then, if necessary, choose a different setting from the Scale pop-up menu in the Property inspector.

Shockwave

As the Internet-ready form of movies created with Macromedia's Director, Shockwave is an older brother to Flash. Director has a longer history as a tool for developing complex interactive presentations. It began life as a program for creating CD-ROMs; but when the Web exploded onto the scene, Director quickly morphed into a Web-authoring tool. Because of its CD background, Shockwave offers far more complex programming possibilities; it's ideal for detailed interactive presentations.

Like Flash, Shockwave requires a plug-in; but unlike the Flash plug-in, this one doesn't generally come preinstalled with Web browsers. If you include Shockwave animations in your Web site, many of your visitors will need to download the Shockwave player—a 3.5-megabyte download!

That annoying requirement is a good argument against using Shockwave for general-audience Web sites. Some of your visitors—especially the ones that don't have cable modems or DSL—may not put in the time and effort required to enable their browsers to view your masterpiece.

But if you just can't do without Shockwave, you insert a Shockwave movie into a Web page just as you would any multimedia format. Click where you want to insert the movie; then choose Insert→Media→Shockwave (or click the Shockwave button on the Objects panel). Either way, a Select File dialog box appears; find and double-click the Shockwave movie file (look for the .dcr extension).

The Shockwave movie appears as a gray rectangle with the Shockwave logo in the center. But Dreamweaver can't automatically calculate the dimensions of Shockwave movies, so you need to type the width and height of the movie in the W and H fields of the Property inspector. Use the same dimensions you specified when creating the file in Director.

Figure 13-4:
This Shockwave game offers animation and interactivity just like a Flash movie. However, for games that require precise timing and action, Shockwave is usually a better choice. Its advanced 3-D features and built-in physics principles (like gravity and collision detection , make it perfect for advanced gaming applications. To sample this technology, go to www. shockwave.com. There you'll find a mixture of Flash and Shockwave movies. (In this figure, only the rectangular area representing the basketball court is the Shockwave movie. The top area and sidebar are just GIFs and plain old HTML.)

You can preview Shockwave files directly in Dreamweaver by selecting the movie and clicking Play on the Property inspector. To stop the movie, click the same button (which is now a Stop button).

You resize a Shockwave movie just as a Flash movie, as described on page 355.

Shockwave Movie Properties

The only Shockwave movie property you have to set by hand is the width and height of the movie. Most of the time, you won't need to bother changing the default properties; the Property inspector does, however, let you change the movie's name (a requirement for using JavaScript to control its playback), substitute a different movie, choose the movie's alignment relative to the text around it, specify a background color, select an ActiveX ID, or specify top/bottom or side/side margins. All of these options work just as they do for Flash movies (see page 354).

Generator Templates

Generator is a server-based Macromedia technology that lets you include auto-updating data into a Flash movie, such as the current time, the user's name, or information from a database. While Generator templates (as they're called) make possible Web pages whose Flash movies address you by name or include the latest news headlines, this level of customization requires some fairly sophisticated software and a high level of technical expertise.

Although you can create Generator templates in Macromedia Flash, the Generator program itself runs on your Web server. When someone requests a Web page with a Generator template in it, the Generator program (on the Web server) processes the template, plugs in the dynamic data, and transmits the results to the visitor's computer. And even though you use Flash to create the template, Generator can actually produce GIF, JPEG, or PNG files as well as QuickTime movies.

To insert a Generator object into a Web page, click where you want to insert the template; then choose Insert→Media→Generator, or use the corresponding Object panel. Browse to, and select, the Generator template file you want (it has a .swt extension in Windows).

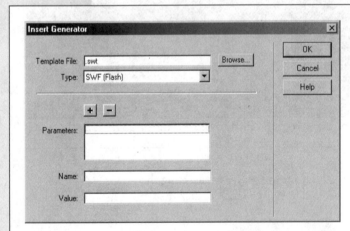

Figure 13-5:
When you insert a Generator template, you can add parameters that the Generator server uses when it creates the Flash movie.

Now you're asked to choose the type of file you want the Generator server to output (see Figure 13-5); whereas Flash lets you include animation, sounds, and interactivity, you can choose GIF, JPEG, or PNG if the Generator template is just a static image. The MOV option informs the Generator server to produce a QuickTime movie.

Also as shown in Figure 13-5, you can click the + button to add a name/value pair. These are technical parameters that let you control the behavior of the Generator template. For example, you might add a *cache* parameter that controls whether or not the Generator server saves the file it creates, so that it doesn't have to create a new file each time someone goes to the page. For information that isn't updated every second, this tactic can really keep the server from being overworked. In this case, the name of the parameter would be *gmc,* and the value (to turn *on* caching) would be *true.*

When you're finished typing in your parameters, click OK to insert the Generator object, which looks just like a Flash movie: a gray box with a Flash logo on it. You can't use the Property inspector to adjust its settings; unfortunately, if you need to edit any of the parameters of the Generator object, you have to go into the HTML source code and do it by hand (see Chapter 9 for information on editing HTML source code).

Generator templates have the same properties as Flash movies. After you insert one into a Web page, you can use the Property inspector to set them (see page 354).

Java Applets

A few years ago, it seemed that the whole world was going Java crazy. Created by Sun Microsystems, this powerful programming language seemed to offer an end to cross-platform problems. Programs written in Java can run on any operating system: Mac, Unix, Windows, whatever. Java also offered programmers the opportunity to write sophisticated applications that could run in the form of a compact file, called an *applet,* within any browser. Java applets can provide sophisticated graphics and user interface elements that go well beyond what HTML can do. In fact, Java can be used not only for graphics and multimedia, but to build complete applications like word processors, spreadsheets, or mortgage calculators that can live right in a Web page. For loads of sample applets, visit *www.javaboutique.com.*

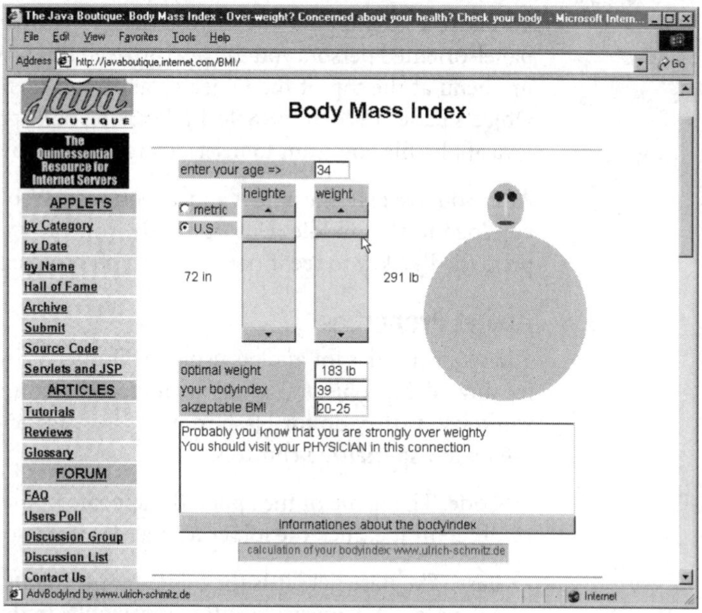

Figure 13-6: *Java applets can perform sophisticated tasks that HTML alone can't. In this example, a Java applet lets you interactively determine whether your body mass is appropriate for your age and height. Through the use of custom interface elements (such as the sliders under the height and weight columns), you control the size of the "man" and receive instant feedback in various form fields. (In this example, only the area between the two horizontal rules is the actual applet. Everything else is HTML.)*

In the end, Applets didn't make as big a splash on Web pages as industry forecasters originally thought. One of Java's limitations is that its applets don't work unless a Web-page visitor has a special software program called a Java Virtual Machine. This program translates the Java code into instructions appropriate for the visitor's particular operating system. As with plug-ins, virtual machines require lengthy downloads and installations that scare off many potential users. In addition, unlike JavaScript, which is fairly easy to learn, Java is not for the faint of heart. It's a complex language that requires a lot of skill and practice to do well.

But when the time comes that you've been handed a Java applet for insertion onto, say, a client's page, here's how to do it.

FREQUENTLY ASKED QUESTION

Java, JavaScript

Is Java the same as JavaScript?

In a word, no. Don't get the two confused.

Java is a full-featured programming language that programmers use to create elaborate programs that can run with or without a Web browser. JavaScript, on the other hand, is a much simpler, *scripting* language that Web designers use to add interactivity to Web pages.

Why are their names so similar? Years ago, Netscape invented a programming language called LiveScript to enhance Navigator with interactive forms, dialog boxes, and so on. When Java appeared on the scene, Netscape renamed LiveScript to JavaScript to cash in on the excitement. However, the two are distinct languages without any technical relationship.

Ah, marketing.

To insert a Java applet, just choose Insert→Media→Applet. (If you're an Object-panel-oriented person, you can also proceed this way: Choose Special from the pop-up menu at the top of the Objects panel, and then click the Applet button on the Objects panel.) When the Select File dialog box appears, find and double-click the Java applet file you want to insert. (Java applets have a .class or .jar extension.)

After you insert it, the applet appears on your Web page as a gray box with a coffee cup logo in the middle. Unfortunately, you can't preview it within Dreamweaver; press the F12 key to see it run in your Web browser.

Applet Properties

You set properties for applets using the Property inspector (see Figure 13-7), just as for any HTML object. The name, margins, alignment, and width/height controls work just as they do for Flash movies (see page 354); JavaScript applets, however, offer a few specialized controls:

- **Code.** The name of the applet file appears in the Code field. If you wish to use a different file, click the folder icon and select another applet.

- **Base.** The Base field lists the folder that contains the applet file. When you insert an applet, Dreamweaver automatically fills in this field.

- **Alt.** For the benefit of visitors whose browsers don't support Java (or who have turned Java off), you can provide an alternative image or text description. Type the text in the Alt field, or click the little folder icon and select a GIF or JPEG file that will appear in place of the Java applet. The image will appear automatically if the Java Virtual Machine isn't installed.

Some applets may have properties in addition to the ones listed in the Property inspector. To add these properties, click the Parameters button. For example, the applet ticker.class shown in Figure 13-7 produces a ticker-tape display on a Web page. In order to let the applet know what message it needs to present, you add a parameter called *message*. The value of that parameter would be the message: "Welcome to my home page. This ticker-tape display is truly annoying, isn't it?"

Figure 13-7:
You set up a Java applet just as you would any other object—using the Properties inspector.

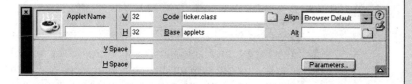

ActiveX Controls

ActiveX controls are miniature applications that work like plug-ins in Web browsers. In fact, the Flash Player for the Windows version of Internet Explorer *is* an ActiveX control.

However, this powerful technology can handle much more than multimedia; it can plug right into your computer, accessing files and other programs, or enabling spreadsheets and other productivity programs, right in a Web page. For links to many different ActiveX controls, visit *http://browserwatch.internet.com/activex.html*.

Unfortunately, this Microsoft technology only works on Windows machines *and* only in Internet Explorer. As a result, it has yet to gain a foothold on the Web—and it may never. But if you're required to incorporate an ActiveX control into your site (perhaps because Microsoft is your client), then here's how to do it.

To insert ActiveX controls that you've programmed in Visual Basic or found on the Web, just choose Insert→Media→ActiveX. An ActiveX icon appears on the Web page, selected so that you can now change its options using the Property inspector.

ActiveX Properties

Some of the settings you can change for ActiveX controls (see Figure 13-9) are the same as you'd find for the other technologies described in this chapter (see page 354): name, width/height, alignment, and margins, for example. A few others are unique to this technology.

ClassID

The ClassID identifies the ActiveX control for the browser. Dreamweaver includes three ClassIDs in the pop-up menu: Real Player, Shockwave, and Flash. (Selecting either of the last two simply changes the ActiveX icon on the page to either Shockwave or Flash.) The Real Player option lets you insert a control for including Real Video or Audio files on a page.

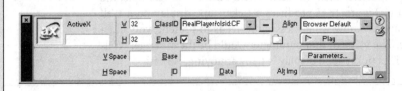

Figure 13-8:
ActiveX controls can vary widely in what functions they perform, so there's no standard set of properties for all controls.

Embed and Src

If there is a comparable Netscape plug-in for the ActiveX control you're adding to the page, you can turn on the Embed checkbox to add the <embed> tag. This way, Netscape and Mac users can also enjoy the benefits provided by the ActiveX control.

The HTML <object> tag specifies the ActiveX control and its properties. Netscape Navigator, on the other hand, uses the <embed> tag for adding plug-ins. Some external multimedia files, such as Flash, Shockwave, and Real Video, can use either an ActiveX control or a plug-in. In order to make both the ActiveX control and the Netscape plug-in available, you need to have both <object> and <embed> tags in the HTML code for your page (see the box on page 353).

If you turn on the Embed checkbox, you'll need to specify a file for the plug-in to use in Netscape. For example, a .swf (Flash movie) file would be used as a Src file for the Flash Player plug-in. To choose a file, click the folder icon and select it from your site folder (if it's not already there, Dreamweaver offers to copy it there for you).

- **Base.** The Base field indicates the URL for the ActiveX control. If the visitor doesn't already have the ActiveX control on her PC, Internet Explorer will go to this URL, download the control, and install it.

- **ID.** An ActiveX control's ID is used to pass information to other ActiveX controls.

- **Data.** Some ActiveX controls require an additional data file. Enter the name of that file in this field. Consult the instructions for your particular ActiveX control to find out if an additional file is necessary.

- **Alt.** For browsers that don't support the <object> tag, you can provide an alternative image. Click the folder icon and select a GIF or JPEG file from your Web site. Because ActiveX only works in one browser and one platform, give strong consideration to providing an Alt image: "Sorry, you're out of luck! Buy a Windows PC and use Internet Explorer next time!" (This option doesn't work if you've turned on the Embed checkbox in the Property inspector.)

Plug-ins

Flash and Shockwave may be among the most popular plug-ins, but they're by no means the only ones (see Figure 13-9). The Web teems with other plug-ins that add new features to a Web browser. The Adobe Acrobat plug-in, for example, lets you view PDF files directly inside a Web browser window; the Real Video lets you watch video in a tiny window.

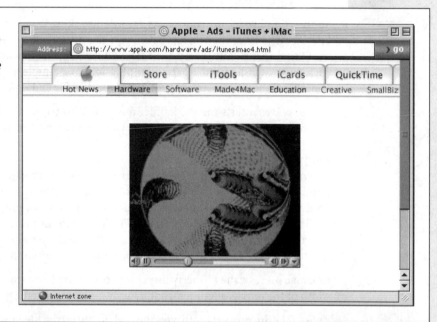

Figure 13-9:
With the QuickTime plug-in for Mac or Windows (available at www.apple.com/ quicktime), *your visitors can view and listen to QuickTime movies embedded directly in a Web page.*

EXTENSION ALERT

Plug-in Support at Macromedia Exchange

The Plug-in object is a simple way to embed code for plug-in files. Unfortunately, because it's designed as a generic method of adding files for any and all plug-ins, it's not pre-tailored for any one plug-in, such as the Real Media Player.

That's not to say that you can't add ready-to-use plug-in objects to your Web pages in software; you can. If you visit the Macromedia Exchange *(www.macromedia.com/exchange/dreamweaver/)*, you can find *extensions* (see page 493) that help you insert media in a variety of different plug-in formats. These extensions help you put the proper code in your page to make the plug-in work.

Once on the Exchange Web site, choose Rich Media from the Browse Extensions menu. You'll find extensions that help you add QuickTime, Real Video and Audio, and other plug-in-dependent media. For more on using the Macromedia Exchange, see Appendix B.

Dreamweaver's Plug-In Object offers a generic method of inserting media that requires a plug-in. It doesn't address any of the specific needs of any one plug-in technology like, say, Real Video (see the sidebar above). As a result, just adding Dreamweaver's Plug-in object to your Web page is no guarantee that the plug-in

---

will work. You may need to set additional properties or information; the software company responsible for the plug-in can provide details.

Then, of course, including any plug-in-dependent media in a Web page is always a risky proposition. If your visitors don't have the plug-in, they may be unwilling to go through the process required for downloading and installing the appropriate software. Before including any media that might discourage visitors, make sure it's absolutely necessary for your site.

To insert a plug-in file, choose Insert→Media→Plug-in; or, if you're viewing the Special category of the Objects panel, you can instead click the Plug-in button on the Objects panel. Either way, the Select File dialog box appears; find and double-click the media file for the particular plug-in. For example, if you're embedding a QuickTime movie into a Web page, you'd locate a file ending in .mov.

Dreamweaver inserts the media file into your Web page. It looks like a light gray square with a jigsaw-puzzle piece on it; you can preview it using the Play button.

Plug-in Properties

When you select a plug-in object in your Web page, the Property inspector displays some basic properties (see Figure 13-10). Since each plug-in is unique, you may need to set additional properties in order to make it work properly. To view these specialized options, click the Parameters button on the inspector. For example, when inserting a QuickTime movie, you can add the parameter *autostart* with a value of *true* to make the movie automatically begin playback when the page loads.

As usual, some of the Property inspector options are fairly standard: name, height/width of the movie, alignment, and margins. The other settings include:

- **Src.** The Src property indicates the path to the media file in your Web site folder; Dreamweaver fills this in automatically when you select a file. The plug-in relies on this path to locate the media file. To swap in a different media file, you can click the folder icon.

- **Plg URL.** If you know the URL of the Web page from which the user can download the necessary plug-in, enter it in this field. If your visitor's browser doesn't have the plug-in, it will automatically attempt to download it from this URL.

- **Border.** To insert a border around the plug-in file, type a line-thickness pixel value in this field. (Unfortunately, not all browsers recognize this property.)

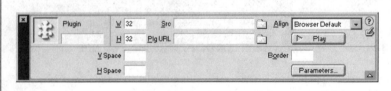

Figure 13-10:
Clicking the Play button plays the file indicated in the Src field–if you have the plug-in.

Part Four:
Building a Web Site

4

Introducing Site Management

As the dull-sounding name *site management* implies, organizing and tracking your Web site's files is one of the least glamorous, most time-consuming and error-prone aspects of being a Web designer. On the Web, your site may look beautiful, run smoothly, and appear to be a gloriously unified whole, but behind the scenes it's nothing more than a collection of varied files—HTML, images, Cascading Style Sheets, Flash movies, and so on—that must all work together. The more files you have to keep track of, the more apt you'll be to misplace one. A single broken link or missing graphic can interfere with the operation of your entire site, causing personal—even professional—embarrassment.

Fortunately, computers excel at tedious organizational tasks; Dreamweaver's site management features take care of the complexities of dealing with a Web site's many files, freeing you to concentrate on the creative aspects of design. In fact, even if you're a hand-coding HTML junkie and you turn your nose up at all visual Web-page editors, you may find Dreamweaver worth its weight in gold just for the features described in this chapter and the next two.

Where the first three parts of this book describe how to create, lay out, and embellish a Web site, this part offers a bird's-eye view of the Web production process as you see your site through to completion and, ultimately, upload it to the Internet.

To get the most out of Dreamweaver's site management features, you need to be familiar with some basic principles for organizing Web files, as discussed in the next section.

Structuring a Web Site

When you build a Web site, you probably spend hours providing your visitors with carefully planned links, helpful labels, and clear, informative navigation tools. You want your *site architecture* to make it easy for them to understand where they are, where they can go, and how to return to where they came from (see Figure 14-1). Behind the scenes, it's equally important to organize your site's files with just as much clarity and care, so that you can find *your* way around when updating or modifying the site later. And, as on your home computer, a Web site's main organizational tool is the humble folder.

Figure 14-1:
A good site has an easy-to-understand structure. Content is divided into logical sections, and a prominent navigation bar–the row of black buttons in this image–gives visitors quick access to information. When building a site, this "information architecture" provides a useful model for naming and creating the folders that will hold the site's files.

You organize files on your computer every day, creating, say, a folder called Personal, within which are folders called Financial Planning and Vacation Pictures. Inside the Vacation Pictures folder, you have separate folders for your memories of Maui, Yosemite, and the Mall of America.

The same principle applies to the folders that make up a Web site: All Web sites have one primary folder—the *root folder*—that holds all of the site's Web pages, graphics, and other files used in the site. The root folder usually contains additional folders for further subdividing and organizing the site's files.

A good structure (see Figure 14-2) speeds up the production and maintenance of your site by giving you quick access to whatever graphic, style sheet, or Flash movie you're looking for. But don't fall into the trap of becoming so obsessed that you put every graphic or Web page you create in its own separate folder; creating a structure for the files in a site should make your job easier, not harder.

Tip: If your already have a Web site that suffers from lack of organization, it's not too late. Dreamweaver can help you reorganize your files quickly and accurately; take the following rules to heart and then turn to "Organizing Site Files" on page 375, to learn how you can use Dreamweaver to knock your current site into shape.

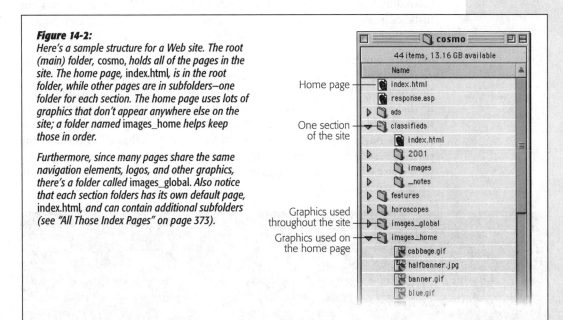

Figure 14-2:
Here's a sample structure for a Web site. The root (main) folder, cosmo, *holds all of the pages in the site. The home page,* index.html, *is in the root folder, while other pages are in subfolders—one folder for each section. The home page uses lots of graphics that don't appear anywhere else on the site; a folder named* images_home *helps keep those in order.*

Furthermore, since many pages share the same navigation elements, logos, and other graphics, there's a folder called images_global. *Also notice that each section folders has its own default page,* index.html, *and can contain additional subfolders (see "All Those Index Pages" on page 373).*

Home page
One section of the site
Graphics used throughout the site
Graphics used on the home page

Here, then, are some guidelines for effective site organization:

- **Plan for future growth.** Like ever-spreading grapevines, Web sites grow. Today you may only have enough words and pictures for ten Web pages, but tomorrow you'll put the finishing touches on your new thousand-page online catalog. It may seem like overkill to create a lot of folders for a small site, but better to start with a solid structure today than find yourself knee-deep in files tomorrow.

  For instance, it's useful to create additional folders for graphics files that appear within each section of the site. If a section of your site is dedicated to promoting your company's products, create a folder called Products for storing product Web pages; create an additional folder called Images to store the pictures of those products. Then, when you add more products or images, you know right where to put them.

- **Follow the site's architecture.** Take advantage of the work you've already done in organizing the content on your site. For instance, Cosmopolitan Farmer's content is divided into six main sections: Features, Projects, Horoscopes, Quiz, Reviews, and Classified Ads, as shown in Figure 14-1. Following this architecture, it makes sense to create folders—features, projects, and so on—in the site's root folder for each section's respective Web pages. If one section is particularly large, add additional subfolders.

- **Organize files by type.** After you create folders for each section of your site, you'll probably need to add folders for storing other types of files like GIFs, JPEGs, Cascading Style Sheets, external JavaScript files, and PDF files. Most sites, for instance, make extensive use of graphics, with several graphics on each page; if that's the case for you, you need to file those images neatly and efficiently.

One way to organize your graphics is to create a folder for images that appear on your home page and another for images that appear elsewhere in the site. Often, the home page is visually distinct from other pages on the site and contains graphics that are unique to it. You can create a folder—images_home, for example—in the root folder for images that only appear on the home page. Create another folder—images_global, for example—to store graphics that all or most of the pages use, such as the company logo, navigation buttons, and other frequently used icons; when you add images to other pages of your site, you'll know to look for them in this folder.

UP TO SPEED

Naming Your Files

The rules for naming files in Windows and Macintosh are fairly flexible. You can use letters, numbers, spaces, and even symbols like $, #, and ! when naming folders and files on these operating systems.

Web servers, on the other hand, are far less accommodating. Because many symbols—such as &, @, and ?—have special significance on the Web, using them in file names can confuse Web servers and cause errors.

The precise list of no-no's varies from Web server to Web server, but you'll be safe if you stick to letters, numbers, the hyphen (-), and the underscore (_) when naming files and folders. Stay away from spaces. File names like *company logo.gif* or *This company's president.html* probably won't work on most Web servers. Replace spaces with underscores or inner caps—*company_logo.gif* or *companyLogo.gif*—and remove all punctuation marks.

- **Use understandable names.** While file names like *1a.gif, zDS.html,* and *f.css* are compact, they aren't very explanatory. Make sure file names mean something. Clear, descriptive names like *site_logo.gif* or *directions.html* will make it a lot easier for you to locate files and update pages.

This principle is especially important if you work as part of a team. If you're constantly explaining to your coworkers that *345g.gif* is the banner for the home page, changing the file name to *home_banner.gif* could save you some aggravation. There's a tradeoff here, however, as long file names can waste precious bytes: a name like *this_is_the_image_that_goes_in_the_upper_right_corner_of_the_home_page.gif* is probably not a good idea.

It's also helpful to add a prefix to related files. For example, use *nav_* at the beginning of a graphic name to indicate that it's a navigation button. In this way, you can quickly identify *nav_projects.gif, nav_quiz.gif,* and *nav_horoscopes.gif* as graphics used in a page's navigation bar. As a bonus, when you view the files on your computer or in Dreamweaver's Site window (see Figure 14-5), they'll appear neatly sorted by name; in other words, all the nav_ files will cluster together in the file list.

Tip: If you use a Mac, you might not be familiar with the three or four letters that follow Web file names. These letters, or *file name extensions,* tell Windows computers what program should open the file; they're used universally as part of all Web files' names.

The trick is that Windows and Macintosh computers use slightly different extensions. For example, in Windows, Web page names are often followed by *.htm,* whereas the Mac uses *.html.* In most cases, the Windows and Macintosh extension versions are interchangeable. The one exception is JPEG files: Some Windows computers don't understand the Mac extension *.jpeg.* It's best to stick to the Windows extension, *.jpg.*

To specify the extension Dreamweaver uses when saving Web pages, choose Edit→Preferences to open the Preferences window. Click the General category, turn on Add Extension When Saving, and type the extension in the box. You can type .html, .htm, or any other extension you wish.

FREQUENTLY ASKED QUESTION

All Those Index Pages

Why are so many Web pages named index.html*?*

If you type *www.cosmofarmer.com/* into a Web browser, the Cosmopolitan Farmer home page opens on your screen. But how did the Web server know *which* page from the site to send to your browser? After all, you didn't ask for a particular Web page, like *www.cosmofarmer.com/ about.html.*

When a Web server gets a request that doesn't specify a particular Web page, it looks for a default Web page—usually named *index.html* or *index.htm.* It does the same thing even when the URL you've typed specifies (with a slash) a folder inside the site root, like this: *www.cosmofarmer.com/ horoscopes/.* In this case, the Web server looks for a file

called *index.html* inside the *horoscopes* folder, and—if it finds the file—sends it to your Web browser.

If the Web server doesn't find an *index.html* file, two things can happen, both undesirable: The Web browser may display either an ugly error message or a listing of all the files inside the folder. Neither result is user-friendly.

While your site will still function without this step, it's good form to give the main Web page inside each folder in your site the proper default page name. Web servers use different names for these default pages—*index.html* or *default.html,* for example—so check with your Web server's administrator or help desk.

- **Be consistent.** Once you've come up with a system that works for you, follow it. Always. If you name one folder *images,* for instance, don't name another *graphics* and a third *pretty_pictures.* And certainly don't put Web pages in a folder named *images,* or Flash movies in a folder named *style_sheets.*

  In fact, if you work on more than one Web site, you may want to use a single naming convention and folder structure for all of your sites, so that switching between them will go more smoothly. If you name all your graphics folders *im-*

ages, then no matter what site you're working on, you already know where to look for GIFs and JPEGs.

Tip: Put only files that will go on your Web site in the root folder and its subfolders. Keep your source files—the original Photoshop, Fireworks, Flash, or Word documents where you created your content—stored elsewhere on your computer. This way, you're much less likely to accidentally transfer a 14.5-megabyte Photoshop file to your Web server (a move that would *not* gain you friends in the IT department).

FREQUENTLY ASKED QUESTION

Bringing Your Own Web Site

I already have a Web site. Will Dreamweaver work with it?

Yes. In fact, Dreamweaver's site management features are an invaluable aid in organizing the files of an existing site. As you can read in "Organizing Site Files" on the facing page, you can use Dreamweaver to rearrange, rename, and reorganize files—tasks that are extremely difficult and time-consuming to do by hand. Furthermore, Dreamweaver lets you clean up and reorganize a site without breaking links. So Dreamweaver can be just as useful for working with a completed site as it is for creating one from scratch.

To work on an existing site, first save a copy of all site files on your computer, all in one folder. When defining the site (page 23), choose this folder for the local root folder.

Defining a Site

Organizing and maintaining a Web site—creating new folders and Web pages; moving, renaming and deleting files and folders; and transferring pages to a Web server—used to require going back and forth between a couple of different programs. With Dreamweaver's site management features, however, you can do it all from within the program. But in order to take advantage of these features, you must first *define* the site; in other words, give Dreamweaver some basic information about it.

Defining the site involves showing Dreamweaver which folder contains your Web site files—which folder, in other words, is your *root folder*—and setting up a few other options. The whole process begins with the Choose Site→New Site command, and it's described in delicious detail on page 23.

EXTENSION ALERT

Site Import Export

When you define a site, Dreamweaver stores that site's information with your copy of the program. This means if you want to work on your site using a different computer, you must define each site again. In a design firm where several people might be working together on many different sites, that's a lot of extra setup. In fact, even if there's just one of you, but you have two computers, this is a pain.

The Site Import Export extension can help. This extension lets you export the site definition information for any or all of the sites you've defined in Dreamweaver. You can then import the file into other copies of Dreamweaver. To get this extension, go to the Macromedia Exchange (see page 493) and search the site for "Site Import Export."

Editing or Removing Defined Sites

Sometimes you need to edit the information associated with a site. Perhaps you want to rename the site, or you've reorganized your hard drive and moved the local root folder to a different location, and you need to let Dreamweaver know what you've done.

To edit a site, open the Define Sites dialog box (choose Site→Define Sites or, in the Site window, choose Define Sites from the Site pop-up menu) and double-click the name of the site you want to edit; the Site Definition window opens (see Figure 14-3). Now you can type a new name in the Site Name box, choose a new local root folder, or make any other changes. Click OK to close the dialog box when you're done.

Once you've finished a site and are no longer working on it, you may wish to remove it from Dreamweaver's list of sites. To delete a site from the list, open the Define Sites dialog box as described above, click to select the site you wish to delete, and click Remove.

A warning appears telling you that this action can't be undone. Don't worry; deleting the site here doesn't actually *delete* the site's images, Web pages, and other files from your computer. It merely removes the site from Dreamweaver's list of defined sites. (You can always go back and define the site again, if you need to, by following the steps above.) Click Done to close the Define Sites window.

Tip: If you do, in fact, want to delete the actual Web pages, graphics, and other site components, you can either switch to the desktop (the Finder or Windows Explorer, for example) and delete them manually—or delete them from within Dreamweaver's Site window, described in this chapter.

Organizing Site Files

Once you've defined your local site, Dreamweaver helps you organize your files, create folders, and add new Web pages to your site using the Site window as your command center. To open the Site window, take your pick:

- Choose Site→Site Files.

- Press F8.

- Click the Open Site button on the Launcher bar (choose Window→Launcher if you don't see it).

The Site window is divided into two sections. On the right, you find the list of files in the current site's local root folder. This list looks and acts just like Windows Explorer or the Macintosh Finder; you see names, file sizes, and folders. You can view the files inside a folder by clicking the + symbol next to the folder, or simply by double-clicking the folder. Double-click a Web page to open it in Dreamweaver.

The left pane of the Site window starts out showing you what's on the Web copy of your site—that is, a list of the files on the remote site. Of course, before you've posted your site on the Web, this list is empty; information appears here only after you connect to your Web server. See Chapter 16 for details on connecting to a Web server and using the Remote site list. (And see page 380 for details on making the Site window show a site map instead of a remote-site listing.)

Tip: You can swap the left and right lists, so that Dreamweaver shows your local files in the *left* pane of the Site window, and remote files on the right. The trick is to choose Edit→Preferences to open the Preferences window. Select the Site category; choose Local Files from the first menu at the top, and choose Left from the second menu. Click OK.

To save screen space when you're not transferring files to the Web server, click the arrow in the lower-left corner of the Site window (Figure 14-3) to hide the Remote Site list. To show the Remote site, just click the arrow again to expand the Site window.

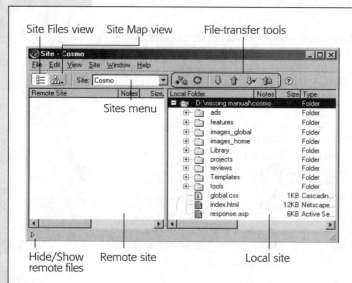

Site Files view   Site Map view   File-transfer tools

Sites menu

Hide/Show   Remote site   Local site
remote files

Figure 14-3:
Dreamweaver can store information on many different sites and switch between them easily. A list of all the Web sites you've defined in Dreamweaver appears in the Sites pop-up menu; to work on a different site, select its name from the list. The Site panel also includes tools for creating a Site Map and for transferring files between the local and remote sites. (These file transfer tools are discussed in Chapter 16.)

Tip: You can even open certain types of files in an outside program of your choice by defining an external editor for the file type. For example, you can tell Dreamweaver to open GIF files in Fireworks, Photoshop, or another image editor. (See "Setting Up an External Editor" on page 104 for more on this feature.)

Adding New Folders and Files

The Site window provides a fast way of adding blank Web pages to your site. With one click, you can create a new page in any folder you like, saving you several steps you'd otherwise have to perform using the File menu.

Adding files

To create a new, blank Web page, open the Site window using one of the methods described on page 375, then right-click (Control-click) a file or folder in the Site window.

In the contextual menu that appears, choose New File. Dreamweaver creates a new, empty Web page. (Actually, the page doesn't have to be empty; you can edit the file Dreamweaver uses as its default new page, as described in the sidebar box below.

The new file appears in the Site window with a highlighted naming rectangle next to it; type a name for the page. Don't forget to add the appropriate extension—.htm or .html—to the end of its name.

POWER USERS' CLINIC

Changing the Default New Page

Whenever you make a new Web page—for example, by choosing File→New or by right-clicking (Control-clicking) an existing file in the Site window—Dreamweaver gives you a blank, white document window. But what if you always want your pages to have gray backgrounds, or mauve?

Every new Web page you create is actually an untitled *copy* of a default template document called Default.html; you'll find it in the Macromedia Dreamweaver 4→Configuration→Templates folder. You can open this file within Dreamweaver and edit it however you like: Change its background color, add a default logo, or whatever, so that all subsequent new pages you create inherit its settings. (You might consider making a backup of this file before editing it, however, so that you can return to the factory settings if you accidentally make a mess of it.)

Adding folders

You can add folders to your site directly in Dreamweaver using the Site window. Just right-click (Control-click) a file or folder in the Local Folder list. If you click a file, Dreamweaver creates the new folder in the same folder as that file; if you click a folder, you get a new folder inside it.

From the contextual menu, choose New Folder.

If you crave variety, you can add a folder another way. Select a file or folder in the Site window and then:

- *Windows:* In the Site window, choose File→New Folder.
- *Macintosh:* Choose Site→Site Files View→New Folder.

Finally, in the naming rectangle that appears in the Site window, type a name for the new folder.

Moving files and folders

Because the Dreamweaver Site window looks and acts so much like the Windows Explorer and Macintosh Finder, you may think it does nothing more than let you move and rename files and folders on your computer. You may even be tempted to

---

work with your site files directly on your Desktop, thinking that you're saving time. However, when it comes to moving the files and folders in your site, Dreamweaver does more than your computer's Desktop ever could.

In your Web travels, you've probably encountered the dreaded "404: File Not Found" error. This "broken link" message doesn't necessarily mean that the page doesn't exist; just that your Web browser didn't find the page at the location (URL) specified by the link you just clicked. In short, someone working on that Web site probably moved or renamed a file without updating the link. Because Web site files are interrelated in such complex ways—pages link to other pages, which include paths to graphics, which in turn appear on other pages—an action as simple as moving one file can wreak havoc on an entire Web site. That's why you shouldn't drag Web site files around on your Desktop or rename them in Windows Explorer or the Macintosh Finder.

In fact, moving and reorganizing Web site files is so headache-ridden and error-prone that some Web designers avoid it altogether, leaving their sites straining under the weight of thousands of poorly organized files. Fortunately, Dreamweaver 4 makes reorganizing a site easy and error-free. The program looks for actions that might break your site's links; when you use the Site window to move files, Dreamweaver can automatically rewrite paths of links, images, and other media.

Note to programmers: If your custom JavaScript programs include paths to images, Web pages, or other files in your site, Dreamweaver won't help you. While the program can update paths in its own JavaScript programs (behaviors), it doesn't track paths or links in *custom* JavaScript programs..

Just be sure to do your moving from within Dreamweaver, like this: In the Site window, drag the folder or file into its new folder (see Figure 14-4). (To move multiple files, Ctrl-click [⌘-click] each of the ones you want to move, then drag them as a group; to deselect a selected file, Ctrl-click or ⌘-click it again. You can also select one folder or file and Shift-click another to select all files and folders in the list between the two.)

When you release the mouse button, the Update Files dialog box appears (see Figure 14-4); just click Update. Dreamweaver updates all the links for you.

Tip: If you accidentally dragged the file or folder to the wrong location, click Don't Update. Then drag the file back to its original location and, if Dreamweaver asks you, click Don't Update once again.

Renaming files and folders

Renaming files and folders poses the same problems as moving them. Because links include file names, altering a file name can break a link just like moving or deleting the file.

For example, say you've created a new site with a home page you named *home.html*. You cheerfully continued building the other pages of your site, linking them to *home.html* as you went along. But after reading this chapter and checking to find out what default file name your Web server requires (see the box on page 373), you found that you need to rename your home page file *index.html*. If you were to rename the file *index.html* using Windows Explorer or the Macintosh Finder, every link to *home.html* would result in a "File Not Found" error.

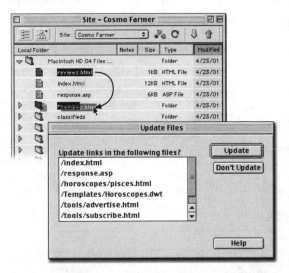

Figure 14-4:
Top left: You can move files and folders within the Site window just as you would in Windows Explorer or the Macintosh Finder. Simply drag the file into (or out of) a folder. But unlike your computer's file system, Dreamweaver constantly monitors the links between Web pages, graphics, and other files. Bottom right: If you move a file using Windows Explorer or the Finder, you'll most likely end up breaking links to that file, or, if it's a Web page, links in that file. Fortunately, Dreamweaver is smart enough to know when moving files will cause problems. The Update Files dialog box lets you update links to and from the file you're moving, so that your site keeps working.

Dreamweaver, on the other hand, handles this potential disaster effortlessly, as long as you rename the file in the Site window instead. To do so, just click the file or folder in the Site window. Pause a moment, and click the *name* of the file or folder. (The pause ensures that Dreamweaver won't think you just double-clicked the file for editing.)

A renaming rectangle appears; type the new name. Be sure to include the proper extension for the type of file you're renaming. For example, GIFs end with .gif, Cascading Style Sheets end with .css. Although Dreamweaver lets you name files without using an extension, the extensionless files won't work when you move them to a Web server.

Finally, in the Update Files dialog box (see Figure 14-4), click Update; Dreamweaver updates all the links to this file or folder to reflect the new name.

Caution: It bears repeating: never rename or move files and folders *outside* of Dreamweaver. If you use Windows Explorer or the Macintosh Finder to reorganize the files in your site, links will break, images will disappear from your pages, and the earth will open underneath your feet. (Well, actually, that last thing won't happen, but it might *feel* that way when your boss comes in and says, "What's happened to our Web site? Nothing works!")

If you've edited files outside of Dreamweaver by accident, see page 396 to learn how to find and fix broken links.

Deleting files and folders

It's a good idea to clean up your site from time to time by deleting old and unused files. Just as with moving and renaming files, you delete files from the Site window.

To delete a file or folder, just select click to select it in the Site window and press Backspace or Delete. (To select multiple files or folders, Ctrl-click [⌘-click] them as described on page 370.) If the doomed file or folder isn't referenced by any other page on the site, a simple "Are you sure you want to delete this file?" warning appears; click Yes.

However, if other files link to the file—or to files within the folder—that you're deleting, then a warning dialog box (Figure 14-5) appears informing you that you're about to break links on one or more pages in your site. The message even lists the first few pages that use the file. If you've made a mistake, click No to leave your site untouched.

If you're sure you wish to delete the file, click Yes; and yes, this move does *break links* in all the pages listed. Repairing those links, which usually means linking them to a new page, requires a separate step: using the Site→Change Links Sitewide command, as described on page 401.

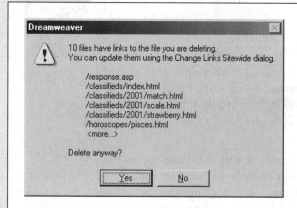

Figure 14-5:
When you delete files in the Site window, Dreamweaver warns you if other pages reference (link to) the file. If you click Yes, you'll have to go back and repair the links. Dreamweaver gives you a convenient way to do it—the Change Links Sitewide command—and reminds you of it in this dialog box.

Viewing a Site Map

While the Site window's list of files and folders is a great aid in managing those files, it doesn't give you a picture of how your site's Web pages are linked together. You can see that the *index.html* file in the root folder is the site's home page, for instance, but you can't see how it relates to the other pages in the site; you can't tell which pages link to or from it. To see those relationships, you need Dreamweaver's Site→Site Map view.

The Site Map is a visual guide to the links in a site (see Figure 14-6). An icon representing the home page appears at the top of the map, and arrows connect the home page to icons representing each of the links it contains. As shown in Figure 14-6, special icons clearly mark external, broken, and email links. Furthermore, the Site Map does more than just provide a visual overview; it also gives you an easy way to rename files and even retitle Web pages.

Figure 14-6:
The Site Map displays icons for each link in a Web site. Symbols provide added information about the pages: The globe icon ( ) indicates an external link such as http://www.yahoo.com. The broken link icon ( ) indicates that the file either doesn't exist or has been misfiled, so the link won't work. Dreamweaver also highlights the name of the missing file in red. For more on finding and fixing broken links, see page 396 in the next chapter.

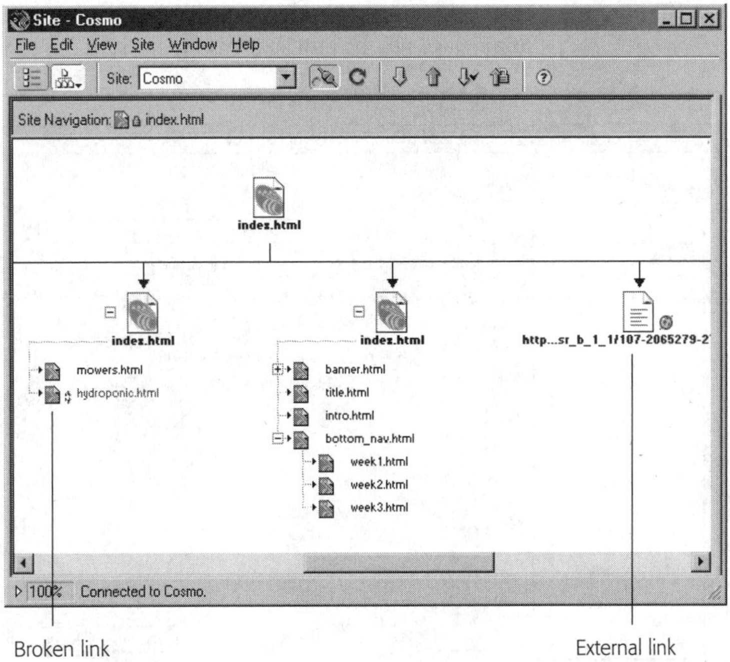

Setting up Site Map View

To view a Site Map, you'll first need to do a little preparation:

1. **Choose Site→Define Sites (or choose Define Sites from the Site menu in the Site window).**

   The Define Sites window appears, listing all of your sites.

2. **In the Define Sites dialog box, click a site name and click Edit (or just double-click the site name).**

   The Site Definition window opens.

   You can also follow these steps when defining a site for the first time, as detailed in the steps starting on page 24.

3. **In the Category list, choose Site Map Layout.**

   You see the dialog box shown in Figure 14-7.

4. **Click the folder icon next to the Home Page field and navigate to the home page file in the site's root folder.**

Click Select (Windows) or Open (Mac) to set this page as the home page. (Remember that your home page must be in the root folder. Technically, you *can* choose a file that's buried several folders deep in your site folder, but don't do it—unless, of course, you really want to tell people to visit your company's home page at *www.mycompany.com/about_us/about_me/my_dog/ralphie.html.* By specifying a home page in the outer level of your root folder, you can assure that the home page will be at *www.mycompany.com.*)

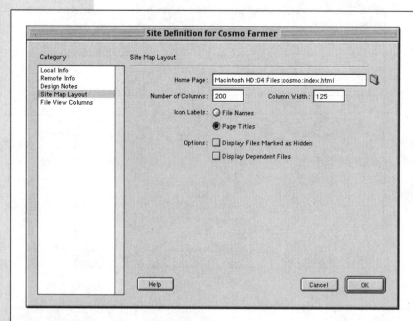

Figure 14-7:
The Site Map Layout category of the Site Definition window lets you define the site's home page and set preferences for using Dreamweaver's Site Map view. But if your home page file is named index.html or index.htm, you don't have to change anything here; Dreamweaver automatically sets it as the home page for you. However, if you use a different file name, such as default.html or index.asp, you must specify it in the Home Page field.

5. **Set any other Site Map preferences you wish.**

The **Number of Columns** field determines how many links can be displayed in a single row of the Site Map (see Figure 14-6). For instance, if you set the number of columns to five, but the home page has ten links on it, the Site Map only has enough columns for the first five links; the remaining five icons get bumped down to a second row directly below the first. Displaying more than one row of links from the home page can be confusing, so it's best to use a number of columns that's at least equal to the number of links on the home page. Dreamweaver's default value of 200 is just fine.

The **Column Width** represents the width, in pixels, of each column. As you can see in the box on page 383, file names and page titles may not fully appear if the column width is too small. Again, stick with Dreamweaver's default value of 125.

Using the **Icon Labels** buttons, choose whether you'll want the Site Map to display the file name *(index.html)* or page title ("Welcome to Cosmopolitan Farmer") next to each page's icon. Ctrl+Shift+T (⌘-Shift-T) toggles between the two views.

Once you've got your Site Map on display, you can hide certain files for the sake of clutter reduction by marking them as hidden. To make sure they stay hidden, leave **Display files marked as hidden** turned off. You can always make the hidden files reappear using the steps described on page 384.

The **Display dependent files** option will make GIF, JPEG, CSS, Flash, and all other non-HTML files show up in the Site Map. Since this can make the site map a confusing jumble of files, it's best to leave this option turned off.

6. Click OK.

You return to the Site window.

Viewing and Customizing Site Map View

Once you've set up Site Map view as described above, just click the Site Map button/pop-up menu in the Site window (shown in Figure 14-8) to see the results.

Figure 14-8:
The Site Map button in the Site window lets you see either a single-pane window (Map Only) or a double-pane window (Map and Files).

GEM IN THE ROUGH

Don't Get Lost in the Site Map

The Site Map clearly displays links between pages, but if you're not careful, you may end up chasing your tail. Very often, Web pages link back and forth to each other. For example, the home page may link to a page in the site that, in turn, links back to the home page.

In this example illustrated here, the Advertising page ("Advertise with Cosmopolitan Farmer") has a link to the home page ("Cosmopolitan Farmer"), which links to the advertising page, which links back to the home page, which links to the advertising page…and so on. All four of the pages indicated

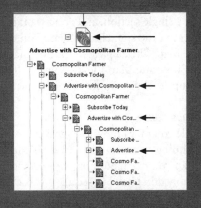

by arrows are, in fact, the same page!

As shown here, the Site Map shows the advertising page as a link from the home page. When you then click the + to expand the advertising page, you see a duplicate icon for the home page (whose original icon appears at the top of the Site Map). When you click the + sign next to the home page icon under the advertising page, you don't get a new level of site links, even though the Site Map displays it that way. What you've done is "re-expand" the home page and display more duplicate icons.

The pop-up menu offers you two options: Map and Files. Files view displays the site's local files in the right pane of the Site window and the Site Map in the left pane. Map Only fills the Site window with the map, as shown in Figure 14-6. (Unfortunately, if you resize the Site window, the Site Files list frequently reappears. To overcome this bug, choose Map Only once again.)

When you first view the Site Map, only the first two levels—the home page and all of the pages linked from it—appear. A small + symbol next to a page indicates that there are additional links on that page; clicking the + expands the list of links on that page. If those pages, in turn, have links, additional + symbols appear. You can continue to follow the links by expanding each page, but viewing too many levels at once can bring a confusing complication; see the box on page 383 for advice.

As in the Site file list, you can open a page by double-clicking its icon in the Site Map. In fact, selecting a page in the Site Map highlights the corresponding page in the File list, and vice versa.

Identifying pages in the Site Map

The Site Map view starts out showing the file name of each Web page, which can be less than informative. If you've structured your site so that the main page for each section of the site is stored in a different folder and is named *index.html,* the Site Map will be an unhelpful sea of *index.html* labels (see Figure 14-6).

A better approach: Use each page's *title* as the icon label. You can do this when you first set up the site, as described on page 381, or you can choose View→Show Page Titles (Windows) or Site→Site Map View→Show Page Titles (Mac). Repeat the same command to see the filenames again. The keyboard shortcut is a fast way to toggle between the two views: Ctrl+Shift+T (⌘-Shift-T).

Viewing just part of a Web site

When viewing large Web sites, you might find the Site Map awkward. Perhaps you're working on just a single section, and don't want to be bothered with the extraneous details of the rest of the site. No problem: You can isolate a particular page when viewing the Site Map. Click a page in the Site Map and choose View→View as Root (Windows) or Site→Site Map View→View as Root (Mac). The page you selected appears as the top-level page in the Site Map (see Figure 14-9).

Hiding extraneous links

Like some people you may know, the Site Map loves detail; it includes *all* links from your pages, including external links and email links. At times, this may be a bit more information than you need. Suppose you provide 200 email addresses on a single page; you probably don't need to see all of those listed in the Site Map.

Fortunately, Dreamweaver lets you hide any links you wish. All you have to do is select the files you want to hide (Shift-click them, or drag across a group of them) and then choose View→Show/Hide Link (Windows) or Site→Site Map View→Show/ Hide Link (Macintosh); Dreamweaver makes them disappear.

To show hidden files again, choose View→Show Files Marked as Hidden (Windows) or Site→Site Map View→Show Files Marked as Hidden (Mac); Dreamweaver makes all hidden files appear with their names italicized, indicating that you've marked them as hidden. You can turn off a file's "hidden" status by selecting it and choosing View→Show/Hide Link (Windows) or Site→Site Map View→Show/Hide Link (Mac).

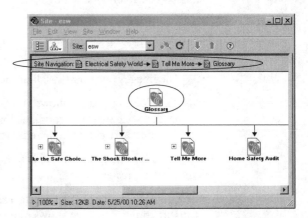

Figure 14-9:
This Site Map is zoomed in on a single page (Glossary), which appears at the top level of the Site Map where the home page normally would be. The path from the home page to this file appears above the map in the Site Navigation bar. The home page is titled Electrical Safety World. A link from the home page leads to a page titled Tell Me More, which in turn links to the glossary page. To once again view the home page as the top level of the Site Map, click its name in the Site Navigation bar.

Renaming Pages in the Site Map

You can rename files in Site Map view, which works similarly to renaming them in the File List view. However, only the Site Map lets you easily change the *titles* of your site's Web pages. In fact, this is one of the best features of the Site Map. While displaying the page titles, you can quickly scan your site for missing or incorrect page titles and fix them in just a few steps.

You rename a file in the Site Map just as you do in the Site window; the steps appear on page 378. In this case, just be sure you're looking at the right kind of data—either page titles or file names—before you begin; press Ctrl+Shift+T (⌘-Shift-T) to switch back and forth.

When you're finished, Dreamweaver rewrites the title in the HTML of the page; the new title also appears next to the page icon.

Site Assets

Web pages integrate lots of different elements: GIFs, JPEGs, links, colors, and Flash and Shockwave movies, to name just a few. In a large site with lots of files, it can be a challenge to locate a particular image or remember an exact color.

To make the process easier, Dreamweaver 4 introduces the Assets panel. For want of a better generic term, Macromedia defines the term *asset* to mean any element you use on a Web page, such as a GIF file, a link, or even an individual color.

Viewing the Assets Panel

Dreamweaver lists your site's assets on the nine category "pages" of the Assets panel (see Figure 14-10). To open the panel, choose Window→Assets, or click the Assets panel button ( ) in the Launcher bar, or press F11.

You select an asset in the list by clicking its name; a miniature preview appears above the Assets list. To preview a movie, click the green arrow that appears in the preview window.

The assets panel highlights nine different categories of site elements. To view the assets in a particular category, click its icon at the left of the Assets panel.

- The **Images** category lists all of the GIF, JPEG, and PNG files in your site.

- The **Colors** category shows all of the colors specified in the Web pages and embedded style sheets of your site: link colors, background colors, and text colors (but not, alas, colors in linked style sheets; see page 210.)

- The **Links** category lists all external links: standard *http://* links, email links, and FTP addresses.

- The **multimedia** categories—Flash, Shockwave, and Movies—are roughly equivalent. Each shows movie files with corresponding extensions: .swf (Flash), .dcr (Shockwave), .mov (QuickTime), or .mpg (MPEG).

- The **Scripts** category lists JavaScript or VBScript files (only external script files that Web pages link to, not scripts that are embedded into a Web page, like those created using Dreamweaver Behaviors).

- These categories—**Templates** and **Library**—are described in Chapter 17.

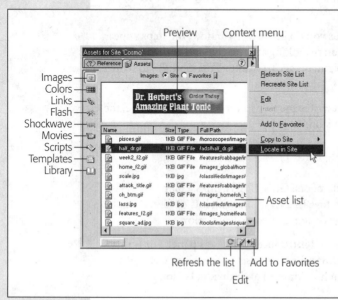

Figure 14-10:
The Context menu (in the upper right corner of the Assets panel) contains frequently used asset commands. Most of them duplicate commands available in the panel itself, but the last two options appear only on this menu: The Copy to Site menu lets you copy the selected asset to another site that you've defined. The Locate in Site command opens the Site window and highlights the file of the asset you selected in the Assets panel. (You can also open a contextual menu by right-clicking [Control-clicking] any asset in the list.)

You can switch between two different views for each asset category—Site and Favorites—by clicking the radio buttons near the top of the Assets panel. The Site option lists all the assets that appear in the Site for the chosen category; Favorites lets you create a select list of your most important and frequently used assets (see page 388).

If, as you work on a site, you add additional assets—for example, you import a new GIF image—update the Assets panel by clicking the Refresh List button (C).

Inserting Assets

The Assets panel's prime mission is to make using assets easier. From the Assets list, you can add graphics, colors, and links to your pages with a click of the mouse. Most of the categories on the panel refer to external files that you can include on a Web page: images, Flash, Shockwave, movies, and scripts.

The easiest way to insert an asset file is to drag it from the Assets panel into the document window. You can drag the asset anywhere on the page you'd normally insert an object—in a table cell, at the beginning or end of a page, or within a paragraph. Script assets can go in the head of a Web page (see Figure 14-11).

(If you're billing by the hour, you may prefer the long way: Click in the document window to plant the insertion point; click the asset's name; and then click Insert at the bottom of the Assets panel.)

Adding color and link assets

Unlike other asset files, color and link assets don't stand on their own. Instead, they *add* color or a link to images or text you've selected. In this way, you can quickly add a frequently used link—the URL to download the Flash player, for example.

To do so, start by highlighting the text (to change its color or turn it into a link) or image (to turn it into a link). In the Assets panel, click the appropriate category button—Colors or Links. Click the color or link you want and then click Apply. (Alternatively, you can drag the color or link asset from the panel to the selection.)

POWER USERS' CLINIC

The Return of Root-Relative Paths

Chapter 4 explains the different types of link paths—absolute, document-relative, and root-relative—that Dreamweaver understands (see page 81). While it's best to use document-relative paths for linking to pages within your own site, or for adding images and other media to a page, you may notice that Dreamweaver frequently displays root-relative paths in its site-management tools.

For instance, the list in the Assets panel includes the full root-relative path of each asset—*/images_home/banner.gif*, for example. The initial "/" indicates the root folder of the site, and the information that follows indicates the rest of the path to that asset. In this example, the graphic asset *banner.gif* is in a folder called *images_home*, which is itself in the site's root folder. Dreamweaver needs to look no further than the root folder to find the asset in question.

Root-relative paths indicate a precise location within a site and let Dreamweaver know where to find a file. This doesn't mean, however, that *you* should use root-relative paths in your Web sites. Use document-relative paths and let Dreamweaver do its own thing.

Note: Applying color to text using the Assets panel simply wraps the selected text in a <font> tag. If you're using style sheets to format your pages, see the box on the next page for another way to use color assets.

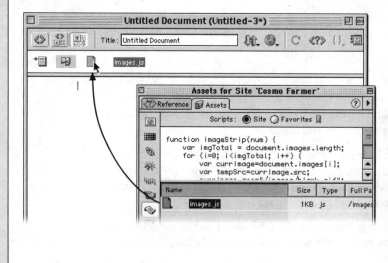

Figure 14-11:
While you'll insert most assets into the body of a Web page, you can (and usually should) place script files in the head of the page. To do this, first choose View→Show Head Content. Then drag the script from the Assets panel into the head pane, as shown here. (Adding a script asset does not copy the JavaScript or VBScript code into the Web page. Instead, just as with external style sheets, Dreamweaver links to the script file so that when a Web browser loads the page, it looks for and then loads the file from the Web site.)

Favorite Assets

On a large site, you may have thousands of image files, movie files, colors, and external links. Because scrolling through long lists of assets can be a chore, Dreamweaver lets you create a compact list of your favorite, frequently used assets.

For example, you might come up with five main colors that define your site's color scheme, which you'll use much more often than the other miscellaneous colors on the Assets list. Add them to your list of *favorite* colors. Likewise, adding graphics files you use over and over—logos, for example—to a list of favorites makes it easy to insert them into your pages. (Dreamweaver's Library and Template features are similar, but more powerful tools for keeping frequently used items at the ready. Turn to Chapter 17 for the details.)

Identifying your Favorites

If the color, graphic, or other element to be added to your Favorites list already appears on your Assets panel, highlight it in the list and then click the Add to Favorites button ( ).

You can also add Favorites as you go, snagging them right from your Web page in progress. Just right-click (Control-click) the image; from the contextual menu, choose Add to Image Favorites. Dreamweaver instantly adds the graphic to your list of favorites. You can do the same with Flash, Shockwave, and QuickTime files, as well as with links. (Unfortunately, this shortcut doesn't work for colors and script files.)

When it comes to colors and links, there's another way to turn them into Favorites: In the Assets panel, select the Color or Links category, click the Favorites radio button, and then click the New Asset button (⊞). Then:

- If you're adding a favorite color, the Dreamweaver color box appears. Select a color using the eyedropper (see page 30).

- If you're adding a favorite link, the Add URL window opens. Type an absolute URL in the first field, either a Web address starting with *http://* or an *email* link— *mailto:subscriptions@cosmofarmer.com.* Next, type a name for the link in the Nickname field—Netscape Download or Subscription Email, for instance—and then click OK.

Your new color or link appears in the Favorites list.

Using your Favorites

You insert Favorites assets just as you would any assets; see page 387.

Removing Favorites

To remove something from the Favorites list, select it and then press Delete (or click the Remove from Favorites button (⊟) on the Assets panel, or use the Context menu [Figure 14-10]).

Don't worry: Removing an asset from the Favorites list *doesn't* delete that asset from the Assets panel—only from the Favorites list. You can still find it listed if you click the Site radio button.

GEM IN THE ROUGH

Better Use of Color Assets

Although color assets are only meant for coloring text, you can use them any time Dreamweaver's eyedropper tool appears, such as when you're about to apply color to tables, table cells, links, pages, and other elements. In other words, anytime you need a frequently used color, you can hop right to the Assets panel rather than pecking around on the color palette or trying to find another occurrence of the color on your screen.

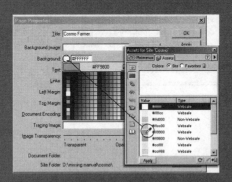

Whenever you click a color box—in the Page Properties window, Property inspector, or Style Definition window, for example—a color palette appears and the cursor changes to an eyedropper. You could, of course, use this eyedropper to pick a color from the palette or to sample a color from the screen. But if you've already used the color in your site—or saved it in the Favorites list (see above)—just grab it from the Assets panel. To do so, move the eyedropper to the colored swatch in the Assets list and click.

Organizing Favorite assets

On a large site with lots of important assets, even a Favorites list can get unwieldy; that's why you can set up folders within the Assets panel. For example, if you use lots of ads on a site, create a folder in the Image assets Favorites called Ads, or even multiple folders for different types of ads—Banner Ads, Half Banners, and so on.

You can then drag assets into the appropriate folders, and you can expand or collapse the folder to show or hide the assets inside (see Figure 14-12). (These folders simply help you organize your Assets panel; they don't actually appear anywhere within the structure of your site. Moving a favorite asset into a folder in the Assets panel doesn't change the location of files within your site.)

To create a Favorites folder, click the appropriate category button at the left edge of the Assets panel (any except the bottom two; you can't create folders for Templates and Library items). Click Favorites at the top of the Assets panel (you can't create folders in Site view). Finally, click the folder button (📁) at the bottom of the Assets panel; when the new folder appears with its naming rectangle highlighted, type a new name for the folder and then press Enter.

To put an asset into a folder, just drag it there from the list. And if you're really obsessive, you can even create subfolders by dragging one folder into another.

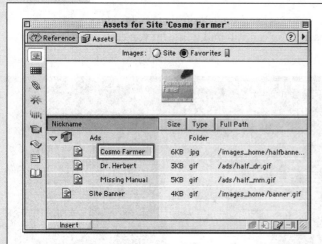

Figure 14-12:
In addition to using folders to organize your favorites, you can also give a favorite asset an easily identifiable nickname. Instead of listing a favorite image using its file name—148593.gif—use an easily understood name like New Product. Naming favorite colors can be particularly helpful—a nickname like Page Background is more descriptive than #FF6633. To name a favorite asset, click to select it, pause a moment, and click again to edit its name. (These nicknames only apply in the Assets panel; they don't rename or retitle your files.)

Testing Your Site

As you've no doubt realized by now, there are quite a few steps involved in building a Web site. At any point in the process, it's easy to introduce errors that affect the performance of your pages. Both small mistakes, like typos, and site-shattering errors, like broken links, occur frequently in the Web development cycle.

Unfortunately, Web designers often don't develop a good procedure for testing their sites. This chapter offers some helpful techniques for testing your site, including using Dreamweaver's wide array of site testing tools.

Site Launch Checklist

Don't wait until you've finished your site before embarking on a thorough strategy of testing. By that time, serious design errors may have so completely infested the pages of your site that you may have to start over, or at least spend many hours fixing problems that could have been discovered early on.

- **Preview early and often.** The single best way to make sure a page will look and function the way you want it to is to preview it in as many Web browsers as possible. Use Dreamweaver's Preview command (see page 37) to preview your page in every browser you can get your hands on. Make sure the graphics look right, that your layout remains the same, and that advanced technologies like Cascading Style Sheets, Dreamweaver Behaviors, and layers work as intended.

  For a thorough evaluation, however, you should preview your pages using every combination of browser *and* operating system you think your site's visitors might use. Enroll co-workers, family members, and household pets, if necessary, in this effort. At the very least, test your pages using Internet Explorer 4 and 5, and Netscape 4, on *both* Mac and Windows. As the population of Netscape 6 and Internet Explorer 6 users grows, add these to your test schedule, too.

Unfortunately, you'll discover that what works on one browser/operating system combination may not work on another. That's why you should preview your designs *early* in the process of constructing your site. If you design a page that doesn't work well in Netscape 4 on the Mac, for example, it's better to catch and fix that problem immediately than discover it after you've built 100 pages based on that design.

- **Check pages in target browsers.** Dreamweaver's Check Target Browsers command (see below) is a helpful diagnostic tool; it analyzes the code of your Web pages and checks for compatibility with various versions of Netscape Navigator and Internet Explorer.

  Once again, take this step early in the process of building your site. After completing a preliminary design for your home page, for example, use this tool to see if the code will work in the browsers you're aiming for.

Some troubleshooting steps should come at the end of the process, when a page (or entire site) is ready to be moved to a Web server:

- **Check spelling on your pages.** Amazingly, this simple step is often overlooked. As a result, it's easy to find otherwise professional-looking Web pages on the Internet that are undermined by sloppy spelling. To learn how to use Dreamweaver's built-in spell checker, see page 52.

- **Check your links.** As the name indicates, a Web site can be a complex and twisted collection of interconnected files. Web pages, graphics, Flash movies, and other types of files all work together. Unfortunately, if one file is moved or deleted, problems can ripple through the entire site. Use Dreamweaver's Check Links command to identify and fix broken links (see page 396).

- **Run site reports.** It's always the little things. When building a Web site, small errors inevitably creep into your pages. While not necessarily life-threatening, forgetting to title a Web page or to add an Alt property to an image does diminish the quality and professionalism of a site. In addition, despite its ability to write good HTML, even Dreamweaver can occasionally write sloppy code. Use Dreamweaver 4's new site-reporting feature to quickly identify these problems (see page 405).

Check Target Browsers

As noted early in this book, different browsers don't always display HTML in the same way. What's worse, older browsers don't even *understand* a lot of the code that Dreamweaver can produce, because it may conform to HTML standards that were developed only in recent years.

The best way to ensure that visitors see your site the way you intend it is to preview your pages frequently in as many browsers on as many computers as possible. In this way, you can identify and fix problems early.

But if you don't happen to have old computers with old browsers lying around your basement, Dreamweaver can identify elements of a page that won't work in older browsers, or that might be supported by only a single browser. For example, the <layer> tag (see page 329) works *only* in Netscape 4, while the <marquee> tag is specific to Internet Explorer.

The File→Check Target Browsers command checks the HTML of pages you've selected and generates a report that tells you if you've used code that doesn't work in various versions of Internet Explorer or Netscape Navigator. You can choose which versions of the browsers you'd like to test, all the way back to the 2.0 version, which is still being used by Jason P. O'Gillicuddy of Muddy Ditch, Kansas.

Dreamweaver then creates a Web page listing any errors it's found (see Figure 15-1). The most common culprits are Cascading Style Sheets, layers, and JavaScript created by Dreamweaver's Behaviors. These relatively new Web technologies work only in the more recent browsers—versions 4 and later.

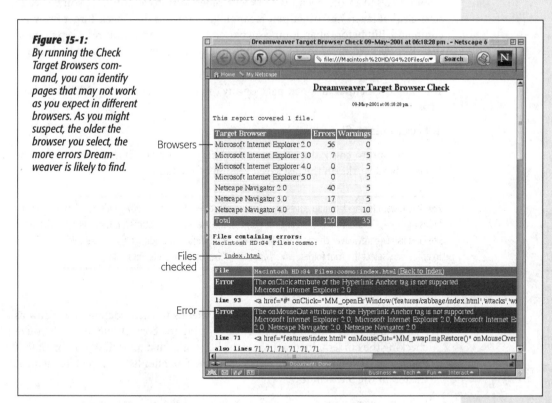

Figure 15-1:
By running the Check Target Browsers command, you can identify pages that may not work as you expect in different browsers. As you might suspect, the older the browser you select, the more errors Dreamweaver is likely to find.

Keep in mind that Dreamweaver doesn't actually *test* your pages in these different browsers. It simply compares the HTML in your page against a series of files—called browser profiles—that identify which HTML tags the various browsers understand. In other words, don't count on this feature to help you with the subtle differences between browsers—such as Navigator 4's troubles with layers (documented in Chapter 12). Just because a browser is programmed to understand a particular piece of HTML doesn't mean it always does the job correctly. Throughout this book, you'll find information on these kinds of problems, but there's no substitute for thoroughly testing your pages in as many browsers as you can.

Once you've identified any errors, you can either choose to remove the offending code—perhaps by getting rid of a rollover effect, or abandoning layers—or live with the fact that not everyone on earth will be able to view your site.

Tip: One effective strategy in solving such problems involves Dreamweaver's Check Browser behavior, which is described on page 299. You can use this feature to direct visitors to pages that are built specifically for their browser version.

If your Web site absolutely must work with older versions of browsers, you'll need to steer clear of layers and other new technologies, and use the Check Target Browsers command. But before abandoning such useful and advanced features, keep in mind that over 90 percent of the Web-surfing public uses version 4 or later of Internet Explorer or Netscape Navigator.

You can check either an open page or any or all pages in a site by following these steps:

1. **Select a file or files to check.**

   If you want to check the file you're working on, just save it and go to step 2 (the command works on the last *saved* version of the file).

Tip: If you want to check multiple files, or an entire site, open the Site window, if it's not already open, by choosing Site→Open Site and choosing the name of the site from the submenu. Then click a folder in the Site Files list; Dreamweaver checks every Web page in this folder, including pages in subfolders. To check an entire site, select the root folder, which appears at the top of the Site Files list.

---

2. **Choose File→Check Target Browsers.**

   For Windows users: Since Windows adds menus to each document window as well as to the Site window, be sure you're using the correct File menu. If you're checking the current document, use the File menu that appears at the top of that document. If you're checking pages using the Site Files list, use the File menu at the top of the Site window.

   Dreamweaver opens the Check Target Browsers dialog box (see Figure 15-2).

3. **Select one or more browsers from the list.**

To select more than one browser, Ctrl-click (⌘-click) their names. (Similarly, Ctrl-click or ⌘-click a browser name to remove it from a selection you've built up.)

Figure 15-2:
You can check the HTML of your pages against the capabilities of any or all of the browsers listed, but limit your choices to the browsers your visitors will be using. If you choose an old browser like Netscape Navigator 2.0, Dreamweaver will generate a long list of errors; most of the HTML commands Dreamweaver generates weren't even around back when Navigator 2.0 was in circulation.

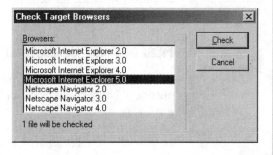

4. **Click Check.**

Dreamweaver checks each page and generates a Web page listing any errors it finds. It then launches your Web browser and displays the results.

Dreamweaver doesn't save this Web page automatically; if you'd like to preserve the results of this check, choose File→Save from within your Web browser to save the Web page onto your hard drive.

5. **Review the results.**

The page Dreamweaver produces (see Figure 15-1) lists which browsers you checked against and which files you checked. You'll also see any errors Dreamweaver found, complete with an explanation of the problem and the line number where the error occurs. (You can identify line numbers in the HTML of your page using the Code view; see page 252.)

An error appears when a browser doesn't understand a particular HTML tag or property. For example, Internet Explorer 3 has a very limited understanding of JavaScript; therefore, you'll see an error listed for every page where you used an image rollover effect (see page 109). The error indicates that IE 3 doesn't understand the JavaScript code, and the rollover won't work.

Don't panic if you run this command on your site and see lots of errors. The errors don't mean that *you* made mistakes; they simply indicate that one of the browsers you selected doesn't understand some of the tags Dreamweaver inserted.

Furthermore, Dreamweaver is often smart enough to use *two* tags—one for Navigator and Internet Explorer—to get the job done. For example, to eliminate the margin at the left edge of a page, you have to set the Left Margin *and* Margin Width properties of the page (see step 9 on page 31). But because Navigator doesn't understand the Left Margin property (it only works in Internet Explorer), you'll still get an error if you check your page against Navigator browsers. In other words, an error reported by Dreamweaver doesn't necessarily mean that your page won't work in a specified browser.

This command is a good way to quickly learn about the different HTML tags each browser supports. In time, you'll probably know enough to avoid using elements that don't work for the browsers your visitors use; eventually, you'll find this command unnecessary.

Find and Fix Broken Links

Broken links are inevitable. If you delete a file from your site, move a page or graphic outside of Dreamweaver, or simply type an incorrect path to a file, broken links and missing graphics may result. In the B.D. era (before Dreamweaver), the only way to fix such problems was to methodically examine every page and every link on every page in your site. Fortunately, Dreamweaver's link-checking features can automate the process of tracking down broken-link problems.

Note: In this context, a *link* doesn't only mean a hyperlink connecting one page to another. Dreamweaver also uses the term to include the paths that identify external files incorporated in your Web page, such as GIFs, JPEGs, external CSS style sheets, and Flash movies. For example, if a graphic is missing or isn't in the place specified by the Web page, Dreamweaver will also report a broken *link*.

Finding Broken Links

The Site→Check Links Sitewide command scans an entire site's worth of files and reports all links and paths that don't lead to a file. (It's one of Dreamweaver's site management features, meaning that you have to define a local site before using this command; see page 23.) Note that Dreamweaver only checks links and paths *within* the local site folder; it doesn't check links that lead to other people's Web sites.

Checking just one page
To check links on an open page, save it in your local site folder. Then choose File→Check Links (or press Shift-F8). Dreamweaver scans the page and opens the Link Checker window, which lists files containing broken links (see Figure 15-3). If Dreamweaver doesn't find any broken links—you HTML god, you—the window comes up empty.

Checking specific pages
You can also check links just on specific pages of your site, like this:

1. Choose Site→Open Site and choose the name of the site you want to check from the submenu.

   If you're already working on the site you want to check, you can skip this step.

2. In the Site window, select the files you'd like to check.

For techniques on selecting files and folders in the Site window, see the sidebar box below.

Tip: Selecting a folder will make Dreamweaver scan all files in that folder.

---

3. **Choose File→Check Links (or press Shift-F8).**

   Alternatively, you can right-click (Control-click) the selected files, and then choose Check Links→Selected Files/Folders from the contextual menu.

   Either way, Dreamweaver scans the pages and opens the Link Checker window (see Figure 15-3).

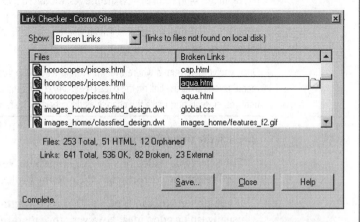

Figure 15-3:
Check your site for broken links using Dreamweaver's Check Links Sitewide command. The command also generates a list of all external links (though it can't check them) and all orphaned files (files that have no links to them). If you wish, click Save to save all of this information into a tab-delimited text file.

Selection Shortcuts in Lists

When using the Link Checker dialog box, you'll often want to select several Web pages from the list. In fact, you'll find yourself staring at similar dialog boxes during many Dreamweaver exercises.

You probably can figure out that you should click a file to select it. But you can also select *several* files that are listed consecutively: click the first one, scroll if necessary, and then, while pressing Shift, click the last one. Dreamweaver highlights all the files between your first and final clicks.

If you want to select several files that aren't consecutive in the list, the trick is to click each one while pressing the Ctrl (⌘) key.

Once you've selected one or more files, you can *de*select one by Ctrl-clicking (⌘-clicking) it once again.

Checking the entire Web site

To check the links on all pages of your Web site, open the Web site you want to check, if it isn't already open (choose Site→Open Site and choose the name of the site you want to check). Then choose Site→Check Links Sitewide, or press Ctrl+F8

(⌘-F8); once again, Dreamweaver scans your site and opens the Link Checker window, which lists files containing broken links (Figure 15-3).

Fixing Broken Links

Of course, simply finding broken links is only half the battle. You also need to *fix* them. The Link Checker window provides a quick and easy way to do this:

1. **In the Link Checker window, click a path in the Broken Links column (see Figure 15-3).**

   The path is highlighted, and a tiny folder icon appears to the right.

Tip: The Link Checker window shows you which pages *contain* broken links, but doesn't show you the text or images of the broken links themselves, which can make it difficult to figure out how you're supposed to fix them ("Was that a button that links to the home page?"). In such a case, *double-click* the file name in the Link Checker window. Dreamweaver opens the Web page, and, even better, highlights the link on the page.

Once you've determined where the link should lead ("Oh yeah. That's the button to the haggis buffet menu"), you can fix the link on the page (see page 92) or jump back to the Link Checker (which stays open until you close it) and make the change as described in the next step.

---

2. **Click the tiny folder icon.**

   The Select File dialog box opens. From here, you can navigate to and (in the next step) select the correct page, the one the broken link *should* open.

   If you prefer, you can type a path directly in the Link Checker window; doing so usually isn't a good idea, however, since it's difficult to understand the path from one page to another by just looking at the Link Checker window. Searching for the proper page using the Select File dialog box is a much more accurate method.

3. **Double-click a Web page.**

   The dialog box disappears, and Dreamweaver fixes the link.

   If your Web site contains other links pointing to the same missing file, Dreamweaver asks if you'd like to update those pages, too—an amazing time saver that can quickly repair broken links on dozens of pages.

Note: Dreamweaver's behavior is a bit odd in this regard, however. Once you fix one link, it remains selected in the Link Checker window. You must click another broken link, or one of the buttons in the window, before Dreamweaver asks if you'd like to fix that same broken link on other pages.

---

4. **Continue to fix broken links, following steps 1 through 3.**

   When you've repaired all the broken links, click Close.

Listing External Links

Although Dreamweaver doesn't verify links to other Web sites on your pages, it does show you a list of such *external links* when you run the link checker. To see this list, choose External Links from the Show menu of the Link Checker window (see Figure 15-4). The list includes absolute URLs leading to other sites (like *http://www.yahoo.com*) as well as email links (like *mailto:Webmaster@cosmofarmer.com*).

This window can be especially useful if, for example, you've created a link to a certain external Web site several times throughout your Web site:

1. **Choose Site→Check Links Sitewide (or press Ctrl+F8 [⌘-F8]).**

    Dreamweaver scans your site and opens the Link Checker window.

2. **From the Show pop-up menu, choose External Links.**

    The window lists links you've created to sites outside your own.

3. **Click the external link you want to change.**

    Dreamweaver highlights the link, indicating that you can now edit it.

4. **Type the new URL; then press Enter or Return.**

    If other pages contain the old URL, Dreamweaver asks if you would like to update them as well. If so, click Update; the deed is done.

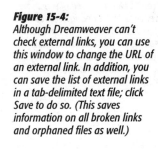

Figure 15-4:
Although Dreamweaver can't check external links, you can use this window to change the URL of an external link. In addition, you can save the list of external links in a tab-delimited text file; click Save to do so. (This saves information on all broken links and orphaned files as well.)

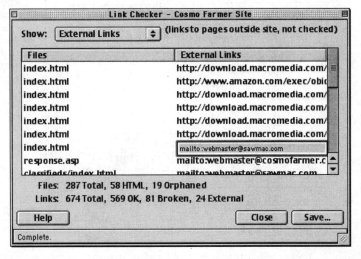

Orphaned Files

The Link Checker window also provides a list of files that aren't used by any Web page in the site—*orphaned* files, as they're called. You wind up with an orphaned graphic file when, for example, you save a GIF into your site folder, but then never use it on a Web page. Or suppose you eliminate the only link to an old page that you don't need any more; it's now an orphaned file. Unless you think you might link to it in the future, you can delete it to clean up unnecessary clutter in your site.

In fact, that's the primary purpose of this feature: to locate old and unused files and delete them. Here's how it works:

1. **Choose Site→Check Links Sitewide, or press Ctrl+F8 (⌘-F8).**

   Dreamweaver opens the Link Checker window.

2. **From the Show menu, choose Orphaned Files.**

   The list of orphaned files appears (see Figure 15-5).

3. **Select the files you want to delete.**

   You can use any of the selection methods described on page 397.

4. **Press Delete.**

   Dreamweaver asks if you really want to delete the files. Click OK if you do, Cancel if you suddenly get cold feet.

5. **Click Close when you're finished.**

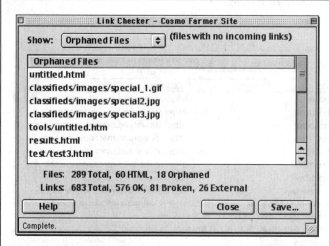

Figure 15-5:
Identify (and delete) unused files using Dreamweaver's Link Checker. Because the Link Checker can find external links and orphaned files as well as broken links, you'll probably use this box a few times, using the Show menu to isolate the different types of link.

Before you get spring-cleaning fever and delete all orphaned files in your site, however, keep a few pointers in mind:

- First, just because a file isn't *currently* being used doesn't mean you may not want it later. For example, say you have an employee of the month page. In March, you included a photo of Brian Albert, your best salesperson. In April, someone else got the award, so you removed Brian's photo. Just because you're not using that photo now—rendering it an orphaned file—doesn't mean that next month you won't need it again, when Brian develops a spurt of motivation. Make sure a file is really useless before deleting it.

- More important, Dreamweaver may flag as orphaned files your site actually needs. For example, some sites include what's called a *splash page:* an introductory page that first appears when someone comes to the site. It might be a page with a bold graphic and the text "Click here to enter the site." Or it might be a fancy Flash movie intended to make a big impact on your visitors. Usually, this page is nothing more than a welcome mat that leads to the *real* home page. Since it's simply an introductory page, no other page in the site links to it. Unfortunately, that's precisely what Dreamweaver considers an orphaned file, and Dreamweaver will identify it as such.

- If you write your own JavaScript code, you may reference graphic files and Web pages. Dreamweaver doesn't keep track of these references, and will identify those files as orphans (unless they're inserted or linked to elsewhere in the page or site).

    Fortunately, Dreamweaver is somewhat smarter when it comes to Behaviors; it can track files referenced as part of its own JavaScript programs—for example, graphic files you use in a rollover effect—and doesn't list them as orphaned files.

The bottom line is that while this report is useful, use it cautiously when deleting files.

Changing a Link throughout a Site

Suppose you've created a page on your site to teach your visitors about the basics of the HTML language. You think this would be really, really helpful to your visitors, so you create links to it from every page on your site. After a while, you realize you just don't have the time to keep this page up-to-date, but you still want to help your visitors get this information. Why not change the link so it points to a more current and informative source? Using Dreamweaver's Change Link Sitewide command, you can do just that.

1. Choose Site→Change Links Sitewide.

    The Change Link Sitewide dialog box opens (see Figure 15-6).

Note for Windows Users: The Site menu appears on the Site window *and* on each document window. However, only the menu on the Site window offers the Change Links Sitewide command. (If the Site window is closed, press F8 to open it.)

This dialog box offers two different fields: Change All Links To and Into Links To. Understanding what you're supposed to do at this point is easier if you imagine that the first label is actually "Change All Links That *Currently* Point To." In other words, first you'll indicate where those links point now; then you'll indicate where you'd like them to go instead.

At this point, you can type the new Web address into the Change All Links To field. For example, if your aim is to round up every link that now points to Yahoo and redirect them to Google, you could start by typing *http://www.yahoo.com* here.

If the links you're trying to change refer to a page in your own site, however, proceed like this:

2. **Click the folder icon to the right of the Change All Links To field.**

   The Select Link to Change dialog box opens. You're about to specify the file that the links point to *now*.

3. **Select a file in the local site folder; click Select (Windows) or Save (Mac).**

   In the following steps, Dreamweaver will change every link that leads to *this file*, whether it's a graphic, Cascading Style Sheet file, or any other external file that can be part of a Web page.

Tip: As a shortcut to following steps 1, 2, and 3, you can select a file in the Site window, *then* choose Site→Change Links Sitewide. Dreamweaver automatically adds the selected file's path to the Change All Links To field.

Now it's time to substitute the new URL or file—the one to which all of those links will be redirected. If you're reassigning them to a different Web site, you can type its URL directly into the Change All Links To field. For example, in the previous example, you can type *http://www.google.com*.

Tip: For a quicker way to change one external link into another, see page 399.

If you'd like the changed links to point to a file on your own Web site instead, proceed like this:

4. **Click the folder icon to the right of the Into Links To field.**

   The Select Link to Change dialog box opens.

5. **Select a file in the local site, and then click Select (Windows) or Save (Mac).**

   You've just selected the new file you wish to link to. In other words, every link that once led to the file you selected in step 3 will now link to this file. You can select graphics, Cascading Style Sheet files, and any other external files you can include in a Web page.

   You'll get unpredictable results, however, if you change a link that points to a graphic file into, say, a link that points to a Web page, or vice versa. Make sure the "before" and "after" links share the same file type: Web page, style sheet, or graphic.

6. **Click OK to make the change.**

The same Update Files dialog box you encountered in the last chapter appears; it lists every page that will be affected.

7. **Click Update to update the pages.**

Dreamweaver scans your site and updates the pages.

Figure 15-6:
Dreamweaver uses a root-relative link to specify the page, as indicated by the slash (/). Don't worry; this doesn't mean Dreamweaver will make the link root-relative; it's just how Dreamweaver identifies the location of the page in the site. See page 83 for more on root-relative links.

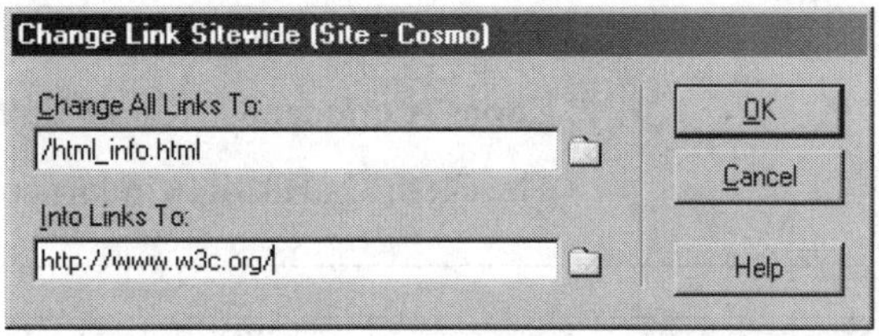

Cleaning up HTML

It's time to come clean.

You've been reading about what great HTML code Dreamweaver writes, and how all you hand-coders need to get on the WYSIWYG bandwagon. In fact, this isn't always true. In the process of formatting text, deleting elements, and—in general—building a Web page, it's quite possible to end up with less-than-optimal HTML coding. While Dreamweaver usually catches potentially sloppy HTML, you may nonetheless run across instances of empty tags, redundant tags, and nested <font> tags in your Dreamweaver pages.

For example, after applying a size and font to a text selection, you may later decide to add some color. The result will be HTML that looks like this:

```
<font face="Arial, Helvetica, sans-serif" size="5"><font
color="#FF0000">Arugula</font></font>
```

See how the <font> tag appears twice? There's no need for this redundancy; the color property from the second tag should be combined with the first tag. Remember, the less code your page uses, the faster it loads, so eliminating redundant tags can improve the download speed of your site.

Fortunately, Dreamweaver is aware of its own limitations. The program comes with a command that's designed to streamline the code in your pages: the Clean Up HTML command. It not only improves the HTML in your page, it can also strip out other nonessential code, such as comments, and even eliminate a specific tag or tags.

Tip: The Clean Up HTML command is extremely useful. Once you've tried it a few times, you'll probably want to use it on all your pages. Unfortunately, it doesn't come with a keyboard shortcut. This is a classic case when Dreamweaver 4's new keyboard shortcuts editor is just the white knight you need; using it, you can add a key combination to trigger this command from the keyboard. See page 489 for details.

To use this command:

1. **Open a Web page to clean up.**

   Unfortunately, this great feature only works on one page at a time. No cleaning up a site's worth of pages in one fell swoop! As a result, you should get in the habit of running this command every time you finish a Web page, or perhaps running it on only problem pages that you round up using Dreamweaver 4's new Site Reports feature (next page).

2. **Choose Commands→Clean Up HTML.**

   The Clean Up HTML window appears (see Figure 15-7).

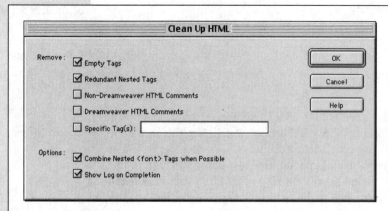

Figure 15-7:
The Clean Up HTML command lets you improve the speed of a Web page by stripping out redundant and useless code. You can even use it to strip out useful tags by specifying a tag in the Specific Tag field (although the Find and Replace command provides a much more powerful method of identifying and removing HTML tags; see page 476).

3. **Turn on the checkboxes for the options you want.**

   Empty Tags deletes any tags that don't actually modify anything. For example, you might delete some text that had been set in boldface, leaving behind opening and closing bold tags without any text in between: <b></b>. Or you might delete an image within a link, leaving behind a useless pair of <a> tags. It's always a good idea to check this option.

   Redundant Nested Tags deletes tags that appear within other tags of the same type, like this: <b>You can't get any <b>bolder</b> than bold</b>. The second set of bold tags does no good, so choosing this option would produce this: <b>You can't get any bolder than bold</b>—an extremely useful option.

   Non-Dreamweaver HTML Comments deletes any comments *not* inserted by someone using Dreamweaver. Comments are notes placed in the code of a page; Web designers use them to give directions or explain parts of the code. (Comments are invisible in a Web browser; they appear only in the Code view, or as a gold comment icon in the document window.) Since comments are often added as an aid for maintaining a Web page, you may not want to choose this option. However, if the page is finished, and you doubt you'll need the information the comments contain, you can decrease the file size of a page by using this option.

Dreamweaver HTML Comments deletes any comments inserted by someone using Dreamweaver. Dreamweaver relies on comments in some of its features, including tracing images (see page 138), Templates, and Libraries (Chapter 17). Choosing this option will eliminate those features from a page, so use this option with care.

Specific Tag(s) deletes HTML tags you specify. Type the name of the tag (without brackets) in the field like this: *font*. To remove multiple tags at once, separate each tag name by a comma like this: *font, blink*.

Be careful with this option. Since it lets you remove *any* tag from a page, it's easy to delete an important and necessary tag (like the <body> tag) from your page by accident. Furthermore, Dreamweaver's Find and Replace command provides much more powerful tools for performing this kind of surgery (see page 476).

Combine Nested <font> Tags when Possible combines multiple font properties into a single tag, as in the example above. This, too, is a useful option to turn on.

If you want to see a report of all the changes Dreamweaver makes to a page, turn on **Show Log on Completion**.

4. **Click OK to clean up the page.**

   If you selected Show Log on Completion, a dialog box then appears, listing the types of changes, and the number of changes, Dreamweaver made to the page.

As long as you keep the page open, you can undo any changes Dreamweaver made. Suppose you asked Dreamweaver to remove any comments, and suddenly realized you really did need them. Ctrl+Z (⌘-Z) will do the trick; you can also use the History panel, which lists this step as Clean Up HTML (see page 55).

Site Reporting

The Clean Up HTML command is a great way to make sure your code is well-written. But what if you forget about it until after you've built all 500 pages of your site? Do you have to open each page and run the command—whether there's a problem or not?

Fortunately, no. Dreamweaver 4 introduces a new feature—Site Reports—that makes identifying problems throughout a site a snap. In addition to locating the problems fixed by the Clean Up HTML command, it makes Dreamweaver check your pages for other problems, such as missing titles and empty Alt properties for images.

After running a report, Dreamweaver displays a list pages with problems. Unfortunately, the Site Reports feature only finds problems; it doesn't fix them. You have to open and fix each page individually.

To run a report on one or more Web pages, proceed like this:

1. **Choose Site→Reports.**

   The Reports window opens (see Figure 15-8).

2. **Select the files to analyze from the Report On menu.**

   Dreamweaver can report on a single Web page, multiple pages, or even an entire site. Choose **Current Document** to check the Web page that's open at the moment. **Entire Local Site** checks every Web page in the local site folder, including folders inside it. This option is great when you want to check your entire site prior to uploading it to a Web server and making it "live" (more on that in the next chapter).

   Selected Files in Site checks only the files you choose in the Site window. You need to open the Site window and select files in the local file list for this to work. See the box on page 397 for methods on selecting files in the Site window. Choose this option when you've modified or added pages to a site, and are ready to move them to the Web server.

   Folder checks all Web pages in a selected folder. After choosing this option, an empty field and a folder icon appear. Click the folder icon; a dialog box gives you the opportunity to locate and select the folder you wish to check, including any folders inside it. You can also use this option when you wish to check pages that aren't actually part of the current site.

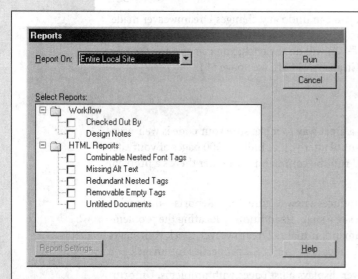

Figure 15-8:
Dreamweaver 4's new Site Reports feature makes quick work of finding common page errors. It's also one of Dreamweaver's many customizable features. You can download additional types of reports from the Macromedia Exchange Web site or even program your own. For more information on customizing Dreamweaver and using the Macromedia Exchange, see page 493.

3. **Select the types of reports you want Dreamweaver to generate.**

   The Reports window is divided into two types of reports. The first set, Workflow reports, deal with features that facilitate working with others as part of a production team (see the following chapter). The second type of reports, HTML reports, are useful for locating common errors, such as forgetting to title a Web page or forgetting to add an Alt property to an image.

Three of the HTML report options—**Combinable Nested Font Tags**, **Redundant Nested Tags**, and **Removable Empty Tags**—search for pages with common code mistakes. These are the same problems fixed by the Clean Up HTML command (see page 403).

Turn on **Missing Alt Text** to search for pages with images that are missing an alternate text description (page 98).

Finally, turn on **Untitled Documents** to identify pages that are either missing a title or still have Dreamweaver's default title ("Untitled Document").

4. **Click Run.**

Dreamweaver analyzes the pages you specified. It then produces a report that lists pages that match your report settings (see Figure 15-9). Each line in the Results window displays the name of the file, the line number where the error occurs, and a description of the error.

Note: Depending on the size of your site and the number of reports you choose to run, this feature can take a while to process. If you decide that the report is taking too long, you can always stop it by clicking the icon in the lower-right corner of the Results window. It looks like a red stop sign with an X through it, and only appears while a report is running.

Figure 15-9:
The Site Report's Results window displays the results of a report. Unfortunately, as part of the reporting process, Dreamweaver also searches files that aren't Web pages, such as the scripts.xml file shown in this illustration—files that Dreamweaver produces behind the scenes, as part of its normal routine. If you encounter files that end in .xml in your reports, you can safely ignore them.

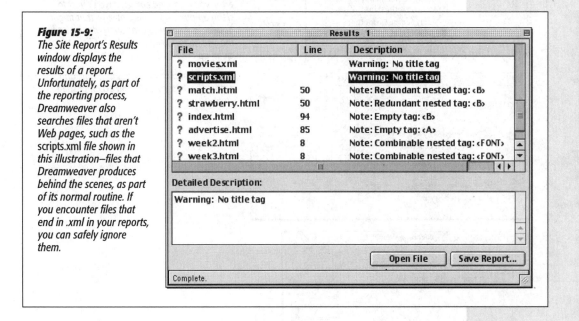

5. **Click a file in the list to select it.**

   A detailed description, if available, appears in the bottom of the window.

6. **Click the Open File button to open the selected file.**

   Double-clicking a file in the results list also opens it.

   Either way, Dreamweaver opens the file; it automatically highlights the offending code.

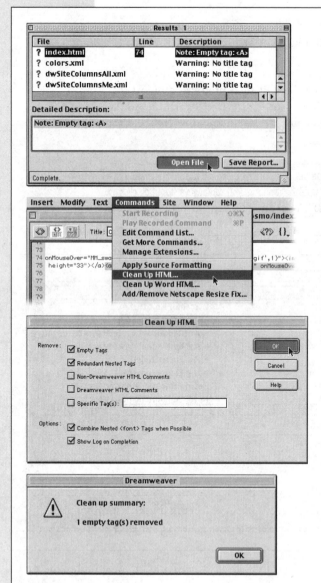

Figure 15-10:
The life cycle of a typical HTML error. Top: After running a report, you might find a common HTML error such as an empty link tag. Select the page in the Results window and click the Open File button.

Second from top: The page opens with the offending code selected in Split view. (Dreamweaver often highlights the problem code in this view, so you can identify the problem in the HTML.) Since you can fix this particular error—and more—with the Clean Up HTML command, choose Commands→Clean Up HTML.

Third from top: The Clean Up HTML window opens. Even though you can just clean up the error you identified earlier, it won't hurt to clean up other possible problems that might appear in your code (and somewhere else in the Site Report Results window). Click OK to clean up the HTML.

Bottom: Dreamweaver does its magic and reports back to you. Mission accomplished—code cleaned.

7. **Fix the problem according to its type.**

For a page containing **Combinable Nested Font Tags**, **Redundant Nested Tags**, or **Removable Empty Tags** errors, use the Clean Up HTML command as described on page 403.

For pages missing a title, add one using the technique described in step 4 on page 28.

You can add **Missing Alt** properties using the Property inspector, as described on page 98, but you may find it faster to use Dreamweaver's powerful Find and Replace command (see page 486).

8. **Continue opening files from the Results window and fixing them until you've corrected each mistake.**

Unfortunately, Dreamweaver doesn't provide a quick, one-step method to fix any of these problems. Except when using the Find and Replace tip for adding missing Alt text, you must open and fix each page individually.

If you want to save the results of your report, click the Save Report button. Dreamweaver opens a Save As dialog box, and lets you save the report as an XML file. When you're finished, click the Results window's close box to close the window.

The moment has come: your site is complete, your pages work, and your HTML is fine-tuned. In the next chapter, you'll learn how to share all or your hard work and beautiful design with the world by moving it onto a Web server.

Download Statistics

Remember the joke that WWW really stands for "World Wide Wait"? Even as more and more people upgrade to speedy DSL and cable modems, file size is the constant foe of the Web designer. What takes only a moment to load from your computer's hard drive could take minutes to travel across the Internet. The more information you put into a Web page, the more time it will take to load.

You can judge how big your page is, and therefore how long it will take to download, by looking at the download stats in the status bar. You'll see something like this: *5k/ 2 sec.*

The first bit of information tells you the total size of your Web page and any files included in the page. That's an extremely helpful statistic, because even though a Web page document itself may only be 1 K in size, a 20 K GIF image actually blows it up to 21 K.

Next to the file size, you see how long, in seconds, it will take to download the page and all its graphics and other elements. Of course, each visitor's connection speed may be different, depending on whether she's using a cable modem, gas-powered 14.4 Kbps dial-up modem, or whatever. By default, Dreamweaver calculates this figure based on the time it would take a 28.8 Kbps modem to download the page.

You can change this setting easily enough, however; open the Status Bar Preferences window by choosing Edit Sizes from the status bar's window-size pop-up menu. Alternatively, choose Edit→Preferences and click the Status Bar category of the Preferences window; either way, proceed as described in Figure 15-11.

Caution: People hate to wait. You may think that the graphic design of your Web site is so compelling that even if it takes a full minute to download that zippy new Flash home page, people will stick around.

Think again. Research shows that 10 seconds is the maximum amount of time that someone will stay focused on a task while waiting. That means if you're designing a Web site for people with 28.8k modems, keep your pages below 34 K in size.

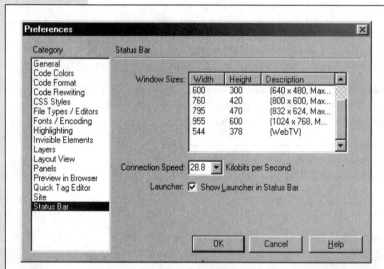

Figure 15-11:
In this dialog box, you can change the connection speed that Dreamweaver uses in calculating how long your page will download. A 34 K Web page will take about 10 seconds to download over a 28.8 modem, but if you choose 56 Kpbs from the pull-down menu, the status bar will list the download time as 5 seconds. Choose the connection speed that you think most visitors to your site will be using. When you aren't sure, err on the side of caution by using a lower speed.

GEM IN THE ROUGH

Caching in

Behind the scenes, Web browsers store the graphics they download onto the computer's hard drive; it's a speed trick. If you click your Back button to return to a Web page whose graphic files the browser has already downloaded, the browser simply pulls them out of the *cache*—off the hard drive, in other words—instead of re-downloading them. This arrangement makes the page load more quickly, since the hard drive is generally much faster than the modem.

As a Web designer, you can capitalize on this standard Web-browser feature by reusing the same graphic files on more than one page of your site. For instance, you might create a navigation bar composed of small graphic buttons (Home, Contact Us, Products, and so on). If you reuse those buttons on other pages of the site, those pages will appear to download more quickly.

If you do capitalize on this trick, be aware that the download stats in Dreamweaver's status bar may not reflect the added speed boost that's provided by cached graphics.

Moving Your Site to the Internet

Building Web pages on your computer is a big accomplishment, but it's not the whole job. Your beautifully designed and informative Web site will simply languish in obscurity on your hard drive unless you move it to a Web server.

Fortunately, once your Web site is ready for prime time, you can put it on a server without ever leaving the comfort of Dreamweaver: the program includes simple commands for transferring files back and forth between the Web server and your desktop.

Depending on how you operate, you can choose one of two methods for transferring your files:

- If you're the sole Web developer for a site, Dreamweaver's Get and Put commands are the easiest way to go.

- If, on the other hand, there's a group of people working on your site, Dreamweaver's Check Out and Check In tools let you move files at will without wiping out others' hard work. In addition, this group feature integrates seamlessly with two other industrial-strength Web-collaboration tools: Microsoft's Visual SourceSafe and WebDAV, an open source file-management tool.

Either way, you'll begin by defining a remote site.

Defining a Remote Site

As you create your Web site on your computer, you keep it in a *local site folder* (see page 23), often called a *local site* for short. You can think of a local site as a work-in-progress. As your site is under construction—whether you're building it from scratch or adding and modifying pages—you'll routinely have partially finished documents sitting on your computer.

Then, when you've perfected and tested your pages using the techniques described in Chapter 15, you're ready to transfer them to a Web server that's connected to the Internet. Dreamweaver refers to the Web-server copy of your files as the *remote site*, and the program provides four methods for transferring files between it and your local site:

- **FTP.** By far the most common method is *FTP*, or File Transfer Protocol. Just as HTTP is the process by which Web pages are transferred from servers to Web browsers, FTP is the traditional method of transferring files over the Internet, and it's the one to use if a Web hosting company or Internet Service Provider (ISP) provides the home for your Web pages.

- **Over the local area network.** If you're working on an intranet, or if your company's Web server is connected to the company network, you may also be able to transfer files just as you would any files on your office network (using the Network Neighborhood, My Network Places, or Chooser tools, depending on your operating system), without even connecting to the Internet.

- The last two options—**SourceSafe and WebDAV**—are advanced file management systems used for collaborative Web development; they're discussed on page 416.

FREQUENTLY ASKED QUESTION

Beyond Dreamweaver

Do I have to use Dreamweaver to move my files to the Web server?

No. If you're used to using another program for this purpose, such as CuteFTP (Windows) or Fetch (Mac), you can continue to use it and ignore Dreamweaver's Remote Site feature.

However, if you've never before used Dreamweaver to move files to a server, you may want to at least try it; you'll find that Dreamweaver simplifies much of the process. For example, when you want to move a file from your computer to the Web server using a regular FTP program, you must first locate the file on your local machine and then navigate to the proper folder on the Web server. Dreamweaver saves you both steps; when you select the file in the Site window and click the Put button, Dreamweaver automatically locates the file on your computer and transfers it to the correct folder on the Web server.

Setting up a Remote Site with FTP

You can set up a remote site only if you've first set up a *local* site on your computer. Even if you're just putting up a temporary site while working on your *real* Web site, you must at least have the temporary site constructed and defined in Dreamweaver (see page 23).

Once that's done, here's how you go about creating an Internet-based mirror of your local site folder:

1. **Choose Site→Define Sites.**

   You can also choose Define Sites from the Site window's Site menu.

   The Define Sites dialog box opens, listing all sites that you've defined so far. You're about to prepare Dreamweaver so it can create an Internet-based *copy* of one of these local sites.

2. **Click the name of the site you want to post on the Internet, and then click Edit.**

   Alternatively, just double-click the site name in the list. The Site Definition window appears for the selected site, as shown in Figure 16-1.

Tip: You can also define the remote site and the local site simultaneously, when you first begin creating a Web site (as described on page 24). Even then, however, Dreamweaver requires that you first give the site a name and choose a local root folder; at that point, you rejoin the steps described here.

---

3. **In the Category panel, click Remote Info. From the Access pop-up menu, choose FTP.**

   The Site Definition window now shows menus and fields for collecting your connection information (see Figure 16-1).

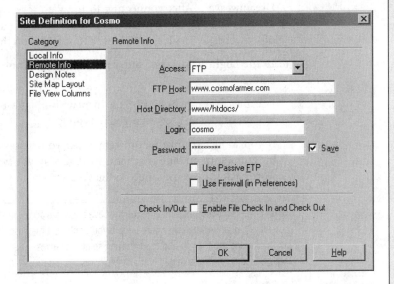

Figure 16-1:
If a Web hosting company or ISP will host your Web site, you'll use FTP to put your site on the Web. To make sure you have all the information you need to connect to the Web server, ask your ISP for these four pieces of information: (1) the FTP host name of the server, (2) the path to the root directory for your site (3) your login name and (4) your password. (If the Web server comes with your email account, your login and password may be the same for both.)

4. **Fill in the FTP Host field.**

   Your FTP host name is probably a name in the format *www.cosmofarmer.com* or *ftp.cosmofarmer.com*. It never includes directories, folders, or slashes (like *www.cosmofarmer.com/home*), never includes codes for the FTP protocol (*ftp:// ftp.cosmofarmer.com*), and is never only a domain name, such as *cosmofarmer.com*.

If you don't know the host name, there's only one way to find out: Call your Web hosting company or ISP or check its Web site.

5. **In the Host Directory field, type the path to the *root directory*.**

   You're specifying which *folder* within your Web hosting account will contain your Web-page files and serve as the root folder for your site.

   Just as on your own hard drive, all the files of your Web site on the Web will be completely contained inside a master folder referred to as the *root folder*. But when you connect to your Web server using FTP, you're rarely connected to the root folder itself. Instead, you usually connect to a folder that isn't accessible over the Web—some administrative folder for your Web account, often filled with folders for log reports of your site's Web traffic, databases, and other files not visible over the Web.

   Your hosting account's root directory folder (or even a folder within it) is where you place your *site's* root folder; that's why you're typing its name here. Common names for the root folder at ISPs or Web-hosting companies are *docs, www, htdocs, public_html,* or *virtual_html.* (Call your Web hosting company or ISP to find out.)

   The information you give Dreamweaver here represents the path from the FTP folder to the root folder. It may look like this: *www/htdocs.* In effect, you're telling Dreamweaver: "After connecting to the Web server, you'll find a folder named *www.* Inside *this* folder is another folder, *htdocs.* Put my site files in there." In other words, *htdocs* is the Web site's root folder on the remote hosting account.

6. **In the Login field, type your user name; type your password in the Password field.**

   Dreamweaver uses bullets (•••) to display your password so that passing evildoers in your office can't see what you're typing.

   If you want Dreamweaver to remember your password each time you use the program, turn on the Save checkbox. This way, you won't have to type your password each time you connect to the Web server.

Note: For security reasons, don't turn on the Save box if you access the Web using computers at, say, your local library, or anywhere else where people you don't trust may use the machine. Otherwise, you might just awake one morning to find the following splattered across your home page: "Hi there! Welcome to Jack's house of illegally acquired and unlawfully distributed music, featuring Metallica's greatest hits."

---

7. **Turn on the Use Passive FTP or Use Firewall boxes, if necessary.**

   If you're building sites from your home, home office, or small company, you'll most likely never need to use these technical options.

   Many corporations, however, use *firewalls*: hardware- or software-based gateways that control incoming and outgoing traffic through a network. Firewalls protect the company network from outside hackers; unfortunately, they also limit how computers inside the network—*behind the firewall*—can connect to the outside world.

If your company's system administrator confirms that you have a firewall, you'll need to also get the name of the firewall host computer and its port number. Enter these in the Site Preferences dialog box (press Ctrl+U or ⌘-U to open Preferences; click the Site category). Your firewall configuration may also require *passive FTP*—a method of connecting using your local software, rather than the firewall server. Check with your administrator to see if this is the case, and, if so, turn on the Use Passive FTP checkbox.

8. **If you and your team of Web developers all use Dreamweaver, turn on Enable File Check In and Check Out and fill in the corresponding options.**

When you turn on Check In and Out, additional options appear at the bottom of the Site Definition window (see Figure 16-2).

Start by turning on the Check Out File when Opening checkbox; now you'll be able to "check out" a file on the remote server just by double-clicking its name in the Site Files list. Fill in your name (which your team members will see when you check out a file) and email address, also as shown in Figure 16-2.

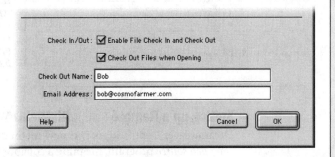

Figure 16-2:
If you work on the site in several different locations (for example, from home and your office), use a different name for each location–BobAtHome and BobAtWork, for example. In this way, you can identify which files you've checked out to your home computer and which to your computer at work.

9. **Click OK to return to the Define Sites dialog box; click Done.**

The Define Sites dialog box closes, and the Site window opens.

At this point, you're ready to connect to the Web server and transfer files. If you're the only person working on the site, Dreamweaver's Get and Put commands will do the trick; turn to page 419. If, however, you're part of a development team, use Dreamweaver's Check In and Check Out feature, described on page 424, instead.

Setting up a Remote Site over a Local Network

If you're working on an intranet, or if your company's Web server is connected to the company network, you may also be able to transfer your Web files just as you'd move any files from machine to machine. Dreamweaver provides the same file transfer functions as with FTP, but setup is simpler.

Follow steps 1 and 2 of the previous instructions; but in step 3, click the Remote Info category, and then choose Local/Network from the Access pop-up menu. Menus and fields for collecting your connection information appear in the Site Definition box (see Figure 16-3).

Now click the folder icon next to the Remote Folder field; in the resulting dialog box, navigate to and select your site's remote root folder. On a local network, this folder functions as the root folder on your company's Web server (see page 23), even though it's actually still within the walls of your building. (For differences on selecting root folders on Windows and Macs, see Figure 14-3 on page 25.)

Wrap up with steps 8 and 9 of the previous instructions. At this point, you're ready to connect to the Web server and transfer files.

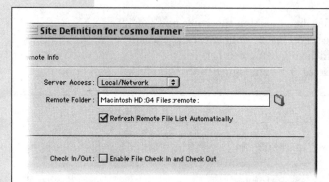

Figure 16-3:
Clicking the Refresh Remote File List Automatically box updates the list of files in the Site window. Changes to the remote site, such as when someone adds a file, are listed automatically. Because automatic updating slows down the process of moving files to the remote site, however, you may want to deselect this option when you begin a session of moving many files. You can always refresh the file list manually by clicking the Refresh button on the Site window (see page 419).

Setting up a Remote Site with WebDAV

Dreamweaver 4 introduces two new methods of accessing a remote site: WebDAV (an *open source* program, meaning a collaborative effort by volunteer programmers all over the world) and Microsoft's Visual SourceSafe. Both technologies are designed to address one of the biggest problems when collaborating on a Web site: file management and version control.

For instance, all kinds of havoc can result if two people edit a page simultaneously; whoever uploads the page to the Web server *second* winds up wiping out the changes made by the first person.

What you need is a way to prevent more than one person from working on the same file at the same time. WebDAV, short for Web-based Distributed Authoring and Versioning, provides one such solution. It integrates seamlessly with Dreamweaver's Check In and Check Out feature, described on page 424.

Note: Both WebDAV and SourceSafe are advanced options used by corporations that require a good deal of technical expertise; consider using them only if you have someone on staff who can guide you in setting them. Note, too, that you need Dreamweaver 4.0.1 or later for these technologies, an update described in the tip on page 3.

Both Microsoft Internet Information Server (IIS) 5.0 and Apache Web Server can work with WebDAV. To find out if your Web server can handle WebDAV (and to find out the necessary connection information), consult your Web server's administrator.

To create a remote site in Dreamweaver that will work with WebDAV, follow steps 1 and 2 on page 413. In step 3, click the Remote Info category, and then choose WebDAV from the Access pop-up menu (see Figure 16-1).

The Site Definition window displays a version number, a short description, and a button labeled Settings. Click Settings to open the WebDAV Connection window, shown in Figure 16-4. In this dialog box, type the URL of the root directory on the WebDAV server (beginning with *http://*), your user name, email address, and password. (If you don't know these three bits of information, ask the server administrator or help desk.) Click OK.

As a final step, turn on the Check Out Files when Opening checkbox in the Site Definition dialog box; Dreamweaver's Check In and Check Out feature will now work seamlessly with the WebDAV connection. Click OK, then Done. You're ready to connect to the Web server and transfer files, as described on page 424.

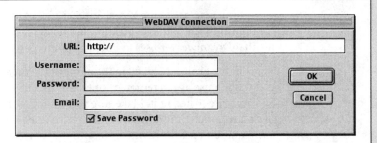

Figure 16-4:
*WebDAV, short for Web-based
Distributed Authoring and
Versioning, is built into several
Web server packages, including
Microsoft Internet Information
Server and Apache. Dream-
weaver 4 provides seamless
integration with this system.*

Setting up a Remote Site with SourceSafe

Microsoft originally created Visual SourceSafe for managing team software development. Like WebDAV, SourceSafe makes sure you don't accidentally stomp on someone else's hard work by overwriting a Web page they just modified. In addition, this sophisticated program tracks different versions of files and lets an administrator "roll back" to previous versions of a Web page, or even an entire site; it's the granddaddy of Undo's.

To take advantage of this power, however, you need a Visual SourceSafe (VSS) server and VSS database already set up. In addition, Windows users need to install Microsoft Visual SourceSafe Client version 6 on their PCs; Mac users need Metrowerks Visual SourceSafe database client. (For detailed directions on setting up a Mac for SourceSafe, see *www.macromedia.com/support/dreamweaver/site/source_safe_mac/*.)

Once you've installed the VSS Client software, and you've created and defined a local site (page 23), you're ready to configure Dreamweaver for SourceSafe using the Site Definition window. Basically, you tell Dreamweaver where to find the SourceSafe database and how to sign on to the server.

Once again, follow steps 1 and 2 on page 413. But in step 3, click the Remote Info category, and then choose SourceSafe from the Access pop-up menu (see Figure 16-1). In the resulting dialog box, click Settings to reveal the Open SourceSafe Database dialog box, shown in Figure 16-5.

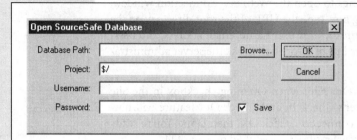

Figure 16-5:
Dreamweaver 4 introduces support for Microsoft's Visual SourceSafe system. Many corporations use this powerful file-control system to control access to files in large projects involving many people.

Click Browse to select the Visual SourceSafe (VSS) database file on your computer (or type in the file path, if you know it, into the Database Path field)—the *srcsafe.ini* file that Dreamweaver uses to initialize SourceSafe.

Then, in the Project field, fill in the name of the *project* within the VSS database that you wish to use as the remote root folder. (A VSS database can have many projects and Web sites listed in it. Make sure you enter the right project name for this site. If in doubt, contact the administrator of the Visual SourceSafe database.) Type your user name and password into the appropriate fields; again, ask the administrator for guidance.

Click OK. But before dismissing the Site Definition dialog box, turn on the Check Out Files when Opening checkbox, so that Dreamweaver's Check In and Check Out feature will work with the VSS system.

Click OK, then Done. You're ready to connect to the Web server and transfer files. Both WebDAV and SourceSafe use Dreamweaver's Check In and Check Out process, described on page 424, for transferring files.

Transferring Files

Once you've told Dreamweaver *how* you plan to ship off your Web-page files to the Net, you can set about *doing* it. Thanks to Dreamweaver's Site window, the whole process takes only a few steps.

Moving Files to the Web Server

To transfer files to your Web server:

1. **Open the Site window.**

   Windows: Choose Window→Site Files. *(Keyboard shortcut: F8.)*
   Mac: Choose Window→Open Site. *(Keyboard shortcut: F8.)*

   Either way, the Site window opens, as shown in Figure 16-6.

2. **From the Site menu, choose the name of the site whose files you wish to move (if it isn't already selected).**

   Note the Site window's split personality: On the right side, you see the folders inside the local site folder on your hard drive. These are the files you've worked so hard to create in Dreamweaver. On the left side, you see (or will eventually see) a mirror image; these are the folders and files you've sent to the Internet, the living copies of the site on your hard drive.

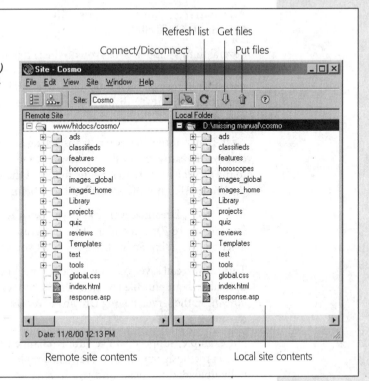

Figure 16-6:
While the Local Folder (right pane) holds all the Web files on your computer, the Remote Site (left pane) lists all of the files on the Web server. As you can see, both sets of files are organized in exactly the same way. They have the same folders and subfolders and pages are stored in the same locations on both computers. Of course, if you're uploading the local files for the first time, launching a new site, then the Remote Site panel will be empty.

Refresh list   Get files
Connect/Disconnect   Put files

Remote site contents   Local site contents

3. **From the file list in the Site window, select the files you wish to upload to the Web server.**

To move a folder and every file inside it, just select the folder. (In other words, you can transfer your *entire* Web site to the server by simply selecting the local root folder—the folder listed at the very top of the Local Folder file list.) When only a few files have changed, you can also select only certain files or folders for uploading, using any of the techniques described on page 378.

When you use do-it-yourself FTP programs like WSFTP or Fetch, you have to specify a folder location for every file you transfer to the Web server. But here's one of the great advantages of letting Dreamweaver do your file-shuffling; it already knows where the files should go on the remote site. The local and remote sites are, after all, mirror images (see Figure 16-6), so Dreamweaver simply puts files in the corresponding folders on the remote site.

For example, suppose you select the file *mayo.html,* which is in a folder called Condiments, which is itself stored in the local root folder. When you transfer the file, Dreamweaver knows to put this file in the Condiments folder in the root folder on the remote site.

A hush falls over the audience; you're ready to go live with your Web page.

4. **Click the Put files button—the up arrow—on the Site window.**

Alternatively, you can choose Site→Put, or use the keyboard shortcut Ctrl+Shift+U (⌘-Shift-U).

Several things happen when you do this: First, if you're using an FTP connection, Dreamweaver attempts to connect to your Web server, dialing your modem if necessary. It may take a minute or so to establish a connection; the Connect button (see Figure 16-6) displays a bright green light when Dreamweaver is connected.

Next, if any of the files you're transferring are currently open and have unsaved changes, Dreamweaver asks if you want to save the files before transferring them to the server. Click Yes to save the file, or, if there are multiple unsaved files, click the Yes To All button to save all of them before posting them online.

In addition, Dreamweaver asks if you wish to also transfer any *dependent files* (see Figure 16-7). Dependent files are graphics, frame pages in a frameset, or external Cascading Style Sheets files that you've placed onto a page.

This feature can save you considerable time and hassle; no need to hunt for and upload each graphic file yourself. On the other hand, if all the dependent files are *already* on the server, having Dreamweaver transfer the same files again is a waste of time.

For example, suppose you've simply changed some words on a Web page that you'd previously put on the server. The graphics were transferred when you originally uploaded the page, and you haven't added any additional graphics to the page. Since all the dependent files are already on the server, you only need to transfer the Web page file itself. Dreamweaver lets you make the choice.

Tip: If you turn on the Don't Ask Me Again box and then click Yes, Dreamweaver will *always* copy dependent files without asking. On the other hand, if you turn on the Don't Ask Me Again box and click No, Dreamweaver will *never* copy dependent files.

If you want the Dependent Files dialog box to appear again after you've turned it off, hold down the Alt (Option) key when you transfer a file, or choose Edit→Preferences→Site Category to turn this feature on or off.

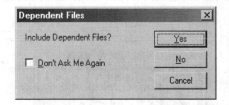

Figure 16-7:
The Dependent Files feature of Dreamweaver's File Transfer command makes sure all necessary files—graphics, Flash movies, and so on—are copied to the Web server along with your Web pages.

5. **Click Yes to transfer dependent files, or No to only transfer the files you selected.**

   Dreamweaver copies the files to the Web server. If you're copying a file that's inside a folder that isn't already on the remote site, Dreamweaver creates the folder as well. In fact, Dreamweaver will create as many subfolders as necessary to make sure every file is transferred to the same folder location on the remote site as it is in the local site. (Try doing *that* with a regular FTP program.)

6. **Continue using the Put button to transfer all files in your Web site to the remote site.**

POWER USERS' CLINIC

Troubleshoot with the FTP Log

If you're having problems moving files using Dreamweaver's FTP command, you may be able to find some clues in the records Dreamweaver keeps when transferring files. If you've used other FTP programs, you may have seen little messages that are sent back and forth between the Web server and the FTP program like this:

```
200 PORT command successful.
LIST
150 Opening ASCII mode data connection
```

```
for /bin/ls.
```

Dreamweaver also sends and receives this information, but keeps it hidden. To see the FTP log, choose Window→FTP Log in the Site window (Windows) or choose Site→FTP log (Mac). Any errors appear in this log.

For example, if you encounter a "cannot put file" error, it may mean that you're out of space on your Web server. Contact your ISP or the administrator of your Web server for help.

Depending on the number of files transferred, this operation can take some time. Transferring files over the Internet using FTP isn't nearly as fast as copying files from one hard drive to another (see the box on page 424).

Other ways to move files to the Web server

In the Site window, you can also *drag* a file from the Local Folder list into the Remote Site list. But don't do it: it's too easy to drag a file into the wrong place. If you drag a file to the wrong folder on the remote site, for example, you'll probably break all the links on the page. It's much better to let Dreamweaver keep track of where files should go in the organization of your site. (However, if you're already in this mess, see "Find and Fix Broken Links" on page 396.)

Figure 16-8:
Dreamweaver 4's toolbar provides a quick way to transfer the current document to a Web server; choose Put from the menu. You can also use this menu to retrieve a copy of this file from the server (Get), use the Check In and Out features, or review Design Notes.

WORKAROUND WORKSHOP

Don't Replace the Wrong File

One strange feature of the Site window's Get and Put commands may get you in trouble. Suppose, having just added new information to the home page (index.html), you want to transfer it to the Web server. You select it in the Local Folder list of files—but then you accidentally click Get instead of Put.

Not knowing your true intention, Dreamweaver dutifully retrieves the index.html file *from* the Web server and prepares to replace (wipe out) the newly updated home page on your computer.

Fortunately, Dreamweaver also opens a warning message asking if you really want to overwrite the local file. Click No.

> **Dreamweaver**
> Do you wish to overwrite your local copy of aries.html?
> [No] [Yes]

The opposite happens if you select a file in the Remote Site list and click the Put button: Dreamweaver tries to replace the remote file with the local version. If that's not what you meant to do, be sure to click No. Remember that the warning message is your last chance to avoid a potentially disastrous mistake.

You can also copy your current document to the Web server without using the Site window at all. You can go directly to the Put command when, say, you finish building or modifying a Web page and want to immediately move it to the Web server. Just choose Site→Put or press Ctrl+Shift+U (⌘-Shift-U); Dreamweaver automatically copies the fresh page to the proper folder online.

The toolbar also provides a quick menu shortcut for this operation, as shown in Figure 16-8.

Getting Files from the Web Server

So far, this chapter has described getting your hard drive-based Web pages *to* the Internet. Sometimes, however, you'll want to download one or more files *from* the Web server. Perhaps you've made a horrible (and irreversible) mistake on the local copy of a file, and you want to retrieve the last version from the Web server, using the remote site as a last-ditch backup system. Or perhaps someone else uploaded some files to the site, and you want to download a copy to your own computer (although the Synchronize feature described on page 430 would also work).

To get files from the remote site, open the Site window (press F8) and proceed as follows:

1. **From the Site pop-up menu, choose the site whose files you wish to retrieve.**

   If only the Local Folder files are visible, click the tiny white triangle in the lower-left corner, and make sure that the Site File view button is selected (see Figure 14-3 on page 376).

2. **Click the Connect Button (see Figure 16-6).**

   Dreamweaver tells you that it's attempting to connect to the Web server. Once the connection has been made, a list of files and folders appears in the Remote Site list, and the Connect button displays a bright green dot. (Dreamweaver will automatically disconnect you after 30 minutes of inactivity, and the green dot will turn black. It's usually a good idea to not stay connected to a server indefinitely; doing so takes processing power away from the server and poses a security risk.)

Tip: By default, Dreamweaver disconnects from the Remote site after 30 minutes of inactivity. If you'd like to change this setting, press Ctrl+U (⌘-U) to open the Preferences window. Click the Site category and change the number listed in the Minutes Idle box. Be aware, however, that some Web servers have their own settings and may disconnect you sooner than you've specified.

   If you're connected to the Web server over a local network as described on page 415, the Connect button is dimmed, and you can skip this step. You only use the Connect button when connecting to the Web server via FTP, Visual SourceSafe, or WebDAV.

3. **From the Remote Site file list at the left side of the Site window, select the files you wish to download from the Web server.**

For techniques on selecting files in the Site window, see page 378. To download a folder and every file inside it, just click the folder. This technique also lets you get your *entire* Web site from the server; just click the remote root folder, which appears at the very top of the Remote Site file list.

4. **Click the Get files button—the down arrow (see Figure 16-6).**

   Alternatively, you can choose Site→Get, or use the keyboard shortcut Ctrl+Shift+D (⌘-Shift-D).

   If the *local* version of any file you are getting from the remote site is currently opened and has unsaved changes, Dreamweaver warns you that those changes will be lost. (No surprise there; copying a file from the remote site automatically replaces the same file in the local site, whether it's open or not.) Dreamweaver also warns you if you're about to replace a local file that's *newer* than the remote one.

   In addition, Dreamweaver offers to transfer any dependent files, as described in Figure 16-7.

5. **Click Yes to transfer dependent files, or No to only transfer the files you selected.**

   Dreamweaver copies the files to the local site folder, creating any folders necessary to replicate the structure of the remote site.

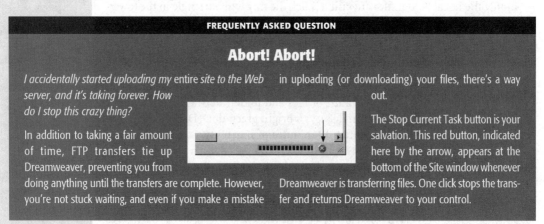

FREQUENTLY ASKED QUESTION

Abort! Abort!

I accidentally started uploading my entire site to the Web server, and it's taking forever. How do I stop this crazy thing?

In addition to taking a fair amount of time, FTP transfers tie up Dreamweaver, preventing you from doing anything until the transfers are complete. However, you're not stuck waiting, and even if you make a mistake in uploading (or downloading) your files, there's a way out.

The Stop Current Task button is your salvation. This red button, indicated here by the arrow, appears at the bottom of the Site window whenever Dreamweaver is transferring files. One click stops the transfer and returns Dreamweaver to your control.

Check In and Check Out

If you're the sole developer for a Web site, the Site window's Get and Put buttons are fine for transferring your files. But if you're on a team of developers, these simple tools can get you in trouble.

For example, suppose your boss emails you an important announcement that he wants posted on the home page immediately. So you download the home page from the Web server and start to edit it. At the same time, your co-worker Bob notices a typo on the home page. He downloads it, too.

You're a much faster worker than Bob, so you've added the critical news to the home page and moved it back to the Web server. But now Bob transfers his corrected home page to the Web server, *overwriting* your edits and eliminating that urgent notice you just uploaded. (An hour later, your phone rings. It's the boss.)

Without some kind of system to monitor who has what file, and to prevent people from overwriting each other's work, collaborative Web development can be a chaotic mess. Fortunately, Dreamweaver's Check In and Check Out system provides a civilized answer to this problem. It works like your local public library: When you check a file out, no one else can have it. When you're finished, you check the file back in, releasing control of it, and allowing someone else on the team to check it out and work on it.

To use the Check In/Check Out feature effectively, it helps to keep a few things in mind:

• When you're developing a Web site solo, your local site usually contains the most recent versions of your files. You make any modifications or additions to the pages on your computer first and *then* transfer them to the Web server.

But in a collaborative environment where many people are working on the site at once, the files on your hard drive may not be the latest ones. After all, your co-workers, like you, have been updating pages and transferring them to the Web server. The home-page file sitting in the local site folder on your computer might be several days older than the file on the remote site. This is why checking out a file from the *remote* site, rather than editing from the copy on your computer, is so important. It guarantees that you have the latest version of the file.

• In a collaborative environment, nobody should post files to the Web server using any method except Dreamweaver's Check In and Check Out system.

The reason is technical, but worth slogging through: When Dreamweaver checks out a file, it doesn't actually *lock* the file. Instead, it places a small, invisible text file (with the suffix *.lck)* on both the remote server and in your local site folder. This text file indicates who has checked out the file. When Dreamweaver connects to a remote site, these .lck files tell it which Web files are in use by others.

But only Dreamweaver understands these .lck files. Other FTP programs, like WSFTP (Windows) or Fetch (Mac), gladly ignore them and can easily overwrite any checked-out files. This risk also applies when you simply copy files back and forth over the office network.

• All Dreamweaver users must configure their remote site to use Check In and Check Out (see step 8, page 415). If just one person doesn't do it, you risk overwritten files.

Note: Visual SourceSafe and WebDAV users are free of these last two constraints. As long as everyone working on the site uses programs that support the Visual SourceSafe client or the WebDAV protocol, they can work seamlessly with Dreamweaver users. And vice versa.

Checking Out Files

When you want to work on a file in a collaborative site, you check it out from the Web server. Doing so makes sure that *you* have the latest version of the file, and that nobody else can make changes to the file.

Note: There's nothing to check out when you're creating a *new* page for the site. Since the only version of the file in the universe is on your computer, there's no fear that someone else might work on it at the same time as you. In this case, you only need to check the file into the site when you're done (see page 424).

You check out a file using the Site window; if it's not open, press F8 or use any of the methods described on page 375. Then choose the remote site you wish to work on from the Site pop-up menu (Figure 16-9).

Now you're ready to begin. From the Local Folder file list in the Site window, click to select the files you wish to check out from the Web server—or, to check out an entire folder and every file inside it, just select the folder.

You may in some instances want to select a file from the Remote Site list as well. For example, maybe you need to modify a page that you didn't create, and which you've never before checked out. In this case, the file isn't *in* your local folder, so you must select it from the Remote Site list. First, connect to the Web server by clicking the Connect button (Figure 16-9). After Dreamweaver connects to the server, the remote files will appear in the Remote Site list. Select the ones you wish to check out.

Tip: If, when you define the remote site (page 411), you select the Check Out File when Opening option, you can also check out (and open) a file by double-clicking it in the Site window. This is a quick way to open a page for editing while still using Dreamweaver's Check Out feature.

In any case, now just click the Check Out files button on the Site window (see Figure 16-9), or choose Site→Check Out, or use the keyboard shortcut Ctrl+Shift+Option+D (⌘-Shift-Option-D). (Not enough fingers? See page 489 to learn how to change Dreamweaver's shortcuts.)

WORKAROUND WORKSHOP

Manual Checkout Override

Occasionally you may wish to erase the checked-out status of a file. Suppose, for example, someone who's checked out a lot of files suddenly catches the plague and can't continue working on the site. In order to free those files so others can work on them, you should undo his checkout (and quarantine his cubicle).

To do this, select the checked-out file in the Site window. Choose Site→Undo Check Out. (Windows users must use the Site menu on the Site window.) As Dreamweaver warns you, doing this also copies the remote site version of the file to your local site; you can stop the process, if necessary, by clicking Cancel. When complete, a padlock icon appears next to the file.

You can also use this technique if, after checking out a file, you've made a horrible mistake on the page and wish to revert to the copy on the Web server.

Dreamweaver asks if you wish to also check out any dependent files (see Figure 16-7). Be careful checking out dependent files; clicking Yes here *locks* all of those files so that nobody else can modify them. If you check out both a page and its linked external style sheet, for example, whoever's responsible for maintaining your site's styles won't have access to the sheet. When she needs to add a new style, she'll be stuck until you check the style sheet back in.

When you check files out, Dreamweaver copies them to your computer and marks them as checked out so others can't change them. As when uploading and downloading files, checking out files can take time, depending upon how fast your computer can communicate with the Internet.

After you've checked out a file, a green "checked-out" checkmark appears next to its name in the Site window (see Figure 16-9). You can now open and edit it, and (when you're done) check the file back in.

If you attempt to check out a file someone else has already checked out, Dreamweaver tells you as much. It also gives you the option to override their checkout; but unless you're the boss, resist the temptation, for two reasons. First, your colleagues may have made some important changes to the page, which will be wiped out by your shenanigans. Second, because you so rudely stole the file, they may decide to stop talking to you.

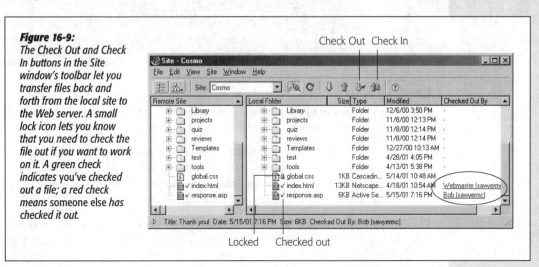

Figure 16-9:
The Check Out and Check In buttons in the Site window's toolbar let you transfer files back and forth from the local site to the Web server. A small lock icon lets you know that you need to check the file out if you want to work on it. A green check indicates you've checked out a file; a red check means someone else has checked it out.

A better way to work with someone who's checked out a file you need is to use Dreamweaver's email feature. You can see who checked out a file by consulting the Checked Out By column (see Figure 16-9). Even better, if you click the name, Dreamweaver opens your email program and addresses an email to that person, so you can say: "Hey Bob, you've had the home page checked out for two days! I need to work on it, so check it back in!"

The name and address Dreamweaver uses depends on the information they provided, just as you did when you configured your computer for remote site use (see Figure 16-2 on page 415).

Get and Put, In and Out

I'm using Dreamweaver's Check In and Check Out buttons to transfer my files. What do the Get and Put buttons do when the Check In/Out feature is enabled?

If you're using Check In and Out, the Get and Put commands function slightly differently than described on page 419. *Get* copies the selected file or files to your local site. However, Dreamweaver draws a small lock icon next to each of these "gotten" files in your Local Folder list. The files are locked, and you shouldn't edit them. Remember, checking out a file is the only way to prevent others from working on it. If you edit a locked file on your computer, nothing is stopping someone else from checking the page out from the Remote site, editing it, and checking it back in.

But using the Get command in such a situation can still be

useful. For example, suppose someone just updated the site's external style sheet. Pages you're editing use this style sheet, so you'd like to get the latest version. You don't want to *edit* the style sheet itself, so you don't need to check it out. By using Get instead of checking out the pages, you can keep a reference copy on your computer without locking it for anyone else and without having to check it back in later.

Put, on the other hand, simply transfers the file on your local site to the remote site. This is usually a bad idea when you're also using the Check In/Check Out feature. The remote site should be your reference copy; several rounds of revisions may have been made to a file since you last checked it out. Your local copy will be hopelessly out of date, and moving it the server using Put will destroy the most recent version of the file.

Checking Files In

When you're ready to move a page you've edited back onto the server, you check it in. (You also check in *new* files you've created.)

To check in files, open the Site window (press F8), choose the site you're checking into from the Site pop-up menu, and (using the Local Folder file list in the Site window) select the files you wish to Check In to the Web server. As always, you can click a folder to check it out, along with every file inside it.

The files you select should be files you've checked out, or brand-new files that have never been on the Web server. If you attempt to check in a file that someone else has checked out, Dreamweaver warns you with a message box. Click Cancel to stop the check-in procedure, so that you won't overwrite the checked-out file on the server.

Dreamweaver also warns you if you try to check in a file that's older than the server copy. Again, unless you're sure this is what you want to do, click Cancel.

Tip: If you want to check the page you're currently working on into the remote site, use the Toolbar in the document window (see Figure 16-8).

You can check in the selected files in any of the usual ways:

- Click the Check In files button (see Figure 16-9).

- Choose Site→Check In.

- Use the keyboard shortcut Ctrl+Shift+Option+U (⌘-Shift-Option-U). (See page 489 to learn how to change the Dreamweaver shortcut to something less cumbersome.)

Dreamweaver asks if you wish to also check in any dependent files (see Figure 16-7). You should transfer dependent files only if you first checked them out, or if the dependent files are new and have never been uploaded to the server. If you attempt to check in a dependent file that someone else has checked out, Dreamweaver warns you with a message box.

After you've clicked through all message boxes, Dreamweaver copies the files to the Remote site. Once you've checked in a file, a padlock icon appears next to its name in the Site window (see Figure 16-9); checking in locks the file so that you don't accidentally change the local copy. If you wish to modify the file in some way, check it out again.

Generating a Report on Checked-Out Files

As described in Chapter 15, Dreamweaver can generate a series of reports on the files in your site. One of those reports lets you see which files a specific person has checked out. In this way, for instance, you can identify all the files you've checked out, or all the files that have been checked out by your co-worker Bob (who has since left the company).

To generate a report, follow the steps described on page 405. Turn on the Checked Out By option when specifying the type of report to run. Then click Report Settings; in the dialog box that appears, type the person's name as it appears in the Checked Out By column (see Figure 16-9). (To find *all* checked-out files, leave the box blank.) Click OK, and then click Run to generate the report.

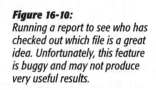

Figure 16-10:
Running a report to see who has checked out which file is a great idea. Unfortunately, this feature is buggy and may not produce very useful results.

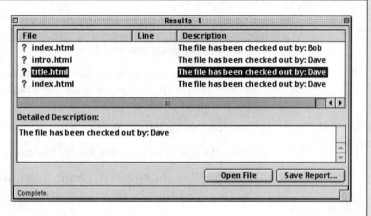

Unfortunately, several issues undermine the usefulness of the "Checked Out By" report. First, if you're connected to the Remote server using FTP, you'll wait quite awhile; Dreamweaver needs to download a lot of information, which, even on a small site, can take a long time. (Even worse, Dreamweaver can hang or crash in this process.)

In addition, the report you finally get isn't very useful (see Figure 16-10). The operations you're most likely to perform on checked-out files—checking them back in, undoing their checkout status, or contacting the person who checked them (see Figure 16-9)—require you to switch to the Site window. Unfortunately, there's no link between the report and the Site window; you can't, for example, make Dreamweaver highlight the reported files in the Site window.

Synchronizing Site Files

As you might suspect when you keep two sets of files—Local Folder and Remote Site—it's easy to lose track of which files are the most recent. For example, say you finish your Web site and move all the files to the Web server. The next day, you notice mistakes on a bunch of Web pages, so you make corrections on the copies in your local site. But in your rush to fix the pages, you didn't keep track of which ones you corrected. So although you're ready to move the corrected pages to the Web Server, you're not sure *which* ones you need to transfer.

When you use the Check In/Check Out feature described on page 424, you avoid this problem altogether. Using that system, the version on the Web server is *always* the latest and most definitive copy—*unless* you or someone else has checked that file out. In that case, whoever checked the file has the most recent version.

But if you're operating solo, for example, and don't use the Check In/Check Out feature, you may get good mileage from the Synchronize command, which lets you compare the remote and local sites and transfer only the newer files in either direction. (In fact, since the Synchronize command uses the Get and Put methods of transferring files, *don't* use it if you're also using Check In and Check Out [see the box on page 428.])

To synchronize your sites:

1. **Choose Site→Synchronize.**

   Windows users should use the Site menu on the Site window; Mac users should choose from the menu bar (with the Site window open and in front of any open documents).

   The Synchronize Files dialog box appears (see Figure 16-11).

2. **Using the Synchronize menu, specify the files to update.**

   You can either synchronize all files in the current Web site, or just files you've selected in the Local Folder list. This last option is good when you have a really big site and you want to limit this operation to just a single section of the site—one folder, for example. For Site file selection techniques, see page 378.

3. **Using the Direction pop-up menu, choose where you'd like to copy newer files.**

   You have three choices. **Put newer files to remote** updates the Web server with any newer files from your local site folder. It also copies any *new* files on the local site to the remote site. Use this option when you've done heavy editing to the local site and you want to move all new or modified pages to the Web server.

   Get newer files from remote does just the reverse: it updates your local site folder with any newer (or new) files from the remote site. Here's one instance where the synchronize feature comes in handy in team-design situations. If you've been out of the office for a while, click this option to download copies of the latest site files. (Note that this doesn't check any files out; it merely makes sure you have the latest files for your own reference.)

   Get and put newer files is a two-way synchronization. Any new files on the local site are transferred to the remote site and vice versa; the result is that both "sides" contain the latest files.

Figure 16-11:
Using the Synchronization command, you can copy newer files from your computer to the Web server, or get newer files from the remote site. Unfortunately, if you are using Visual SourceSafe, the Synchronization command is not available.

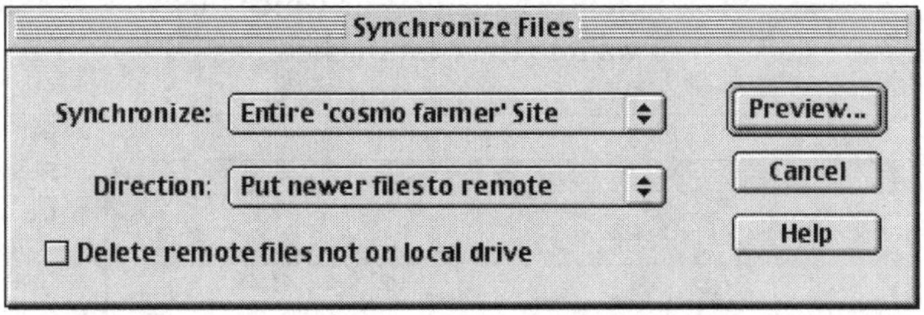

4. **Turn on the Delete checkbox, if desired.**

   The wording of this option reflects the option you selected in the previous step. If you're moving newer files *to* the remote site, it says "Delete remote files not on local drive." It's a useful option when, for example, you've spent the afternoon cleaning up the local copy of your site, deleting old, orphaned graphics files and Web pages, for example, and you want Dreamweaver to update the Web server to match.

   If you chose to transfer newer files *from* the remote site, Dreamweaver lets you "Delete local files not on remote server." Use this feature when your local site is hopelessly out of date with the remote site. Perhaps you're working on the site with a team, but you've been on vacation for two months (this is, of course, a hypothetical example). The site may have changed so significantly that you want to get your local copy in line with the Web site.

Note: Of course, you should proceed with caution when using *any* command that automatically deletes files. This operation cannot been undone, and you don't want to accidentally delete the only copy of a particular page, graphic, or external Cascading Style Sheet.

If you chose the "Get and put new files" option in step 3, the Delete checkbox is dimmed and unavailable. This option truly synchronizes the two; Dreamweaver copies newer files on the remote site (including files that exist on the Web server but not on your computer) to your local site, and vice-versa.

5. **Click Preview to begin the synchronization process.**

Dreamweaver connects to the remote site and compares the two sets of files—if your site is large, a time-consuming process. When it finishes, the Synchronize preview window appears (see Figure 16-12), listing which files Dreamweaver will delete and which it will transfer.

6. **Turn off the Action boxes next to any files you don't want Dreamweaver to touch.**

For example, if you realize that Dreamweaver is going to delete a file that you *know* you need, uncheck the box next to that file. When you do this, "skip" appears next to the file in the Status column (see Figure 16-12). This is your last chance to determine which files you want to transfer and delete, and which you want to leave untouched.

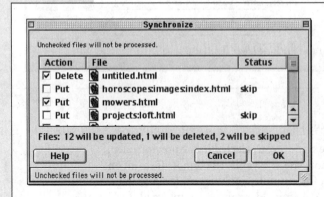

Figure 16-12:
The Synchronize window lets you preview any actions Dreamweaver intends to take to synchronize the files on your local and remote sites. You can deselect any actions you don't want, or simply back out of the whole process without making any changes by clicking Cancel.

7. **Click OK to proceed, or Cancel to stop the synchronization.**

If you click OK, Dreamweaver commences copying and deleting the chosen files. If you want to stop this process, click the red Stop icon in the Synchronize window (see the box on page 424).

8. **Click Close.**

Tip: If you just want to *identify* newer files on the local site without synchronizing them (to run a report on them, for example), choose Edit→Select Newer Local in the Site window menu bar (Windows) or choose Site→Site Files View→Select Newer Local (Mac). Dreamweaver connects to the remote site and compares the files, then, in the Site window's Local Folder list, highlights files on the Local site that are newer than their remote counterparts.

You can also identify newer files on the remote site: Choose Edit→Select Newer Remote from the Site window menu bar (Windows) or choose Site→Site Files View→Select Newer Remote (Mac). As with the Synchronization command, these options are unavailable if you're using Visual SourceSafe (page 417).

Communicating with Design Notes

Lots of questions arise when a team works on a Web site: Has this page been proof-read? Who is the author of the page? Where did this graphic come from? Usually, you must rely on a flurry of emails to ferret out the answers.

But Dreamweaver's Design Notes dialog box (Figure 16-14) eliminates much of that hassle by letting you attach information, such as a Web page's status or author, to a file. You can open these notes (from the Site window or from a currently open document), edit them, and even share them with others. In this way, it's easy to leave notes for other people—such as, "Hey Bob, can you make sure that this is the most recent photo of the Anodyne 1000?" You can even add notes to files other than Web pages including folders, images, Flash movies, and external Cascading Style Sheets—anything, in fact, that appears in the Site window.

Setting Up Design Notes

You can't use Design Notes unless the feature itself is turned on. To find out, open the Site Definition dialog box by double-clicking the site's name in the Define Sites dialog box (choose Define Sites from the Site menu or the pop-up menu in the Site

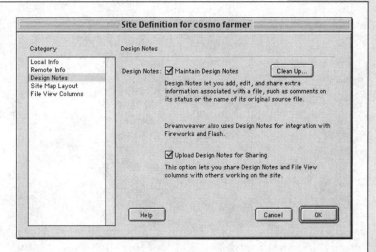

Figure 16-13:
The Clean Up button deletes any notes that were attached to now-deleted files. (To avoid stray notes files in the first place, always delete pages in Dreamweaver's Site window, rather than just deleting them on your computer.) If you turn off the Design Notes feature by unchecking the Maintain Design Notes box, clicking Clean Up removes all Design Notes files for the site. (Unfortunately, Dreamweaver still spews the ubiquitous _notes folders all over your hard drive.)

window). In the Category list, click Design Notes; as shown in Figure 16-13, two checkboxes pertain to the notes feature:

- **Maintain Design Notes.** This checkbox lets you create and read notes using Dreamweaver's File→Design Notes command (see the next section).

- **Upload Design Notes for Sharing.** If you're using Design Notes as part of a team, turn on this checkbox, which makes Dreamweaver upload design notes to the remote site, so that your fellow team members can read them.

Note: Design Notes are especially useful for keeping track of pages that are built and maintained by a team of developers. But if you're a solo operator and still want to use them—maybe you're the type with a hundred Post-it notes taped to the edges of your monitor—then turn off Upload Design Notes for Sharing. You'll save time and server space by preventing Dreamweaver from transferring note files to the Web server.

Click OK to close the Site Definition dialog box; you can double-click another site in the Define Sites dialog box to turn on its Design Notes feature, or click Done.

Adding Design Notes to a File

To add a design note to a document you're working on, choose your favorite method:

- Choose File→Design Notes.

- Choose Design Notes from the File Status menu in the toolbar (see Figure 16-8).

POWER USERS' CLINIC

Create Your Own Status Menu

The Status pop-up menu in Design Notes is a great feature. With a flick of the mouse, you can assign a status to a page or file, letting others know if a page is finished or just a rough draft. But the preset status options may not exactly fit your process. Your team may not use the terms "alpha" or "beta"; instead, you may have other stages you'd like to add, such as "copy edit" to signify that a page is ready to be proofread and tested.

With a little sly hacking, you can change the status categories to suit your needs. The file Design Notes.htm, in the Dreamweaver 4→Configuration→Commands folder, holds the key to this puzzle. Start by making a safety copy of the file; you can always return to it if something goes wrong.

Then open this file in a text editor like NotePad or Simple-Text, or even within Dreamweaver's Code view (page 243).

Find line 28 in the file, which looks like this:

```
var STATUS_ITEMS = new
Array("","draft","revision1","revision2","revision3",
"alpha","beta","final","needs atten-
tion");
```

The words between the double-quotes are the choices that appear in the Status menu. You can change or delete them as you see fit (if you delete one, be sure to delete the word, both sets of quotation marks, and the following comma). Then, after saving changes to the file, quit and restart Dreamweaver, where you'll see your new, improved Status pop-up menu ready for action.

To make sure you and your co-workers see the same choices, give each of them the modified Design Notes.htm file; advise them to put it in their own Dreamweaver 4→Configuration→Commands folders.

• Right-click (Control-click) a file in the Site window (or an external object, such as a graphic or Flash movie, in the document window), and choose Design Notes from the contextual menu.

In any case, the Design Notes window now opens (Figure 16-14). If you like, you can use the Status pop-up menu to let your team members know where the file stands. For example, is it ready to move to the Web server? Is it just a draft version? Or is there something wrong with it that requires specific attention? Dreamweaver provides eight different options: draft, revision1, revision2, revision3, alpha, beta, final,

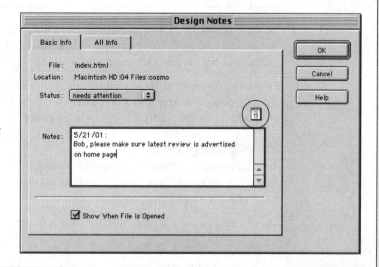

Figure 16-14:
If you want the Design Notes window to open whenever someone opens the page, turn on Show When File is Opened. This option makes sure no one misses an important note attached to a Web page. When the page is opened in Dreamweaver, the Design Notes window appears automatically. (This option has no effect when adding notes to GIFs, JPEGs, Flash movies, or anything other than a Web page.)

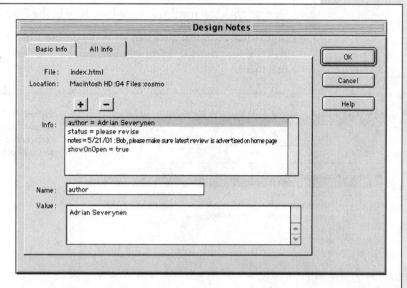

Figure 16-15:
Dreamweaver lets you create your own types of notes in the All Info tab of the Design Notes window. This lets you add more information to a page such as its author or designer. If you want to delete a note you've added, it's a simple matter of clicking on the note in the Info box and clicking the – (minus) button.

and needs attention; if these categories don't match your workflow—for example, you want a "needs proofing" flag—you can change them; see the box on page 434.

The note itself, which you type into the Note box, could be a simple question you have for the author of the page ("Are you sure 'Nsync: Defining a New Musical Language for the Modern Age' is an appropriate title for this article?") or more information about the status of the page ("Still need studio shot of apartment sod kit").

Tip: Click the calendar icon (circled in Figure 16-14) to pop the date into your note—a great way to keep a running tally of notes and the dates they were made.

When you click OK, Dreamweaver creates a file with all note information in it. This file ends with the extension .mno and begins with the name of the file; for the file *index.html,* for example, the note would be called *index.html.mno.*

Dreamweaver stores notes in a folder called *_notes* that it keeps in the same folder as the page or file. For example, if you add notes to the home page, Dreamweaver stores the notes file in the *_notes* folder inside the root folder.

Viewing Design Notes

You can view design notes in a number of ways. If the note's author turned on Show When File Is Opened (see Figure 16-14), of course, the Design Notes window opens automatically when you open that page.

Otherwise, to look at a note, you have any number of options:

- Choose File→Design Notes.

- Choose Design Notes from the document window's toolbar (see Figure 16-8).

- Double-click the small yellow balloon icon in the Site window (Figure 16-16).

- Right-click (Control-click) an embedded object like a graphic or Flash Movie, right there in the document window, and choose Design Notes from the contextual menu.

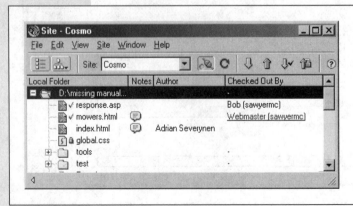

Figure 16-16:
A yellow speech bubble in the Notes column of the Site window indicates a Design Notes file.

Organizing the Columns in the Site Window

The Site window's columns identify a file's name, file size, modification date, type, and so on.

Tip: You can adjust the relative widths of these columns by dragging the dividing line between the column names. You can also sort all the pages listed in this window by clicking the relevant column's name; clicking Modified, for example, sorts the files so that the newest appear first. Click a second time to reverse the sort, placing oldest files first.

This may be more information than you're interested in—or it might not be enough. Fortunately, Dreamweaver lets you show or hide these various columns, change their order, or even create new columns with information retrieved from a file's Design Notes (see page 434).

When you're setting up a Web site in the Site Definition window, you can view the column setup by clicking the File View Columns category (see Figure 16-17). If you're already working on a Web site, you may find it faster to choose View→File View Columns in the Site window (Windows) or Site→Site Files View→File Views Column (Mac).

Once you're looking at the display shown in Figure 16-17, you can perform any of these stunts:

- **Reorder columns.** Click a column name in the Site Definition window to select it. Then click the up and down arrow buttons to move the column one spot to the left or right, respectively, in the Site window.

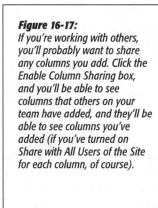

Figure 16-17:
If you're working with others, you'll probably want to share any columns you add. Click the Enable Column Sharing box, and you'll be able to see columns that others on your team have added, and they'll be able to see columns you've added (if you've turned on Share with All Users of the Site for each column, of course).

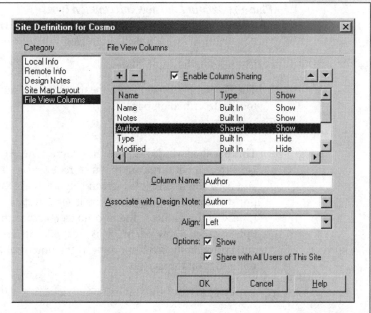

- **Hide columns.** You may not care what date a file was last modified or whether it's a folder or Web page; to hide a column, click its name in the Site Definition window and then turn off the Show checkbox (see Figure 16-17). (You can always return to the Site Definition window and turn the column back on.)

- **Share a column.** If you work with a team of designers, you might want to make newly added columns (see the next section) visible to them, too; see Figure 16-17 for details.

- **Adding Columns.** You can add new columns of your own, as described next.

- **Deleting columns.** Click the column name, and then click the minus (–) button to delete the column. (Dreamweaver doesn't let you delete the built-in columns: Name, Notes, Type, Modified, and so on.)

"All Info" Design Notes in Column Views

Your Site window offers columns for all the usual information bits: Name, Checked Out, and so on. But you may someday wish there were a column that showed each page's status, so that your Site window could show you which files need proofreading, or who wrote each article, or which pages are being held until a certain blackout date.

You can indeed add columns of your own design, although the process isn't streamlined by any means. It involves two broad efforts: First, using an offshoot of the Design Notes feature described earlier, you set up the new columns you'll want displayed; then, using the column-manipulation dialog box shown in Figure 16-17, you make them visible in the Site window.

Phase 1: Defining the new information types

You create new kinds of informational flags—primarily for use as new columns in the Site window—using the Design Notes dialog box. Here's the rundown:

1. **Choose File→Design Notes.**

   The Design Notes window appears. (You can summon it in various other ways, too, as described on page 436.)

2. **Click the All Info tab.**

   This peculiar window shows the programmery underbelly of the Dreamweaver Notes feature; it turns out that it stores every kind of note as a name/value pair. If you used the main Notes screen (Figure 16-14) to choose Beta from the Status pop-up menu, for example, you'll see a notation here that says "status=beta." (*Status* is the name of the info nugget; *beta* is the value.) If you turned on the option called Show When File is Opened, you'll see "showOnOpen=true." And if you typed *Badly needs updating* as the note itself, you'll see "notes=Badly needs updating" on this screen.

   But those are just the built-in info types; you're free to create your own.

3. **Click the + button.**

You may wonder why you'd do this; after all you can type a lot of information in the Notes box under the Basic Info tab. The primary benefit of creating new types of notes is that you can display that information in the Site window.

4. **Type the name of the new note in the Name field.**

It might be Author, for example, so that you can note who wrote the text of each page. Or it could be Artist, if you wish to add a note to each image specifying who created it. Maybe you need a column called Hold Until, which lets you know when certain information is OK to publish online.

5. **Press Tab (to jump to the Value field); type the contents of the note.**

This might be the actual name of the author or artist—Jane Stevens, for example— or the actual "Hold Until" date.

Tip: Keep the value short—one or two words. Otherwise, the narrow Site window column will chop off the latter part of it.

Repeat steps 3 through 5 if you want to add more notes to the page or file.

6. **Click OK.**

The dialog box closes.

Phase 2: Adding the column

Just creating a new note type gets you only halfway home; now you have to tell Dreamweaver that you want to *see* that information in the Site window, like this:

1. **Choose View→File View Columns in the Site window (Windows) or Site→Site Files View→File Views Column (Mac).**

The File Views dialog box appears.

2. **Click the + button (Figure 16-17).**

A new, untitled column is added to the list, complete with three fields that need filling in (they now say "untitled").

3. **In the Column Name box, type the column heading name you want to appear in the Site window.**

Make it short and descriptive. If possible, it should match the note type (Author, Artist, Hold Until, or whatever).

4. **Press Tab. Type the name of the Design Note you wish to use for this column.**

This is the name part of the name/value pair described in step 4 of the previous instructions. For example, if you added a note named Author to a file, you would type *author* in this field. Capitalization doesn't matter.

There's a pop-up menu here, too, but it always lists the same four options: Status, Assigned, Due, and Priority. If you choose Status, you'll get a column that reflects your choice from the Status pop-up menu shown in Figure 16-14. The other three options do nothing *unless* you created a matching note type in step 4 of the previous instructions. (It would be nice if this pop-up menu listed *all* of the note names you've created, so that you didn't have to remember them. Maybe in Dreamweaver 5.)

Before you wrap up the column-adding procedure, you can, if you wish, choose an alignment option for the text in the Site column (left, right, or center); check to make sure that the Show checkbox is turned on (otherwise, your new column won't appear, and you've just defeated the purpose of this whole exercise); and turn on Share with All Users of the Site, if you like.

The Share feature works like this. The next time you connect to the remote site, Dreamweaver uploads a file containing your newly defined column information. The next time another member of the team connects to the remote site, *his* copy of Dreamweaver downloads this file, so that his Site window shows the same columns yours does.

Note: The column-sharing feature is very handy; it lets everyone working on a site share the same note information. But it works properly only if everyone on the team has the Enable Column Sharing box turned on (see Figure 16-17).

---

5. **Click OK.**

   You should now see the new information column in your Site window, as shown in Figure 16-18. (If not, you may need to widen the window to reveal the additional column.)

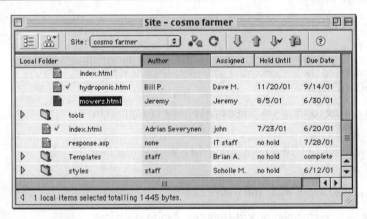

Figure 16-18:
The Site window can show newly created kinds of status information. Each is actually a Design Note you've invented. To sort the list, click the gray column heading.

Part Five:
Dreamweaver Power

5

Libraries and Templates

You've finished the design for your company's new Web site. It looks great and your boss is ecstatic. But you've only just begun. There are hundreds of pages to build before you launch the site. And once it's online, you'll make endless updates to keep it fresh and inviting. This is where Dreamweaver's site management features come into play, making the sometimes tedious work of building and updating Web pages much easier.

On most sites, many pages may have certain elements in common: a copyright notice, a navigation bar, or a logo. In fact, dozens of Web pages may be identical except for the text; for instance, a company Web site with an employee directory may dedicate a single Web page to each employee. Each of those pages probably has the same navigation bar, banner, footer, and layout; only a few particulars differ, such as the employee name, photo, and contact information.

For any of these situations, your first instinct should be to exploit Dreamweaver's Library items and Templates.

Library Basics

Imagine this situation: You manage a relatively large Web site consisting of thousands of Web pages. At the bottom of each page is a simple copyright notice: "Copyright MyBigCompany. We reserve all rights—national, international, commercial, noncommercial, and mineral—to the content contained on these pages." Each time you add another page to the site, you could retype the copyright message, but this approach invites both typographic errors and carpal tunnel syndrome. And if you must *format* this text too, then you're in for quite a bit of work.

Fortunately, Dreamweaver's Library can turn any selection in the document window (a paragraph, an image, a table) into a reusable chunk of HTML that, later, you can easily drop into any Dreamweaver document. The Library, in other words, is a great place to store copyright notices, navigation bars, or any other snippet of HTML you use frequently.

But this is only half of the Library's power. When you add a Library item to a Web page, it's actually only a copy that remains linked to the original. That means whenever you update the original Library item, you may choose to update every page that uses that item.

Suppose your company is bought, for example, and the legal department orders you to change the copyright notice to "Copyright MyBigCompany, a subsidiary of aMuchBiggerCompany" on each of the Web site's *10,000 pages*. If you had cleverly inserted the original copyright notice as a Library item, you could take care of this task in the blink of an eye. Just open the item in the Library, make the required changes, save it, and let Dreamweaver update all the pages for you (Figure 17-1).

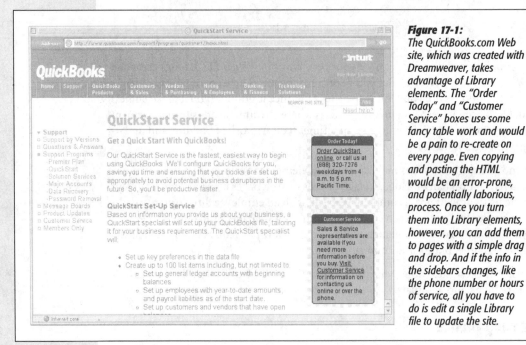

Figure 17-1:
The QuickBooks.com Web site, which was created with Dreamweaver, takes advantage of Library elements. The "Order Today" and "Customer Service" boxes use some fancy table work and would be a pain to re-create on every page. Even copying and pasting the HTML would be an error-prone, and potentially laborious, process. Once you turn them into Library elements, however, you can add them to pages with a simple drag and drop. And if the info in the sidebars changes, like the phone number or hours of service, all you have to do is edit a single Library file to update the site.

Create and Use Library Items

To create a Library item, start by opening the Library window itself. Choose Window→Library, or, if the Assets panels is already open, click the Library items button (it looks like an open book, as shown in Figure 17-2) to reveal the Library category.

Now select the part of your document that you wish to save as a Library item: a blob of text, a graphic, or whatever.

Note, however, that Library items can only contain page elements that appear in the document window—in other words, only HTML from the <body> of a Web page. You can't include anything that appears in the *head* of a page, like timelines (see page 337), Cascading Style Sheets, Dreamweaver Behaviors (Chapter 11), or meta tags. Furthermore, Library items must include a complete set of HTML tags—both an opening and closing tag—and include all tags necessary to complete the original object. For example, Dreamweaver won't let you turn just a single cell, row, or column in a table into a Library item. If you try, Dreamweaver will add the *entire* table to the Library.

Tip: Use the tag selector (page 16) to make sure you select precisely what you want.

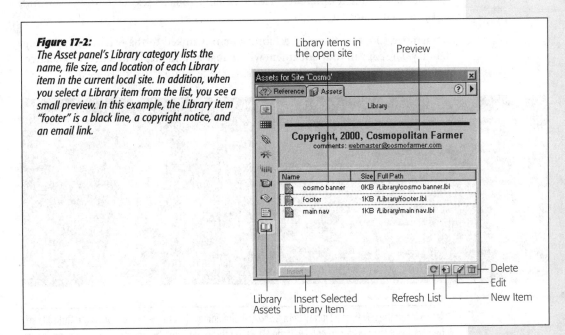

Figure 17-2:
The Asset panel's Library category lists the name, file size, and location of each Library item in the current local site. In addition, when you select a Library item from the list, you see a small preview. In this example, the Library item "footer" is a black line, a copyright notice, and an email link.

Next, add the selection to the Library. As you may expect, Dreamweaver provides several ways to do this:

- Drag the highlighted selection into the list of Library items.
- Click the New Library Item button (Figure 17-2).
- Choose Modify→Library→Add Object to Library.
- Press Ctrl+Shift+B (⌘-Shift-B).

The new item appears in the Assets panel, bearing the jaunty name "untitled." Just type to replace that proposal with a more useful name, such as *Copyright notice* or *Logo*. Your new Library element is ready to use.

Add Library Items to a Page

To add a Library item to a Web page, just drag it directly out of the Assets panel onto your page. (The long way: Click to plant your insertion point in the Web page, click the Library item you want in the Assets panel, and click the Insert button on the Assets panel, shown in Figure 17-2.)

When you insert a piece of Library item into a Web page (or turn a selected item *into* a Library item), it sprouts a light yellow background color—or, in the case of non-transparent graphics, it takes on a gray, darkened look. The highlighting indicates that Dreamweaver intends to treat the Library item as a single object, even though it may be made of many different HTML elements. You can select it or drag it around, but you can't change it.

Remember, too, that the placed Library item is linked to the original copy in the Library. The copy in your document will change automatically to reflect any changes you make to the copy in the Library, using the technique described next.

Under the Hood of Library Items

Behind the scenes, Dreamweaver stores the HTML for Library items in basic text files. Those files' names end with the extension *.lbi,* and they stay in the Library folder inside your local site folder.

When you insert a Library item into a Web page, Dreamweaver inserts the item's HTML and adds a set of *comment* tags. These tags refer to the original Library file and help Dreamweaver remember where the Library item begins and ends. For instance, if you turned the text "Copyright 2001" into a Library item called *copyright* and inserted it into a Web page, Dreamweaver would add the following HTML to the page:

<!--#BeginLibraryItem "/Library/copyright.lbi"-->Copyright 2001<!--#EndLibraryItem-->

Tip: To insert the HTML of a Library item *without* maintaining a link to the Library, press the Ctrl (⌘) key when adding it to your document. Now the HTML on this page won't be updated when you change the original Library file.

You can also break the link between the Library and a Library item you've already placed onto a Web page. Select the item on the page and then click Detach from Original in the Property inspector (Figure 17-3). Dreamweaver removes the comment tags (see the box above), thus breaking the link to the Library.

Edit Library Items

You'll appreciate the real power of Library items when it's time to make a change. When you update the file in the Library, all the pages that you've graced with that item update themselves, too.

Start by opening the Library, as described on page 444. Then:

1. **Open the Library item that you want to edit.**

   You can do this by double-clicking the Library item in the Assets panel, by highlighting it and then clicking the Edit button (Figure 17-2), or by highlighting a Library item on a Web page and then clicking the Open button on the Property inspector (Figure 17-3).

   Dreamweaver opens what looks like a miniature Web page document, containing nothing but the text, graphics, or other elements of the Library file.

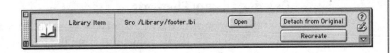

Figure 17-3:
The Property inspector shows that the selected Library item (a .lbi file) is in the site's Library folder. (The path appears after the word Src.)

2. **Edit away.**

   A Library item is only a selection of HTML; it's not a complete Web page. That means you can't edit page properties like the title or background color. Also, Library items can only be inserted in the body of a Web page, so stick with objects that would normally appear in the document window, such as links, images, tables, and text. Don't add any code that appears in the head of a Web page, such as Cascading Style Sheets, meta tags, behaviors, or timelines.

3. **Choose File→Save.**

   Dreamweaver checks to see if there are any pages that use the Library item, and if there are, opens the Update Library Items window. A list of all pages in the site that use that Library item appears.

4. **Click Update.**

   Dreamweaver opens the Update Pages window, updates the HTML in all the pages that use the Library item, and then lists all of the files that it changed.

   On the other hand, you don't necessarily have to click Update. Perhaps you have a lot of changes to make to the Library item, and you just want to save the work you've done so far. You're not done editing it yet, so you don't want to waste time updating pages that you'll just have to update again. You can always update later (see the box on page 459); in that case, click Don't Update.

5. **Click Done.**

   As you can see, the Library is an incredible timesaver that greatly simplifies the process of changing common page elements.

Renaming Library Elements

To rename something in your Library, click its name on the Assets panel (Figure 17-2). On the Mac, the name immediately becomes highlighted for editing; on Windows, you must pause briefly, click again, and *then* type the new name.

If you've already added the item to your Web pages, Dreamweaver prompts you to update those pages. Click the Update button; otherwise, the link will break between those pages and the Library.

Tip: If you accidentally click Don't Update, don't panic. Simply change the Library item back to its original name, and then *re*-rename it; don't forget to click Update this time!

Deleting Library Elements

You can delete unnecessary elements from your Library at any time—but do so with caution. When you delete something from the Library, Dreamweaver leaves behind every copy of it that you've already placed onto your Web pages—complete with links to the now deleted Library item!

In other words, you won't be able to edit the copies on your Web pages until you break those links. If you do indeed want to edit them, you'll have to do that manually on each page where the Library item appears, first selecting the item and then clicking the Detach from File button (see Figure 17-3).

You've been warned; now here are the instructions. To get rid of a Library item, click it in the Assets panel, and then do one of the following:

- Click the Trash can icon in the Assets panel.
- Press the Delete key.
- Right-click (Control-click) the item's name and choose Delete from the contextual menu.

Tip: If you ever accidentally delete an item from the Library, you can re-create it, provided you've used it somewhere on one of the Web pages in the site.

Open the page containing the Library item; click the Library item to select it. Click Recreate on the Property inspector (Figure 17-3) to make it anew. (It means "re-create"; it has nothing to do with recreation at, say, the local community center.) A new Library item appears in the Library, using the name and HTML from the item you selected.

Template Basics

Some Web designers handcraft sites with loving care, changing layouts, colors, fonts, banners, and navigation from page to page. But that kind of approach isn't always practical—or desirable. Consistency is a good thing. Web pages that look and act similarly reassure visitors; when only important material changes from page to page, readers can concentrate on finding the information they want. Even more importantly, a handcrafted approach is often unrealistic when you're designing on a deadline.

This is where *templates* come in. As noted earlier, the underlying design of many pages on many Web sites is identical, as shown in Figure 17-4.

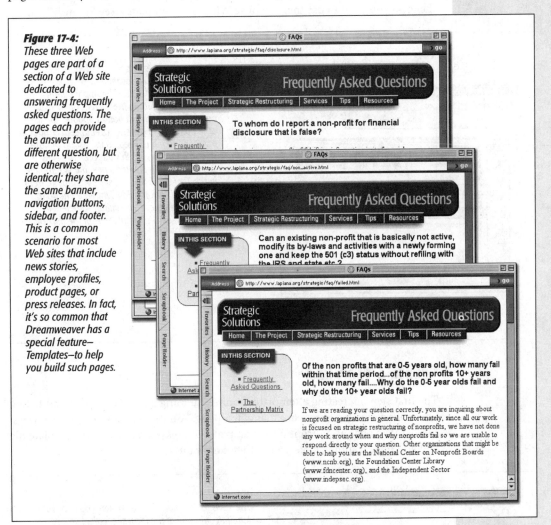

Figure 17-4:
These three Web pages are part of a section of a Web site dedicated to answering frequently asked questions. The pages each provide the answer to a different question, but are otherwise identical; they share the same banner, navigation buttons, sidebar, and footer. This is a common scenario for most Web sites that include news stories, employee profiles, product pages, or press releases. In fact, it's so common that Dreamweaver has a special feature—Templates—to help you build such pages.

Templates help you take advantage of this fact to quickly build pages. A new page based on a template looks just like the template, but you can only edit certain areas of the page, called, logically enough, *editable regions*. In the example shown in Figure 17-4, the editable region includes the question-and-answer text area; the rest of the page remains untouched and is, in fact, locked. Templates let you build pages that share a similar structure and graphic identity, quickly and without having to worry about accidentally deleting or changing elements.

Like Library items, pages based on templates retain a reference to the original Template file. Any changes made to the template can be automatically passed on to all pages created from it, which can save you tons of time and trouble when it comes time to update the look or structure of your site.

Also like Library items, Templates live on the Assets panel. To see the Templates and the tools you need to use them, choose Window→Templates (see Figure 17-5).

Templates in the current site
Preview

Figure 17-5:
The Asset panel's Templates category lists the name, file size, and location of each template in the current local site. The Apply button applies a template to the current open Web page. The Refresh List button updates the list of templates. (In general, Dreamweaver does a very good job of keeping the list up to date, so you'll rarely need this button.) The New Template button creates a new blank template in the Templates folder. Select a template from the list and click the Edit Template button to open the template for editing. To delete a template, select a template from the list and click the Delete button.

Delete
Edit
New Item

Template Assets
Apply Selected Template to Page
Refresh List

Create a Template

The first step in creating a template requires building a basic Web page and telling Dreamweaver you'd like to use it as a Template. You can go about this in two ways: Build a Web page and turn it into a template, or create a blank empty Template file and add text, graphics, tables, and other content to it.

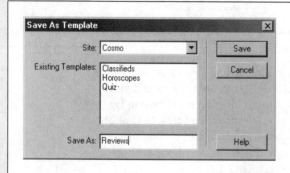

Figure 17-6:
The Save As Template dialog box lets you save your template into any of the local site folders you've defined within Dreamweaver. Stick to your current local site to avoid broken links and other problems.

Turning a Web Page into a Template

The easiest way to create a template is simply to base it on a Web page in your current site folder. Although you can create templates based on Web pages that *aren't* part of the current local site, you may run into problems with links and paths to images, as described in a moment.

Once you've opened the Web page, just choose File→Save As Template. In the Save As Template window (Figure 17-6), the name of the current local site appears in the Site pop-up menu; you see all templates for that site listed in the Existing Templates field.

Note: At this point, you could theoretically use the Site menu to save a template into any local site folder you've defined (see Chapter 14 for a discussion of local sites), but be careful with this option. If your page contains images and links, and you save it as a template for another local site, Dreamweaver won't copy the images from the first site folder into the other one; as a result, the paths to the image files and links won't work correctly.

If you must use a page from one site as a template for another, *copy* the Web page *and graphics* into the new site's root folder, open the page from there, and then create a template as described here.

FREQUENTLY ASKED QUESTION

The Broken-Link Blues

Why aren't links in my templates working?

When you created the link, you must have *typed* a path into the Property inspector's Link field—a recipe for heartbreak. Instead, always select the target Web page for a link by clicking the folder icon in the Property inspector, or by pressing Ctrl+L (⌘-L); in other words, link to pages within the site by *browsing* to the desired file.

Dreamweaver saves templates in the Templates folder inside the local root folder; all *relative* links need to be relative to this location (absolute links, like those to other Web sites, aren't a problem; see page 81 for the difference). The reason you should browse to, rather than type in, your links is so that Dreamweaver can create a proper relative link.

Imagine this situation: You create a template for your classified ads. You'll store all classified ads for April 2001 inside a series of folders like this: *classifieds→2001→april,*

as shown in the site diagram here.

A link from a page in the *april* folder to the home page would follow the path marked 1 here. So when creating a link on your template, you might create a link to the home page by typing the path *../../../index.html.*

That's a logical choice if you're thinking about the page (in the *april* folder) you'll create *from* the template—but it won't work. Dreamweaver stores templates in the Templates folder, so the correct path would be path 2, or *../index.html.* When you create a new page *based on* the template and save it in the *april* folder, Dreamweaver, in its wisdom, automatically rewrites all paths in the page so that the links function correctly.

The beauty of Dreamweaver is that *you* don't have to understand how all this works. Just remember to use *relative* links in your templates; create your links by clicking the folder icon in the Property inspector.

Finally, type a name for the new template, and then click Save. Dreamweaver saves the page in the Templates folder of your local site root folder; it adds the extension .dwt to the file to indicate that it's a Dreamweaver template.

Building a Template from Scratch

It's easiest to create a Web page first and then save it as a template, but you can also build one from scratch. Once you've opened the Asset panel's Templates category (see page 450), click the New Template button at the bottom of the Assets panel; once Dreamweaver adds a new, untitled template to the list, type a new name for it. Something descriptive, like "press release" or "employee page," will help you keep track of your templates.

After you've created a blank template for the site, you can open it by double-clicking its name in the Assets panel (or select its name and then click the Edit Template button at the bottom of the Assets panel). It opens just like any Web page, so that you can get busy designing it as you would any Web page.

POWER USERS' CLINIC

Under the Hood of Templates

Dreamweaver saves templates as HTML files in the Templates folder inside your current local site folder (see Chapter 14 for information on local sites); each template has the filename extension .dwt to distinguish it from regular Web pages. The program treats files in the Templates folder differently than normal Web pages, so don't save anything but .dwt files there. In addition, since Dreamweaver expects the Templates folder to be in the local root folder of your site, don't *move* the Templates folder. If you do, your templates won't work.

As with Library items, Dreamweaver uses HTML comment tags to indicate the name of the template. If you inspect a template-based document's HTML code (see Chapter 9), you'll see that, immediately following the opening <html>

tag, Dreamweaver inserts a comment tag with the text *#BeginTemplate* followed by the location and name of the template. Additional comment tags indicate areas of the page that you can modify. For instance, the title of a page based on a template is always editable; its comment tag might look like this:

```
<!--#BeginEditable "doctitle"-->
<title>My New Page</title>
<!--#EndEditable-->
```

The first comment indicates the editable region's beginning and also includes the editable region's name. When editing pages based on the template, you can change only the HTML between these comment tags. Everything else on the page is locked.

Define Editable Regions

Your next project is to specify which parts of your template are locked, and which are editable. By default, *everything* on a page is locked. After all, the main reason to use templates is to keep a consistent, unchanging design and structure between pages. To make a template usable, you must define the area or areas you *can* change.

To add an editable region to a template, start by selecting the part of the page you want to be able to change. You can incorporate anything in the document window (any HTML between the <body> tags); HTML that appears in the <head> of a page, such as meta tags, Cascading Style Sheets, and JavaScript, is always locked.

Drag across your page to select the elements you wish to make editable, or, for greater precision, you can use the tag selector (page 16) to make sure you select the exact HTML you want.

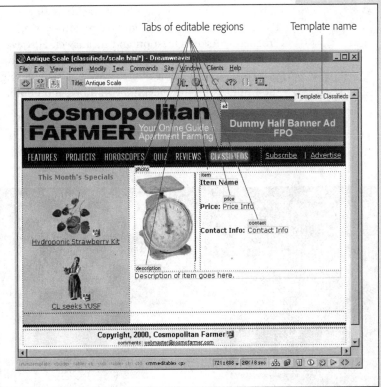

Figure 17-7:
This page is based on a template called Classifieds, as you can tell from the little tab in the document window's upper-right corner. You can modify editable regions; they're labeled with small tabs. In this example, the editable regions are called ad, photo, price, item, contact, *and* description. *You can also edit the title of any page created from a template. All the other parts of the page are locked; you can only make changes by re-opening the original template file.*

Tabs of editable regions

Template name

Now tell Dreamweaver that the selected elements are to be editable. You can use any of these techniques:

- Choose Modify→Templates→New Editable Region.

- Press Ctrl+Alt+V (⌘-Option-V).

- Right-click (Control-click) the selection and choose New Editable Region from the contextual menu.

When the New Editable Region dialog box appears, type a name for the region (you can't use the same name twice) and click OK. You return to your template, where the name you gave the region appears in a small blue tab above the editable region (see Figure 17-7).

Tip: If you use tables to lay out your pages (see Chapter 6), you'll often assign one table cell as the main area to hold the primary content of the page. For example, in the pages shown in Figure 17-4, the Frequently Asked Question and its answer appear in a single cell on the page. This cell makes a perfect editable region for a template. In the tag selector, just click the <td> tag associated with that cell and use any of the techniques discussed here to convert it to an editable region.

You may find that a single editable region is all you need. For example, the pages in Figure 17-4 have only one editable region—a single table cell where you can add a Frequently Asked Question and its answer. However, if you need to edit *multiple* areas of a Web page, add more editable regions to the template. For instance, when you create a template for an employee page, you might create editable regions for the employee's name, telephone number, and photo.

If you change your mind and want to lock a region again, simply choose Modify→Templates→Remove Editable Region. The Remove Editable Region dialog box appears, listing all of the editable regions in the template. Select the name of the region you wish to lock and click OK.

FREQUENTLY ASKED QUESTION

Hindered by Highlighting

I'm distracted by the tabs and background colors that Dreamweaver uses to indicate Library items and Templates. How do I get rid of them?

When you use Library items or Templates, you'll see blue tabs and yellow backgrounds to indicate editable regions and Library items. Although these visual cues don't appear in a Web browser, they can still make your page harder to read while working in Dreamweaver. Fortunately, you can alter the background color of these items and even turn highlighting off altogether.

Choose Edit→Preferences or press Ctrl+U (⌘-U). In the Preferences Category list, click Highlighting . To change the

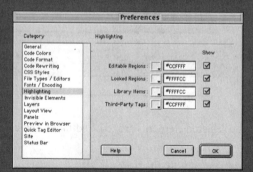

background color for editable regions, locked regions, and Library items, use the color box (page 30) or type in a hexadecimal color value. To remove the highlighting, turn off the Show box next to the appropriate item.

However, it's often useful to keep highlighting on; it's a good way to keep track of Library items and editable regions. If you want to turn off highlighting temporarily, simply choose View→Visual Aids→Invisible Elements, or use the keyboard shortcut Ctrl+Shift+I (⌘-Shift-I) to toggle these visual cues off and on. This technique has the added benefit of hiding table borders, layer borders, and image maps, as well as other invisible elements.

Building Pages From a Template

Building a template is only a prelude to the actual work of building your site. Once you finish your template, it's time to produce pages.

To create a new document based on a template, choose File→New from Template. If the Assets panel is open, right-click (Control-click) the template and choose New from Template from the contextual menu.

Either way, the Select Template dialog box appears (Figure 17-8), listing the templates you've created.

Tip: If you don't want your new Web page linked to the template (so that changes to the template would also affect the Web page), turn off the Update Page when Template Changes checkbox. The result is a new page that looks just like the template, but has no locked regions, so you can edit the entire page. This is useful, for example, when you want to start with the general design and structure of a certain template, but still want to add Cascading Style Sheets or meta tag information.

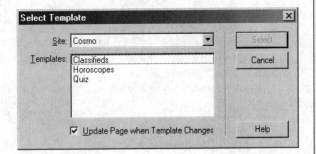

Figure 17-8:
You can use the Site pop-up menu to choose another site you've defined and reveal the list of templates it uses. However, choosing a template stored in a different site is not a good idea. Dreamweaver doesn't copy any images on the template to the current site and can't translate relative links correctly. The result is broken links aplenty.

Finally, double-click the template you want. A new Web page document opens, based on the template, bearing a tab in the upper-right corner that identifies the underlying template name. Dreamweaver outlines any editable regions in blue; a small blue tab displays each region's name (see Figure 17-7).

Dreamweaver makes it painfully obvious which areas you aren't allowed to edit; your cursor changes to a forbidden symbol (⊘) when it ventures into a locked area.

To add content to an editable region, you must first select it, using any of these methods:

- Click anywhere inside the editable region.
- Click the blue tab that holds the region's name.
- Choose Modify→Templates, then choose the region's name from the submenu.

After you select the region, you can type inside it, add graphics, or add any other objects or HTML you can normally add to a document. However, you can't add

Cascading Style Sheets, meta tags, layers, or timelines (items that go in the <head> of an HTML document). You can, however, change the document's title and add Behaviors (see Chapter 11).

Note: Dreamweaver doesn't let you use the Layer tool to draw a layer into an editable region. That's because using this method, Dreamweaver tries to add the code for the layer at the very beginning of the page, which is usually a non-editable region. Instead, click somewhere in an editable region and choose Insert→Layer. You can then work with the layer as you normally would (see Chapter 12).

Furthermore, it's best to not insert the code into a table cell; Netscape Navigator 4 has trouble with that arrangement. The best solution is to add a single paragraph to the template file, and mark *it* as editable. Then use this region in your templated files to insert layers.

FREQUENTLY ASKED QUESTION

Editable Region Errors

When I'm in some editable regions, Dreamweaver beeps and doesn't do anything if I hit Enter to create a new paragraph. Why?

If the editable region doesn't include a paragraph or block-level element, Dreamweaver won't allow you to create a new paragraph. This usually happens when you've created an editable region from too little text.

Look at these two examples of HTML in a template:

```
<p><b><!-#BeginEditable "item"-
    >Item Name<!-#EndEditable-></
    b> </p>
<!-#BeginEditable "description"->
    <p>Description</p><!-
    #EndEditable->
```

The problem is technical, but logical. In the first example, the HTML comment tags (<!-#Begin Editable "item"-> and <!-#EndEditable->) that Dreamweaver uses to mark editable regions enclose nothing but the words "Item Name." Both the bold (<b>) and paragraph (<p>) tags lie *outside* of these comments, so they're locked. You can't modify HTML that's outside an editable region, so in this example, you can't add more paragraphs or change the paragraph to another block-level element such as a header or list.

In the second example, however, the paragraph tag *is* inside an editable region. This time, Dreamweaver will let you add more paragraphs, change the paragraph into a heading, and use any block-level formatting you wish.

If you ever encounter this problem, open the original template file, remove the editable region, and then create a new editable region. Make sure to select at least one paragraph before defining the new region.

You can use this behavior to enforce strict design control over pages created from templates. For example, imagine that you've created a template for your company's personnel pages. You want each employee's name to be a red Heading 1 that uses the font Arial. You also want to make sure that your boss's not-so-attentive nephew (who, unfortunately, has been assigned to your department during his summer break from film school) doesn't accidentally apply the wrong formatting as he builds all of the pages from the template you designed.

All you have to do is turn the text itself into an editable region, but *not the HTML formatting* surrounding it. This technique can prove tricky, because Dreamweaver assumes that you *want* to make the text formatting editable. If you run into trouble, select the text in your template and turn it into an editable region. Next, choose View→Code to view the HTML code. Locate the HTML for the editable region and, if necessary, move the beginning and ending comment tags so that they surround the text but not the formatting.

Applying a Template to a Page You Already Made

What happens if you create a Web page and *then* decide you want it to share the look of a template? No problem. Dreamweaver lets you apply a template to any Web page in your site, as long as that page isn't already based on a template.

To apply a template to a page you've already created:

1. **Choose File→Open to open the page you want to alter.**

   The Web page opens.

2. **Choose Window→Templates.**

   The Assets panel appears and reveals a list of the site's templates.

3. **Click a template in the list on the Assets panel, and then click Apply.**

   The clumsily named Choose Editable Region for Orphaned Content dialog box opens.

4. **Choose what to do with the material that's already on the page.**

   The dialog box lists all of the editable regions of the template. You have to put the Web page's current contents into *one* of them—or get rid of the current contents.

   If you want to keep the content, select the name of an editable region from the list in the dialog box; otherwise, choose (none), which, in effect, creates new blank page based on the template.

   Unfortunately, you can only select a single editable region; if several content regions are in the original, Dreamweaver merges them all into a single editable region. Also, since the <head> region of a template is locked, Dreamweaver will replace the document's Cascading Style Sheets, JavaScript, and meta tags with those from the template.

WORKAROUND WORKSHOP

Add Meta Tags to Pages Created from Templates

You can't change anything in the head of a page created from a template except its title. This restriction is a real pain if you use meta tag information to add page descriptions and keywords to your pages (see page 249).

Fortunately, there's a workaround. Switch to Code view (see page 249) and locate the <title> tag near the top of the page. Notice that the title lies between comment tags that denote an editable region. Here you can take advantage of the fact that Dreamweaver lets you *add* content to an editable region and won't attempt to change this material even if you update the original template file.

Thus, all you have to do is add whatever head content you want to this area. Click immediately after the closing <title> tag and press Enter to create a new line. While you're still in Code view, you can use the Insert menu or the Objects panel to insert meta tags. In fact, you can insert any tags that can go in the head of a Web page, including JavaScript tags.

Note: Although a Library item can't include elements from the <head> of a Web page, you can add HTML that has a Dreamweaver Behavior attached to it. For example, you can turn a navigation bar, complete with rollover buttons, into a Library item. Dreamweaver 4 doesn't store the JavaScript code in the library, but when you insert the Library item into a page, it's smart enough to add the appropriate code to the page so that the behaviors work.

5. **Click OK.**

   Your new page appears.

Updating a Template

Templates aren't just useful for building pages rapidly; they also make quick work of site updates. Pages created from templates maintain a link to the original template file; you can automatically pass changes to a template along to every page built from it. If you used templates to build your site, you probably won't cry on your keyboard when the boss says you must add an additional button and link to the navigation bar. Instead of rebuilding every page, you can simply open the template file, update the navigation bar, and let Dreamweaver apply the update to all the pages.

You update a template (and all the pages based on it) like this:

1. **Choose Window→Templates.**

   The Assets panel appears and reveals a list of the site's templates.

2. **Double-click the template's name to open it.**

   Alternatively, you can select the template in the Assets panel and click the Edit button to open the original template (.dwt) file (see Figure 17-5).

   The template opens.

3. **Edit the template as you would any Web page.**

   Since this is the original template file, you can edit any of the HTML in the document, including Cascading Style Sheets, meta tags, timelines, and layers. You can also add additional editable regions to the page or remove editable regions (see "Adding Editable Regions" earlier in this chapter).

   Take care, however, to edit *only* the areas that you did *not* mark as editable regions. The reason: When you update your pages, any region marked as editable in a template file isn't passed on to pages built from that template. After all, the template is only supposed to dictate the design of those pages' *non*-editable regions.

Note: Be careful when you remove editable regions from a template. If you've already built some pages based on the template, Dreamweaver warns you when you save the template. As described below, you can either *delete* the content that was added to that region in each of the pages you created, or move it to another editable region in the page.

4. **Choose File→Save.**

If you've already created pages based on this template, Dreamweaver opens the Update Template Files dialog box. It lists all the files that use the template.

5. **Click Update to update all files based on the template.**

Dreamweaver automatically applies the changes you made to the pages based on the template. Then, the Update Pages dialog box opens and displays a log of all changes Dreamweaver made to the files in your site.

On a large site, this automatic update feature can be an incredible timesaver, but you may *not* want to click Update, at least not right now. Perhaps you're just saving some of your hard work on the template, but aren't quite finished perfecting it—why waste your time updating all those pages more than once? In such a scenario, click the Don't Update button. You can always update the pages later (see the box below).

6. **Click Close.**

The Update Pages dialog box closes.

You'll need to update all your files even if you make a simple change to the template, such as changing its name.

POWER USERS' CLINIC

Wait to Update

Whenever you modify and save a Library item or a template, Dreamweaver gives you the option to update any pages in the site that are descended from it. Very often, you'll say Yes.

But there are times when you might wait to update the site. If you're making a lot of changes to multiple Library items or Templates, for example, you may wish to wait until you've finished all your edits before letting the changes ripple through your pages. After all, it can take some time to update large sites that have lots of pages.

Dreamweaver lets you update pages that use Library items and templates at any time. Just choose Modify→ Library→Update Pages or Modify→Templates→Update

Pages. Both menu options open the same dialog box.

At this point, you can update pages that use a specific Library item or template by choosing Files that Use from the Look In menu and then selecting the appropriate name from the pop-up menu. If you want to update all pages in the site, choose Entire Site, and select the name of the local site from the pop-up menu. Turn on both the Library Items and Templates checkboxes to update all pages.

When you click Start, Dreamweaver does its work, reporting the results of the update in the Log field at the bottom of the dialog box. If you find the log useless, just turn off Show Log to hide the report. Click Close after Dreamweaver finishes.

Unlinking a Page from a Template

If you're confident that you won't be making any further changes to a page's template, and you'd like to be able to edit the page's locked regions, you can break the link between a page and its template; just choose Modify→Templates→Detach from Template.

All of the HTML in the page is now editable, just as on a regular Web page—which is what it is. You've removed all references to the original template; changes to the template will no longer have any effect on this page.

Library and Template Tutorial

In this tutorial, you'll turn the Cosmopolitan Farmer copyright notice into a reusable Library item and add it to several pages in the site. In addition, you'll create a template for the classified ads and build a page based on it.

Note: The tutorial in this chapter requires the example files from this book's Web site, *www.sawmac.com/ missing/.* Click the Tutorials link to go to the tutorials page. Click to download <u>Library and Template Tutorial– Mac Files</u> or <u>Library and Template Tutorial–Windows Files</u>, depending on the kind of machine you're using.

After your browser downloads and decompresses the files, you should have a DWLibTemp (short for Dreamweaver Libraries and Templates) folder on your computer, containing the Web pages and graphics needed for this tutorial. If you're having difficulties, the Web site contains detailed instructions for downloading the files you'll be using with this book.

Creating a Library Item

Keep track of the location of the DWLibTemp folder; you'll need it in the next step.

1. **Following the instructions on page 24, create a local site in Dreamweaver, choosing the DWLibTemp folder as the root folder.**

    Name the site and set the root folder in the Local Info category of the Site Definition window; don't worry about the Remote Info, Design Notes, or any of the other categories.

2. **In the Site window, double-click the file *index.html*.**

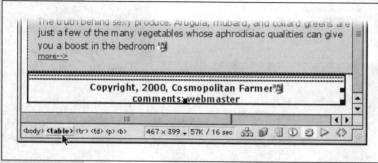

Figure 17-9:
The tag selector at the bottom of the Document window is a great way to select an HTML tag. Here, clicking <table> selects the table containing the site's copyright notice.

The home page opens.

3. **Scroll to the bottom of the page and select the copyright.**

   Copyright information should be on every page of the site, so it makes a perfect candidate for a Library item. Notice that the copyright information is more than just text; it's actually a small table. The best way to select it is to click inside the text, and then click the <table> tag in the status bar of the document window.

4. **Choose Window→Library.**

   The Assets panel opens and displays the Library category.

5. **Click the New Library Item button on the Assets panel.**

   A warning message appears, saying that the Library item may not look the same in other pages. Dreamweaver is trying to tell you that Library items can only contain HTML from the body of a Web page—not Cascading Style Sheets. (You can still include HTML, such as this table, that's had a style applied to it; just make sure that any *pages* to which you add the Library item have the appropriate style sheets.)

   The text in this example *is* formatted using a style sheet, so sure enough, it won't look the same in pages that don't have the same style sheet. In this exercise, however, that won't be a problem; all the pages in the site share the same linked external style sheet (see page 210).

   Click OK to dismiss the warning. The copyright-notice item appears in the Library list, with an "untitled" naming rectangle next to it.

6. **Type *footer* next to the new item on the Assets panel.**

   You've just checked this standard blob of text into your Library. It's ready to use anywhere else on your site.

7. **In your Site window, double-click the file in the *horoscopes* folder called *pisces.html*.**

   Notice that this page is missing a copyright notice at the bottom of the page.

8. **Drag the *footer* Library item from the Assets panel to the bottom of the Pisces page, as shown in Figure 17-10.**

   You can recognize the newly inserted Library item by its yellow background. Click the text in the item and notice that you can't edit it; Dreamweaver treats it like a single object.

9. **Add the footer Library item to the other pages in the *horoscopes* folder.**

   There are eleven other pages in this folder. Open each page (by double-clicking its name in the Site window) and repeat step 8. All right, you don't have to do *all* of the pages, but at least do three or four to experience the full impact of what's next.

(You can close and save the pages as you go, or leave them open. Leave at least one open at the end and go on to step 10.)

10. **Notice the mistake!**

    The copyright notice has the wrong date. The year 2000 is long gone! Oh, great—you'll have to change the date on every page. Fortunately, you've used a Library item; making the change will be a breeze.

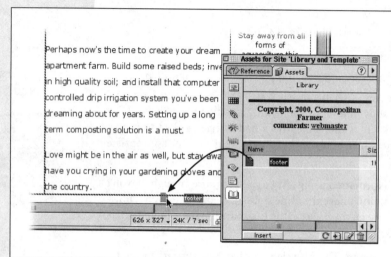

Figure 17-10:
In addition to dragging a Library item into the document window, you can also insert the item, by placing the insertion point in the document window and clicking the Insert button on the Assets panel.

11. **Double-click the footer item's icon (not its name) in the Assets panel.**

    The Library item opens up, ready for editing.

12. **Change *2000* to the current year. Choose File→Save.**

    The Update Library Items dialog box appears, listing all of the pages in the site that use the footer item.

13. **Click Update.**

    Dreamweaver opens the Update Pages dialog box and updates all the Web pages that use the footer item.

14. **Click Close to close the Update Pages dialog box.**

    And *now* if you open a file in the *horoscopes* folder, you'll find that the copyright date is correct.

    Now imagine that you just used this auto-update feature on a 10,000-page site. Sit back and smile.

Creating a Template

This tutorial guides you through the creation of a template, the creation of a page *based* on that template, and then an editing-and-auto-update procedure.

These instructions assume that you've downloaded the necessary tutorial files and selected the resulting DWLibTemp folder as your root folder (both steps are described on page 460).

1. **In the Site window, find and double-click the page *classified_design.html* in the root folder.**

   It's usually easier to start with an already designed Web page and then save it as a Template. For the purposes of getting to bed before midnight tonight, pretend that you've just designed this beautiful, half-finished Web page.

2. **Choose File→Save as Template.**

   The Save as Template dialog box opens.

3. **Name the template *Classified*; click Save.**

   Behind the scenes, Dreamweaver saves the file with the name Classified.dwt in the DWLibTemp→Templates folder, and a new template is born; you can see it in the Templates page of the Assets panel, as well as in the Site window.

   The template is a model for other pages. But although they'll be *based* on its design, they won't be identical; the next step is to identify those areas of the design that will change from page to page—the editable regions.

4. **Click the graphic labeled "Dummy Half Banner Ad" at the top right of the page.**

   For placement purposes, suppose you've put a dummy graphic on the page. When you add new classifieds to the site, you can replace this graphic with a real half-banner ad. To make it possible to replace this dummy graphic with a real ad in the resulting Web pages, you need to mark this graphic as editable, like this:

5. **Choose Modify→Templates→New Editable Region.**

   The New Editable Region dialog box appears.

   Here, as in the following steps, you can also right-click (Control-click) the selected item and choose New Editable Region from the contextual menu, or press Ctrl+Alt+V (⌘-Option-V).

6. **Type *banner ad* and click OK.**

   A small tab, labeled *banner ad,* now appears on the placeholder ad. Now you should define another graphic as replaceable: the one where a photo of the advertised item will go.

7. **Click the black square graphic. Choose Modify→Templates→New Editable Region.**

   Once again, the New Editable Region dialog box appears.

8. Type *photo*; click OK.

There are two more things you'll want to replace every time you create a Web page based on this template: the item name and its description.

9. Select the text "Item Name." Choose Modify→Templates→New Editable Region.

The easiest way to select the text is to click inside it, then click the <p> tag at the bottom edge of the document window (the tag selector), which neatly highlights the entire (one-line) paragraph.

10. Type *item name* and click OK. Make the Description text editable, too.

That is, repeat step 9 (but select the text "Description") and step 10 (but name the new region *description*).

11. Choose File→Save and then close the file.

Congratulations! You've created your first template.

Creating a Page Based on a Template

Now it's time to get down to business and build Web pages. Check the Site menu to make sure you've selected the site that you defined in step 1 (page 460). Then:

1. Choose File→New From Template.

The Select Template dialog box opens. Make sure Update Page when Template Changes is turned on.

2. Double-click Classified in the list.

And lo, a new, untitled Web page document appears, one that looks exactly like the template (Figure 17-11).

3. Choose File→Save. Save the file as *scale.html* in the DWLibTemp→classifieds folder.

(On the Mac, remember the .html extension; Windows adds it automatically.)

Figure 17-11:
In pages based on a template, not only do blue tabs identify editable areas of the page, but a yellow tab appears in the upper-right corner of the document window to indicate that this page is based on a template. Its name appears inside this tab.

To indicate that it's the offspring of your template, a yellow tab in the upper-right corner of the document window reads Template: Classified. You can see your four editable regions indicated by blue tabs.

4. **Make sure the document window's toolbar is visible (View→Toolbar); type** *Antique Scale for Sale* **into the Title field.**

You've just named your page, saving you from the ignominy of showing up in search engines as "Untitled." Next stop: replacing the dummy ad with a real one.

5. **Click the banner graphic to select it. Press the Delete or Backspace key.**

It was useful to include placeholders for your text and graphics, like this fake banner ad, in your templates, to give your page shape and make clear what the "real" content should look like. But you won't be needing this dummy ad; now you'll replace it with an ad graphic from an actual paying advertiser.

6. **Insert the new ad graphic.**

Choose Insert→Image, for example. Navigate to the DWLibTemp→ads folder; double-click the file called *half_dr.gif*. When you return to your document, you'll discover that Dreamweaver has replaced the placeholder ad with one for Dr. Herbert's Amazing Plant Tonic.

Now you'll insert a proper photo into that black placeholder square.

7. **Click the black square graphic to select it. Press Delete or Backspace to remove it. Insert the product photo.**

Once again, you can choose Insert→Image. Navigate to the DWLibTemp→ classified→images folder; double-click the file called *scale.jpg*.

If you had no trouble replacing the placeholder graphics, replacing the dummy text should be a piece of cake:

8. **Click the blue** *item name* **tab to select the editable region. Type** *Antique Scale.*

If Dreamweaver doesn't select the editable region when you click the blue tab—it occasionally doesn't—click inside the editable area and click the <mm:editable> tag in the tag selector instead. Similarly, you'll have to replace the description:

9. **Click the blue tab labeled "description" to select its editable region. Type** *This antique produce scale dates back to well before disco. Call Ado at 555-245-9870 for more information.*

This classifieds page is really starting to look like something.

10. **Choose File→Save and then close the** *scale.html* **document window.**

Congratulations! You've just created your first page based on a template. You could, of course, continue, building page after page of template-based pages.

Updating a Template

Now the fun begins. Remember, this page links to the original template. In the final phase, you're going to edit the template. Choose Window→ Templates to open the Assets panel and reveal the Templates category, if it wasn't already visible.

1. **In the Assets panel, double-click the classified template to open it.**

   Double-click the icon, not the name. The original template—the *classifieds.dwt* file—opens.

2. **On the template, click the left-hand column below the words "This month's specials." Type *Antique Produce Scale*.**

   For added realism, you can link this text to the *scale.html* file like this:

3. **Select the text you just typed; press Ctrl+L (⌘-L).**

   This shortcut is a quick way to add a link. The Select File dialog box appears.

4. **Navigate to the *classifieds* folder; double-click the file *scale.html*.**

   The Select File dialog box closes, and the text "Antique Produce Scale" turns into a link. While you're polishing up your template, you should probably add the copyright notice to this page:

5. **On the Assets panel, click the Library button to display the site's Library items.**

   There's only one item listed: the footer you created earlier.

6. **Scroll to the bottom of the template page. Drag the footer from the Assets panel to the bottom of the page.**

   If you followed the steps on page 461, this routine should seem familiar; this time, however, you're adding a Library item to a template, not to a document.

7. **Choose File→Save.**

   The Update Template Pages dialog box appears, listing all of the pages in the site based on this template.

8. **Click Update.**

   Dreamweaver opens the Update Pages dialog box and updates the appropriate Web pages, adding your link and copyright-notice footer to each one. In this case, you based only one page on the template, so Dreamweaver updates only one page, as indicated by the list of changes Dreamweaver shows when it's finished.

9. **Click Close to close the Update Pages dialog box. Finally, open the file *scale.html*.**

   Notice that the "Antique Produce Scale" link now appears in the *scale.html* document and the copyright notice appears at the bottom of the page, because you changed the template to which it was genetically linked. Ah, the power!

Feel free to compare the results of your work with the professionally completed version at *www.sawmac.com/missing/tutorials/*.

Automating Dreamweaver

O ne of Dreamweaver's greatest selling points is that it makes you more productive. You've experienced this firsthand if you ever labored over tables in an HTML text editor. What once took many keystrokes now takes one click of the Object panel's Table object.

If you're looking for even *more* ways to cut time off your day, Dreamweaver doesn't disappoint. In addition to its Library and Template features (see Chapter 17) the program offers two tools that let you automate common and time-consuming tasks.

The History panel lets you reuse actions you've taken in the document window. With a single click, you can replay one, two, three, or more steps—for example, you could assign an identical alignment, margin, and border for each of 20 images on a page, with a single click each. You can even save frequently used actions and access them from the Command menu.

In the same vein, the powerful Find and Replace command lets you quickly make site-wide changes—not just to text in the Web-page body, but even to specific HTML tags.

The History Panel Revisited

As you work on a Web page, Dreamweaver keeps track of everything you do. You can see a list of your actions, or *history*, in the History panel. Each document has a separate history; Dreamweaver discards it when you close the document or quit the program.

You can use the History panel to quickly undo or redo multiple actions (see page 55), but that's only the tip of the iceberg. You can also use it to replay and record a series of actions you wish to repeat. If you've ever used macros in Word or actions in Adobe Photoshop, you'll probably get the hang of this feature quickly.

To open the History panel, choose Window→History, or press Shift-F10 (see Figure 18-1). You may also be able to open the History panel by clicking the Open History icon (▷) on the Launcher or Launcher bar, depending on how you set them up (see page 18).

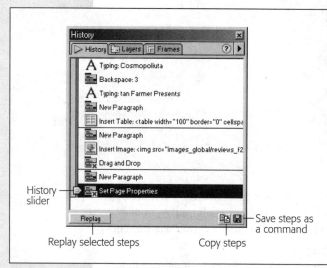

History slider

Replay selected steps

Copy steps

Save steps as a command

Figure 18-1:
The History panel lists every little step you've taken while working on the current document—even typos. You can replay one or more actions on the list, copy them for use in another document, or save them as a command in the Commands menu. If an action can't be replayed, it appears with a red X next to it. The History slider indicates where you are in the document's history.

Replay Your Steps

To replay a step in the History panel, click its name to highlight it. You can also select multiple steps by using one of these methods:

- To select a group of consecutive steps, drag from one to another. You can drag your mouse across either the labels or icons. Take special care not to move your cursor into the History slider on the left edge of the window; clicking there will undo or redo steps (see page 55).

- You can also select consecutive steps by holding down the Shift key as you click down the list.

- To select steps that aren't consecutive, Ctrl-click (⌘-click) only the ones you want. For example, say you hit Return, typed *hello,* and then inserted a horizontal rule. If you wanted to omit the step where you typed *hello,* you could Ctrl-click (⌘-click) the other two. Dreamweaver will ignore a step that isn't selected.

Now, when you click Replay (see Figure 18-1), Dreamweaver replays the selected steps. Unfortunately, you can't reorder the steps; they always play from the top of the list to the bottom.

Once you've created a series of steps, you can reuse it. For example, say you select a word and format it as red, bold, and italic. Once Dreamweaver records these steps in the History panel, you can select more text and replay those steps to format it the same way. Now imagine that instead of a three-step process, you have a ten-step chore that involves not only key strokes, but multiple visits to the Objects panel and Property inspector; you can begin to see the power of this feature.

Tip: You probably know that you can repeat your last action by pressing Ctrl+Y (⌘-Y) or choosing Edit→Repeat. For example, if you type the word *hello* in the document window, pressing Ctrl+Y (⌘-Y) will type the word *hello* again. Unless you're Jack Nicholson's character in *The Shining*, this feature may sound less than useful, but used in combination with the History panel's Replay feature, it can be a real time-saver. When you use the History panel to replay several steps, you'll notice the last item in the History list is Replay Steps. Dreamweaver treats all of these steps as a *single action*. Now if you press Ctrl+Y (⌘-Y), you'll replay all of the steps again.

Exceptions and Errors

Unfortunately, Dreamweaver can't record and play back everything. The exceptions generally involve making changes in certain dialog boxes or moving objects with the mouse. For example, you can't record tasks you perform in the Modify Page Properties dialog box. And you're left to your own devices when you want to click, drag, or drop a graphic in the document window.

On the other hand, not everything you do with the mouse is off-limits to the History panel. It can track most common tasks, like clicking the Objects panel, choosing a menu item, or clicking in the Property inspector to set a property. Also, you can avoid using many mouse movements by using equivalent keystrokes, which Dreamweaver *can* record. (See the box below.)

FREQUENTLY ASKED QUESTION

Keyboard to the Rescue

If Dreamweaver can't track mouse movements, how can I replay an action that involves selecting something?

It's easy to use the mouse to make selections and move items around the screen, but you can do much of the same with the humble keyboard. That's a good thing, because if you can type it, Dreamweaver can record it.

To move up one line, for instance, press the up arrow key; to move down a line, press the down arrow. You can move to the top or bottom of the document window with the Page Up and Page Down keys, or move to the beginning or end of a line by pressing Home or End. Press Shift while pressing the right or left arrow key to select the object or

letter to the right or left of the insertion point. Add the Ctrl (⌘) key to that combination to select one *word* at a time.

Unfortunately, Dreamweaver doesn't record the keystrokes you use for moving between table cells (Tab and Shift-Tab). However, there's a workaround: To move from one cell to the cell on its right, press End, followed by the right arrow key. To move to the cell to the left, press Home, followed by the left arrow key; these are keystrokes the History panel can track.

(You don't have to memorize all of this. You can print out a complete list of keyboard shortcuts from within Dreamweaver, as described on page 489.)

If you take a step, such as a mouse drag, that Dreamweaver can't replay, a red X appears next to it in the History panel (see Figure 18-1). A line between two actions also indicates a step that can't be repeated. This problem usually arises when you've clicked in the document window (to deselect a selected image, for example). If you get into the habit of deselecting an object in the document window by pressing the keyboard's arrow keys instead, you'll find your History steps more fully replayable.

Since Dreamweaver just reapplies your steps, sometimes you'll get strange results. For example, suppose you select a table cell and set its background to dark gray. If you select a paragraph of *text* and replay the set background step, Dreamweaver adds a background property to the paragraph like this: <p bgcolor="#666666">. Dreamweaver did what you asked: It set the background color property. The problem is that there *isn't* a Bg color property for the <p> tag in HTML; when you preview your page in a browser, the paragraph won't have a background color at all.

The bottom line: If you have problems replaying your steps, take a moment to make sure they can be applied to whatever you selected.

Copying and Pasting Actions

Each document has its own history; if you work on one page and then switch to another, the History panel changes to reflect only the actions you performed on the new document. The biggest drawback of this quirk is that you can't make a series of steps in one document to replay in another.

For example, while working on your home page, you might click the Date object in the Objects panel to insert the current date (see page 46) and then choose a format for the date in the dialog box. You want to place the date on another page using the same format. But when you switch to that page and click Replay on the History panel, your steps aren't there!

POWER USERS' CLINIC

Copy (and Study) Actions

Dreamweaver is relatively easy to customize, because the objects that appear in the Objects panel, the behaviors available from the Behaviors panel, and even the Property inspector are all, behind the scenes, combinations of HTML pages and JavaScript programs. If you understand JavaScript, you can add your own commands, behaviors, and objects.

When *learning* JavaScript, however, you may need all the help you can get. The History panel's Copy Steps feature is a good place to start.

To study how Dreamweaver's built-in commands, behaviors, and objects have been programmed, copy one or more actions using the method described above. In Dreamweaver's Code view (or any HTML text editor), choose Edit→Paste.

What you see is the JavaScript code that Dreamweaver uses to carry out those actions. You'll find out, for example, that while you perceive adding a new paragraph to your Web page as a matter of hitting Enter, to Dreamweaver it looks like this: dw.getDocumentDOM().newBlock().

Fortunately, there's a workaround: ye olde copy/paste routine. Select the steps you want to copy (see "Replay Your Steps," page 468, for selection techniques), and then click the Copy Steps button (see Figure 18-1) on the History panel. (The regular copy shortcut, Ctrl+C or ⌘-C, *doesn't* work in this situation.) Now switch to the new document; select an object (or click to place the insertion point), and then choose Edit→Paste or press Ctrl+V (⌘-V).

Dreamweaver responds by playing the copied steps.

Note: You can't reliably copy certain actions, most notably Copy and Paste. If the actions you wish to reuse include a copy or paste step, save the actions as a command instead (see below).

Save Steps as Commands

It's quick and easy to replay and copy steps to automate repetitive tasks, but if you close the document or quit Dreamweaver, your recorded actions disappear—and with them, any chance you had of replaying them in the future. What if you come up with a great sequence of steps that you'd like to use over and over again?

The solution: Before it disappears forever, turn it into a *custom command*. Dreamweaver adds your command to the bottom of the Commands menu; you can choose it from here anytime.

To save steps as a command, select the steps you want to copy (see "Replay Your Steps," page 468, for selection techniques), then click the Save Steps button (its icon looks like a little floppy disk) on the History panel.

The Save as Command dialog box pops open. (If you've selected steps that Dreamweaver can't replay, such as mouse movements, a warning appears. Click Yes to continue without those steps; the valid steps will work just fine.) Type a short, descriptive name and click OK. Now take a look at the Commands menu; sure enough, your command now appears at the bottom.

To use your custom command, simply select its name from the Commands menu.

Tip: If you decide you want to delete your command or change its name, choose Commands→Edit Command List. In the dialog box that appears, click the command's name to select it. Type a new name or click Delete.

Recording Commands

You can also create a command by telling Dreamweaver to watch and record your actions. This time, Dreamweaver won't *let* you perform mouse movements while you're recording, so you can be sure recorded commands will play back properly.

To record a command, make sure the relevant Web page document is frontmost, then choose Commands→Start Recording, or press Ctrl+Shift+X (⌘-Shift-X). The cursor turns into a cassette-tape icon to indicate the command is recording; now's your chance to do whatever you want Dreamweaver to memorize. (If you try to use the mouse to move or select anything in the document window, Dreamweaver will complain via dialog box.)

When you're finished, choose Commands→Stop Recording, or press Ctrl+Shift+X (⌘-Shift-X). Your cursor returns to normal, and Dreamweaver saves the sequence as a command, which you can replay in any document by pressing Ctrl+P (⌘-P). (If you're totally mouse-driven, choose Commands→Play Recorded Command.)

Note, however, that this command disappears when you quit Dreamweaver or record another command. (Dreamweaver can only save one recorded command at a time.) If you want to preserve it for posterity, you'll have to save it to the Commands menu, like this:

1. Press Ctrl+P (⌘-P) to play the command.

The History panel lists this action as Run Command.

WORKAROUND WORKSHOP

Pasting Bullet Points

All of this business about creating your own software-robot macro commands in Dreamweaver pays off in plenty of eccentric circumstances. Here's a prime example: When you copy and paste bulleted text from a word processing program (shown here, top) into Dreamweaver (bottom), you don't end up with a bulleted list. Instead, Dreamweaver pastes the list as a single paragraph. Each list item ends in a line break, and is preceded not with an HTML bullet, but with a bullet *character* (which won't display properly on the Web). If you use a Mac, you're even worse off—you get the Greek letter Sigma instead of a bullet character!

Fortunately, you can whip up a quick little command to get that text in shape. Here's how:

Click just before the first item in the list, and then choose Commands→Start Recording. As usual, the cursor turns into a cassette-tape icon to show that Dreamweaver is recording.

Press Delete (Windows) or Del (Mac) to delete the bullet

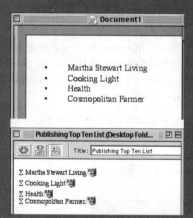

symbol. (That's the *forward*-delete key; if your older Mac keyboard lacks one, press Shift-right arrow, then the regular Delete key.) Now press End to make the insertion point jump to the end of the line; then press Backspace (Windows) or Delete (Mac) to nuke the unnecessary line-break character.

Press End, and then Return, to create a new paragraph. Finally, choose Commands→Stop Recording.

Now you're ready to replay the newly created command: Click before the next problem line in the list, and then press Ctrl+P (⌘-P) to trigger the cleanup command. Continue until you've applied the command to each item in the list.

After you've gotten rid of the bad formatting, all you need to do to transform your information into a proper HTML bulleted list. Select the list items and click the Bulleted List button in the Property inspector (see page 63). You may want to save this command permanently to your Commands menu (see page 471 for instructions).

---

2. **Choose the Run Command step from the History panel.**

   The step highlights to indicate you've selected it.

3. **Click the Save Steps button (its icon looks like a little floppy disk).**

   The Save as Command dialog box appears.

4. **Type a name for the command; click OK.**

   Dreamweaver adds your new command to the Commands menu, where it's ready for action in this or any future Dreamweaver session.

Create Web Photo Album

So you took your digital camera to your nephew's wedding. Your phone's ringing off the hook with family wanting to see those pictures. Using Dreamweaver's Create Web Photo Album command, you can quickly generate a simple showcase for your digital masterpieces. (This command works only if you have Macromedia Fireworks on your computer.)

Figure 18-2:
Use Dreamweaver's built-in Create Web Photo Album command to whip up a set of Web pages that showcase your photos. The command creates a simple index for your photo album (left), including clickable thumbnail images; each opens up an individual page that showcases a larger version of the photo (right).

To create a photo album, put all the graphics you want featured into a single folder. (It doesn't have to be in your site folder.) Then choose Commands→Create Web Photo Album. The dialog box that appears (see Figure 18-3) offers these controls:

- **Photo Album Title, Subheading Info.** The title you type will appear in a gray box on the thumbnail page, and at the top of each photo page (see Figure 18-2). If you type a subheading, it will appear in smaller type on the thumbnail page, below the title.

- **Other Info.** Use this optional box to provide a short description of the photos; this text will appear as plain paragraph type below the subhead.

• **Browse.** Click the top Browse button (next to the Source Images Folder box) to find and select your folder of graphics files. The graphics files themselves don't have to be in a Web-ready format (GIF, JPEG or PNG); Fireworks can process GIF, JPEG, PNG, Photoshop (.psd), or TIFF files. In the next step, the program will convert them into a Web-friendly graphics file format.

Click the lower **Browse** button (next to the Destination Folder box) to find and highlight the folder where you'll want the converted graphics (and the album Web pages) stored. This should be an empty folder in your site folder.

Dreamweaver creates a new *index.html* page for the album's thumbnail page, as well as additional folders for the thumbnail images, larger images, and photo pages.

• **Size pop-up menu.** You can choose from five preset sizes for the thumbnail images: 36 x 36, 72 x 72, 100 x 100, 144 x 144, or 200 x 200 pixels. These sizes represent the *maximum* size of the height and width of the thumbnail image. For example, if a photo in its original format is 785 pixels wide and 405 pixels tall, the 100 x 100 option will create a miniature image that's 100 pixels tall by 52 pixels wide. (Fireworks doesn't distort the image by turning it into a 100 x 100 pixel square.)

• **Columns.** Specify the number of columns you want for the thumbnail page layout. If you have nine photos, for example, type *3* in the column box; Dreamweaver produces a page that displays your images three across and three down.

• **Thumbnail Format pop-up menu.** Choose the graphics format for both the thumbnail images and larger photo images. Fireworks converts the photos in the folder you've specified into either JPEG or GIF images.

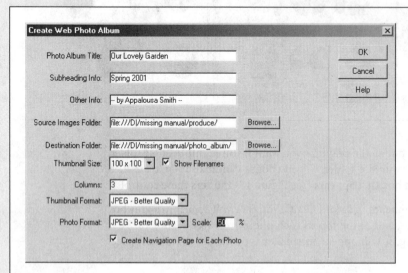

Figure 18-3:
The Create Web Photo Album dialog box lets you define the properties of your photo album. The Show Filenames box tells Dreamweaver to add the actual file name of the image under each thumbnail. If your images are from a photo CD or stock image disc, you'll probably get uninformative names such as DS3746F7.jpg.

- **Scale.** Here, you can type a percentage for scaling the original images. If the original photos are very large, for example, you might want to create smaller versions that fit on a Web page better and are small enough to download quickly. For example, say your original digital photos are 1,000 pixels wide—really huge for a Web page—you might type *40* (percent) to bring the images on the resulting Web pages down to a reasonable size. *Try 25%*

- **Create Navigation Page for Each Photo.** This useful option creates a separate page for each photo, complete with its title, filename, and previous/next links (Figure 18-2, bottom). If you turn off this box, Dreamweaver will merely link the thumbnail images directly to each larger photo; when a visitor clicks the thumbnail, the full-size image will still appear, but without the title or navigation controls.

When you click OK, Fireworks opens and creates the thumbnail and larger photo images. This may take a few minutes depending on how many image files Fireworks must process (and how big they are). When it's done, Dreamweaver steps in and creates the pages themselves; an "Album Created" message appears when your new photo gallery is ready to preview. Press F12 to open it in your Web browser.

EASTER EGG HUNT

Would You Like to Play a Game?

As today's software programs go, Dreamweaver is delightfully brimming with Easter eggs (see page 103). But there's one particular Easter egg that's never before been seen outside of Macromedia—a software surprise so delicious, it was revealed for inclusion in this book only on the promise that the actual trigger wouldn't be explicitly printed here. But experimenting until you find it is worth the time; the result is a full-fledged *color game,* a full-blown version of an old classic board game. It's a fun little diversion when you want a break from the daily grind.

It goes like this: Summon the Create Web Photo Album dialog box. Type the secret, three-word password into the Photo Album Title box with no spaces. (And what's the password, you may well ask? Here's a hint: It's a key phrase in the 1983 Matthew Broderick movie *WarGames,* and it appears somewhere in this chapter.)

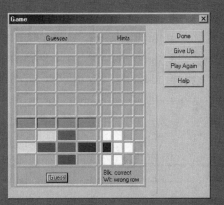

To play the game once it appears, your challenge is to guess the secret four-color pattern that Dreamweaver has dreamed up. Click each of the squares on the bottom left row; click a square repeatedly until it shows the color you want. When you've arranged the four rectangles in the colors that represent your guess, click Guess. The smaller squares at the right side show you how many of your guesses were "right colors, right positions" (black) and how many were "right colors, wrong positions" (white). Use these clues to guide you in your next guess—in the second row of left-side rectangles. Keep going until you've unveiled Dreamweaver's secret—its *second* secret, that is.

Find and Replace

You've probably encountered find and replace tools in word processing programs and even some graphics programs. As the name implies, the command finds a piece of text (*Webmaster,* for example) and then *replaces* it with something else (*Webmistress*). Like Microsoft Word, Dreamweaver can search and replace text in the body of your Web pages. But it also offers variations on this feature that enhance your ability to work within the tag-based world of HTML.

What's more, Dreamweaver lets you find and replace text on *every* page of your Web site, not just the current, open document. In addition, you can *remove* every appearance of a particular HTML tag, or search and replace text that matches very specific criteria. For example, you can find every instance of the word Aardvark that appears within a center-aligned paragraph. These advanced find and replace options are some of the most powerful—and underappreciated—tools in Dreamweaver's toolbox. If you learn how to use them, you'll be able to make changes to your pages in a fraction of the time it would take using other methods.

Find and Replace Basics

To start a search, press Ctrl+F (⌘-F), or choose Edit→Find and Replace. The Find and Replace window opens (see Figure 18-4). Now all you have to do is fill in the blanks and set up the search.

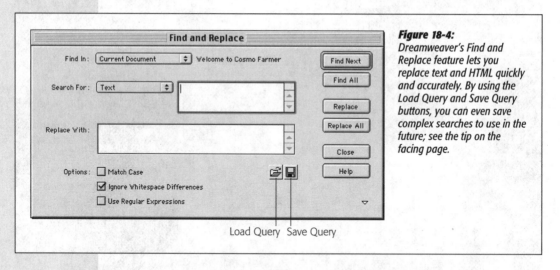

Figure 18-4:
Dreamweaver's Find and Replace feature lets you replace text and HTML quickly and accurately. By using the Load Query and Save Query buttons, you can even save complex searches to use in the future; see the tip on the facing page.

Load Query   Save Query

Whether you perform a simple text search or a complex tag-based search and replace, the procedure for using the Find and Replace command is basically the same. First, you need to tell Dreamweaver *where* to search (in a file, a folder, or an entire Web site). Next, tell it what to search for (text, HTML, or a particular tag with a specific attribute). Finally, you can decide what to replace the item with. This last step is optional; you can use the Find and Replace window as a way to locate an item on the page, or in your site, without actually changing it to anything.

Tip: After you've entered the Find and Replace criteria, click the Save Query button (see Figure 18-2). A Save dialog box appears; you can type in a name for your query, which Dreamweaver saves as a .dwr (Dreamweaver replace query) file in the Dreamweaver 4→Configuration→Queries folder. To reuse a query, simply click the Load Query button and locate the .dwr file. The search and replace criteria will load, and you can click any of the four action buttons—Find Next, Find All, Replace, or Replace All.

Basic Text and HTML Searches

Dreamweaver can either search all of the HTML source code in a page or simply focus on text that appears in the document window. If you've used Find and Replace in other programs, this routine will seem familiar:

- A **source code** search lets you find and replace any character in the HTML of a page, including words, letters, and symbols.

- **Text** searches are more refined. They look only for text that appears within the body of a page. That is, Dreamweaver ignores HTML tags, properties, and comments when searching—in short, it ignores anything that doesn't appear as actual words in the document window. By using a text search when you want to change the word "center" to "middle," for example, you won't accidentally alter the center *alignment* option of a table cell—<td align="center">—by setting the alignment value of its HTML tag to "middle" (an invalid value that Web browsers would just ignore).

Figure 18-5:
The Find and Replace command is not limited to the current document. You can also search multiple Web pages or even an entire site.

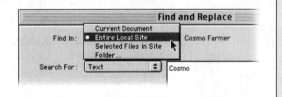

Phase 1: Determine the scope of your search

Using the Find In menu (see Figure 18-5), choose any of these options:

- **Current Document.** Searches the Web page you're working on.

- **Entire Local Site.** Searches every Web page in the site folder, including pages in folders *inside* the site folder. This option is invaluable when some basic piece of information changes throughout your site; for instance, when your boss's sex-change operation requires you to replace every instance of "Mark Jones" with "Mary Jones" throughout your company's site.

Warning: Using the Find and Replace command is one of the best ways to quickly make changes to an entire site, but it's also one of the easiest ways to *wreck* a site's worth of Web pages. Dreamweaver can't undo changes made by the Find and Replace command to files that aren't open on your computer. So be careful. If you plan on making extensive changes, make a backup copy of your files first!

- **Selected Files in Site.** Searches files you select in the Site window. This option assumes, of course, that you've opened the Site window and selected files in the local file list for this to work. (See page 375 for details.)

- **Folder.** Search all Web pages in a particular folder. Dreamweaver also searches Web pages in all folders *within* the selected folder. You can use this option to search pages that aren't part of the current site.

Phase 2: Specify what to search for

For your next trick, you'll tell Dreamweaver what you want to search for. Use the Search For pop-up menu to choose one of these two options:

- **Text.** Dreamweaver will search for a certain word or phrase of text that appears in the body of the documents you've specified. Type the text you want to find into the Search For field. (If you're searching for a pattern in your text, enter a *regular expression* here and turn on the Use Regular Expressions box (described below).

- **Source Code.** Basic text searches are very useful, but they're limited to text that appears in the body of the page (what you see in the document window). If you want to search and replace HTML code, you need the Source Code option.

  Source code searches work identically to text searches. The only difference is that Dreamweaver searches *everything* within the file—text, HTML, JavaScript, Cascading Style Sheets (CSS) and so on—and replaces any part of the file. Using this option, you could search your document for any instance of the tag <img src= "mark_jones_photo.jpg">, for example, and replace it with <img src= "mary_jones_photo.jpg">.

  (If you're in Code View, Dreamweaver automatically selects the Source Code option for you.)

  As you fill in the Search For field, be aware that some plain-English words are also special words in HTML, JavaScript, or CSS. If you try to replace *table* with *desk* using a source-code find and replace, you'll completely destroy any <table> tags on the page.

  You can also enter a regular expression to search for patterns in your HTML source code (see the box on the facing page).

Phase 3: Provide the replacement text

If you want to change the text that Dreamweaver finds, type the replacement text into the Replace With box. It may be the word or words you'd like to swap in if you chose a Text search as described above, or actual HTML code if you're performing a source-code search.

If you only want to find the text without replacing it, you can skip this step.

Tip: If you want to find the specified text and replace it with *nothing* (that is, deleting every occurrence of the text), leave the Replace With field blank and perform a replace operation, as described below.

Phase 4: Choose the search settings

Dreamweaver gives you three options that govern its search and replace option; some of them are quite complex.

- The **Match Case** option limits the Find command to text that exactly matches the capitalization you used in the Search For field. If you search for the text *The End* with the Match Case box turned on, Dreamweaver will find a match in "The End is near," but not "You're almost at the end." Use this trick to find every instance of *web* and replace it with *Web*.

- The **Ignore Whitespace Differences** option treats multiple spaces, tabs, nonbreaking spaces and carriage returns as a single space when searching. For instance, if you search for *the dog* and turn on this option, Dreamweaver matches "the dog" as well as "the   dog".

The HTML of a page can contain lots of extra spaces, line breaks, and tabs that don't appear in a Web browser or in Dreamweaver's document window. For ex-

---

POWER USERS' CLINIC

Turbocharge Your Searches

If you want to find the phone number 555-123-5473, no problem; just type *555-123-5473* into the search field. But what if you wanted to find any and *every* phone number—555-987-0938, 555-102-8870, and so on—on a Web page or in a site?

In such a case, you need to use *regular expressions,* the geeky name for a delightfully flexible searching language carried over from early UNIX days: wildcard characters that let you search for patterns of text instead of actual letters or numbers. Each phone number above follows a simple pattern: three numbers, a dash, three more numbers, another dash, and four more numbers.

To search for a pattern, you use a variety of symbols combined with regular text characters to tell Dreamweaver what to find. For example, \d, in the world of regular expressions, stands for *any number.* To find three numbers in a row, you could search for \d\d\d, which would find 555, 747, 007 and so on. There's even shorthand for this: \d{3}. The number between the braces ({}) indicates how many times in a row the preceding character must appear to match. To finish up the example of the phone numbers, you could use a regular expression like this: \d{3}-\d{3}-\d{4}. The \d{3} finds three numbers; the hyphen (-) fol-

lowing it is just the hyphen in the phone number.

Here are some of the other symbols you'll encounter when using regular expressions:

. (period) stands for *any* character, letter, number, space, and so on.

\w stands for any letter or number

* represents the preceding character zero or more times (and is always used after another character). This is best explained with an example: the regular expression *colou*r,* for instance, matches both *colour* and *color.* The * following the *u* indicates that the *u* is optional (it can appear zero times). This would also match *colouuuuur* (handy for those times when you've fallen asleep at the keyboard).

To see a complete list of the regular expression characters Dreamweaver understands, launch the Dreamweaver online Help system (press F1) and search for the topic "About Regular Expressions." A full-length discussion of regular expressions could fill a book of its own—and does, in fact; check out *Mastering Regular Expressions* by Jeffrey E. F. Friedl. (For an example of Regular Expressions in action, see page 486.)

---

ample, in the HTML of a document, it's possible to have two lines of code that look like this:

```
<p>This sentence will appear on one
line in a Web browser</p>
```

Even though this text would appear on a single line in the document window, a search for "one line" *without* the Ignore Whitespace Differences would find no match. The carriage return at the end of "one" is not an exact match for the space character in "one line." In other words, it's best to keep this option turned on.

• **The Use Regular Expressions option** is used for matching patterns in text. For a discussion of this advanced technique, see the box on page 479.

Phase 5: Take action

Finally, you're ready to set the search in motion by clicking one of the four action buttons in the Find and Replace window (see Figure 18-6):

• **Find Next** locates the next instance of the search term. If you're searching the current document, Dreamweaver highlights the matching text. If you're searching an entire Web site or a folder of pages, Dreamweaver opens the file *and* highlights the match. You can cycle through each instance of the search term by repeatedly clicking this button or by pressing Ctrl+G (⌘-G).

Note: In some programs (notably Microsoft Word), you can press Enter to repeat the Find Next function. Not so in Dreamweaver; even with the Find window open, Enter or Return starts a new paragraph. You must either click Find Next or press F3 (⌘-G).

• **Find All** locates every instance of the search terms, all at once, and shows them to you in a list at the bottom of the Find and Replace window (see Figure 18-6). Unlike the Find Next action, Find All doesn't automatically open any of the Web pages containing matches. Instead, to open a matched page, double-click its name in the results list. Only then does the Web page open; Dreamweaver highlights the match.

• **Replace** locates the next instance of the search term *and* replaces it with the text in the Replace With field, leaving the replaced text highlighted for your inspection.

You can use this button in combination with Find Next to selectively replace text. First, click Find Next. Dreamweaver locates and highlights the next match. If you want to replace the text, click Replace. If not, click Find Next to search for the next match, and repeat the cycle.

• **Replace All** is the ultimate power tool. It finds every instance of the search term and replaces it with the text entered in the Replace With field. Coupled with the Find in Entire Local Site option, you can quickly make site-wide changes (and mistakes).

When you click this button, Dreamweaver warns you that this operation cannot be undone on any closed files. You can erase any mistakes you make with the Find and Replace in *open* documents, by choosing Edit→Undo, but Dreamweaver *permanently* alters files that are closed—be careful! (On the other hand, changes to open documents aren't permanent until you save those files.)

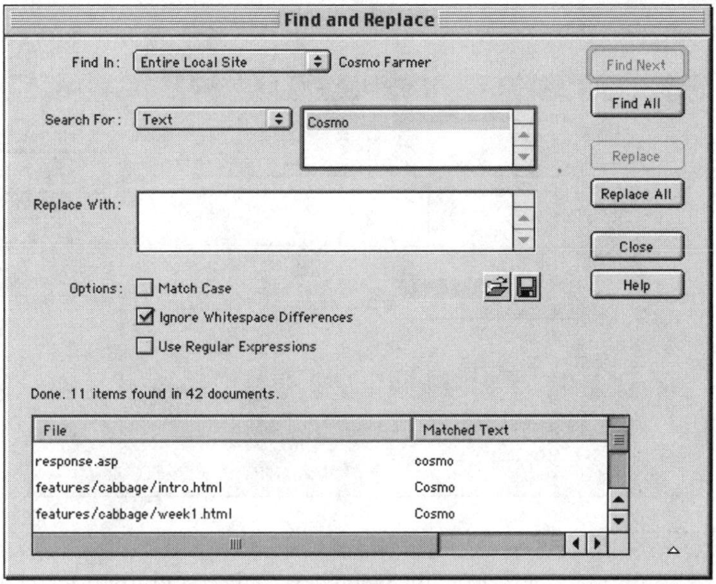

Figure 18-6:
If you click Find All, Dreamweaver displays a list of all matches at the bottom of the Find and Replace window. The name and location of the file (if multiple files are searched) appears to the left, and the matched text appears to the right. If you double-click a file in the list, Dreamweaver opens the document and highlights the matched text. You can also click a listed file to select it and then click Replace to replace its matched text. To hide or show this panel, click the arrow in the lower right corner of the window.

The Find and Replace window stays open in the foreground (floating above open documents) until you close it, so that you can jump back and forth between documents and the Find and Replace window.

Advanced Text Searches

If you want greater control over a text search, you can use the Find and Replace command's *advanced* text-search option, which lets you confine a search to text either inside or outside of a specific tag.

For example, when Dreamweaver creates a new blank document, it sets the page's Title property to *Untitled*. Unfortunately, if you forget to change it, a site can quickly fill up with untitled Web pages. A basic text search won't identify this problem, because it searches only the body of a page, while titles appear in the *head*. And a source-code search for *Untitled* would turn up the word "untitled" *wherever* it appeared in the page, not just inside the <title> tag.

In cases like this, an Advanced Text Search is your best choice. Simply set the Find and Replace command to search for *Untitled* whenever it appears within the <title> tag.

To use the advanced text search, use the same general routine as described on the previous pages. But before using one of the action buttons, you can make a few additional setup changes to the dialog box:

Limiting the search by tag

Choose Text (Advanced) from the Search For pop-up menu to make the expanded, new controls appear (see Figure 18-7).

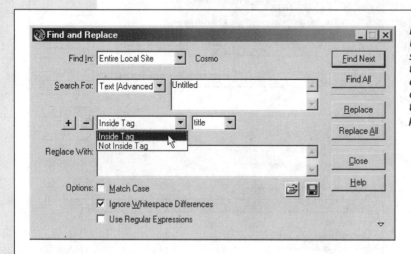

Figure 18-7:
Use an advanced text search to limit your search to text that appears within a particular HTML tag. Or, conversely, search for text that *doesn't* appear in a particular tag.

Now, from the menu next to the + and – buttons, choose either "Inside Tag" or "Not Inside Tag." For example, consider this line of code: "Stupid is as <b>stupid</b> does." The first instance of "stupid" isn't inside the <b> tag, but the second one is.

Note: A more descriptive name for the first option would be "*Enclosed* By Tag"; Dreamweaver actually searches for text that's between opening *and closing* tags. In fact, an advanced text search using this option doesn't identify text that's literally inside a tag. For example, it won't find "vegetable" in this line of code: <img src="cabbage.jpg" alt="Beware this vegetable.">, but it would find "vegetable" in this one: <b>Beware this vegetable.</b>. In the first example, *vegetable* appears as part of the <img> tag, while in the second, *vegetable* is enclosed by the opening and closing <b> tags.

Once you've specified whether you're looking for text inside or outside of tags, you can choose a specific HTML tag from the Tag menu identified in Figure 18-7.

The menu lists all qualifying tags—that is, those with both an opening and closing tag. For example, the image tag (<img>), is not included, since it has no closing tag.

Tip: A great way to search for text in both the title and body of a Web page is to choose the HTML tag from this menu. That way, you can search for any text that appears within the opening <html> and closing </html> of the page—which, since those tags start and end any Web document, is *all* text on a page.

Limiting the search by attribute

To limit the search further, click the + button (see Figure 18-8); yet another new set of fields appears.

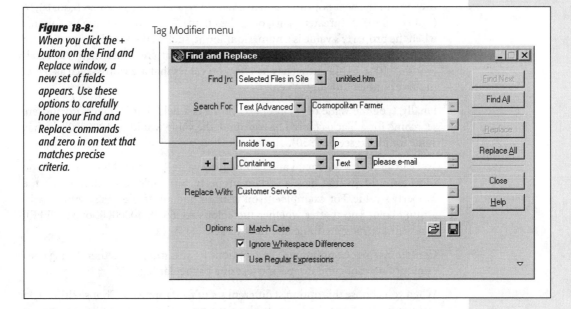

Figure 18-8:
When you click the + button on the Find and Replace window, a new set of fields appears. Use these options to carefully hone your Find and Replace commands and zero in on text that matches precise criteria.

Tag Modifier menu

Using the tag modifier menu—next to the + and – buttons (Figure 18-8)—you can choose from any of six options that break down into three groups:

• **With Attribute/Without Attribute.** To limit the search, you can specify that a tag must either have (With Attribute) or not have (Without Attribute) a specific property.

For example, say the following line of code appears throughout a Web site:

```
<p>For assistance, please email
<a href="mailto:mail@cosmofarmer.com">
Cosmopolitan Farmer.</a></p>
```

But you need to change it to say, "For assistance, please email Customer Service." A basic text find and replace would incorrectly change the words "Cosmopolitan Farmer" to "Customer Service" *everywhere* on the site.

However, an advanced text search using the With Attribute option would do the trick. You could look for the text "Cosmopolitan Farmer" wherever it appears inside an <a> tag whose *href* attribute is set to "mailto:mail@cosmofarmer.com." (To learn about the different HTML tags and attributes, use Dreamweaver's built-in code reference; see page 257.)

After you choose With Attribute, use the menu on the right to select *which* of the tag's properties you want to find (Dreamweaver automatically lists properties that are appropriate for the tag you've specified). For example, if you search inside a <table> tag, the menu will list such properties as Align, Background, Bg color, and so on.

Advance to the next pop-up menu to choose a type of comparison: = (equals), != (not equal to), > (greater than), or < (less than). These options are useful only when the property's value is a numeric amount, such as the Width property of an image. In this way, you could locate all images that are wider than 100 pixels (width > 100). (This setting has no effect on values that are words, such as *center* in this example: <td align="center">.

Finally, type the value of the property in the last field. For instance, if you were searching for a black-colored background, the value would be #000000 (the hex value for black; see page 30).

You can also click the menu and choose [any value]—a useful option when you want to find tags that have a certain property, but you're not interested in the property's value. For example, if you want to find all <table> tags with a background color (no matter whether the color's #336699, #000000, or #FFFFFF), choose the *bgcolor* attribute and [any value].

- **Containing/Not Containing.** These options let you specify whether the tag contains, or does not contain, specific text or a particular tag.

  When you choose this option, a different set of fields appears. Choose either Text or Specific Tag from the menu to the right, and then either enter some text or select a tag in the last field in the row.

  For example, another solution to the problem above would be to search for the text "Cosmopolitan Farmer" wherever it appears inside a <p> (paragraph) tag that *also contains* the text "please email" (see Figure 18-8).

- **Inside Tag/Not Inside Tag.** These last two choices are identical to those described on page 482. They let you specify whether the tag is inside or not inside a specific tag. Use these to limit a search, for example, to text that appears only within a <font> tag that's *inside* a Heading 1 (<h1>) tag.

If you like, you can add even more restrictions to your search, adding new rules by clicking the + button and repeating the setup just described. When you're really on a roll, it's even possible to add so many modifiers that the Find and Replace window actually grows past the bottom of your monitor. To remove a modifier, click the – (minus) button.

Advanced Tag Searches

If you find the number of options an advanced text search offers overwhelming, you haven't seen anything yet. Dreamweaver's tag search adds more choices to help you quickly search for, and modify, HTML tags. You can use a tag search to strip out unwanted HTML tags (think <blink>), transform one tag into another (for example, you could turn unreadable italics [<i>] into eye-catching bold [<b>]), and perform a host of other powerful actions.

In its basic outline, a tag search is much like the regular text search described on page 477. But this time, from the Search For menu, you should choose Specific Tag.

Now a tag menu appears next to the Search For menu, and the dialog box expands to display a new set of fields (see Figure 18-9). Some of them are the same as the controls you see when performing an advanced text search (see page 481), such as the tag modifier menu and the + button that lets you add additional restrictions to the search.

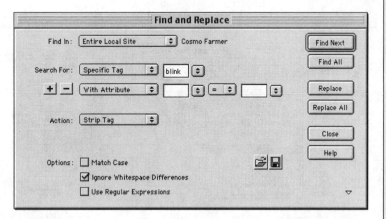

Figure 18-9:
Remember the nasty old <blink> tag that makes text flash on and off like the outside of a Las Vegas casino? It's a snap to remove unwanted (or obnoxious) tags when you use the "Specific Tag" option in Dreamweaver's Find and Replace command. This option is also handy if you're replacing old-style text formatting with cascading style sheets; use it to strip out unwanted <font> tags.

But a key difference here is the Actions menu (see Figure 18-10), which lets you specify the action Dreamweaver will perform on tags that match the search criteria when you click Replace or Replace All (if you intend to search but not replace, these options don't apply):

- **Replace Tag & Contents** replaces the tag, and anything enclosed by the tag (including other tags), with whatever you put into the With box to the right of this menu. You can either type or paste text or HTML here.

- **Replace Contents Only** replaces everything enclosed by the tag with text or HTML that you specify. The tag itself remains untouched.

- **Remove Tag and Contents** deletes the tag and *everything* inside.

- **Strip Tag** deletes the tag from the page, but leaves anything inside the tag untouched.

- **Set Attribute** *adds* an attribute to the tag. For example, you could set the Alt property of your images this way (see the example on page 486).

- **Remove Attribute** removes an attribute from a tag. For example, you could remove the not-so-useful *lowsrc* attribute from all image tags on your pages (see page 98).

- **Add Before (After) Start (End) Tag.** The last four actions in the menu simply offer variations on the same theme. They each let you place content in a Web page just before or after the tag you're searching for.

  To understand how these actions work, remember that most HTML tags come in pairs. The paragraph tag, for example, has an opening tag, <p>, and a closing tag, </p>. Say you searched for a paragraph tag; you could add text or HTML *before* or *after* the start tag (<p>) or *before* or *after* the end tag (</p>). (For an example of this action at work, see "Convenient Copyright Notices" at the end of this chapter.)

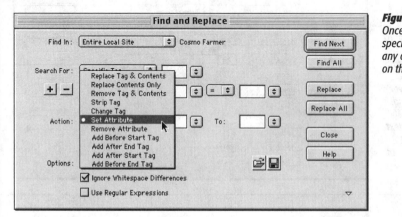

Figure 18-10:
Once Dreamweaver finds a specific tag, it can perform any of eleven different actions on the tag or its contents.

A Powerful Example: Adding Alt Text Fast

You've just put the finishing touches on the last page of your brand-new, 1,000-page site. You sit back and smile—and then snap bolt upright when you notice you forgot to add an Alt description for the site's banner graphic (see page 98). This graphic, called *site_banner.gif*, appears on every single one of the 1,000 pages; with rising dread, you realize that you'll have to open each page, select the graphic, and add the Alt property by hand.

And then you remember Dreamweaver's advanced tag-based find and replace.

Here's what you do. Press Ctrl+F (⌘-F) to open the Find and Replace window. Set up the dialog box like this:

1. **From the Find In menu, choose Entire Local Site.**

   You want to fix *every* page on your site.

2. **From the Search For pop-up menu, choose Specific Tag; from the pop-up menu to its right, choose *img*.**

   You'll start by identifying every image (the <img> tag).

3. **On the next row, use the three pop-up menus to choose With Attribute, *src*, and the equals sign (=).**

This tells Dreamweaver to look for specific images—in this case, images with a *src* attribute (the path that tells a Web browser where to find the image file on the Web server) with a specific value.

4. **Type .*site_banner.gif in the box next to the = sign.**

The name site_banner.gif is the name of the image file. The .* is the magic, and it'll be explained in a moment.

5. **Click the + button.**

Another row of tag modifier menus appears.

6. **From the new row of menus, choose Without Attribute and *alt*.**

You've further limited Dreamweaver's search to only those images that don't already have the *alt* attribute (after all, why bother setting the Alt property on an image that already has it?). The dialog box should look like the one in Figure 18-11.

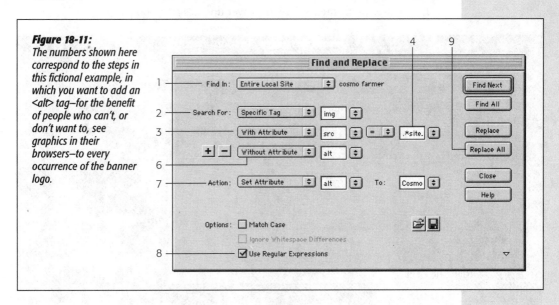

Figure 18-11:
The numbers shown here correspond to the steps in this fictional example, in which you want to add an <alt> tag—for the benefit of people who can't, or don't want to, see graphics in their browsers—to every occurrence of the banner logo.

7. **From the Action menu, choose Set Attribute; from the tag menu, choose *alt*.**

You've just told Dreamweaver what to do when you click the Replace or Replace All button. When Dreamweaver finds an <img> tag that matches the search criteria, it will then *add* an Alt property to that tag.

In this example, you might type *Cosmopolitan Farmer* in the To field; you've just specified the Alt text that Dreamweaver will add to the image.

8. **Turn on Use Regular Expressions.**

Regular expressions, described on page 479, let you search for specific patterns of characters, and in this case, will help you accurately identify the banner graphic file everywhere it appears.

You know you're looking for the file *site_banner.gif,* wherever it appears in the site. Unfortunately, if you just type *site_banner.gif* as the value of the *src* property of step 3, Dreamweaver won't succeed in its task. That's because the *src* attribute, the part of the <img> tag that includes the name of the file, varies from page to page. Depending on where a page is relative to the graphic, the *src* might be *site_banner.gif, images/site_banner.gif,* or even *../../../images/site_banner.gif.* What you need is a way to match every *src* attribute that *ends* in *site_banner.gif.*

A simple regular expression, .*site_banner.gif,* does the trick. The period stands for *any* character (6, g, or even %, for example), while the * (asterisk) means *zero or more times.* When you add these codes to the graphic name, *site_banner.gif,* you instruct Dreamweaver to find every *src* value that ends in *site_banner.gif.*

9. **Click the Replace All and sit back.**

In a matter of moments, Dreamweaver updates all 1,000 pages.

FREQUENTLY ASKED QUESTION

Convenient Copyright Notices

I want to add a copyright notice to the bottom of each page in my Web site. Is there a way to automate this process so I don't have to edit every page in my site by hand?

Of course there is. Use Dreamweaver's Find and Replace command to add text or HTML to the bottom of any Web page. The trick is knowing how to use the command's Specific Tag option.

First, choose Edit→Find and Replace to open the Find and Replace window. Next, choose Entire Local Site from the Find In menu, and choose Specific Tag from the Search For menu. Choose *body* from the tag menu. Remember, the <body> tag in HTML encloses everything that appears inside a browser window; it's equivalent to what you see

in the document window.

From the Action menu, choose Add Before End Tag. The end tag in this case is </body>. Since </body> marks the end of any content in a Web page, whatever appears *directly* before this closing tag will appear at the bottom of the Web page (you can probably see where this is going).

Now, in the text field next to the Action menu, type (or paste) the copyright notice you'd like to use on each. You may want to first design the copyright message using Dreamweaver, then copy and paste the HTML into this field.

Click Replace All; Dreamweaver handles the rest.

Customizing Dreamweaver

Whether you're a hard-core HTML jockey who prefers to be knee-deep in Code view or a visually oriented, drag-and-drop type who never strays from the document window, Dreamweaver lets you work your way.

Not only are the tools built into the program incredibly flexible, the program *itself* can be customized. Dreamweaver gives you the power to add, change, and share keyboard shortcuts. If that's not enough of an efficiency boost, you can add features that even Macromedia's engineers never imagined, from new Flash button designs to additional Behaviors. Dreamweaver's design allows amateur and professional programmers alike to write new features and functions using HTML, JavaScript, and XML (Extensible Markup Language). There are hundreds of these extras, called *extensions*, for you to explore. Best of all, you can try most them for free.

Keyboard Shortcuts

As you use Dreamweaver, you'll hit the same keyboard shortcuts and travel to the same palettes and menus time and again. But you may find that, after the thousandth time, Ctrl+Alt+F (⌘-Option-F) to insert a graphic hurts your pinkie. And some things you do all the time (inserting text fields into forms, for instance) may not have shortcuts at all, so you're forced to go to a menu.

To speed up your work and save your tendons, Dreamweaver 4 comes with a special editor that lets you define or redefine the program's keyboard shortcuts.

Dreamweaver stores keyboard shortcuts in sets. It's easy to switch between them (see Figure 19-1)—a useful feat when you share your computer with someone who likes different keystrokes. Four sets come with the program:

- **Macromedia Standard.** When you first fire up Dreamweaver 4, this is the set that's turned on. The latest versions of Macromedia products, including Fireworks and Flash, share these shortcuts, meaning that you can switch between Macromedia programs without missing a keystroke.

- **Dreamweaver 3.** Some keyboard shortcuts have changed since Dreamweaver 3— for example, F8 instead of F5 now opens the Site window—so if you're comfortable with the older shortcuts, you may prefer this set.

- **BBEdit.** This set is for Mac users with a code-editing past who have spent a lot of time learning shortcuts for Bare Bones Software's popular BBEdit.

- **HomeSite.** Likewise, if you're adept at the Windows HTML text editor HomeSite, you may choose to use its keyboard shortcuts.

Make Your Own Shortcut Set

What if you want a set that *combines* BBEdit shortcuts with your most used Dreamweaver 3 ones? You can easily create keyboard shortcut sets that fit the way you work. Dreamweaver doesn't let you alter any of the four standard sets, so if you want to create your own, the first step is to make a copy of an existing one.

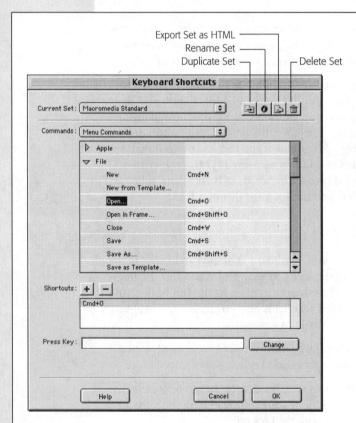

Export Set as HTML
Rename Set
Duplicate Set
Delete Set

Figure 19-1:
The Keyboard Shortcuts window lets you select or duplicate a shortcut set, as well as add and remove keyboard shortcuts for every menu item in Dreamweaver 4.

You can access the shortcut sets from the Keyboard Shortcuts window. Choose Edit→Keyboard Shortcuts. Be patient; it can take some time for the sets to load. Once the dialog box appears, you can switch sets by choosing a new one from the Current Set menu shown here.

To do so, choose Edit→Keyboard Shortcuts; in the Keyboard Shortcuts window, use the Current Set pop-up menu to choose the set you wish to copy, and then click the Duplicate Set button (see Figure 19-1). Dreamweaver asks you to name the new set; do so, then click OK.

You can rename or delete any set you create, once you figure out that the button in the Shortcuts window with the cryptic icon is the Rename Set button (see Figure 19-1). The Trash can button, of course, deletes the current set. (You can't rename or delete any of the four shortcut sets that come preinstalled in Dreamweaver.)

Changing Keyboard Shortcuts

Once you've created a new set, you can select any command and alter its shortcut. Start by choosing Edit→Keyboard Shortcuts to open the Shortcuts window, if it's not already open. Then:

1. **From the Commands pop-up menu, choose the command type.**

   Dreamweaver organizes shortcuts into three (Macintosh) or five (Windows) primary categories. These categories don't always make sense; for example, Copy and Paste appear under the Code Editing category, even though you use them at least as frequently while editing a document in Design view. Browse to see which commands have (or could have) keyboard shortcuts associated with them.

   Menu Commands are the commands in Dreamweaver's menus, such as Insert→Image.

   You might presumably use the **Code Editing** commands when editing HTML code. However, you could just as easily use them in Design view. They include Cut, Paste, and Move to Top of Page, to name a few.

   Document Editing commands are for selecting text and objects on a page, as well as previewing a page in a Web browser.

   Site Menu Commands (Windows only) are the commands available from the Site menu on the Site window, such as Site→Change Link Sitewide. (On the Mac, these commands are listed with the others in the Menu Commands category.)

   Site Window Commands (Windows only), available when working in the Site window, include Cancel FTP. On the Mac, these commands are listed in the Document Editing group.

2. **In the scrolling list, click the command whose keyboard shortcut you want to change.**

   You'll find menu commands grouped by menu name: Commands available in the File menu, like Open and Save, fall under File. Click the + (Windows) or flippy triangle (Mac) next to the menu name to display the list of commands hidden underneath (see Figure 19-1). If the command already has a keyboard shortcut, it appears in the right-hand column. If it isn't assigned a shortcut, you see an empty space.

3. **Click inside the Press Key field, and then press the new keystroke.**

Unless you're assigning the shortcut to an Fkey, you must begin your shortcut with the Ctrl key (⌘ key). For example, the F8 key is a valid shortcut, but the letter R is not. Press Ctrl+R (⌘-R) instead.

Of course, many commands already have shortcuts. If you choose a key combination that's in use, Dreamweaver tells you which command has dibs. You can pick a different key combination, or simply click the Change button to reassign the shortcut to your command.

4. **Click the Change button.**

Dreamweaver saves the new shortcut in your custom set.

Repeat from step 1 if you want to make other keystroke reassignments; when you're finished, click OK to close the dialog box.

What if a command you use often doesn't have a shortcut at all? It's no problem to create one. As a matter of fact, Dreamweaver lets you assign *two* keyboard shortcuts to every command—one for you, and one for your left-handed spouse, for example.

To give a command an additional shortcut (or its first):

1. **Choose the command.**

Follow the first two steps of the preceding instructions, for example.

2. **Click the + button next to the word Shortcuts.**

The cursor automatically pops into the Press Key field.

3. **Press the keys of your additional shortcut, and then click the Change button again.**

Repeat from step 1 if you want to make other keystroke reassignments; when you're finished, click OK.

Deleting shortcuts is just as easy. Simply click the command in the list, and then click the – button next to the word Shortcuts.

Create a Shortcut Cheat Sheet

Unless your brain is equipped with a 40-gig hard drive, you'll probably find it hard to remember all of Dreamweaver's keyboard shortcuts.

Fortunately, Dreamweaver offers a printable cheat sheet for your reference. At the top of the Shortcuts window, there's a handy Export Set as HTML button. (It's labeled with a cryptic icon; see Figure 19-1.) Click this button to name and save a simple HTML page that lists all of the commands and keyboard shortcuts for the currently selected set. Once you've saved the file, print it out or use it as an online reference—a great way to keep a record of your shortcuts for yourself or a team of Web page designers (see the box on the facing page).

Dreamweaver Extensions

While keyboard shortcuts provide an easy way to access frequently used commands, they're not much help if the command you want doesn't exist. Suppose, for example, that you use the Validate Form behavior to make sure visitors to your site properly fill out your forms (see page 278). However, you wish that in addition to just checking for an email address or number, that it could check for phone numbers, Zip codes, and social security numbers. What's a Web designer to do? You could dash off a quick email to *wish-dreamweaver@macromedia.com,* asking the bustling team of programmers to add the command to the next version. But you'd have to wait (and there's no guarantee that Macromedia will do it).

The legions of hard-core Dreamweaver fans have taken this feature-wish-list issue into their own hands. As it turns out, amateur (and pro) programmers can enhance Dreamweaver relatively easily by writing new feature modules using the basic languages of the Web: HTML, JavaScript, and XML (Extensible Markup Language). (In fact, HTML forms, JavaScript programs, and XML documents constitute much of the program. The objects in the Objects panel, for example, are actually HTML pages stored within Dreamweaver's Configuration folder, and all of Dreamweaver's menus have actually been written as an XML file.)

Because of this "open architecture," you can add new functions and commands, called *extensions*, to Dreamweaver by downloading the work of all of those programmers. (Macintosh fans shouldn't confuse these plug-in software modules with *system* extensions, the kind that drop into the System Folder and sometimes cause troubleshooting headaches.)

A Dreamweaver extension can take many forms and work in a variety of ways to change the way the program works. It can be an icon on the Objects panel, a behavior listed on the Behaviors panel, or a command in the Commands menu. It might even be an entirely new floating window, like the Property inspector, that you use to alter some aspect of your page.

Best of all, whereas programming ability may be required to *create* extensions, none at all is necessary to use them. You can download hundreds of extensions from the Web and install them on your computer for free.

FREQUENTLY ASKED QUESTION

Sharing Shortcuts

How do I share my keyboard set with other people?

Dreamweaver stores your keyboard shortcuts as a file in the Macromedia Dreamweaver 4→Configuration→Menus→Custom Sets folder. Each keyboard set lives in an XML file; the file's name ends with the extension .xml.

You can copy these files and place them in the Custom Sets folder on other computers. Once you've done so, the Dreamweaver users on those machines can use the Keyboard Shortcuts window (Edit→Keyboard Shortcuts) to select the new set, just as though it had been created in that copy of Dreamweaver.

Browse the Exchange

The best spot to find Dreamweaver extensions is the Macromedia Exchange Web site, which offers hundreds of free extensions. Although some come from Macromedia itself, the majority are written by an army of talented Dreamweaver users.

Using the Exchange is a straightforward process.

1. **In your Web browser, go to *www.macromedia.com/exchange/*.**

   Alternatively, in Dreamweaver, choose Commands→Get More Commands.

2. **Click the Macromedia Exchange for Dreamweaver link.**

   Two other programs can be enhanced with extensions. Macromedia's Flash and UltraDev also have exchange sites, so you need to specify that you're using Dreamweaver.

3. **Log in (see Figure 19-2).**

   You can *browse* the site without logging in, but to *download* any of the extensions, you need to get a Macromedia ID and sign in, using the Exchange Login form.

4. **Browse the extensions.**

   Once you've logged into the site, the home page highlights new and popular extensions. Unfortunately, as of this writing, the site is poorly organized; finding an extension takes some work.

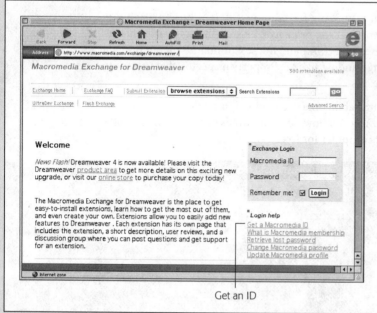

Get an ID

Figure 19-2:
To take advantage of the Exchange, you must get a Macromedia ID and log into the site. Fortunately, the information you need to provide for membership is rather benign: name, email address, and preferred password. You needn't fill out a long questionnaire about your high-tech shopping habits or submit a DNA sample.

You have two ways to look. First, near the top of each page, you'll see a pop-up menu that lists different categories of extensions: Accessibility, DHTML/layers, Navigation, Productivity, Flash media, Scripting, Tables, Text, eCommerce, and so on. When you choose a category, you go to a page listing all of the extensions within that category (see Figures 19-3 and 19-4).

If you're looking for a *particular* extension, the search command is your best bet. Type the extension's name, or a few descriptive words, into the Search Extensions field, and then click the Go button. (Unfortunately, this is the only way you can direct someone to a particular extension. At this point, the Exchange doesn't provide each one with a unique URL.)

5. **Click an extension's name to go to its Web page.**

On an extension's page, you'll find a description of it, a link for downloading it, as well as a discussion board where you can post questions, comments, compliments, and criticism (see Figure 19-3).

Find a Good Extension

How do you figure out which extensions are worth checking out? First, you can find some recommendations of the best ones scattered through this book in special sidebars labeled Extension Alert (see pages 111 and 374, for example).

The Exchange also provides information to help you separate the wheat from the chaff. Macromedia tests each new extension before posting it. Extensions that pass a basic set of tests—it installs OK, it works, it doesn't blow up your computer—are given a Basic approval rating. Some extensions also pass a more rigorous test that

Figure 19-3:
At the Exchange, you can choose a category to see a list of extensions. Sort the list by clicking the headings at the top of each column. For example, click Date to sort the extensions by how recently they were posted.

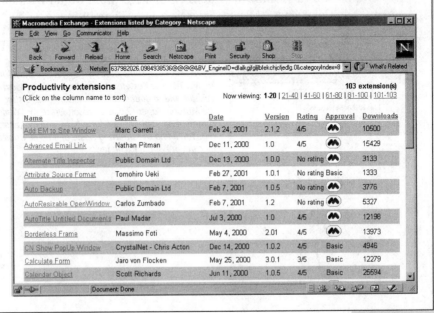

determines if the extension works in a way that's "Dreamweaver-like." In other words, these extensions are designed to look, feel, and act like the program. These extensions get a Macromedia Approved rating, indicated by the Macromedia logo.

Of course, these approval ratings only let you know if an extension works; they don't tell you that it's *useful*. As an extra aid, Dreamweaver aficionados (including you) can rate each extension on a scale of 1 (worst) to 5 (best). An extension's average rating gives you a good indication of how handy it is. When you're browsing the Exchange, look for the column labeled Rating to the right (see Figure 19-3). Click the header to organize the extensions from most to least recommended.

Download and Install Extensions

Once you've found a great extension, download it by clicking the appropriate link: Mac or Windows. You can save the resulting downloaded file anywhere on your computer, but the Dreamweaver 4→Downloaded Extensions folder is a logical place.

A downloaded extension file's name ends with .mxp, which stands for Macromedia Exchange Package. That's a special file format that works with the Extension Manager—the program, described next, that installs the extension into Dreamweaver.

The Extension Manager

To add and remove a Dreamweaver extension, you use the Extension Manager, a stand-alone program that's integrated with Dreamweaver 4. It's designed to let you manage extensions for Dreamweaver by installing them, turning them on and off, and removing them. If you also use Macromedia Flash or UltraDev; this feature gives you a handy single access point for managing *all* your extensions.

You can launch the Extension Manager from within Dreamweaver by choosing Commands→Manage Extensions (see Figure 19-5).

Figure 19-4:
If you ever need some destructive criticism, download the Dreamweaver Assistant extension. The "assistant," a cigarette-smoking pushpin with a goatee and an attitude (and a stinging spoof of Clippy the Moronic Paper Clip in Microsoft Office for Windows), will gently comment on your site, ask for a beer, and make time with a paper clip. You'll find this amusing waste of time in, ironically, the Productivity category of the Exchange.

To add an extension you've downloaded, proceed like this:

1. **In Dreamweaver, choose Commands→Manage Extensions.**

   The Extension Manager launches, listing all installed extensions (Figure 19-5).

2. **Choose Dreamweaver 4 from the pop-up menu.**

   Since the Extension Manager handles extensions for several different programs, you need to specify which program you're using. Of course, if you don't have UltraDev, Flash 5, or Dreamweaver 3 installed on your machine, Dreamweaver 4 is the only option.

3. **Choose File→Install Extension.**

   If you're using Windows, you can also click the Install Extension button. The Select Extension window appears, listing the folders on your hard drive.

4. **Navigate to and select the extension package (.mxp file) you wish to add.**

   A disclaimer appears with a lot of legal text. In brief, it holds Macromedia free of liability if your computer melts as a result of installing the extension.

Figure 19-5:
The Extension Manager window lists each extension you've installed along with its version number, type, and author. If you select an extension from the list, a description displays in the bottom half of the window. The Windows and Macintosh versions differ slightly; the Windows version (top) includes four buttons for easy access to common tasks. The same functions can be accessed on the Mac (bottom) from the File and Help menus.

Install Extension
Delete Extension
Go to Exchange
Help

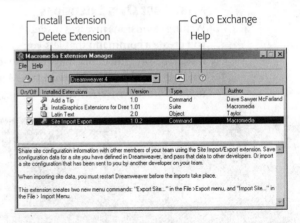

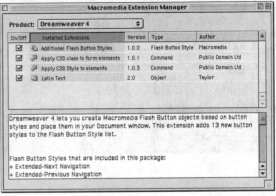

5. **Click Accept.**

A message may appear that asks you to quit and restart Dreamweaver; do so.

Tip: You can also install an extension simply by double-clicking the .mxp file after you download it, which saves you a few steps.

To remove an extension, select it from the list and choose File→Remove Extension (or, in Windows, click the Trash can button).

Warning: If you install a lot of extensions, Dreamweaver may take longer than usual to load. It needs to process every extension file as it launches. If you want to temporarily turn off an extension (as opposed to deleting it forever), open the Extension Manager and uncheck the On/Off box next to the extension name.

If you had downloaded and installed a bunch of extensions back when you used Dreamweaver 3, you can import them into Dreamweaver 4 by choosing File→Import Extensions. Select Dreamweaver 3 from the menu and click OK; Dreamweaver 4 will copy all installed extensions from Dreamweaver 3.

Make Your Own Extensions

Writing extensions involves in-depth knowledge of JavaScript and HTML. But when you create a command that lets you complete a weekly task in a fraction of the time it took before, the effort may just be worth it. For more information, visit the Extending Dreamweaver page on the Macromedia Web site: *www.macromedia.com/support/dreamweaver/extend.html.*

POWER USERS' CLINIC

The Secret Life of Extensions

Where do extensions go? The basic answer is: inside the Dreamweaver 4→Configuration folder.

The Configuration folder holds many of the files that control the look and operation of the program. For instance, the entire menu structure, including menu items and submenus, is described in a file called *menus.xml.* When Dreamweaver starts, it reads this file and uses the information inside it to draw the menus on the screen.

The Configuration folder holds many subfolders, each with a special purpose. For instance, the Objects folder contains files that tell Dreamweaver which icon buttons appear on the Objects panel and how each one works.

Depending on the type of extension you've downloaded—command, object, behavior, or whatever—the extension manager stores the file (or files) required by the extension in one or more folders inside the Configuration folder. Because all of the files inside the Configuration folder are crucial to the way Dreamweaver works, don't delete the folder or any of the files inside it. In fact, because the Extension Manager automatically makes any required changes to the Configuration folder, there's no reason for you to even look inside it.

Getting Help

Hard as it may be to believe, even this book may not answer all your questions about Dreamweaver. Fortunately, a wide range of other resources awaits when a particular feature doesn't work for you.

Getting Help From Dreamweaver

There's plenty of assistance built right into the program, from beginning tutorials to a complete browser-based help system. You can open these aids and more by using the Help menu (Figure A-1).

Getting Started

If you're brand-new to Dreamweaver, consider taking the program's guided tour, which gives you a good overview of the Dreamweaver landscape and prepares you for more learning. To launch it, choose Help→Guided Tour.

Dreamweaver also includes seven step-by-step lessons for specific Web-creation tasks, ranging from creating an image map to using Cascading Style Sheets. You'll find them to be fairly basic, and they don't include tutorials on the more routine tasks you'll face in day-to-day Web design work, but they're a start. Choose Help→Lessons to access them.

Detailed Assistance

For detailed information on specific features of the program, turn to the Using Dreamweaver reference. This browser-based help system includes everything in the printed manual, and more. Press F1 to view the first page of this manual in your Web browser.

This electronic manual is made up of Web pages (which sit in the Dreamweaver 4 folder on your computer). You can navigate them using a Table of Contents, Index, or Search engine. The Search feature makes finding certain topics easier than flipping through the manual. Better yet, the content of this Web-based reference is an expanded version of the printed manual, so you'll find extra information (and much better indexing) here.

If you're getting into writing your own Web code, the Reference window (Help→Reference) provides in-depth information on HTML, CSS, and JavaScript.

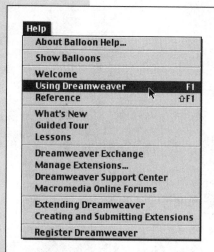

Figure A-1:
Dreamweaver's Help menu provides quick access to a guided tour, lessons, a browser-based help system, and several online support sites.

Getting Help from Macromedia

You can also get more up-to-date and personalized support offerings from Macromedia, ranging from technical notes posted on the Macromedia Web site to pay-as-you-play support plans.

Free Email Support

www.macromedia.com/support/email/complimentary/

You're entitled to 90 days of free Dreamweaver help by email. The clock starts clicking when you make your first request for help, and it's available only if you've registered your copy of the software first (by choosing Help→Register Dreamweaver). To post a question, go to Macromedia's Web site, where you'll find a support form to fill out. Macromedia says it will usually send you an answer within one business day.

Paid Support

www.macromedia.com/support/programs/priority.htm

Once your free email-help period expires, you can turn to two types of personalized fee-based support. Priority Access Support ($100 for one year) gives you the right to contact Macromedia's tech-help department via email or 800 number. For more information on this program, go to the URL above or call 800-457-1774.

If you just have a single nagging question, you can also pay $25 per call, which gives you up to 15 minutes of a Macromedia technician's undivided attention. Call 415-252-9080 weekdays, Friday, 7 a.m. to 4 p.m., Pacific time. This service is only available to North American customers.

Macromedia Web Site

www.macromedia.com/support/dreamweaver/

If you don't mind hunting around for the right information, you'll find plenty of good, *free* information on Macromedia's Web Site. If you've got a question or problem, the best place to start is at the Dreamweaver support (that's another word for help) area of Macromedia's Web site. Here you'll find useful tips, techniques, and tutorials, along with a searchable archive of tech notes (short articles on specific, tweaky problems) that may just hold the answer you're seeking.

Quick Reference Guide

www.macromedia.com/support/dreamweaver/documentation/dreamweaver4_ref.html

Cheat sheets are always a blessing when learning a program. Macromedia supplies Mac and Windows reference guides in PDF format (and in multiple languages). Keyboard shortcuts are neatly organized by topic in this handy two-page reference.

Newsgroup

news://forums.macromedia.com/macromedia.dreamweaver

The Macromedia Newsgroup is a terrific source of information, offering almost real-time answers on Dreamweaver and related Web-design techniques. (Among the experts manning the messages there: Murray Summers, this book's technical editor.)

A newsgroup is an Internet bulletin board; a popular one like Macromedia's can generate hundreds of replies-to-replies a day. Using a newsgroup reader like the one in Outlook Express, you can post questions here. Odds are one of the many knowledgeable experts who always seem to be hanging around will come back with an answer, sometimes within hours or even minutes. (If you're a newsgroup first-timer, *www.macromedia.com/support/forums/using.htm* explains how to use them. You'd be wise to visit *www.macromedia.com/support/forums/etiquette.htm,* too, to learn the proper etiquette for using newsgroups.)

Help from the Real World

If Macromedia doesn't have the answer, there's probably a Web site out there that does. In fact, you're likely to find more honest critiques of the program at some of these sites. Here are a few of the best non-Macromedia sites providing answers to your questions.

Dreamweaver FAQ and Resource Site

www.roubaixinteractive.com/dwfaq/

www.dreamweaverfaq.com/index.asp/

The Dreamweaver FAQ and Resource Site is a compendium of fabulously useful links to Dreamweaver tutorials and information. It's the best place to start for answers to most routine questions about Dreamweaver.

The PattySite–Dreamweaver Resources

www.thepattysite.com/dreamweaver/

This site, produced by Macromedia Evangelist Patty Ayers, contains information of use to the Dreamweaver Web developer.

Newsgroup FAQs

www.cauzway.net/dreamweaver/faq.asp

This site's FAQ list holds the answers to some very common Dreamweaver questions.

Help with Extensions

If you're excited by the possibilities of Dreamweaver extensions discussed in Chapter 19, you'll find plenty of sites dedicated to extension development. On the Web, you'll be able to find hundreds of extensions to supercharge your copy of Dreamweaver; most are free. Here's a sampling of some of the best Dreamweaver extension sites.

The Exchange

www.macromedia.com/exchange/Dreamweaver/

Of course, the most comprehensive source of extensions is Macromedia's own Exchange Web site. It's dedicated to providing Dreamweaver users access to hundreds of (mostly) useful add-ons; see page 493 for more detail.

Massimo's Corner

www.massimocorner.com/

Massimo Foti, one of the premier extension developers in the Dreamweaver community, hosts this site full of useful extensions, tips, and tricks.

Yaromat

www.yaromat.com/dw/

Another great developer, Jaro van Flocken, provides his extensions at this site.

Project Seven

www.projectseven.com/Dreamweaver/

Project Seven has developed some truly remarkable, very advanced extensions especially for animation and interactivity. This site also offers tutorials and a line of commercial (as in, you have to pay for them) Dreamweaver templates.

Creating Your Own Extensions

If you've got the programming bug and are well versed in JavaScript you might want to take a crack at creating your own Dreamweaver Extensions. To help you out, Dreamweaver includes a *detailed* set of Web pages covering every aspect of Extension development. Choose Help→Extending Dreamweaver (see Figure A-1). Your Web browser opens, and the first page of the reference appears.

After creating an extension, you can learn how to prepare it for public consumption by choosing Help→Creating and Packaging Extensions (see Figure A-1). This opens your Web browser and loads a page explaining how to prepare your extensions in the .mxp format (the format used by the Extension manager), and how to submit them to the Macromedia Exchange for review.

Colophon

The book was written in Word 2000 and 2001, whose revision-tracking features made life far easier as drafts were circulated from authors to technical and copy editors.

The screen images in this book were captured by Ambrosia Software's Snapz Pro *2* *(www.ambrosiasw.com)* on the Mac and TechSmith's SnagIt *(www.techsmith.com)* on Windows. Adobe Photoshop *(www.adobe.com)* and Macromedia Freehand *(www.macromedia.com)* were called in as required for touching them up.

The book was designed and laid out in Adobe PageMaker 6.5 on a Power Mac 8500, Power Mac G3, and Power Mac G4. The fonts include Formata (as the sans-serif family) and Minion (as the serif body face). To provide the ⌘ and ⌘ symbols, a custom font was created using Macromedia Fontographer.

Index entries were typed into a custom FileMaker database, then collated and formatted by a custom indexing program written in MacPerl. The book was then generated as Adobe Acrobat PDF files for proofreading, "beta reading," and final transmission to the printing plant.

Index